D0079085

COST AND MANAGERIAL ACCOUNTING

COST AND MANAGERIAL ACCOUNTING

Jack Gray
Professor of Accounting
University of Minnesota, Minneapolis

Don Ricketts
Professor of Accounting
University of Cincinnati

McGraw-Hill Book Company

New York St. Louis San Francisco Auckland Bogotá Hamburg Johannesburg London Madrid Mexico Montreal New Delhi Panama Paris São Paulo Singapore Sydney Tokyo Toronto

COST AND MANAGERIAL ACCOUNTING

1 2 3 4 5 6 7 8 9 0 DODO 8 9 8 7 6 5 4 3 2

ISBN 0-07-024220-8

This book was set in Century Schoolbook
by Monotype Composition Company, Inc.
The editors were Donald G. Mason,
Michael Elia, and Edwin Hanson;
the designer was Robin Hessel;
the production supervisor was Charles Hess.
The drawings were done by VIP Graphics.
R. R. Donnelley & Sons Company was printer and binder.

Library of Congress Cataloging in Publication Data

Gray, Jack C., date
Cost and managerial accounting.

Includes index.
1. Cost accounting. I. Ricketts, Don.
II. Title.
HF5686.C8G685 657′.42 81-20710
ISBN 0-07-024220-8 AACR2

CONTENTS

PREFACE

In the early 1960s, a major step in the evolution of accounting occurred. Cost accounting books appeared which gave predominant emphasis to managerial accounting rather than traditional cost accounting topics. These textbooks facilitated teaching how accounting information was prepared for and used by managers. The new emphasis gained considerable popularity because managerial accounting is both interesting and useful to students of accounting and of management.

Twenty years later, many books emphasizing managerial accounting are available. And other books which previously emphasized traditional topics have been modified to include material on managerial accounting along with their traditional emphasis.

Why, then, a new book on cost and managerial accounting? Because all the earlier books are, in a sense, captives of their origins. None facilitate a *balanced* coverage of traditional cost accounting and of managerial accounting topics. The objective of this book is to provide balanced coverage. We want to help the student to learn cost and managerial accounting concepts to understand practice.

OBJECTIVE OF THE BOOK

The book has been written to provide all students with a basis for learning. This has not been done by avoiding difficult topics. Rather, extensive learning aids have been provided. The first example of this is the careful writing and illustrations of each chapter. In doing this, we had the aid of Michael Elia, whose suggestions, demands for additional illustrations, and comments often stretched over more pages than the chapter drafts we had provided him. Thanks, Michael.

At the beginning of each chapter we have provided learning objectives to indicate the concepts the students should know after completing their study of the chapter. Throughout each chapter we have included marginal notes to emphasize important concepts. At the end of each chapter we have provided a glossary, defining all important terms included in the chapter. A review problem with a complete solution is provided at the end of each chapter to reinforce the learning objectives.

Before the writing of the book began, McGraw-Hill Book Company did a substantial market research study which guided us on the topics to be included and the problems to be provided. No topic which market research showed was used by many professors was omitted. Further, the problem set was built around the market study. The types of problems professors told us they wanted were included in double measure—with appropriate variations in difficulty level.

ORGANIZATION OF THE BOOK

We believe that the traditional subject of cost accounting, centering on the determination of inventory costs, is a subject worthy of serious study by students of accounting and management. Almost any system encountered in practice has its origins in traditional cost accounting. Understanding how that system functions is important. At the same time, managerial accounting is a subject of considerable interest and utility which deserves solid, coherent coverage.

This book is organized to help students understand the different roles of cost accounting and managerial accounting. In the first chapter, we define cost accounting (primarily inventory valuation) and managerial accounting (primarily reporting for planning and control). We explain that the choice of cost accounting methods is based mainly on "generally accepted accounting principles" because the output of cost accounting (inventory costs) is used in preparation of balance sheets and income statements. Like all of financial accounting, cost accounting must conform to generally accepted accounting principles to result in acceptable balance sheets and income statements.

In contrast, the choice of managerial accounting methods is based primarily on the concept of relevance to the planning or control decision for which the report is prepared. Of course, choice of both cost and managerial accounting methods is also governed by the cost-benefit principle—more refined accounting methods of any kind should be chosen only when the benefit of the added refinement exceeds the cost of the additional accounting effort.

It has been our experience that students are often confused in their study of cost and managerial accounting methods because they are not sure whether the topic being considered is cost accounting or managerial accounting. With this distinction made in Chapter 1, the student is better equipped to follow any pattern of study of cost and managerial accounting topics. More important, in this book, each chapter has a distinct focus on either cost or managerial accounting, which establishes a clear frame of reference for the study of the chapter.

Chapter 2 defines cost terms and cost-volume behavior which are important to both cost and managerial accounting. We have chosen to follow the two opening chapters with the study of traditional cost accounting. Overhead allocation and predetermined overhead rates are followed by job order costing and process cost accounting. Accounting for defective units and joint costs are next. Finally, the cost accounting section of the book introduces standard costing, flexible budgeting, and direct costing as cost accounting systems. This seems appropriate because of their heavy use in practice as cost accounting systems, quite apart from their potential contribution to the planning and control reporting of managerial accounting. Later in the book, their managerial accounting applications are discussed.

Managerial accounting is introduced with Chapters 12 and 13, on budgeting (the planning decision) and responsibility accounting (the basic ideas of control). This introduction is followed by the planning topics of cost-volume-profit analysis and relevant costs and nonrecurring planning decisions. The control topics then considered include cost centers (engineered, managed, and capacity), revenue centers, profit centers, investment centers, and transfer pricing.

Because of individual preferences for introduction of quantitative materials and capital budgeting, they are grouped at the end of the book in Chapters 21 through 26. They are written to be used as a group at the end of the course, to be moved forward and integrated with earlier subject matter, or to be omitted if they are covered elsewhere in the curriculum.

COURSE ORGANIZATIONS

The balance between cost and managerial accounting and the structure of the book should not be seen as a barrier to alternate organizations of the course. Because each chapter is focused on either cost accounting or managerial accounting, they can be arranged to fit the course objectives without danger that students will confuse the objective.

Illustrations of course organizations follow:

One-year course (two semesters or three quarters):

Chapters 1 and 2	Introduction, definitions, and cost behavior
Chapters 3–11	Traditional cost accounting
Chapters 12–20	Managerial accounting
Chapters 21–24	Quantitative materials
Chapters 25 and 26	Capital budgeting

One-year course for students with strong quantitative backgrounds:

Chapters 1, 2, and 23	Introduction, definitions, cost behavior, and statistical cost estimation
Chapters 3–11	Traditional cost accounting
Chapters 12, 13, and 21	Introduction to managerial accounting and decision making
Chapters 14, 15, and 24	Planning decisions
Chapters 22, 16–20	Reporting for managerial control
Chapters 25 and 26	Capital budgeting

A two-quarter course could follow the same patterns as above, omitting material students will learn in other courses. A one-semester course balancing cost accounting and managerial accounting could include:

Chapters 1 and 2	Introduction, definitions, and cost behavior
Chapters 3–7	Traditional cost accounting
Chapters 12 and 13	Introduction to managerial accounting
Chapters 14 and 15	Planning decisions
Chapters 8 and 16, 9 and 17	Reporting for cost control

A one-semester course introducing cost accounting but emphasizing managerial accounting could be as follows:

Chapters 1 and 2	Introduction, definitions, and cost behavior
Chapters 3–5	Basics of traditional cost accounting
Chapters 12 and 13	Introduction to managerial accounting
Chapters 14 and 15	Planning decisions
Chapters 8 and 16, 9 and 17	Reporting for cost control
Chapters 18 and 19	Revenue profit and investment centers

Single quarter courses can be designed omitting some of the material in the semester courses.

ACKNOWLEDGMENTS

The authors wish to acknowledge the help of many persons who contributed to the book. Early contributors include people who responded to the market survey and John J. Willingham, Peat Marwick Mitchell & Company. Paul Dierks, the University of Texas–Arlington, has contributed extensive review of several drafts of the book and is the author of an excellent study guide to accompany this book.

The following professors reviewed chapter drafts and we appreciate the improvements resulting from their suggestions: James Adler, Checkers, Simon & Rosner CPA, Chicago, Illinois; K. Edwin Bailey, University of Florida; Donald E. Bostrom, The University of North Dakota; Charles Brandon, University of Central Florida; Samuel Chesler, University of Lowell; Jackson F. Gillespie, University of Delaware; Joseph F. Goetz, Jr., Oklahoma State University; L. R. Loschen, University of Southern California; Elzy V. McCollough, The Ohio State University; Jon R. Nance, The University of Nebraska–Lincoln; Joseph R. Razek, University of New Orleans; Alan R. Senn, California State Polytechnic University; and David Shields, University of Florida.

At McGraw-Hill, we are grateful for the help of Stephen Dietrich, Donald Chatham, and Donald Mason. The contribution of Michael Elia was mentioned earlier. Ed Hanson kept the project moving in the production stages.

Problems identified by the designation (CPA) are used with permission of the American Institute of Certified Public Accountants. The Institute of Management Accountants of the National Association of Accountants permitted use of problems labeled (CMA). The assistance of both these organizations has added to the quality of the book and is appreciated.

A special note of acknowledgment is extended to Patty Shick for her excellent typing of the final draft.

Finally, we wish to acknowledge publicly our appreciation of our wives, consultants and proofreaders, Pat Ricketts and Marlys Gray. Throughout the process they continually exhibited the qualities of love, patience, and support which greatly eased the burdens we had to carry.

Jack Gray
Don Ricketts

1

COST ACCOUNTING AND MANAGERIAL ACCOUNTING

AFTER COMPLETING YOUR STUDY OF THIS CHAPTER, YOU SHOULD HAVE LEARNED:

1 The differences and similarities between cost accounting and managerial accounting. You will find that the primary difference is associated with the use of the data by managers.

2 How managerial accounting relates to planning and control decisions, and how cost accounting relates to the preparation of income statements and balance sheets.

3 The importance of evaluating alternative accounting procedures from a cost-benefit viewpoint.

4 How cost accounting and managerial accounting rely on a common data base to accomplish their objectives.

The first chapter of a textbook is often the hardest chapter to write. When authors begin a book, there is so much to say it is difficult to know where to start or when to stop. We have tried to make our beginning chapter worth reading and studying. The things you can expect to learn have been suggested in the list of objectives which begins each chapter. We use these objectives to help you know in advance what you can expect to learn by studying each chapter.

Here is a list of questions which are answered through the use of cost accounting and managerial accounting:

Questions cost and management accounting can help answer.

1 If McGraw-Hill Book Company has 8,000 copies of this book in inventory at year-end, at what cost will they be reported in the company balance sheet?

2 How many copies of this book must McGraw-Hill sell before a profit is made?

3 What does it cost a company when its union goes on strike?

4 What does it cost a company to stop polluting the air?

5 What will it cost Ford Motor Company to meet the minimum fuel economy standards for 1985?

6 If a university is considering offering a new Master of Accounting degree, what will it cost?

7 What does it cost to audit the financial statements of New York City?

This book is about accounting methods which can be used to answer these and many other similar questions.

Cost defined.

Profit defined.

The word "cost" was used in all questions except number 2, which used the word "profit." **Cost** is defined as the resources consumed to accomplish a specific objective. McGraw-Hill Book Company consumed several different types of resources in publishing this book. They consumed dollars by paying wages to people who worked to make this the best book possible. They also consumed paper, ink, and partially consumed (wore out) machinery in the setting and printing of the book. *Profit* is the difference between sales revenues and the expired costs (or, more technically, expenses) of earning those revenues. Thus, cost must be measured to answer each question, including the question that mentioned profit rather than cost.

You calculate the cost of something with a specific purpose in mind.

Notice that the definition of cost referred to accomplishing a "specific objective." Each of the questions implies a specific objective or purpose. Question 1 implied the purpose of preparing a balance sheet for McGraw-Hill Book Company. Question 2 implied a purpose of deciding whether it would be profitable to produce and sell this book. (Neither McGraw-Hill nor the authors would have put the required amount of effort into preparing this book for literary recognition alone.) Exhibit 1-1 lists the implied specific purposes of each question.

COST ACCOUNTING SYSTEMS

Cost accounting system defined.

A **cost accounting system** is used to record, summarize, and report cost information. Some cost information is reported in income statements and balance sheets which are presented to external users such as shareholders and creditors. Other cost information is given in special reports to managers within the firm for use in

EXHIBIT 1-1
The Purpose of Cost Information

Question Number	Implied Specific Purpose
1	Prepare a balance sheet.
2	Will producing the book be profitable?
3	Should the company offer a higher settlement to avoid a strike?
4	Should the company close the plant or install pollution control equipment?
5	How will Ford Motor Company obtain the needed resources?
6	Will the new degree produce enough tuition to make it feasible?
7	Is improved quality of information worth the cost of an audit?

deciding how to operate the organization. Those *decisions* are simply the choices managers make about how their organizations should do things.

Managerial accounting provides cost information to managers to assist them in making decisions.

Exhibit 1-1 shows that most of the implied specific objectives are decisions or choices to be made by managers. Providing cost information to managers to assist them in making decisions is the part of accounting called **managerial accounting** or **management accounting.** Providing cost information for income statements and balance sheets is called **cost accounting.**

Cost accounting systems were developed many years ago to meet the needs of cost information for income statements and balance sheets. Only later did the development of more complex organizations demand that cost information also be collected and reported for management decisions. Cost accounting systems have evolved so that today they provide cost information for both cost accounting (for income statements and balance sheets) and managerial accounting.

The kind of information provided has also expanded so that in addition to cost information it may include sales and production information in dollars and units. We will continue to use the term "cost information" because it is convenient, but you should remember that for some decisions it will also include revenue (sales) information.

Cost-accounting means developing cost data for income statements and balance sheets.

Let us make the distinction again. When we use the term "cost accounting" we mean developing cost data for use in income statements and balance sheets, the kind of data suggested in question 1 above. When we use the term "managerial accounting" we mean data prepared specifically for managers within the organization to help them make the decisions or choices which are needed for their part of the organization to achieve its objectives. But a cost accounting *system* provides cost data for both cost accounting and managerial accounting.

The reason for distinguishing between cost accounting and managerial accounting is that in many situations different information is needed for each. You may make mistakes if you use cost accounting reports for management decisions. A good example of this is sales orders. Marketing managers and production managers want to know about sales orders as they are received (before the products are shipped). Orders received help the marketing manager decide if sales are being made on schedule or whether increased sales efforts are needed. Orders received help the production manager decide what products and how many units of product should be produced. Are orders received managerial accounting or cost accounting information? If you chose managerial, you were right, because this information is being used by managers within the organization to make decisions. When the sales orders are shipped to the customers they influence cost accounting. The cost of the order is

EXHIBIT 1-2
The Relation between Cost Accounting Systems, Managerial Accounting, and Cost Accounting

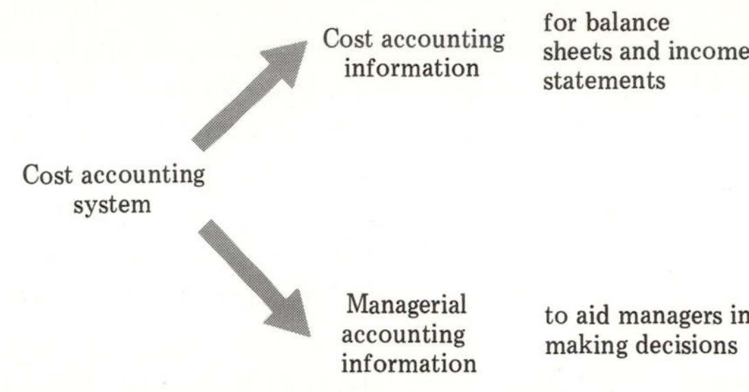

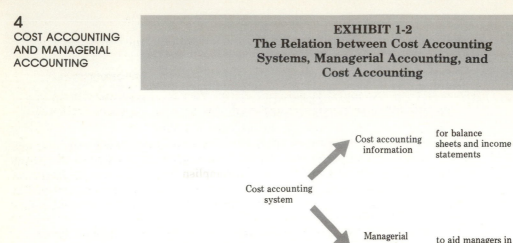

deducted from the sales revenue in the income statement. Thus, the shipment of the order is important to cost accounting.

Examples of the difference between cost accounting and managerial accounting information.

If a production manager made production decisions based only on amounts of products shipped rather than orders received, the wrong products might be produced. The production department would be producing products needed last month for shipment to customers, but it might not be producing the products which customers will need this month and next month. A production manager needs managerial accounting information. This discussion can be summarized graphically as shown in Exhibit 1-2.

We shall next discuss managerial accounting and then cost accounting in more detail.

Managerial Accounting

In managerial accounting the accountant accumulates, summarizes, and reports information which managers need to make specific decisions; thus the name managerial accounting.

Planning decisions defined.

Control decisions defined.

Planning and Control The decisions managers are concerned with can be categorized as *planning* and *control* decisions. Planning decisions establish goals for the organization and choose plans (feasible sets of actions) to accomplish the goals. Control decisions result from implementing the plans and monitoring the actual results to see if goals are being achieved. If goals are not being achieved, control decisions must be made either to do things differently or to alter plans or goals to attainable levels.

Typical planning decisions for which managerial accounting information is needed include:

Examples of planning decisions.

- Should a new product line be marketed?
- Should the production and sale of an existing product line be terminated?
- How many units of each product should we produce this year?

- Should our production facilities be expanded? Contracted?
- What are our cash needs for the year? Should we negotiate a revolving line of credit with the bank?
- How much should we spend on advertising? Research and development?
- Is it more economical to purchase a part from an outside supplier or to manufacture it in our own production facilities (the make or buy decision)?

Planning is based on estimated future costs and revenues, but often historical data provides a good base for the estimates.

All the planning decisions listed above will require *estimates* of future costs and in some cases *estimates* of future revenues. Planning decisions establish the course of action the organization will follow to accomplish its goals. These decisions are based on what management *expects* to occur in the future, not what has occurred in the past. However, we will learn that the historical cost data provides a good base to estimate the future costs.

Typical control decisions for which cost accounting data are needed include:

Examples of control decisions.

- What can be done to make actual sales equal to budgeted sales?
- How can labor be used more efficiently so that actual costs do not exceed planned costs?
- Is a change in research and development projects needed to achieve planned results?
- Does actual production volume need to be changed to equal planned volume?

Control decisions involve comparing actual results with expected results.

All the control decisions listed above require the comparison of actual results with expected results where the expected results are developed from the planning decisions made by management. The actual results represent data collected by the cost accounting system from the actual events that have occurred during the implementation of the plans. This comparison of actual and expected results may necessitate *additional management* decisions to assure that either the original plan is attained or that modifications are made to the original plan in an acceptable way in order to match the actual conditions being encountered.

To illustrate, Melia Company planned to introduce a new product because managerial accounting analysis suggested that the new product could be produced for $3 per unit. Marketing managers believed that 1,000 units of product could be sold each month for $5 per unit. Melia's top management believed that these plans would lead to a satisfactory return on investment so the plan was accepted.

Implementation began but it was found that the cost of producing each unit was $3.50. The higher cost meant lower profit and return on investment. Melia was faced with control decisions. Some of the choices considered were:

Illustrations of control decisions.

1 Can different production methods be used to bring the cost per unit down to $3?

2 Can the product be sold for $5.50 per unit so that the profit per unit will be as planned even with the higher cost per unit?

3 Can the product be redesigned with less expensive materials so that the cost will be $3 per unit?

4 Can more than 1,000 units be sold per month so that even with the planned $5 selling price and the $3.50 cost, the total profit will yield a satisfactory return on investment?

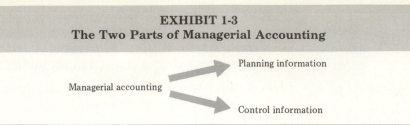

EXHIBIT 1-3
The Two Parts of Managerial Accounting

The methods of obtaining the needed information will be discussed in later chapters of this book, but seeking answers to questions like these is the essence of control. Graphically, the parts of managerial accounting are shown in Exhibit 1-3.

Relevance As you study this textbook you will learn that a great variety of accounting information is available to managers. For example, we previously learned that sales orders received and sales orders shipped are used for different purposes. How does an accountant know what information should be reported to managers to aid them in making their planning and control decisions? The accountant chooses information to be reported to a manager by (1) identifying the specific purpose, decision model, or technique the manager will use to make the decision and then (2) determining the **relevant information.**

The first part of the process, identifying the specific purpose, decision model, or technique in which the information will be used, was discussed earlier. Information that is important to one decision may not be important to another decision. This is why it is crucial to know the specific purpose or decision to be made before information is gathered.

The main topic of this section is relevance of information. Only relevant information can improve a decision. Information is *relevant* if it:

Relevant information (1) affects the accomplishment of objectives, and (2) will change as a result of the decision.

1 Affects the accomplishment of the objectives of the decision maker

2 Will change as a result of the decision or choice made by the decision maker

Relevance is important in managerial accounting because it is the main determinant of what the accountant will do and what information will be collected and reported. We will illustrate relevance with a personal example and then with a business example.

A personal illustration of the meaning of relevance.

Suppose that the specific decision to be made is to choose a pair of shoes to purchase. In the first illustration let us assume that the shoes are to be used for job interviews. Also assume that the shoestore at which we are shopping has a big rack of shoes available for a single price, \$60 per pair. We are sure we can find a suitable pair on the rack. Since we are choosing shoes to be used in an interview, appearance and color are both very important. We want to project a well-dressed appearance so we will rule out casual shoes. The style of the shoe is *relevant* because we must avoid certain styles if we are to appear well dressed. The color is relevant because it must coordinate with the rest of the clothes we expect to wear in the interview.

In this special case the price of the shoes is not relevant.[1] Regardless of which pair we select, the price will be \$60. So we ignore price in making this decision and consider only color and style. The information we use in making the choice is the relevant information.

[1] We have asked you to assume that all the shoes are the same price. This may seem somewhat unrealistic, but we ask you to do so to make an important point.

Consider one other shoe example. Suppose that we are buying some jogging shoes and that we have no more than $25 to spend on them. Make one further assumption, that we jog in an isolated place and do not care about our appearance. In this case color and style are probably not relevant. What is relevant? Probably comfort and durability. Price is relevant also because we cannot consider a pair that costs more than $25. Further, we would probably prefer the lowest priced pair that promises good comfort and reasonable durability.

A business illustration of the meaning of relevance.

By now you should be getting the idea of relevance. Let us see how relevance applies to a business decision. Assume a company owns a manufacturing machine with a remaining useful life of 10 years and is depreciating the machine at a rate of $12,000 per year. The machine is used to produce three different plastic products: A, B, and C; during the past year 1,000 units of each product were produced. The historical costs incurred and sales revenue generated are shown in Exhibit 1-4.

Assume the supplier of the direct materials for product A has notified management the unit cost will increase to $5 for each unit of A produced. Management had

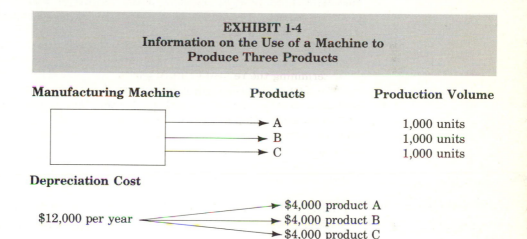

EXHIBIT 1-4
Information on the Use of a Machine to Produce Three Products

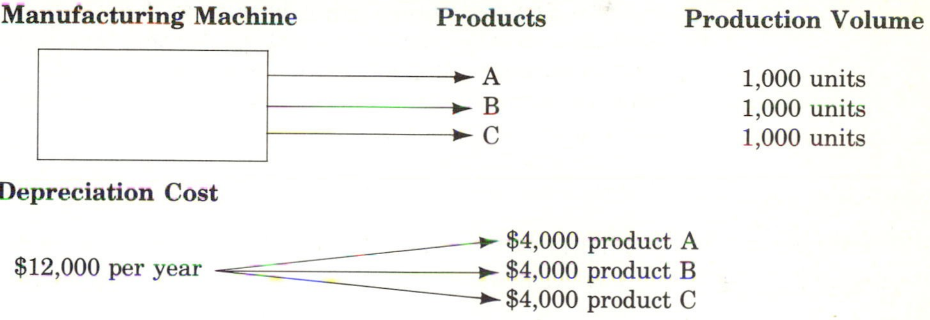

Since the machine is automatic, only a small amount of permanent labor is needed to produce the products. It is divided equally among the products.

Operating Profits for the Year 19X1

	Products			
	A	**B**	**C**	**Total**
Sales revenue	$9,000	$13,000	$12,000	$34,000
Direct materials cost*	4,000	4,000	6,000	14,000
Depreciation	4,000	4,000	4,000	12,000
Labor and other costs	1,000	1,000	1,000	3,000
Total expenses	9,000	9,000	11,000	29,000
Operating profit	$ 0	$ 4,000	$ 1,000	$ 5,000

* Direct materials are the materials that become a part of the finished product. In a desk, it would include lumber, varnish, screws, etc. This definition is considered in more detail in Chapter 2. In these products the direct materials are the plastic in each product.

planned to produce 1,000 units of each product which is the maximum they anticipate could be sold. However, this increase in direct materials cost for product A will cause product A to show an operating loss of $1,000 computed as follows:

Expected Operating Loss—Product A

Sales revenue	$ 9,000
Direct materials cost	
1,000 units @ $5	5,000
Depreciation	4,000
Labor and other costs	1,000
Total expected expense	$10,000
Operating loss	($ 1,000)

Assuming management's goal is to maximize total profits, they are now considering eliminating production and sale of product A because of the projected operating loss. The decision management must make is whether product A should be continued or eliminated.

The data relevant to the decision include any data item that will change as a result of the decision to continue or to eliminate product A and which relates to the company objective of making as much profit as possible. The expected sales revenue of product A *is relevant* since if product A is eliminated the total sales revenue will become $25,000 ($13,000 + $12,000) rather than the $34,000 ($9,000 + $13,000 + $12,000) if product A is continued. The *historical* direct material cost of $4,000 is irrelevant since it will not change no matter what the decision.[2] The expected direct material cost of $5,000 is *relevant* since this is a cost management will incur if product A is produced. If the product is eliminated the direct material cost for product A will be zero. The depreciation cost of $4,000 assigned as product A's share is not relevant since depreciation of the machine will be incurred whether product A is continued or eliminated. As long as the company continues to own the machine the depreciation cost of $12,000 per year will be incurred. The labor and other costs of $1,000 assigned to product A are irrelevant since the full $3,000 of labor and other costs will be incurred if products B and C are produced. To summarize, the relevant data are shown in Exhibit 1-5.

EXHIBIT 1-5
Evaluating the Decision to Drop Product A

	Continue A, B, C	Eliminate A Continue B, C	Changes
Expected sales	$34,000	$25,000	$9,000
Expected raw materials cost	15,000	10,000	5,000
Depreciation	12,000	12,000	—
Labor and other costs	3,000	3,000	—
Expected operating profit	$ 4,000	$ 0	($4,000)

[2] Generally, historical costs are not relevant for most planning decisions since these decisions are based on future expectations. However, in many cases historical costs are the best basis for predicting the future costs. An exception is the tax effects of write-offs of historical costs.

Reporting data which is not relevant may lead to decisions which reduce profit rather than maximize it.

The example shows that not all cost data are relevant to the decision of whether to continue or eliminate product A. In fact, if the data which are not relevant to this decision are reported, managers might choose to eliminate product A which would reduce the organization's total profit rather than maximizing its profit. Of course, in this case the increase in the direct materials cost of product A from $4,000 to $5,000 will reduce the total profit of the firm. But profit will be reduced more severely if product A is eliminated. Management will probably seek some other plan, such as increasing the sales price of product A or selling more of products B and C; eliminating product A is not the solution, as the relevant data show. Notice that the right decision can be made by focusing on the total profit from each alternative (the first two columns of Exhibit 1-5) or by looking only at the changes, the relevant information (the last column of Exhibit 1-5).

In summary, managerial accounting is concerned with the development and reporting of information to aid management in making their planning and control decisions. Reporting issues are decided on the basis of the relevance of the information to a particular decision. This is illustrated graphically as follows:

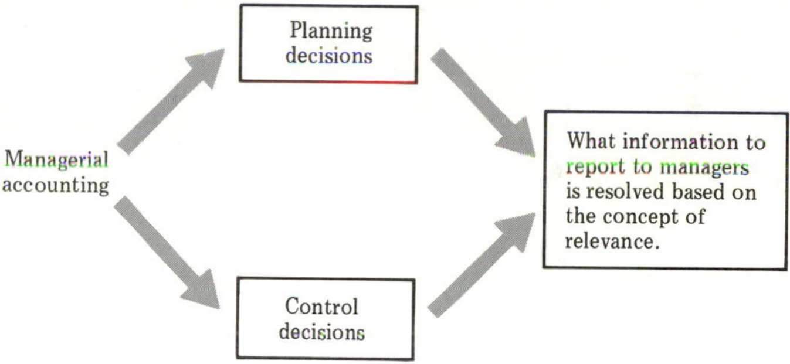

As we shall see in the next section, reporting issues in cost accounting are resolved on the basis of "generally accepted accounting principles."

Cost Accounting

Cost accounting is primarily concerned with data for financial reports to external parties.

Cost accounting is primarily concerned with accumulating, summarizing, and reporting cost data for the preparation of financial reports for external parties, such as shareholders, bankers, government agencies, and financial analysts. The cost data is used to determine:

1 The cost for inventories reported on the balance sheet

2 The cost of goods sold, selling costs, and administrative costs for the computation of net income

Cost accounting relies on generally accepted accounting principles.

How does the accountant know what costs should be included in the inventory on the balance sheet and the cost of goods sold on the income statement? These issues are resolved based on generally accepted accounting principles (GAAP). Today, changes in generally accepted accounting principles are mainly formulated by the Financial Accounting Standards Board. Based on GAAP, a major objective of inventory accounting is the proper determination of income through the process of matching costs against revenues. The concept of matching costs and revenues suggests that if there is a cause-and-effect relationship between costs and revenues, they should be matched by reporting the revenue (the effect) and the cost (the cause) in the income statement for the same period. The cost that is to be assigned to inventory for financial reports is the cost of the resources utilized directly or indirectly to bring an item to its current condition and location.[3]

Cost accounting information is different than relevant information.

In the example used to illustrate relevance for managerial cost accounting (Exhibit 1-4), the relevant information for the decision to continue or eliminate product A was expected future costs and revenues. Cost accounting deals with the recording of *historical* events. Therefore, the appropriate cost data for inventory valuation and income determination for the past year would be the depreciation cost of $4,000 assigned to product A, the $4,000 of direct material cost, and the $1,000 of labor and other costs. These are the costs incurred to bring product A to its current condition and location.

In retail or wholesale organizations that you studied in elementary accounting, the major cost accounting problem you probably encountered was should the organization use LIFO, FIFO, weighted average, or specific identification to assign costs to inventories? The problem is not so much the choice between LIFO, FIFO, etc., because the choice is largely an arbitrary one, but the problem for the accountant is to assure that the chosen method is applied correctly and consistently. The cost assigned to a particular inventory item is basically the purchase price plus handling and transportation charges.

For a manufacturing organization there are additional problems we will have to solve to assign costs to inventories. For example, the depreciation cost of $12,000 in Exhibit 1-4 was arbitrarily assigned evenly to products A, B, and C. The $12,000 depreciation cost is really a joint cost of producing all three products. Later in this book you will learn that there are a number of arbitrary but accepted accounting procedures for allocating joint costs among the several products receiving benefits from the cost. As with the problem of choice among LIFO, FIFO, etc., once the choice has been made the accountant must be sure the method is applied correctly and consistently.

In summary, relevance to the decision is the primary criterion for identifying data appropriate for managerial accounting. The primary criterion for identifying data appropriate for cost accounting is the proper determination of income through the process of matching historical costs and revenues. The accounting methods to accomplish the proper determination of income are chosen in accordance with cost accounting—what information to report based on GAAP.

COST-BENEFIT OF INFORMATION

In the design of a cost accounting system for accumulating cost accounting and managerial accounting information, you will be faced with choosing among alternative accounting methods. We have already discussed how the concept of *relevance* guides the accountant's choice for managerial accounting and how GAAP guides the accountant's choice for cost accounting. However, you must also recognize that accounting information is a commodity just like automobiles, food, or clothing. Accounting information is not free—the cost of information includes salaries of accountants, supplies, and costs of using equipment. An organization makes a decision to "buy" more or less information, and, like any purchase decision, information should be purchased only if it is worth the cost.

Accounting information should be purchased only if it is worth its cost.

The basic idea of the **cost-benefit of information** is that information has a cost and that it also has a benefit through improving decisions. The first step is to remember that information is not free, even though it seems that way until you think about it. When you buy a newspaper, you are paying for information. The cost is the price you pay for the paper, and perhaps the value of the time you spent

[3] *Accounting Research Bulletin* No. 43, p. 28, published by the American Institute of Certified Public Accountants.

buying and reading the paper. You may have bought the paper in order to have information about the movies that are currently showing. You may have bought the paper to obtain information about what is currently on sale so that you may make the most economical purchases. You may get most of your information from the radio or television. But even these sources of information cost you your time.

If you need technical information it may be necessary to conduct a survey. Market researchers incur considerable cost to provide information about customer needs and purchasing plans. If you are considering an investment in stock, you may take the time to go to the library and read annual reports and special reports on the companies that interest you. Again you are incurring a cost equal to the value of the time you spend in your research. Investors who manage large amounts of investment funds often subscribe to investment advice services and pay considerable costs for this information.

A management accountant may hire engineers to make a study to predict the cost of producing a new product. A company might incur the cost of placing electric meters in each department in order to "buy" the information of how much electricity is used in each department. The point of all these illustrations is that information has a cost and that managers must buy information carefully just as they buy materials, labor, or other things.

Information usually also has a benefit. The benefit can be described as improving the decision made. If you buy a newspaper to see which movies are currently showing, the benefit is having a more enjoyable evening. In the business sense, the benefit is usually making more profit which can be done by increasing revenues or reducing costs. By paying the cost of an engineering study on methods of producing a new product, we are more likely to make the most profitable decision, either to produce or not to produce the new product. If we pay the cost of metering electricity into each department, we may have the benefit of knowing where conservation efforts are most likely to produce the greatest cost savings. Or knowing how much electricity is used in each department may produce more accurate cost information used in reporting inventories on the balance sheet and permit better matching of costs and revenues according to GAAP on the income statement.

Usually the accountant and the decision maker jointly decide how much information to "buy." In general, information has benefit if it has the potential of changing the decision. To illustrate, assume a manager has a choice of accounting method 1 or accounting method 2. If the decision to be made will not change as a result of the accounting method chosen, then the lowest cost accounting method should be chosen. If the decision to be made will change, the accounting method is then *decision significant*. In this case the accounting method that produces the greatest positive difference between the benefits and cost (profits) should be chosen.

THE COMMON DATA BASE FOR COST AND MANAGERIAL ACCOUNTING

Cost and management accounting are linked by the data base.

To this point, emphasis has been placed on the differences between cost accounting and managerial accounting. The link between the two areas lies in the fact that they both utilize the same basic data to a significant degree. Much of the data used to generate cost accounting reports is also used to prepare managerial accounting reports.

The relationships are illustrated in Exhibit 1-6. At the top of the diagram are representative sources of data entered into the accounting data base. The first row represents files in which data are stored until they are needed to be combined and summarized into accounting reports. Cost accounting draws on data about sales, production, personnel, and facilities to determine the cost of inventories on hand at

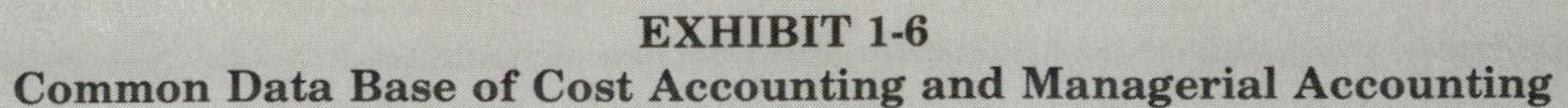

EXHIBIT 1-6
Common Data Base of Cost Accounting and Managerial Accounting

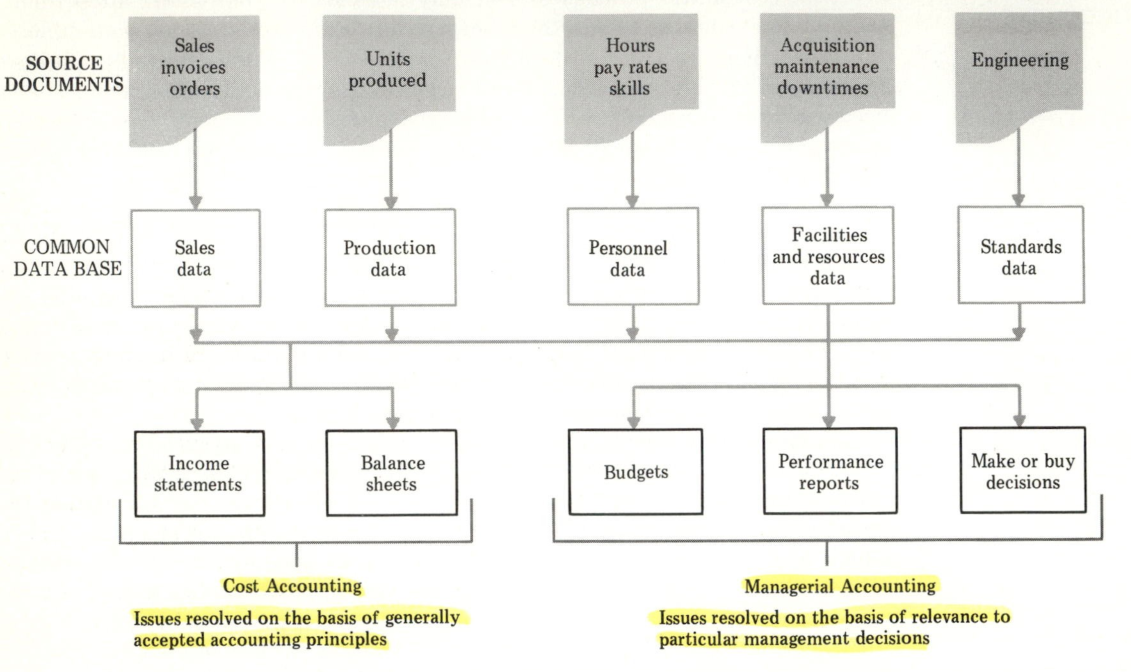

the end of the period and the cost of goods sold during the period. Managerial accounting draws on the same data to develop budgets, performance reports, and analyses for other decisions.

The data base contains data that is common to cost and managerial accounting and also data that is special to each.

The data base includes common data, i.e., the same data are used by managerial accounting and by cost accounting, but in different ways. For example historical data on labor costs are used by cost accounting to determine inventory values and cost of goods sold. The historical data on labor cost might be used to *estimate* the labor cost for the coming year to determine the size of workforce needed to meet anticipated production requirements and to *estimate* the cash requirements to meet weekly payrolls. This represents the use of cost accounting data to develop managerial accounting data for planning decisions. The historical data on labor costs might be compared with the estimated labor costs to determine if labor is being used effectively and efficiently. This represents the use of cost accounting data to develop managerial accounting data for control decisions. The data base also includes what we might consider special data for cost accounting and special data for managerial accounting, obviously called special because they are data used only by either cost accounting or by managerial accounting. For example, the marketing managers and the production managers in a firm would have to know about unfilled orders received—the production backlog of orders which customers have committed to purchase and will become sales as soon as the firm can produce the product. Managerial accounting would report these unfilled orders to marketing managers and production managers. Unfilled orders do not mean anything to cost accounting. Cost accounting does not record and report a sale until the order is shipped to the customer. Once the goods are shipped to the customer the unfilled order becomes a filled order, that is, it becomes a sale, and because it is now a sale, cost accounting records it by removing

A cost accounting system manages the data base to provide both cost accounting information and managerial accounting information.

the cost from the inventory account on the balance sheet and adding it to the cost of goods sold account on the income statement.

Because of the common data collected and stored in files, generally one group of accountants in an organization is concerned with both cost accounting and managerial accounting. This book deals with the subject of cost accounting *systems* which manage the data base to provide both cost accounting and managerial accounting information. The primary emphasis of Chapters 2 through 11 is on cost accounting, with the remainder of the book devoted to managerial accounting.

SUMMARY

This chapter has emphasized that a cost accounting system is used to record, summarize, and report cost information. Some cost information is reported in the financial statements to external parties, such as shareholders, creditors, and government agencies. The development of cost information for financial reports is called cost accounting. In deciding what cost information to report the accountant is guided by generally accepted accounting principles.

Other cost information is reported to the internal managers of the organization for their planning and control decisions. The development and reporting of information for managerial planning and control is referred to as managerial accounting. In deciding what information to report to managers, the accountant is guided by the relevance of the information to the decision. Information is relevant if it affects the accomplishment of the objectives of the decision maker and will change as a result of the decision.

In choosing among alternative accounting methods for cost or managerial accounting, the accountant must remember that information is not free. In deciding which set of information to "buy," the accountant should compare the cost of the information with the benefits of the information.

The major concepts discussed in this chapter are summarized as follows:

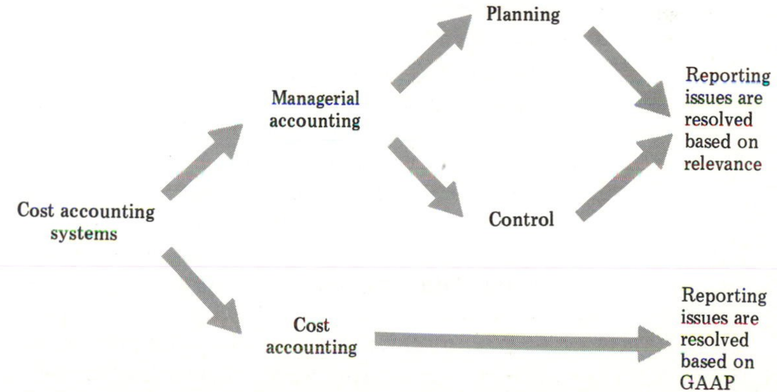

Both cost accounting and managerial accounting share a common data base. Because of this, a single group of accountants within an organization is usually concerned with both cost and managerial accounting problems.

Glossary

Cost The total resources consumed to accomplish a specific objective.

Cost accounting system The procedures used to record, summarize, and report cost information.

Cost accounting That part of the cost accounting system used to determine the cost of the products for external financial reports.

Cost-benefit of information Evaluation of accounting methods by comparing the cost of the method with the benefits associated with the information provided. The accounting method that produces the greatest positive difference between benefits and cost should be chosen.

Managerial (or management) accounting That part of the cost accounting system used to accumulate information for managerial planning and control decisions.

Relevant information Information that will affect the accomplishment of the objectives of the decision maker and will change as a result of the decision.

Questions and Problems

1-1 Distinguish between cost accounting and managerial accounting.

1-2 Distinguish between planning decisions and control decisions.

1-3 What criteria are used to resolve cost accounting reporting problems?

1-4 What criteria are used to resolve managerial accounting reporting problems?

1-5 Compare your answer to question 1-3 with your answer to 1-4. Why is there a difference?

1-6 What factors make information relevant?

1-7 A production manager is considering the replacement of a drill press currently operated by two employees with a drill press that contains an automatic feeding device. The operation of the new drill press will require only one employee. List the relevant costs for this decision.

1-8 In the collection of data does the accountant separate cost accounting and management accounting?

1-9 Computing Total Cost A professor is planning a trip. She expects to drive 1,500 miles and average 28 miles per gallon. The expected gasoline price is $2.00 per gallon.

The automobile to be used on the trip originally cost $9,100 and she expects to keep the car for nine years at which time she expects to have driven 108,000 miles. She estimated the salvage value nine years hence at $100. The automobile is presently four years old. At the start of the trip it has a market value of $3,100. At the end of the trip the market value remained $3,100.

The annual license fee for the automobile is $45. The insurance costs $240 per year. The professor has the car lubricated, the oil changed, and oil filter replaced every 6,000 miles at a cost of $12.60. The car engine was recently tuned at a cost of $40. The engine is tuned twice a year. The tires presently on the car cost $300 and have an estimated life of 40,000 miles. Other maintenance cost on the car runs about $120 annually.

On the trip, the professor actually drove 1,624 miles, including a side trip of 44 miles and a detour of 11 miles. The actual gasoline consumption was 56 gallons at a cost of $109.20.

She could have made the trip by airplane at a fare of $194. Taking the side trip by air would raise the air fare to $250. She decided that by taking the car she could bring her bicycle which she decided would be too much of a hassle on the airplane.

Required

1 Calculate the cost of the trip by air and by car.

2 Develop one other piece of cost information which you find interesting. Explain why you find it interesting.

1-10 Identifying Relevant Information Bearlights, Inc., operates a small factory in which two products, piece and gris, are produced. The production process employs a number of skilled workers operating general-purpose lathes, grinders, and similar machines. On January 1, company management expected the following results for 19X1:

	Piece	Gris	Total
Units produced	10,000	12,000	
Material cost	$30,000	$30,000	$ 60,000
Labor cost	$60,000	$48,000	$108,000
Other costs			$ 48,600

The average labor wage rate was expected to be $4 per hour.

By June 30, management felt that operations had generally proceeded according to plan. The following data had been collected by the accounting system for the period of January 1 to June 30:

	Piece	Gris	Total
Units produced	2,500	4,000	
Material cost	$ 7,500	$10,000	$17,500
Labor cost	$15,000	$16,000	$31,000
Other costs			$21,712

Required

Answer the following questions, treating each question as independent of the others.

1 Do you believe that the cost control has been effective so far in 19X1? (Show any computations you may have made in reaching your conclusion.)

2 A foreign retailer has offered to buy 3,000 units of piece at a price of $11. Factory capacity will permit the production of the extra units. Bearlights has never sold in foreign markets and does not plan to enter these markets in the foreseeable future. What is the relevant information for this decision? Should Bearlights sell the additional pieces?

3. Gris is a lower-quality product and at December 31, Bearlights management had decided to discontinue production of this product effective December 31. At December 31, there were 1,000 unsold units in inventory. What is the minimum sales price which Bearlights would be willing to accept for these units?

COST CLASSIFICATIONS AND FLOWS

AFTER COMPLETING YOUR STUDY OF THIS CHAPTER, YOU SHOULD HAVE LEARNED:

1 Why determining cost of goods sold for International Business Machines Inc., and other manufacturing firms differs from determining cost of goods sold for Macy's department store and other merchandising firms.

2 To apply the definition of direct materials, direct labor, and overhead costs. Why the salary of the person who sweeps the factory floor is part of manufacturing overhead cost and not direct labor cost.

3 How to get a mental picture of what is happening in the factory by looking at how the costs move through the cost accounting system.

4 How cost behavior differs from human behavior. (Cost behavior depends only on activity changes.)

5 Why a company like McGraw-Hill Book Company uses a "job order" cost accounting system while a company like Coca-Cola Bottling Company in Miami uses a "process" cost accounting system, and what the differences are between job order and process costing systems.

Note: As you may have guessed, in this chapter you will learn a lot of the vocabulary you will need to talk to and about cost accountants. Perhaps even enough to make people think you are one.

17
PRODUCT COSTS AND PERIOD COSTS

In Chapter 1, cost accounting was explained as the part of the cost accounting system which develops the cost data used in the inventory section of the balance sheet. We pointed out that if McGraw-Hill had 8,000 copies of this book in inventory at the end of the year, generally accepted accounting principles require that the book be reported in inventory at its historical cost. As you will see later in this chapter, when each book is sold, the inventory account must be reduced by the cost of the book and the cost of goods sold account must be increased by the cost of the book.

Chapter 1 also illustrated how managerial accounting provides data to answer such questions as whether it is more profitable to install pollution control equipment or to replace an entire plant, and whether a new master's degree program will cost more to offer than it can generate in tuition. (No relation between pollution and a master's degree is implied.) Some of the concepts of this chapter, particularly the cost behavior definitions, will also apply to managerial accounting, but the main focus of this and the next several chapters is cost accounting.

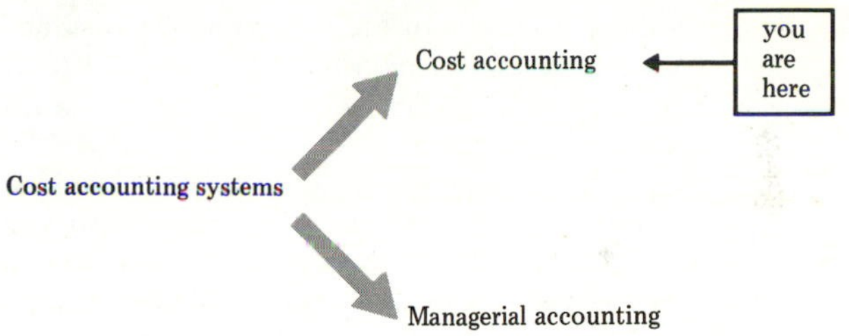

This chapter is also full of definitions which will be used throughout the book and in your business life. Some people find learning a foreign language is fun, others don't. But whether fun or not, if you are going to communicate, you need to know the language. You will have a much better grip on the language after you study this chapter.

Definition of cost.

Let us start at the beginning. In Chapter 1 we defined the term **cost** as the total resources consumed to accomplish a specific objective. Perhaps we have to start before the beginning to note that the specific objective to be accomplished might be the production of a product, the acquisition of a service, the measurement of net income, or any other objective. Depending on the objective to be accomplished there are different ways of classifying costs.

This chapter will concentrate on only the most basic cost classifications needed at this juncture of your study of cost and managerial accounting. As we progress through our presentation of cost accounting, we will introduce other classifications of costs.

PRODUCT COSTS AND PERIOD COSTS

Unexpired costs are assets and appear on the balance sheet.

Expired costs are expenses and appear on the income statement.

The accumulation of data for the preparation of balance sheets and income statements is a major objective of cost accounting. To accomplish this objective you will need to know the difference between unexpired costs and expired costs. Unexpired costs are assets that can be associated with revenues of future time periods. Since unexpired costs are assets, they will appear in the balance sheet. They include items such as the cost of unsold inventory and prepaid insurance or rent. Expired costs, on the other hand, are expenses that are deducted from revenues to compute net income. They include cost of goods sold expense and selling and administrative expense.

How do we determine whether a cost is unexpired or expired? To answer this question we need an additional classification of costs: period costs and product costs.

Definition of period costs.

Definition of product costs.

Period costs are those costs that can be associated with a particular accounting period rather than with the products delivered to the customers. **Product costs** are the costs of inventory purchased for resale or manufactured for sale. They remain an asset (inventory) until the unit of inventory is sold; then they become cost of goods sold expense.

Examples of period cost.

Period costs include the wide variety of selling and administrative costs needed to keep the business operating. Most period costs are necessary to generate revenue but they cannot be directly associated with particular sales units. For example, the rental of a store is certainly a way of selling products, but the rent is generally a specific sum each month. Suppose the rent of a store is $1,000 per month. The $1,000 of rent will have to be paid each month independent of the amount of sales activity. There is no such thing as a unit of rent which can be associated with a particular sale. It is important to have a president to do planning for the organization, but the salary of the president can rarely be associated with the sale of a particular product. The accountant's approach to income determination is to place the rent and salary cost in the month it is consumed (expired). Thus, these costs are deducted from revenues in the period the resources are consumed. Hence, the name period costs.

Any unexpired period costs are classified on the balance sheet as prepaid or deferred costs. For example assume a company buys a two-year fire insurance policy on January 1, 19X1 for a cost of $2,000. At the end of 19X1, $1,000 of the cost has expired and would be deducted from the revenues in calculating 19X1 net income. The other $1,000 of the cost covers the year 19X2 and would be an unexpired cost. The unexpired cost would appear on the December 31, 19X1 balance sheet as prepaid fire insurance.

Product costs, in contrast, are associated with the inventory which is sold to the firm's customers. Since product costs are assigned to inventory units they are sometimes referred to as "inventoriable" costs. These costs are held as assets on the balance sheet (inventory) until the units of product are sold. Then the product costs are transferred to cost of goods sold expense and deducted from the revenue generated by the sale of the product.

A product cost illustration.

To illustrate the accounting for product costs, assume on June 1 a company is started with a $10 investment by the owner. During June the company pays cash to purchase 2 units of inventory for $3 each. During the month of July one of those units is sold for $5 cash. To keep the example simple, assume that no other activity occurs in these two months and that there will be no expenses other than cost of goods sold. During June an exchange of $6 of one asset (cash) was made for $6 worth of another asset (inventory). There were no sales or expenses during the month of June. During July there is revenue of $5 resulting from the sale of 1 unit of inventory. This requires that the inventory be reduced by the cost of 1 unit and that cost of goods sold expense be increased by the corresponding amount. The income statement for July shows net income of $2, the difference between the $5 of sales revenue and the $3 cost of goods sold expense. This can be illustrated as follows:

Balance Sheets

	June 1	June 30	July 31
Cash	$10	$ 4	$ 9
Inventory		6	3
Total assets	$10	$10	$12
Total equities	$10	$10	$12

Income Statements

	June	July
Revenue	$0	$5
Cost of goods sold expense	0	3
Net income	$0	$2

It would have been incorrect to record the cost of the inventory purchased in June as an expense in June. Since there had been no sales so far, there are no expenses to be matched to the revenue. In July, it would have been incorrect to not record any expense, because 1 unit of inventory was transferred to the customers for the $5 cash. It would have been equally incorrect to record the cost of both units of inventory as expense, because the benefit of only 1 unit of inventory has expired. The benefit of the second unit will not expire until that unit is sold in some later month.

The process of associating product costs with the sale of product and period costs with the accounting period in which they expire is called matching of expenses and revenues.

This process of income determination by associating product costs with the sale of the product and period costs with the accounting period in which they expire is called the *matching* of revenues and expenses. Matching means that expenses of earning revenues are reported in the same period in which those revenues are reported.

To summarize the classifications you have learned in this section, we have developed the following diagram:

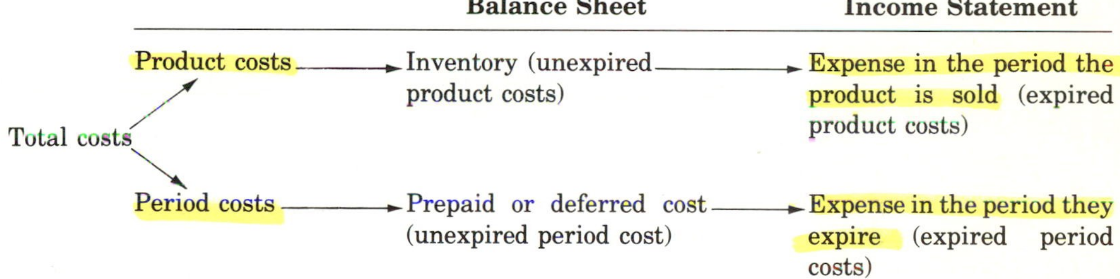

In the next two sections we will distinguish between product costs in merchandising companies and manufacturing companies.

Product Costs in a Merchandising Company

Merchandising companies, such as department stores, grocery stores, or drug stores, purchase merchandise to sell to their customers. The purchase price of the merchandise is a product cost. The purchase price is recorded as an asset (unexpired cost) in the balance sheet at the time of purchase. When the revenue from the sale of the product is reported in the income statement, the cost of the product (expired cost) is removed from the balance sheet and reported in the income statement.

Exhibit 2-1 shows an income statement for a merchandising company. The product costs are used to calculate cost of goods sold. The objective in calculating cost of goods sold is to match the cost of the inventory with the sales revenue in the income statement. The difference between the sales revenues and cost of goods sold is the *gross margin*. The gross margin is the excess of sales revenues over the cost of the products sold. Next, the selling and administrative expenses are deducted

Gross margin defined.

EXHIBIT 2-1
STEINWAY MERCHANDISING COMPANY
Income Statement
For the Year Ended December 31, 19X1

	Sales revenues		$1,230,000
PRODUCT COSTS	Merchandise inventory January 1, 19X1	$120,000	
	Purchases of inventory	650,000	
	Total goods available for sale	$720,000	
	Merchandise inventory December 31, 19X1	150,000	
	Cost of goods sold*		570,000
	Gross margin		$ 660,000
	Selling and administrative expenses		
PERIOD COSTS	Salaries	$ 80,000	
	Sales commissions	90,000	
	Rent	80,000	
	Advertising	70,000	
	Utilities	35,000	
	Supplies	15,000	
	Insurance	10,000	
	Total selling and administrative expenses		$ 380,000
	Net income		$ 280,000

* Technically this should be labeled cost of goods sold expense since it represents an expired cost; however given the wide use of the term cost of goods sold we will use it to mean the expense associated with the goods that have been sold.

from the gross margin to obtain the net income for the year. The selling and administrative expenses are *expired* period costs. These expenses represent resources consumed in operating the business during 19X1. Since the resources were consumed during 19X1, they are included in calculating 19X1 net income.

To summarize, product costs in a merchandising company consist of the purchases of inventory for resale to its customers. All selling and administrative costs are classified as period costs. These basic ideas are illustrated below:

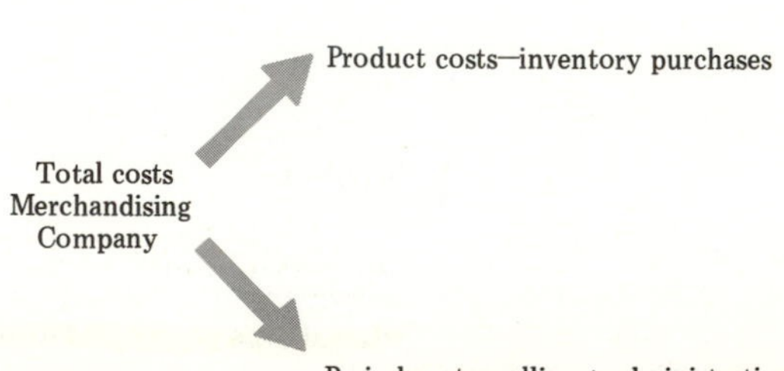

Product Costs in a Manufacturing Company

Product costs in a manufacturing company include all costs necessary for the manufacture of the product.

Manufacturing companies, such as International Business Machines and General Motors, must also deal with product costs. However, product costs are more difficult to deal with in a manufacturing company than a merchandising company. In a manufacturing company materials and other resources are purchased and converted into finished products through the manufacturing process. *Product costs* in a manufacturing company include *all costs necessary for the manufacture of the product.* These costs are recorded as assets until the product is sold and the revenue from the sale of the product is reported in the income statement. Then the product costs are transferred to cost of goods sold for the calculation of net income.

To illustrate, suppose that during September some materials are purchased to produce a batch of product. The product is actually manufactured in October and sold in November. The cost of materials is recorded as an asset (materials inventory) at the end of September. In October, other manufacturing costs are incurred—labor, electricity, and supplies—to manufacture the completed product. These costs are also recorded as assets. At the end of October, no sales of this product have been made. The product costs, now including material, labor, electricity and supplies, are still recorded as an asset on the balance sheet (now finished goods inventory). In November, the products are sold and then all the costs associated with these products are removed from the finished goods inventory account and transferred to cost of goods sold. The important point to understand is that product costs do not reach the income statement until the products are sold, which may be several months after

EXHIBIT 2-2
MICRO-TOOL MANUFACTURING COMPANY
Income Statement
For the Month Ended January 31, 19X9

	Sales revenues		$140,000
PRODUCT COSTS	Beginning finished goods January 1, 19X9	$14,000	
	Cost of goods manufactured	52,000	
	Total goods available for sale	$66,000	
	Ending finished goods January 31,19X9	6,000	
	Cost of goods sold		60,000
	Gross margin		$ 80,000
	Selling and administrative expenses		
PERIOD COSTS	Salaries	$ 8,000	
	Sales commissions	15,000	
	Rent	5,000	
	Advertising	10,000	
	Utilities	6,000	
	Supplies	3,000	
	Insurance	8,000	
	Total selling and administrative expenses		55,000
	Net income		$ 25,000

The only difference between the income statement of a merchandising company and a manufacturing company is in the product cost section of the statement.

the costs are incurred. However, period costs go directly to the income statement in the month when they expire.

Exhibit 2-2 is an income statement for the Micro-Tool Manufacturing Company. On the surface it appears very similar to the income statement for the Steinway Merchandising Company (Exhibit 2-1). In fact, the only difference is in the section on product costs. The section on period costs is exactly the same in both statements. The section on product costs differs since a manufacturing company acquires materials and other resources and converts them into a salable product. You might think that finished goods inventory is a new account, but it is not. Merchandising companies have inventories of finished product ready to sell to their customers. But they simply call it merchandise inventory. They have only one kind of inventory so they do not need to call it finished goods inventory to distinguish it from materials inventory. But it is the same thing. The cost of goods manufactured is similar to purchases for a merchandising company. "Purchases" in a merchandising company represents the cost of the goods *bought* for sale to customers. The cost of goods manufactured in a manufacturing company represents the cost of the goods *produced* for sale to customers. How do we determine the cost of goods manufactured? Basically by knowing what costs are product costs in a manufacturing company and by understanding the flow of costs through the accounts. As defined previously product costs in a manufacturing company include all costs necessary for the manufacture of the product. These costs are classified in several different ways. The next section discusses the various classifications of manufacturing product costs. The flow of costs through the accounts will be discussed later in the chapter.

Classifying Manufacturing Product Costs

Costs are classified different ways for different purposes.

We have discussed several examples of product costs. Because there is a wide variety of product costs it is often useful to classify them in various ways. This section of the chapter will note several ways of classifying product costs. Remember that the classifications overlap and are not mutually exclusive. The usefulness of these classifications may not be clear right now, but as we use the categories later in this chapter and later in the book, you will see their usefulness.

The first classification of product costs we will consider is (1) direct material (2) direct labor, and (3) manufacturing overhead.

Direct Materials, Direct Labor, and Manufacturing Overhead **Direct materials cost** refers to the cost of all the *important* materials used in the production of the product. Since they are used in the production of the product, they are physically traceable to the product. You can go into the factory and see the direct materials going into the product. Examples of direct materials are the cloth used in the manufacture of a suit (but not the thread–it is not important enough), the sheet steel used in the manufacture of an automobile (but not the bolts), or the wood used in the production of a golf club (but not the screws). Clearly the thread, bolts, and screws are used in the manufacture of these products. In theory, they should also be treated as direct materials. But the cost of these items is small, relative to the important direct materials. Further, record keeping would be considerably more expensive if it was necessary to trace each bolt to each automobile produced, or to measure the amount of thread used in each suit. While theoretically these could be considered direct materials, their low cost means that there would be very little benefit in accounting for them as direct materials and the cost of such accounting would be very high. They are classified as manufacturing overhead. As a practical matter, the definition of direct materials is restricted to the important materials.

Important in this context means costly enough to justify the expense of accounting for it as direct material.

Direct labor costs refer to the cost of all *important* labor performed on the product itself. Direct labor is physically traceable to the product in the sense that you can go into the factory and see direct labor being performed on a particular unit or batch of product. Examples of direct labor are the work of people who operate the sewing machine used in manufacturing a suit (but not the persons who sweep the floor of the sewing room), the work of people who weld the body of the automobile together (but not the people who bring the welding supplies to the welder), or the work of the person who cuts the wood for the golf club (but not the person who keeps the time records in the factory). Again in theory, very detailed record keeping would permit more labor cost being classified as direct. For example, the wages of the person bringing the welding supplies to the car could be classified as direct labor cost if the company wanted to ask the person to record how much time was spent in taking welding supplies to each automobile. But again the cost of making this kind of refinement in the cost accounting system would be very high and undoubtedly higher than any potential benefit.

It would be possible to classify more costs as direct labor cost, but the added expense of the accounting is not worth it.

To see if you are keeping track of where we are, let us ask you a slightly tricky question. Is the sales commission paid to the sales representative who sells the automobile a direct labor cost? The answer is no. Certainly the sales commission is easily traced to a particular car sold. But direct labor cost is a subdivision of product cost and sales commission is not a product cost: it is a __ __ __ __ __ __ cost.

Manufacturing overhead refers to all costs necessary for the production of a product *except* direct materials cost and direct labor cost. A more mechanical definition is:

manufacturing overhead = total product costs
− direct materials costs − direct labor costs.

Examples of manufacturing overhead include all the materials and labor cost previously mentioned which were too small to be counted as direct materials or direct labor. The materials and labor costs included as part of manufacturing overhead are called *indirect* materials costs and *indirect* labor costs. In addition, the costs of depreciation of plant and its equipment, factory maintenance costs, property taxes on the factory and machinery, factory insurance, and utilities are all examples. Their primary characteristic is that they cannot be physically traced to particular units of finished product but were incurred in the manufacture of the product. These manufacturing overhead costs are sometimes referred to as *indirect* manufacturing costs.

Let us summarize the classifications of the total costs for a manufacturing company we have made so far. They are probably the most important ones we will make. The diagram will be the summary.

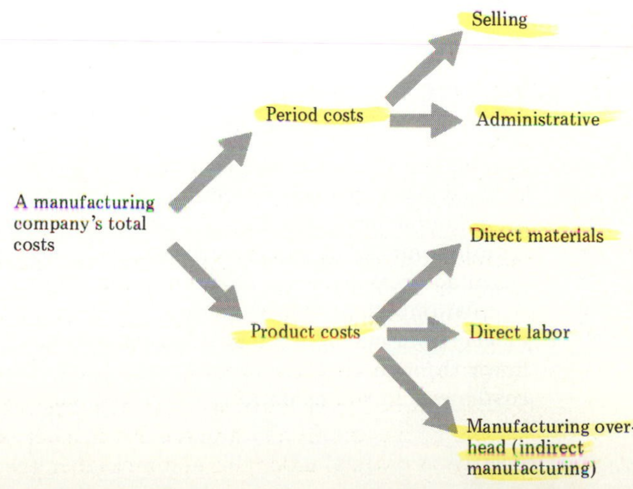

To identify prime cost you must be able to identify direct materials and direct labor.

Prime Costs and Conversion Costs This section introduces two additional cost classifications. The first, prime costs, is mainly of historical interest, although the term is sometimes used today. **Prime costs** are the sum of the direct materials cost and the direct labor cost. When cost accounting first developed, it concentrated on direct materials and direct labor costs, because of their physical traceability. The accounting for these categories of product costs is fairly simple as you will see in Chapter 4. It was much later that techniques of accounting for manufacturing overhead costs were developed. During this time, only direct materials and direct labor were accounted for as product costs. Manufacturing overhead was accounted for as a period cost. The word "prime" is probably derived from the idea of being first.

To identify conversion costs you must be able to identify direct labor cost and manufacturing overhead cost.

The second definition, for conversion costs, is quite frequently used today. **Conversion costs** are the sum of the direct labor cost and the manufacturing overhead cost. At first it might strike you as strange that direct labor and manufacturing overhead would be lumped together in this definition, because we have emphasized that direct labor cost is physically traceable to products, whereas manufacturing overhead cost provides general benefits to manufacturing but is *not* physically traceable to products. But you will see in Chapter 3 that there is an important reason why direct labor cost and manufacturing overhead cost are associated under the heading of conversion costs. The word "conversion" is used because direct labor and manufacturing overhead are the costs of *converting* direct materials to finished products.

These two classifications can be illustrated as follows:

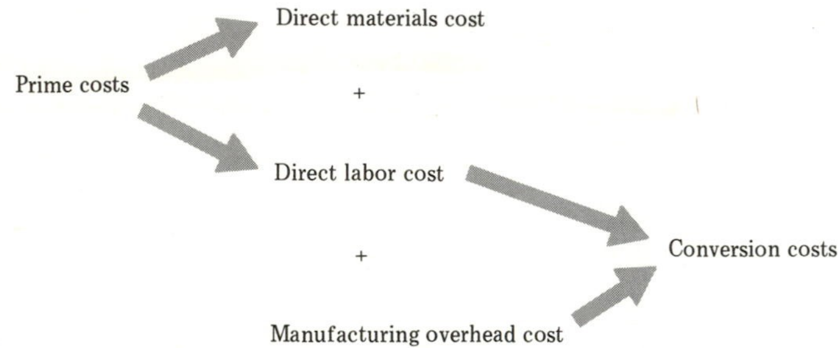

Never add prime costs to conversion costs.

Notice that the two classifications overlap. It would never be sensible to add prime costs to conversion costs, because you would be double counting direct labor cost.

Now that we have defined product costs for a manufacturing company, how do we determine the cost of goods manufactured? The cost of goods manufactured is determined by tracing the flow of manufacturing product costs through the accounts.

FLOW OF COSTS THROUGH THE ACCOUNTS

Manufacturers need the set of accounts illustrated in Exhibit 2-3 to account for product costs while merchandisers need only the finished goods account.

Exhibit 2-3 illustrates the flow of costs through the manufacturing accounts to the finished goods inventory account and on to the cost of goods sold account. What are the manufacturing accounts? They are the accounts which record the product costs. Retailers and wholesalers need only be concerned with one inventory account. All manufacturers use a set of accounts like those shown in Exhibit 2-3.

An important feature to notice is that the costs flow through the accounts (are moved from one account to the next) in the same sequence as the actual product flows through the factory and out of the company when the product is sold to customers. Before examining the flow of costs more carefully, note that a manufac-

EXHIBIT 2-3
Manufacturing Cost Flow through the Balance Sheet and Income Statement

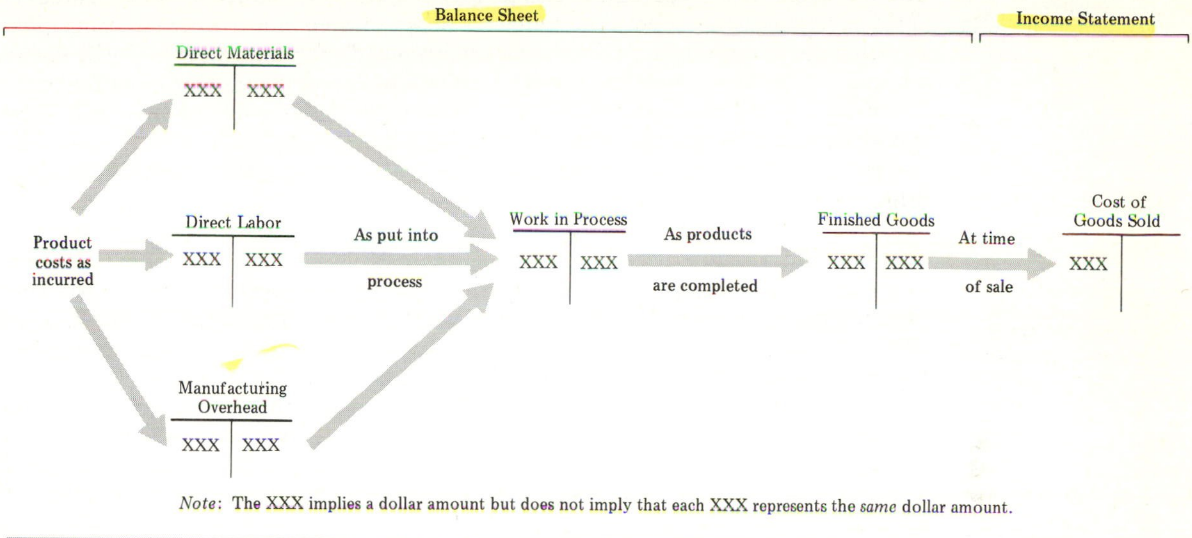

Note: The XXX implies a dollar amount but does not imply that each XXX represents the *same* dollar amount.

A manufacturer has two types of inventory accounts which a merchandiser does not have.

turer has two inventory accounts on its balance sheet which do not appear on the balance sheet of a retailer or wholesaler. They are direct materials inventory and work in process inventory. We have earlier defined direct materials, so you can see that a direct materials inventory account simply records the amount of direct materials (unprocessed materials) which happen to be on hand at the balance sheet date. The work in process inventory account records the costs assigned to units of product which are started but not completed at the balance sheet date. The finished goods account represents the cost of the goods that are ready for shipment to the customers. As noted earlier in this chapter, this account is similar to the merchandise inventory account of a merchandising firm.

Now back to the flow of costs through the manufacturing accounts. The starting point is when direct materials are purchased and placed in the direct materials storeroom. As direct materials are placed in the storeroom, their cost is added to the direct materials inventory account. As direct labor costs and manufacturing overhead costs are used, they are recorded in the appropriate accounts. It would be possible to add direct labor costs and manufacturing overhead costs directly to the work in process inventory account, but then some detail might be lost which would later be wanted for analysis of operations. As direct materials are taken from the direct materials storeroom to the production area, the direct materials inventory account is reduced and the work in process account is increased. Direct labor costs and manufacturing overhead costs are recorded in their original accounts, and are moved to the work in process account as the labor and manufacturing overhead items are used to produce the products. As products are completed, they are moved from the production area to a finished goods warehouse. The accountant responds by taking the cost of completed units out of the work in process account and adding the cost to the finished goods inventory account. Finally, as the products are shipped to customers, the cost of the goods sold is transferred from the finished goods account to the cost of goods sold account.

Statement of Cost of Goods Manufactured and Sold

The statement of cost of goods manufactured and sold describes the activity in the manufacturing accounts.

As you know from your earlier study of financial accounting, income statements and balance sheets are prepared by listing the balances in the accounts in a customary fashion. The fact that a manufacturer has additional manufacturing accounts gives rise to a new statement which is used to show how the cost of goods sold is calculated. This new statement is called a statement of cost of goods manufactured and sold. It simply reports the activity which took place in the accounts shown in Exhibit 2-3. A sample statement is shown in Exhibit 2-4.

To the left side of the exhibit have been added some notes explaining how the statement relates to the accounts. If you compare the statement, you see that as it moves from top to bottom it generally follows the flow of costs through the accounts from left to right as in Exhibit 2-3.

To understand the statement of cost of goods manufactured and sold, go with the flow.

At the start of Exhibit 2-4 is the beginning work in process inventory of $15,000. Direct materials used, direct labor incurred, and manufacturing overhead were added to the beginning work in process and will be shown on the statement. But first, the amount of direct materials used must be calculated.

Direct materials purchases of $17,000 are added to a beginning inventory of direct materials of $9,000. The resulting $26,000 is the total direct materials available to be used during the period. But since there was an ending inventory of $11,000, only $15,000 of direct materials were used in production during the month. Also direct labor cost of $20,000 was incurred during the month. To this is added the manufacturing overhead which totals $10,000. Finally, the ending work in process inventory is subtracted, leaving the cost of goods manufactured, the cost of goods completed during the month.

The final section of the statement calculates the cost of goods sold for reporting on the income statement. This section of the statement is really an analysis of the activity in the finished goods inventory account. It starts with the beginning inventory of finished goods which was $14,000. To this is added the cost of goods manufactured of $52,000 calculated in the upper part of the statement. In other words, $52,000 worth of products were completed during the month and this amount of cost was therefore transferred out of the work in process account and added to the finished goods account. The beginning inventory of finished goods plus the cost of goods manufactured provided a total of $66,000 of finished goods which might have been sold during the month. However, since the ending inventory of finished goods was $6,000, the cost of the goods which were sold must have been only $60,000. As noted earlier, the $60,000 cost of the goods which were sold will be reported as cost of goods sold expense on the income statement in the usual manner.

Total Costs and Unit Costs

Unit costs are used extensively to determine the amount of manufacturing product costs that should be assigned to cost of goods sold (expired product costs) and the amount that should be assigned to the ending inventory (unexpired product costs). For example, assume the following:

Total cost of goods manufactured	$100,000
Total units completed	20,000
Unit cost ($100,000 ÷ 20,000)	$5.00

EXHIBIT 2-4
ILLUSTRATION OF A COST OF GOODS MANUFACTURED AND SOLD STATEMENT
MICRO-TOOL MANUFACTURING COMPANY
Statement of Cost of Goods Manufactured and Sold
For the Month Ended January 31, 19X9

Analysis of the work in process account	Work in process—January 1, 19X9		$15,000
Analysis of direct materials account	Direct materials inventory January 1, 19X9	$ 9,000	
	Plus: Direct materials purchases	17,000	
	Cost of direct materials available	$26,000	
	Less: Direct materials inventory January 31, 19X9	11,000	
	Cost of direct materials used in production		15,000
	Direct labor		20,000
	Manufacturing overhead		
	Factory utilities	$ 3,000	
	Factory supervision	2,500	
	Property taxes on factory equipment	$ 500	
	Factory maintenance and repairs	2,000	
	Depreciation of plant and equipment	2,000	10,000
	Total		$60,000
	Less: Work in process—January 31, 19X9		8,000
	Cost of goods manufactured		$52,000
Analysis of finished goods account	Finished goods—January 1, 19X9		$14,000
	Plus: Cost of goods manufactured		52,000
	Total		$66,000
	Less: Finished goods— January 31, 19X9		6,000
	Cost of goods sold		$60,000

Unit costs are just costs per unit which are useful in accounting for inventories and cost of goods sold.

Assume further that 15,000 units are sold and that 5,000 units are in the ending finished goods inventory. The unit cost can be used to calculate the amount of the $100,000 total cost that should be assigned to cost of goods sold and the ending finished goods inventory as follows:

Cost of goods sold 15,000 units × $5.00 =	$ 75,000
Ending finished goods inventory 5,000 units × $5.00 =	25,000
	$100,000

In the next section you see how the unit cost and total cost change when the production volume changes.

COST BEHAVIOR

Cost behavior refers to how costs change (or do not change) as volume changes.

In addition to the classification of cost already discussed in this chapter, costs can be classified according to how they change (or do not change) when the volume of activity changes. This classification is generally referred to as classifying costs according to their cost behavior. Let us provide two basic definitions and then we can carry this discussion further. **Variable costs** are costs for which the total amount of cost changes in direct proportion to changes in volume of activity. Another way to state the definition which is exactly equivalent is to say that a variable cost is one where the *per unit* cost remains constant as volume changes. **Fixed costs** are costs for which the total amount is *independent of* changes in volume of activity. Independence means that the changes in the volume of activity do not change the total amount of a fixed cost. Total fixed costs may and do change, but as a result of other changes, not volume changes.

Some product costs are fixed and some are variable. The same is true of period costs.

These classifications are independent of the classifications discussed earlier in the chapter. Some product costs are fixed, and some are variable. For example, property taxes, depreciation, insurance, and heating costs are usually classified as fixed costs. They are also classified as manufacturing overhead. Direct materials cost, direct labor cost, and electricity used to run machinery are usually classified as variable costs. They are also classified as product costs. Some period costs are variable and some are fixed. For example, sales commissions are usually variable and the salary of the president is usually fixed.

Knowing the amount of variable and fixed costs helps to estimate future costs.

If these classifications overlap the old ones, why do we need them? For a very important reason. They help us estimate future costs. Consider the situation where you want to estimate the cost of keeping your automobile for another year. If you keep it, you will drive 12,000 miles during the year. Last year when you drove 8,000 miles, you incurred the following costs.

Cost of Driving an Automobile 8,000 Miles during 19X8

Depreciation	$2,000
Insurance	350
License	50
Maintenance done every three months (4 × $30)	120
Maintenance done every 4,000 miles (2 × $40)	80
Gasoline	600
Total	$3,200

What is fixed and what is variable?

You estimate that the first three items are fixed expenses. It is true that if you drove an extraordinary number of miles your depreciation and insurance might increase, but for the normal mileages you drive, they are fixed, they will not change with the amount of miles driven. You have talked to a car dealer about how much your car will depreciate in value next year and have received an estimate of $1,500. You think that your insurance might go up a bit, but that your license will probably go down by about the same amount because the car is older. You expect maintenance costs to remain about the same for next year, but that there may be a 20% increase in the cost of gasoline. Your miles per gallon should stay about the same, because you maintain your car carefully. You did not have to spend anything on tires last year, but you expect that you will probably have to replace all four next year at a cost of $300. You decide that the variable expenses are the last two items. Variable maintenance was 1 cent per mile ($80/8,000 miles) and gasoline was 7½ cents per mile ($600/8,000 miles). If gasoline increases 20%, it will be 9 cents per mile (7½ cents × 1.20). With this information you are ready to estimate your cost for next year.

Estimated Automobile Costs, 12,000 Miles during 19X9

Depreciation (from dealer estimate)	$1,500
Insurance and license (same total as last year)	400
Maintenance done every three months (same as last year)	120
Maintenance done every 4,000 miles (12,000 miles × 1 cent)	120
Gasoline (12,000 miles × 9 cents)	1,080
Tires (per estimate)	300
Total	$3,520

The total estimated cost of operating your car next year has increased, partly because of increased estimated mileage, and partly because of changes in prices of both fixed and variable items. It would have been very difficult to estimate next year's cost without applying the ideas of fixed and variable cost. Perhaps the whole estimating process seemed to you like just plain common sense. If so, great. The things that a cost accountant does should make sense. But as the problems become more complex, it is necessary to have an organized way of approaching them.

Estimated future costs will provide the basis for determining manufacturing overhead rates which will be discussed in Chapter 3. In later chapters, we will illustrate the use of cost-volume analysis in planning and control of operations.

Accountants generally assume that a graph of a total cost will follow a straight line.

One assumption made by accountants in classifying costs is that their behavior with respect to volume is linear rather than nonlinear. This assumption makes the arithmetic of analyzing and estimating costs considerably easier. It permits graphs of costs to be drawn using straight lines. This simplifying assumption generally results, in practice, in reasonably accurate estimates of future costs.

Variable Costs

Direct materials cost and direct labor cost are usually variable costs because a constant amount is required per unit of product.

Direct materials cost and direct labor cost are two costs which are generally variable costs. Exhibit 2-5 shows how direct labor cost, for example, varies as production output varies. Notice that the cost of direct labor is $2 *per unit* for each unit produced and that this labor cost per unit is constant no matter how many units are produced. Of course, this means that total direct labor costs increase in direct proportion to increases in units produced. Exhibit 2-5 illustrates these points. Note that it is the total variable costs that change as more units are produced: the per unit variable cost remains constant. This is illustrated below:

Number of Units Produced	Direct Labor Cost per Unit	Total Direct Labor Cost
1,000	$2.00	$2,000
2,000	$2.00	$4,000
3,000	$2.00	$6,000

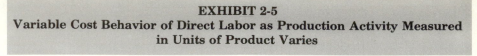

EXHIBIT 2-5
Variable Cost Behavior of Direct Labor as Production Activity Measured in Units of Product Varies

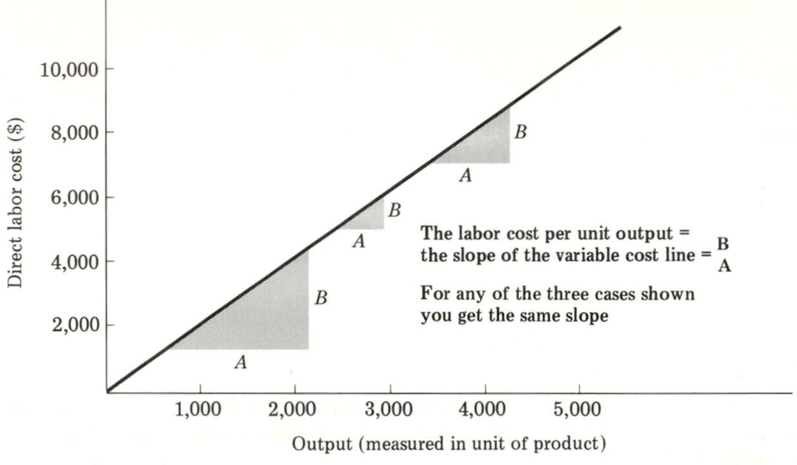

Fixed Costs

Costs, such as insurance, depreciation, and property taxes, are fixed costs for a given level of capacity, and, in fact, for a range of capacity. The range of capacity over which management does not expect the cost to change is called the **relevant range.** It is true that if a firm somehow overnight tripled its plant, machinery, etc., these costs would rise. But, first, a firm cannot do this very easily: it takes planning and time to build the new plant and get it ready for production. Second, the planning that went into the plant would include estimating what the new fixed costs would be at the new level of capacity. No one would try to use the existing level of fixed costs to estimate the fixed costs of a significantly expanded plant.

Suppose that a plant can produce a maximum of 25,000 video cassettes per month. The insurance is $Z per year, the property taxes are $Y per year, and the depreciation is $X per year. These are fixed and do not change whether the firm produces 10,000 video cassettes per month or 25,000 cassettes per month. Now suppose that everyone seems to be able to afford to buy home video recorders and the sales of video cassette recorders increase sharply. Company management senses a demand for as many as 50,000 video cassettes per month. They cannot produce them in the existing plant, but decide to build another much larger (and more efficient) plant. Their plans show that a plant with three times the capacity will incur insurance cost of $2Z, property taxes of $2Y per year, and depreciation of $2X per year. After the new plant is built, these costs will still be fixed, but at a new higher level. This change does not make these costs variable costs.

Exhibit 2-6 illustrates the fixed depreciation costs of the original plant assuming that $x = \$70{,}000$. Fixed costs are constant in total, regardless of the production volume. However the production volume can influence the fixed cost per unit. For example, consider the video cassettes in the following table.

Number of Video Cassettes Produced	Total Fixed Cost	Fixed Cost per Unit
10,000	$70,000	$7.00
15,000	$70,000	$4.67
20,000	$70,000	$3.50

Fixed costs per unit change as volume changes and are therefore not useful in estimating future fixed costs.

If 10,000 video cassettes are produced the fixed cost per unit is $7 but if 20,000 video cassettes are produced the fixed cost per unit becomes $3.50. This variation in unit costs presents problems for the cost accountant which will be discussed in Chapter 3. It also has the potential for confusing the manager. It is better for estimating future fixed costs to concentrate only on total fixed costs rather than fixed costs per unit.

Mixed Costs

Mixed costs combine a fixed and a variable cost component.

In practice, many costs are impossible to classify as strictly fixed or variable because they are a combination of both. These costs are referred to as **mixed costs.** An example of a mixed cost would be the earnings of a sales representative who is compensated with a fixed annual salary plus a sales commission of a specified percentage of the sales dollars generated. Exhibit 2-7 illustrates a mixed cost with a fixed cost component of $6,000 and a variable cost of 10% of each sales dollar generated. How was the graph in Exhibit 2-7 drawn? From the compensation agreement, we knew the basic facts. Further, since accountants normally assume that costs behave in a straight-line fashion, if we can find any two points on the line, we can draw the straight line between them. It really does not make any difference which two points are chosen. They should all give the same result.

Before we get too far on the graph, it is a good idea to make a rough estimate of the scale of the graph. Starting with the activity axis, we would like someone to tell us how much in sales this sales representative is likely to make in a year.

EXHIBIT 2-6
Fixed Depreciation Cost of a Manufacturing Plant

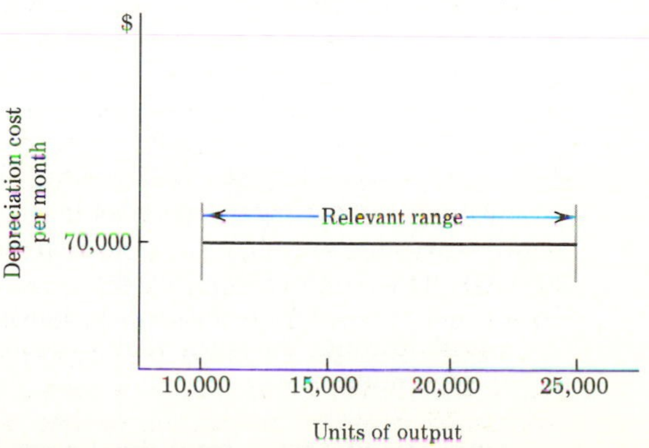

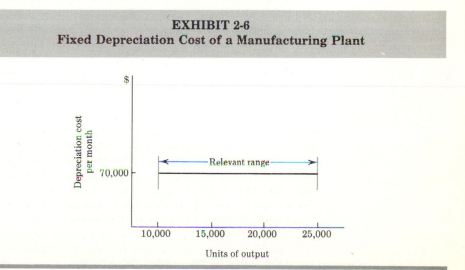

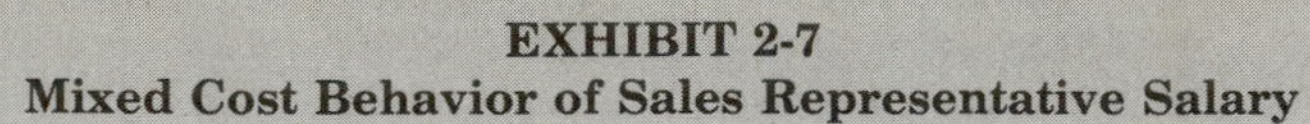

EXHIBIT 2-7
Mixed Cost Behavior of Sales Representative Salary

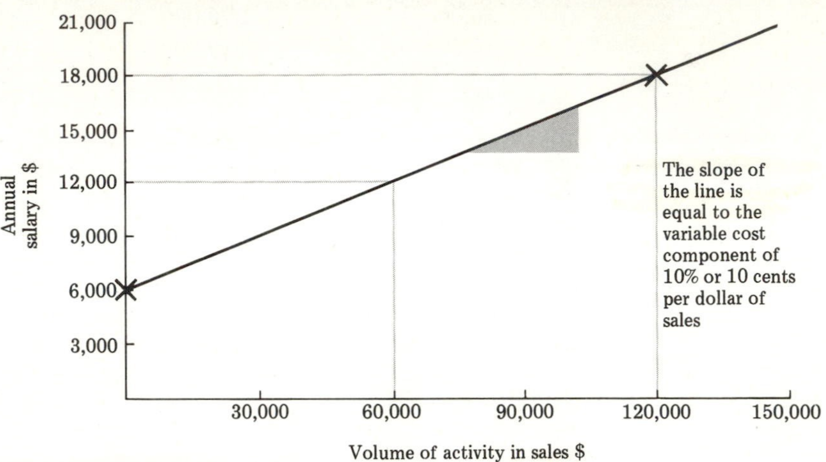

Suppose that someone tells us that $150,000 is the likely maximum. The minimum, of course, is zero. That tells us what must be on the horizontal axis to represent the salesperson's output. The vertical axis will show the total salary of the sales representative. In this case, the sales representative gets a minimum salary of $500 per month or $6,000 per year even if nothing is sold. We could make our minimum $6,000, but it is customary to have the vertical axis start at zero as well as to have the horizontal axis start at zero.

While we can pick any two points, one point is easier than the rest. It is the point where volume of output (sales) is zero. We just said that the sales representative will earn $6,000 salary. We then pick another point, but one which will be easy to plot (why not?). Let us take $120,000. The question is: What will the sales representative earn if sales of $120,000 are achieved during the year? It will be the $6,000 base salary plus 10% of the sales achieved (10% × $120,000) or $6,000 + $12,000 = $18,000. The second point on the line is therefore $120,000 sales, $18,000 salary. Putting these two points on our graph (shown by "X" on Exhibit 2-7) we draw a straight line between them. We can then use this straight line to estimate salary at any other sales volume between zero and $150,000.

Using the cost behavior graph to estimate the sales representative's annual earnings.

To illustrate how it would work, let us pick another point to estimate total salary of the sales representative. Again, let us pick a relatively easy one to read on the graph. Suppose we wonder what the salary would be if the sales representative sold a total of $60,000 during the year. We draw a vertical line from $60,000 sales up to our estimating line. From that point, we draw a horizontal line until it hits the vertical axis. It hits at $12,000, which is the estimated annual salary.

Just one further point before we leave this illustration. The whole concept can be expressed algebraically, which is often easier than drawing lines on a graph (and probably more accurate too). Remember how we located the two points used to draw the estimating line. We took the fixed expense which we knew to be $6,000 per year and added 10 cents times the dollar amount of sales. We can express this in the algebraic formula below.

Expressing the cost behavior algebraically.

Total mixed cost = total fixed cost
+ (variable cost per unit × units of activity)

Those of you who have had an algebra course within recent memory may recognize this as the familiar equation of a straight line, $Y = a + bX$, with a, the vertical intercept, and b, the slope of the line. Nevertheless, let us see how it works. Let us try the sales volume of $60,000, as we did just a few minutes ago, graphically

$$\textbf{Total mixed cost} = \$6{,}000 + (10 \text{ cents} \times \$60{,}000)$$
$$= \$6{,}000 + \$6{,}000 = \underline{\underline{\$12{,}000}}$$

Using the algebraic expression of cost behavior to estimate the sales representative's annual earnings.

and *voilá!*, the same result we got graphically. Check out the formula with the $120,000 volume level we used in plotting the graph. You know that the answer should be $18,000. In fact, you can try as many points as you need to be comfortable with the formula, because you can get a check answer by reading the graph.

As a final check on how well this is sinking in, consider the two graphs shown in Exhibit 2-8. Each represents a different plan for compensating sales representatives. Both are like the plan discussed earlier in that they are a combination of a flat salary and a sales commission. There are purposely no dollar amounts shown on the two graphs so that you have to do this by thinking about the problem rather than making calculations. You do know that both graphs are drawn to the same scale. Now the question: Which compensation plan would be preferred by a good sales representative?

The choice really does depend on how good the sales representative is, because plan B produces higher total compensation if sales volume is high. Therefore, the better sales representative would likely prefer plan B. As a final note: Which plan has the highest fixed cost component? Which pays a higher percentage sales commission?

Separating the Fixed and Variable Cost Components of a Mixed Cost To get a better idea of what mixed costs are all about, let us first return for a moment to variable costs. In an industry which produces large quantities of product, variable costs, such as direct materials and direct labor, accumulate to very large amounts and are therefore watched and analyzed very carefully. Certainly you can appreciate that an industry such as automobile manufacturing would want to know precisely how much direct material and direct labor should go into producing the 12 million or so vehicles which are produced each year in the United States. So industries like this put a lot of effort into time studies (where workers are timed doing various tasks) and analyses of the production process to see if there are more efficient ways of producing the product with the minimum waste of material and time. A lot of

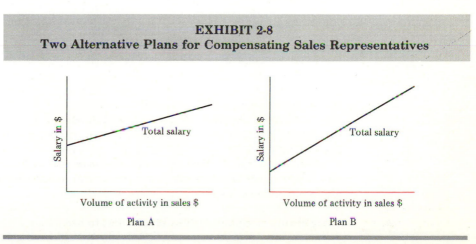

EXHIBIT 2-8
Two Alternative Plans for Compensating Sales Representatives

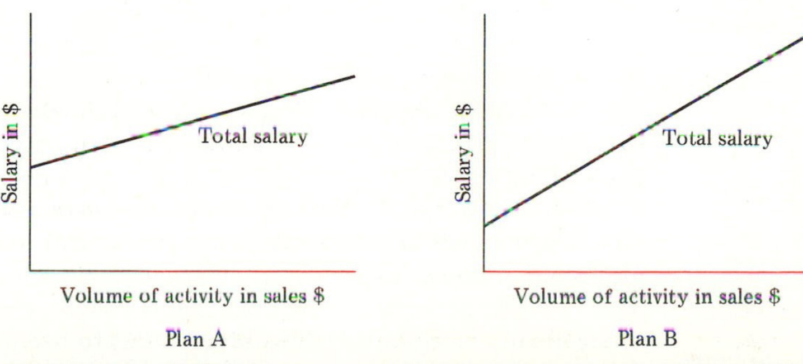

engineering talent is used to develop accurate estimates of the major variable costs that go into each product. All this is done because direct labor and direct materials costs of a product can be enormous.

Mixed costs, when taken on an item by item basis, are generally not large enough to warrant a detailed industrial engineering study. Generally, accountants and managers rely on analysis of historical data to estimate the fixed and variable cost components of mixed costs.

Estimating the variable and fixed cost components of some mixed costs is relatively easy because they are determined by agreement or custom. For example, the salary of the sales representative was determined by a contract which provides for a flat monthly salary (fixed cost component) and a sales commission (a variable cost component). Other similar agreements exist and can be used to determine the fixed and variable cost components fairly easily.

But most mixed costs are a little more complicated to analyze. For example, consider the cost of electricity used to operate machines and to light the building. The electricity used to light the building is probably a fixed cost (the building has to be lighted whether we operate at 60% of capacity or 80% of capacity). The electricity used in the machines, however, is probably variable. The more we produce, the more we use the machines; the more we use the machines, the more electricity we use. Unless we have separate wiring and electric meters for lights and machinery, our electric bill will be for all electricity used, both for lighting and machinery. Determining the fixed and variable cost components in this situation requires analysis of historical data. It is required for many mixed costs. The graphic method of making the analysis is discussed next.

The graphic method of using historical data to estimate the fixed and variable cost components of a mixed cost has five steps.

There are five steps in the graphic method. We will list the steps and then discuss and illustrate them.

1 Get the data from the accounting records for a number of recent months. For each month we must know the total amount of the mixed cost incurred and the volume of activity for that same month.

2 Plot the points on a graph which show volume of activity on the horizontal axis and total amount of the mixed cost on the vertical axis.

3 Draw a straight line on the graph which comes close to as many points as possible.

   Note: As soon as we get the line drawn we ignore the points and work only with the line for the remaining steps.

4 Estimate the variable cost component (which is the same as determining the slope of the line).

5 Determine the fixed cost component by taking any volume, estimating the total cost, and then subtracting the variable cost at that volume from the total cost to get the fixed cost.

The accountant must be alert to changes which would make historical costs not representative of future costs.

Step 1 Getting the data from the accounting records is not difficult as long as the accounting records have been properly organized in the first place. Suppose we are estimating the fixed and variable cost component of electricity used in the factory. If our accounts have a separate account for electricity, it is a matter of copying down the amounts for perhaps the last 24 months. We must be careful that there was not some important change in our electricity cost in the months we use. For example, if we bought some new machines 18 months ago which were much more efficient than the old machines, we would not want to use 24 months of data. Only the data from the last 18 months would be relevant to estimating future electricity usage.

Also, if there have been changes in the electrical rates in the last 18 months, we would want to go back and make adjustments for the changes. It would be a matter of taking the electricity bills and figuring what the electricity would have cost at the current rates. The other data we need is the volume of activity for each of the last 18 months. Since we believe that the variable component of electricity cost depends on the number of hours we operate the machines, we might use machine-hours as the measure of volume of activity. If our records have not kept track of the machine hours operated, we might have to use direct labor hours as a substitute.

The data needed for analysis consists of a pair: (1) the total mixed cost and (2) the volume of activity.

One important thing to remember is that we want pairs of numbers. For each month we use, we want to know how much the electricity cost and how many machine hours were worked. We need the pairs of data for plotting on the graph in step 2.

Step 2 When we have the pairs of data, the next step is to plot them on a graph. Having collected the data, we know what range of numbers is needed on a graph. On the horizontal axis we wish to lay out a scale for volume of activity. If the highest monthly number of machine hours is 4,000, we want a scale which runs from zero to 4,000 on the horizontal axis. For the vertical axis we do the same thing. If our highest monthly electric bill was $750, we want the vertical scale to run from zero to $750.

With the graph ready, we then simply take each month and plot the activity and electric bill on the graph. If, for example, in one month we worked 2,200 machine hours and had an electric bill for that month of $600, we would go out on the horizontal scale to 2,200 machine hours and then straight up to $600 on the vertical scale and mark the first point on the graph. We would do this with the data from each month for which we have data.

You may notice when you are done that you will not know which point represents which month. For our purposes, this is not too important. There are some statistical analyses in which this would be important, but it is not important to us at the moment. When we are done with step 2, we have something that looks like Exhibit 2-9, part A.

Step 3 The next step is to draw a line on the graph which is a reasonable approximation of the points, that is, it is reasonably close to most of the points. There are statistical methods of doing this, but we will not take time to discuss

EXHIBIT 2-9
Steps 2 and 3 in Finding the Fixed and Variable Cost Components of a Mixed Cost

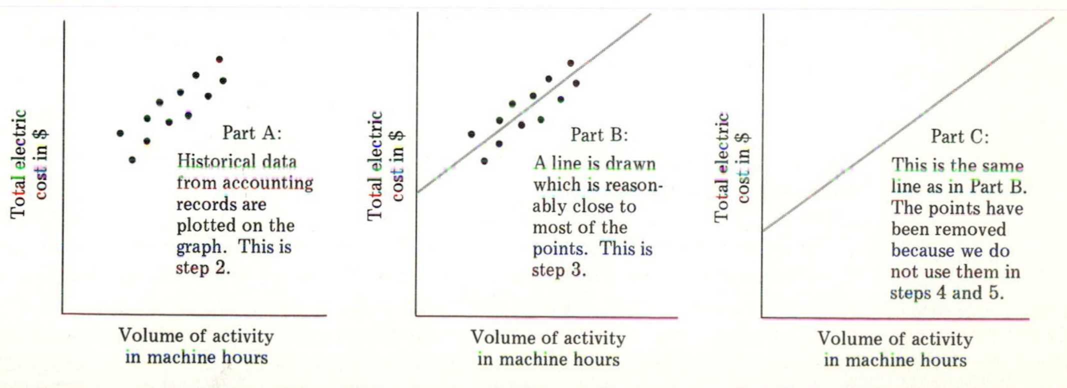
Total electric cost in $
Part A:
Historical data from accounting records are plotted on the graph. This is step 2.
Volume of activity in machine hours
Total electric cost in $
Part B:
A line is drawn which is reasonably close to most of the points. This is step 3.
Volume of activity in machine hours
Total electric cost in $
Part C:
This is the same line as in Part B. The points have been removed because we do not use them in steps 4 and 5.
Volume of activity in machine hours

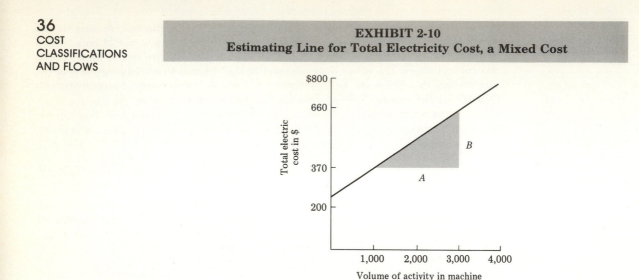

EXHIBIT 2-10
Estimating Line for Total Electricity Cost, a Mixed Cost

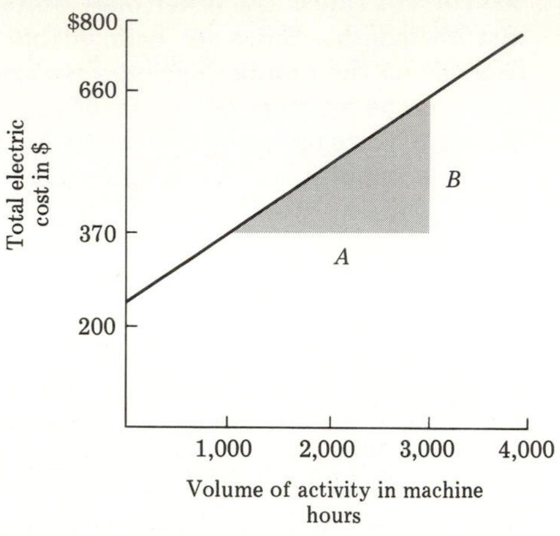

Since drawing the line involves judgment each analyst might get a slightly different result.

them in this chapter. Since judgment is involved, each of us might get a slightly different result. But we should all come reasonably close. Part B of Exhibit 2-9 shows the graph from part A with a line drawn in. Since we told you earlier that as soon as you have drawn the line, you ignore the points, part C of the exhibit shows the same graph, with the points removed. It is the graph in part C which we will use in steps 4 and 5.

Step 4 In step 4, we determine the slope of the line we have just drawn. The slope of this line is equal to the variable cost per unit, in this case the variable electricity cost per machine hour of operation. This is the point at which we would like to have a large graph drawn accurately. If we determine the slope incorrectly, our estimating formula will be wrong.

We illustrated in Exhibit 2-5 how the slope of the line was simply the amount of increase on the vertical axis divided by the amount of increase on the horizontal axis. In that graph we show a number of small differences. To minimize the error, we will use relatively large changes in step 4. The graph from part C of Exhibit 2-9 is reproduced as Exhibit 2-10 with a scale shown (the scale would have had to be there when we plotted the points, but was left out in Exhibit 2-9 to avoid cluttering the graph any more than needed). Also, the levels of activity for finding the slope are drawn.

The slope of the line and the variable cost per machine hour is the distance B divided by the distance A.

As we see in Exhibit 2-10, the slope of the line (and the variable cost per machine hour) is *B* divided by *A*. We chose our points so that the length of *A* is easy to read. It is simply 3,000 machine hours minus 1,000 machine hours, or 2,000 machine hours. The length of *B* is a bit harder to read on a small graph, but we estimate that the upper end of *B* is at $660 and the lower end is at $370. Thus *B* = $660 − $370 = $290.

Slope = variable electricity cost per machine hour
= *B*/*A*
= $290/2,000 hours
= $0.145 per machine hour

And step 4 is complete.

Step 5 For step 5, we simply take the total cost at any volume of activity and estimate the amount of variable cost included using the result of step 4. The rest has to be total fixed cost. While we can take any volume of activity, we might as well use one of the two we already have. You take 1,000 machine hours where we estimated total cost to be $370 and we will take 3,000 machine hours, where we estimated total cost to be $660. We should get the same answer.

Total cost at 3,000 hours	$660	
Variable cost at 3,000 hours ($0.145 × 3,000 hours)	435	
Total fixed cost	$225	per month

By the way, how did we know that the fixed cost is the fixed cost per *month* rather than fixed cost per quarter or fixed cost per year? Easy, because we started out with monthly data. If we had started with quarterly or annual data, we would have ended with total fixed cost per quarter or per year.

If we want to express our prediction as a formula it is the following:

Total electricity cost per month = $225 + ($0.145 × number of machine hours)

This is one approach to estimating the variable and fixed components of a mixed cost. Other approaches, including regression analysis, are discussed in Chapter 23.

Step Costs

A step cost is fixed for a short range of activity and changes abruptly to a new fixed level.

Another type of cost which frequently occurs is a step cost. It is so called because a graph of a step cost looks a bit like a set of steps (if you do not wonder what is holding the steps up). A **step cost** is fixed for a short range of activity, changes abruptly, and then remains fixed for another short range of activity.

Supervision costs generally are in this category. Assume that a plant is operated with a supervisor for each shift. The number of shifts operated depends on the demand for the product. Assume that 20,000 units of product per month can be produced on one shift and that the salary of the shift supervisor is $2,000 per month. If the demand for product is between zero and 20,000 units for a given month, one shift will suffice and the shift supervisor salary will total only $2,000 for the month. If demand between 20,000 and 40,000 units is anticipated, then the second shift will be operated and a second supervisor will be paid a salary of $2,000 for the month. The total shift supervisor salary for the month will be $4,000. If a third shift is required, the shift supervisor salary will total $6,000 for the month.

Exhibit 2-11 contains a graph of the shift supervisor cost under the circumstances just outlined.

PRODUCT COSTING SYSTEMS

By now, you are probably getting the idea that there are a lot of things which must be done to determine the cost of products produced by a manufacturing company. Are you ready for another? Cost accounting also depends on the nature of the manufacturing process. That really is not so surprising. The accountant is simply reporting in financial terms what is happening in the factory. If one factory operates

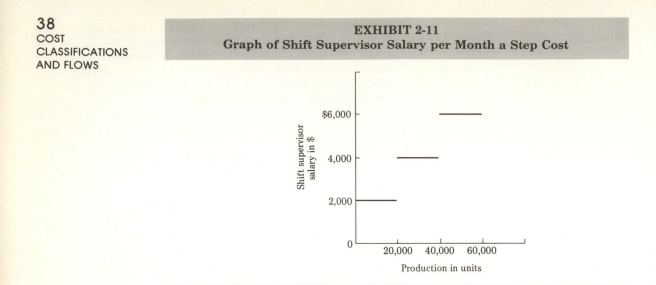

EXHIBIT 2-11
Graph of Shift Supervisor Salary per Month a Step Cost

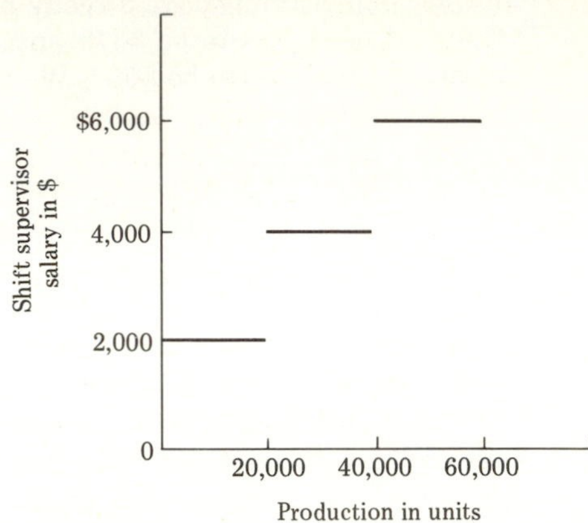

differently from another factory, it is logical that there will be differences in the cost accounting system.

We mentioned before the idea of assigning costs to units of product. The word "assign" implies that the process is not too precise. We have already seen that manufacturing overhead costs cannot be physically traced to each unit of product—it is necessary to assign (or allocate, the more technical term) manufacturing overhead costs to each unit of product. Direct material and direct labor are physically traceable to units of product, but we still make some assumptions, because it would be too costly to weigh every pound of material used in a product or to have workers record the amount of time spent on each unit of product. If a production line were running at 200 units per day, the worker would have to make that many recordings of his or her time. More time would be spent recording time than producing products.

The assumptions we make in assigning costs to units of products depend on the nature of the production process. There are two main types of manufacturing systems. Any other system is a combination of the two. We will discuss them in the next section.

Types of Manufacturers

The two main types of manufacturers are job order and process manufacturers.

The two main types of manufacturers are job order manufacturers and process manufacturers. Job order manufacturers produce goods in batches or jobs. Often a job order manufacturer does not start a batch until an order is received because each customer may want the batch or job produced to particular specifications.

A process manufacturer is one that produces a relatively standard product in large quantities on an assembly-line basis. Most consumer products, ranging from toothpaste to automobiles, are produced by process manufacturers. *Job order* manufacturers produce many of the components of the goods produced on assembly lines. Thus it is not unusual for one company to do both job order and process production.

Job Order Cost Accounting Systems A furniture company is an example of a job order manufacturer. It manufactures various items of furniture to the retailer's or to the final customer's specifications. Each time a manufacturer receives an order, an identifying number is assigned to the order. When production is started, a cost sheet is started for the order. The cost of direct materials used for a particular order is recorded on its cost sheet, and so also is the direct labor cost recorded for that order. The direct labor cost is recorded through the use of a time ticket—any employee who works directly on that job order is required to keep track of the time put in on that job. By multiplying the hours worked times the wage rate, the direct labor cost is determined and entered on the job cost sheet. Finally, each job going through the plant will be assigned a proportion of the total manufacturing overhead costs.

For job order manufacturers, costs are collected for each job.

The end result is a total job cost—let us say for five identical colonial-style dining room sets—and the average cost per set is computed by dividing the total cost by the number of units produced. The important point is that the cost data is collected by job. Job order costing is the subject of Chapter 4.

Process Cost Accounting Systems A typical process manufacturer might produce automobiles, toasters, television sets, or any other product that is produced in large quantities of identical units. The process manufacturer will not have a series of jobs of different description passing through the plant. Rather, this type of company will have a more or less continuous stream of several standard products flowing through several production departments. Each department will operate on an assembly-line basis. The objective of the cost system used by a process manufacturer, like that of a job order manufacturer, is to record and assign direct material, direct labor, and manufacturing overhead costs to the products in order to calculate a cost per unit. When materials are taken from the storeroom, a record is made of which department used them. Similarly, direct labor workers use a time clock to record how much time was spent working in each department. Finally, each department is assigned a portion of the total manufacturing overhead. At the end of the month, the total direct material, direct labor, and manufacturing overhead recorded for each department is added together and divided by the number of units produced in the department during the month.

For a process manufacturer, costs are collected for each department.

Whether a manufacturer is a process manufacturer or a job order manufacturer, the calculation of cost per unit of product requires recording total cost and dividing it by the number of units of product produced. The distinction is that the job order manufacturer totals and averages by job, whereas the process manufacturer totals and averages by department. Process costing is the subject of Chapter 5.

SUMMARY

The two most important things discussed in this chapter were: the various ways costs are classified, and the flow of product costs through the accounts of a manufacturing company.

How you will use the cost determines how you will classify that cost. By familiarizing ourselves with different cost classifications, it is easier to determine what costs are appropriate for specific decisions which require cost information.

- Costs can be classified as product costs or period costs.
- Period costs include all selling and administrative costs that are matched

against the revenue in the period for which the accounting report is prepared.

- Product costs are the cost of inventory purchased for resale or manufactured for sale. They remain an asset (inventory) until the unit of inventory is sold, then they become cost of goods sold expense.

- Manufacturing product costs are subdivided into direct materials, direct labor, and manufacturing overhead costs. Direct materials and direct labor can be physically traced to units of product, but manufacturing overhead must be assigned to products by some proportional means since overhead is not physically traceable to units of product.

Manufacturers record product costs in direct materials, direct labor, and manufacturing overhead accounts. As work is performed, costs are transferred to a work in process inventory account. When the products are completed, the costs assigned to them are transferred from the work in process inventory account to the finished goods inventory account. When the products are sold, their cost is transferred from the finished goods inventory account to the cost of goods sold account for reporting in the income statement.

A statement of cost of goods manufactured and sold is customarily prepared to show how the cost of goods sold was calculated. This statement is nothing more than an analysis of what happened in the manufacturing cost accounts during the period.

When a firm makes plans for future operations and for controlling costs, those planning and control decisions must be based on estimated future costs. The most helpful way of estimating those costs is to break them into their fixed cost and variable cost components.

A cost which in total varies in direct proportion to changes in the volume of activity is a variable cost. Another way of stating this is to say that if the per unit amount of a cost is constant as volume varies, the cost is a variable cost.

A cost which in total remains constant as volume of activity varies is a fixed cost. That is, the amount of the total fixed cost is independent of fluctuations in volume of activity.

Accountants usually make the simplifying assumption that costs are linear and can be graphed as straight lines.

Mixed costs contain both fixed and variable cost components. The fixed and variable components can be separated by analysis of historical data from the accounting records. A graphical method was illustrated in the chapter.

Manufacturing cost data are collected using either a job order cost accounting system or a process cost accounting system.

A manufacturer who produces products or services to customer specifications in distinct batches (jobs) will use a job order cost accounting system. Generally, a large number of jobs will be worked on during the year. Costs are assigned to each job and then to products.

A manufacturer using a process cost accounting system is generally mass producing a standardized product and the costs are assigned to departments and then to products.

Review Problem

The following data pertain to the manufacturing operations of the Burns Company for the year 19X1.

Materials balance January 1, 19X1	$ 10,000
Direct labor	170,000
Factory insurance	5,000
Depreciation—plant	20,000
Depreciation—machinery	40,000
Lubricants for machinery	2,000
Cleaning rags for factory	200
Cutting tools used	800
Work in process balance December 31, 19X1	90,000
Finished goods balance January 1, 19X1	100,000
Supervision salaries—factory	55,000
Indirect labor salaries	14,000
Overtime premiums—indirect labor	3,000
Materials balance December 31, 19X1	5,000
Work in process balance January 1, 19X1	85,000
Heat, light, and power—factory	6,000
Finished goods December 31, 19X1	95,000
Property taxes—plant	5,000
Materials purchases	40,000

Required Prepare a cost of goods manufactured and sold statement.

Solution

BURNS COMPANY
Cost of Goods Manufactured and Sold Statement
For the Year Ended December 31, 19X1

Work in process January 1, 19X1			$ 85,000
Materials January 1, 19X1		$10,000	
Purchases		40,000	
Cost of materials available for use		$50,000	
Materials December 31, 19X1		5,000	
Cost of materials used in production			45,000
Direct labor incurred			170,000
Manufacturing overhead			
Factory insurance	$ 5,000		
Lubricants	2,000		
Cleaning rags	200		
Cutting tools	800		
Supervision salaries	55,000		
Indirect labor	14,000		
Overtime premiums	3,000		
Heat, light, and power—factory	6,000		
Property taxes—plant	5,000		
Depreciation—plant and machinery	60,000		151,000
Total			$451,000

Work in process December 31, 19X1	90,000
Cost of goods manufactured	$361,000
Finished goods January 1, 19X1	100,000
Cost of goods available for sale	$461,000
Finished goods December 31, 19X1	95,000
Cost of goods sold	$366,000

Glossary

Conversion costs The sum of the direct labor and manufacturing overhead costs.

Cost Resources consumed to accomplish a specific objective.

Direct labor cost The cost of all important labor that is physically and economically traceable to a single product.

Direct materials cost The cost of all important materials used in production that are physically and economically traceable to a single product.

Fixed cost A cost whose total does not change with change in activity within the relevant range.

Manufacturing overhead All production costs necessary for the production of the product other than direct materials and direct labor.

Mixed cost A cost that contains both a fixed and variable component.

Period cost A cost that is recognized as an expense in the period it expires.

Prime cost The sum of direct materials and direct labor costs.

Product cost A cost necessary to obtain or produce a product. It is recognized as an expense in the period the product is sold.

Relevant range The range of activity over which management does not expect the cost to change.

Step cost A cost that is fixed for a short interval of activity, changes abruptly, and then remains fixed for another short range of activity.

Variable cost A cost whose total changes in direct proportions to changes in activity.

Questions and Problems

2-1 Distinguish between an expired and unexpired cost.

2-2 Define the following costs: variable cost, fixed cost, mixed cost, and step cost.

2-3 Distinguish between period and product costs.

2-4 Define the major types of manufacturing costs. Which are prime costs? Conversion costs?

2-5 What are the characteristics of a company that would use a job order cost system? A process cost system?

2-6 Are all unexpired costs inventoriable costs? Discuss.

2-7 Distinguish between product costs in a merchandising company and a manufacturing company.

2-8 Describe how the rent for production facilities in July may not be charged against income until September.

2-9 What is the difference between cost of goods manufactured and cost of goods sold?

2-10 Why are mixed costs separated into their fixed and variable components?

2-11 What is the "relevant range"? Why is it important to cost accountants?

2-12 **Cost Classifications** Classify each of the following costs using the following classes:

a Direct materials
b Direct labor
c Manufacturing overhead
d Nonmanufacturing expense

1. The company president's salary
2. Oil for a milling machine
3. Salary of the milling machine operator
4. Salary of the supervisor of assembly department, for products A, B, and C
5. Depreciation on the factory building
6. Federal income tax expense
7. Depreciation on the direct materials warehouse
8. Depreciation on the administrative office building
9. Rent on the finished goods warehouse
10. Rent on the sales office
11. Insurance on the truck used for delivery of finished goods sold
12. Gasoline for the truck used for transfer of work in process from one department to another
13. Cost of the batteries installed in product C
14. Contribution to the United Fund
15. Interest on notes payable

2-13 **Cost Classifications** Classify each of the following manufacturing costs using the following classes:

a Fixed
b Variable
c Mixed

1. Rent on the factory building
2. Salary of the supervisor of the casting department
3. Wages of the lathe operators
4. Cost of tires installed on one of the products produced
5. Overtime premium for lathe operators
6. Fire insurance on the factory equipment
7. Cost of water used to cool production machinery
8. Depreciation on production machinery
9. Cost of paint used on products
10. Cost of electricity used to operate production machinery

2-14 **Cost Classifications** Classify the following manufacturing costs as direct or indirect product costs.

1. Rent on the factory building
2. Salary of the supervisor of the casting department
3. Salary of the machining department's supervisor
4. Fire insurance on the factory equipment

5 Labor cost for material handling
6 Power cost for operating plant machinery
7 Storage costs for raw materials
8 Major raw materials used to manufacture the product
9 Lubricants for machinery
10 Wages for tool and die makers

2-15 Separating Mixed Costs The Backrat Company has collected the following data concerning material handling costs for the past six months:

Period	Material Handling Costs	Direct Labor Hours
1	$4,180	1,510
2	4,500	1,750
3	3,480	1,450
4	4,000	1,500
5	4,800	1,800
6	4,600	1,850

Required

1 Graph the data on material handling costs as a function of direct labor hours.

2 Visually fit a line through the data and compute the fixed and variable components of the cost.

2-16 Calculations of Net Income The following information pertains to Bing Company:

Sales	$127,000
Cost of goods manufactured:	
Variable costs	$ 38,000
Fixed costs	$ 32,000
Selling and administrative expense (fixed)	$ 30,000
Beginning inventory of finished goods	0
Actual production	8,000 units
Ending inventory of finished goods	2,000 units
Beginning and ending inventory of work in process	0

Required Calculate the net income for Bing Company for the period.

2-17 Preparation of a Cost of Goods Manufactured and Sold Statement The following data are from the accounts of Waldo Manufacturing Company. Figures are for the month of August or as of August 31, as appropriate, except where otherwise stated. (Data are 1,000s of dollars, but the zeroes may be omitted.)

From the data prepare a cost of goods manufactured and sold statement.

Accounts receivable	19
Sales	89
Production wages	21
Factory heat and power	4

Factory superintendent	1
Finished goods August 31	6
Plant and equipment	110
Taxes on factory	1
Income taxes	10
Materials August 1	8
Materials August 31	10
Finished goods August 1	17
Work in process August 1	17
Factory maintenance	3
Advertising expense	2
Material purchases	19
Sales commissions	4
Accumulated depreciation—plant and equipment	60
Selling expenses	11
Administrative expense	9
Work in process August 31	7
Depreciation of plant and equipment	5

2-18 Preparation of a Cost of Goods Manufactured and Sold Statement The Ganite Company manufactures a single product. The beginning and ending inventories for the current year's production are given below, along with the actual manufacturing costs.

Inventories	January 1, 19X9	December 31, 19X9
Materials	$53,576	$47,860
Work in process	75,650	62,420
Finished goods	84,250	75,600

During the year the company purchased $250,000 of materials, and used 36,500 hours of direct labor at $6.75 per hour. The actual overhead costs for the year are summarized below:

Supervision salaries	$ 45,000
Indirect labor	60,000
Lubricants	40,000
Depreciation	200,000
Property taxes—plant	80,000
Other manufacturing expenses	160,000
Total	$585,000

Required Prepare a cost of goods manufactured and sold statement for 19X9.

2-19 Identification of Cost Behavior Patterns Assume that each graph shown below has *either* the cost per unit or total cost on the vertical axis and volume on the horizontal axis. For each of the following costs identify the appropriate graph.

1 Direct labor cost per unit
2 Total fixed cost
3 Straight-line depreciation per unit
4 Total direct materials cost
5 Depreciation per unit—units of production method
6 Total property taxes
7 Total supervision salaries
8 Total heat, light, and power cost
9 Total manufacturing overhead
10 Supervision salaries per unit
11 Total direct labor cost
12 Material cost per unit
13 Total manufacturing cost
14 Total insurance cost

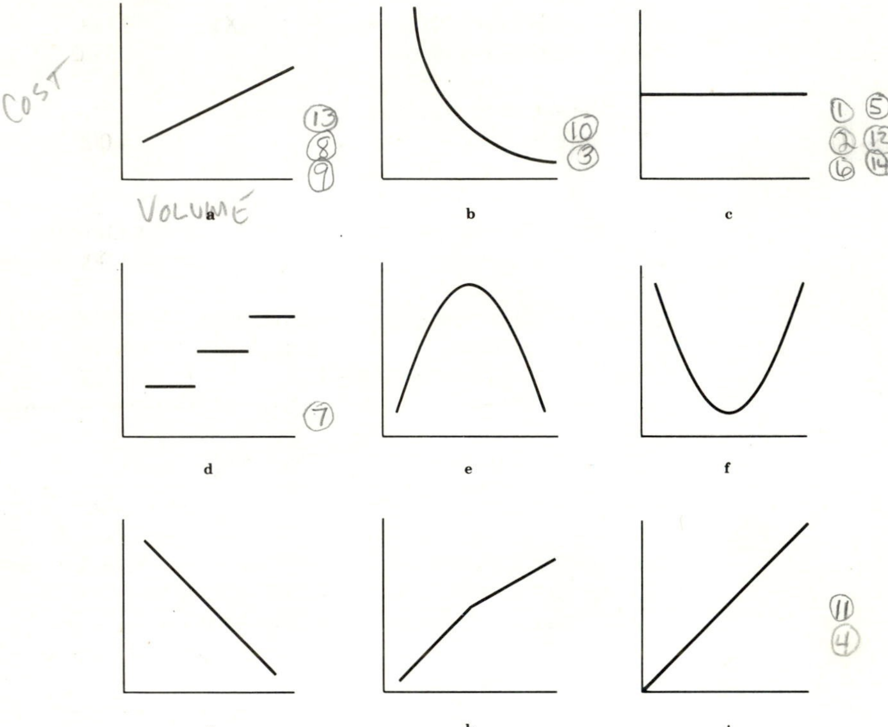

2-20 Separating Mixed Costs The ABC Company incurred the following manufacturing overhead costs during the past four-month period:

Month	Direct Labor Hours	Manufacturing Overhead Costs
April	2,000	$20,000
May	2,500	22,500
June	4,000	30,000
July	3,500	27,500

Required

1 Using the graphical method calculate the fixed cost and variable cost per direct labor hour.

2 If the company expects to work 3,000 direct labor hours in August, what is the estimated total manufacturing overhead cost?

2-21 Find the Unknowns For each case listed below calculate the unknowns indicated by ?. Each case is independent.

	Case 1	Case 2	Case 3
Sales	$20,000	$30,000	$?
Finished goods January 1, 19X1	?	4,000	2,000
Cost of goods manufactured	$10,000	?	$12,000
Finished goods December 31, 19X1	3,000	5,000	?
Cost of goods sold	9,000	?	12,000
Gross margin	?	16,000	3,000
Selling and administrative expenses	5,000	?	1,000
Net income	?	8,000	2,000
Work in process January 1, 19X1	1,000	?	4,000
Direct materials used	3,000	4,000	3,000
Direct labor	4,000	5,000	3,000
Manufacturing overhead	?	7,000	?
Total costs added to work in process	?	?	14,000
Work in process December 31, 19X1	1,000	4,000	?
Cost of goods manufactured	10,000	?	?

2-22 Statement of Cost of Goods Manufactured The Helper Corporation manufactures one product. You have obtained the following information for the year ended December 31, 19X3, from the corporation's books and records:

Total manufacturing cost added during 19X3 (sometimes called cost to manufacture) was $1,000,000 based on direct materials, direct labor, and factory overhead.

Cost of goods manufactured was $970,000 also based on direct materials, direct labor, and factory overhead.

Factory overhead was 75% of direct labor dollars. Factory overhead for the year was 27% of the total manufacturing cost.

Beginning work in process inventory, January 1, was 80% of ending work in process inventory, December 31.

Required

Prepare a formal statement of cost of goods manufactured for the year ended December 31, 19X3, for Helper Corporation. Show supporting computations in good form.

(CPA)

2-23 Manufacturing Statement and Income Statement The following information was taken from the records of the Zing Company:

Account Balances	December 31 19X1	December 31 19X2
Direct materials	20,000	25,000
Work in process	30,000	40,000
Finished goods	50,000	40,000

During the year 19X2 the following transactions were recorded:

Direct materials purchased	$ 85,000
Direct labor cost incurred	90,000
Factory indirect labor	10,000
Factory supplies	5,000
Factory utilities	15,000
Depreciation—factory	30,000
Factory maintenance	10,000
Total selling and administrative expenses	60,000
Sales	340,000

Required

1 Prepare a cost of goods manufactured and sold statement.

2 Prepare an income statement.

2-24 Product Cost, Unit Cost, and Profit Computation The Dudley Company produces golf balls and during the year 19X8 incurred the following costs:

	Fixed	Variable	Total
Direct materials used	$	$ 50,000	$ 50,000
Direct labor		50,000	50,000
Indirect labor—factory	30,000	40,000	70,000
Supplies—factory		30,000	30,000
Depreciation—factory	15,000		15,000
Heat, Light, and power—factory	10,000	5,000	15,000
Other indirect—factory		10,000	10,000
Sales salaries	40,000		40,000
Commissions—salesmen		90,000	90,000
Advertising	30,000	20,000	50,000
Other selling	10,000	5,000	15,000
	$135,000	$300,000	$435,000

At the end of the year 5,000 dozen golf balls were in finished goods inventory valued at $24,000. The finished goods inventory is valued at the average production cost for 19X8. The work in process inventory was zero at the end of 19X8. The sales price is $12.00 per dozen. All beginning inventories were zero.

Required

1 Calculate the number of dozen golf balls produced in 19X8.

2 Compute the number of dozen golf balls sold in 19X8.

3 Prepare an income statement for 19X8.

MANUFACTURING OVERHEAD COST ACCOUNTING FOR PRODUCT COSTING

AFTER COMPLETING YOUR STUDY OF THIS CHAPTER, YOU SHOULD HAVE LEARNED:

1 How to calculate the actual manufacturing overhead cost per unit in a single product firm and the problems associated with using the actual manufacturing overhead cost per unit.

2 How to compute a predetermined manufacturing overhead rate and how it is used to compute the manufacturing overhead cost per unit.

3 How in a multiple product production situation some manufacturing overhead costs benefit more than one product and how to find a common denominator to measure the production activity for all products.

4 The difference between plantwide and departmental manufacturing overhead rates. We will find that in some situations departmental manufacturing overhead rates provide us with a better measure of the relationship between the manufacturing overhead costs and the production of the products.

Your first step in this chapter is to review Chapter 2 to be sure you understand the classification of manufacturing product costs into direct materials, direct labor, and manufacturing overhead.

Direct manufacturing costs—direct materials costs and direct labor costs—are matched with revenues in this way: The direct costs incurred in producing the products are added up and divided by the total number of each product manufactured to get a "direct material and direct labor cost per unit of each product manufactured." As each unit of these products is sold, each cost per unit of products manufactured becomes a part of "per unit cost of goods sold." And, in this way, direct costs are matched to revenues.

Calculating direct materials and direct labor cost per unit of output is fairly simple because of their physical link to output.

The calculation for matching direct costs to revenue is fairly easy because there is a physical link between direct costs and the units produced as a result of these direct costs. That is, it is relatively simple to physically trace the direct materials and direct labor, and thus their costs, to each manufactured unit. The main thing to realize here is that you can measure rather precisely the direct costs needed to produce a particular unit. For example, you can measure the pounds of materials needed and you can measure the amount of direct labor needed using a clock and thus the cost of direct materials and direct labor to produce that unit. But you cannot do that with manufacturing overhead costs.

The calculation of manufacturing overhead per unit of output is more complex because there is no physical link to output.

All manufacturing costs not classified as direct manufacturing costs are classified as indirect manufacturing costs—**manufacturing overhead costs.** These costs are also matched to revenue by calculating their cost per unit manufactured. We will find later in this chapter that the computation is more complex, however, because indirect manufacturing costs cannot be physically traced to the units manufactured. Finally, it should be noted that some minor direct costs, such as supplies, may be treated as indirect costs because treating them as direct costs does not provide significantly more accurate accounting information and to do so would cost more than it would be worth.

For example, each stereo receiver has a few screws in its chassis. Let us assume that it costs the producer $142.76 for all direct costs not including the screws. To include the screws in direct costs might provide more accurate accounting information—the total direct costs might amount to $142.78—but it might cost the producer several thousands of dollars to collect information on the costs of screws and how many of each type of screw go into each stereo chassis. So the producer accounts for the costs of the screws in manufacturing overhead instead.

In this chapter, you will be concerned with all kinds of manufacturing overhead costs, such as the depreciation cost of a factory building, as well as minor overhead costs such as supplies, or the screws in the preceding example. We will show you how to calculate manufacturing overhead costs per unit, and then in Chapters 4 and 5 how to match unit manufacturing overhead costs to revenue.

PREDETERMINED OVERHEAD[1] RATES

An example of the actual overhead cost per unit.

If our sole objective was to calculate the overhead cost per unit in a single-product manufacturing firm for the preparation of end of the year financial statements, the computations would be fairly easy. We would simply accumulate the *actual* overhead costs incurred throughout the year and divide by the *actual* number of units produced to compute the *actual* overhead cost per unit.

[1] Rather than using the term "manufacturing overhead," we will use the term "overhead" to simplify the discussion in this chapter. Remember, when you see the word overhead it is manufacturing overhead.

EXHIBIT 3-1
HOLDER MANUFACTURING COMPANY
Actual Overhead Costs
For the Year 19X3

Item	Cost
Indirect materials	$ 80,000
Indirect labor	120,000
Heat, light, and power	90,000
Depreciation	180,000
Property tax	60,000
Supervision	120,000
Repairs and maintenance	70,000
Total	$720,000

$$\text{Actual overhead cost} = \frac{\$720{,}000}{100{,}000 \text{ units}} = \$7.20 \text{ per unit}$$

Overhead cost of goods sold = 90,000 units × \$7.20 =	\$648,000
Overhead cost of ending inventory = 10,000 units × \$7.20 =	72,000
	\$720,000

For example, consider Exhibit 3-1 for the Holder Manufacturing Company. At the end of year 19X3, the company had incurred $720,000 of overhead costs and produced 100,000 units of product, resulting in an overhead cost per unit of $7.20. This amount can be used to compute the overhead included in the cost of goods sold of $648,000 (90,000 units at $7.20 per unit) and the overhead cost of ending inventory of $72,000 (10,000 units at $7.20 per unit). The cost of goods sold is matched with the revenues in 19X3 in calculating the net income, and the ending inventory value is used in preparing the end of year balance sheet.

The above computations average the actual overhead cost for the year over the actual production, and the computation can only take place at the end of the year. However, managers in manufacturing firms desire unit cost information throughout the year for the purposes of preparing monthly income statements and balance sheets. Also, the unit cost information is used to prepare bids for job orders and to evaluate product prices. For these reasons the overhead cost per unit is calculated at the *beginning* of the year rather than at the end of the year. The computation is based on the *estimated* annual overhead cost and *estimated* annual production volume, and the result is referred to as a **predetermined overhead rate.** The computation is as follows:

With a predetermined overhead rate, the overhead cost per unit can be calculated before year-end.

$$\textbf{Predetermined overhead rate} = \frac{\textbf{estimated annual overhead cost}}{\textbf{estimated annual production volume}}$$

Predetermined overhead rates require the accountant to estimate future overhead costs not just record what they were in the past. Past overhead costs are simple to deal with; all an accountant has to do is to look at the bills, record all costs, and then perform some arithmetic. But, even when estimating future overhead cost—the record of past actual costs—past overhead costs are important because the accountant analyzes and uses them as the basis for the estimate.

Seasonal Variations in Overhead Costs and Production Volume

At this point you should be wondering why we do not compute an actual overhead rate at the end of each month to prepare monthly financial statements. There are two reasons:

Two factors keep an actual monthly overhead rate from being useful.

1 The seasonal nature of some overhead costs

2 The fixed nature of some overhead costs and seasonal changes in production volume

Seasonal Overhead Costs A number of overhead costs are seasonal. Heating and lighting costs are higher in the winter months than in the spring months. Snow removal costs will be incurred only during the winter months. Social security taxes tend to decrease late in the year as the employees reach the maximum taxable income. Vacation pay tends to be incurred primarily during summer months when children are out of school. If we use actual overhead costs from individual months, the overhead cost per unit would vary because of seasonal costs. In some months heating would be part of the overhead cost per unit and in other months it would not.

Seasonal costs would lead to different costs for identical products.

Consider a company that makes broom handles in Maine where it is very cold and snowy in the winter. If the overhead cost per unit were calculated on a monthly basis, the heating and snow removal costs would be included in the winter months and, consequently, broom handles made in the winter would cost more than broom handles made in the spring. These types of variations in unit costs of identical units might mislead readers of financial statements into believing management is less efficient in winter. But the cost variations just reflect the time of year the units were produced, a factor outside the control of management. Accountants try to average out these variations through the use of a predetermined overhead rate calculated on an annual basis. All these seasonal costs are lumped together and spread over the production for the entire year.

Predetermined overhead rates average seasonal cost over the entire year's production.

Fixed Costs and Seasonal Production Volume The objective of the accountant is to calculate an *average* annual overhead cost per unit. Fixed overhead costs, such as depreciation, supervision, property taxes, etc., are constant in total from month to month. However, when this constant total is divided by differing production volumes a different per unit overhead cost results. For example, consider Exhibit 3-2 for the Fauver Manufacturing Company. The company's management has committed itself to incurring $20,000 of fixed overhead cost each month to provide the capacity to satisfy the maximum production requirements which occur in the summer months. Variable overhead costs are $1.20 per unit. Should inventory produced in the summer months be reported using an overhead cost of $2.53 per unit, while an identical unit produced in the winter months is reported at $5.20 per unit? Most people would answer no to this question since the fluctuations in the fixed overhead cost per unit are the result of expected seasonal changes in production volume.

The total amount of fixed cost remains constant at $20,000 per month, but as the number of units produced varies the fixed cost per unit varies. A fixed cost per unit that fluctuates provides little information to management, especially if it fluctuates because production volume variations are expected seasonal changes. A fixed cost per unit should be just that, fixed, and it should not be affected by anything that does not provide any useful information. Notice that the variable cost per unit is a constant $1.20 per unit.

EXHIBIT 3-2
FAUVER MANUFACTURING COMPANY
Impact of Production Volume on the Overhead Cost per Unit

Month	Fixed Cost	Variable Cost	Production	Unit Cost
January	$ 20,000	$ 6,000	5,000 units	$5.20
February	20,000	6,000	5,000 units	5.20
March	20,000	6,000	5,000 units	5.20
April	20,000	6,000	5,000 units	5.20
May	20,000	12,000	10,000 units	3.20
June	20,000	18,000	15,000 units	2.53
July	20,000	18,000	15,000 units	2.53
August	20,000	18,000	15,000 units	2.53
September	20,000	12,000	10,000 units	3.20
October	20,000	6,000	5,000 units	5.20
November	20,000	6,000	5,000 units	5.20
December	20,000	6,000	5,000 units	5.20
	$240,000	$120,000	100,000 units	

$$\text{Average (normal) overhead cost per unit} = \frac{\$360,000}{100,000} = \$3.60$$

Predetermined overhead rates average the fixed overhead costs per unit over the entire year's production.

Normal overhead costs are calculated by use of an annual predetermined overhead rate.

The accountant averages out these variations in production volume, and their impact on the fixed overhead cost per unit, through the use of a predetermined overhead rate calculated on an annual basis. When this is done the resulting product cost per unit is referred to as a "normal" cost rather than an "actual" cost. Normal cost means that the total product cost per unit contains a normal amount of overhead costs based on estimated annual overhead costs and estimated annual production volume. In the Fauver manufacturing example the normal overhead cost is $3.60 per unit.

The Impact of Joint Overhead Costs on Predetermined Overhead Rates

Many overhead costs are joint to several products.

In the above examples and discussions we assumed the Fauver Manufacturing Company was producing a single product. This allowed us to calculate the normal overhead cost per unit using the estimated units of production as a denominator. However, most companies produce more than one product and many overhead costs benefit the production of more than one of those products. Such overhead costs are called **joint costs.** With joint overhead costs it is not feasible to directly measure the portion of the cost that applies to a particular unit of production.

For example, the cost of maintaining a machine benefits all products produced on that machine; the benefit is not just for one particular product. Thus, the cost of maintenance is a benefit to all products produced on that machine—that is, the cost of maintenance of this machine is a joint overhead cost.

Joint overhead costs may be fixed or variable.

All other costs of owning or operating this same machine, such as depreciation costs and property taxes, are joint costs. These last two examples are fixed costs, and that means they are the same cost no matter how many units of product or which product are produced on the machine.

Another example of a joint overhead cost is the salary of the factory manager which benefits the production of all products produced in the factory. If more than one product is produced in a factory, the salary of the factory manager is joint among the products. You might wonder, why not ask the factory manager to keep a record of how much time is spent working on the problems of each product? Probably some of the manager's time could be divided this way. But a major element of the manager's time would inevitably be related to problems which affect all products, such as working on union negotiations for the entire workforce.

Jointness exists with many costs other than the plant manager's salary, depreciation, and maintenance. The cost of heating and maintaining the factory building benefits all products produced in the building. These costs are seasonal in addition to being joint. The cost of having factory timekeepers and production schedulers is joint to all products. The cost of operating the materials storeroom is another joint cost.

The problem joint costs create is that in the denominator of the predetermined overhead rate computation we cannot add together units of production of different products. It would not make sense to add together bars of Ivory soap and boxes of Tide laundry detergent produced in the same maufacturing plant to determine the total units of production. The reason for this is that a box of Tide might take three times the number of machine-hours to produce as one bar of Ivory.

The joint overhead cost problem is solved by selecting a common denominator which reflects overhead usage by each product.

To solve this problem, the accountant selects a measure of production activity that represents a common denominator across all products being produced. We cannot add together bars of Ivory and boxes of Tide but we can add together the machine-hours, direct labor hours, direct labor dollars, or direct materials dollars which are used in the production of both products. The measure of production activity that we choose to compute a denominator for the predetermined overhead rate computation is referred to as an **activity base.**

The common denominator is called an activity base.

Now, to understand what we mean by activity base, consider that there are a number of activities that take place in making a product. Let us consider machined wooden yo-yos. There is the activity of machining (cutting and shaping) the parts of the yo-yos; there is also the activity of processing—sanding, painting, lacquering—the parts of the yo-yos; finally there is the activity of assembling the yo-yo parts together to make the whole yo-yo. The direct labor that goes into all the yo-yos is a measure of the amount of some of the activities. The hours of machining is a measure of the amount of another activity required to make the yo-yos. Sometimes, the cost of the direct materials used to make different products is the best measure of the amount of some activity required for each product.

An activity base should be measurable for each product and have a cause-and-effect relation to the overhead cost.

Selection of an Activity Base An activity base should be (1) directly measurable for each product and should have, at least indirectly, (2) a cause-and-effect relation to the overhead cost. These relationships are illustrated in Exhibit 3-3. The two-way arrow on the left indicates the cause-and-effect relationship between the base and the overhead cost while the two-way arrow on the right indicates the relation of the activity base to each product. These two relationships are used to calculate a predetermined overhead rate which is then used to assign overhead costs to products based on the amount of the activity base included in each product. The amount of overhead assigned to the products using the predetermined overhead rate is referred to as *applied overhead* to distinguish it from actual overhead.

Applied overhead rather than actual overhead is assigned to the products.

In selecting an activity base our objective is to find one that has a *cause-and-effect relationship* with the incurrence of the overhead costs and can be physically related to the production of the products. The most commonly used activity bases

EXHIBIT 3-3
Relationship between Overhead Costs, Activity Base, and Overhead Cost per Unit of Product

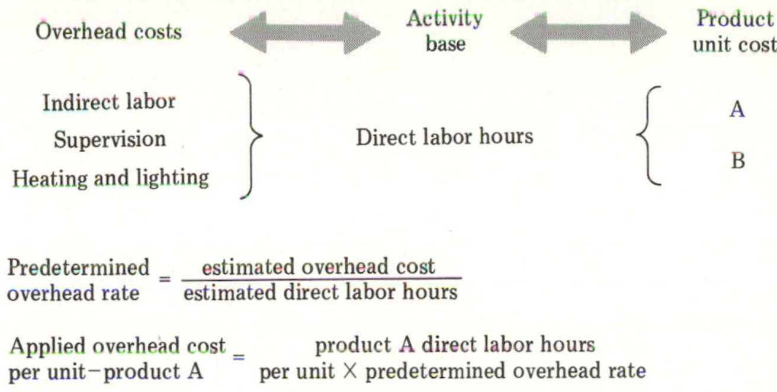

$$\text{Predetermined overhead rate} = \frac{\text{estimated overhead cost}}{\text{estimated direct labor hours}}$$

$$\text{Applied overhead cost per unit–product A} = \text{product A direct labor hours per unit} \times \text{predetermined overhead rate}$$

in practice are direct labor hours and machine hours. In some situations, however, direct labor dollars and direct material dollars are used.

Direct labor hours are used in situations where the overhead costs are primarily related to the amount of time used in producing the product. Overhead costs, such as indirect labor, heating and lighting, and supervision, are related to the number of direct labor hours worked.

Machine hours are used in situations where the overhead costs are primarily related to equipment usage. This would include overhead costs such as depreciation, material handling, cutting tools, and lubricants for cooling the equipment.

Direct labor dollars is used in situations where more overhead cost is incurred the higher the employee's wage rate. This situation would exist mainly for overhead costs such as fringe benefits. If the wage rates are about the same for all employees, direct labor dollars will provide about the same overhead product unit cost as direct labor hours and the most convenient measure would be selected.

Direct materials dollars or direct materials units would be an appropriate activity base for overhead costs involving the storing of direct materials and the transportation of the materials to the work stations in the plant.

Predetermined Overhead Rates Illustrated

To illustrate the computation of predetermined overhead rates we use the Brazos Aluminum Company. Brazos is a manufacturing company that makes aluminum windows and door frames and sells them to wholesalers or contractors in the construction industry. The window and door frames, used in home and apartment construction, are made with a highly automated extruding and finishing process. Since the company is producing multiple products with a single manufacturing process, total units of production would not be an appropriate measure for calculating a predetermined overhead rate. Therefore, the company must choose some activity base to act as a common denominator across both products being produced.

An illustration of the development and use of a predetermined overhead rate.

Exhibit 3-4 presents the estimated production costs, estimated production volume measured by alternative activity bases, and the predetermined overhead rates for each activity base. To apply overhead costs to the windows and door frames

EXHIBIT 3-4
BRAZOS ALUMINUM COMPANY
Estimated Cost of Goods Manufactured
For the Year Ended December 31, 19X3

Estimated production costs:			
Direct materials	$817,000		
Direct labor	200,000		
Total direct costs		$1,017,000	
Overhead			
Supplies	$ 47,000		
Indirect labor	60,000		
Electricity	58,000		
Plant supervisory salary	40,000		
Property taxes and insurance	35,600		
Depreciation	138,600		
Total overhead		379,200	
Total manufacturing cost			$1,396,200

Estimated Production Volume with Different Activity Bases
Direct Labor Hours (DLH)

Windows	10,000 Units × 1.0 DLH =	10,000
Door frames	5,000 Units × 2.0 DLH =	10,000
	Total direct labor hours =	20,000

Machine Hours (MH)

Windows	10,000 Units × 1.5 MH =	15,000
Door frames	5,000 Units × 2.5 MH =	12,500
	Total machine hours =	27,500

Alternative Predetermined Overhead Rates

Overhead cost per direct labor hour	= $379,200 ÷ 20,000 DLH	= $18.960/DLH
Overhead cost per machine hour	= $379,200 ÷ 27,500 MH	= $13.789/MH
Overhead cost per material dollar	= $379,200 ÷ $817,000	= $.464/M$
Overhead cost per direct labor dollar	= $379,200 ÷ $200,000	= $1.896/DL$

the company must select the most appropriate predetermined overhead rate from among the four alternative computations in Exhibit 3-4. The appropriate rate is the one for the activity base that most closely relates the overhead cost to the final product.

Brazos management chose machine hours as the activity base for its predetermined overhead rate because they believed it followed the cause-and-effect idea. They noted that material prices and direct labor rates could vary without changes in production volume. And because they were seeking a way of relating overhead cost to production volume they eliminated direct materials dollars and direct labor dollars as the activity base. They did that somewhat reluctantly because both direct materials cost and direct labor dollars were already accumulated by the accounting system and since that information was already in the system it was available without additional accounting costs.

Direct labor hours was also eliminated because it does not closely reflect changes in activity. The manufacturing process uses highly automated machinery. Thus, the machinery could produce great amounts or small amounts of products, all with the same amount of labor.

The use of machine hours as an activity base for determining the overhead rate is appealing for two reasons: it does not have the defects noted of the activity bases already eliminated, and it seems best to apply the cause-and-effect idea which we will see as we examine the nature of the overhead costs in this example. Return to Exhibit 3-4 and observe that all the overhead costs except indirect labor and plant supervisor salary are closely related to the machines. The supplies are used mainly for oiling and cooling the machines. The electricity is used primarily to operate the machines. The property taxes, insurance, and depreciation are all related to the number of machines owned by Brazos. These costs together amount to $279,200, or about 74% of the total overhead costs; they are all related either to how much the machines are operated or how many machines the company has. Thus, the accountants concluded that the cause-and-effect relationship was strongest between total overhead costs and machine hours.

Brazos has selected a predetermined overhead rate of $13.789 per machine hour. For each actual machine hour used in producing a window or door frame Brazos will apply $13.789 of overhead to the window or door frame. To illustrate the use of the predetermined overhead rate, assume that it takes 1.5 machine hours (MH) to produce a window and 2.5 machine hours (MH) to produce a door frame. The overhead applied to a window and a door frame is calculated as follows:

Product	**Activity Base**		**Predetermined Overhead Rate**		**Applied Overhead Cost per Unit**
Windows	1.5 MH	×	$13.789/MH	=	$20.684
Door frames	2.5 MH	×	$13.789/MH	=	$34.473

The overhead cost applied to windows is $20.684 per unit and to door frames is $34.473 per unit. These are the overhead cost per unit figures that will be used to compute cost of goods sold and to determine the cost of the ending finished goods inventory.

The predetermined overhead rate is based on estimated overhead costs and estimated machine hours. Now let us jump ahead in time and look back at the actual overhead costs and actual machine hours and see how well that predetermined overhead rate applied overhead costs to the products. If there are any large differences between the way we expected to apply overhead costs to the products and the way they were indeed applied, what do we do about them?

Over- or Underapplied Overhead

Suppose that during the past year Brazos operated at an activity level of 26,000 machine hours and incurred $366,361 of actual overhead costs according to the accounting records. The total applied overhead, the overhead costs assigned to the windows and door frames, would be calculated as follows:

$$\text{Total applied overhead costs} = \$13.789 \text{ per machine hour} \times 26{,}000 \text{ machine hours} = \$358{,}514$$

Since the actual overhead cost was $366,361, Brazos *underapplied* overhead for the year by $7,847, computed as follows:

Actual overhead cost	$366,361
Applied overhead cost	358,514
Underapplied overhead cost	$ 7,847

Differences between actual and applied overhead costs result from either volume differences or differences in the amount of overhead costs themselves.

There are two possible reasons for the difference between actual overhead cost and the applied overhead cost. One reason is that the production volume during the year was slightly below estimated volume; for example, 26,000 actual machine hours versus 27,500 estimated machine hours. The second possible reason is that Brazos might have misestimated their overhead costs in calculating the predetermined overhead rate. For the moment, we simply want to make the point that there will be differences between applied overhead and actual overhead. We also want you to know the two things that affect this difference. You should also be aware that accountants do not ignore this difference; they are indeed sensitive to it, and they report it in the financial statements. We will have to withhold further discussion and explanation about what to do with the difference between applied overhead and actual overhead until Chapter 4, where we will study a complete cost system called "job order costing."

Selection of a Production Volume for the Predetermined Overhead Rate

Up to this point in the chapter we have emphasized the use of the expected annual production volume as the denominator in the calculation of the predetermined overhead rate. The major reason for using an annual rather than a monthly production volume was to smooth the cost per unit impact of seasonal overhead costs and seasonal changes in production volume. In addition to expected annual production volume here are two other production volumes that we need to consider:

Practical volume is the maximum production volume which can realistically be attained.

1 **Practical production volume,** which represents the maximum production volume that can be attained, giving consideration to uncontrollable machine breakdowns, delays in material delivery, and other factors that could cause a reduction in production volume.

Normal volume is the average volume which will satisfy demand over a relatively long time span.

2 **Normal production volume,** which represents the average production volume that will satisfy the average demand on the production facility for a particular time span. The time span is usually several years, enough to smooth out cyclical and trend factors in demand.

To illustrate the impact on the overhead cost per unit of these three different measures of production volume, let us assume that management has constructed a manufacturing facility that can produce 100,000 units—practical volume—of product per year. The expected production, based on product demand, is 70,000 units in year 1 and increases by 10,000 units per year up to 100,000 units in years 4 and 5. The average expected production—normal volume—is therefore 88,000 units per year. These facts are summarized in Exhibit 3-5. The fixed overhead cost associated with

EXHIBIT 3-5
Impact of Practical Production Volume, Normal Production Volume, and Expected Production on the Fixed Overhead Cost per Unit

	Fixed Overhead	Practical Production		Normal Production		Expected Production	
Year	Cost	Volume	Cost per Unit	Volume	Cost per Unit	Volume	Cost per Unit
1	$100,000	100,000	$1.00	88,000*	$1.136	70,000	$1.429
2	$100,000	100,000	$1.00	88,000	$1.136	80,000	$1.250
3	$100,000	100,000	$1.00	88,000	$1.136	90,000	$1.111
4	$100,000	100,000	$1.00	88,000	$1.136	100,000	$1.000
5	$100,000	100,000	$1.00	88,000	$1.136	100,000	$1.000

* Normal production volume = average expected production

$$= \frac{70{,}000 + 80{,}000 + 90{,}000 + 100{,}000 + 100{,}000}{5}$$

= 88,000 units

the manufacturing facility is expected to be $100,000 per year.[2] This would include depreciation costs, supervision costs, property taxes, insurance, etc. We have included only fixed overhead in the illustration, since variable overhead is expected to change in direct proportion to changes in production volume. Thus the point of this illustration is the impact of production volume on the fixed overhead cost per unit.

The use of practical volume for the overhead base will almost always underapply the overhead.

In examining Exhibit 3-5 we can see that the production volume we chose to calculate the predetermined overhead rate will influence the cost per unit. Practical volume provides the lowest cost per unit since it assumes the company is operating at the maximum attainable production volume. Realistically though, the demand for the product will keep production below this level for the first three years and using a predetermined overhead rate based on practical volume during that time the company will underapply the fixed overhead. Very few companies use a measure of volume to calculate predetermined overhead rates if they do not expect to attain that volume of production since it will "build in" underapplied overhead and understate the cost of the inventory. In this example the average production volume over the five-year period is 12,000 units less than practical volume (100,000 − 88,000). Management expected this result and decided to build the facility of this size anyway.

Normal volume smoothes out the effects of cyclical and trend fluctuation in production volume.

Normal volume smoothes out cyclical and trend factors associated with product demand and production relationships. The concept behind normal volume is that the fixed costs of the manufacturing facility are to be "recovered" over a long period of time. The constant fixed cost per unit resulting from normal volume is effectively spreading the fixed cost for all five years over the production for all five years. This is what management expected when they built the facility. When it is feasible to develop accurate forecasts over a five-year period, normal volume provides a "fair" measure for calculating the overhead cost per unit. The use of normal volume will result in the underapplication of fixed overhead in the years when actual volume is less than normal volume and overapplication of fixed overhead in the years when actual volume is greater than normal volume. This presents the accountant with

[2] Effects of inflation are omitted from consideration in this illustration.

The rationale for use of expected annual volume is that each year's overhead costs should be applied to that year's production.

some financial reporting questions that will be discussed in Chapter 10. A number of companies do use normal volume for calculating predetermined overhead rates. The major reason many companies do not use it is the difficulties involved in forecasting the production volume and fixed costs over a period of several years into the future.

The most widely used measure of volume for calculating predetermined overhead rates is the expected production volume for the coming year. The reason for this, in addition to the forecasting problems with normal volume, is the idea that the accounting period for financial reports is one year and that each year must stand alone. Therefore, the expected fixed overhead costs for each year should be applied to the production for that year.

One final point to keep in mind is that if total production volume does not change greatly from year to year then normal volume and expected volume will be about the same. The choice between the measures of volume for the most part depends on the judgment of management. We will study extensively how to analyze differences between actual and applied overhead costs in Chapter 9.

PLANTWIDE VERSUS DEPARTMENTAL PREDETERMINED OVERHEAD RATES

Brazos Company, in our illustration of predetermined overhead rates, used one overhead rate for both products it produces—a single plantwide overhead rate. All overhead costs were grouped together and a single overhead rate was used to apply the overhead to each of the products. This single plantwide overhead rate provided an acceptable estimate of the overhead cost per unit since we assumed that Brazos only had one manufacturing process or department. Also, in manufacturing situations where only one product is produced in multiple departments, a single plantwide overhead rate provides an acceptable estimate of the overhead cost per unit since all overhead cost is assigned to one product. However, in more complex manufacturing situations— multiple departments and multiple products—we would want to consider having a **departmental predetermined overhead rate** for each department involved in producing the products. However, like anything else, a more complex accounting system costs more money than a simple accounting system. For many firms, like Brazos, a single **plantwide predetermined overhead rate** is a sufficiently accurate match of overhead costs to products and their revenues. A more complex and more costly accounting system would not provide any increase in benefit. Other firms, usually much larger firms, need a more complex accounting system because a single plantwide overhead rate is not satisfactory. It provides a poor match between all overhead costs and all products and their revenues.

Department Predetermined Overhead Rates

All but the very smallest firms in all industries today find that they can operate more efficiently if they are divided into groups or departments, each department usually defined by its function. Many manufacturing processes have been divided into departments according to the major production function performed by each department. Such production departments might include a foundry department, a machining department, an electronics department, an assembly department, and a finishing department. Each manufacturing department has specialized workers and equipment to do its own particular type of work.

Departmental overhead rates permit different activity bases in each department.

The cost accounting problems arise because different products make different use of the production departments. One product may make no use of the foundry, heavy use of the electronics department, some use of machining, and major use of the assembly department. Another product may use only the foundry and machining departments. This kind of situation creates two problems for a firm that would use only a single predetermined plantwide overhead rate.

> First, with a single rate, each product is allocated a share of the overhead cost of *all* departments, including departments which are not used in the manufacture of that product.
>
> Second, the cause-and-effect idea suggests that each department should use an activity base which best applies the cause-and-effect idea to its own operations and overhead costs.

For example, kilograms of materials might be appropriate for the foundry, machine hours for the machining department, and direct labor hours for the electronics and assembly departments.

Departmental overhead rates provide the two following advantages: First, each department uses its own activity base that best relates the department's overhead cost to the products. Second, only products worked on in a particular department are assigned a share of that department's overhead, which means that each product is assigned a more representative share of the overhead costs needed to produce it, and no more than its fair share of the overhead costs.

At one time, most firms used only a single plantwide overhead rate because it was considered too expensive for the more complex accounting system needed to make it possible to predetermine overhead rates for each department. Because of the way organizations are now structured and because of the use of computers in accounting, it is no longer expensive to predetermine departmental overhead rates.

To illustrate the difference between plantwide and departmental overhead rates, consider the Hook Manufacturing Company in Exhibit 3-6. This company produces two products in two manufacturing departments, extruding and finishing. The estimated overhead costs are larger in extruding because of the machinery necessary to fabricate the products. Product A requires a considerable amount of machining in the extruding department and very little time in the finishing department. Product B, on the other hand, requires little machining time in the extruding department but a great deal of time in the finishing department.

If we use the plantwide overhead rate of $6 per direct labor hour, both products will be assigned an overhead cost per unit of $72. However, this does not recognize the fact that product A requires considerably more time than product B in the department (extruding) that is expected to incur the largest amount of overhead costs. To recognize this fact we need to use departmental overhead rates. They produce an overhead cost per unit of $104 for product A and $40 for product B. Thus, the departmental overhead rates provide a better measure of the relationship between the production activity, the overhead costs, and the product unit costs. They better match overhead costs to products and their revenue. The expense of a more complex accounting system to collect data and establish the "multiple" overhead rates is warranted and would pay off the benefit that overhead costs would be more effectively and proportionately allocated among the different products.

A review problem and its solution, covering plantwide overhead rates, is provided on page 71.

EXHIBIT 3-6
A Comparison of Plantwide with Departmental Overhead Rates
Hook Manufacturing Company

	Departmental Rates		Plantwide Rate
	Extruding	**Finishing**	**Total**
Estimated overhead cost	$500,000	$100,000	$600,000
Estimated direct labor hours (DLH)	÷ 50,000	÷ 50,000	÷ 100,000
Predetermined overhead rates	$ 10.00	$ 2.00	$ 6.00

Unit overhead cost—plantwide rate
Product A—(10 DLH extruding + 2 DLH finishing) × $6.00 = $72.00
Product B—(2 DLH extruding + 10 DLH finishing) × $6.00 = $72.00

Unit overhead cost—departmental rates

Product A—	10 DLH extruding × $10.00 =	$100.00
	2 DLH finishing × $ 2.00 =	4.00
		$104.00
Product B—	2 DLH extruding × $10.00 =	$ 20.00
	10 DLH finishing × $ 2.00 =	20.00
		$ 40.00

Note: One might prefer to use machine hours in the extruding department, but management found that it took one direct labor hour for each hour a machine was operated. This meant that machine hours equaled direct labor hours and it was unnecessary to do the additional accounting to record the machine hours. Direct labor hours were already recorded for payroll purposes.

ALLOCATION OF SERVICE DEPARTMENT COSTS TO PRODUCING DEPARTMENTS

Service departments aid the production departments but do no direct work on the product.

Not only are manufacturing operations divided into departments according to production activities, like the ones just mentioned, but service operations in the factory are also divided into departments according to the major service performed by each department. Service departments support the production departments; it is more efficient to have one central department provide support services to each of the production departments than to have each production department provide its own support services. Examples of service departments are the factory office, plant cafeteria, maintenance, engineering, building and grounds, and materials handling. Service departments do no direct work on the product.

Overhead costs can be applied to products worked on in production departments through the use of a predetermined overhead rate. Overhead costs cannot be applied

Service department costs are allocated to production departments for inclusion in the predetermined overhead rates.

to products in service departments because there is no physical link between service departments and products. There is no direct materials cost and no direct labor cost in service departments. The entire cost of a service department is overhead. The cost of operating service departments must be included in the overhead cost per unit of the products because they are costs of producing a product just like any other overhead cost. So the cost of the service departments must first be *allocated* to the producing departments and then included in the predetermined overhead rates of the production departments.

Selecting a Basis for Allocating Service Department Costs to Production Departments

The function of service departments is to serve other departments. The cause-and-effect idea is again used in selecting a basis of allocating service department costs to other departments. Usually the nature of the service supplied by the service department provides the best measure. If the department provides services for people in other departments, the number of people working in the other departments would probably be used. For example, an employment office will screen applicants for the factory departments; therefore, costs of an employment department are usually allocated to production departments based upon the estimated number of employees in each department. It is assumed that departments with a large number of employees will consume more of the time of the employment department than departments with fewer employees, and should therefore receive more of the cost. Likewise, the cost of a repair and maintenance department may be allocated to production departments based on the number of machines or machine hours in each department. The assumption underlying the use of this base is that more repair and maintenance time will be expended in departments with many machines than in departments with few machines. Finally, some costs, such as those for a central heating plant, might be allocated on the basis of number of square feet in each department on the assumption that it costs more to heat a large area than a small area.

Determination of Production Department Overhead Rates

After allocating all estimated service department costs to each of the production departments, the share of service department costs are added to the other overhead costs which are incurred in each of the production departments. Then a predetermined departmental overhead rate can be determined using the same approach previously described. Thus, the predetermined overhead rate for a production department can be thought of as follows:

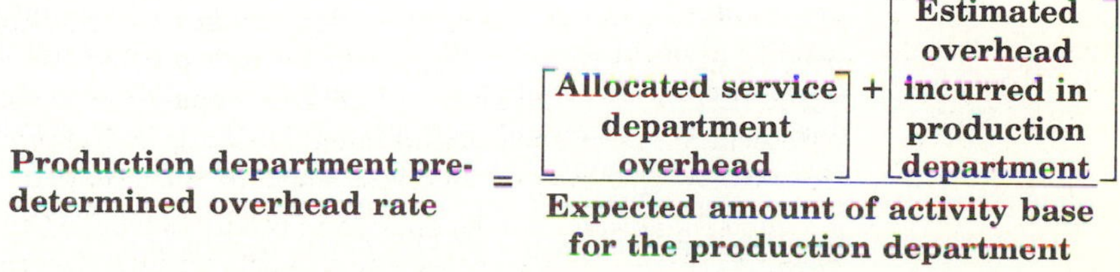

$$\text{Production department predetermined overhead rate} = \frac{\begin{bmatrix}\text{Allocated service}\\\text{department}\\\text{overhead}\end{bmatrix} + \begin{bmatrix}\text{Estimated}\\\text{overhead}\\\text{incurred in}\\\text{production}\\\text{department}\end{bmatrix}}{\text{Expected amount of activity base for the production department}}$$

Three Methods to Allocate Service Department Cost to Producing Departments

To calculate departmental predetermined overhead rates, the service department costs must be allocated to the producing departments. We will consider three methods of allocating service department costs to producing departments:

1. Direct allocation
2. Step allocation
3. Reciprocal allocation

An example requiring allocation of service department costs.

To illustrate how service department costs are allocated to production departments with each method, let us return to the Brazos Aluminum Corporation. For purposes of illustration, assume the Brazos production process and factory organization is more complex than our original description. The company is divided into two service departments and two producing departments. The two service departments are the maintenance department, which includes minor repairs and janitorial services, and the factory office department, which handles plant payroll and factory cost accounting. The company's two production departments are the extruding department, where the aluminum is shaped into the required forms for window frames and door frames, and the assembly department, where the frames are assembled and finished.

The cause-and-effect principle suggests to management that the maintenance department costs be allocated on the basis of the number of square feet in each production department and that factory office department costs be allocated based upon the number of employees in each production department. The rationale for allocating maintenance using square feet would be based upon the type of service rendered by the maintenance department. In Brazos, the maintenance department is primarily a janitorial service as well as a minor repair service. (The company brings in outside repairmen for major repairs.) Since it takes maintenance personnel longer to clean and maintain physically larger departments, allocation based upon the number of square feet follows cause and effect.

Because the factory office department keeps payroll records, cause and effect suggests that the relative number of employees in each production department be the basis of allocating factory office department costs. Payroll, which is a large portion of their work, is based upon the number of employees. The factory office department also does all the interviewing and testing of prospective employees. Thus cause-and-effect reasoning is used in allocating cost based on the number of employees in each department.

The direct method of allocating service department costs is the easiest method.

Direct Allocation The direct allocation of the service department costs to the producing departments is illustrated in Exhibit 3-7. The first part of the exhibit presents the number of square feet and the number of employees in each of the production departments in the Brazos plant. This exhibit also shows the percentages used to allocate service department costs to the extruding and assembly production departments. Direct allocation of service department costs to production departments does not recognize any services provided by one service department to another service department. Therefore, even though there are employees in all four departments and all departments occupy some portion of the plant, we did not show the total square feet in the service departments and the total number of employees in the service departments in Exhibit 3-7.

Using the percentages presented in Exhibit 3-7, the direct allocation of service

EXHIBIT 3-7
BRAZOS ALUMINUM CORPORATION
Direct Method for Allocating Service Department Costs

	Service Departments		Producing Departments		
	Maintenance	Factory Office	Extruding	Assembly	Total
Square feet			30,000	30,000	60,000
Percentage			50%[a]	50%[b]	100%
Number of employees			9	36	45
Percentage			20%[c]	80%[d]	100%
Overhead costs before allocation	$94,000	$48,000	$188,000	$ 49,200	$379,200
Allocation of maintenance	($94,000)		50% ($94,000) 47,000	50% ($94,000) 47,000	
Allocation of factory office		(48,000)	20% ($48,000) 9,600	80% ($48,000) 38,400	
Overhead costs after allocation			$244,600	$134,600	$379,200
Estimated machine hours			20,000		
Predetermined overhead rate			$ 12.23		
Estimated direct labor hours				10,000	
Predetermined overhead rate				$ 13.46	

[a] $\left(\frac{30,000}{30,000 + 30,000}\right)$
[b] $\left(\frac{30,000}{30,000 + 30,000}\right)$
[c] $\left(\frac{9}{9 + 36}\right)$
[d] $\left(\frac{36}{9 + 36}\right)$

department costs to production departments is presented in the second part of the exhibit.

Using direct allocation of service department costs to production departments, Brazos allocated (divided) the total estimated maintenance cost—$94,000—directly to the extruding and assembly departments and allocated the total estimate of factory office department costs—$48,000—directly to the extruding and assembly departments. After the allocation of the service department costs, all service department costs are associated with either the extruding or assembly departments. Instead of using one plantwide predetermined overhead rate to apply overhead to the two products—window frames and door frames—the company can now develop departmental predetermined overhead rates—one for the extruding department and one for the assembly department—and use each of these rates to apply overhead costs to the products.

In the plantwide predetermined overhead rate illustrated earlier in the chapter, management decided to base the single rate on machine hours, since the overhead costs were mostly machine related. With departmental rates, management can recognize that the machinery is primarily in the extruding department. The assembly operation depends primarily on labor hours rather than machine hours. Therefore, management chose to use machine hours as the basis for the predetermined overhead rate in the extruding department and direct labor hours in assembly. At expected annual volume, Brazos estimated that 20,000 machine hours would be worked in extruding and 10,000 direct labor hours would be worked in assembly. The predetermined overhead rates for each department are calculated by taking the total overhead costs in each production department, after allocation of service department cost, and dividing it by the expected amount of the appropriate activity base.

The step method is slightly more complicated because it recognizes more service relationships.

Step Allocation The step method of allocating service department costs recognizes that some service departments provide services to other service departments, as well as to production departments, and some service department costs can be allocated to other service departments. Therefore, the step method recognizes more of the relationships among the service and manufacturing departments than the direct method. Thus, more cause-and-effect relationships are incorporated into the computation of the predetermined overhead rate. Of course, like any situation where we can choose between alternative accounting methods, the step versus the direct method has to be evaluated on a cost-benefit basis.

The first thing you must do in the step method is to decide the order in which the steps are to be taken. In the case of only two service departments, this means deciding which service department's costs will be allocated first and which will be allocated second. There are general rules about the order, and they are quite arbitrary rules. The most frequently used rule is the department which serves the most other departments is allocated first. Next, the department which serves the most remaining departments is allocated, and so on until all service department costs have been allocated.

In many cases a number of departments serve an equal number of other departments, and the rule just described gives no guidance about the order of steps of allocation. In that situation, the rule is: the department with the greatest amount of cost is allocated first. Remember that any rule for choosing the order of allocation is arbitrary.

An example of the step method.

In the Brazos Company illustration, the maintenance department provides services for the factory office and the factory office provides services for the maintenance department. That means each service department serves another service department as well as the two production departments. Thus, the order of allocation must be decided on the basis of the amount of cost in each department. Since the maintenance department has $94,000 costs before allocation and the factory office has only $48,000, maintenance department costs will be allocated first to the factory office and the extruding and assembly departments. After this first step is done, factory office costs—including its share of the maintenance department cost, which we will explain—will be allocated to the extruding and assembly departments.

Important: Notice that once the costs of a department are allocated, no further costs are allocated *back* to that department. That is why no factory office costs are allocated to the maintenance department.

After the costs are allocated out of a service department, no costs are allocated back into it.

After service department costs are all allocated, predetermined overhead rates are computed for each production department. These predetermined overhead rates are used to assign overhead cost to individual products.

Exhibit 3-8 shows the calculation of the percentages used for allocating the service department costs using the step method. Notice that the percentages for the maintenance department change from those used in the direct method because some of the maintenance department cost will be allocated to factory office. The percentages for factory office allocation do not change because its cost will be allocated only to the two production departments as in the direct illustration. But the dollar amounts allocated from factory office change because factory office cost will contain a share of maintenance cost.

Exhibit 3-8 shows the allocation of service department costs by the step method and the calculation of the predetermined overhead rate for each production department.

If Brazos had many service departments, the step method of allocating service department costs would require a more lengthy set of computations but the basic procedure is the same.

Comparison of the results of the step method of allocation in Exhibit 3-8 to the results of the direct allocation method in Exhibit 3-7 show that the predetermined overhead rates are different. The extruding department's rate is $12.23 per machine hour with the direct method and has been lowered to $11.877 per machine hour with the step method. The assembly department's rate, on the other hand, has increased with the step method. If the cost of performing the computations with the step method are not much greater, then it would be preferred in this situation since it incorporates more of the relationship between the service departments, production departments, and the products being produced.

The reciprocal method recognizes all services between all departments.

Reciprocal Allocation The step method recognized and incorporated in the allocation the fact that some service departments provide services to other service departments. However, once a service department's costs were allocated, no further costs could be allocated back to that service department. The reciprocal allocation method allows costs to be allocated back to a service department once its costs have been allocated. For example, Brazos maintenance department provides services to the factory office, and the factory office provides services to the maintenance department. The reciprocal method allows us to allocate maintenance department costs to the factory office department *and* to allocate factory office department costs to the maintenance department. This incorporates more of the cause-and-effect relationship in the calculation of the predetermined overhead rate than the step method. Again, whether we use the reciprocal, step, or direct method depends on the additional benefit versus the added cost.

Exhibit 3-9 illustrates the reciprocal method for the Brazos Company. In the first part of the exhibit notice that the percentages for the maintenance department do not change from the step method because we allocated its cost to the factory office

EXHIBIT 3-8
BRAZOS ALUMINUM CORPORATION
Step Method for Allocating Service Department Costs

	Service Departments		Producing Departments		
	Maintenance	Factory Office	Extruding	Assembly	Total
Square feet		20,000	30,000	30,000	80,000
Percentage		25%[a]	37.5%[b]	37.5%[c]	100%
Number of employees			9	36	45
Percentage			20%[d]	80%[e]	100%
Overhead costs before allocation	$94,000	$48,000	$188,000	$ 49,200	$379,200
Allocation of maintenance	($94,000)	25% ($94,000) 23,500	37.5% ($94,000) 35,250	37.5% ($94,000) 35,250	
Allocation of factory office		($71,500)	20% ($71,500) 14,300	80% ($71,500) 57,200	
Overhead costs after allocation			$237,550	$141,650	$379,200
Estimated machine hours			210,000		
Predetermined overhead rate			$ 11.877		
Estimated direct labor hours				10,000	
Predetermined overhead rate				$ 14.165	

[a] $\left(\frac{20,000}{20,000 + 30,000 + 30,000}\right)$

[b] $\left(\frac{30,000}{20,000 + 30,000 + 30,000}\right)$

[c] $\left(\frac{30,000}{20,000 + 30,000 + 30,000}\right)$

[d] $\left(\frac{9}{9 + 36}\right)$

[e] $\left(\frac{36}{9 + 36}\right)$

IMPORTANT

EXHIBIT 3-9
BRAZOS ALUMINUM CORPORATION
Reciprocal Method for Allocating Service Department Costs

	Service Departments		Producing Departments		
	Maintenance	Factory Office	Extruding	Assembly	Total
Square feet		20,000	30,000	30,000	80,000
Percentage		25%[a]	37.5%[b]	37.5%[c]	100%
Number of employees	5		9	36	50
Percentage	10%[d]		18%[e]	72%[f]	100%
Overhead costs before allocation	$94,000	$48,000	$188,000	$ 49,200	$379,200
Allocation of maintenance	(101,333)*	25% ($101,333) 25,333	37.5% ($101,333) 38,000	37.5% ($101,333) 38,000	
Allocation of factory office	10% ($73,333) 7,333	(73,333)*	18% ($ 73,333) 13,200	72% ($ 73,333) 52,800	
Overhead costs after allocation	0	0	$239,200	$140,000	$379,200
Estimated machine hours			20,000		
Predetermined overhead rate			$ 11.96		
Estimated direct labor hours				10,000	
Predetermined overhead rate				$ 14.00	

[a] $\left(\frac{30,000}{20,000 + 30,000 + 30,000}\right)$

[b] $\left(\frac{30,000}{20,000 + 30,000 + 30,000}\right)$

[c] $\left(\frac{30,000}{20,000 + 30,000 + 30,000}\right)$

[d] $\left(\frac{5}{5 + 9 + 36}\right)$

[e] $\left(\frac{9}{5 + 9 + 36}\right)$

[f] $\left(\frac{36}{5 + 9 + 36}\right)$

* Let M = Total maintenance costs

F = Total factory office costs

$$M = 94,000 + .1F$$
$$F = 48,000 + .25M$$
$$M = 94,000 + .1\ (48,000 + .25M)$$
$$M = 94,000 + 4,800 + .025M$$
$$.975M = 98,800$$
$$M = 101,333$$
$$F = 48,000 + .25M$$
$$F = 48,000 + .25\ (101,333)$$
$$F = 73,333$$

department and the producing departments. The percentages for the factory office department do change, since now we will allocate a part of its cost to the maintenance department.

An illustration of the reciprocal method.

The total maintenance department cost and factory office department cost that has to be allocated is determined with simultaneous equations as illustrated at the bottom of Exhibit 3-9. The simultaneous equations are structured to represent the total overhead cost of each service department after factory office costs have been allocated to the maintenance department and maintenance costs have been allocated to the factory office department. For more complex situations, involving more than two service departments, matrix algebra is used to solve the equations.[3]

The second part of Exhibit 3-9 shows the allocation of the service department costs to each other and to the producing departments along with the calculations of the predetermined overhead rates. The overhead rates calculated using the reciprocal method are not much different than the results of the step method. Generally, this will be the case; consequently the reciprocal method is not widely used in practice. However, situations will arise where significant differences could occur, and if management is using the data for decision making, the accountant should ascertain whether the decisions could be changed by the results of the allocation method. If the decisions are sensitive to the allocation method, the reciprocal method provides the most accurate estimate of the predetermined overhead rates.

In this chapter we have only been concerned with overhead cost allocations for product costing, i.e., cost accounting. Since our concern was with product costing, we concentrated on accounting methods that would apply the overhead to the product in such a manner that net income would be reported in accordance with GAAP. We have not discussed overhead cost allocation for management planning and control decisions, i.e., managerial accounting. This topic will be explored in Chapter 17, where you will learn that relevance to the decision will guide the procedures we will use to allocate or not to allocate manufacturing overhead costs.

SUMMARY

The main discussion of this chapter concerned how accountants determine the amount of overhead cost to be applied to each unit of product. We started the chapter by illustrating how the actual overhead cost per unit could be calculated for a single-product firm. However, since managers desire unit cost information during the year for interim financial statements and decision making, the overhead cost per unit is predetermined at the beginning of the year. A year was used as the time period for predetermining the overhead rate for two reasons:

1. To smooth out the seasonal variations in overhead costs, such as heating and snow removal costs incurred only in the winter months
2. To smooth out the impact of seasonal changes in production volume on the fixed overhead cost per unit

When a company is producing more than one product some of the overhead costs are joint costs. Joint overhead costs benefit the production of more than one

[3] For an illustration of the calculations for more than two service departments, see John K. Shank, *Matrix Methods in Accounting,* Addison-Wesley Publishing Co., Inc., Reading, Mass., 1972.

product. To assign joint costs to the products, we must select a measure of production activity that is a common denominator for all products and relates the cause and effect for the overhead costs. The measure of production chosen is referred to as an activity base. The most widely used activity bases in practice are direct labor hours, machine hours, direct labor dollars, and direct material units or dollars.

Often the use of a predetermined overhead rate will result in an amount of overhead cost applied which is different from the actual overhead cost incurred. This overapplied or underapplied overhead can be caused by two things—production at above or below expected volume, and greater or lesser overhead cost than was anticipated when the overhead cost was estimated. The accounting for over- or underapplied overhead is discussed in Chapter 4.

In complex manufacturing situations—multiple products and multiple production departments—companies will use departmental predetermined overhead rates. The advantages of departmental predetermined overhead rates over a plantwide overhead rate are:

1 Each department can use the activity base that best relates the department's overhead cost to the products.

2 Only products worked on in a particular department are assigned a share of that department's overhead cost.

In calculating departmental overhead costs we have to allocate manufacturing service department costs to the producing departments. Three methods were discussed and illustrated to accomplish this: direct allocation, step allocation, and reciprocal allocation. The most theoretically correct method is the reciprocal method. However, its use is rarely justified by the benefit of improved information and one of the simpler methods is most often used in practice.

Review Problem

The cost accountants of Kustom Order Company established the following basis for applying manufacturing overhead to jobs:

$$\frac{\textbf{Estimated manufacturing overhead}}{\textbf{Estimated direct labor cost}} = \frac{\$75{,}000}{\$100{,}000}$$

$$= \$.75 \text{ of overhead for each direct labor dollar}$$

During the following period actual direct labor cost was $90,000 and the actual manufacturing overhead was as follows:

Factory supplies	$ 7,000
Rent	26,000
Heat, light, and power	12,000
Indirect labor	7,000
Indirect materials	5,000
Depreciation on machinery	15,000
Factory insurance	2,000

Required 1 Did the company apply more or less overhead to production than it actually incurred during the period?

2 Describe some of the factors that could have caused the over- or underapplication of manufacturing overhead during the period.

Solution

1 Manufacturing overhead applied to production	$90,000 × .75 =	$67,500
Actual manufacturing overhead	=	74,000
Underapplied overhead		$ 6,500

The company charged less overhead to production than it actually incurred during the period.

2 a The estimate of direct labor cost could have been in error because of a misestimate of production volume.

b The estimate may not have considered the rate of inflation.

c Changes may have taken place which affect the overhead to direct labor ratio, such as:

1 Laborers became more efficient
2 A machine replaced a number of laborers
3 Wage rates may have changed

Review Problem

The Space Production Company manufactures components for radio and television satellites using two service departments and two production departments. The interdepartmental relationships and estimated overhead costs are given below:

		Percentage of Services Provided to			
		Maintenance	**Scheduling**	**Molding**	**Assembly**
From	Maintenance	—	10%	40%	50%
	Scheduling	20%	—	50%	30%
	Total overhead cost	$750,000	$400,000	$378,000	$276,000

Required 1 Use the direct method to allocate the service department cost to the producing department and calculate the overhead cost for molding and assembly.

2 Repeat **1** using the step method and allocating maintenance first.

3 Repeat part **1** using the step method allocating scheduling first.

4 Repeat part **1** using the reciprocal method.

Solution

1

SPACE PRODUCTION COMPANY
Direct Allocation of Service Department Costs

	Maintenance	Scheduling		Molding		Assembly
Total cost	$ 750,000	$ 400,000		$378,000		$276,000
Allocation of maintenance	(750,000)		(4/9)*	333,333.33	(5/9)	416,666.67
Allocation of scheduling		(400,000)	(5/8)	250,000	(3/8)	150,000
Total cost after allocation				$961,333.33		$842,666.67

* (40%/90%)

2

SPACE PRODUCTION COMPANY
Step Allocation of Service Department Costs
Allocation of Maintenance First

	Maintenance		Scheduling		Molding		Assembly
Total cost	$ 750,000		$400,000		$378,000		$276,000
Allocation of maintenance	(750,000)	(10%)	75,000	(40%)	300,000	(50%)	375,000
Allocation of scheduling			($475,000)	(5/8)	296,875	(3/8)	178,125
Total cost after allocation					$974,875		$829,125

3

SPACE PRODUCTION COMPANY
Step Allocation of Service Department Costs
Allocation of Scheduling First

		Maintenance	Scheduling		Molding		Assembly
Total cost		$750,000	$400,000		$378,000		$276,000
Allocation of scheduling	(20%)	80,000	(400,000)	(50%)	200,000	(30%)	120,000
Allocation of maintenance		($830,000)		(4/9)	368,888.88	(5/9)	461,111.12
Total cost after allocation					$946,888.88		$857,111.12

4 The equations for total cost using the reciprocal method are:

Maintenance	$M = 750{,}000 + .2S$
Scheduling	$S = 400{,}000 + .1M$

Using substitution the values of M and S are calculated as follows:

$$M = 750{,}000 + .2\,(400{,}000 + .1M)$$
$$M = 750{,}000 + 80{,}000 + .02M$$
$$.98M = 830{,}000$$
$$M = 846{,}938.77$$
$$S = 400{,}000 + .1\,(836{,}938.77)$$
$$S = 484{,}693.88$$

SPACE PRODUCTION COMPANY
Reciprocal Allocation of Service Department Costs

		Maintenance		Scheduling		Molding		Assembly
Total cost		$750,000		$400,000		$378,000		$276,000
Allocation of maintenance		(846,938.77)	(.1)	84,693.88	(.4)	338,775.51	(.5)	423,469.38
Allocation of scheduling	(.2)	96,938.77		(484,693.88)	(.5)	242,346.94	(.3)	145,408.17
Total cost after allocation		0		0		$949,122.45		$844,877.55

Glossary

Activity base A measure of production volume used to relate manufacturing overhead to the product. Common activity bases are material dollars, direct labor dollars, direct labor hours, and machine hours.

Annual volume The expected production activity for the coming year. Annual volume smoothes out the seasonal fluctuations in overhead cost and production volume.

Departmental predetermined overhead rates A predetermined overhead rate calculated for each production department. This provides a better matching of overhead costs with the products than a plantwide overhead rate.

Direct allocation A method for allocating service department overhead to producing departments that does not recognize any services provided by one service department to another service department.

Joint cost A cost whose incurrence necessarily benefits more than one cost object. Many overhead costs are joint.

Manufacturing overhead (Indirect manufacturing costs) All manufacturing costs except direct material and direct labor.

Normal volume The expected average production activity which will satisfy product demand for several years. Normal production volume smoothes out the cyclical and trend factors in demand.

Plantwide predetermined overhead rate A single predetermined overhead rate that is used by all production departments to assign overhead to the products.

Practical volume The maximum production activity that can be attained, giving consideration to uncontrollable machine breakdowns, delays in material delivery, and other uncontrollable factors that could reduce production.

Predetermined overhead rate An overhead rate calculated from estimated overhead costs and estimated production volume.

Reciprocal allocation A method for allocating service department overhead to producing departments that recognizes all the service provided by one service department to other service departments.

Step allocation A method for allocating service department overhead to producing departments that recognizes some of the service provided by service departments to other service departments.

Questions and Problems

3-1 What is the purpose of calculating a predetermined overhead rate?

3-2 Discuss the procedures involved in determining a predetermined overhead rate for a manufacturing company.

3-3 Discuss the criteria for the selection of an activity measure for the allocation of overhead to the products or jobs.

3-4 What are the advantages of normal volume and annual volume for the calculation of predetermined overhead rates?

3-5 Describe a situation where a plantwide predetermined overhead rate would be preferred over departmental predetermined overhead rates.

3-6 Describe a situation where departmental predetermined overhead rates would be preferred over a plantwide predetermined overhead rate.

3-7 List the procedures that are necessary for the calculations of departmental predetermined overhead rates.

3-8 Describe the methods for allocating service department costs to producing departments.

3-9 What criteria are often used for selecting the sequence of departmental allocations with the step method?

3-10 Why is the reciprocal method considered the preferred method for cost allocations from service to producing departments?

3-11 **Predetermined Overhead Rates and Product Cost per Unit** The Whynot Company produces two products: whys and nots. At the beginning of 19X5 the manufacturing manager supplied the cost accounting department with the following *estimates:*

Manufacturing overhead	$400,000
Machine hours	100,000
Direct labor hours	50,000

Required

1 Calculate a predetermined overhead rate using machine hours as the activity base.

2 Calculate a predetermined overhead rate using direct labor hours as the activity base.

3 Assume that during 19X5 it takes the following machine hours and direct labor hours to produce 1 unit of each product:

	Whys	**Nots**
Machine hours	4	2
Direct labor hours	2	2

Calculate the overhead cost per unit for whys and nots assuming the company used a predetermined overhead rate based on:

a Machine hours

b Direct labor hours

4 What criteria should the company use to select an activity base for applying overhead to their products?

3-12 Working Backwards to Calculate Actual and Estimated Direct Labor Hours The Bonham Company incurred $150,000 of manufacturing overhead during 19X4. This was $30,000 less than the applied overhead. The applied overhead is based on direct labor hours using a rate of $1.50 per direct labor hour.

Required

1 Calculate the actual direct labor hours worked during 19X4.

2 Assuming the actual manufacturing overhead cost is equal to the estimated manufacturing overhead cost for 19X4, calculate the estimated direct labor hours for 19X4.

3-13 Predetermined Overhead Rates The Acme Manufacturing Company has *estimated* the following data for 19X5:

	Fabricating	**Assembly**
Manufacturing overhead	$800,000	$400,000
Machine hours	200,000	80,000
Direct labor hours	50,000	100,000

The company uses a predetermined overhead rate for applying the overhead to the products. The overhead rate is based on machine hours in fabricating and direct labor hours in assembly.

Required

1 Calculate the predetermined overhead rate for the fabricating and assembly departments.

2 Assume the *actual* results for the year 19X5 are:

	Fabricating	Assembly
Manufacturing overhead	$820,000	$398,000
Machine hours	210,000	75,000
Direct labor hours	55,000	110,000

Calculate the over- or underapplied overhead for each department and for the company as a whole.

3-14 Comparison of Plantwide and Departmental Predetermined Overhead Rates The Bailey Fabricating Company produces two products, XY10 and XY13, in two manufacturing departments. For the year 19X4, the following estimated data have been prepared:

	Machining	Assembly
Estimated overhead cost	$400,000	$100,000
Estimated direct labor hours	100,000	100,000

Required

1 Calculate a plantwide predetermined overhead rate using direct labor hours.

2 Calculate departmental predetermined overhead rates using direct labor hours.

3 Assume that during 19X4 it takes the following direct labor hours to produce 1 unit of each product:

	Machining	Assembly
XY10	15	5
XY13	5	15

Calculate the overhead cost per unit for XY10 and XY13 using:
a The plantwide overhead rate
b The departmental overhead rate

4 Which of the predetermined overhead rates would you choose to determine the product cost of XY10 and XY13? Why?

3-15 Direct versus Step Method for Allocating Service Department Costs The Parker Manufacturing Company has two production departments (fabrication and assembly) and three service departments (factory administration, factory maintenance, and factory cafeteria). A summary of costs and other data for each department prior to allocation of service department costs for the year ended June 30, 19X1, appears below:

	Producing Departments	
	Fabrication	Assembly
Direct labor costs	$1,950,000	$2,050,000
Direct materials costs	3,130,000	950,000
Manufacturing overhead costs	1,650,000	1,850,000
Labor hours	562,500	437,500
Number of employees	280	200
Square footage occupied	88,000	72,000

	Service Departments		
	Factory Administration	Factory Maintenance	Factory Cafeteria
Direct labor costs	—	—	—
Direct materials costs	—	—	—
Manufacturing overhead costs	$160,000	$203,200	$240,000
Labor hours	31,000	27,000	42,000
Number of employees	12	8	20
Square footage occupied	1,750	2,000	4,800

The costs of the general factory administration department, factory maintenance department, and factory cafeteria are allocated on the basis of labor hours, square footage occupied, and number of employees, respectively. Round all final calculations to the nearest dollar.

Required

1 Using the direct method, allocate the service department costs to the two producing departments.

2 Using the step method and starting with the service department that has the greatest total cost, allocate the service department costs to the producing departments.

3-16 Step and Reciprocal Allocations The ABC Company has two main products, Y and Z. Product Y is produced in department I and product Z is produced in department II. To produce the main products the producing departments utilize the services of two service departments, P and Q. An analysis of the work done by the service departments yields the following data.

		Units of Service Department Output Transferred to:				
		P	Q	I	II	Total
From	Department P	0	30	70	100	200
	Department Q	20	0	40	40	100

The total costs incurred by P are $100,000 and by Q are $200,000.

Required

1 Using the step method and allocating P first, determine the total service department cost charged to Y and Z.

2 Using the reciprocal method of allocation determine the total service department cost charged to Y and Z.

3-17 Direct and Reciprocal Allocation and Computation of Overhead Rates The Grant Specialty Manufacturing Company has two service and three producing departments. A schedule showing the percentage of service department resources provided to each user is shown below:

		To					
		S1	**S2**	**P1**	**P2**	**P3**	**Total**
From	S1	—	40%	20%	10%	30%	100%
	S2	20%	—	30%	40%	10%	100%

The overhead has been estimated and resulted in the following figures for the year:

Department	Overhead
S1	$126,000
S2	200,000
P1	350,000
P2	215,000
P3	240,000

The overhead is assigned to production based on machine hours in P1 and direct labor hours in P2 and P3.

The estimated annual activity for all three producing departments in both machine and labor hours is shown below:

	Estimated	
Department	**Machine Hours**	**Direct Labor Hours**
P1	100,000	40,000
P2	30,000	85,000
P3	15,000	120,000

Required

1 Using the direct method, allocate the service department costs to the producing departments.

2 Compute the predetermined overhead rates in the production departments.

3 Repeat parts 1 and 2 using the reciprocal method.

3-18 Comparison of Expected Annual, Maximum, and Normal Volume The Net Corporation is trying to decide whether to use the maximum production capacity, expected annual production, or normal capacity to assign overhead costs to their products. Normal capacity is defined as the average expected activity over a five-year period. The production statistics and estimated overhead cost are given below:

	Year				
	19X1	**19X2**	**19X3**	**19X4**	**19X5**
Estimated direct labor hours	120,000	130,000	120,000	140,000	150,000
Maximum direct labor hours	150,000	150,000	150,000	150,000	150,000
Estimated overhead costs*	$460,000	$490,000	$460,000	$520,000	$550,000

* Based on estimated production.

Required

1 Calculate the overhead per direct labor hour using expected actual, maximum capacity, and normal capacity as the activity base for each of the five years.

2 Which activity level would you recommend to management for the assignment of overhead to the products? Why?

3-19 Comparison of Direct and Step Methods The Anso Company produces a complete line of plastic toys in three producing departments: molding, cutting, and assembly. These departments are supported by two service departments, maintenance and personnel. For the coming year the overhead costs in all departments have been estimated as follows:

Department	Estimated Overhead
Maintenance	$ 50,000
Personnel	20,000
Molding	175,000
Cutting	120,000
Assembly	75,000

The service department overhead is allocated to the producing departments based on machine hours for maintenance and number of employees for personnel. The overhead is then assigned to the products using machine hours in molding and cutting and labor hours in assembly. Data for allocating the service department overhead to the producing departments and from the producing departments to the product are given below:

Department	Number of Employees	Machine Hours	Direct Labor Hours
Maintenance	50	—	—
Personnel	5	—	—
Molding	50	50,000	20,000
Cutting	50	40,000	20,000
Assembly	100	10,000	60,000

Required

1 Allocate the service department overhead cost to the producing departments using the direct method.

2 Calculate the predetermined overhead rate for each production department.

3 Repeat parts 1 and 2 using the step method allocating the personnel department first.

3-20 Calculation of Overhead Rate Using the Step Method The Bottle Company has three service departments and two producing departments. Data concerning the overhead cost and selected production statistics are given below:

	Service Departments		
	Personnel	**Maintenance**	**Scheduling**
Overhead cost	$100,000	$350,000	$200,000
Number of employees	5	25	10
Number of work orders	—	500	—
Machine hours	—	—	—
Labor hours	—	—	—

	Producing Departments	
	Fabricating	**Assembly**
Overhead cost	$900,000	$620,000
Number of employees	50	75
Number of work orders	1,500	2,000
Machine hours	30,000	15,000
Labor hours	20,000	50,000

The company uses the step method to allocate the service department cost to the producing departments. The order of allocation is personnel department first using number of employees, the scheduling department second using work orders, and last the maintenance department using machine hours. The predetermined overhead rate is based on machine hours in fabricating and labor hours in assembly.

Required

Allocate the service department costs and calculate the predetermined overhead rate for both producing departments.

3-21 Direct and Step Allocations The Dimeri Manufacturing Company has two production departments and two service departments. The cost data and relevant statistics for a normal year are summarized below:

	Producing Departments	
	Fabrication	Assembly
Direct labor hours	50,000	100,000
Direct labor cost	$412,500	$645,000
Overhead cost	$820,000	$467,000
Number of employees	20	50
Machine hours	75,000	25,000

	Service Departments	
	Factory Maintenance	Factory Administration
Indirect labor hours	20,000	5,000
Indirect labor cost	$186,000	$49,000
Other overhead cost	$210,000	$70,000
Number of employees	10	2
Machine hours	—	—

The factory maintenance department and factory administration cost are allocated on the basis of machine hours and number of employees respectively. The overhead in both producing departments is assigned to the products based on direct labor hours:

Required

1 Using the direct method of allocation, compute the overhead rates for the two producing departments.

2 Using the step method and allocating the factory administration department first, compute the overhead rate for the two producing departments.

3-22 Comparison of Plantwide versus Departmental Overhead Rates The Patex Company consists of two service departments and two production departments. The estimated overhead cost and selected production statistics are given in the following table:

	Service Depts.		Production Depts.	
	Power	Maintenance	1	2
Square feet		10,000	30,000	40,000
Machine hours	20,000		50,000	30,000
Labor hours			30,000	50,000
Overhead cost	$80,000	$90,000	$150,000	$110,000

During the year the company completed three projects requiring the following amount of machine hours and labor hours in the production departments.

	Machine Hours		Labor Hours	
	Dept. 1	Dept. 2	Dept. 1	Dept. 2
Project A	10,000	8,000	3,000	15,000
Project B	20,000	6,000	8,000	30,000
Project C	25,000	4,000	9,000	17,000
	55,000	18,000	20,000	62,000

Required

1 Using the step method and allocating the power department overhead first, calculate the total overhead cost assigned to each producing department. Square feet should be used to allocate power costs and machine hours for maintenance costs.

2 Calculate the predetermined overhead rate using machine hours in department 1 and labor hours in department 2.

3 Compute the total overhead applied to each of the three projects.

4 Using direct labor hours as the activity base compute a plantwide predetermined overhead rate.

5 Using the plantwide predetermined overhead rate, calculate the total overhead applied to each of the three projects.

6 Compare the answer to question 5 with the answer to question 3.

3-23 Reciprocal Method A manufacturer's plant has two service departments (designated below as S_1 and S_2) and three production departments (designated below as P_1, P_2, and P_3) and wishes to allocate all factory overhead to production departments. The company makes the allocation of overhead from service departments to production departments on a reciprocal basis, recognizing the fact that services of one service department are utilized by another. Data regarding costs and allocation percentages are as follows:

Service Department	Service Department Overhead Cost Allocation Percentages to be Allocated to Departments				
	S_1	S_2	P_1	P_2	P_3
S_1	0%	10%	20%	40%	30%
S_2	20	0	50	10	20

Service Department	Manufacturing Overhead to Be Allocated				
	S_1	S_2	P_1	P_2	P_3
Cost	$98,000	$117,600	$1,400,000	$2,100,000	$640,000

Required

Using the reciprocal method, calculate the total overhead cost of each production department.

(CPA)

JOB ORDER COSTING

AFTER COMPLETING YOUR STUDY OF THIS CHAPTER, YOU SHOULD HAVE LEARNED:

1 The production situations which would use job order costing to accumulate the product costs for the preparation of income statements and balance sheets.

2 Why the job cost sheet is a basic accounting document used to accumulate the cost of manufacturing a product in a job order costing system.

3 How to record the manufacturing costs in the general and subsidiary ledgers of a manufacturing firm.

4 How to calculate the average cost per unit of the products manufactured and how to use it in costing the finished goods inventory and determining the cost of goods sold.

5 How to account for the differences between the actual overhead cost and the applied overhead cost, a topic carried over from Chapter 3.

Determining the average cost per unit to manufacture a product is the primary objective of cost accounting. The average cost per unit is important in cost accounting since it is used to determine the cost of the inventories on the balance sheet and the cost of goods sold on the income statement.

Job order costing is one of two major product cost accounting systems for assigning manufacturing costs to the products and then matching the average cost per unit with the revenues recognized from the sale of the product.

Job order costing and process costing are the two major systems for assigning manufacturing costs to products.

The other major product cost accounting system is process costing, and we shall discuss it in Chapter 5. Nevertheless, as we begin this chapter, you should keep in mind that both job order costing and process costing are two different ways to assign manufacturing costs to a product. For example, how do we assign the cost of sheet metal to the automobiles produced by General Motors or Datsun? How do we assign the labor cost of assembling furniture to a customer's order for a living room set? How do we assign the manufacturing overhead of Acme Printing Company to each textbook or magazine produced? If you fully understand the operation of job order costing and process costing you will be able to answer these questions.

JOB ORDER COSTING AND PROCESS COSTING

The product cost accounting system a company should use depends primarily on how the product is produced.

There are basically two categories of product cost accounting systems, **job order costing** and **process costing.** They are two different ways of recording the manufacturing costs and assigning them to products for calculating the average cost per unit. The product cost accounting system a company should use depends primarily on how the product is produced.

Job order costing is used by companies whose products are produced in distinct batches.

Job order costing is used by companies whose products are produced in distinct batches. Examples of industries where job order costing is the main cost accounting system include construction, management consulting, public accounting, printing, furniture manufacturing, and machine tool manufacturing.

The firms in these industries supply their customers with products or services that are unique to each particular customer. Let us assume you suddenly come into enough money to do something you have always wanted. You can afford to have a sauna installed in your bedroom. You call a contractor, whose product is saunas, specify that you want timers installed which will turn on the sauna to be ready every evening when you get home and every morning when you get out of bed. You also want a stereo system, a cassette deck, and a TV set installed and several spigots added that can be turned on to produce your favorite beverage when you are in the sauna. Early one Monday morning the contractor appears and begins to hack at the walls in your bedroom where you want the sauna put. Two weeks later you come home in the evening and find the sauna is finished. It is ready to relax your muscles and your mind.

The sauna the contractor constructed for you is unique—it was produced to your specifications. Let us further assume the contractor is producing a sauna for a local health club. Most likely it will be much larger than yours; certainly it will be different. Thus, the builder's accountant will accumulate the separate costs for your sauna and for the one in the health club.

Each of the saunas described above would be defined as a *job* by the contractor. Since the two jobs are different, the contractor wants to know the cost of each job. This is what job order costing is all about—determining the cost of a specific job.

A job order costing system determines the cost of each individual job.

The jobs described above consisted of 1 unit of the contractor's product—one sauna for your bedroom and one sauna for the health club. A job can consist of more than 1 unit of product. Assume the sauna contractor also produces saunas for building contractors. A local building contractor might order 10 identical saunas for 10 homes currently under construction. This order for 10 saunas would be considered a single job by the sauna contractor.

Job order costing is not appropriate for continuous production of a large quantity of identical products. For this kind of production, the appropriate cost accounting system is process costing, which we will cover in the next chapter. Until then you should at least be aware that process costing is used when there is a large degree of product standardization. Industries where process costing is the predominant cost accounting system include chemicals, oil refining, paint manufacturing, beer brewing, and meat packing. In each of these industries the firms regularly produce large quantities of standardized products. Many of the products are produced on a continuous basis 24 hours a day.

The two determinants of whether to use job order or process costing are the production process and the degree of product standardization.

The idea we want you to remember from the discussion up through this point is that there are two things that determine whether a job order cost system should be used to assign the costs to a product—and those determinants are the production process and the degree of product standardization. So that you will form that idea, we may have given you the impression that a product is produced only by either job order or process manufacturing. Unfortunately, it is not that simple. Many products are produced using various combinations or blends of job order and process manufacturing. That is one of the things that makes life interesting for accountants—to determine which cost accounting system to use for products that are produced through blends of the two production methods. You might look at it this way, job order and process cost accounting are on opposite ends of a continuum of different cost accounting systems as illustrated below:

Continuum of Cost Accounting Systems

Job Order Cost Accounting System	Blends of Job Order and Process Cost Accounting Systems	Process Cost Accounting System
All jobs are produced to customer specification and each is unique Example: Kenneth Smith's golf clubs based on the customer's height, weight, swing, length of arms, etc.	Components produced in batches where job costing is appropriate and final products are produced on an assembly-line basis Example: Production of motorcycles	All products are standardized and production is continuous Example: The production of Crest toothpaste by Procter & Gamble. Each tube of toothpaste is identical to all other tubes; all are produced on a continuous basis

MANUFACTURING COST FLOWS—JOB ORDER COSTING

Having learned the nature of the production process that would cause you to use a job order cost system, you are now prepared to study how the manufacturing costs are assigned to jobs and how to calculate the average cost per unit for each job.

To illustrate the assignment of manufacturing costs to jobs and the calculation of the average cost per unit for each job, we will use the Acme Printing Company as our illustration. Acme prints advertising brochures and circulars to customers' specifications. The company consists of two departments: a composing department where rubber mats are prepared, and a press department which uses the rubber mats to print the brochures and circulars. Our illustration will cover the month of November 19X0.

Computing the Average Cost per Unit in Job Order Costing

You calculate the average cost per unit in any cost accounting system just as you might expect. You divide the total cost for all units produced by the total number of units produced. The result—average cost per unit. Simple enough. But what is not so simple is to be sure that you are using the correct total cost and the correct total number of units. After you are certain you have collected the correct total costs, you simply divide by the correct number of total units. *Or*:

Cost per unit is simply the total manufacturing cost of the job divided by the number of units in the job.

$$\textbf{Average cost per unit} = \frac{\textbf{total manufacturing cost to produce the job}}{\textbf{total number of units produced for the job}}$$

To be sure that you have the correct total manufacturing cost, you must remember that it is the sum of direct materials costs, direct labor costs, and applied overhead. The accuracy of your total manufacturing cost will be as accurate as your component costs. The way to obtain the correct manufacturing costs for a job is to keep a record of each of these types of costs for that job. Such a record of costs is called a **job cost sheet.** Take a look at Exhibit 4-1 which is a job cost sheet for the Acme Printing Company.

A job cost sheet specifies the following basic information: identifies the customer; the date the customer wants the finished job; the date the job is started and the date the job is actually completed; the assigned job number; the name or title of the product; and the number of units requested. The **direct materials, direct labor,** and **applied overhead** costs of completing the job are recorded on the job cost sheet. Once the job is completed, all the component costs are added together at the bottom of the job cost sheet and shown as total manufacturing cost. The total manufacturing cost is then divided by the total units produced and the result of all this, of course, is the average manufacturing cost per unit at the very bottom of the job cost sheet.

We have just briefly shown you the procedure of where the data comes from and how the average unit cost is calculated. Now we have to be concerned about how the cost data got there in the first place. The next three sections of this chapter will respond to these important questions:

1 Exactly how do we obtain the cost data that are recorded on the job cost sheet and how can we be sure to record the correct costs?

2 How are the cost data recorded in the general and subsidiary ledgers of the firm?

Material Accounting

Accounting for the cost of the materials that go into a job is perhaps the easiest of the three manufacturing costs to deal with. Remember that materials are classified as either direct materials (materials that are necessary for the production of a job and are physically traceable to the job) or indirect materials (which are not traceable

EXHIBIT 4-1
ACME PRINTING COMPANY
Job Cost Sheet

Customer name ______ Job number ______

Date requested ______ Product ______

Date started ______ Number of units ______

Date completed ______

DIRECT MATERIALS

Date	Department	Requisition No.	Total

DIRECT LABOR

Date	Department	Labor Time Ticket Number	Total

APPLIED OVERHEAD

Date	Department	Basis for Overhead Application	Units of Base	Rate	Total

Total manufacturing cost ______

Units produced ______

Unit cost ______

to the job and, hence, are treated as a part of manufacturing overhead cost). Indirect materials include items such as nails, thread, glue, and miscellaneous supplies as described in Chapter 2. If we use these basic ideas as a guide, that will be sufficient to assure that we will accumulate the correct amount of costs for direct materials and indirect materials.

Purchase of Materials The materials necessary to produce the jobs are purchased from Acme's suppliers. The receipt of the materials is recorded in the general ledger with entry (1) as follows:

Material purchases are recorded as an addition to the materials inventory account in the general ledger and also recorded on a materials stock card.

		Debit	Credit
(1)	**Materials Inventory**	**$37,400**	
	Accounts payable		**$37,400**
	(To record the purchase of 2,000 rubber mats at $10 per mat and other materials necessary for production.)		

"Materials Inventory" is an asset account on the balance sheet. The cost of any unused materials will be included in the materials inventory account at the end of the accounting period.

In addition to the above journal entry, the acquisition of materials is also recorded on a **materials stock card.** The materials stock card, illustrated in Exhibit 4-2, is the subsidiary ledger supporting the journal entries to the materials inventory account. A separate materials stock card is prepared for each type of material used by the company. The materials stock card contains a column to record the receipts of each material, materials issued, and the balance of materials remaining to be used.

The materials stock card contains details on each type of material. The group of materials stock cards are a subsidiary ledger containing the details of the materials inventory account in the general ledger.

Issuance of Materials Let us assume that Acme has just received an order for 20,000 copies of Brochure no. 50. The production manager assigns job no. A-3201 to this job to distinguish it from the other jobs expected during the month. To obtain the rubber mats to start job A-3201, the production manager prepares a **materials requisition,** as illustrated in Exhibit 4-3.

The materials requisition shows the date the materials are issued, the inventory item name and number, the quantity of materials required and issued from the materials storeroom, unit cost of the materials, and the signature of the production manager acknowledging receipt of the materials. In addition, in the bottom left-hand corner of the materials requisition the production manager indicates whether the material is to be used directly in the production of a job or whether the material is for general use in manufacturing all jobs—indirect materials. If the material is direct materials, the number of the job it is to be used on is recorded by

EXHIBIT 4-2
ACME PRINTING COMPANY
Materials Stock Card

Item name Rubber Mats — Item number 742

	Receipts				Issued				Balance		
Date	Invoice No.	Quantity	Unit Cost	Total	Requisition Number	Quantity	Unit Cost	Total	Quantity	Unit Cost	Balance
November 1, 19X0	XO-1078	2,000	$10.00	$20,000					2,000	$10.00	$20,000
November 15, 19X0					XO-123	10	$10.00	$100.00	1,990	$10.00	$19,900
November 30, 19X0					⋮ XO-148	⋮ 20	⋮ $10.00	⋮ $200.00	⋮ 1,000	⋮ $10.00	⋮ $10,000

Other material stock cards would be increased for $17,400 to show the total increase in materials of $37,400 as recorded in journal entry number 1.

EXHIBIT 4-3
ACME PRINTING COMPANY
Materials Requisition

Materials Requisition

Date November 15, 19X0 Requisition number X0-123

Inventory item name Rubber Mats Inventory item number 742

Quantity	Unit Cost	Total Cost
10	$10.00	$100.00

Job number A-3201 Issued by

Manufacturing overhead account number Received by

Department Composing

the production manager on the material requisition. In Exhibit 4-3 the cost of the 10 rubber mats is charged to job no. A-3201. If the material is indirect materials, the manufacturing overhead account number is entered by the production manager on the materials requisition.

A materials requisition identifies the amount of materials needed to produce a job or for overhead. It is the basis on which the general ledger materials inventory account and the materials stock card is reduced.

To start job A-3201 the production manager identifies which materials and how much of each are needed by preparing a materials requisition and presenting it to the materials storeroom clerk. The materials storeroom clerk supplies the materials and signs the requisition as "issued." Once the materials are issued a copy of the requisition is sent to the accounting department to show that these materials have been used and that the materials inventory has been reduced. The materials storeroom clerk uses the data from the materials requisition to reduce the inventory level on the materials stock card as illustrated in Exhibit 4-2.

The journal entry to record the issuance of materials in the general ledger is based on a compilation of the materials requisitions. An example of such a compilation is shown in Exhibit 4-4. This compilation is prepared by the accounting department using the materials requisitions received from the storeroom clerk. As can be seen in Exhibit 4-4, the accounting department sorts the materials requisitions between direct materials and indirect materials. Next, each category of materials requisitions is sorted by department. The direct materials cost and indirect materials cost, by department, are determined by adding together the cost recorded on each materials requisition. This information is then used to record the cost of materials used in the general ledger.

EXHIBIT 4-4
ACME PRINTING COMPANY
Compilation of Material Requisitions
For November 19X0

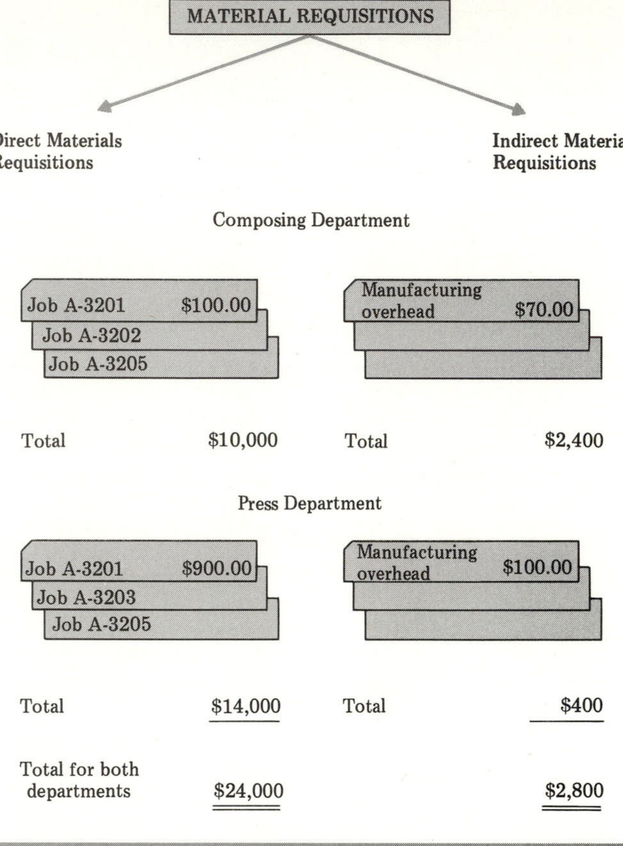

To summarize, the main cost accounting information provided by the materials requisition is the direct materials cost by job (for the cost per unit calculation) and the indirect material cost by department (in case the company wishes to use departmental overhead rates).

To illustrate the journal entry for materials used assume the accounting department of Acme Printing Company during the month of November 19X0 collected all of the material requisitions and performed the compilation illustrated in Exhibit 4-4. The results of compiling the material requisitions showed that direct material costs were $24,000 and indirect material costs were $2,800. The general ledger journal entry to record the issuance of materials is shown in entry (2) below:

		Debit	Credit
(2)	**Work in Process**	**$24,000**	
	Actual Manufacturing Overhead	**2,800**	
	Material Inventory		**$26,800**
	(To record the issuance of materials to the manufacturing departments of the Acme Printing Company for November 19X0.)		

In addition to providing information for the general ledger and the materials stock card, the requisition is the basis for recording direct material on the job cost sheet.

The materials cost charged to work in process represents direct materials cost assignable to specific jobs. Since our objective in job order costing is to calculate the average cost per unit of each job produced, these direct materials costs must be assigned to specific jobs. This is the reason the job order number is recorded on the materials requisitions for direct materials. Using the job order numbers on the direct materials requisitions to identify the specific job the accounting department records the direct materials cost on the job cost sheet. The total direct materials cost recorded on the job cost sheets will be equal to the direct materials cost charged to the work in process account.

To illustrate the recording of the direct materials cost on the job sheet, assume that two direct materials requisitions were for job A-3201 in the Acme Printing Company. One requisition is from the composing department for $100 and one requisition is from the press department for $900. Exhibit 4-5 shows how the information from the direct materials requisition is recorded on the job cost sheet of job A-3201.

Summary: Materials Cost and Documents Exhibit 4-6 summarizes the materials cost flows in the general ledger of the Acme Printing Company. The total cost of materials used during November 19X0 is $26,800. Of this $26,800, the indirect materials cost is $2,800 and the direct materials cost is $24,000. The boxes show that direct materials cost is also assigned to specific job cost sheets. Job A-3201 is assigned $1,000 for direct materials and all other jobs are assigned $23,000. The indirect materials used may also be recorded by department as shown in the lower set of boxes.

As you can see from a glance at Exhibit 4-7, the information on the materials requisition is eventually used in three different places.

Summary of use of information from the materials requisition.

1 The information is used by the storeroom clerk to record the amount of the materials that have been used. This helps them to determine the amount of materials currently available and whether additional materials should be ordered.

2 The information is used to compile the cost of direct materials and indirect materials for the journal entry in the general ledger recording the use of materials.

3 The information is used to record the cost of the direct materials on the job cost sheet. The information is recorded on the job cost sheet because the job cost sheet is where accountants accumulate the cost of producing a particular job.

Manufacturing Labor Accounting

Manufacturing labor costs are accounted for in a manner similar to the accounting for materials costs. Remember that manufacturing labor costs are classified as either direct labor or indirect labor.

We have already explained that direct labor includes all major labor costs that can be physically traced to the production of a particular job. If you have any doubts about how to classify labor costs, remember that the labor you can observe performed on a job is direct labor.

Direct labor is work which can be physically traced to a product because it is performed directly on the product.

Any labor that you see going on in manufacturing but which is not directly on a job (product) is indirect labor. Indirect labor is necessary to make the production process possible but it is not performed directly on the products. Examples of indirect labor are factory supervision, materials transportation within the factory, stockroom

EXHIBIT 4-5
ACME PRINTING COMPANY
Job Cost Sheet

Customer name A. Simon
Job number A-3201
Date requested November 30, 19X0
Product Brochure No. 50
Date started November 15, 19X0
Number of units 20,000
Date completed ____

DIRECT MATERIALS

Date	Department	Requisition No.	Total
Nov. 15, 19X0	Composing	X0-123	$ 100.00
Nov. 26, 19X0	Press	X0-132	$ 900.00
			$1,000.00

DIRECT LABOR

Date	Department	Labor Time Ticket Number	Total

APPLIED OVERHEAD

Date	Department	Basis for Overhead Application	Units of Base	Rate	Total

Total manufacturing cost ____
Units produced ____
Unit cost ____

activities, maintenance and repair crews, and similar types of labor needed to make a factory function. Indirect labor also includes "idle time" of the employees who normally work directly on the jobs.

The cost of direct labor is assigned to specific jobs and is charged to the work in process account. The cost of indirect labor is not assignable to specific jobs and is treated as a part of actual manufacturing overhead costs.

A clock card keeps track of the number of hours the employee works so that the worker can be properly paid.

Recording the Liability for Manufacturing Wages To understand the accounting for labor costs, you must first understand how the accounting process records the firm's liability for the work performed by its employees. The document that is used to record the hours worked by each employee is the **clock card.** Exhibit 4-8 illustrates a clock card employees must use to record the time they arrive for work, leave for lunch, return from lunch, and leave at the end of their work shift. At the end of each week, the payroll department uses the information on the clock cards to calculate each employee's pay. The payroll information for all manufacturing employees, both direct laborers and indirect laborers, is compiled and a journal entry is made in the general ledger to record the firm's payroll liability. The journal entry is generally made on a weekly or monthly basis depending on when the payroll is recorded.

To illustrate the journal entry, assume the total manufacturing payroll, during the month of November 19X0, for the Acme Printing Company is $80,700. This total was determined by adding up the total pay on the clock cards for the manufacturing employees. Of the $80,700, $70,600 is to be paid to the employees and $10,100 is withheld for social security (FICA) taxes, federal income taxes, state income taxes, city income taxes, and other deductions from the pay. The journal entry to record the payroll is entry (3) which follows:

(3) Payroll	**$80,700**	
Wages Payable		**$70,600**
Other credits		**$10,100**
(To record the payroll costs for the month of November 19X0.)		

EXHIBIT 4-6
ACME PRINTING COMPANY
Materials Cost Flows in the General Ledger

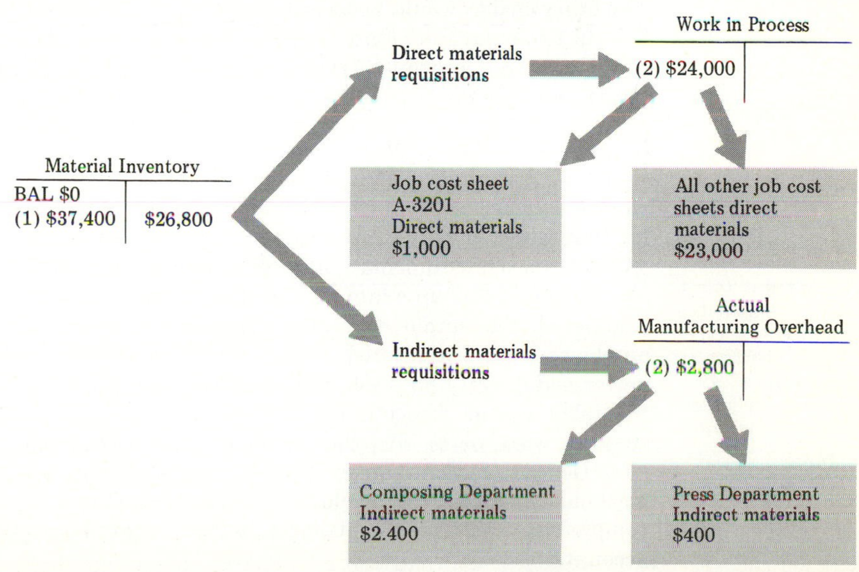

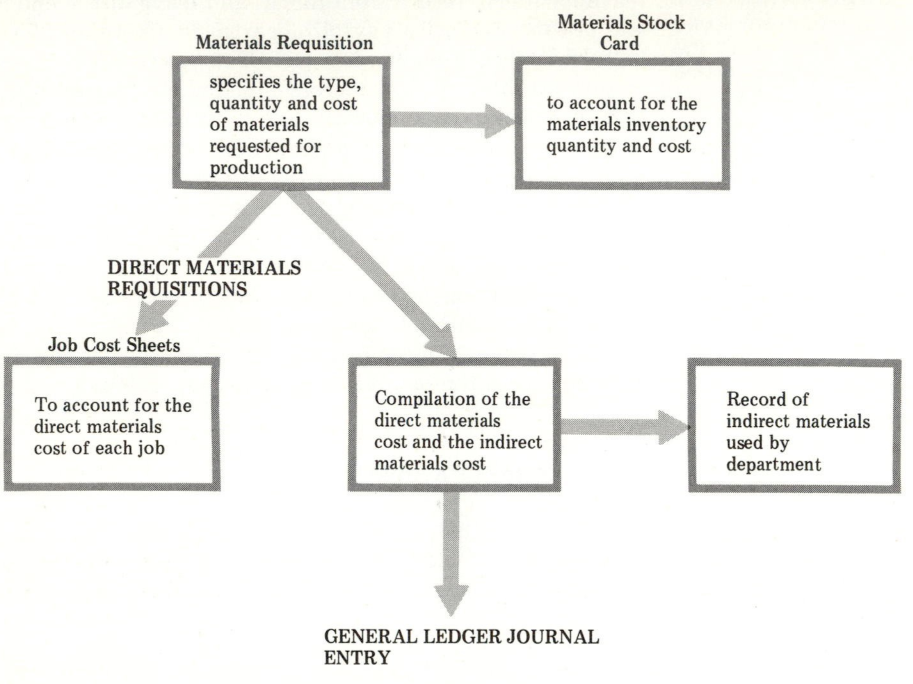

The other credits would be to various liability accounts, such as FICA taxes payable, federal taxes payable, state and city taxes payable, etc.

The payroll journal entry is a record of the firm's liability for the work performed by its employees.

Recording the Use of Manufacturing Labor The clock card only records the total time worked by each employee. It is used by the employee to tell how much time he worked in a period and by the employer to determine how much to pay the employee for that work. A clock card does not record how much time each employee worked on each job. That information is recorded by the employees on a *time ticket*.

A time ticket is like a materials requisition except that it records direct labor used on a job or indirect labor for a particular department.

Exhibit 4-9 is an example of a **time ticket** and it shows the date the work was completed, the employee name, department, operation performed, the time the employee started and finished the work, and the total elapsed time. If the work is performed directly on a job, the employee would record the job number, indicating the labor cost is direct labor. If the worker is performing general maintenance, cleanup work, or is idle, the overhead account number would be recorded on the time ticket to indicate an indirect labor cost. These time tickets represent an hour by hour summary of employee activities during the day. An employee might complete several time tickets for a day to charge time to the proper jobs or overhead accounts.

The accounting department collects all the labor time tickets, records the pay rate of the employee on the ticket, and calculates the labor cost of the operation. Next, the tickets are sorted by department between direct labor and indirect labor, as illustrated in Exhibit 4-10. The direct labor cost and indirect labor cost can then be determined by adding together the labor cost recorded on each time ticket. This information is then used to record the labor cost in the general ledger. The direct labor cost is charged to the work in process account and the indirect labor cost is charged to the actual manufacturing overhead account.

To illustrate the accounting for manufacturing labor, assume the Acme Printing Company has collected all the labor time tickets and performed the compilation illustrated in Exhibit 4-10. The results show a total direct labor cost of $60,000 and an indirect labor cost of $20,700. The general ledger journal entry to record the labor cost is shown in entry (4) below:

(4)	**Work in Process**	**$60,000**	
	Actual Manufacturing Overhead	**20,700**	
	Payroll		**$80,700**
	(To record the manufacturing labor costs for the Acme Printing Company for November 19X0.)		

EXHIBIT 4-8
ACME PRINTING COMPANY
Clock Card

Name: Sam Jones

Week Ending: November 15, 19X0 Department: Composing

Date	Morning In	Morning Out	Afternoon In	Afternoon Out	Hours
Nov. 11	7:56	12:01	12:59	5:03	8
Nov. 12	7:58	11:59	12:58	5:01	8
Nov. 13	7:57	11:59	1:01	5:02	8
Nov. 14	8:01	12:00	1:02	5:04	8
Nov. 15	7:59	12:01	12:58	5:03	8

Total hours: 40

Pay rate: $12/hr.

Total pay: $480

EXHIBIT 4-9
ACME PRINTING COMPANY
Time Ticket

Date	November 18, 19X0	Ticket number	1056
Employee name	S. Benson	Department	Composing
Operation	Stencil	Job number	A-3201
		Overhead account number	
Start time	8:00		
Finish time	11:00	Labor rate	$20/hr.
Total time	3 hrs. 0 min.	Labor cost	$60.00

Time tickets are also summarized to record direct labor cost on job cost sheets.

The labor cost charged to the work in process account represents direct labor cost assignable to specific jobs. Using the job number on the labor time tickets, the accounting department determines the direct labor cost for each job by department. The direct labor cost is recorded on the job cost sheet and will be equal to the direct labor cost charged to the work in process account.

To illustrate the recording of the direct labor cost on the job cost sheet, we will continue job A-3201 for the Acme Printing Company. Assume November direct labor time tickets for job A-3201 in the composing department showed a total direct labor cost of $1,002 and the direct labor time tickets in the press department showed a total direct labor cost of $6,998. Exhibit 4-11 shows how this information is recorded on the job cost sheet of job A-3201.

Summary: Manufacturing Labor Costs and Documents Exhibit 4-12 summarizes the manufacturing labor cost flows in the general ledger of the Acme Printing Company. The total cost of manufacturing labor during November 19X0 is $80,700, of which $20,700 represents indirect labor cost and $60,000 represents direct labor cost. The direct labor cost is assigned to specific job cost sheets. Job A-3201 is assigned $8,000 and all other jobs are assigned $52,000. Records of indirect labor by department will be kept if departmental overhead rates are used. Indirect labor might also be broken down by type such as idle time, materials transportation, supervision, etc.

Exhibit 4-13 summarizes the documents which are used as the basic source of information to account for labor costs. The clock cards are used by the firm to determine the total payroll cost, which represents the firm's liability for employee wages. The time tickets have two different purposes:

1. They are used to determine how much of the payroll cost is direct labor cost and how much is indirect labor cost. With this information the accountant can prepare the journal entry to charge work in process for the direct labor cost and actual manufacturing overhead for the indirect labor cost.
2. They are also used to assign the direct labor cost to the individual jobs. This information is recorded on the job cost sheets to be used in calculating the cost per unit when the job is completed.

Manufacturing Overhead Accounting

Accounting for direct materials and direct labor was relatively straightforward. You simply had to determine the materials and labor that were used directly to produce a job. Any materials and labor not used directly to produce a job were classified as manufacturing overhead.

Manufacturing overhead cost accounting is conceptually more problematical than direct materials and direct labor cost accounting. What makes overhead cost accounting so difficult is that the actual overhead costs are not physically traceable to a specific job—lack of a physical link—and many overhead costs benefit the production of a number of jobs—a joint cost. We can resolve the probems of traceability and jointness in overhead costs by following the generally accepted accounting procedures we discussed in Chapter 3.

Actual Manufacturing Overhead We have already illustrated how the actual cost of indirect materials and indirect labor are recorded in the general ledger using materials requisitions and labor time tickets. In addition to indirect materials and

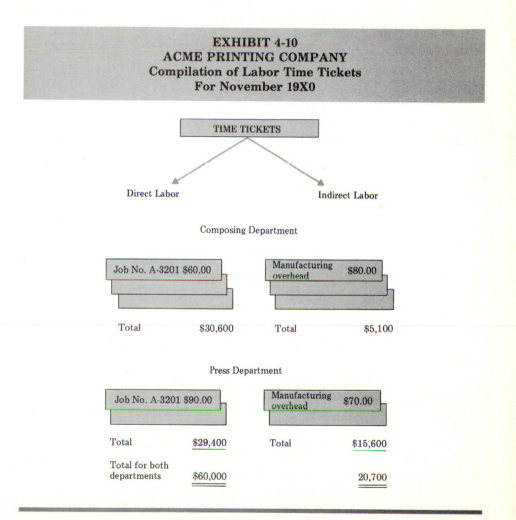

EXHIBIT 4-10
ACME PRINTING COMPANY
Compilation of Labor Time Tickets
For November 19X0

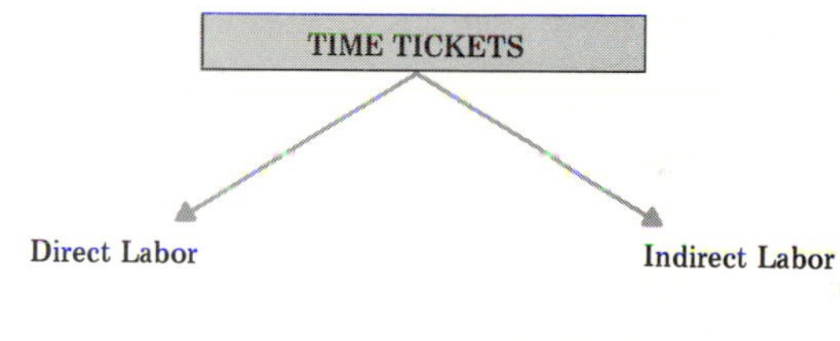

Composing Department

Direct Labor		Indirect Labor	
Job No. A-3201 $60.00		Manufacturing overhead $80.00	
Total	$30,600	Total	$5,100

Press Department

Direct Labor		Indirect Labor	
Job No. A-3201 $90.00		Manufacturing overhead $70.00	
Total	$29,400	Total	$15,600
Total for both departments	$60,000		20,700

EXHIBIT 4-11
ACME PRINTING COMPANY
Job Cost Sheet

Customer: A. Simon
Job number: A-3201
Date requested: November 30, 19X0
Product: Brochure No. 50
Date started: November 15, 19X0
Number of units: 20,000
Date completed: November 29, 19X0

DIRECT MATERIALS

Date	Department	Requisition No.	Total
Nov. 15, 19X0	Composing	X0-123	$ 100.00
Nov. 26, 19X0	Press	X0-132	$ 900.00
			$1,000.00

DIRECT LABOR

Date	Department	Labor Time Ticket No.	Total
Nov. 29, 19X0	Composing	1056-1079	$1,002.00
Nov. 29, 19X0	Press	1120-1197	6,998.00
			$8,000.00

APPLIED OVERHEAD

Date	Department	Basis for Overhead Application	Units of Base	Rate	Total

Total manufacturing cost ______

Units produced ______

Unit cost ______

labor, the production of the jobs requires other overhead costs, such as telephone, electricity, heat, and services provided by the company's suppliers. The amounts of those overhead costs are determined from invoices received from the suppliers. Other overhead costs include amortization of costs incurred in prior accounting periods, such as insurance, property taxes, and depreciation of plant and equipment.

The amounts of these overhead costs are determined from amortization schedules prepared by the accounting department. All these overhead costs are charged to the actual manufacturing overhead account in the general ledger.

Actual overhead costs in addition to indirect materials and indirect labor enter the cost accounting system from invoices and from accounting depreciation schedules.

To illustrate the journal entry to record actual manufacturing overhead costs, assume the Acme Printing Company incurred the following overhead costs during November 19X0.

Electricity cost for production	$ 4,350
Telephone cost for production offices	2,000
Insurance cost for production facilities	8,000
Property taxes on production facilities	9,800
Depreciation on production facilities and equipment	$20,800

The journal entry to record the overhead costs in the general ledger is entry (5) below:

(5) Actual Manufacturing Overhead	**$44,950**	
Accounts payable (Electricity and Telephone)		**$ 6,350**
Prepaid Insurance		**8,000**
Property Taxes Payable		**9,800**
Accumulated Depreciation		**$20,800**
(To record the overhead costs for the Acme Printing Company for November 19X0.)		

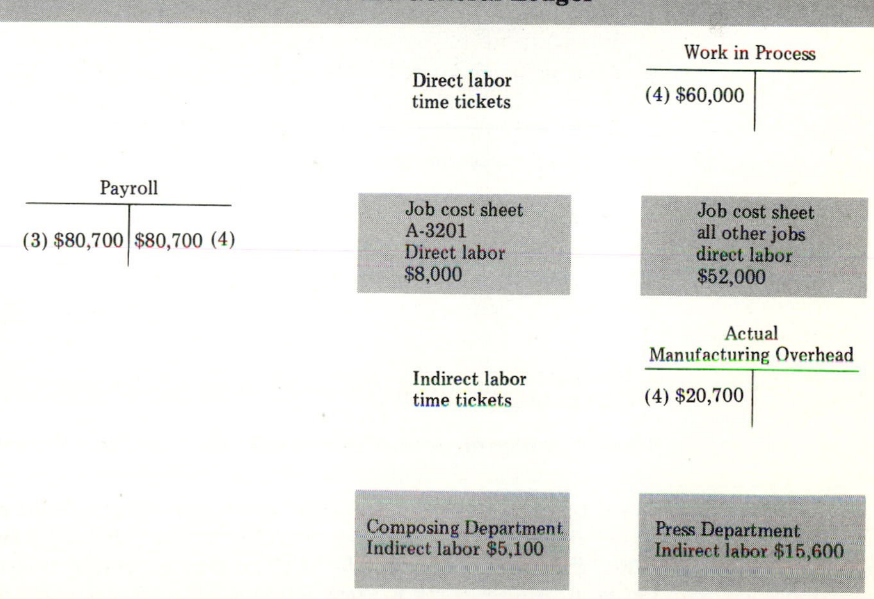

EXHIBIT 4-13
ACME PRINTING COMPANY
Summary of Document Flows
Manufacturing Labor

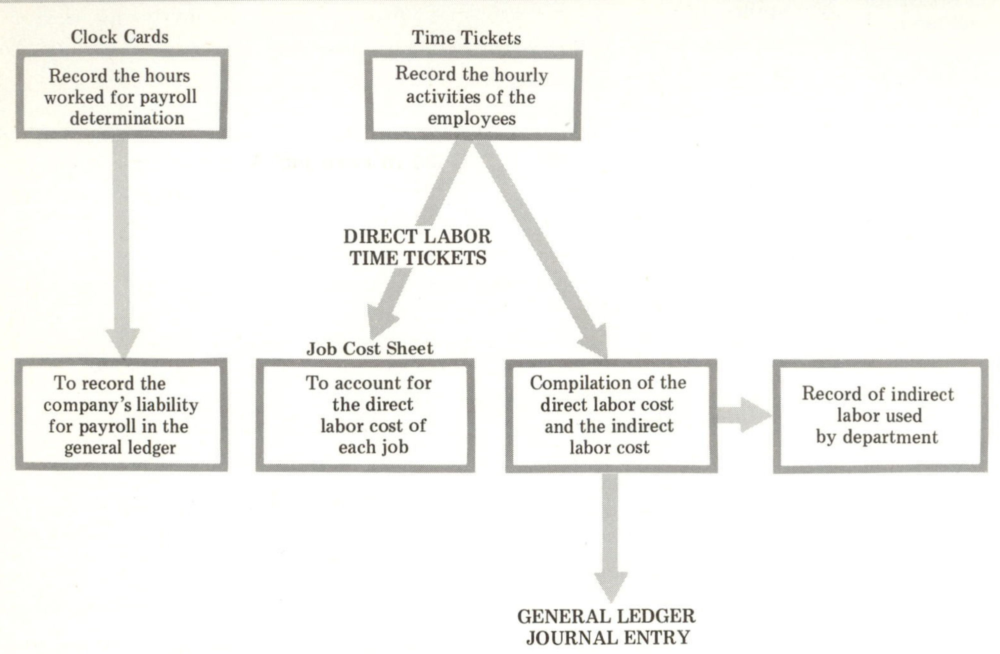

In addition to recording the actual overhead costs in the accounts, most manufacturing firms will maintain a departmental overhead cost sheet—to record the actual overhead costs of each department by item. Such a cost sheet, for the Acme Printing Company, is illustrated in Exhibit 4-14. The departmental overhead cost sheet represents the subsidiary ledger supporting the entry in the general ledger recording the actual overhead costs. These actual overhead costs by department are used to develop the basic inputs for estimating the overhead costs on a departmental basis, as illustrated in Chapter 3. You will see in Chapter 9 how the actual departmental overhead costs will be used to calculate variances from the expected overhead costs. This use of the actual overhead costs provides management with information for controlling the overhead costs.

Actual overhead cost by department is recorded on a departmental overhead cost sheet.

Applied Manufacturing Overhead In the previous section we recorded the actual overhead cost incurred during November 19X0 for the Acme Printing Company. This recording of **actual overhead cost** had no impact on the work in process account. How do we apply the overhead cost to work in process and assign it to the specific jobs? The answer, of course, is through the use of a **predetermined overhead rate.** Remember, the predetermined overhead rate is calculated at the beginning of the year by estimating the total overhead cost for the year and then dividing this estimate by some measure of production activity for the year, such as direct labor dollars. Then, throughout the year the overhead is applied to work in

Applied overhead rather than actual overhead is entered in the work in process account and on the job cost sheets.

process by multiplying the predetermined overhead rate times the direct labor dollars. The applied overhead is assigned to each job by multiplying the predetermined overhead rate times the number of direct labor dollars required to complete the job.

If direct labor dollars is the activity base for the predetermined overhead rate, the amount of overhead cost applied to a job is the direct labor cost of that job times the predetermined overhead rate.

To illustrate this accounting for the applied overhead, we will continue our Acme Printing Company example. Assume that by analyzing the past year's overhead costs and adjusting for expected changes in this coming year's methods of production, prices, and volume, management concluded that the total estimated overhead cost for the year would be $876,000. Suppose further that management decided to use a plantwide rate and to apply overhead cost in proportion to the amount of direct labor cost contained in each job. Management studied production methods, production volume, and the union wage settlements expected for the coming year and estimated the total direct labor cost to be $700,800. The predetermined overhead rate for the year was computed as follows:

Predetermined overhead rate

$$= \frac{\text{total estimated overhead cost for the year 19X0}}{\text{total estimated direct labor cost for the year 19X0}}$$

$$= \frac{\$876{,}000}{\$700{,}800} = \$1.25 \text{ per direct labor dollar}$$

The rate could also be expressed as 125% of the direct labor cost.

This predetermined overhead rate is used to calculate the applied overhead cost

EXHIBIT 4-14
Departmental Overhead Cost Sheet
For the Month of November 19X0

Cost Items	Total	Departments	
		Composing	Press
Indirect materials	$ 2,800	$ 2,400	$ 400
Indirect labor	20,700	5,100	15,600
Electricity for heat, light, and power	4,350	2,250	2,100
Telephone	2,000	1,200	800
Insurance	8,000	3,000	5,000
Property taxes	9,800	6,000	3,800
Factory depreciation	20,800	5,800	15,000
	$ 68,450	$ 25,750	$ 42,700

we will charge to the work in process account in the general ledger and to assign the overhead cost to the specific jobs worked on in each department.

The total direct labor cost for the Acme Printing Company, determined from the labor time tickets for November 19X0, is $60,000. Using the predetermined overhead rate of $1.25 per direct labor dollar, we can calculate the total applied manufacturing overhead as follows:

Manufacturing overhead applied = 60,000 × $1.25 = $75,000

The journal entry in the general ledger to record the application of overhead is shown below as entry (6).

(6) Work in Process	**$75,000**	
Applied Manufacturing Overhead		**$75,000**
(To record the application of overhead to jobs with $60,000 of direct labor cost at $1.25 per direct labor dollar.)		

This journal entry is generally made periodically, on a weekly or monthly basis.

The applied overhead charged to the work in process account represents the overhead cost assigned to specific jobs. Since Acme Printing Company uses direct labor cost to apply overhead, the direct labor cost recorded on the job cost sheets can be used to apply overhead to the specific jobs.

To illustrate the application of overhead to a specific job, consider Exhibit 4-15, the job cost sheet for job A-3201. The direct labor cost recorded on the job cost sheet is transferred to the appropriate column of the applied overhead section of the job cost sheet. The direct labor cost is then multiplied by the predetermined overhead rate to calculate the amount of applied overhead assigned to job A-3201. In this example a total of $10,000 of applied overhead is assigned to job A-3201.

Summary: Manufacturing Overhead Accounting Exhibit 4-16 summarizes the manufacturing overhead cost flows in the general ledger of the Acme Printing Company. The total manufacturing overhead incurred during November 19X0, of $68,450, is charged to the actual manufacturing overhead account. The manufacturing overhead applied to work in process is calculated by multiplying the predetermined overhead rate times the direct labor cost in the Acme Printing Company. The manufacturing overhead applied to work in process is assigned to the individual jobs based on their direct labor cost.

Exhibit 4-17 summarizes the documents and other sources of information which are used to account for manufacturing overhead. Materials requisitions for indirect materials, labor time tickets for indirect labor, vouchers, invoices, and amortization schedules are used to record the actual manufacturing overhead in the general ledger and to assign the actual manufacturing overhead to the specific departments. The predetermined overhead rate and the activity base for applying manufacturing overhead are used to record the applied manufacturing overhead in the general ledger and to assign the applied manufacturing overhead to the specific jobs.

Calculating the Average Cost per Unit

Now that you have been introduced to some of the basic concepts of how to collect actual direct materials and direct labor costs for each job, and how to assign applied manufacturing overhead costs to each job, you are prepared to learn how to use these costs to calculate the average cost of each unit in a job—the per-unit cost.

EXHIBIT 4-15
ACME PRINTING COMPANY
Job Cost Sheet

Customer: A. Simon
Job number: A-3201
Date requested: November 30, 19X0
Product: Brochure No. 50
Date started: November 15, 19X0
Number of units: 20,000
Date completed: November 29, 19X0

DIRECT MATERIALS

Date	Department	Requisition No.	Total
Nov. 15, 19X0	Composing	XO-123	$ 100.00
Nov. 26, 19X0	Press	X0-132	$ 900.00
			$1,000.00

DIRECT LABOR

Date	Department	Labor Time Ticket No.	Total
Nov. 29, 19X0	Composing	1056-1079	$1,002.00
Nov. 29, 19X0	Press	1120-1197	6,998.00
			$8,000.00

APPLIED OVERHEAD

Date	Department	Basis for Overhead Application	Units of Base	Rate	Total
Nov. 29, 19X0	Composing	Direct labor dollars	$1,002.00	$1.25	$ 1,252.50
Nov. 29, 19X0	Press	Direct labor dollars	$6,998.00	$1.25	$ 8,747.50
					$10,000.00

Total manufacturing cost	$19,000.00
Units produced	20,000
Unit cost	$0.95

EHIBIT 4-16
ACME PRINTING COMPANY
Manufacturing Overhead Cost Flows in the General Ledger

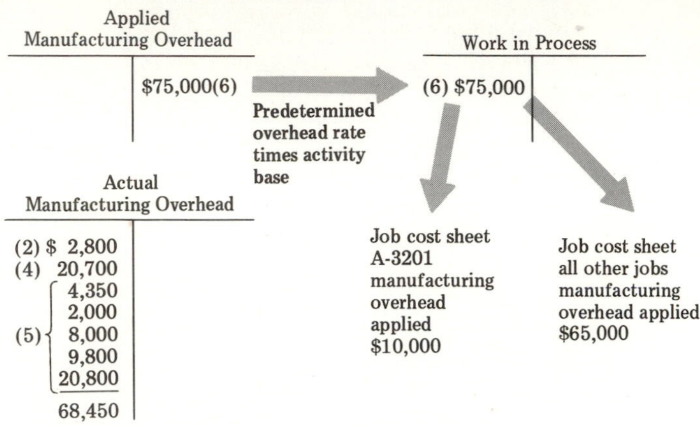

The costs used to calculate the cost per unit cost for a job are recorded on the job cost sheet, like the one shown in Exhibit 4-15. As you can see in the exhibit, the job cost sheet consists of three parts:

1 *Direct materials costs* The costs entered here originate from the materials requisition forms which show the cost of the direct materials used on the job.

2 *Direct labor costs* The costs here originate from the time tickets which show the direct labor cost incurred on the job.

3 *Applied manufacturing overhead* The costs here originate with the predetermined overhead rate and the activity base used to assign the applied manufacturing overhead to each job.

The cost per unit of a product is found when the job is complete by totaling the direct materials, direct labor, and applied overhead shown on the job cost sheet and dividing by the number of units in the job.

When a job is completed and all the above costs have been recorded on the job cost sheet, you can calculate the average cost per unit of a job by adding together the three categories of cost and dividing by the number of units in the job.

To illustrate, assume the Acme Printing Company has completed job A-3201 and the production records show that 20,000 units were produced. Using the data from the job cost sheet, Exhibit 4-15, the cost per unit in this job would be calculated as follows:

Total direct materials cost	$ 1,000
Total direct labor cost	8,000
Applied overhead cost	10,000
Total cost of job A-3201	$19,000

$$\textbf{Cost per unit} = \frac{\$19{,}000}{20{,}000 \text{ units}} = \$0.95 \text{ per unit}$$

As you may have noticed in Exhibit 4-15, this calculation is also shown on the job cost sheet.

Cost of Goods Completed

When a job is completed, its total cost as shown on the job cost sheet is transferred from the work in process account to the finished goods account in the general ledger.

When a job is completed and the units are ready for sale, they are transferred from the manufacturing area to the finished goods storeroom. The manufacturing costs assigned to the completed job must be moved from the work in process account to the **finished goods** account in the general ledger. This transfer of the manufacturing costs from one asset account to another asset account reflects the physical movement of the job to the finished goods storeroom.

To illustrate the journal entry, assume the only job completed by the Acme Printing Company during the month of November 19X0 is job A-3201 whose total cost is $19,000. The journal entry to record the completion of job A-3201 is shown below as entry (7):

		Debit	Credit
(7)	**Finished Goods**	**$19,000**	
	Work in Process		**$19,000**
	(To record the completion of job A-3201.)		

You can always confirm the work in process account balance at the end of any accounting period by totaling the costs recorded on the job cost sheets for all uncompleted jobs.

This entry is also shown in Exhibit 4-18. Included in the exhibit is a balance in the work in process account of $140,000. This $140,000 represents the direct materials, direct labor, and applied overhead costs for all uncompleted jobs. The details of the ending work in process balance can be found on the job cost sheets for the uncompleted jobs. These job cost sheets for the uncompleted jobs represent the subsidiary ledger for the work in process account.

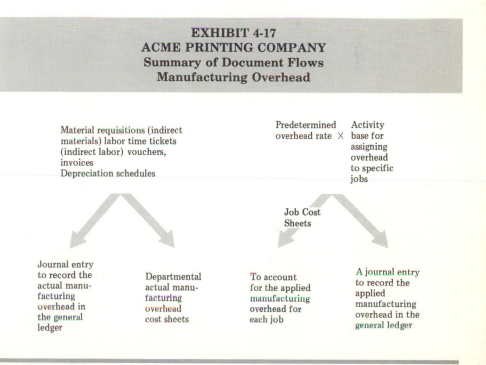

EXHIBIT 4-17
ACME PRINTING COMPANY
Summary of Document Flows
Manufacturing Overhead

Material requisitions (indirect materials) labor time tickets (indirect labor) vouchers, invoices
Depreciation schedules

Journal entry to record the actual manufacturing overhead in the general ledger

Departmental actual manufacturing overhead cost sheets

Predetermined overhead rate × Activity base for assigning overhead to specific jobs

Job Cost Sheets

To account for the applied manufacturing overhead for each job

A journal entry to record the applied manufacturing overhead in the general ledger

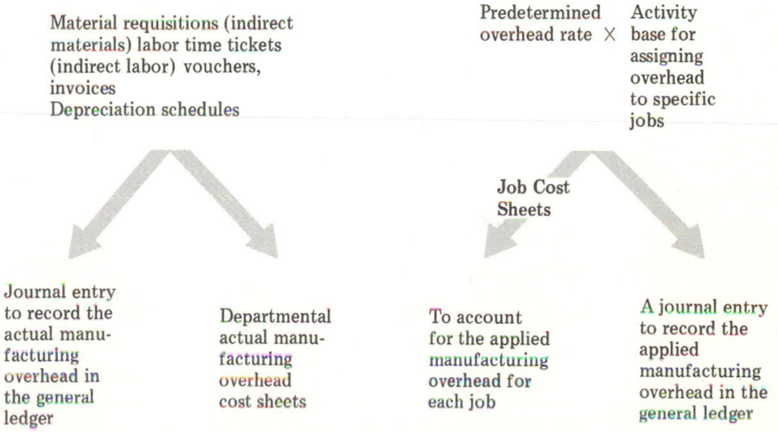

When the units from a completed job are received in the finished goods storeroom, the number of units and cost per unit are recorded on a finished goods stock card.

When the job is received in the finished goods storeroom, the clerk prepares a **finished goods stock card,** as shown in Exhibit 4-19. The clerk in the finished goods storeroom uses the finished goods stock card to record the receipts of finished units, shipment of units to customers, and the unit balance available for future shipments. The finished goods stock card is the subsidiary ledger for the finished goods inventory account.

Cost of Goods Sold

Shipments of finished goods to customers are recorded on the finished goods stock card which also provides the information needed for the cost of goods sold journal entry.

When units are shipped to the firm's customer, the finished goods storeroom clerk reduces the inventory level on the finished goods stock card as shown in Exhibit 4-19. The cost accountant then transfers the cost of the units shipped from the finished goods inventory account to the cost of goods sold account in the general ledger. To calculate the cost of the units shipped we multiply the units shipped times the cost per unit recorded on the finished goods stock card.

To illustrate the journal entry, assume that Acme shipped 12,000 units of job A-3201 during November 19X0. The total sales price of the 12,000 units was $16,000. At a unit cost of $.95 per unit, the journal entry to record the cost of goods sold is shown below as entry (8):

(8)	**Cost of Goods Sold**	**$11,400**	
	Finished Goods		**$11,400**
	(To record the sale of 12,000 units of job A-3201 at a cost of $.95 each.)		

The journal entry to record the sales revenue is shown as entry (9).

(9)	**Accounts Receivable**	**$16,000**	
	Sales		**$16,000**
	(To record the sale of 12,000 units of job A-3201.)		

EXHIBIT 4-18
ACME PRINTING COMPANY
Completion of Job A-3201: Cost Flows in the General Ledger

		Work in Process (Dr.)	Work in Process (Cr.)	Finished Goods (Dr.)	Finished Goods (Cr.)
Direct materials	(2)	$ 24,000			
Direct labor	(4)	60,000	$19,000 (7)→	(7) $19,000	
Applied overhead	(6)	75,000			
		$140,000			

The details of the ending balance in the Work in Process account are reflected in the job cost sheets of all uncompleted jobs.

EXHIBIT 4-19
ACME PRINTING COMPANY
Finished Goods Stock Card

Product name: Brochure No. 50												
	Receipts				Shipments				Balance		
Date	Job Number	Quantity	Unit Cost	Total	Invoice Number	Quantity	Unit Cost	Total	Quantity	Unit Cost	Balance
Nov. 29,X0	A-3201	20,000	$0.95	$19,000							
Nov. 30,X0					X0-1078	12,000	$0.95	$11,400	8,000	$0.95	$7,600

Summary: Cost Flows and Documents

Exhibit 4-20 summarizes all the journal entries for the Acme Printing Company in T account form. The numbers identifying the journal entries correspond to the numbered journal entries on the previous pages.

The documents required to operate a job order cost system and the subsidiary ledgers that support the journal entries in the general ledger and how the accounting information flows among the documents and ledger are shown in Exhibit 4-21. In reviewing Exhibit 4-21 one of the important things for you to see is that the basic documents are listed in the T accounts and the subsidiary ledgers are shown at the bottom of the T accounts.

OVERAPPLIED OR UNDERAPPLIED OVERHEAD

In the previous chapter and earlier in this chapter, we introduced you to the basic ideas of a "predetermined overhead rate." We showed you how to estimate the total overhead costs, based on recent past overhead costs, how to select an activity base and finally how to calculate the predetermined overhead rate itself which can then be used to assign overhead costs to jobs produced in the factory. In other words, we showed you how to develop and use a predetermined overhead *rate* to apply overhead costs to jobs.

In this chapter you learned that applied overhead is recorded in the general ledger as a credit to the *applied* manufacturing overhead account and a debit to the work in process account. You also saw how overhead is applied to the specific jobs being produced and recorded on the job cost sheet.

Review of what you have learned about manufacturing overhead.

It is important to notice that *actual* overhead costs incurred to produce the job are not assigned to specific jobs. Rather actual overhead costs are accumulated in a general ledger account called actual manufacturing overhead. As the actual overhead cost is incurred you debit the actual manufacturing overhead account and credit accounts such as materials inventory (indirect material), payroll (indirect labor), accounts payable, and accumulated depreciation.

EXHIBIT 4-20
ACME PRINTING COMPANY
T Accounts Illustrating the Operation of a Job Order Cost Accounting System

Accounts Receivable

(9) 16,000	

Accumulated Depreciation

	(5) 20,800

Payroll

(3) 80,700	(4) 80,700

Prepaid Insurance

	(5) 8,000

Accounts Payable

	(1) 37,400
	(5) 6,350

Applied Manufacturing Overhead

	(6) 75,000

Materials Inventory

Bal. 0	
(1) 37,400	(2) 26,800
10,600	

Wages Payable

	(3) 70,600

Actual Manufacturing Overhead

(2) 2,800	
(4) 20,700	
(5) 44,950	
68,450	

Work in Process

Bal. 0	
(2) 24,000	
(4) 60,000	(7) 19,000
(6) 75,000	
140,000	

Other Credits

	(3) 10,100

Sales

	(9) 16,000

Finished Goods

Bal. 0	
(7) 19,000	(8) 11,400
7,600	

Property Taxes Payable

	(5) 9,800

Cost of Goods Sold

(8) 11,400	

1 Purchase of materials
2 Issue of direct and indirect materials
3 Manufacturing payroll liability
4 To record direct and indirect labor costs
5 To record actual manufacturing overhead costs
6 Application of manufacturing overhead
7 Completion of job A-3201
8 Cost of units shipped
9 Sales revenue

EXHIBIT 4-21
Major Documents Used to Operate a Job Order Costing System

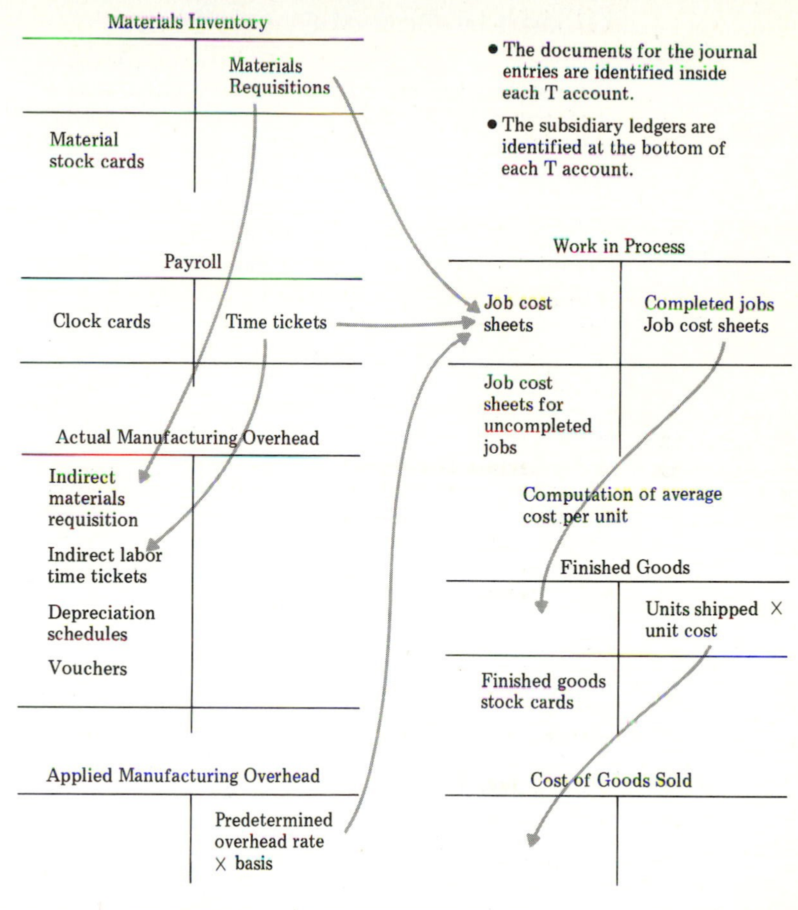

By this point, you should be quite aware that the overhead costs applied to the jobs being produced in the factory are based on estimates because the predetermined rates are. At the end of the year we will know what the actual overhead costs are for *all* jobs worked on during the year. What we will do now is to take a look at how to compare the estimated overhead costs applied to the jobs with the actual overhead costs, and what to do about any differences between applied overhead costs and actual overhead costs. The overhead costs are *overapplied* when the applied overhead costs are greater than actual overhead costs. The overhead costs are *underapplied* when the applied overhead costs are less than the actual overhead costs.

Over- and underapplied overhead defined.

There are two main accounting methods for handling the difference between applied overhead costs and actual overhead costs at the end of the year. They are:

There are two main methods of accounting for over- or underapplied overhead.

1 The difference is closed to the cost of goods sold account.

2 The difference is allocated between work in process, finished goods, and cost of goods sold.

Closed to Cost of Goods Sold

If the difference between applied overhead costs and actual overhead costs is small, most firms will close the difference to cost of goods sold since this method is simpler than the allocation method. The general ledger journal entry to accomplish this closes the applied manufacturing overhead account and the actual manufacturing overhead account to each other and the difference is closed to cost of goods sold.

To illustrate this journal entry, assume at the end of the year Acme Printing Company shows the following data in their general ledger:

	Actual Manufacturing Overhead			Applied Manufacturing Overhead	
Jan. 31	$ 81,200			$ 76,000	Jan. 31
Feb. 28	77,400			79,200	Feb. 28
Mar. 31	79,200			83,200	Mar. 31
.	.			.	.
.	.			.	.
.	.			.	.
Dec. 31	77,000			74,400	Dec. 31
Total	$850,000			$820,000	

The overhead for the year is underapplied by $30,000 ($850,000 − $820,000). At first $30,000 may seem like a large amount, but it represents less than 4% of applied overhead and is probably less than 1% of cost of goods sold. The journal entry to close the underapplied overhead to cost of goods sold is:

Illustration of closing underapplied overhead to cost of goods sold.

Cost of Goods Sold	**$ 30,000**	
Applied Manufacturing Overhead	**$820,000**	
Actual Manufacturing Overhead		**$850,000**

(To close the actual manufacturing overhead and the applied manufacturing overhead accounts and assign the difference to cost of goods sold.)

Allocation between Work in Process, Finished Goods, and Cost of Goods Sold

Throughout the year we use a predetermined overhead rate to assign overhead costs to specific jobs. As you have learned, the overhead cost assigned to the jobs was referred to as applied overhead cost to distinguish it from actual overhead cost.

At the end of the year the total applied manufacturing overhead for the year is found in three accounts: cost of goods sold (jobs shipped to customers), finished goods (jobs completed but not shipped to customers), and work in process (jobs that are not yet completed).

113

OVERAPPLIED UNDERAPPLIED OVERHEAD

At year-end we know the actual overhead cost and it is different from the applied overhead cost. Assuming our rate was based on expected annual activity, the difference between applied and actual overhead exists due to errors we made at the beginning of the year in the estimates used to calculate the predetermined overhead rate (after all, nobody is perfect). If the difference is large, we might want to recompute so that cost of goods sold, ending work in process inventory, and finished goods inventory contain the same amounts as they would have if we had estimated with 100% accuracy. If we had estimated with 100% accuracy, the applied overhead would have equaled the actual overhead. Since we know the difference between the actual overhead and the applied overhead at the end of the year we can allocate this difference to the work in process, finished goods, and cost of goods sold accounts and have the same result as if our estimates had been 100% accurate.

To illustrate the allocation for the Acme Printing Company, assume the $820,000 of applied overhead is distributed as follows:

	Applied Overhead	Ratio	Percentage
Work in process	$ 82,000	82/820	10%
Finished goods	164,000	164/820	20%
Cost of goods sold	574,000	574/820	70%
Total	$820,000		100%

The underapplied overhead would be allocated based on the percentage of applied overhead in each account. The computation is shown below:

	Percentage		Underapplied Overhead		Allocation	+	Applied Overhead	=	Actual Overhead
Work in process	10%	×	$30,000	=	$ 3,000		$ 82,000		$ 85,000
Finished goods	20%	×	$30,000	=	$ 6,000		164,000		170,000
Cost of goods sold	70%	×	$30,000	=	$21,000		574,000		595,000
	100%				$30,000		$820,000		$850,000

The journal entry to close the actual manufacturing overhead account and the applied manufacturing overhead account and to allocate the underapplied overhead is shown below:

Work in Process	**$ 3,000**	
Finished Goods	**6,000**	
Cost of Goods Sold	**21,000**	
Applied Manufacturing Overhead	**820,000**	
Actual Manufacturing Overhead		**$850,000**

(To close the actual and applied overhead accounts and to allocate the difference to work in process, finished goods, and cost of goods sold.)

While the allocation of the over- or underapplied overhead between the work in process, finished goods, and cost of goods sold accounts provides account values based on actual cost, it is generally only used when the amount of over- or underapplied overhead would have a significant impact on net income. If the amount of over- or underapplied overhead is relatively small, most firms simply close the actual and applied overhead accounts to cost of goods sold.

In preparing monthly or quarterly financial statements, the over- or underapplied factory overhead is generally reported on the balance sheet as a debit balance (underapplied) or a credit balance (overapplied). The rationale for this treatment is that the predetermined overhead rate is calculated on an annual basis to eliminate the impact of seasonal fluctuations in actual overhead costs and production volume on the actual monthly overhead rate. Thus we would not expect the actual and applied overhead to be approximately equal until the end of the year. This topic will be discussed in more depth in Chapter 10.

SUMMARY

Job order costing is appropriate for manufacturing situations where the products are produced in batches and each product may be distinctly different from other products.

Each order for the firm's product is referred to as a job and each job is identified by a job number. Direct material cost and the direct labor cost information is originally collected on materials requisitions and time tickets, and is periodically transferred to the job cost sheet.

Overhead cost is assigned to the job using a predetermined overhead rate and is recorded on the job cost sheet.

When a job is completed the direct costs and applied overhead costs are added, giving a total manufacturing cost for the job. The total cost is divided by the number of units in the job; the result is the average cost per unit. The average cost per unit is used to determine the cost of the units in the finished goods inventory and the cost of goods sold.

Overhead costs must be applied to work in process, and the best way to do that is to use a predetermined overhead rate which is based on estimates. At the end of the year you can then determine the accuracy of your estimates. Very likely, the actual overhead costs will not be identical to the estimated overhead costs.

The difference between the actual overhead cost and applied overhead cost is commonly treated as an adjustment to cost of goods sold. If the difference would have a significant impact on net income it is allocated between the work in process, finished goods, and cost of goods sold accounts.

Review Problem

The Caldon Company started business in January 19X8. During the month of January the following transactions occurred:

1	Purchase of materials on account	$35,000
2	Issuance of materials for job order no. 101	3,000
3	Factory depreciation cost	3,000
4	Factory heat, light, and power cost	1,000
5	Issuance of materials for job order no. 102	2,000

6	Manufacturing labor charges from clock cards	9,000
7	Factory maintenance cost	800
8	Direct labor charges for job order nos. 101 and 102 are $4,000 and $3,000 respectively. Indirect labor charges are $2,000	—
9	Factory overhead is charged to the job orders at a rate of 100% of direct labor cost	—
10	Job order no. 101 was completed and transferred to finished goods	—

Required

1 Prepare journal entries to record the above transactions.

2 Calculate the overapplied or underapplied overhead.

Solution

1 Journal entries

1	**Materials Inventory**	**$35,000**	
	Accounts Payable		**$35,000**
	(To record the purchase of raw materials.)		
2	**Work in Process Inventory**	**3,000**	
	Materials Inventory		**3,000**
	(To record issue of raw materials for job order no. 101.)		
3	**Actual Manufacturing Overhead**	**3,000**	
	Accumulated Depreciation		**3,000**
	(To record depreciation for January 19X8.)		
4	**Actual Manufacturing Overhead**	**1,000**	
	Miscellaneous Payables		**1,000**
	(To record utilities for January 19X8.)		
5	**Work in Process Inventory**	**2,000**	
	Materials Inventory		**2,000**
	(To record issue of raw materials for job order no. 102.)		
6	**Payroll**	**9,000**	
	Wages Payable		**9,000**
	(To record labor payroll for January 19X8.)		
7	**Actual Manufacturing Overhead**	**800**	
	Miscellaneous Payables		**800**
	(To record factory maintenance.)		
8	**Actual Manufacturing Overhead**	**2,000**	
	Work in Process Inventory	**7,000**	
	Payroll		**9,000**
	(To charge job order nos. 101 and 102 with direct labor cost and balance to actual overhead.)		
9	**Work in Process Inventory**	**7,000**	
	Applied Manufacturing Overhead		**7,000**
	(To charge job order nos. 101 and 102 with factory overhead at 100% of direct labor cost.)		
10	**Finished Goods Inventory**	**11,000**	
	Work in Process Inventory		**11,000**
	(To transfer the cost of job order no. 101 to finished goods inventory.)		

Supporting computations—job order no. 101

Direct materials	$ 3,000
Direct labor	4,000
Factory overhead at 100% of direct labor	4,000
Total cost of job order no. 101	$11,000

2 Computation of January overapplied manufacturing overhead:

Actual Overhead	
Factory depreciation cost	$3,000
Factory heat, light, and power	1,000
Factory maintenance cost	800
Indirect labor	2,000
Total	$6,800
Manufacturing overhead applied	7,000
Overapplied overhead	$ 200

Glossary

Actual overhead cost All manufacturing costs necessary for the production of products except for direct materials and direct labor. Actual overhead costs are accumulated in the actual manufacturing overhead account in the general ledger as incurred.

Applied overhead cost The overhead cost charged to the work in process account and recorded on the job cost sheets of specific jobs. The applied overhead cost is calculated by multiplying the predetermined overhead rate times the activity base for the month and for the job.

Clock card A document used by employees to record the total hours worked per week. It is used by the employer to determine the total payroll cost.

Direct labor Manufacturing labor that is used directly in the production of a job. This labor can be physically traced to a particular job.

Direct materials Materials that are used directly in the production of a job. These materials are physically traceable to a particular job.

Finished goods The account in the general ledger used to record the cost of completed jobs.

Finished goods stock card A record of the receipts, shipments, and balance of each completed job produced by the company.

Job cost sheet The document used in job order costing to record the direct materials, direct labor, and applied factory overhead cost for each job.

Job order costing A cost accounting system that assigns the manufacturing costs to specific jobs produced by the company. Job order costing is used by companies that produce unique products to customer specifications.

Materials requisition A document that shows the type, quantity, and cost of materials used in the production of jobs. It is used to determine the direct and indirect materials cost.

Materials stock card A record of the receipts, issues, and balance of each type of material used in production.

Predetermined overhead rate The total annual estimated overhead cost divided by the total annual estimated production activity. The rate is used to calculate the applied overhead cost.

Process costing A cost accounting system that assigns the manufacturing costs to departments and then to products. Process costing is used by companies that mass produce standardized products.

Time ticket A document the employees use to record their activities during the work shift. The time tickets are used by the accounting department to determine the total direct and indirect labor cost and to assign the direct labor cost to specific jobs.

Work in process The account in the general ledger used to record the manufacturing costs incurred for the production of jobs. When a job is completed its cost is removed from work in process and charged to the finished goods account.

Questions and Problems

4-1 What are the characteristics of the production process that would suggest a job order cost system be used to collect the cost data?

4-2 Is job order costing appropriate for companies in service industries? Explain.

4-3 What source documents are used to collect direct material and labor costs? List the essential information each document contains and also how it is used.

4-4 What data are collected on the job cost sheet?

4-5 How is the average cost per unit computed and used in job order costing?

4-6 Discuss the reasons manufacturing overhead cannot be assigned directly to jobs.

4-7 What alternatives are available to account for overapplied and underapplied overhead at the end of the year?

4-8 Computation of Overhead Rates The Lawson Company uses direct labor cost to assign the manufacturing overhead to the production jobs. For the coming year the estimated manufacturing overhead cost is $500,000 for a normal volume of $400,000 direct labor dollars. During the month of March the following jobs were completed:

	Job No. 6876	Job No. 7530
Direct materials cost	$1,000	$1,500
Direct labor cost	$2,000	$2,500
Units completed	40	60

Required

1 Calculate the predetermined overhead rate for the Lawson Company.

2 Compute the total overhead cost for jobs no. 6876 and no. 7530.

3 What is the cost per unit for jobs no. 6876 and no. 7530.

4-9 Journal Entries The following transactions relate to the manufacturing operations of the Blue Ridge Company:

1	Purchase of materials on account	$85,000
2	Purchase of factory supplies on account	40,000
3	Materials issued directly for production orders	56,000
4	Direct labor cost incurred	60,000
5	Materials returned to the storeroom	7,000
6	Supplies issued to the factory	20,000
7	Indirect labor cost incurred	30,000
8	Factory depreciation cost	24,000
9	Factory heat, light, and power cost	12,000
10	Factory overhead is applied at a rate of 150% of direct labor cost	—

Required

1 Prepare journal entries to record the transactions.

2 Compute the over- (under-) applied overhead.

4-10 Recording Manufacturing Transactions The following accounts were taken from the books of the Baldwell Company at January 1, 19X3.

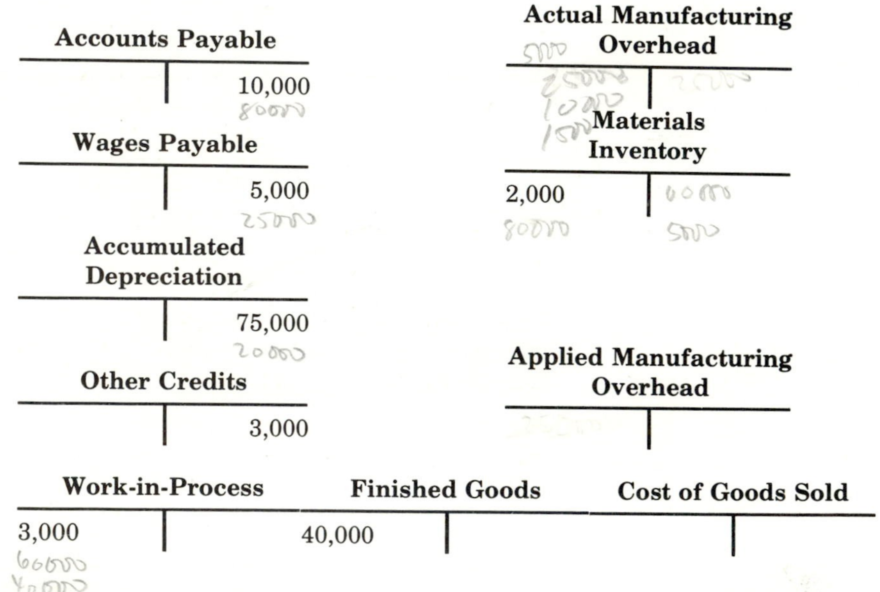

During the month of January the following transactions occurred:

1	Purchase of materials	$80,000
2	Issuance of direct materials for production orders	60,000
3	Indirect wages incurred	25,000
4	Direct labor cost incurred	40,000
5	Factory depreciation	20,000
6	Property tax bill on plant and equipment received	10,000
7	Heat, light, and power cost for January	1,500
8	Indirect materials issued to production	5,000
9	Direct materials returned to storeroom	3,000

10 Manufacturing overhead is applied at a rate of 200% of direct labor cost	—
11 Cost of production orders completed	150,000
12 Cost of production orders shipped	130,000

Required

1 Record the above transactions in the T accounts.

2 Compute the balances for January 31.

4-11 Calculation of Overhead Rates and Job Costing The Hunter Company began operation on January 1, 19X0, producing products to customer specification in a two-department machine shop. The factory overhead is assigned to the jobs using machine hours in department one and direct labor dollars in department two. For the year 19X0, the company has prepared the following estimates:

	Department	
	One	Two
Total factory overhead	$150,000	$120,000
Direct labor cost	$100,000	$200,000
Machine hours	10,000	4,000

During the month of January only one job was completed, job no. X758. The cost card for job X758 revealed the following information:

Direct materials cost	$5,000
Direct labor—department one	$4,000
Direct labor—department two	$9,000
Machine hours—department one	200
Machine hours—department two	90

Required

1 Calculate the predetermined overhead rates for departments one and two.

2 Calculate the total cost of job X758. Assuming 175 units of product are included in job X758, what is the cost per unit?

3 Assume for the year 19X0 actual machine hours in department one are 10,700, actual direct labor cost in department two is $185,000, and actual overhead costs were $155,000 and $115,000 for departments one and two respectively. What is the over- or underapplied overhead for each department?

4-12 Recording Transactions in T Accounts During the month of September the Bar Company purchased $80,000 of direct materials, paid $75,000 direct labor cost, and incurred $100,000 of manufacturing overhead costs. The company assigns overhead to the product at a rate of 120% of direct labor cost. The balances in the inventory accounts are as follows:

	Balance Sept. 1, 19X1	Balance Sept. 30, 19X1
Direct materials	$20,000	$35,000
Work in process	60,000	80,000
Finished goods	70,000	60,000

Required

1 Set up the necessary T accounts to record the above data.

2 Record the transactions for the month of September.

3 What is the cost of goods sold?

4 How much is the over- (under-) applied overhead?

4-13 Identifying General Ledger Relationships from Incomplete Data The Scent Company has provided you with the following information for the month of March.

Materials		Work in Process		Finished Goods	
3/1 12,000		3/1 20,000		3/1 20,000	
3/31 15,000		3/31 15,000		3/31 24,000	

Payroll		Applied Overhead		Cost of Goods Sold	
50,000			29,000	80,000	

Other Information

a Materials in the amount of $7,000 are classified as indirect and should be charged to the actual overhead account.

b The indirect labor and supervision cost was $20,000.

Required

1 Determine the cost of direct materials, direct labor, and applied overhead charged to work in process.

2 Calculate the cost of materials purchased.

4-14 Working from Incomplete Data Given the following facts:

	Beginning	Ending	
Direct materials inventory	$4,000	$2,800	
Work in process inventory	1,600	1,300	
Finished goods inventory	7,000	?	
Purchases of direct materials			$12,000
Total credits to factory payroll account			31,000
Cost of goods sold			56,400
Overhead applied			24,000
Direct labor cost incurred			20,000
Cost of goods manufactured			57,500

Overhead is applied on the basis of direct labor cost. During the period overhead was overapplied by $2,000. The overapplied overhead is *not* closed to cost of goods sold.

Required

1 What was the cost of direct materials used during the period?

2 What was the ending finished goods inventory?

3 What was the actual overhead cost incurred during the period?

4 What was the predetermined overhead rate?

5 What was the amount of indirect labor cost incurred during the period?

4-15 Cost Flows—T Accounts The ABC Company has presented you with the following information concerning the operations for the month of August.

Materials

8/1 5,000	
32,000	
8/31 10,000	

Work in Process

8/1 10,000	

Finished Goods

8/1 12,000	

Payroll

47,000	

Manufacturing Overhead Applied

Actual Manufacturing Overhead

30,000	

Cost of Goods Sold

Additional Information

1 Total material requisitions for jobs worked on during the month is $25,000.

2 The direct labor cost for the month amounted to $40,000 for 8,000 hours. All employees receive the same hourly wage.

3 Overhead is applied to jobs at a rate of $6 per direct labor hours.

4 The only unfinished job for the month has assigned to it $3,000 for direct materials and 750 direct labor hours.

5 The debit to the actual manufacturing overhead account represents all overhead costs except indirect labor and indirect materials.

6 The cost of the jobs shipped during the month is $108,750.

Required

1 Calculate the ending inventory of work in process and finished goods.

2 How much was the overhead over- (under-) applied?

4-16 Journal Entries for Cost Flows The Ace Specialty Company manufactures furniture to customers' specifications. For the month of June, the following data have been collected concerning the material, labor, and manufacturing expenses.

Materials purchases	$45,750
Materials requisitions	
Production jobs	30,000
Production supplies	5,000

Maintenance	4,750
Labor Cost—factory	
Time tickets—direct labor	60,000
Foreman's salary	15,000
Set-up cost—indirect	6,000
Maintenance	8,000
Administrative	12,000
Additional manufacturing expenses	
Depreciation	20,000
Property taxes	3,000
Insurance	1,000
Heat, light, and power	1,500
Payroll taxes	10,000
Other supplies	4,000
Cost summary—completed jobs	

	Job XK74	**JobXK76**	**Job XK77**
Units in job	1,000	2,000	2,000
Direct materials cost	$ 5,000	$10,000	$ 4,600
Direct labor cost	$15,000	$20,000	$10,000
Units shipped	1,000	1,200	1,300

The manufacturing overhead is assigned to the jobs at a rate of 150% of direct labor cost.

Required Prepare journal entries to record the cost flow information.

4-17 Job Order Costing—Service Company The Sauer and Sauer CPA firm requires each of its employees to complete a weekly time card specifying the hours they worked on each job, the hours spent on professional development, and the unassigned hours. This information is then transcribed to job cost sheets for each of the clients and used for costing and billing purposes. The time cards for the past week are summarized below.

Employee	**Rank**	**Client**	**Hours**
J. Jones	Senior	101	15
		102	25
S. Send	Senior	103	20
		104	20
P. Maska	Junior	101	10
		102	20
B. Bucks	Junior	101	10
		102	20
		104	5
T. Whitehall	Junior	103	10
		104	15

Q. Faxon	Junior	102	10
		103	5
		104	25
P. Bills	Junior	101	15
		103	10
		104	10
P. Rabit	Manager	101	10
		102	15
		103	5
		104	20
J. Sauer	Partner	101	10
		104	15
S. Sauer	Partner	102	16
		103	15

The weekly pay rates for the employees are:

Junior	$260
Senior	300
Manager	500
Partner	700

These rates represent the pay for 40 hours. To allocate the salary cost to the clients an hourly rate is calculated and used to assign the salary cost to the clients. Any professional development time and unassigned time is charged to an overhead account. The overhead cost is allocated to the client at a rate of 200% of the salary cost.

The clients are billed for the services based on the following rates:

Partner	$50 per hour
Manager	40
Senior	30
Junior	20

Required

1 Calculate the salary and overhead cost assigned to each client.

2 Assuming the audit is completed for clients 102 and 104, calculate the amount of each bill that will be submitted to the client.

3 Comment on the use of the job cost data calculated in part 1 for estimating the cost of future audits.

4-18 Calculation of Job Costs, Inventory Values, and Cost of Goods Sold The Morgan Manufacturing Company has two departments, fabricating and assembly, for the production of automotive parts. The overhead in each department is applied to the jobs based on direct labor hours (DLH). The cost of the beginning work in process and a summary of the direct materials and direct labor cost for the month of June 19X9 are provided below. A schedule for the estimated annual overhead for each department is provided. During the month all jobs were completed except job X765.

Beginning Work in Process

Job	Direct Materials	Direct Labor	Applied Overhead	Total
X751	$2,000	$3,050	$6,200	$11,250
X761	$3,000	$4,755	$9,500	$17,255

Summary of Direct Material Requisitions

Requisition	Job	Quantity	Cost per Unit	Total
R1008	X762	100 lbs	$3.50	$350
R1009	X763	120 lbs	4.20	504
R1010	X763	60 lbs	4.20	252
R1011	X764	85 lbs	5.00	425
R1012	X764	70 lbs	1.00	70
R1014	X765	160 lbs	4.00	640
R1013	X762	30 lbs	3.50	105

Direct Labor Data Summary—Fabricating

Work Order	Job	Hours	Cost per Hour	Total
F 75	X751	8	7.00	$ 56
F 76	X762	45	7.00	315
F 77	X763	70	7.00	490
F 78	X764	45	7.00	315
F 79	X765	20	7.00	140
F 80	X762	10	7.00	70

Direct Labor Data Summary—Assembly

Work Order	Job	Hours	Cost per Hour	Total
A 96	X751	10	$5.00	$ 50
A 97	X761	15	5.00	65
A 98	X762	30	5.00	150
A 99	X763	45	5.00	225
A 100	X764	25	5.00	125
A 101	X765	15	5.00	75

Annual Budgeted Overhead

Item	Department: Fabricating	Department: Assembly
Supervision	$18,000	$15,000
Indirect labor	7,500	5,000
Depreciation	20,000	6,000
Miscellaneous supplies	4,000	2,000
Total	$49,500	$28,000

Estimated Activity (DLH)	2,500	1,600
Predetermined overhead rate	$19.80 per DLH	$17.50 per DLH

The production and shipping records for the month provided the following information:

Completed Jobs

Job	Units Produced	Units Shipped
X751	100	80
X761	150	150
X762	100	60
X763	160	160
X764	150	70

Required

1 Calculate the total cost of producing each job.

2 Prepare schedules showing the cost of the ending work in process, finished goods, and cost of goods sold.

4-19 Overhead Assignment to Jobs The Grant Specialty Manufacturing Company has three producing departments. The overhead has been estimated and resulted in the following figures for the year:

Department	Estimated Overhead
P_1	$435,000
P_2	311,950
P_3	307,200

The overhead is assigned to the jobs in the producing departments based on machine hours in P_1 and direct labor hours in P_2 and P_3. The estimated annual activity for all three producing departments in both machine and direct labor hours is shown below:

Department	Estimated Machine Hours	Estimated Direct Labor Hours
P_1	100,000	40,000
P_2	30,000	85,000
P_3	15,000	120,000

During the month of June 10 jobs were started in the plant and the following machine and direct labor hours were used in fabricating the jobs:

	Machine Hours			Direct Labor Hours		
Job	P_1	P_2	P_3	P_1	P_2	P_3
1	50	20	20	20	38	44
2	100	34	18	40	60	100
3	30	10	8	10	18	22
4	200	78	50	75	100	120
5	150	50	20	50	98	110
6	80	25	10	30	70	130
7	100	45	20	40	85	150
8	300	100	60	130	270	400
9	150	70	40	70	180	230
10	40	15	10	20	40	55

At the end of the month, jobs 3, 4, 6, 8, 9, and 10 were completed and shipped to the customers. All other jobs require more work prior to shipping them to the customers.

Required

1 Calculate the overhead rate for each department.

2 Calculate the amount of overhead assigned to each job.

3 Calculate the amount of overhead that will be included in cost of goods sold and in work in process.

4-20 Multiple Choice. Job Costing Department 203—Work in Process—Beginning of Period

Job No.	Direct Material	Direct Labor	Applied Overhead	Total
1376	$17,500	$22,000	$33,000	$72,500

Department 203 Costs for 19X7

Incurred by Jobs	Material	Labor	Other	Total
1376	$ 1,000	$ 7,000	—	$ 8,000
1377	26,000	53,000	—	79,000
1378	12,000	9,000	—	21,000
1379	4,000	1,000	—	5,000

Not Incurred by Jobs

Indirect materials and supplies	15,000	—	—	15,000
Indirect labor	—	53,000	—	53,000
Employee benefits	—	—	$23,000	23,000
Depreciation	—	—	12,000	12,000
Supervision	—	20,000	—	20,000
Total	$58,000	$143,000	$35,000	$236,000

Department 203 Overhead Rate for 19X7

Budgeted overhead	
Indirect materials	$ 16,000
Indirect labor	56,000
Employee benefits	24,000
Supervision	20,000
Depreciation	12,000
Total	$128,000
Budgeted direct labor dollars	$ 80,000
Rate per direct labor dollar ($128,000 ÷ 80,000)	160%

1 The actual overhead for department 203 for 19X7 was
a $156,000 b $123,000 c $70,000 d $112,000
e none of the above

2 Department 203 overhead for 19X7 was
a $11,000 underapplied d $44,000 overapplied
b $11,000 overapplied e none of the above
c $44,000 underapplied

3 Job no. 1376 was the only job completed and sold in 19X7. What amount was included in cost of goods sold for this job?
a $72,500 b $91,700 c $80,500 d $19,200 e none of the above

4 The value of work in process inventory at the end of 19X7 was
a $105,000 b $180,600 c $228,000 d $205,800
e none of the above

5 Assume that overhead was underapplied in the amount of $14,000 for department 203. If underapplied overhead was distributed between cost of goods sold and inventory, how much of the underapplied overhead was charged to the year-end work in process inventory?
a $9,685 b $4,315 c $12,600 d $1,400 e none of the above

(CMA)

PROCESS COST ACCOUNTING

AFTER COMPLETING YOUR STUDY OF THIS CHAPTER, YOU SHOULD HAVE LEARNED:

1 What process cost accounting is and how it differs from job order cost accounting.

2 How manufacturing costs are recorded and assigned to products using process cost accounting.

3 How to calculate the average manufacturing cost per unit and how it is used in a process cost accounting system.

4 The concept of equivalent finished units, and why it is used as a measure of the output of a process manufacturing system.

5 How the average manufacturing cost per unit is used to calculate the cost of the work in process inventory, finished goods inventory, and cost of goods sold.

Job versus process production situations.

In a job order production system, there is a definite beginning and completion for each job, each job is different from another, they are produced in small quantities, and each is produced to specifications. A process production system is different in each respect: products are produced continuously, there is no beginning or end; products are built to standard specifications, that is, they are identical, produced continuously, and in enormous quantities.

Process production is used extensively in the oil, chemical, steel, electronics, and food industries. In each of these industries standardized products are produced on a continuous basis and warehoused. For example, gasoline is produced by the oil industry, ammonia is produced by the chemical industry, sheet metal is produced by the steel industry, pocket radios and calculators are produced by the thousands by the electronics industry, breakfast cereals by the food industry. There is a continuous flow of these kinds of products from the manufacturer to their warehouses, and then on to customers when and in quantities they request.

COST FLOWS IN PROCESS COSTING

Job Order Costing: A Reprise

In job order cost accounting we used materials requisitions to collect direct and indirect materials cost, time tickets to collect direct and indirect labor costs, and voucher and amortization schedules to collect the actual manufacturing overhead costs for each department. The information from the materials requisitions and labor time tickets was used to assign the direct materials cost and direct labor cost to the individual jobs worked on in each department. The manufacturing overhead was applied to each job using a predetermined overhead rate. Since each job was different, we could not calculate the average cost per unit for a particular job until the job was completed. A job might extend over a number of accounting time periods, but this was of no concern to us. Any uncompleted job at the end of a time period represented work in process. The cost of the work in process could be determined from the job cost sheets for the uncompleted jobs.

And Now: Process Costing

With **process costing** we will use materials requisitions and labor time tickets to collect the direct materials and direct labor cost by department. The actual manufacturing overhead costs will be collected by department, using material requisitions for indirect materials, labor time tickets for indirect labor, vouchers, and amortization schedules for the remaining overhead costs. The applied manufacturing overhead is also determined for each department using a predetermined overhead rate.

The direct materials, direct labor, and applied manufacturing overhead are accumulated by department for a weekly or monthly accounting period. Also accumulated during the accounting period is the number of units produced by the department. Because the department is producing a standard product, we can calculate the average cost per unit for the accounting period simply by dividing the total manufacturing costs assigned to the department by the number of units it produced. And that is the basic difference between the cost per unit in job order costing and the cost per unit in process costing.

The basic difference between job order and process costing.

EXHIBIT 5-1
Timing of Cost per Unit Calculation
Job Order and Process Cost Accounting

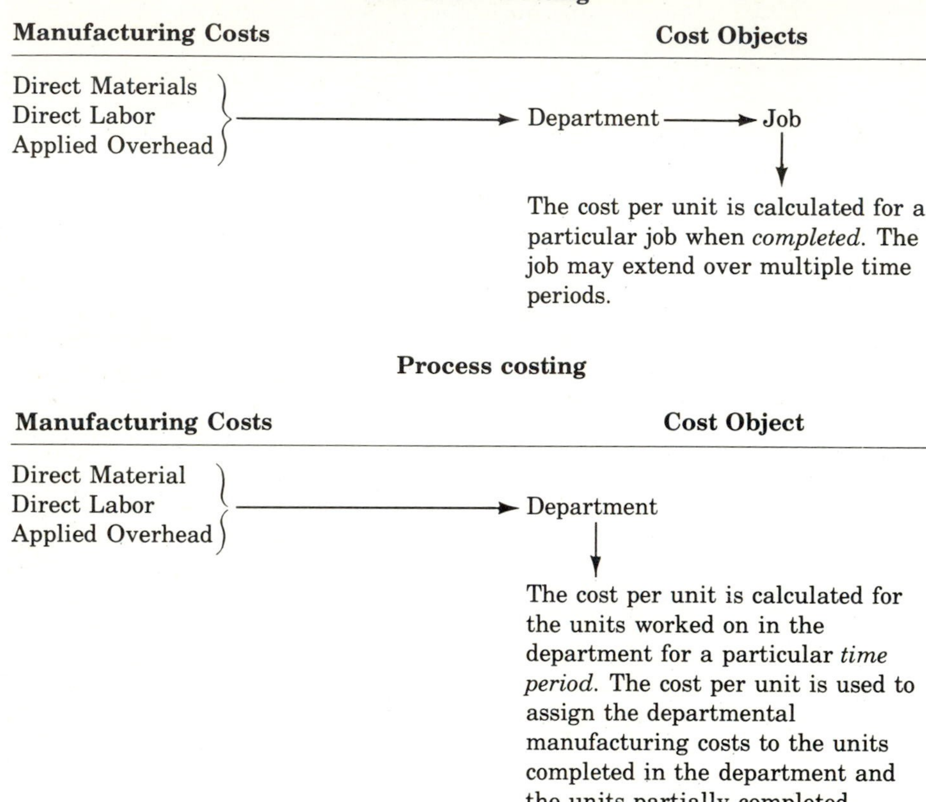
Job Order Costing
Manufacturing Costs
Cost Objects
Direct Materials
Direct Labor
Applied Overhead
Department
Job
The cost per unit is calculated for a particular job when *completed.* The job may extend over multiple time periods.
Process costing
Manufacturing Costs
Cost Object
Direct Material
Direct Labor
Applied Overhead
Department
The cost per unit is calculated for the units worked on in the department for a particular *time period.* The cost per unit is used to assign the departmental manufacturing costs to the units completed in the department and the units partially completed.

In job order costing the manufacturing costs were initially assigned to the department and then reassigned to individual jobs and the unit cost was calculated when each job was completed. In process costing the manufacturing costs assigned to departments are used to calculate a departmental unit cost at the end of an accounting time period. The unit cost in process costing is used to assign the departmental manufacturing costs to the units completed in the department and the units partially completed during the accounting period. Exhibit 5-1 summarizes these basic differences between job order and process cost accounting systems.

Product Flows in Process Costing

Example of process production.

Companies that use process costing to account for their manufacturing costs are usually organized into various producing departments with the product being worked on in each department. For example, the Acme Company, a manufacturer of electronic calculators, has the following product flow through three producing departments:

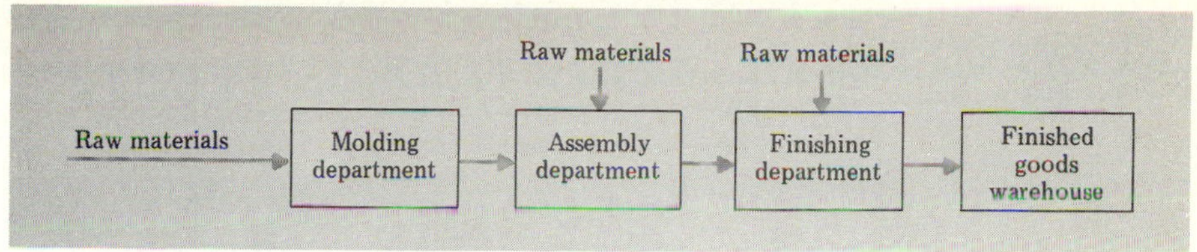

The molding department melts raw plastic, forms it into the calculator case, and hardens the case. When this process is completed the case is transferred to the assembly department. Since the molding department is operating on a continuous basis, the cases are transferred to the assembly department probably on an hourly or daily basis.

The assembly department installs all the electronic components in the case. When this process is completed the calculator is transferred to the finishing department. Again this transfer occurs on an hourly or daily basis.

The finishing department glues the decals showing the operating instructions to the back of the case and packages the calculator in cardboard containers. The product, a packaged calculator, is then transferred to the finished goods warehouse to await shipment to the customers.

Cost per unit Calculations

To determine the total cost per packaged calculator, we will accumulate the manufacturing costs for each department—molding, assembly, and finishing—for the accounting period. Then we will calculate the cost per unit in the molding department to transfer the cost of the plastic cases to the assembly department. Next, we will calculate the cost per unit in the assembly department to transfer the cost of the plastic cases and electrical components to the finishing department. Finally, we will calculate the cost per unit in the finishing department to transfer the cost of the packaged calculators to the finished goods warehouses. The process is illustrated below:

Building up the cost per unit.

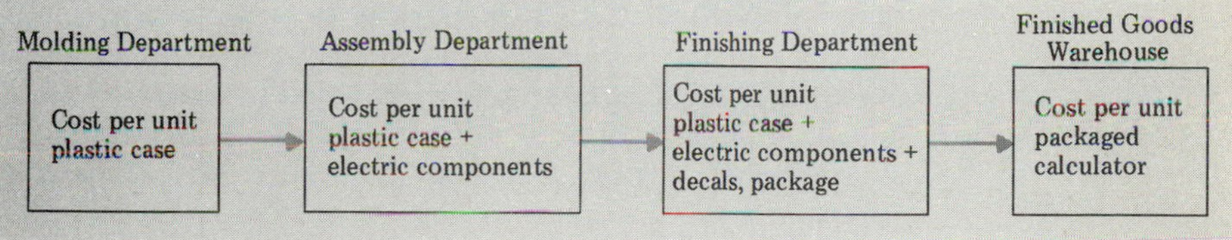

Let us begin by taking a look at the units processed through the molding department and the costs incurred there during the month of June as shown below:

Molding Department—June

Units	
Beginning work in process	0
Units started	10,000
Units completed	10,000
Ending work in process	0

Costs Added for June

Direct materials	$ 9,000
Direct labor	8,000
Applied overhead ($8,000 × .50)*	4,000
Total costs	$21,000

* The predetermined overhead rate is assumed to be 50% of direct labor cost in the molding department.

In the molding department sufficient plastic materials were started in June to complete 10,000 calculator cases. During the month of June the workers in the molding department processed the plastic and completed 10,000 cases. As these cases were completed during June they were transferred to the assembly department. That is, cases were transferred to the assembly department each day during June and the total transferred for the month was 10,000.

The total costs for the molding department in June amounted to $21,000 for the production of 10,000 units. The journal entry to charge these costs to the molding department is given as entry (1) below:

(1)	**Work in Process—Molding Department**	**$21,000**	
	Materials Inventory		**$9,000**
	Payroll		**8,000**
	Applied Manufacturing Overhead		**4,000**
	(To record the total manufacturing costs for the Molding Department—for June.)		

Since in process costing we calculate a cost per unit figure for each department, we use a separate work in process account for each department.

Cost of processing one unit through the molding department.

To determine the cost of processing 1 unit through the molding department, we can simply divide the $21,000 by the 10,000 units. This gives us a unit cost of $2.10 for the molding department, as shown in Exhibit 5-2. Exhibit 5-2 also shows that we have $21,000 of costs to be accounted for in the molding department. Since the molding department physically transferred 10,000 completed units to the assembly department, we need to make a journal entry to transfer the total cost of these 10,000 units to the assembly department. The total cost is calculated by multiplying the 10,000 units times the unit cost of $2.10. The journal entry to transfer the costs from the molding department to the assembly department is entry (2) below:

(2)	**Work in Process—Assembly Department**	**$21,000**	
	Work in Process—Molding Department		**$21,000**
	(To transfer the cost of completing 10,000 units at $2.10 per unit in the molding department to the assembly department.)		

At this point process costing appears to be relatively simple. However, you will find out that when a department has **partially completed units** in the beginning and ending work in process the unit cost computation is more complex.

EXHIBIT 5-2
ACME COMPANY
Cost Summary—Molding Department
For the Month of June

	Cost	Units Produced	Cost per Unit
Costs to account for			
Direct materials	$ 9,000		
Direct labor	8,000		
Overhead applied (50% × $8,000)	4,000		
Total	$21,000	10,000	$2.10
Costs Accounted for			
Transferred to assembly department	10,000 units @ $2.10		$21,000

THE IMPACT OF PARTIALLY COMPLETED UNITS IN THE ENDING WORK IN PROCESS

In the previous example, the per-unit cost calculation was easy to do because in the molding department all units were started during the month and all were completed by the end of the month. But that is hardly the way it is in real life. In a more realistic example, the company will very likely have partially completed units at the beginning as well as at the end of the month. This is to be expected because in a process production system where large quantities of standard products are manufactured continuously over time, there is no reason why the process should begin at the beginning of the month and be completed by the end of the month. If you visualize a production line, at any time if the line is stopped, there will be, all along the line, units which have not been completed.

These partially completed units and the completed units must have some of the total departmental manufacturing costs assigned to them as illustrated below:

Work in process inventory is the cost of partially completed units.

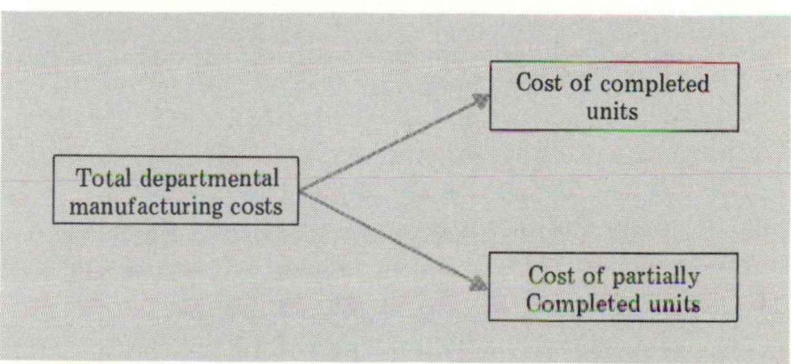

In process costing what we have to do is calculate the manufacturing cost per completed unit and use this to assign the total departmental manufacturing costs to the completed units and the partially completed units. And what this problem boils down to is that you cannot add the quantity of completed units to the quantity of partially completed units; such a total would be a meaningless mixture of units.

However, there is a way of accounting for partially completed units—**equivalent finished units**—which can be meaningfully added to the number of completed units yielding a total quantity that can be used to calculate unit costs.

Equivalent Finished Units

If we understand the concept of equivalent finished units, we can calculate the unit cost for a manufacturing department, no matter how many completed units and how many partially completed units there are at the beginning and the end of an accounting period.

To begin to get an idea of what equivalent finished units is all about, consider this example. A department had no completed units at the start of the month. During an accounting period A department started 7,000 units in the production process and at the end of the accounting period 5,000 of these units were completed leaving an ending work in process of 2,000 units as follows:

	Beginning work in process	0
plus:	Units started	7,000
less:	Units completed	5,000
	Ending work in process (partially completed units)	2,000

Output of the department is the total equivalent units for the period.

The department completed 5,000 units, but we cannot say the output of the department is only 5,000 units. Remember, the employees in the department also worked to some extent on 2,000 units. The work that they did on these 2,000 partially completed units must also be included as part of the total output of the department for the accounting period.

Now, how can we represent, meaningfully, these 2,000 partially completed units as "equivalent finished units" so that we can calculate the total output of the department during the accounting period? Basically, we examine the partially completed units and determine the percentage of the total effort necessary to complete a unit that has been expended on the partially completed units. Total effort would include all the resources of production—materials, labor, and overhead.

Let us assume that an examination of these 2,000 partially completed units revealed that sufficient effort had been performed to physically get the units 60% complete. To calculate the department's output, the accountant assumes that the amount of effort required to get 2,000 units 60% complete is equivalent to the amount of effort required to start and completely finish 1,200 units, that is, .60 × 2,000 units.

The department's output in terms of equivalent finished units can then be calculated as follows:

	Units completed	5,000
plus:	Equivalent finished units—ending work in process, 2,000 units 60% complete	1,200
equals:	Total equivalent finished units of output	6,200

The 6,200 equivalent finished units of output is what we will use as the total output quantity—the denominator for the unit cost calculation for this department.

Now that you know what an equivalent finished unit is and how to calculate it, let us back up for a moment and take a look at how resources are consumed in a production process and how this affects the calculation of equivalent finished units.

Direct labor and overhead are added uniformly throughout the period.

Resources are consumed in two ways: uniformly throughout the production process and in discrete lumps at particular points in the production process. Generally speaking, direct labor and overhead are resources that are assumed to be consumed uniformly during the production process. While this may not be completely accurate physically, it is quite accurate enough for cost accounting. Workers regularly perform direct labor on the product throughout the production process. Likewise, overhead costs, such as supervision, machine costs, and supplies are used regularly and consumed evenly throughout the production process.

Direct materials are most often added as a lump at some stage of the production process.

In contrast, direct materials are most often added in a lump at some stage of the production process. For example, the direct materials required to manufacture the product are added at the start of the process; thus, the direct materials for these processes are consumed as a lump at the start of the process. Of course, there are many processes where one kind of direct material is needed at the start of the process and other kinds of direct materials are needed at various stages of the process to complete the product. The cost of each type of material is simply accounted for at the point during the process when the lump of each material is introduced into the process.

Direct materials are occasionally added uniformly throughout the period.

Occasionally, a production process requires direct materials uniformly throughout the production process. An example of this would be a mixing process where some type of ingredient is continuously added during the entire production process. This type of direct material is treated in the same way as direct labor and overhead are treated.

Why is it important to distinguish between how resources are consumed in manufacturing a product? It is important because, when it comes to determining equivalent finished units, you must first be able to determine how the resources were consumed in producing the product. For resources consumed continuously, the equivalent finished units are proportional to the stage of completion. For resources consumed in a lump, the equivalent finished units are the number of units that have passed the stage where the resource is consumed.

For example, assume 8,000 units are started in a department and all direct materials necessary to complete the units are added, in a lump, at the start of the process, and direct labor and overhead are consumed continuously throughout the process. At the end of the accounting period, assume that none of the units are completed but that they have physically been processed 70% of the way through the department. That is, 30% of the total effort to complete the units will be performed in the next accounting period. The equivalent finished units are calculated as follows:

	Equivalent Finished Units	
	Direct Materials	**Direct Labor and Overhead**
Ending work in process		.7 × 8,000
8,000 units	8,000	5,600

The equivalent finished units for direct materials are 8,000 units since all the direct materials necessary to complete the units have been consumed. The equivalent finished units for direct labor and overhead are 5,600 (.7 × 8,000) since the units have only been processed 70% of the way toward becoming a completed unit.

What this means is that when there is a department where resources are consumed in lumps and uniformly, you no longer work with total costs for the department during the accounting period and total number of units produced during that accounting period. What you have to do then is work with individual costs per equivalent finished unit per cost item. You must calculate the equivalent finished units for each of the lump resources and simply divide the total cost of the lump by the number of equivalent finished units produced after that lump. You also must figure the cost per equivalent finished unit for the uniform costs. Then, having costs per unit, which are now independent of lumps and uniform costs, you can add up the cost per unit for each cost item to get a total cost per unit.

Cost Calculations with Partially Completed Units in the Ending Work in Process

Let us return to the earlier illustration of the Acme Company. During the month of June, the molding department processed 10,000 calculator cases and transferred them to the assembly department. The assembly department installs the electronic components in the cases.

In the assembly department we will assume that all direct materials are consumed at the start of the process and that direct labor and overhead are used uniformly throughout the process. Now, let us calculate the unit cost for the assembly department in a situation where not all the units are completed at the end of the accounting period. We will assume that we have collected the following data for the month in the assembly department:

Assembly Department—June

Units	
Beginning work in process (Work already in process at the start of the accounting period)	0
Units received from the molding department	10,000
Units completed	7,000
Ending work in process (100% finished for direct materials, 70% finished for conversion)	3,000
Costs for June 19X2	
Prior department	$21,000
Direct materials	20,000
Direct labor	9,100
Applied overhead ($9,100 × .30)*	2,730
	$52,830

* The predetermined factory overhead rate is 30% of direct labor cost in this department.

The journal entry to charge the new costs to the assembly department is shown as entry (3):

(3) **Work in Process—Assembly Department**	**$31,830**	
Material Inventory		**$20,000**
Payroll		**9,100**
Applied Manufacturing Overhead		**2,730**
(To record the total manufacturing costs for the Assembly Department for June.)		

Prior department costs include direct material, direct labor, and applied overhead costs of the molding department.

The prior department costs were charged to the department as journal entry number 2. In the assembly department, there are four groups of costs to keep track of: direct materials, direct labor, applied overhead, and **prior department costs.** Prior department cost is a new category. It is the total costs of the direct materials, direct labor, and applied overhead for processing the units in the prior department. There is no particular need to keep separate track of the direct materials, direct labor, and applied overhead costs incurred in a prior department; instead these costs are grouped as a total under the heading of "prior department" costs. In this company, as is often the case, the prior department costs are like a direct materials cost which is added in a lump at the start of the process.

Because the direct materials are added in the assembly department in a lump at the start of the process, and direct labor and overhead are added uniformly throughout the process, we must calculate two types of equivalent finished units. There are equivalent finished units for costs added as a lump at the start of the process, and equivalent finished units for costs which are added uniformly throughout the process.

The flow of the units through the assembly department can be represented graphically as in the following scale of completion:

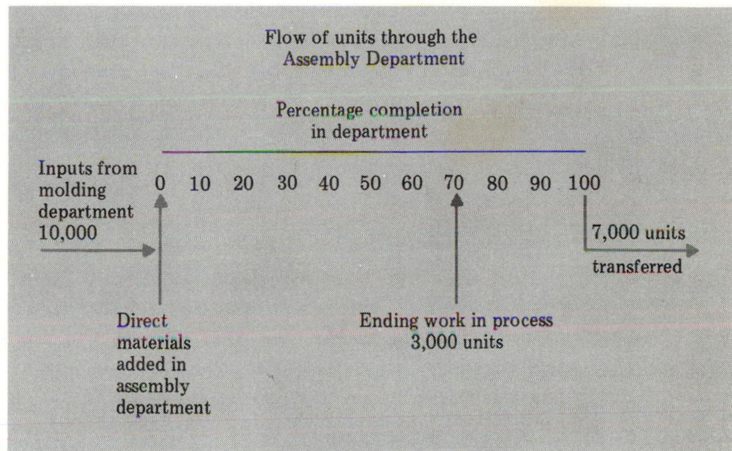

In this example the equivalent finished units for the assembly department for the costs added in a lump—prior department costs and direct materials costs—is 10,000 units computed as follows:

Equivalent units for costs added as lump sum.

7,000 units started and completed × 100%	=	7,000
3,000 units started and 100% completed for prior department cost and direct materials costs × 100%		3,000
Total equivalent finished units for costs added in a lump		10,000

The equivalent finished units for costs added uniformly—direct labor and applied overhead—is calculated as follows:

Equivalent units for costs added uniformly.

7,000 units started and completed × 100%	=	7,000
3,000 units started and 70% completed (3,000 × 70%)	=	2,100
Total equivalent finished units for costs added uniformly		9,100

With this basic information, we can now follow along the steps in Exhibit 5-3 to see how to calculate the total **cost per equivalent finished unit** at the completion of an accounting period for the assembly department.

Exhibit 5-3 described.

Part A shows the total number of actual physical units which were started in the assembly department and must be accounted for through to the end of the process in that department.

Part B shows the total number of actual physical units completed and still in work in process. The total of the completed and partially completed actual physical units at this step must equal the total number of physical units in part A. Also, in part B are the equivalent finished units for each of the cost categories—prior department cost, direct materials, direct labor, and applied overhead—in the assembly department.

In part C, you see a tabulation of each of the four cost items, the costs incurred for each cost item, the total, \$52,830, and the equivalent finished units for each cost, as well as the cost per equivalent finished unit for each cost item. The sum of the individual costs per equivalent finished unit is \$5.40, the total cost per equivalent finished unit through the end of the accounting period for units processed through the assembly department.

Part D shows the number of total physical units completed and transferred to the finishing department, and the total cost of those units, also transferred to the finishing department. For the units still to be completed in the assembly department, part D shows the equivalent finished units for each cost item and the costs expended on these units as of the end of the accounting period.

Note that the total costs for all cost items and all units, \$52,830 in part C, must equal the total cost of transferred units, \$37,800, plus cost of the ending work in process, \$15,030, still in the assembly department.

It is very important that you understand the data and information in part D of Exhibit 5-3. Each unit transferred out of the assembly department (and, of course, all units transferred out of a department are fully completed units) is assigned all the costs expended to get it to the point where it is completed. Those costs include the full prior department cost (molding department), and the assembly department's direct materials cost, direct labor cost, and applied overhead. The partially completed units remaining in the assembly department work in process have the full prior department and assembly department direct materials cost added at the start of the process, but only their proportional share of the direct labor and applied overhead which were added uniformly in the assembly department.

The journal entry to record the transfer of costs to the finishing department from the assembly department is entry (4) below:

(4)	**Work in Process—Finishing Department**	**\$37,800**	
	Work in Process—Assembly Department		**\$37,800**
	(To transfer the cost of completing 7,000 units at \$5.40 per unit in the assembly department to the finishing department.)		

EXHIBIT 5-3
ACME COMPANY
Cost Summary—Assembly Department
For the Month of June

A Units to Account for	Physical Units
Received from molding department	10,000

B Units Accounted for	Physical Units	Equivalent Finished Units: Prior Dept.	Direct Material	Direct Labor	Applied Overhead
Completed	7,000	7,000	7,000	7,000	7,000
Ending work in process	3,000	3,000	3,000	2,100	2,100
Total	10,000	10,000	10,000	9,100	9,100

C Costs to Account for	Cost	Equivalent Units	Cost per Unit
Prior department	$21,000	10,000	$2.10
Direct material	20,000	10,000	2.00
Direct labor	9,100	9,100	1.00
Applied overhead (30% × $9,100)	2,730	9,100	.30
Total	$52,830		$5.40

D Costs Accounted for			
Completed and transferred to finishing department 7,000 units @ $5.40			$37,800
Ending work in process			
Prior department	3,000 @ $2.10	$6,300	
Direct material	3,000 @ $2.00	6,000	
Direct labor	2,100 @ $1.00	2,100	
Applied overhead	2,100 @ $ .30	630	15,030
Total			$52,830

THE IMPACT OF PARTIALLY COMPLETED UNITS IN THE BEGINNING WORK IN PROCESS

In earlier accounting courses, you no doubt were introduced to the basic principles of **first-in, first-out (FIFO) cost** flow and average cost flow and how to use these methods to calculate the cost of inventories. In our example, in the molding and assembly departments, either of these methods of costing inventory at the end of an accounting period would have resulted in the same cost per unit because there were no beginning inventories in either department. That is, there were no partially completed units in the department at the beginning of the accounting time period and we only had current period costs to deal with.

However, it is not quite as simple with the partially completed units in the beginning inventory. We have already calculated a cost per equivalent finished unit for these partially completed units in the prior accounting period but what makes life for the accountant a bit more difficult is that during the next accounting period, the manufacturing costs will very likely change. That is, the total costs for materials, labor, and overhead for 1,000 equivalent finished units in the beginning inventory may add up to $8,000. During the next accounting period, costs for materials, labor, and overhead might very well go up to $9,000 to produce the same 1,000 equivalent finished units at the end of that period. How do we account for this difference? This is where the FIFO or **average cost methods** of costing inventory are used to resolve per-unit cost determinations.

Either FIFO or average inventory costing assumption is required when there are beginning work in process inventories.

The purpose of these next two sections is to enable you to calculate the cost per unit using either the average cost method or the FIFO method. To illustrate the process costing computations for FIFO and average cost methods, we will use the finishing department of the Acme Company.

Average Cost Calculations

As the name suggests, the average cost method combines the costs assigned to the beginning work in process with the costs incurred during the current period, and combines the units in the beginning work in process with the units started in the current period; the result is a cost per unit that is an average between the costs incurred in the prior period and assigned to the beginning work in process and the costs incurred during the current period. The average cost per unit is used to determine the cost of the units completed in the department and the cost of the ending work in process as illustrated below:

Average costing uses an average of the beginning work in process costs and the costs incurred in the current period.

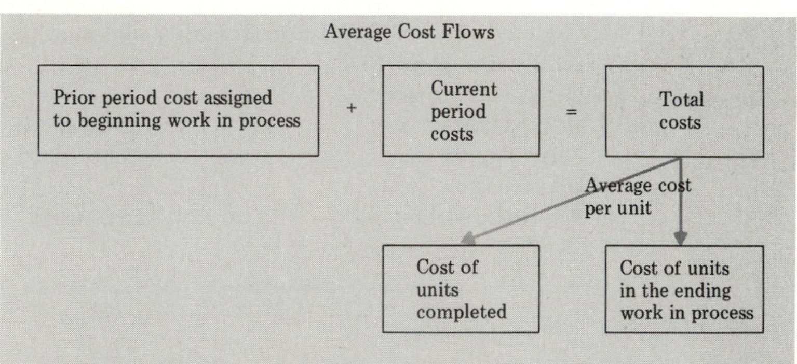

Let us move along now with the 7,000 fully completed units transferred out of the assembly department to the finishing department. During the month of June for the process in the finishing department, these 7,000 units will require a lump of direct materials, and they will also require direct labor and overhead, which will be consumed evenly as the units are processed through the finishing department.

At the beginning of June for the finishing department, we have a beginning inventory of 4,000 partially completed units; more exactly they are 100% completed for direct material and 40% completed for direct labor and applied overhead.

With those basic facts in mind, let us take a look at the following data to see what happened in the finishing department during the accounting period.

Finishing Department, June

Units	
Beginning work in process (100% finished for direct materials; 40% finished for conversion costs)	4,000
Units received from the assembly department	7,000
Total	11,000
Units completed	8,000
Ending work in process (100% finished for direct materials; 70% finished for conversion)	3,000

Costs	
Beginning work in process (prior department $21,050, direct materials $3,780; conversion; $1,895)	$26,725
Costs Incurred during June	
Prior department	$37,800
Direct materials	$ 7,000
Conversion (direct labor $6,375; applied overhead $6,375*)	12,750
Total costs to account for	$84,275

* The predetermined overhead rate is assumed to be 100% of direct labor cost in the finishing department.

Direct labor and applied overhead can be combined into conversion cost to simplify calculations.

Note how we have combined direct labor and applied overhead into one figure called **conversion costs**. We did this because, in this example, we assumed that direct labor and applied overhead are consumed at the same uniform rate. Therefore, calculations can be simplified a bit if we add together direct labor costs and applied overhead costs because both direct labor and applied overhead will always cover the same number of equivalent finished units for the accounting period in the finishing department.

The journal entry to charge these costs to the finishing department is entry (5) below:

(5) Work in Process—Finishing Department	**$19,750**	
Material Inventory		**$7,000**
Payroll		**6,375**
Applied Manufacturing Overhead		**6,375**
(To record the manufacturing costs assigned to the finishing department for June.)		

Exhibit 5-4 summarizes, for the accounting period in the finishing department, the flow of units into and out of the department, the cost per unit computation, and the disposition of the total costs.

Exhibit 5-4 described.

Part A shows the total physical units we have to account for in the finishing department. This consists of the 4,000 units in the beginning work in process, which were worked on in the prior month, plus the units received from the assembly department during June.

EXHIBIT 5-4
ACME COMPANY
Cost Summary—Finishing Department
Average Cost Flow for the Month of June

A Units to Account for	**Physical Units**
Beginning work in process	4,000
Received from assembly department	7,000
Total	11,000

		Equivalent Finished Units		
B Units Accounted for	**Physical Units**	**Prior Department**	**Direct Material**	**Conversion**
Completed	8,000	8,000	8,000	8,000
Ending work in process	3,000	3,000	3,000	2,100
Total	11,000	11,000	11,000	10,100

C Costs to Account for	**Beginning Work in Process**	**Current period**	**Total**	**Equivalent Units**	**Average Cost per Unit**
Prior department	$21,050	$37,800	$58,850	11,000	$5.35
Direct material	3,780	7,000	10,780	11,000	.98
Conversion	1,895	12,750	14,645	10,100	1.45
Total	$26,725	$57,550	$84,275		$7.78

D Costs Accounted for

Completed and transferred to finished goods 8,000 units @ $7.78		$62,240
Ending work in process:		
Prior department 3,000 @ $5.35	16,050	
Direct material 3,000 @ $.98	2,940	
Conversion 2,100 @ $1.45	3,045	$22,035
Total		$84,275

Part B shows the number of units that were completed and the number of units in the ending work in process. Also shown in part B are the equivalent finished units for each cost category—prior department cost, direct materials cost, and conversion cost. It is important that you notice in the part B calculations of the physical flow and equivalent finished units how the units in the beginning work in process have been combined with the units received from the assembly department. Since we are calculating an average cost per unit, the work done in the prior month and included in the beginning work in process has to be combined with the work done in the current month.

In part C is a tabulation of the costs assigned to the beginning work in process and the costs incurred in the current period. The total cost by cost category—prior department cost, direct materials cost and conversion cost—is the sum of the cost assigned to the beginning work in process plus the current period cost. It is this total cost, by cost category, that is divided by the equivalent finished units to obtain the average cost per unit. The total average cost per unit finished through the end of the finishing department is $7.78.

Part D shows the number of units completed and transferred to finished goods and the total cost of those units, $62,240. For the units remaining in the ending work in process, the equivalent finished units for each cost item are multiplied times the average cost per unit to determine the cost assigned to these units, $22,035.

The journal entry to transfer the cost of the completed units to finished goods is entry (6) below:

(6)	**Finished Goods**	**$62,240**	
	Work in Process—Finishing Department		**$62,240**
	(To transfer the cost of completing 8,000 units at $7.78 per unit to the finished goods inventory.)		

FIFO Cost Flows

With a FIFO cost flow our accounting for the physical units is different than with the average cost method. The finishing department completed 8,000 units during June. With the FIFO cost flow we account for the units completed in two batches. One batch consists of the 4,000 units in the beginning work in process started in May and completed in June. The other batch consists of the 4,000 units started and completed in June. Of course this may not be the true physical flow of units through the finishing department but it is what accountants assume with FIFO.

FIFO cost flow accounts for completed units in two batches.

The costs we assign to the beginning work in process, which we assume is completed in June, consists of the prior period cost of $26,725 plus the *current period cost* to complete the units. The units started-and-completed in June are assigned the *current period* cost per unit for June. Since with a FIFO cost flow the work on the ending work in process is assumed to be done in June, these units are costed using the *current period,* June, cost per unit. These concepts are summarized as follows:

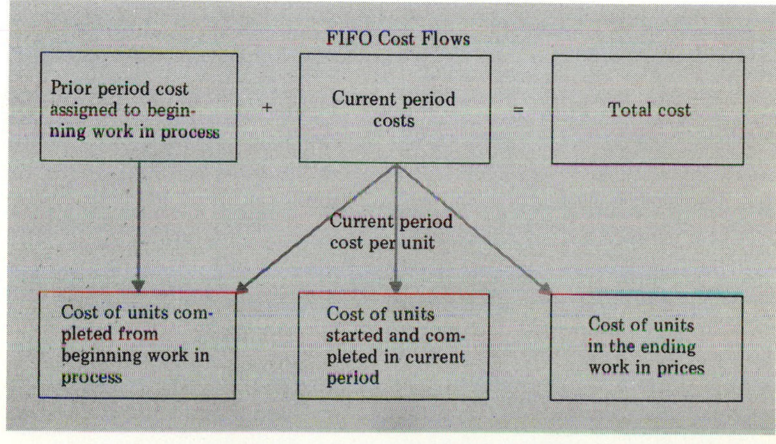

Since we know the total prior period cost, $26,725, assigned to the beginning work in process, we have to compute the *current period* cost per unit to determine the cost of completing the beginning work in process, the cost of the units started-and-completed in the current period, and the cost of the ending work in process. And to calculate only the cost per equivalent finished unit during the current period, the denominator of the cost per unit calculation should only contain the equivalent finished units of work performed in the current period.

Exhibit 5-5 summarizes for the accounting period in the finishing department the flow of units into and out of the department, the cost per unit computation, and the disposition of the total costs.

Exhibit 5-5 described.

Part A shows the total number of physical units we have to account for. This consists of the 4,000 partially completed units in the beginning work in process plus the units received from the assembly department during June.

Part B shows the total number of physical units completed and transferred to finished goods and the units in the ending work in process. In part B of Exhibit 5-5 we also show the calculation of the *current period* equivalent finished units. The current period equivalent finished units for the beginning work in process is 2,400—.6 × 4,000 units—equivalent finished units of conversion costs. The beginning work in process—4,000 units—had been assigned in the prior period, prior department costs of 100% and the direct materials costs of 100% but only 40% of the conversion costs. To complete the beginning work in process, 60% of the conversion work—that is, direct labor and applied overhead—was performed in the current period.

The computation of the current period equivalent finished units for the units started-and-completed—4,000 units—and the ending work in process—3,000 units—follows the same procedure as in the assembly department. Do you see how the 2,100 equivalent finished units for conversion costs in the ending work in process is calculated? If not, go back to the discussion of the assembly department.

Part C shows a tabulation of the total costs to account for in the finishing department and the calculation of the current period cost per unit. It is important to understand that with FIFO, only the current period cost per equivalent finished unit is being calculated, and that is why costs assigned to the beginning work in process are not included in the calculation because they represent prior period costs.

Part D shows how the total costs of $84,275 assigned to the finishing department are accounted for. In distributing the costs to the goods completed, all the costs assigned to the beginning work in process, $26,725, are transferred to finished goods along with the current period conversion costs, $3,600, required to complete them.

The cost of the units started and completed, $31,600, is added to the total cost of the beginning work in process for a total of $61,925 transferred to finished goods. The ending work in process inventory, $22,350, is valued at the current period cost per unit.

As before, you should notice that the physical units accounted for in part B must agree with the physical units to account for in part A. Likewise, the total costs accounted for in part D must agree with the total costs accounted for in Part C. If these totals do not agree, there must be an error in the analysis.

The journal entry to transfer the cost of the units completed in the finishing department is shown below as entry (7):

(7)	**Finished Goods**	**$61,925**	
	Work in Process—Finishing Department		**$61,925**
	(To transfer the cost of the 8,000 units completed in the finishing department to the finished goods inventory.)		

EXHIBIT 5-5
ACME COMPANY
Cost Summary—Finishing Department
FIFO Cost Flow for the Month of June

A Units to Account for	**Physical Units**	
Beginning work in process	4,000	(100% complete for prior department and direct material. 40% complete for conversion)
Received from assembly department	7,000	
Total	11,000	

B Units Accounted for	**Physical Units**	**Current Period Equivalent Finished Units** Prior Department	Direct Materials	Conversion Costs
Completed from beginning work in process	4,000	0	0	2,400
Started and completed	4,000	4,000	4,000	4,000
Ending work in process	3,000	3,000	3,000	2,100
Total	11,000	7,000	7,000	8,500

C Costs to Account for	**Cost**	**Current Period Equivalent Units**	**Current Period Cost per Unit**
Beginning work in process	$26,725		
Prior department	37,800	7,000	$5.40
Direct materials	7,000	7,000	1.00
Conversion cost	12,750	8,500	1.50
Total	$84,275		$7.90

D Costs Accounted for		
Completed from beginning work in process:		
Prior period costs 4,000 units	$26,725	
Current period costs to complete:		
Conversion cost 2,400 × $1.50	3,600	
	$30,325	
Started and completed from current production:		
4,000 @ $7.90	$31,600	
Total costs transferred to finished goods		$61,925
Ending work in process inventory		
Prior department 3,000 @ $5.40	$16,200	
Direct materials 3,000 @ $1.00	3,000	
Conversion Cost 2,100 @ $1.50	3,150	22,350
Total costs accounted for		$84,275

EXHIBIT 5-6
ACME COMPANY
Cost Flow Summary for June

Materials Inventory

Debit	Credit
	(1) 9,000
	(3) 20,000
	(5) 7,000

Payroll

Debit	Credit
	(1) 8,000
	(3) 9,100
	(5) 6,375

Applied Manufacturing Overhead

Debit	Credit
	(1) 4,000
	(3) 2,730
	(5) 6,375

Work in Process Molding Department

Debit	Credit
(1) 21,000	(2) 21,000
bal. 0	

Work in Process Assembly Department

Debit	Credit
(2) 21,000	(4) 37,800
(3) 31,830	
bal. 15,030	

Average Cost

Work in Process Finishing Department

Debit	Credit
bal. 26,725	
(4) 37,800	(6) 62,240
(5) 19,750	
bal. 22,035	

Finished Goods

Debit	Credit
(6) 62,240	

FIFO Cost

Work in Process Finishing Department

Debit	Credit
bal. 26,725	(7) 61,925
(4) 37,800	
(5) 19,750	
bal. 22,350	

Finished Goods

Debit	Credit
(7) 61,925	

1 To charge June manufacturing cost to the molding department.
2 To transfer the cost of completed units from molding to assembly.
3 To charge June manufacturing cost to the assembly department.
4 To transfer the cost of completed units from assembly to finishing.
5 To charge June manufacturing cost to the finishing department.
6 To transfer the cost of complete units from finishing to finished goods using an average cost flow.
7 To transfer the cost of completed units from finishing to finished goods using a FIFO cost flow.

When the units are received in the finished goods storeroom, the FIFO distinction is usually dropped and the entire 8,000 units are accounted for at a single average cost per unit of $7.74 ($61,925/8,000 units). The reason is that it simplifies the accounting procedures. Because the distinction of separate FIFO batches is lost when the completed units are transferred out of the department, some accountants refer to this costing method as "modified" FIFO.

COST FLOW SUMMARY

Exhibit 5-6 summarizes the cost flows for the Acme Company for the month of June in T accounts. The numbers identifying the entries in the T accounts refer to the numbered journal entries in the chapter.

SUMMARY

Process costing is used to determine the cost per unit of manufactured products in situations where there is continuous mass production of a standardized product. The fundamental computation, as always, is to divide a total cost by a number of units to obtain the required cost per unit. In job order costing this was done by identifying the total costs for a job and dividing it by the number of units in the job. In process costing the total costs are identified with a particular department for a time period, typically a month, and the cost total for the month is divided by the number of units for the month.

The use of arbitrary boundaries of a time period for the cost per unit computation leads to the complications of partially completed units appearing as beginning and ending work in process inventories. The accounting for the partially completed units requires adoption of a cost flow assumption and the calculation of equivalent units to convert the physical units to units of equivalent effort.

The cost flow assumptions most widely used in practice are average cost and FIFO.

Review Problem

The Mikek Company manufactures a cleaning compound by processing direct materials through two departments. One direct material is introduced at the beginning of the process in department 1 and additional direct materials are added 80% of the way through department 2. The conversion costs are incurred uniformly throughout both departments. The work in process is valued using the average cost method in department 1 and the FIFO method in department 2. The beginning work in process and current production statistics are as follows:

Unit Data	Department 1		Department 2	
Beginning work in process	40,000	(70% complete)	30,000	(50% complete)
Units started	90,000		—	
Units completed	100,000		110,000	
Ending work in process	30,000	(50% complete)	20,000	(90% complete)

Costs	Department 1	Department 2
Beginning work in process		
Prior department	—	$ 5,100
Direct materials	$4,400	—
Conversion	1,400	1,365
Current period		
Direct materials	9,900	10,660
Conversion	4,465	10,170

Required Prepare cost summaries for departments 1 and 2.

Solution

MIKEK COMPANY

Cost Summary—Department 1
Average Cost Method

A Units to Account for:	Physical Units
Beginning work in process	40,000
Started	90,000
Total	130,000

		Equivalent Units	
B Units Accounted for:	**Physical Units**	**Direct Materials**	**Conversion**
Completed	100,000	100,000	100,000
Ending work in process	30,000	30,000	15,000
Total	130,000	130,000	115,000

C Costs to Account for:	Beginning Work in Process	Current Period	Total	Equivalent Units	Unit Cost
Direct materials	$4,400	$ 9,900	$14,300	130,000	$.110
Conversion	1,400	4,465	5,865	115,000	.051
Total	$5,800	$14,365	$20,165		$.161

D Costs Accounted for:		
Completed and transferred to Department 2 100,000 units @ $.161		$16,100
Ending work in process		
Direct materials 30,000 @ $.110	$ 3,300	
Conversion 15,000 @ $.051	765	4,065
Total costs accounted for		$20,165

MIKEK COMPANY
Cost Summary—Department 2
FIFO Cost Method

A Units to Account for:	Physical Units
Beginning work in process	30,000
Received from department 1	100,000
Total	130,000

B Units Accounted for:	Physical Units	Current Period Equivalent Units: Prior Department	Material	Conversion
Completed from beginning work in process	30,000	0	30,000	15,000
Started and completed	80,000	80,000	80,000	80,000
Ending work in process	20,000	20,000	20,000	18,000
Total	130,000	100,000	130,000	113,000

C Costs to Account for:	Cost	Equivalent Units	Unit Cost
Beginning work in process	$ 6,465		
Prior department	16,100	100,000	$.161
Materials	10,660	130,000	.082
Conversion	10,170	113,000	.090
Total	$43,395		$.333

D Costs Accounted for:		
Completed from beginning work in process (30,000 units)		
Prior period costs	$ 6,465	
Current period costs to complete:		
Materials 30,000 @ $.082	2,460	
Conversion 15,000 @ $.090	1,350	
	$10,275	
Completed from current production 80,000 @ $.333	26,640	
Total costs transferred to finished goods inventory		$36,915
Ending work in process		
Prior department 20,000 @ $.161	$ 3,220	
Material 20,000 @ $.082	1,640	
Conversion 18,000 @ $.090	1,620	
		6,480
Total costs accounted for		$43,395

Glossary

Average cost method A cost flow assumption where the beginning work in process in units and dollars is combined with the units started and current costs to calculate an average cost per unit.

Conversion costs The sum of the direct labor and applied overhead costs. In many manufacturing situations direct labor and manufacturing overhead are both incurred uniformly through the manufacturing process. The accounting process can be simplified by combining the costs into one cost category.

Cost per equivalent finished unit The direct materials, direct labor, and applied manufacturing overhead cost of processing 1 unit completely through a cost center.

Costs accounted for The distribution of the costs to account for to the units completed and the ending work in process.

Costs to account for The beginning inventory costs plus the costs incurred during the current period in a department.

Equivalent finished units A measure of the production in a given period which converts the physical number of units worked on to a measure of the amount of effort expended during the period.

First-in, first-out (FIFO) cost A cost flow assumption used in process costing where units in the beginning work in process are assumed to be the first units completed.

Partially completed units Production units that are not completed at the end of the accounting period. These units are converted to equivalent finished units for unit cost calculations.

Prior department costs The costs assigned to the units transferred into a department from another department.

Process costing A procedure for assigning manufacturing costs to a product or subassembly that is standardized and usually produced in large volumes. The unit cost is calculated at the end of each accounting period by dividing the total cost of a department by the equivalent finished units of production.

Units accounted for The disposition of the units to account for at the end of the period. The units can be completed or in the ending work in process.

Units to account for The sum of the physical units in the beginning work in process plus the units started during the period.

Questions and Problems

5-1 What industries would tend to use a process costing system to collect their cost data?

5-2 Why do partially completed units have to be converted to equivalent finished units prior to the calculation of unit costs?

5-3 Distinguish between the unit cost calculation in job order costing and process costing.

5-4 Distinguish between prior department costs and direct materials costs.

5-5 The EU Company started 6,000 units into production during the month of January. At the end of the month, the production records showed 5,000 units completed and the remaining 1,000 units 30% completed for conversion costs. All materials were added at the start of the production process. Required: Calculate the equivalent units for materials and conversion costs.

5-6 How does the first-in, first-out (FIFO) cost method of process costing differ from the average cost method of process costing? Explain.

5-7 Calculate the FIFO equivalent units for cases A, B, and C given below:

	Case A	Case B	Case C
Beginning work in process	500 units	1,000 units	2,000 units
% completed materials	100%	60%	0%
% completed conversion	75%	80%	40%
Units started	5,000 units	6,000 units	10,000 units
Ending work in process	1,500 units	2,000 units	1,000 units
% completed materials	100%	80%	60%
% completed conversion	80%	80%	60%

5-8 Repeat 5-7 using the average cost method.

5-9 Equivalent Units—Multiple Choice The Jorcano Manufacturing Company uses a process-cost system to account for the costs of its only product, product D. Production begins in the fabrication department where units of direct materials are molded into various connecting parts. After fabrication is completed, the units are transferred to the assembly department. There is no material added in the assembly department. After assembly is complete, the units are transferred to a packaging department where packing material is placed around the units. After the units are ready for shipping, they are sent to a shipping area.

At year-end, June, 30, 19X3, the following inventory of product D is on hand:

- No unused raw materials or packing material.
- Fabrication department: 300 units, ⅓ complete as to raw material and ½ complete as to direct labor.
- Assembly department: 1,000 units, ⅖ complete as to direct labor.
- Packaging department: 100 units, ¾ complete as to packing material and ¼ complete as to direct labor.
- Shipping area: 400 units.

Required

1 The number of equivalent units of raw materials in all inventories at June 30, 19X3, is

a 300. **b** 100. **c** 1,600. **d** 925.

2 The number of equivalent units of fabrication department direct labor in all inventories at June 30, 19X3, is

a 1,650. **b** 150. **c** 300. **d** 975.

3 The number of equivalent units of packing material in all inventories at June 30, 19X3, is

a 75. **b** 475. **c** 100. **d** 425.

(CPA)

5-10 **Average Cost Method** The Martin Company uses a process cost system. At the beginning of the month of April, the work in process consisted of 2,000 units with all materials added and 40% of the conversion costs added. The beginning work in process was valued at $5,600 (materials $4,000 and conversion, $1,600). During the month 15,000 units were completed and 3,000 units remained in work in process with all materials and 70% of the conversion work completed. The current period costs included:

Materials	$33,800
Conversion	$36,020

Required Prepare a cost of production report using the average cost method of process costing.

5-11 Repeat 5-10 using the FIFO method of process costing.

5-12 **FIFO Method** The ANNR Company had work in process inventories at the beginning and end of 19X7 as follows:

	Materials	Conversion Costs
January 1, 19X7 6,000 units	100%	60%
December 31, 19X7 7,000 units	100	70

During the year the company started 30,000 units and completed 29,000 units. The manufacturing costs incurred during the year amounted to $89,900 for materials and $142,380 for conversion. The beginning work in process was carried at a cost of $33,600 (materials, $19,200 and conversion, $14,400).

Required Assuming a FIFO cost flow, prepare a cost of production report showing the equivalent units, cost per unit, cost of goods transferred, and cost of the ending work in process.

5-13 Repeat 5-12 using the average cost method of process costing.

5-14 **Average Cost Method—Journal Entries** Roy Company manufactures product X in a two-stage production cycle in departments A and B. Materials are added at the beginning of the process in department B. Roy uses the average cost method. Conversion costs for department B were 50% complete as to the 6,000 units in the beginning work in process and 75% complete as to the 8,000 units in the ending work in process. There were 12,000 units completed and transferred out of department B during February. An analysis of the costs relating to work in process (WIP) and production activity in department B for February is as follows:

	Costs		
	Trans-ferred in	Materials	Conversion
WIP, February 1:			
Costs	$12,000	$2,500	$1,000
February activity:			
Costs added	29,000	5,500	5,000*

* Direct labor is $3,000.

Required

1 Calculate the cost of the ending work in process and the units completed during February.

2 Prepare journal entries to record the costs of department B for February. (CPA)

5-15 Average Cost; Missing Information The Kjelberg Company manufactures a chemical compound in a single operation. All direct materials are added at the beginning of the process and conversion costs are incurred uniformly throughout the process. The company uses the average cost method for calculating unit costs.

At the end of March, Jim Kjelberg was contemplating his scheduled ski trip to Colorado and accidentally dropped his pipe on the cost of production report, recently prepared by the cost department. Since Jim was wearing his ski boots he could not act very quickly and most of the report went up in smoke. Fortunately some fragmentary information still appeared on the report and having been trained in accounting Jim wanted to see if he could reconstruct the report.

The information Jim was able to obtain from the burned report follows:

Total costs to account for	$162,000
Unit cost divisor—conversion costs	54,000
Total cost per unit	$2.90
Costs transferred to finished goods	$145,000
Ending work in process—equivalent units-material	10,000
Ending work in process—material	$ 9,000

Required

Using the fragmentary information calculate:

1 Unit cost divisor—materials cost

2 Total materials cost

3 Total conversion cost

4 Unit cost for materials and conversion

5 Number of units transferred

6 Equivalent units of conversion in ending work in process

5-16 FIFO Cost Flows BST, Inc., manufactures a single product in a single continuous process. You are given the following data.

	Direct Materials	Work in Process	Finished Goods
Beginning inventory	$420	$225 (150 units)	None
Purchases	623		
Ending inventory	380	? (300 units)	?

Materials are added to work in process at the start of processing. The beginning work in process was one-third complete as to processing costs. The ending work in process was one-fourth complete as to processing costs. During the period, 825 units were completed.

Direct labor cost incurred during the period was $1,275 for 425 hours. The overhead rate is $1.80 per direct labor hour. The company uses the FIFO inventory method for both work in process and finished goods.

Sales for the period were 650 units at $6 per unit.

Required

1 What were the equivalent units of production for processing costs?

2 What was the processing cost per unit for the current period?

3 What was the materials cost per unit for the current period?

4 What is the cost of completing the beginning work in process inventory?

5-17 Average Cost and FIFO Cost Hugh Corporation produces bases for stains in a mixing process. All materials for the base are added at the start of the process. Tints are added to the stain as the final step of the process when the stain is put into cans.

For July, the company started 10,000 gallons of stain. The beginning work process inventory was 400 gallons, one-half complete as to conversion costs. The ending work in process inventory consisted of 300 gallons, one-third complete as to conversion costs. The cost of the beginning inventory included $216 of base and $304 of conversion costs.

The following costs were incurred during July:

Materials for base	$5,400
Tint	1,313
Direct labor	7,000
Overhead costs incurred*	8,816

* The corporation uses a predetermined overhead rate of 120% of the direct labor cost.

Required

1 How many gallons of stain were completed during the month?

2 What is the equivalent units for conversion cost:
On the average cost basis?
On the FIFO basis?

3 What is the equivalent units for tint:
On the average cost basis?
On the FIFO basis?

4 On the average cost basis, what is the:
Base cost per equivalent unit?
Tint cost per equivalent unit?
Conversion cost per equivalent unit?

5 What is the cost of goods completed on the average cost basis?

6 What is the cost of goods completed on the FIFO basis?

5-18 Average Cost: Materials Added at End of Process Information concerning department B of the Toby Company is as follows:

	Units	Costs
Beginning work in process	5,000	$ 6,300
Units transferred in	35,000	58,000
	40,000	$64,300
Units completed	37,000	
Ending work in process	3,000	

	Costs			
	Transferred in	Materials	Conversion	Total Costs
Beginning work in process	$ 2,900	$ —	$ 3,400	$ 6,300
Current period	17,500	25,500	15,000	58,000
	$20,400	$25,500	$18,400	$64,300

Conversion costs were 20% complete as to the beginning work in process and 40% complete as to the ending work in process. All materials are added at the end of the process. Toby uses the average cost method.

Required

Prepare a cost of production report showing the equivalent units, unit costs, the cost of the goods transferred, and the cost of the ending work in process.

(CPA)

5-19 Nonuniform Cost Flows—No Beginning Inventory The Walsch Company manufactures a single product, a mechanical device known as "Klebo." The company maintains a process cost type of accounting system.

The manufacturing operation is as follows:

Material K, a metal, is stamped to form a part which is assembled with one of the purchased parts, "X." The unit is then machined and cleaned, after which it is assembled with 2 units of part "Y" to form the finished device Klebo. Spray priming and enameling is the final operation.

Time and motion studies indicate that of the total time required for the manufacture of a unit in the first operation required 25% of the labor cost, the first assembly an additional 25%, machining and cleaning 12.5%, the second assembly 25%, and painting 12.5%. Manufacturing overhead expense is considered to follow the same pattern by operations as does labor.

The following data are presented to you as of October 31, 19X8, the end of the first month of operation:

	Costs
Material K purchased —100,000 lbs	$25,000
Part X purchased—80,000 units	16,000
Part Y purchased—150,000 units	15,000
Primer and enamel used	1,072
Direct labor—cost	45,415
Manufacturing cost (overhead)	24,905
	Unit Quantity
Units finished and sent to finished goods warehouse	67,000
Units assembled but not painted	5,000
Units ready for the second assembly	3,000
Inventories at the end of the month:	
Material K (pounds)	5,800
Part X (units of part X)	5,000
Part Y (units of part Y)	6,000
Klebos in process (units)	8,000

Required

1 A schedule of equivalent production.

2 A schedule of total and unit costs incurred in production for:
  a Each kind of material
  b Direct labor cost
  c Manufacturing overhead
  d Total cost of production

3 A schedule of detailed material, labor, and manufacturing overhead costs assigned to the units left in process.

(CPA)

5-20 FIFO Cost Method An audit of Gem Manufacturing Co.'s financial statements indicate the following ending inventories:

Finished goods	86,000 units
Work in process	72,000 units 80% complete as to direct labor and 40% complete as to overhead

The examination reveals that materials are added to production at the start of the process and that overhead occurs primarily during the last 20% of the process. The company prices inventories at cost on a first-in, first-out basis. Overhead is applied at a rate of $1 per equivalent unit of overhead.

Other information revealed during the audit indicated:

- Beginning Inventory work in process—100,000 units, 90% complete as to labor and 70% complete as to overhead
- Additional units started during the period—400,000 units with prime costs of $756,040, including material $400,000 and direct labor $356,040.

Required

Compute:

1 Equivalent units of production

2 Unit costs of production for each prime cost

3 Ending inventory values of finished goods and work in process

(John Moore)

5-21 Average Cost Method You are engaged in the audit of the December 31, 19X8, financial statements of Spirit Corporation, a manufacturer of a digital watch. You are attempting to verify the costing of the ending inventory of work in process and finished goods which were recorded on Spirit's books as follows:

	Units	Costs
Work in process (50% complete as to labor and overhead)	300,000	$ 660,960
Finished goods	200,000	1,009,800

Materials are added to production at the beginning of the manufacturing process and overhead is applied to each product at the rate of 60% of direct labor costs. There was no finished goods inventory on January 1, 19X8. A review of Spirit's inventory cost records disclosed the following information:

	Units	Costs	
		Materials	Labor
Work in process January 1, 19X8 (80% complete as to labor and overhead)	200,000	$ 200,000	$ 315,000
Units started in production	1,000,000		
Material costs		1,300,000	
Labor costs			1,995,000
Units completed	900,000		

Required

1 Prepare schedules as of December 31, 19X8, to compute the following:
Equivalent units of production using the average cost method
Unit costs of production of materials, labor, and overhead
Cost of the finished goods inventory and work in process inventory

2 Prepare the necessary journal entry to correctly state the inventory of finished goods and work in process, assuming the books have not been closed.

(CPA)

5-22 Journal Entries; FIFO and Average Cost Flow The King Process Company manufactures one product, processing it through two processes; no. 1 and no. 2.

For each unit of process no. 1 output, 2 units of raw material X are put in at the *start* of processing. For each unit of process no. 2 output, three cans of raw material Y are put in at the *end* of processing. Two pounds of process no. 1 output are placed in at the start of process no. 2 for each unit of finished goods started.

In process accounts are maintained for material, conversion costs, and prior department costs.

The company uses FIFO cost for inventory valuation for process no. 1 and finished goods, and average cost for inventory valuation for process no. 2. Data for March:

1 Units transferred: From process no. 1 to process no. 2 — 2,200 pounds
From process no. 2 to finished goods 1,000 gallons
From finished goods to cost of goods sold 700 gallons

2 Raw material unit costs: X – $1.51 per unit;
Y – $2.00 per can

3 Conversion costs: process no. 1 – $3,344;
process no. 2 – $4,010

4 Inventory data:

	Process no. 1		Process no. 2		Finished Goods	
	Initial	Final	Initial	Final	Initial	Final
Units	200	300	200	300	700	1,000
Fraction complete conversion costs	½	⅓	½	⅔		
Valuation					$13,300	
Materials	$560		0			
Conversion costs	$108		$ 390			
Prior department costs			$2,200			

Required

Journalize March entries to record the transfer of costs from process no. 1 to process no. 2, from process no. 2 to Finished Goods, and from Finished Goods to Cost of Goods Sold. Prepare schedules of computations to support entries.

(CPA)

ACCOUNTING FOR DEFECTIVE PRODUCTS

AFTER COMPLETING YOUR STUDY OF THIS CHAPTER, YOU SHOULD HAVE LEARNED:

1 Why companies are willing to accept a certain quantity of defective products.

2 That defective products are classified either as normal spoilage, abnormal spoilage, or units that can be reworked.

3 The accounting procedures for defective products in job order and process costing.

4 The accounting procedures for scrap.

In Chapters 4 and 5 we assumed that all units started in the manufacturing process were eventually fully processed into good products salable to the firm's customers. But this is hardly what we can expect to find in actual practice. In most manufacturing processes some portion of the total units produced will be defective and have to be disposed of because they do not meet company quality specifications.

DEFECTIVE UNITS IN GENERAL

To get an idea of what **defective units** are, let us assume you schedule production of 10,000 wooden yo-yos and by the time you complete the yo-yos you find out that only 9,500 of them are acceptable. That is, only 9,500 yo-yos are salable; for one reason or another, the other 500 were defective, which can happen during the production of any good. These 500 yo-yos must be either junked, that is, they must be disposed of because they are not acceptable to your customers, or they might be disposed of at a low price, called a disposal value. Or possibly you might be able to **rework** some of the defective yo-yos and sell them to your regular customers.

Spoilage is when finished products are of unacceptable quality.

If the 500 defective yo-yos are junked or sold for their disposal value, they are referred to as spoiled units. Spoilage occurs when units do not meet quality standards and must be junked or disposed of at a low price. Spoilage is evidenced by the presence of units of unacceptable quality. Spoilage may occur because parts are cut to the wrong dimensions, air bubbles are found in foundry products, finishes are misapplied, or units break or are deformed in the production process.

Shrinkage or evaporation means using more materials than theoretically required.

In addition to spoilage, companies can lose units of product due to shrinkage or evaporation. Shrinkage or evaporation occurs when the quantity of materials necessary to produce a given job is greater than the quantity theoretically required. In contrast to spoilage, no goods of unacceptable quality result. The prime example of this is a chemical process where variations in temperatures may cause higher than expected rates of evaporation, resulting in a lower number of finished units than might be expected. Since the accounting for spoilage and shrinkage is the same, the balance of the discussion will refer only to spoilage.

Spoilage can be classified as either normal spoilage or abnormal spoilage as shown below:

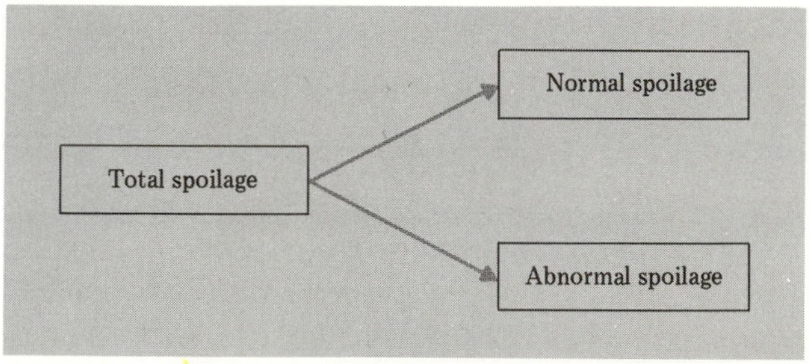

Total spoilage → Normal spoilage
Total spoilage → Abnormal spoilage

In the next two sections we will define and discuss these two types of spoilage.

Normal Spoilage

Normal spoilage is spoilage that is *expected* by management. Why would anyone expect to have spoilage? Because it could very well cost more not to have any spoilage than the spoilage itself costs.

To get an idea of what we mean by "the cost of not having any spoilage" versus accepting some spoilage and, thus, the "cost of the spoiled units," consider the yo-yos, once again. Let us assume that there are two ways to machine the parts of the yo-yos. In one way the parts are machined entirely automatically; the automatic machine can produce completed parts in seconds, producing thousands per hour. However, there is about a 10% spoilage rate from this method. The total cost of producing 1,000 "good" units with the automatic machine is $900. The other way is to use a semiautomatic machine, requiring a worker to place individual blocks of wood in a fixture which then machines each block into a very accurate yo-yo part. The spoilage rate with this method is less than ½%, but remember that a worker is required to do something with each part. The total cost of producing 1,000 "good" units with the semiautomatic machine is $1,100 since more labor cost is incurred.

In the above example management would be willing to accept a 10% spoilage rate from the automatic machine to minimize the total cost of production. This 10% spoilage rate would be considered a normal cost of the manufacturing process.

Normal spoilage is accepted because it minimizes the total cost of production.

Similarly, to avoid shrinkage because of evaporation from a chemical process, a sensitive thermostatic system might be installed to monitor temperatures and control heaters to keep evaporation to a precisely controlled minimum. But the accountant must consider the cost of the temperature control equipment and compare it to the cost of the materials that otherwise would be lost to evaporation. If the equipment is expensive and the cost of the materials lost to shrinkage relatively low, the accountant would recommend that management instead plan to permit acceptable amounts lost to evaporation and to account for them as expected shrinkage cost, that is, just as **normal spoilage.**

Management considers the normal spoilage or shrinkage rate in scheduling the number of units to be started in production. If you know that 10% of the units started will be spoiled or lost through evaporation, then you would start more units into production than you will eventually need.

The cost of normal spoilage is included in the cost of acceptable units.

How do we account for normal spoilage costs? Since normal spoilage is expected from the manufacturing process, we treat the cost of normal spoilage as part of the cost of *good* production. That is, the cost of normal spoilage is considered a product cost and assigned to the acceptable units produced.

Abnormal Spoilage

Abnormal spoilage is spoilage above the normal expected spoilage.

Abnormal spoilage is all spoilage which is *unexpected* and should have been avoided by management. In other words, abnormal spoilage is considered controllable by management. For example, if we use the automatic machine to produce yo-yo parts we expect a normal spoilage rate of 10%. If, however, the actual spoilage rate is 15%, the first 10% would be considered normal spoilage and 5% (15% − 10%) would be considered abnormal spoilage. Abnormal spoilage is a residual; it is the difference between the total spoilage rate and the normal spoilage rate.

How do we account for abnormal spoilage? Since abnormal spoilage is unexpected spoilage, we treat the cost of abnormal spoilage as a loss in the income statement for the period in which it occurs.

To summarize, normal spoilage costs are treated as a product cost and assigned to the good units produced. These costs are inventoried. Abnormal spoilage costs are treated as a loss in the income statement for the period in which they occur. Abnormal spoilage costs are not inventoried.

Rework

If 500 defective yo-yos can be reworked to meet quality standards, they become salable and are included as part of the regular inventory of yo-yos. In reworking the

500 defective yo-yos, additional direct materials, direct labor, and overhead costs will be incurred.

We account for these additional manufacturing costs as part of the cost of good production. That is the cost of rework is considered a product cost and assigned to the good products.

ACCOUNTING FOR DEFECTIVE UNITS IN JOB ORDER COSTING

In a job order manufacturing company many different jobs are being manufactured throughout the year to customers specifications. Because of the machinery, personnel, or raw materials used to manufacture all jobs, management expects a certain amount of normal spoilage which could happen on any job. The cost of this normal spoilage is associated with *all jobs* produced during the year and consequently it is assigned to all jobs produced during the year rather than to the particular job on which it occurred.

In job order costing the cost of normal spoilage is included in the predetermined overhead rate.

The most common method of assigning the normal spoilage cost to all jobs produced during the year is to include an allowance for normal spoilage costs in the predetermined overhead rate. This is done by estimating the cost of normal spoilage at the beginning of the year and including this cost as part of the total estimated overhead costs used to calculate the predetermined overhead rate.

To illustrate the accounting for normal and abnormal spoilage costs in job order costing, assume management of the J. O. Company has estimated the normal spoilage for all jobs to be 5% of the units started and allows for this cost of normal spoilage in the predetermined overhead rate. Further, assume the company has completed work on job no. 271.

The job cost sheet shows direct material cost of $400, direct labor cost of $500, and applied overhead of $500 for a total cost of $1,400.

Sufficient direct materials were started to complete 100 units of job 271.

Now assume that when the job was completed, the units were inspected and it was found that 91 units met quality standards. Thus 9 of the 100 units started are spoiled units. We will assume that there is no disposal value for the spoiled units. Of the 9 spoiled units we can calculate that normal spoilage is 5% of the 100 units started or 5 units (.05 × 100). Abnormal spoilage, therefore, would be 4 units; the total spoilage of 9 units less the normal spoilage of 5 units.

The unit cost for job 271 including the spoiled units is calculated as follows:

$$\textbf{Unit cost job 271} = \frac{\$1{,}400}{100 \text{ units}} = \$14.00$$

This unit cost of $14 includes an allowance for the cost of normal spoilage from the use of the predetermined overhead rate to apply the $500 of overhead cost to job 271.

The cost of the "good" units completed, the normal spoilage and abnormal spoilage is calculated as follows:

"Good" units completed	**= 91 units × $14 per unit =**	**$1,274**
Normal spoilage	**= 5 units × $14 per unit =**	**70**
Abnormal spoilage	**= 4 units × $14 per unit =**	**56**
Total job 271 cost		**$1,400**

The journal entry to record the completion of job 271 and the spoilage costs is:

Finished Goods (91 units at $14 per unit)	**$1,274**	
Actual Manufacturing Overhead (normal spoilage)	**70**	
Loss from Abnormal Spoilage	**56**	
Work in Process		**$1,400**
(To record the completion of job 271 and the cost of normal and abnormal spoilage.)		

Note in the above journal entry the cost of normally spoiled units is charged to the actual manufacturing overhead account since the estimated normal spoilage cost is being taken out and applied to good units by the predetermined overhead rate.

Disposal Value for Spoiled Units

In the above example we assumed the disposal value for the spoiled units was zero. Now let us assume the spoiled units can be sold for $2 each. This disposal value of $2 per spoiled unit reduces the cost of normal and abnormal spoilage from $14 per unit to $14 − $2 = $12 per unit.

The revised journal entry to record the disposal value of the spoiled units, the completion of job 271, and the spoilage costs is:

Inventory (9 spoiled units at $2 per unit)	**$ 18**	
Actual Manufacturing Overhead (5 units of normal spoilage at $12 per unit)	**60**	
Loss from Abnormal Spoilage (4 units of abnormal spoilage at $12 per unit)	**48**	
Finished Goods (91 good units at $14 per unit)	**1,274**	
Work in Process		**$1,400**
(To record the completion of job 271, the disposal value of the spoiled units and the cost of normal and abnormal spoilage.)		

Job-Related Normal Spoilage

You have just learned the accounting procedures for normal spoilage that is related to the manufacture of *all jobs* during the year. Now, let us call this **process-related normal spoilage** since it is expected to affect all jobs. Another type of normal spoilage is **job-related normal spoilage.**

To illustrate job-related normal spoilage, assume the J. O. Company receives a special job which requires some very complicated machining operations. For most jobs, management had previously estimated, from past experience, the normal rate of spoilage is 5% of the units started. However, for this special job management anticipates a spoilage rate of 15%. Because of this higher spoilage rate it is reasonable for management to require a higher price for this special job.

Thus, for this special job we have three types of possible spoilage:

1 Process-related normal spoilage—5%
2 Job-related normal spoilage—10%
3 Abnormal spoilage—any spoilage above 15%

When the special job is completed, the job cost sheet shows direct materials, $296, direct labor, $500, and applied overhead, $500, for a total cost of $1,296. Enough materials were started to produce 120 units.

Management estimates process-related normal spoilage for all jobs to be 5% of the units started and allows for this cost of process-related spoilage in the predetermined overhead rate.

When the job was completed, the units were inspected and it was found that 95 units met quality standards. Management calculated that process-related normal spoilage for all jobs would be 5% of 120 units started, or 6 units. The job-related spoilage allowed for this job would amount to 10% of the 120 units started, or 12 units. But total spoilage was 25 units; that is, 120 units started minus 95 good units completed. Thus, management concluded that abnormal spoilage was 7 units; the total spoilage of 25 units less the sum of process related plus job related spoilage, or 25 − (6 + 12) = 7 units. Using this data, management calculated a cost per unit as follows:

$$\textbf{Cost per unit} = \frac{\$1{,}296}{120} = \$10.80$$

The cost of the "good" units completed, the process-related normal spoilage, and abnormal spoilage are calculated as follows:

The average cost per completed unit is increased by the job related normal spoilage.

Good units completed 95 units × $10.80	=	**$1,026.00**
Job related normal spoilage		
12 units × $10.80	=	**129.60**
Costs charged to finished goods for 95 units		**$1,155.60**
Process related normal spoilage		
6 units × $10.80	=	**$ 64.80**
Abnormal spoilage 7 units × $10.80	=	**75.60**
Total job cost		**$1,296.00**

The 95 units transferred to finished goods inventory are assigned a total cost of $1,155.60, to include the cost of job-related normal spoilage. This increases the average cost per completed unit to $12.16, $1,155.60/95, from $10.80 to reflect the additional costs of producing this specific job.

The journal entry to record the transfer of the costs out of work in process is:

Finished Goods (95 units at $12.16 per unit)	**$1,155.60**	
Actual Manufacturing Overhead		
(6 units at $10.80 per unit)	**64.80**	
Loss from Abnormal Spoilage		
(7 units at $10.80 per unit)	**75.60**	
Work in Process		**$1,296.00**
(To transfer the cost of the completed units to finished goods and to record the cost of normal and abnormal spoilage.)		

Rework

Not all the spoiled units will be disposed of. Some units can be reworked and sold as a regular product. How do we account for the extra direct materials, direct labor, and overhead cost incurred to rework defective units? The cost of rework that is process related is charged to the actual manufacturing overhead account and assigned to all jobs produced during the year as part of the predetermined overhead rate.

To illustrate the journal entry to record the cost of process related rework, assume for job 281 we incurred the following rework costs: direct materials $20; direct labor $40; applied overhead $40. The journal entry is shown below:

Actual Manufacturing Overhead	**$100**	
Materials Inventory (direct material)		**$20**
Payroll (direct labor)		**40**
Applied Manufacturing Overhead		**40**
(To record $100 of process related rework cost for job 281.)		

The accounting for rework cost depends on whether it is process related or job related.

If the rework had been caused by the special characteristics of the job, it would be classified as job related and charged to the specific job. If this were the case in the above illustration, the debit would be to the work in process account and the rework cost would be recorded on the job 281 cost sheet, increasing the cost of the completed units in this job.

ACCOUNTING FOR DEFECTIVE UNITS IN PROCESS COSTING

A process manufacturing company mass produces a standardized product; consequently, we will not have any job related normal spoilage. All spoilage in process costing is either normal spoilage related to the manufacturing process or abnormal spoilage.

In job order costing the expected cost of normal spoilage was included in the predetermined overhead rate. This is not done in process costing where the cost of normal spoilage is calculated at the end of the accounting period and allocated to the units completed and the work in process, depending on the stage of the manufacturing process where the normal spoilage is detected.

Spoilage is generally detected at inspection points in the manufacturing process. The cost of normal spoilage is allocated only to the good units that have passed the inspection point.

To illustrate this consider the following diagram:

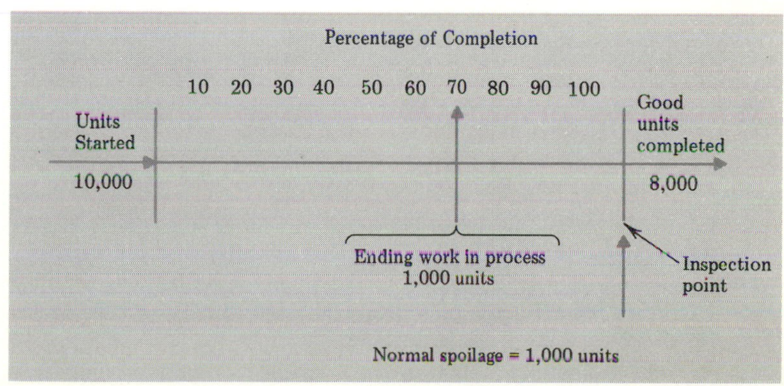

There was no beginning work in process. The diagram shows that 10,000 units were started: at the end of the period 1,000 units are partially completed, 1,000 units of normal spoilage were detected at the end of the process, and 8,000 good units were completed. In this situation the entire cost of the 1,000 normally spoiled units is allocated to the 8,000 good units completed. The 1,000 units in work in process would not be allocated any normal spoilage cost because they have not reached the inspection point.

In process costing the cost of normal spoilage is allocated to all good units which have passed the inspection point.

If, however, the inspection point in the above example was at the start of the process, then the cost of the normally spoiled units would be allocated to the 1,000 units in the work in process and the 8,000 good units completed. In this situation 8/9 (the 8,000 good units completed divided by the 9,000 good units) of the normal spoilage cost would be added to the cost of the goods completed. The balance of the normal spoilage cost, 1/9, would be added to the cost of the work in process.

In the next two sections we will illustrate the accounting for spoilage cost using the average cost method and the FIFO method.

Average Cost Method

To illustrate the accounting for spoilage cost in a process cost system, consider the following facts for the Hunter Company for the month of July:

Hunter Company, July

Units	
Beginning work in process (100% finished for direct material; 50% finished for conversion)	4,000
Units started	8,000
Total	12,000
Good units completed	6,000
Spoiled units* (normal spoilage is 10% of the units completed)	1,000
Ending work in process (100% finished for direct material; 60% finished for conversion)	5,000

* The spoiled units are detected when inspection occurs at the end of the process.

Costs	
Beginning work in process (direct materials: $8,000; conversion: $2,800.)	$10,800
Costs for July	
Direct materials	16,000
Conversion (direct labor $6,000, applied overhead $6,000)	12,000
Total	$38,800

Exhibit 6-1 contains the July cost activity for the Hunter Company; unit costs were calculated using the average cost method. The physical units are first balanced in parts A and B and then the total costs are balanced in parts C and D.

In part B, the physical units are separated into four categories: completed, ending work in process, normal spoilage, and abnormal spoilage. The 600 units of normal spoilage are calculated as 10% of the good units completed, or .10 × 6,000. The 400 units of abnormal spoilage are calculated as the difference between total spoilage, 1,000 units, and normal spoilage, 600 units.

EXHIBIT 6-1
HUNTER COMPANY
Cost Summary
Average Cost Method
Month of July

A Units to Account for	Physical Units	
Beginning work in process	4,000	(50% complete for conversion)
Started	8,000	
Total	12,000	

B Units Accounted for	Physical Units	Equivalent Finished Units: Material	Equivalent Finished Units: Conversion
Good units completed	6,000	6,000	6,000
Ending work in process	5,000	5,000	3,000
Normal spoilage	600	600	600
Abnormal spoilage	400	400	400
Total	12,000	12,000	10,000

C Costs to Account for	Beginning Work in Process	Current Period	Total	Equivalent Finished Units	Cost per Unit
Direct material	$ 8,000	$16,000	$24,000	$12,000	$2.00
Conversion	2,800	12,000	14,800	10,000	1.48
Total	$10,800	$28,000	$38,800		$3.48

D Costs Accounted for		
Abnormal spoilage 400 @ $3.48		$ 1,392
Completed and transferred 6,000 @ $3.48	$20,880	
Normal spoilage 600 @ $3.48	2,088	
Total costs transferred to finished goods		22,968
Ending work in process:		
Direct materials 5,000 @ $2.00	$10,000	
Conversion 3,000 @ $1.48	4,440	14,440
Total costs accounted for		$38,800

Spoiled units are included in the equivalent units based on their percentage of completion at inspection.

In part B the equivalent finished units to be accounted for are calculated as in Chapter 5 for each of the two cost categories. The calculation of equivalent finished units for the spoiled units is based on the stage of the manufacturing process when the spoilage is detected. For this example we assumed that the spoilage was detected at the end of the process. Therefore, the full amount of direct materials and conversion work had been consumed in completing the spoiled units.

In part C, since the average cost method is used, the cost of the beginning work in process is added to the current costs and divided by the equivalent finished units to obtain the average cost per unit.

Part D in Exhibit 6-1 presents the same information as part D of Exhibit 5-4 but in addition presents the cost of abnormal and normal spoilage. Because the spoiled units were completed before the spoilage was detected, 100% of all costs were included and costs are therefore assigned to the spoiled units at $3.48 per unit.

In accounting for the costs of spoiled units, the cost of abnormal spoilage is treated as a loss and is deducted in calculating net income in the period when the spoilage occurs.

The cost per unit of units past the inspection point is increased by the normal spoilage.

The costs of normal spoilage—600 units × $3.48 = $2,088—are considered part of the cost of good units and are assigned to the good units that have passed the spoilage point. In the Hunter Company, these are the units that have been completed and transferred to finished goods. Therefore, the cost of normal spoilage, $2,088, is added to the costs of the completed units, increasing the total cost of the 6,000 completed units to $22,968. That means the cost of the 6,000 units transferred to finished goods is $22,968/6,000 = $3.828 per unit, not $3.48 per unit. This is the result of adding the normal spoilage costs to the cost of the units completed and transferred to finished goods.

The journal entry to record the loss from abnormal spoilage and the completion of 6,000 units is:

Loss from Abnormal Spoilage (400 units × $3.48)	**$ 1,392**	
Finished Goods (6,000 units × $3.828)	**22,968**	
Work in Process		**$24,360**
(To record the cost of abnormal spoilage and the cost of the goods completed.)		

FIFO Cost Method

Now, let us see how to calculate the cost of spoilage using the FIFO cost method. Exhibit 6-2 contains the cost summary for July for the Hunter Company assuming a FIFO cost flow. Part A shows the total units to account for are 12,000. Part B shows how these units are accounted for and the current period equivalent finished units. With the FIFO method we assume the units completed are in two distinct batches: one batch from the beginning work in process—4,000 units—and one batch started-and-completed in the current period—2,000 units. The ending work in process—5,000 units, normal spoilage—600 units, and abnormal spoilage—400 units are assumed to be produced during the current period. Part C shows the total costs to account for, $38,800, and the calculation of the current period cost per finished unit, $3.50.

Part D shows the cost of abnormal spoilage and normal spoilage; otherwise, it is the same as part D of Exhibit 5-5. Since all spoilage is assumed to have occurred from current period production, it is costed using the current period cost per unit, $3.50. The total cost assigned to the 6,000 units transferred to finished goods inventory consists of $13,800 assigned to the beginning work in process; $7,000 assigned to the units started-and-completed; and normal spoilage cost of $2,100, for a total cost of $22,900. This means the cost per unit of the 6,000 completed units is $22,900/6,000 = $3.8167.

The journal entry to record the loss from abnormal spoilage and the cost of the units completed is:

EXHIBIT 6-2
HUNTER COMPANY COST SUMMARY
FIFO Cost Method
Month of July

A Units to Account for	**Physical Units**	
Beginning work in process	4,000	(50% complete for conversion)
Started	8,000	
Total	12,000	

B Units Accounted for	**Physical Units**	**Equivalent Finished Units**	
		Material	**Conversion**
Completed from beginning work in process	4,000	0	2,000
Started and completed	2,000	2,000	2,000
Ending work in process	5,000	5,000	3,000
Normal spoilage	600	600	600
Abnormal spoilage	400	400	400
Total	12,000	8,000	8,000

C Costs to Account for	**Cost**	**Equivalent Finished Units**	**Cost per Unit**
Beginning work in process	$10,800		
Direct material	16,000	8,000	$2.00
Conversion	12,000	8,000	1.50
	$38,800		$3.50

D Costs Accounted for		
Abnormal spoilage 400 @ $3.50		$ 1,400
Completed from beginning work in process:		
Prior period costs 4,000 units	$10,800	
Current period costs to complete:		
Conversion 2,000 × $1.50	3,000	
	$13,800	
Completed and transferred from current production 2,000 @ $3.50	$ 7,000	
Normal spoilage 600 @ $3.50	2,100	
	$ 9,100	
Total costs transferred to finished goods		$22,900
Ending work in process:		
Direct materials 5,000 @ $2.00	$10,000	
Conversion 3,000 @ $1.50	4,500	14,500
Total		$38,800

Loss from Abnormal Spoilage		
(400 units × $3.50)	**$ 1,400**	
Finished Goods (6,000 units × 3.8167)	**22,900**	
Work in Process		**$24,300**
(To record the cost of abnormal spoilage and the units transferred to finished goods.)		

SCRAP

In most manufacturing processes, both job order and process, there are shavings or chips from the machining of metals and residual pieces of wood from the cutting of lumber. These residual pieces of wood and metal shavings or chips are referred to as **scrap.**

Scrap is the residual pieces of wood and metal shavings resulting from the production process.

Typically, scrap has very little market value so accountants do not record its value as an asset in an inventory account. However, when the scrap is sold its disposal value is credited to the actual manufacturing overhead account using the following journal entry:

Accounts Receivable	**$50**	
Actual Manufacturing Overhead		**$50**
(To record the credit sale of $50 worth of scrap.)		

Since the disposal value of scrap is used to reduce the actual manufacturing overhead cost, it would be considered in estimating the total overhead cost when calculating the predetermined overhead rate.

SUMMARY

Defective units can be classified as normal spoilage, abnormal spoilage, or rework.

Spoilage is considered normal when the cost of avoiding the spoilage is greater than the cost of spoilage itself. The cost of normal spoilage is treated as a part of the cost of good production.

Abnormal spoilage is unexpected spoilage which should have been avoided by management. The cost of abnormal spoilage is treated as a loss in the period in which the abnormal spoilage occurred.

Reworked units become salable to the company's customers and are included as part of the regular inventory. The additional manufacturing costs to rework the defective units are charged to the actual manufacturing overhead account.

In job order costing, the cost of process-related normal spoilage is assigned to all jobs worked on during the year by including it in the predetermined overhead rate. The cost of job-related normal spoilage is added to the cost of the specific job that caused the spoilage.

In process costing the cost of normal spoilage is calculated at the end of the accounting period and allocated between the units completed and the work in process.

Scrap is the residual metal shavings or wood chips resulting from the processing of raw materials. Any disposal value of scrap is credited to the actual manufacturing overhead account.

Review Problem

The UDI Company produces furniture to buyers' specifications. During June 19X8, an order for a maximum shipment of 90 custom chairs was received and a production order was issued immediately. The production manager estimated that in addition to the process-related normal spoilage rate of 5% an additional 5% should be allowed because of the unusual specifications of this job. The cost of the process-related normal spoilage is allowed for in the predetermined overhead rate. The production order specified 100 units be started for this job. At the end of the month all operations were completed and 83 finished chairs were transferred to the shipping dock. The job cost sheet showed direct materials $3,500, direct labor $2,000, and applied overhead $4,000.

Required

1 Calculate the units of process-related and job-related normal spoilage and the units of abnormal spoilage.

2 Calculate the unit cost and prepare a journal entry to record the completion of the job and spoilage cost.

Solution

1 Calculation of spoilage units

Total spoilage = 100 − 83	=	17 units
Process-related normal spoilage = .05 × 100	=	5 units
Job-related normal spoilage = .05 × 100	=	5 units
Abnormal spoilage		7 units

2 Calculation of unit cost and journal entries

$$\textbf{Cost per unit} = \frac{\$9{,}500}{100 \text{ units}} = \$95 \text{ per unit}$$

The journal entry is

Loss from Abnormal Spoilage (7 units × $95)	**$ 665**	
Actual Manufacturing Overhead (5 units × $95)	**475**	
Finished Goods (83 units × $100.72*)	**8,360**	
Work in Process		**$9,500**

* The cost of the finished goods is:

Good units completed 83 × $95	=	$7,885
Job-related normal spoilage 5 × $95	=	475
Total cost		$8,360
Cost per unit $8,360/83	=	$100.72

Review Problem

The Mikek Company manufactures a cleaning compound by processing direct materials through one department. Direct material is introduced at the beginning of the process. The conversion costs are incurred uniformly throughout the process.

Any spoilage occurs at the end of processing when the compound is inspected. The normal spoilage amounts to 10% of *good* output. The work in process is valued using the average cost method. The beginning work in process and current period production statistics are as follows:

Unit Data	Department 1	
Beginning work in process	40,000	(70% complete)
Units started	90,000	
Good units completed	100,000	
Ending work in process	15,000	(50% complete)
Total spoilage	15,000	
Costs	**Department 1**	
Beginning work in process		
Direct materials	$ 4,400	
Conversion	$ 1,400	
Current period		
Direct materials	$ 9,900	
Conversion	$ 4,847.50	

Required Prepare a cost summary report for the Mikek Company.

Solution

MIKEK COMPANY
Cost Summary Average Cost Method

A Units to Account for	Physical Units
Beginning work in process	40,000
Started	90,000
	130,000

		Equivalent Units	
B Units Accounted for	**Physical Units**	**Direct Materials**	**Conversion**
Good units completed	100,000	100,000	100,000
Ending work in process	15,000	15,000	7,500
Normal spoilage (.10 × 100,000)	10,000	10,000	10,000
Abnormal spoilage	5,000	5,000	5,000
	130,000	130,000	122,500

C Costs to Account for	Beginning Work in Process	Current Period	Total	Equivalent Units	Unit Cost
Direct materials	$4,400	$ 9,900	$14,300	130,000	$.110
Conversion	1,400	4,847.50	6,247.50	122,500	.051
	$5,800	$14,747.50	$20,547.50		$.161

D Costs Accounted for

Abnormal spoilage	5,000 @ $.161		$ 805.00
Completed and transferred	100,000 @ $.161	$16,100.00	
Normal spoilage	10,000 @ $.161	1,610.00	
Total cost transferred to finished goods			$17,710.00
Ending work in process			
Direct materials	15,000 @ $.110	$ 1,650.00	
Conversion	7,500 @ $.051	382.50	$ 2,032.50
Total costs accounted for			$20,547.50

Glossary

Abnormal spoilage Spoilage that is not expected from normal operations. The cost of abnormal spoilage is treated as a loss in the period incurred.

Defective units Units of product that do not meet the quality standards of salable products. These units are either reworked or disposed of as spoiled units.

Job-related normal spoilage Normal spoilage that results from the special characteristics of a specific job.

Normal spoilage Spoilage that is expected to result from normal operations. The cost of normal spoilage is assigned to the units that have passed the location where the spoilage is identified.

Process-related normal spoilage Normal spoilage that is expected in job order manufacturing because of the condition of the machinery, personnel, or materials needed to manufacture all jobs.

Rework Defective units that can be repaired and sold as good products.

Scrap Residual materials such as metal shavings or wood chips. The disposal value of scrap is credited to the actual manufacturing overhead account.

Questions and Problems

6-1 Distinguish between normal and abnormal spoilage.

6-2 Why would a company allow normal spoilage to continue?

6-3 Discuss the difference between job-related normal spoilage and process-related normal spoilage in job order costing.

6-4 Define scrap. How is the disposal value of scrap accounted for?

6-5 How are the additional manufacturing costs for units reworked into good products accounted for?

6-6 Calculate the FIFO equivalent units for cases A, B, and C below assuming that all spoilage is normal spoilage.

	Case A	**Case B**	**Case C**
Beginning work in process	500 units	1,000 units	2,000 units
% completed materials	100%	60%	0%
% completed conversion	75%	80%	40%
Units started	5,000 units	6,000 units	10,000 units
Ending work in process	1,500 units	2,000 units	1,000 units
% completed materials	100%	80%	60%
% completed conversion	80%	80%	60%
Normal spoilage	0 units	500 units	1,000 units
% completed materials	100%	100%	80%
% completed conversion	20%	100%	80%

6-7 Repeat 6-6 using the average cost method.

6-8 **Job Order Costing and Spoilage** The Cattel Manufacturing Company produces a number of products to customers' specifications. Based on past experience management estimates that 5% of the units started will be spoiled.

During the month of May, 500 units were started for job no. X107. At the end of the month, only 465 units for job X107 passed inspection. The remainder of the units were junked for no disposal value. The cost of completing job X107 consisted of $1,000 for direct materials, $800 for direct labor, and $600 for applied overhead.

Required

1 Calculate the cost of normal and abnormal spoilage and the cost of the units completed.

2 Prepare a journal entry to record the spoilage costs and the completion of job X107.

6-9 **Job Order Costing and Job Related Spoilage** At the beginning of June, 10,000 units were started in production for job 1058. Since job 1058 required a special cutting operation, management estimated that the total spoilage rate for this job would be 15%. Generally, management allows for a spoilage rate of 7% on all jobs started and includes the cost of the 7% spoilage rate in the predetermined overhead rate.

In the month of June, total manufacturing costs of $200,000 were assigned to job 1058.

During June, 8,500 units of job 1058 passed inspection and were shipped to the customer. The other 1,500 units were disposed of for $10 per unit.

Required

1 Calculate the cost of the 8,500 units of job 1058 shipped during June.

2 Prepare a journal entry to record:

a The cost of spoilage, the completion of job 1058, and the sale of the spoiled units.

b The shipment of 8,500 units of job 1058.

6-10 Rework The Ace Specialty Company started 900 units of job 853 at the beginning of May. During the month of May, the company incurred the following costs in processing job 853:

Direct materials	$ 8,000
Direct labor	10,000
Applied overhead	10,000
Total cost	$28,000

At the end of the month it was found that 50 units had to be disposed of as junk and 40 units required rework. During June, the rework was completed at the following costs:

Direct materials	$100
Direct labor	300
Applied overhead	300
Total cost	$700

The Ace Specialty Company charges rework to the actual manufacturing overhead account.

Required

Assuming a process-related normal spoilage rate of 5%, prepare journal entries to record the rework cost and the completion of job 853.

6-11 No Beginning Work in Process—Normal and Abnormal Spoilage The Quebec Manufacturing Company produces a single product. There are two producing departments, 1 and 2, and the product passes through the plant in that order.

There were no work in process inventories at the beginning of the year. In January, materials for 1,000 units were issued to production in department 1 at a cost of $5,000. Direct labor and factory overhead costs for the month were $2,700. During the month, 800 units were completed and transferred to department 2. The work in process inventory at the end of the month contained 200 units complete for material and one-half completed for labor and overhead. Direct labor and overhead in department 2 amounted to $6,250 in January. During the month, 500 units were completed and transferred to finished stock. At the end of the month, 200 units remained in process, one quarter complete. Ordinarily, in department 2, spoilage is recognized on inspection at the end of the process, but in January there was an abnormal loss of 50 units when production was one-half complete. All other spoilage is normal.

Required

Calculate the cost of the normal and abnormal spoiled units for the month of January.

6-12 No Beginning Inventories – Spoilage The Dexter Production Company manufactures a single product. Its operations are a continuing process carried on in two departments—machining and finishing. In the production process, materials are added to the product in each department.

For the month of June 19X5, the company records indicated the following production statistics for each department:

	Machining Department	Finishing Department
Units in process, June 1, 19X5	0	0
Units transferred from preceding department	0	60,000
Units started in production	80,000	0
Units completed and transferred out	60,000	50,000
Units in process, June 30, 19X5*	20,000	8,000
Units spoiled in production	0	2,000

* Percent of completion of units in process at June 30, 19X5:		
Materials	100%	100%
Labor	50	70
Overhead	25	70

The units spoiled in production had no scrap value and were 50% complete as to materials, labor, and overhead. The company's policy is to treat the cost of spoiled units in production as a separate element of cost in the department in which the spoilage occurs. All spoilage is considered abnormal. Cost records showed the following charges for the month of June:

	Machining Department	Finishing Department
Materials	$240,000	$ 88,500
Labor	140,000	141,500
Overhead	65,000	25,700

Required

For both the machining and finishing departments, prepare in good form the following reports for the month of June:

1 Quantity of production report.

2 Cost of production report, using the following columnar headings:

Machining Department		Finishing Department	
Cost	Per Unit	Cost	Per Unit

(CPA)

6-13 No Beginning Work in Process; Normal Spoilage The Incredible Gadget Corp. manufactures a single product. Its operations are a continuing process carried on in two departments—the machining department and the assembly and finishing department. Materials are added to the product in each department without increasing the number of units produced.

In the month of May 19X8, the records showed that 75,000 units were put in production in the machining department. Of these units, 60,000 were completed and transferred to assembly and finishing, and 15,000 were left in process with all materials applied but with only one-third of the required labor and overhead.

In the assembly and finishing department, 50,000 units were completed and transferred to the finished stockroom during the month. There were 9,000 units in process on May 31, 1,000 units having been destroyed in production with no scrap value. All required materials had been applied to the 9,000 units and two-thirds of the labor and overhead, but only one-half of the prescribed material, overhead, and labor had been applied to the 1,000 units lost in process.

There was no work in process in either department at the first of the month.

The cost of units lost in production should be treated as normal spoilage in the assembly and finishing department.

Cost records showed the following charges during the month:

	Materials	Labor	Overhead
Machining department	$120,000	$ 87,100	$39,000
Assembly and finishing department	41,650	101,700	56,810

Required

1 Prepare in good form a statement showing the unit cost for the month.

2 Prepare a schedule showing the details of the work in process inventory in each department.

(CPA)

6-14 FIFO Equivalent Production; Spoilage Poole, Inc., produces a chemical compound by a unique chemical process which Poole has divided into two departments, A and B, for accounting purposes. The process functions as follows:

1 The formula for the chemical compound requires 1 pound of chemical X and 1 pound of chemical Y. In the simplest sense, 1 pound of chemical X is processed in department A and transferred to department B for further processing where 1 pound of chemical Y is added when the process is 50% complete. When the processing is complete in department B, the finished chemical compound is transferred to finished goods. The process is continuous, operating 24 hours a day.
2 Normal spoilage occurs in department A. In the first few seconds of processing 5% of Chemical X is lost.
3 No spoilage occurs in department B.
4 In department A conversion costs are incurred uniformly throughout the process and are allocated to good pounds produced because spoilage is normal.

5 In department B conversion costs are allocated equally to each equivalent pound of output.
6 Poole's unit of measure for work in process and finished goods inventories is pounds.
7 The following data are available for the month of October 19X4:

	Department A	Department B
Work in process, October 1	8,000 pounds	10,000 pounds
Stage of completion of beginning inventory	¾	$^3/_{10}$
Started or transferred in	50,000 pounds	?
Transferred out	46,500 good pounds	?
Work in process, October 31	?	12,000 pounds
Stage of completion of ending inventory	⅓	$^1/_5$
Total equivalent pounds of material added in department B	—	44,500 pounds

Required

Prepare schedules computing equivalent unspoiled pounds of production (materials and conversion costs) for department A and for department B for the month of October 19X4 using the first-in, first-out method for inventory costing.

(CPA)

6-15 Journal Entries; Spoilage; FIFO Cost Flow The King Process Company manufactures one product, processing it through two processes, no. 1 and no. 2.

For each unit of process no. 1 output, 2 units of raw material X are put in at the *start* of processing. For each unit of process no. 2 output, three cans of raw material Y are put in at the *end* of processing. Two pounds of process no. 1 output are placed in at the start of process no. 2 for each unit of finished goods started.

Spoilage generally occurs in process no. 2 when processing is approximately 50% complete. All spoilage is considered abnormal.

In process accounts are maintained for materials, conversion costs, and prior department costs.

The company uses FIFO basis for inventory valuation for process no. 1 and finished goods, and average cost for inventory valuation for process no. 2. Data for March:

1 Units transferred:	From process no. 1 to process no. 2	2,200 pounds
	From process no. 2 to finished goods	900 gallons
	From finished goods to cost of goods sold	600 gallons

2 Units spoiled in process no. 2—100 gallons

3 Raw material unit costs: X—$1.51 per unit; Y—$2.00 per can

4 Conversion costs: Process no. 1—$3,344; Process no. 2—$4,010

5 Inventory data:

	Process No. 1		Process No. 2		Finished Goods	
	Initial	Final	Initial	Final	Initial	Final
Units	200	300	200	300	700	1,000
Fraction complete conversion costs	½	⅓	½	⅔		
Valuation					$13,300	
Materials	$560		0			
Conversion costs	$108		$ 390			
Prior department costs			$2,200			

Required Journalize March entries to record the transfer of costs from process no. 1 to process no. 2, from process no. 2 to finished goods, and from finished goods to cost of goods sold. Prepare schedules of computations to support entries.

(CPA)

6-16 Two Departments; Spoilage Calculation The Mantis Manufacturing Company manufactures a single product that passes through two departments: extruding and finishing-packing. The product is shipped at the end of the day in which it is packed. The production in the extruding and finishing-packing departments does not increase the number of units started.

The cost and production data for the month of January are as follows:

	Extruding Department	Finishing-Packing Department
Work in process, January 1:		
Cost from preceding department	—	$60,000
Materials	$ 5,900	—
Labor	1,900	1,500
Overhead	1,400	2,000
Costs added during January:		
Materials	20,100	4,400
Labor	10,700	7,720
Overhead	8,680	11,830
Percentage of completion of work in process:		
January 1:		
Materials	70%	0
Labor	50	30
Overhead	50	30

January 31:		
Materials	50	0
Labor	40	35
Overhead	40	35
January Production Statistics		
Units in process, January 1	10,000	29,600
Units in process, January 31	8,000	6,000
Units started or received from preceding department	20,000	22,000
Units completed and transferred or shipped	22,000	44,000

In the extruding department materials are added at various phases of the process. All lost units occur at the end of the process when the inspection operation takes place.

In the finishing-packing department the materials added consist only of packing supplies. These materials are added at the midpoint of the process when the packing operation begins. Cost studies have disclosed that one-half of the labor and overhead costs apply to the finishing operation and one-half to the packing operation. All lost units occur at the end of the finishing operation when the product is inspected. All of the work in process in this department on January 1 and 31 was in the finishing operation phase of the manufacturing process.

(The Company uses the average costing method in its accounting system.)

Required

1 Compute the units lost, if any, for each department during January.

2 Compute the output divisor for the calculation of unit costs for each department for January.

3 Prepare a cost of production report for both departments for January. The report should disclose the departmental total cost and cost per unit (for materials, labor, and overhead) of the units (1) transferred to the finishing-packing department and (2) shipped. Assume that January production and costs were normal.

(CPA)

6-17 Normal Spoilage; FIFO Cost Flow Crews Company produces a chemical agent for commercial use. The company accounts for production in two cost centers: (1) Cooking and (2) Mix-Pack. In the first cost center liquid substances are combined in large cookers and boiled; the boiling causes a normal decrease in volume from evaporation. After the batch is cooked, it is transferred to Mix-Pack, the second cost center. The batch is mixed with additional liquids which doubles the volume and bottled in 1-gallon containers.

Material is added at the beginning of production in each cost center and labor is added equally during production in each cost center. Overhead is applied on the basis of 80% of labor cost.

The FIFO method is used to cost work in process inventories, and transfers are at an average unit cost, i.e., the total cost transferred divided by the total number of units transferred.

The following information is available for the month of October 19X7:

	Cooking	Mix-Pack
Work in process, October 1, 19X7		
Materials	$ 990	$ 120
Labor	100	60
Prior department cost		426
Month of October		
Materials	39,600	15,276
Labor	10,050	16,000

Inventory and production records show that Cooking had 1,000 gallons 40% processed on October 1 and 800 gallons 50% processed on October 31; Mix-Pack had 600 gallons 50% processed on October 1 and 1,000 gallons 30% processed on October 31.

Production reports for October show that Cooking started 50,000 gallons into production and completed and transferred 40,200 gallons to Mix-Pack, and Mix-Pack completed and transferred 80,000 1-gallon containers of the finished product to the distribution warehouse.

Required

1 Prepare in good form a quantity report for the Cooking cost center and for the Mix-Pack cost center which accounts for both actual units and equivalent unit production.

2 Prepare in good form a production cost report for each of the two cost centers which computes total cost and cost per unit for each element of cost in inventories and October production. Total cost and cost per unit for transfers should also be computed.

All spoilage is considered normal in both cost centers and occurs at the end of the process after the materials are added.

(CPA)

6-18 Spoilage Ballinger Paper Products manufactures a high-quality paper box. The box department applies two separate operations—cutting and folding. The paper is first cut and trimmed to the dimensions of a box form by one machine group. One square foot of paper is equivalent to four box forms. The trimmings from this process have no scrap value. Box forms are then creased and folded (i.e., completed) by a second machine group. Any partially processed boxes in the department are cut box forms that are ready for creasing and folding. These partly processed boxes are considered 50% complete as to labor and overhead. The materials department maintains an inventory of paper in sufficient quantities to permit continuous processing, and transfers to the box department are made as needed. Immediately after folding, all good boxes are transferred to the finished goods department.

During June 19X1 the materials department purchased 1,210,000 square feet of unprocessed paper for $244,000. Conversion costs for the month were $226,000. A quantity equal to 30,000 boxes was spoiled during paper cutting and 70,000 boxes were spoiled during folding. All spoilage has a zero salvage value, is considered normal and cannot be reprocessed. All spoilage loss is allocated to the completed units. Ballinger applies the average cost method to all inventories. Inventory data for June are given on page 182.

		June 1, 19X1		June 30, 19X1
	Physical Unit	Units on Hand	Cost	Units on Hand
Materials department:				
paper	square feet	390,000	$76,000	200,000
Box department:				
boxes cut, not folded	number	800,000	55,000*	300,000
Finished goods department:				
Completed boxes on hand	number	250,000	18,000	50,000
*Materials	$35,000			
Conversion cost	20,000			
	$55,000			

Required Prepare the following for the month of June 19X1.

1 A report of cost of paper used for the materials department.

2 A schedule showing the physical flow of units (including beginning and ending inventories) in the materials department, in the box department, and in the finished goods department.

3 A schedule showing the computation of equivalent units produced for materials and conversion costs in the box department.

4 A schedule showing the computation of unit costs for the box department.

5 A report of inventory valuation and cost of completed units for the box department.

6 A schedule showing the computation of unit costs for the finished goods department.

7 A report of inventory valuation and cost of units sold for the finished goods department.

(CPA)

6-19 Cost Allocation; FIFO Cost Flows In the course of your examination of the financial statements of the Zeus Company for the year ended December 31, 19X1, you have ascertained the following concerning its manufacturing operations:

- Zeus has two production departments (fabricating and finishing) and a service department. In the fabricating department polyplast is prepared from miracle mix and bypro. In the finishing department each unit of polyplast is converted into six tetraplexes and three uniplexes. The service department provides services to both production departments.
- The fabricating and finishing departments use process cost accounting systems. Actual production costs, including overhead, are allocated monthly.
- Service department expenses are allocated to production departments as follows:

Expense	Allocation Base
Building maintenance	Space occupied
Timekeeping and personnel	Number of employees
Other	½ to fabricating, ½ to finishing

- Raw materials inventory and work in process are priced on a FIFO basis.
- The following data were taken from the fabricating department's records for December 19X1:

Quantities (units of polyplast):	
In process, December 1	3,000
Started in process during month	25,000
Total units to be accounted for	28,000
Transferred to finishing department	19,000
In process, December 31	6,000
Lost end of process (normal)	3,000
Total units accounted for	28,000
Cost of work in process, December 1:	
Materials	$ 13,000
Labor	17,500
Overhead	21,500
	$ 52,000
Direct labor costs, December	$154,000
Departmental overhead, December	$132,000

- Polyplast work in process at the beginning and end of the month was partially completed as follows:

	Materials	Labor and Overhead
December 1	66⅔%	50%
December 31	100	75

- The following data were taken from raw materials inventory records for December:

	Miracle Mix		Bypro	
	Quantity	Amount	Quantity	Amount
Balance, December 1	62,000	$62,000	265,000	$18,550
Purchases:				
December 12	39,500	49,375		
December 20	28,500	34,200		
Fabricating department usage	83,200		50,000	

- Service department expenses for December (not included in departmental overhead above) were:

Building maintenance	$ 45,700
Timekeeping and personnel	27,500
Other	39,000
	$112,200

- Other information for December 19X1 is presented below:

	Square Feet of Space Occupied	Number of Employees
Fabricating	75,000	180
Finishing	37,500	120
	112,500	300

Required

1 Compute the equivalent number of units of polypast, with separate calculations for materials and conversion cost (direct labor plus overhead), manufactured during December.

2 Compute the following items to be included in the fabricating department's production report for December 19X1, with separate calculations for materials, direct labor, and overhead. Prepare supporting schedules.
   a Total costs to be accounted for.
   b Unit costs for equivalent units manufactured.
   c Transfers to finishing department during December and work in process at December 31. Reconcile your answer to part **2a.**

(CPA)

7

JOINT PRODUCTS AND BY-PRODUCTS

AFTER COMPLETING YOUR STUDY OF THIS CHAPTER, YOU SHOULD HAVE LEARNED:

1 How to allocate the manufacturing costs of a single manufacturing process to the multiple products resulting from the process.

2 What kinds of products are allocated a portion of the joint manufacturing costs, what kinds are not (they get a free ride), and the basis for determining which is which.

3 There are two basic methods for allocating the manufacturing costs among the multiple products: one method is based on a physical measure of output; the other method is based on the relative market value of the output.

4 The relevance of joint costs to managerial decisions concerning joint products and by-products.

In the preceding several chapters, we learned how direct materials, direct labor, and applied manufacturing overhead costs were collected and assigned to individual jobs or products. The manufacturing method itself indicated to us whether we should collect cost data using a job order or process cost system. We will see in this chapter how the nature of the manufacturing method will determine the specific cost accounting procedure we will use.

As you already learned, when you collect costs, whether for job order or process manufacturing, what you are basically doing is collecting the manufacturing costs and assigning them to a particular product, as illustrated below:

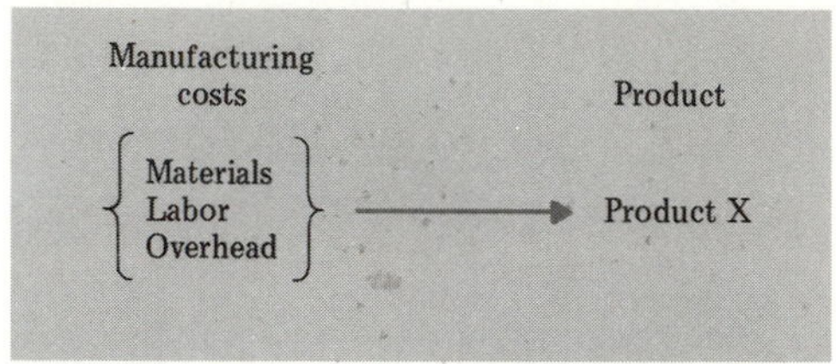

Exactly how you collect and assign costs is determined by how the product is manufactured.

Now we are prepared to consider industries where multiple products are produced from the same set of inputs and the same manufacturing process (as shown below), and how to collect and assign costs to each of the multiple products.

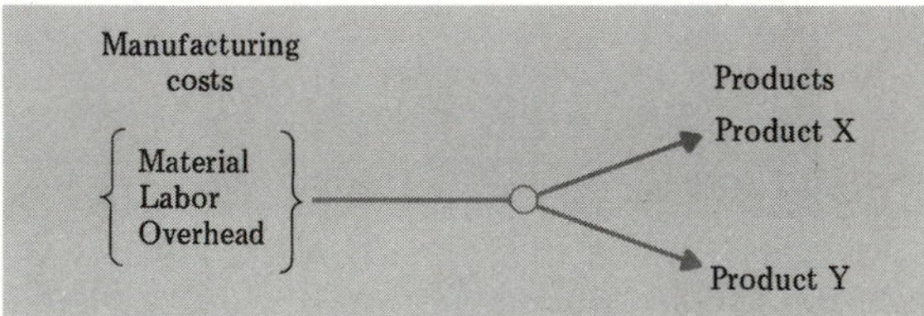

To get an idea of what we mean by multiple products, consider the cracking of crude oil which results in gasoline, heating oil, kerosene, and many other oil-base products. In cracking crude oil, multiple products are a necessary output of the cracking process, that is, they always naturally result from the oil cracking process. Although they always result, the relative proportions of each of the multiple output products can be controlled to some extent.

Multiple products are a natural result of the process. You have no choice of whether or not to have them.

Another familiar industry where multiple products are a natural result of the manufacturing process is meat packing. In processing a cow you necessarily get a cowhide and ground beef along with steaks and other products. You cannot process a cow and produce all steaks.

In the lumber industry, the processing of a tree necessarily yields bark which is used for fuel and soil mulch, boards with few knots which are used for clear lumber, and lumber with many knots which is used for planks and beams.

Multiple products can be either **joint products** or **by-products,** and which they are depends on their market value.

Joint and by-products defined.

> A joint product is any output of a manufacturing process producing multiple products that adds significantly to the total market value of all outputs.
>
> A by-product is an output of a manufacturing process which adds a relatively small amount to the total market value of all outputs.

For example, in processing a tree through a sawmill, the boards ("clear" lumber with few knots) and the planks and beams (lumber with many knots) would be considered joint products. The bark from the tree and the sawdust from processing the tree would be considered by-products.

There is no precise percentage of total market value that we can give you to determine whether a product is a joint product or a by-product. The decision is based on the professional judgment of the accountant. Many accountants feel that if a product represents above 5% of total market value it should be considered a joint product.

Since market values of products can change depending on the supply and demand conditions, a multiple product which was once considered a by-product may become a joint-product. Or, a multiple product currently considered a by-product may eventually come to be considered a joint product. For example, in the early days of the petroleum industry, kerosene was an important joint product because there was much demand for its use in lighting and heating. With the advent of electricity for lighting and furnaces that burn oil or natural gas for heat, the demand for kerosene declined—it was no longer a joint product, it was considered a by-product. But that changed again when the development of jet aircraft engines established a new market for kerosene; the increased demand, greater than before, made it once again a joint product.

In the early days of the lumber industry, sawdust was not even considered a product; it was considered a nuisance because there was the cost of getting rid of it. But then an inventor saw the possibility of using newly available adhesives to shape sawdust into logs which could be burned in fireplaces. These sawdust logs are now sold in many stores in climates where fireplaces are used. The increasing popularity of this multiple product has changed sawdust from an output which once had a negative value (disposal cost) to a by-product.

The split-off point is where the individual products are clearly identifiable.

In any manufacturing process that yields multiple products, there is a point in the process before which it is not possible to identify each of the individual multiple products; beyond that point, the individual products are clearly identifiable. The point in the manufacturing process where the individual products are clearly identifiable is called the **split-off point.**

Cost incurred before the split-off point are called joint costs.

The costs incurred up to the split-off point are referred to as **joint costs.** Joint costs consist of all the materials, labor, and overhead costs necessary to process the multiple products up to the split-off point, as shown below:

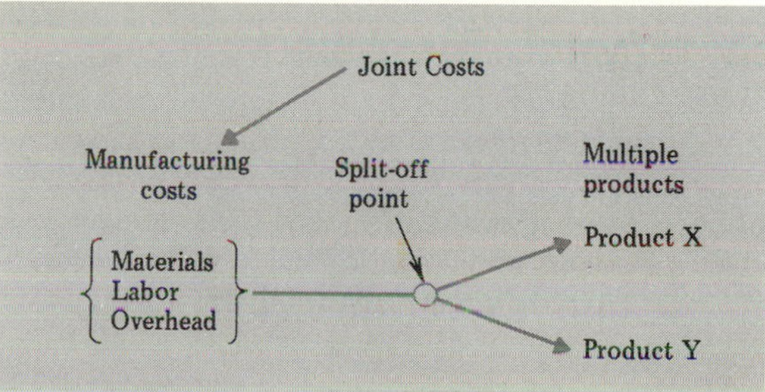

The basic cost accounting problem we face is how do we allocate the joint costs to the multiple products produced by a single manufacturing process.

The plan of this chapter is: First, explain and illustrate how to allocate the joint costs to each of the joint products. That is, we will initially assume that all of the multiple products are joint products. Second, we will explain and illustrate the accounting procedures for by-products. Third, we will briefly examine the managerial decisions that affect joint products.

ALLOCATING JOINT COSTS TO JOINT PRODUCTS

There are two basic methods for allocating joint costs to the joint products. One method uses a physical measure of the joint products produced at the split-off point. The physical measure might be pounds, as in the meat packing industry, or gallons, as in the chemical industry, or board feet, as in the lumber industry. The other method uses the market value of the joint products at the split-off point. To illustrate the basic concepts behind these two methods we will use the following example:

> The Emery Chemical Company processes a single material into two separate products, X and Y. Both products are salable immediately at the split-off point. Product X sells for $6 per gallon, product Y for $3 per gallon. During the month of June 19X2, 1,500 gallons of materials were processed at a joint manufacturing cost of $6,000 for materials, labor, and overhead. The production process yielded 900 gallons of X and 600 gallons of Y. All production was sold in the month of June 19X2.
>
> The cost accounting problem we face is how to allocate the $6,000 of joint costs between products X and Y.

The most helpful way to begin to analyze problems in allocating joint costs is to draw a diagram summarizing the basic facts. For this example such a diagram would be constructed as follows:

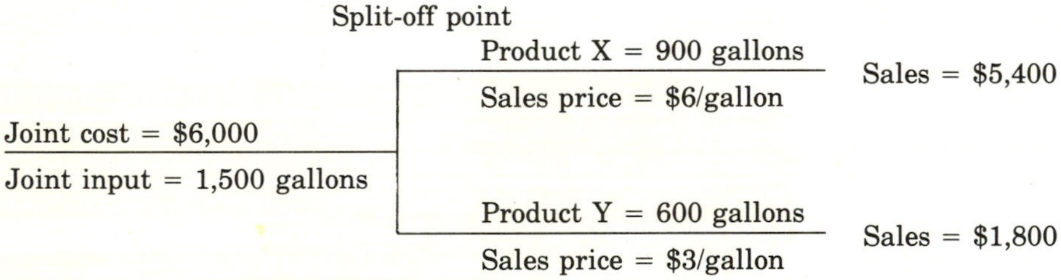

Split-off point

	Product X = 900 gallons / Sales price = $6/gallon	Sales = $5,400
Joint cost = $6,000 / Joint input = 1,500 gallons		
	Product Y = 600 gallons / Sales price = $3/gallon	Sales = $1,800

Physical Measure Method

The facts relevant to the **physical measure method** are that a total of 1,500 gallons of product was produced, 900 gallons of X and 600 gallons of Y. The physical measure method allocates the joint costs to each product in proportion to the gallons of the products produced. Product X will be allocated 60% (900/1,500) of the joint costs and product Y will be allocated 40% (600/1,500), as illustrated below:

The physical measure method divides the joint costs in proportion to gallons of each product.

Product	Production	Propor-tion		Total Joint Cost	Share of Joint Cost		Cost per Gallon
X	900 gallons	900/1,500	×	$6,000	$3,600	÷ 900 =	$4.00
Y	600 gallons	600/1,500			2,400	÷ 600 =	$4.00
	1,500 gallons				$6,000		

EXHIBIT 7-1
EMERY CHEMICAL COMPANY
Product Line Income Statement
Physical Measure Method for Allocating Joint Costs

	Products		
	X	Y	Total
Sales	(900 × $6) = $5.400	(600 × $3) = $1,800	$7,200
Joint costs	(900 × $4) = (3,600)	(600 × $4) = (2,400)	(6,000)
Gross margin	$1,800	$ (600)	$1,200
Gross margin percentage of sales	33%	−33%	16.6%

The physical measure results in different gross margin percentages at the split-off point.

Exhibit 7-1 is an income statement showing gross margins from the two products, assuming all units produced are sold. Note the fourth line in the exhibit, gross margin percentage. The gross margin percentage for each of the joint products is different, which happens because the sales price per unit for each product is different and the unit cost is the same.

The physical measure method always results in the same cost per unit of measure for each of the joint products at the split-off point. In the illustration, product X costs $4 per gallon and so does product Y.

Now, in most situations it does not make sense to allocate costs by the physical measure method because it always results in identical cost per unit for each of the joint products. Our example is just such a case; it does not make sense to do it this way. As you can see from Exhibit 7-1, using the same cost per unit results in a whopping profit for product X and a whopping loss for product Y, yet the two products taken together yield a reasonable combined profit.

For example, as in the case of the meat packing industry, it would not make much sense to cost steak and ground beef, which are joint products of a typical process in this industry, identically at $4 per pound. Obviously a higher price can be charged for steaks than for ground beef and it would, therefore, seem reasonable to allocate the joint costs to the joint products in such a way that the costs correspond somewhat proportionally with the revenue produced by each product.

Thus, viewing the profit (or loss) picture from joint costs resolved to unit costs through the physical measure method causes a distortion in the way we look at the profit of each of the joint products.

There must be a more meaningful way of allocating joint costs. And there is. It is the relative market value method.

Relative Market Value Method

The relative market value method allocates joint costs on the basis of each product's revenue potential.

The objective of the **relative market value method** is to allocate the joint costs on the basis of the potential of each product to generate sales revenue. Advocates of this method point out that the joint costs were incurred with the expectation they will be recovered along with some acceptable level of profit when the joint products are sold. By allocating the joint costs to the joint products based on their market value at the split-off point, each product will have the same gross margin percentage.

To illustrate the relative market value method, we return to the Emery Chemical Company and use the same facts: joint cost of $6,000, the production of 900 gallons of product X salable for $6 per gallon, and 600 gallons of product Y salable for $3 per gallon. The allocation of the joint costs to product X and Y is based on their relative market values at the split-off point. Since both products X and Y are sold at the split-off point, their sales value is the market value we use to allocate the joint costs. The allocation of the joint costs is shown below:

Product	Production		Selling Price at Split-off Point	Market Value at Split-off Point	Proportion	Total Joint Cost	Share of Joint Cost		Cost per Gallon
X	900 gal.	×	$6.00	$5,400	$5,400 / $7,200		$4,500	÷ 900 =	$5.00
						× $6,000 =			
Y	600 gal.	×	$3.00	$1,800	$1,800 / $7,200		$1,500	÷ 600 =	$2.50
	1,500 gal.			$7,200			$6,000		

The relative market value method results in the same gross margin percentage for all joint products at the split-off point.

Exhibit 7-2 is a product line income statement showing the results of using the relative market value method for allocating joint costs, assuming that all products have been sold. Notice in Exhibit 7-2 that product Y shows a positive gross margin percentage by the relative market value method. Using exactly the same data in the physical measure method, Exhibit 7-1, product Y shows a gross margin percentage reflecting a loss.

Additional Processing Costs

In many manufacturing processes that produce joint products, some of the products are not sold at the split-off point, as in the Emery Chemical Company illustrations. Rather, the products are processed further before they are sold. For example, in the

EXHIBIT 7-2
EMERY CHEMICAL COMPANY
Product Line Income Statement
Relative Market Value Method for Allocating Joint Costs

	Products				
		X		Y	Total
Sales	(900 × $6) =	$5,400	(600 × $3) =	$1,800	$7,200
Joint costs	(900 × $5) =	4,500	(600 × $2.50) =	1,500	6,000
Gross margin		$ 900		$ 300	$1,200
Gross margin percentage of sales		16.6%		16.6%	16.6%

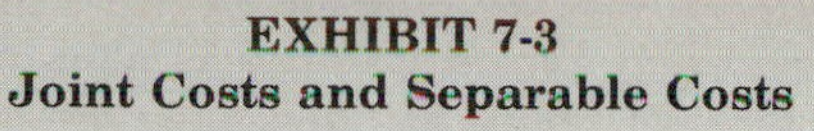

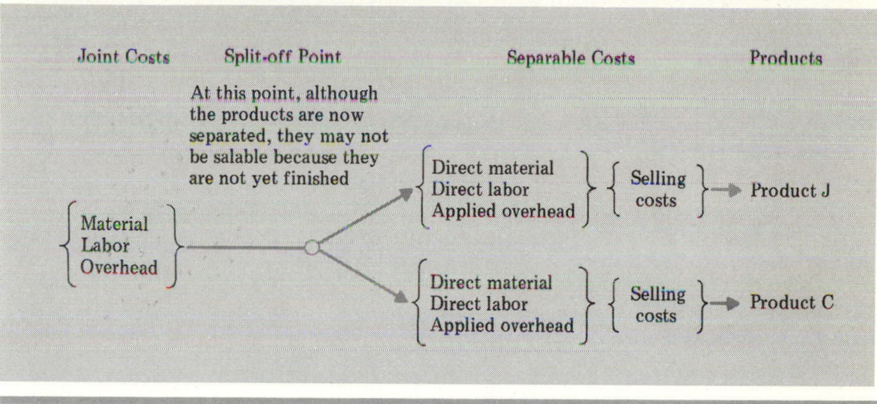

meat packing industry the cowhide and carcass could be sold at the split-off point, or the cowhide could be processed further and tanned and the carcass could be processed further into roasts, steaks, and ground beef.

Separable costs occur after the split-off point and are assigned to the individual products.

These **further processing** costs are referred to as **separable costs** because they are indeed separable and can be assigned to each of the joint products using job order or process costing concepts.

We can now extend our basic diagram to show the relationship among joint costs, separable costs, and joint products as shown in Exhibit 7-3. Notice in Exhibit 7-3 that there is also a separable selling cost for each product in addition to separable production costs.

If we were to use the physical measure method of allocating costs to each of the joint products, there is no need to know the market value of those products at the split-off point. However, if we want to use the relative market value method of allocating joint costs, we will have to determine a market value for each joint product at the split-off point.

If a market exists for the joint product at the split-off point, then, of course, we would use the actual sales price for the joint product at the split-off point to determine market value. This is what we did in our previous illustration.

Approximating a Market Value at the Split-Off Point

If no market exists for the joint product at the split-off point, then we have to approximate a market value. The simplest way to approximate the market value is to look at the values and separable costs of the joint products. We should have a very good idea of what the selling price will be once the units are finished and ready for sale. Thus, we know the sales value of the finished units. We can also easily determine the separable costs, which are costs incurred beyond the split-off point. All we need do is to subtract the separable costs from the sales value, and the result is an approximate market value of each of the joint products at the split-off point. With this market value, we can now allocate the costs prior to the point of separation, that is, the joint costs, to each of the joint products, using the relative market value. This might seem working backwards, and in a way it is, but it is the way to do it. The market value is approximated since it is computed from facts known about the product rather than using an actual sales price at the split-off point.

If joint products cannot be sold at the split-off point without further processing a market value at the split-off point must be approximated.

The following example will illustrate how to approximate market values of joint products at the split-off point.

The Amex Chemical Company produces two products, J and C, using a single material input in their manufacturing process. No market exists for either product at the split-off point. Additional manufacturing and selling costs must be incurred prior to the final point where either product is ready for sale. During the month of June 19X2, 50,000 gallons of materials were processed at a joint cost of $100,000. All units have been completed at the end of June. The following table shows how many gallons of each product resulted from the process, and, for each product, the quantity sold, the selling price per unit, as well as the separable cost per unit.

	Product	
	J	**C**
Production in gallons	25,000	25,000
Sales in gallons	20,000	15,000
Ending inventory—gallons	5,000	10,000
Sales price	$8/gallon	$14/gallon
Separable costs		
Manufacturing	$3/gallon	$6/gallon
Selling	$1/gallon	$2/gallon

These facts can be diagrammed as follows:

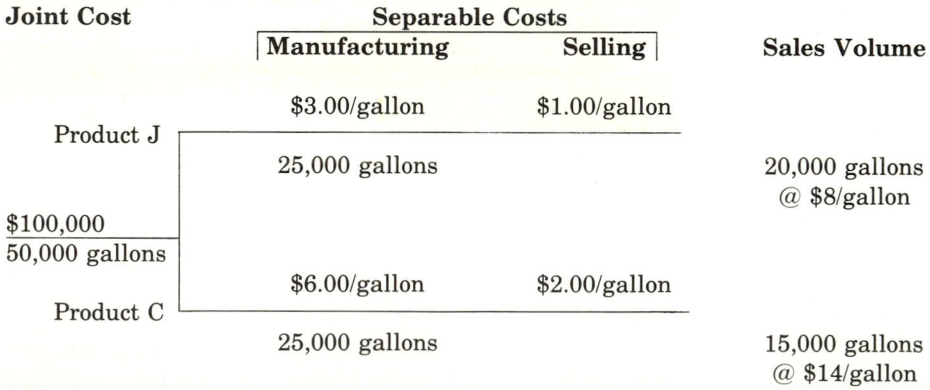

Joint Cost	**Separable Costs**		**Sales Volume**
	Manufacturing	**Selling**	
	$3.00/gallon	$1.00/gallon	
Product J	25,000 gallons		20,000 gallons @ $8/gallon
$100,000 / 50,000 gallons			
	$6.00/gallon	$2.00/gallon	
Product C	25,000 gallons		15,000 gallons @ $14/gallon

Since no actual sales price exists at the split-off point for products J and C, we must first approximate the relative market values of the total production volume of each of the joint products at the split-off point. Once we know those values, we can allocate the joint cost, as shown on page 193.

	Product J	Product C	Total
Production volume	25,000 gal.	25,000 gal.	50,000 gal.
Sales price	× $8/gal.	× $14/gal.	—
Total sales value of production	$200,000	$350,000	$550,000
Less separable costs			
Manufacturing	75,000	150,000	225,000
Selling	25,000	50,000	75,000
Approximate market value at separation	$100,000	$150,000	$250,000
Proportion	$(\frac{100}{250})$ 40%	$(\frac{150}{250})$ 60%	100%
Share of joint cost	$ 40,000	$ 60,000	$100,000

The approximate market value at the split-off point is the final selling price minus the separable costs.

Examine the illustration above and note that we first calculated the market value of the total production volume of each product.

Next, we deducted the separable costs (manufacturing and selling) to approximate the market values of the total production volume of each product at the split-off point. These approximate market values were then used to allocate the joint costs to products J and C.

To obtain the total manufacturing cost for the purpose of calculating a cost per unit for each product, the separable manufacturing costs (but not the separable selling costs) are added to the allocated joint costs, as shown below:

Inventory cost per unit includes a share of the joint cost plus the separable manufacturing costs but not the selling costs.

	Product J	Product C	Total
Allocated joint costs	$ 40,000	$ 60,000	$100,000
Add separable manufacturing costs	75,000	150,000	225,000
Total manufacturing cost	$115,000	$210,000	$325,000
Total units produced	25,000 gal.	25,000 gal.	
Cost per unit	$4.60/gal.	$8.40/gal.	

The separable selling costs are not included since they are *period* costs which are expensed in the period they expire. The costs per unit, $4.60 per gallon and $8.40 per gallon, are used to value the ending inventories of products J and C, respectively.

Exhibit 7-4 is a product line income statement showing the results of the joint cost allocation for Amex Chemical Company's two products. Notice that the gross margin percentage on the two products is no longer equal because the separable costs as a percentage of sales are different for each product.

EXHIBIT 7-4
AMEX CHEMICAL COMPANY
Product Line Income Statement
Approximate Relative Market Value
for Allocating Joint Costs

		Products				
		J			**C**	**Total**
Sales (20,000 gallons × $8)		$160,000	(15,000 gallons × $14)		$210,000	$370,000
Total manufacturing costs*	$115,000			$210,000		$325,000
Ending inventory (5,000 gallons × $4.60)	23,000		(10,000 gallons × $8.40)	84,000		107,000
Cost of sales (20,000 gallons × $4.60)		$ 92,000	(15,000 gallons × $8.40)		$126,000	$218,000
Gross margin		$ 68,000			$ 84,000	$152,000
Gross margin percentage		43%			40%	41%
Selling expense (20,000 gallons × $1.00)		20,000	(15,000 gallons × $2.00)		30,000	50,000
Profit before taxes		$ 48,000			$ 54,000	$102,000
Profit per unit		$ 2.40			$ 3.60	

* For all units produced.

ACCOUNTING FOR BY-PRODUCTS

The distinction between joint products and by-products is based on the market value of the multiple products. By-products do not add significantly to the total market value of all multiple products. Examples of by-products would be the bark and sawdust resulting from the processing of a tree. Because the market value of by-products is not significant compared to the total market value of the multiple products, accountants usually follow simple methods in accounting for by-products.

By-products are often valued at their net realizable value.

One method of accounting for by-products is to value the quantity of by-products produced at their net realizable value. Net realizable value is defined as the final sales price less separable costs. Then the total joint cost of producing all the multiple products is reduced by the net realizable value of the by-product. The reduced joint (total joint cost less net realizable value of by-product) cost is then allocated to the joint products in the usual manner.

To illustrate, assume that a company produces three multiple products in a process, and, by our definitions, two of the products are joint products and one is a by-product. A typical batch produces the following:

Outputs	**Quantity**	**Sales Price at Split-off Point**
Product A	9,000 kilograms	$4 per kilogram
Product B	4,000 kilograms	3 per kilogram
By-product	500 kilograms	0.40 per kilogram

All products are sold at the split-off point. The material cost for the batch is $12,000. The labor cost is $10,000; the predetermined overhead rate is 80% of the labor cost. The applied overhead is, therefore, $8,000 (80% × $10,000) and the total joint costs are $30,000.

The situation can be diagrammed as follows:

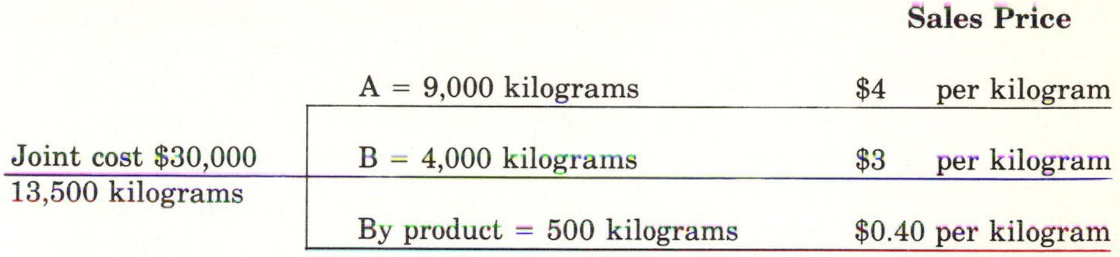

		Sales Price
	A = 9,000 kilograms	$4 per kilogram
Joint cost $30,000 13,500 kilograms	B = 4,000 kilograms	$3 per kilogram
	By product = 500 kilograms	$0.40 per kilogram

The first step in accounting for the joint costs is to determine the **net realizable value** of the by-product and deduct it from the total joint cost. In this example, the net realizable value is equal to the sales price since no additional costs are necessary to complete and sell the by-product. This leaves $29,800 ($30,000 − 500 kg × $.40) of joint costs to be allocated between products A and B in the usual manner.

Material	$12,000
Labor	10,000
Applied overhead (80% × $10,000)	8,000
Total joint cost	$30,000
Less: Net realizable value of by-product 500 kilogram × $0.40	200
Joint cost to be divided between products A and B	$29,800

Product	Units Produced	Selling Price at Split-off Point	Market Value Split-off Point
A	9,000	$4	$36,000
B	4,000	$3	$12,000
			$48,000

Propor-tion	Total Joint Cost	Share of Joint Cost		Cost per Kilogram
$\frac{\$36{,}000}{\$48{,}000}$	× $29,800 =	$22,350	÷ 9,000 =	$2.4833
$\frac{\$12{,}000}{\$48{,}000}$	× $29,800 =	$ 7,450	÷ 4,000 =	$1.8625

Each kilogram of product A in inventory will be reported at $2.4833 on the balance sheet. Each kilogram of B will be reported at $1.8625 per kilogram. The by-product will be reported at $.40 per kilogram. As the units of any of the three products are sold, both the revenue and the appropriate cost of goods sold will be reported on the income statement.

Occasionally by-products are valued at zero cost and the entire joint cost is allocated only to the joint product.

Another way to account for by-products at the split-off point is to value the units of by-product at zero cost. Because it is assumed to have zero cost, at the split-off point the entire joint cost, in our illustration $30,000 (instead of $29,800), would be allocated between the two joint products. The total joint cost would be allocated as if the by-product did not even exist. When the by-product is sold for $.40 per kilogram, revenue of $.40 per kilogram would be shown in the income statement and the cost of the by-product shown in the cost of goods sold would be zero.

Separable Manufacturing Costs for By-Products

This illustration of by-products and joint products assumed no separable manufacturing costs were necessary to complete the by-product. If there were separable manufacturing costs needed to complete the by-product, the first method would add the separable by-product costs to the net realizable value of the by-product to determine the total inventory cost of the by-product.

If we use the method where we assumed no cost is assigned to the by-products at the split-off point, the separable manufacturing costs would represent the total inventory cost of the by-product. This is the cost that would be matched with the revenues from the sale of the by-product.

JOINT COSTS AND MANAGEMENT DECISIONS

There are two types of decisions relating to joint products. One type is whether to process the inputs which produce the joint products at all. The second type of decision is whether to process the joint products further beyond the split-off point.

The first decision is made by comparing the total revenue from all products to the total costs of producing them. Since the decision maker cannot choose to produce some products and not others, the only decision is all or nothing. Because total revenues and total costs are compared to make this all-or-nothing decision, it is not necessary to allocate joint costs to each of the products.

Allocations of joint costs are not relevant to management decisions.

The decision to process a joint product further beyond the split-off point is made by comparing the added revenue resulting from the processing beyond the split-off point to the added separable cost for the joint product. If the additional revenue is greater than the separable cost, the further processing will increase total profits. Again, allocating joint costs to each of the joint products is not relevant to the decision, because it is only the separable costs and the added revenue from additional processing which are considered.

Both of these types of decisions will be developed and illustrated more fully in Chapter 15. Nevertheless, we should make you aware that traditionally decisions relating to joint products are discussed in this chapter. Decision making is what managerial accounting is all about. You may recall from the early pages of this book that we elected to keep cost accounting apart from managerial accounting. Besides, as you probably already surmised for yourself from your study of cost accounting thus far, there is not much relevance between allocating joint costs and managerial decision making, at least not with respect to learning the methodology of how to allocate joint costs and how to report these costs as inventories on the balance sheet. More on all this later.

SUMMARY

A joint process simultaneously produces more than one product from a single set of inputs. Joint costs are the total costs incurred in the process up to the point where the multiple products of the process are separable. Joint costs consist of the materials, labor, and overhead costs.

Products which contribute only a small amount to the total revenue from the total output of the process are called by-products. Other products are called joint products; joint products do contribute significantly to the total revenue of all output from a single process. Because by-products are by definition immaterial, cost accounting for them is simple; usually they are inventoried either at their net realizable value at the split-off point or at zero.

Usually, each of the joint products is inventoried at a cost determined by allocating the joint costs among the joint products. One way to allocate joint costs is based on a physical measure, such as pounds or gallons. However, the most common way accountants allocate joint costs is in proportion to the relative market values of the joint products at the split-off point.

Where a product must be processed further beyond the split-off point before it has any market value, the way to determine its value at the split-off point (although it is a fictional value) is to estimate its value at the point of sale (where it surely has a market value) and subtract from it the separable costs required (beyond split-off) to process it from the split-off point to the point of sale.

Review Problem

The Teto Reclamation Company purchases garbage from the city of Cincinnati; through the use of a special process they can transform the garbage into three salable products, GX, GY, and GZ. GX can only be sold at the split-off point. GY and GZ can either be sold at the split-off point or processed further and then sold. The Teto Reclamation Company decided to process GY and GZ further. The sales price and additional processing costs for the three products are as follows:

Product	Sales Price Split-off Point	Additional Processing Costs	Sales Price After Split-off
GX	.50/pound	—	—
GY	.75/pound	.25/pound	1.10/pound
GZ	1.00/gallon	.50/gallon	1.65/gallon

During the past month, the reclamation company processed 150,000 pounds of garbage at a cost of $60,000. The process yielded 60,000 pounds of GX, 40,000 pounds of GY, and 30,000 gallons of GZ. Both GY and GZ were processed further prior to their sales.

Required Using relative market values for allocating the joint cost, prepare product line income statements assuming all units produced are sold.

Solution

Market Value at Split-off Point		Allocation of Joint Cost	
GX = 60,000 × $ .50 =	$30,000	1/3 × $60,000 =	$20,000
GY = 40,000 × $ .75 =	30,000	1/3 × $60,000 =	20,000
GZ = 30,000 × $1.00 =	30,000	1/3 × $60,000 =	20,000
	$90,000		$60,000

Product Line Income Statements

	GX	GY	GZ	Total
Sales	$30,000	$44,000	$49,500	$123,500
Joint cost	20,000	20,000	20,000	60,000
Separable cost	-0-	10,000	15,000	25,000
Gross margin	$10,000	$14,000	$14,500	$38,500

Note that the sales price at the split-off point is used to calculate the total market value at this point. Since a sales price existed at the split-off point, no approximation of the sales price was required.

Review Problem

The Burns Company produces two joint products, X and Y. In separating products X and Y a by-product is also produced. During the month of July, 20,000 gallons of input were processed producing 12,000 gallons of X, 7,000 gallons of Y, and 1,000 gallons of the by-product. The materials and conversion costs incurred to process and separate the products amounted to $57,000. Before any of the products can be sold, additional manufacturing processing costs are incurred in the following amounts:

Product	Additional Manufacturing Processing Cost
X	$.50/gallon
Y	.75/gallon
By-product	.10/gallon

During July all of the products were fully processed and sales were in the following amounts.

Product	Sales Price	Sales Units
X	$6.50	10,000
Y	5.50	5,000
By-product	2.00	700

Required

1 Using physical measure to allocate the joint costs, compute the total manufacturing cost per unit for the joint products assuming:
   a The by-product is valued at zero cost at the split-off point.
   b The by-product net realizable value is treated as a reduction in the production costs of the joint products.

2 Calculate the cost of the ending inventories using the assumptions in 1 (**a**) and (**b**).

Solution

1a Computation of total manufacturing cost per unit assuming the by-product is valued at zero cost at the split-off point.

Product	Gallons Produced	Proportion		Total Joint Cost		Share of Joint Cost	Joint Cost per Gallon	Separable Cost per Gallon	Total Cost per Gallon
X	12,000	12/19	×	$57,000	=	$36,000	$3.00	$.50	$3.50
Y	7,000	7/19	×	$57,000	=	21,000	$3.00	$.75	$3.75
	19,000					$57,000			

1b Computation of total manufacturing cost per unit assuming the by-product net realizable value is treated as a reduction in the production cost.

Product	Gallons Produced	Proportion		Total Joint Cost		Share of Joint Cost	Joint Cost per Gallon	Separable Cost per Gallon	Total Cost per Gallon
X	12,000	12/19	×	$55,100*	=	$34,800	$2.90	$.50	$3.40
Y	7,000	7/19	×	$55,100	=	20,300	$2.90	$.75	$3.65
	19,000					$55,100			

*Computation of net joint production costs

Total joint cost	=	$57,000
Net realizable value of by-product ($2 − $.10) × 1,000 gallons)	=	1,900
Cost to allocate to joint products		$55,100

2 Computation of ending inventory values.

Product	Ending Inventory Values			
	Part 2a		Part 2b	
X	2,000 @ $3.50 =	$ 7,000	2,000 @ $3.40 =	$ 6,800
Y	2,000 @ $3.75 =	7,500	2,000 @ $3.65 =	7,300
By-product	300 @ $0.10 =	30	300 @ $2.00* =	600
		$14,530		$14,700

* Net realizable value = $1.90
+ Additional processing cost = .10
$2.00

Glossary

By-products Outputs from a manufacturing process whose market value at the separation point does not add significantly to the total market value of all outputs from the process.

Further processing The manufacturing operations performed on joint or by-products after the split-off point.

Joint cost A cost incurred by an organization that necessarily benefits more than one accounting period, product, or project. In this chapter, it is the materials, labor, and manufacturing overhead costs incurred in processing the materials to the split-off point.

Joint products Products produced from a manufacturing process that necessarily yields multiple outputs each of whose market value adds significantly to the total market value of all outputs at the split-off point.

Net realizable value A costing procedure that assigns the sales price less any separable costs to the by-product at the split-off point.

Physical measure cost allocation method A procedure for allocating joint costs to each joint product based on some physical description of the products such as pounds or gallons.

Relative market value cost allocation method A procedure for allocating joint costs to each joint product based on the relative market value of each product at the split-off point.

Separable cost The costs incurred to complete the manufacture and sale of a joint product after the split-off point. The manufacturing costs are collected using job order or process costing procedures and assigned to the individual products.

Split-off point The point in the manufacturing process where the joint products are separated and can be identified as separate items.

Questions and Problems

7-1 Distinguish between joint products and by-products.

7-2 Describe the basic nature of the manufacturing process that gives rise to joint products.

7-3 How are separable manufacturing processing costs accounted for?

7-4 Discuss how the physical measure method and the relative market value method affect the gross margin percentage of the joint products.

7-5 What advantages does the relative market value method have over the physical allocation method?

7-6 Discuss the alternative accounting treatments for by-products.

7-7 Discuss the relevance of allocating joint costs for managerial decisions regarding joint products.

7-8 Joint Costs—Relative Market Value Allocation Gilbert Manufacturing Company manufactures two products, Alt and Bat. Initially, they are processed from the same raw material and then, after split-off, they are further processed separately. Additional information is as follows:

	Alt	Bat	Total
Final sales value	$9,000	$6,000	$15,000
Joint costs prior to split-off point	?	?	6,600
Costs beyond split-off point	3,000	3,000	6,000

Required

Using the relative market value approach, what are the assigned joint costs of Alt and Bat, respectively?

(CPA)

7-9 Joint Cost Allocation Using Relative Market Values The Threepro Co. manufactures three products, Mapro A, Mapro B, and Bypro (a by-product). Threepro incurred a joint cost of $100,000 during December 19X5 in producing the three products. You are given the following information for December:

	Units Produced	Selling Price per Unit	Units Sold	Additional Processing Cost
Mapro A	8,000	$10	7,000	$10,000
Mapro B	12,000	$ 5	9,000	30,000
Bypro	10,000	$ 0.50	5,000	2,000

In addition, selling costs of $1,000 were associated with the sale of Bypro. Threepro treats by-product net realizable value as a reduction in the cost of the joint products.

Required

1 Allocate the joint costs based on the relative market value of the products.

2 Calculate the cost of the ending inventory assuming all products are complete and ready for sale.

(S. Adams)

7-10 Joint Cost Allocation Using Relative Market Value The All-Star Dairy produces two main products, powdered milk and butter, and one by-product which is sold to farmers as hog feed. The production department incurred the following costs for March, 19X6, all of which are joint costs:

Direct Labor	$20,000
Direct Materials	50,000
Applied Overhead	30,000

Additional information on each product is as follows:

	Separable Manufacturing Cost	Packaging Cost	Selling Cost	Sales Revenue
Butter	$30,000	$20,000	$ -0-	$150,000
Powdered milk	60,000	10,000	-0-	190,000
Hog feed	-0-	5,000	5,000	20,000

Required

Compute the joint cost assigned to butter and powdered milk, using the relative market value method and treating hog feed as a by-product whose net realizable value is deducted from the cost of the main products.

(S. Adams)

7-11 Joint Cost Allocation Illustrating Physical Units Method and Relative Market Value Method Vreeland, Inc., manufactures products X, Y, and Z from a joint process. Joint product costs were $60,000. Additional information is as follows:

			Sales Values and Additional Costs if Processed Further	
Product	Units Produced	Sales Value at Split-off	Final Sales Values	Additional Costs
X	6,000	$40,000	$55,000	$9,000
Y	4,000	35,000	45,000	7,000
Z	2,000	25,000	30,000	5,000

Required

1 Using the physical measure method, allocate the joint costs to the three products.

2 Repeat part 1 using the relative market value method.

(CPA)

7-12 Joint Cost Allocation Using Relative Market Values Forward, Inc., manufactures products P, Q, and R from a joint process. Additional information is as follows:

Do Tax Research By 10/13.

	Product			
	P	Q	R	Total
Units produced	4,000	2,000	1,000	7,000
Joint cost				$ 60,000
Sales value at split-off	—	—	$15,000	
Additional costs if processed further	$ 7,000	$ 5,000	$ 3,000	$ 15,000
Sales value if processed further	$67,000	$30,000	$20,000	$117,000

Required Using the relative market value method allocate the joint cost to the three products.

(CPA)

7-13 Allocating Joint Costs and Calculating Unit Costs Rico produces and sells three products, Ape, May, and Jun. The production process starts with a refining of crude crud which yields Ape and Bim. Bim is processed further to yield May and Jun. There is an active market for Ape, May, Jun, and Bim. All may be purchased or sold at these prices:

	Per Gallon
Ape	$ 2.00
May	8.00
Jun	20.00
Bim	4.00

During March, 10,000 gallons of crud costing $20,000 were placed into production. The conversion costs in the refining department amounted to $16,000. The operating costs of the other processing department were $9,000. Production outputs for the month of March were:

Ape	4,000 gallons
Bim	6,000 gallons
Jun	1,000 gallons
May	5,000 gallons

There were no beginning or ending work in process inventories.

Required

1 Compute the cost per unit of Ape using the physical allocation method.

2 Using part 1 results compute the cost per unit of Jun using the market value method.

7-14 Joint Cost Allocation for Valuing the Ending Inventory Miller Manufacturing Company buys zeon for $.80 a gallon. At the end of processing in department 1, zeon splits off into products A, B, and C. Product A is sold at the split-off point, with no further processing. Products B and C require further processing before they can be sold; product B is processed in department 2 and product C is processed in department 3. Following is a summary of costs and other related data for the year ended June 30, 19X3.

	Department		
	1	2	3
Cost of zeon	$96,000	—	—
Direct labor	$14,000	$45,000	$65,000
Manufacturing overhead	$10,000	$21,000	$49,000

	Products		
	A	B	C
Gallons sold	20,000	30,000	45,000
Gallons on hand at June 30, 19X3	10,000	—	15,000
Sales in dollars	$30,000	$96,000	$141,750

There were no inventories on hand at July 1, 19X2, and there was no zeon on hand at June 30, 19X3. All gallons on hand at June 30, 19X3 were complete as to processing. Miller uses the relative sales value method of allocating joint costs.

Required

1 Calculate the manufacturing cost of each product.

2 Calculate the value of the ending inventory for products A and C.

(CPA)

7-15 Joint and By-Products—Gross Margin and Ending Inventory Computations The Harrison Corporation produces three products—Alpha, Beta, Gamma. Alpha and Gamma are joint products while Beta is a by-product of Alpha. No joint cost is to be allocated to the by-product. The production processes for a given year are as follows:

In department One, 110,000 pounds of material, Rho, are processed at a total cost of $120,000. After processing in department One, 60% of the units are transferred to department Two and 40% of the units (now Gamma) are transferred to department Three.

In department Two, the material is further processed at a total additional cost of $38,000. Seventy percent of the units (now Alpha) are transferred to department Four and 30% emerge as Beta, the by-product, to be sold at $1.20 per pound. Selling expenses related to disposing of Beta are $8,100.

In department Four, Alpha is processed at a total additional cost of $23,660. After this processing, Alpha is ready for sale at $5 per pound.

In department Three, Gamma is processed at a total additional cost of $165,000. In this department, a normal loss of units of Gamma occurs which equals 10% of the good output of Gamma. The remaining good output of Gamma is then sold for $12 per pound.

Required

1 Prepare a schedule showing the allocation of the $120,000 joint cost between Alpha and Gamma using the relative sales value approach. The net realizable value of Beta should be treated as an addition to the sales value of Alpha.

2 Prepare a statement of gross margin for Alpha using the following facts:

> During the year, sales of Alpha were 80% of the pounds available for sale. There was no beginning inventory.
>
> The net realizable value of Beta available for sale is to be deducted from the cost of producing Alpha. The ending inventory of Alpha is to be based on the net cost of production.

(CPA)

7-16 Joint Cost; Product Line Income Statements The Savage Chemical Company processes one basic material into three products referred to as A, B, and C. The costs of processing the raw materials prior to the separation of the products for a typical month are:

Materials 100,000 pounds	$20,000
Labor	30,000
Overhead	40,000
Total	$90,000

The 100,000 pounds of raw materials yield the following quantities of A, B, and C.

A	50,000 pounds
B	30,000 pounds
C	20,000 pounds
	100,000 pounds

After the products are separated each must be processed further before they are in marketable condition. The additional processing costs are itemized below.

	A	B	C
Material	$3,000	$2,000	$2,000
Labor	2,000	2,000	1,000
Overhead	2,000	2,000	1,000
Total	$7,000	$6,000	$4,000

During the month all units produced were sold generating $152,000 in sales.

A	$75,000
B	45,000
C	32,000
Total	$152,000

Required

1 Using the relative market value approach, allocate the joint costs to the products.

2 Prepare a product line income statement for the products using the results of 1.

3 Repeat parts 1 and 2 using the physical method to allocate the joint costs.

7-17 Joint and By-Products; Valuation of Ending Inventories During 19X8, the Juno Chemical Company started a new division whose operation consists of processing a mineral into commercial products A, B, C, and D. Each product passes through the same processing operation. However, product D is classified as a second, or reject, and is sold at a lower price.

The following information is available regarding the company's operations for 19X8:

Sales (including product D)	$24,480
Production costs	$49,769

	Total	A	B	C	D
Quantity (tons)					
Beginning inventory	—	—	—	—	—
Production	634	305	137	22	170
Sales	285	132	83	10	60
Ending inventory	349	173	54	12	110
Sales price per ton (Constant throughout the period)	—	$100	$100	$100	$33

Required

1 Compute the inventory valuation at December 31 assuming D is a joint product using the physical method of allocating the joint cost.

2 Compute the inventory valuation at December 31 assuming D is a by-product. The company has elected to reduce the cost of the joint products by the by-product revenue.

(CPA)

7-18 By-Products; Alternative Accounting Treatments The Martin Company produces a chemical compound called Martex. As part of the manufacturing process a by-product Amtex is produced. During the month of January 40,000 pounds of Martex and 2,000 gallons of Amtex were produced. The total manufacturing costs during January amounted to $80,000.

In January, 35,000 pounds of Martex were sold at a price of $4 per pound. Fifteen hundred gallons of Amtex were sold at a price of $2.50 per gallon after incurring marketing costs of $.50 per gallon.

In addition to the marketing cost of Amtex, the selling and administration expenses for January amounted to $40,000.

Required

1 Prepare income statements for the month of January assuming:
   a The by-product is valued at zero cost at the split-off point.
   b The by-product net realizable value is treated as a reduction in the joint product costs.

2 Calculate the cost of the ending inventories using the assumptions in **1a** and **b**.

7-19 Joint and By-Products; Calculation of Unit Costs Amaco Chemical Company manufactures several products in its three departments.

In department 1 the materials amanic acid and bonyl hydroxide are used to produce Amanyl, Bonanyl, and Am-Salt. Amanyl is sold to others who use it as a direct material in the manufacture of soap. Bonanyl is not salable without further processing. Although Am-Salt is a commercial product for which there is a ready market, Amaco does not sell this product, preferring to submit it to further processing.

In department 2 Bonanyl is processed into the marketable product, Bonanyl-X. The relationship between Bonanyl used and Bonanyl-X produced has remained constant for several months.

In department 3 Am-Salt and the material colb are used to produce Colbanyl, a liquid propellant which is in great demand. As an inevitable part of this process Demanyl is also produced. Demanyl was discarded as scrap until discovery of its usefulness as a catalyst in the manufacture of glue; for two years Amaco has been able to sell all of its production of Demanyl.

In its financial statements Amaco states inventory at the lower of cost (on the first-in, first-out basis) or market. Unit costs of the items most recently produced must therefore be computed. Costs allocated to Demanyl are computed so that after allowing for packaging and selling costs of $.04 per pound no profit or loss will be recognized on sales of this product.

Certain data for October 19X2 follow:

	Pounds Used	Total Cost
Amanic acid	6,300	$5,670
Bonyl hydroxide	7,700	6,370
Colb	5,600	2,240

Conversion costs (labor and overhead):

	Total Cost
Department 1	$33,600
Department 2	3,306
Department 3	22,400

Products	Pounds Produced	Inventories, Pounds		Sales Price per Pound
		September 30	October 31	
Amanyl	3,600			$ 6.65
Bonanyl	2,800	210	110	
Am-Salt	7,600	400	600	6.30
Bonanyl-X	2,755			4.20
Colbanyl	1,400			43.00
Demanyl	9,800			.54

Required Prepare for October 19X2 the schedules listed below. Assume the cost of Am-Salt produced was $3.40 in September 19X2.

1 Cost per pound of Amanyl, Bonanyl and Am-Salt produced using the relative sales value method.

2 Cost per pound of Amanyl, Bonanyl and Am-Salt produced using the physical measure method.

3 Cost per pound of Colbanyl produced using the results of part 1.

(CPA)

7-20 By-Products—Gross Profit Calculations The McLean Processing Company produces a chemical compound, Supergro, that is sold for $4.60 per gallon. The manufacturing process is divided into the departments listed below:

1 Mixing department. The materials are measured and mixed in this department.
2 Cooking department. The mixed materials are cooked for a specified period in this department. In the cooking process there is a 10% evaporation loss in materials.
3 Cooling department. After the cooked materials are cooled in this department under controlled conditions, the top 80% in the cooling tank is syphoned off and pumped to the packing department. The 20% residue, which contains impurities, is sold in bulk as a by-product, Groex, for $2.00 per gallon.
4 Packing department. In this department special 1 gallon tin cans costing 60 cents each are filled with Supergro and shipped to customers.

The company's research and development department recently discovered a new use for the by-product if it is further processed in a new boiling department. The new by-product, Fasgro, would sell in bulk for $5 per gallon.

In processing Fasgro the top 70% in the cooling tank would be syphoned off as Supergro. The residue would be pumped to a new boiling department where one-half gallon of materials, SK, would be added for each gallon of residue. In the boiling department process there would be a 40% evaporation loss. In processing Fasgro the following additional costs would be incurred.

Material SK	$1.00 per gallon
Boiling department variable processing costs	$1.00 per gallon of input
Boiling department fixed processing costs	$2,000 per month

In recent months, because of heavy demand, the company has shipped Supergro and Groex on the same day that their processing was completed. Fasgro would probably be subject to the same heavy demand.

During the month of July, which was considered a typical month, the following materials were put into process in the mixing department:

Material FE—10,000 gallons @ $.90 per gallon
Material QT—4,000 gallons @ $1.50 per gallon

July processing costs per gallon of departmental input were:

Mixing department	$.40
Cooking department	.50
Cooling department	.30
Packing department	.10

For accounting purposes the company assigns costs to its by-products equal to their net realizable value

Required Prepare a statement computing total manufacturing costs and gross profit for the month of July that compares (1) actual results for July, and (2) estimated results if Fasgro had been the by-product.

(CPA)

7-21 Process Costing and By-Products The Adept Company is a manufacturer of two products known as "Prep" and "Pride." Incidental to the production of these two products, it produces a by-product known as "Wilton." The manufacturing process covers two departments, grading and saturating.

The manufacturing process begins in the grading department when materials are started in process. Upon completion of processing in the grading department, the by-product "Wilton" is produced, which accounts for 20% of the material output. This by-product needs no further processing and is transferred to finished goods.

The net realizable value of the by-product "Wilton" is accounted for as a reduction of the cost of materials in the grading department. The current selling price of "Wilton" is $1 per pound and the estimated selling and delivery costs total 10 cents per pound.

The remaining output is transferred to the saturating department for the final phase of production. In the saturating department, water is added at the beginning of the production process which results in a 50% gain in weight of the materials in production.

The following information is available for the month of November:

	November 1		November 30
Inventories	**Quantity (pounds)**	**Amount**	**Quantity (pounds)**
Work in process:			
Grading department	None	—	None
Saturating department	1,600	$17,600	2,000
Finished goods:			
Prep	600	$14,520	1,600
Pride	2,400	37,110	800
Wilton	None	—	None

The work in process inventory (labor and overhead) in the saturating department is estimated to be 50% complete both at the beginning and end of November.

Costs of production for November are as follows:

Costs of Production	Materials Used	Labor and Overhead
Grading department	$265,680	$86,400
Saturating department	—	86,000

The material used in the grading department weighed 36,000 pounds. Adept uses the first-in, first-out method of process costing.

Required

Prepare a cost of production report for both the grading and saturating departments for the month of November. Show supporting computations in good form.

The answer should include:

- Equivalent units of production (in pounds)
- Total manufacturing costs
- Cost per equivalent unit (pounds)
- Dollar amount of ending work in process
- Dollar amount of inventory cost transferred out

(CPA)

7-22 Joint Products—Working Backwards Stellar Corporation manufactures products R and S from a joint process. Additional information is as follows:

	Product		
	R	S	Total
Units produced	4,000	6,000	10,000
Joint costs	$36,000	$ 54,000	$ 90,000
Sales value at split-off	?	?	?
Additional costs if processed further	$ 3,000	$ 26,000	$ 29,000
Sales value if processed further	$63,000	$126,000	$189,000
Additional margin if processed further	$12,000	?	$ 40,000

Required

Assuming that joint costs are allocated on the basis of relative sales value at split-off, what was the sales value at split-off for products R and S?

(CPA)

7-23 Relative Sales Value and By-products Superior Company manufactures products A and B from a joint process which also yields a by-product,

X. Superior accounts for the revenues from its by-products sales as a deduction from the cost of the joint products.

Additional information is as follows:

	Products			
	A	B	X	Total
Units produced	15,000	9,000	6,000	30,000
Joint costs	?	?	?	$264,000
Sales value at split-off	$290,000	$150,000	$10,000	$450,000

Required

Assuming that joint product costs are allocated using the relative sales value at split-off approach, what are the joint costs allocated to products A and B?

(CPA)

STANDARD COSTS: DIRECT MATERIALS AND DIRECT LABOR

AFTER COMPLETING YOUR STUDY OF THIS CHAPTER, YOU SHOULD HAVE LEARNED:

1 What a standard cost is, how it differs from actual cost, and how to use it.

2 A standard cost per unit consists of two components: a quantity standard and a price standard. We will explain both and how to use them to calculate differences between total actual costs and total standard costs.

3 How standard costs are used in cost accounting, as well as in managerial accounting.

4 The different types of standards that can be used to establish standard costs.

5 The concept of a variance, which is basically the difference between a standard cost and its corresponding actual cost.

6 How standard costs are recorded in the general ledger.

Standards of one kind or another are used to evaluate many different activities. For example universities set standards that you must achieve to graduate—a 2.00 grade point average—and to graduate with honors—a 3.50 grade point average. When you play golf the standard your score is compared with is par for the golf course. In both of these situations a standard is used to evaluate an individual's performance.

Standards are also used to determine the price you pay for some services. Automotive repair shops determine the price you are charged based on the estimated (standard) hours for the mechanic to perform the repair work. For example, the price to tune a V-8 engine might be based on 1 hour of mechanic time. Your bill is calculated using the standard time of 1 hour even though the actual mechanic time to tune your engine may be 1 hour and 15 minutes. The automotive repair shop evaluates their mechanics by comparing the actual time to perform a job with the standard time.

Standards are used in manufacturing companies to inform management what the manufacturing cost per unit of each product *should be* before the product is produced. So far we have focused on accounting systems that accumulate actual input costs of direct materials and direct labor and thus yield the actual cost of each unit produced. We explained how to collect actual direct materials and direct labor costs for both job order and process cost accounting systems.

Now we will focus on **standard costs** and how they are used in the job order and process cost accounting systems. Of course, we will also explain the difference between a cost per unit produced using standard costs and a cost per unit produced using actual costs.

STANDARD COST PER UNIT OF FINISHED PRODUCT

A standard cost per unit of finished product is a predetermined cost consisting of two components:

Standard cost components.

1 A cost component based on a **quantity standard** per unit of finished product. The quantity standard is expressed in terms of input measures such as pounds, gallons, board feet, or yards per unit of output.

2 A cost component based on a price standard for each measure of the quantity standard. The **price standard** is expressed in terms such as dollars per pound, dollars per gallon, or dollars per board feet of input.

The quantity standard specifies the expected amount of direct material and the expected number of direct labor hours necessary to produce *1 unit* of finished product. We can think of the quantity standard as the expected direct materials and direct labor inputs necessary to produce 1 unit of output as shown below:

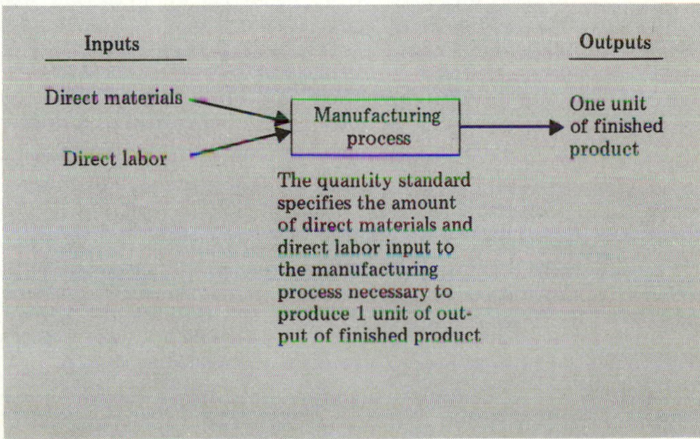

The price standard specifies the amount we expect to pay for the cost of each measure of direct materials and the cost of each hour of direct labor used in manufacturing 1 unit of finished product.

The standard cost of 1 unit of finished product is calculated by multiplying the quantity standard times the price standards for each input and then totaling the standard cost of all inputs.

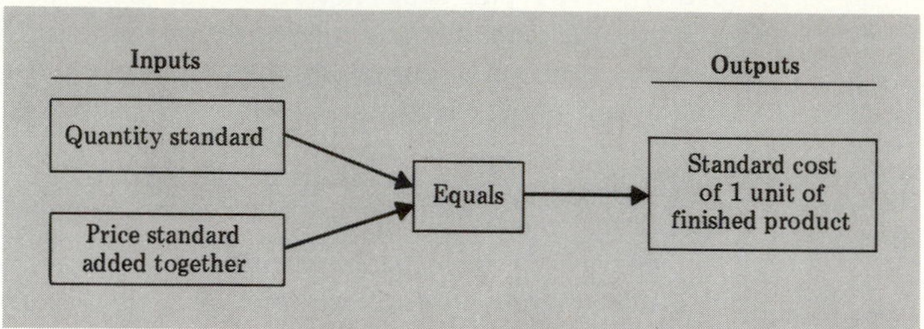

The information describing the quantity standard and price standard for each product is summarized on a standard cost card for that product. To illustrate a standard cost card, assume we are manufacturing a wood cabinet that requires the following direct materials inputs:

18 board feet of oak lumber
4 hinges
8 braces
32 sets of nuts and bolts

Manufacturing the cabinet requires the following direct labor operations:

1. The lumber is cut to the required sizes and shapes.
2. The parts are assembled to form the cabinet.
3. The cabinet is hand sanded to a smooth finish.
4. Varnish is applied to the cabinet.

A standard cost card lists the quantity and price standards for each product.

Exhibit 8-1 illustrates the standard cost card for the wood cabinet. The standard cost card contains a description of the standard quantities of direct materials and the standard price of each type of direct materials required to produce one oak cabinet. Multiplying the standard direct materials quantity times the standard direct materials price provides us with the standard cost for each item of direct materials input necessary to produce one oak cabinet. The total standard direct materials cost per oak cabinet of $92.96 is calculated by summing the standard cost for each direct materials item.

The standard cost card also contains a description of the direct labor operations necessary to produce one oak cabinet. For each direct labor operation the standard quantity is expressed in terms of the number of direct labor hours management expects it to take an employee to perform the operation. The standard price is the expected pay rate for the operation. Again the standard cost is the product of the standard quantity times the standard price. The total standard direct labor cost per oak cabinet is $29.50.

The overhead costs included on the standard cost card specify the basis for applying overhead costs for each operation and the predetermined overhead rate. We will explain in more detail this standard overhead cost later in Chapter 9.

EXHIBIT 8-1
Standard Cost Card
Oak Cabinet

Direct Materials

Item	Standard Quantity		Standard Price per Measure		Standard Cost
Oak lumber	18 board feet	×	$5.00	=	$90.00
Hinges	4	×	.20	=	.80
Braces	8	×	.15	=	1.20
Nut and bolt sets	32	×	.03	=	.96
Total standard direct materials cost per oak cabinet					$92.96

Direct Labor

Operation	Standard Quantity		Standard Price per Hour		Standard Cost
Cutting	2.0 hours	×	$6.00	=	$12.00
Assembly	2.0 hours	×	4.50	=	9.00
Sanding	1.5 hours	×	4.00	=	6.00
Painting	0.5 hours	×	5.00	=	2.50
Total standard direct labor cost per oak cabinet					$29.50

Overhead

Operation	Application Basis		Predetermined Rate/Labor Hour		Standard Cost
Cutting	2.0 direct labor hours	×	$ 12.00	=	$ 24.00
Assembly	2.0 direct labor hours	×	9.00	=	18.00
Sanding	1.5 direct labor hours	×	6.00	=	9.00
Painting	.5 direct labor hours	×	8.00	=	4.00
Total standard overhead cost					$ 55.00
Total standard cost per oak cabinet					$177.46

OBJECTIVES OF STANDARD COSTS

Standard cost is one of the basic tools for cost accounting, as well as for managerial accounting. From the perspective of cost accounting, the most basic use of standard costs is to simplify procedures for determining the costs that are ultimately used to value inventory and also to determine the cost of goods sold. From the perspective of managerial accounting, the most basic use of standard costs is as a cost indicator for decisions in planning and controlling the operations of a company.

Standard Costs and Cost Accounting

In a standard cost system, inventories are recorded at their standard cost.

From the cost accounting viewpoint, the most important feature of standard costs is that standard costs make it unnecessary to choose FIFO or LIFO methods in valuing inventory. In a standard cost system, inventories are recorded at their standard cost. Since standard costs do not change frequently, all units of a given type are recorded at the same cost. With all inventory at the same unit cost, the cost of the ending inventory and cost of goods sold are all the same whether you use FIFO, LIFO, or average costing. You can use standard costs for partially completed units, as well as fully finished units. For the partially completed units, you must be able to come up with a reasonably accurate degree or percentage of completion. For example, if the standard cost for an item is \$5 for direct materials and \$15 for conversion costs and there are 100 units in inventory, 100% complete for materials but 75% complete for conversion cost, the inventory value is (\$5 × 100% × 100) + (\$15 × 75% × 100) = \$1,625. Let us take a further look at standard costs and partially completed units.

To illustrate, let us return to the oak cabinet in our example. Let us assume that it has been in production for the past month. At the end of the month we have 1 unit remaining in work in process. All materials have been used and the cutting and assembly operations have been completed but the sanding operation is only two-thirds complete. No other operations have been started. At what cost would the semifinished cabinet be carried in work in process if standard costs are being used? With the facts just given and the standard cost card shown in Exhibit 8-1, we can calculate the inventory value of the partially completed oak cabinet.

Inventory Value of Partially Completed Cabinet at Standard Cost

	Standard Cost	Percentage Completed		
Direct materials	\$92.96	100%		\$ 92.96
Direct labor				
Cutting	12.00	100	\$12.00	
Assembly	9.00	100	9.00	
Sanding	6.00	66.7	4.00	
Painting	2.50	0	0	25.00
Applied overhead				
Cutting	24.00	100	24.00	
Assembly	18.00	100	18.00	
Sanding	9.00	66.7	6.00	
Painting	4.00	0	0	43.00
Total inventory value at standard cost				\$160.96

Standard costs are considered acceptable for the valuation of inventories so long as they approximate actual costs. As stated in Accounting Research Bulletin No. 43 of The American Institute of Certified Public Accountants:

> Standard costs are acceptable if adjusted at reasonable intervals to reflect current conditions so that at the balance sheet date standard costs reasonably approximate costs computed under one of the recognized bases. In such cases, descriptive language should be used which will express this relationship, as, for instance, "approximate costs determined on the first-in first-out basis," or if it is desired to mention standard costs, at standard costs, approximating "average costs."

This statement says that in order for us to report inventories on the balance sheet at the standard cost rather than the actual cost, the standard cost must be reasonably close to the actual cost.

Standard Costs and Managerial Accounting

In managerial accounting, standard costs are used to aid management in the following ways:

Management uses of standard costs.

1 Preparation of budgets
2 Developing product strategy
3 Measuring performance

Preparing Budgets The **quantity standards** specify the quantity of direct materials and the hours of direct labor required to produce 1 unit of our finished product. To prepare a budget we have to determine the quantity of direct materials and the amount of direct labor needed to produce a given level of output. Using quantity standards, we simply multiply the quantity standard times the expected level of output. For example, if we plan to produce 1,000 units of the wood cabinets described in Exhibit 8-1, the quantity requirements for direct materials—the oak lumber—would be:

Quantity standard for 1 unit × output = standard input quantities
18 board feet × 1,000 units = 18,000 board feet

We can next determine the total cost of oak lumber by multiplying the total standard input quantities by the price standard as follows:

An example of budgeting material cost.

Standard input quantities × price standard = standard cost of oak lumber for 1,000 cabinets
18,000 board feet × \$5.00 per board foot = \$90,000

Using these same ideas we can calculate the direct labor for the cutting operation required to produce 1,000 oak cabinets as follows:

Quantity standard for 1 unit × output = standard input quantities
2 direct labor hours × 1,000 units = 2,000 direct labor hours

Next, we can determine the total cost of the direct labor in the cutting operation by multiplying the total standard input quantities times the price standard as follows:

An example of budgeting direct labor cost.

Standard input quantities × price standard = standard cost of direct labor—cutting operation for 1,000 cabinets

2,000 direct labor hours × $6.00 per hour = $12,000

These computations can be performed for all direct materials requirements and direct labor operations necessary to manufacture the wood cabinets. How these estimated costs are combined with other cost estimates and revenue estimates to form a budget will be illustrated in Chapter 12 on budgeting. In Chapter 9 we will discuss the use of standard overhead costs for budgeting.

Developing Product Strategy As you may have learned in economics (or from grocery shopping), in a competitive market the price which you can charge for a product depends on the competition's products and prices. If one product is exactly like another in every respect, it will have to sell at the same price as the other product. If a product is different from competing products, it may sell at a different price, a price which reflects the differences (at least in the customer's mind) between the two products, but still related to the price of similar products.

Management must compare estimated costs to estimated revenue to decide which products to produce.

Management must decide which of many possible products they will manufacture and sell. Naturally, they want to use available production resources to sell the most profitable products. This is where cost accounting helps managerial accountants guide management. If the product can be manufactured for a cost which is far enough below the competitive price to yield a satisfactory profit, management will choose to manufacture the product. Standard costs can be very helpful in estimating the cost of manufacturing the product. Usually, there are similar products whose standard costs can be adapted to estimate the cost of producing the new product under consideration.

Similarly, management can use standard costs when modifying a product is being considered. Management would estimate the additional price which customers might be willing to pay for the modified product, and compare the added revenue to the estimated additional cost of making the modification. If added revenue exceeds added cost by a sufficient amount, management would probably modify the product.

Measuring Performance The cost of producing a job or product is affected by many variables, most of which management is expected to control. Without a target or yardstick against which to compare actual cost, management will not know whether or not it is operating efficiently. Since a standard cost represents the cost *we expect to incur to produce 1 unit of our product,* we can compare the actual cost with the standard cost to see if there is a variance (or difference). Any variance from standard cost will indicate to management whether the operations are proceeding as planned or if some corrective action should be initiated. This use of standard costs will be discussed in further detail later in this chapter and in Chapter 16.

Standards provide management with a means of measuring production efficiency

TYPES OF STANDARD COSTS

How difficult should it be for management and the employees to attain the standard cost? Should the standard cost be set at a level that is rarely attained? Or should the standard cost be set at a level that is attainable with a reasonable degree of effort by the employees? Opinions about setting levels for standard costs differ among managers, but standard costs have been classified into three types:

1 A standard cost based on past cost information, referred to as a *historical standard*

2 A standard cost based on "perfect" operating conditions, referred to as a *theoretical standard*

3 A standard cost based on "efficient" operating conditions, referred to as a *currently attainable standard*

Historical Standard

A **historical standard** is based on the quantities and prices which were current at the time the standard cost was developed. It is a historical standard in the sense that the prices or quantities, or both, may have changed since the time the standard cost was calculated. The same quantity standards and price standards (remember, these are the two components of any standard cost) may be used for several years even though there may be gradual changes in production methods and prices. Nevertheless, even though the historical standard is no longer currently exact, it may still identify performance trends and it does simplify the collection of cost data.

A historical standard is less expensive but also less useful.

If production methods and prices have not changed much, the historical standard may be acceptable for inventory valuation. It is less acceptable for budgeting or product strategy. The major advantage of this type of standard cost (which is also called a basic standard) is that it is the least expensive of the three types to establish and once established it is inexpensive to maintain because it is seldom revised.

Theoretical Standard

Theoretical standards represent the lowest possible cost that could be attained under "ideal conditions"; by ideal conditions we mean using the least amount of materials and labor at the lowest possible available prices, the most efficient possible production methods, and assuming that everything goes right and nothing goes wrong in production—thus a "theoretical" standard.

A theoretical standard is expensive and still has limited use.

A theoretical standard cost would simplify cost collection and some managers feel that employees will perform efficiently if they strive toward a "high" goal. But because theoretical standard costs represent in theory the lowest costs that can be attained in a world of perfect performance and highest efficiency, which is certainly not the way it is in the real world, you would not want to use theoretical standard costs for valuing inventories, preparing budgets, or developing a product strategy. A theoretical standard represents an extreme limit, the opposite of a historical standard.

Currently Attainable Standard

Currently attainable standards represent standard costs that fall somewhere between theoretical standards and historical standards. Currently attainable standards represent current costs to be expected from efficient operations; these standards do not anticipate ideal performance of operations implicit in theoretical standards. Currently attainable standards include an allowance for the cost of normal spoilage, the cost of idle time due to machine breakdowns, and the costs of other events which are unavoidable in normal efficient operations.

A currently attainable standard is expensive but has the most uses.

Currently attainable standards require much effort and are expensive to develop. They are based on engineering estimates, including allowances for less than ideal operations to the extent that they can be anticipated and quantified. Currently attainable standards are the most expensive of the three types of standards to develop, but they are the most accurate and useful, serving both cost accounting inventory valuations as well as the estimates, analyses, and decision making in managerial accounting.

Since currently attainable standards provide the most benefits to management you should assume throughout this book that when we refer to standards we mean currently attainable standards.

DIRECT MATERIALS STANDARDS

A direct material standard cost, like all standard costs, consists of two components—a quantity standard and a price standard. The quantity standard represents the quantity of direct materials that goes into making 1 unit of the product. The price standard represents the dollars the company expects to pay per measure of direct materials. The standard cost per unit of finished product is the quantity standard times the price standard.

Establishing the Quantity Standards for Direct Materials

Quantity standards for direct materials are generally based on information provided by the design department or the engineering department which specifies how the product is to be produced. These engineering or design specifications are analyzed by engineers to determine what kind of material is needed, how much of it, and which production methods are necessary to produce the product.

The quantity standard for direct materials includes allowances for normal shrinkage and spoilage. For example: In a chemical process 1.2 gallons of input might be necessary to produce 1 gallon of output. The shrinkage of 0.2 gallons is the result of normal evaporation in the manufacturing process. The quantity standard in this example would be 1.2 gallons of input for each gallon of output.

For new products a pilot run of the manufacturing process may be required to establish the quantity standard. A pilot run is a test of the manufacturing process before full-scale production is started. For products that have already been manufactured in prior periods, the historical pattern of how much material was used during normal operations can be used to check the reasonableness of a quantity standard established by engineering analysis.

Establishing the Price Standards for Direct Materials

The materials price standard represents the price the company expects to pay per measure of direct materials during the current period. The price standard is usually set by the purchasing department which bases it on discounts expected on the quantities of direct materials the company intends to purchase; also included in the price standard are any freight or shipping costs the company will have to pay to obtain the materials.

Because prices are subject to many factors, establishing price standards for direct materials requires keen forecasting of quantities of direct materials needed, an awareness of the current supply and demand conditions affecting the prices of direct materials, as well as the most economical ways of shipping the materials needed.

Calculating Variances for Direct Materials

Once the quantity standard and price standard have been established, you then have a basis for judging actual costs. You can compare actual costs with costs that were planned through the standards. This comparison is an essential part of the performance measurement objective. (We discussed this earlier and will again in Chapter 16 in more detail.) This comparison is also necessary to calculate variances—differences between actual cost and standard cost—for the journal entries in the general ledger.

Variances from direct materials standards can result only from either or both of two sources:

Direct materials variances can result only from price differences or quantity differences.

1 Differences between actual prices paid for direct materials and previously established standard prices for direct materials

2 Differences between total actual quantities of direct materials used to manufacture the product and previously established standard quantities to manufacture the product

Each of these variances is isolated from the other and calculated separately, and (not surprisingly) one is called the **price variance** and the other the **quantity variance.**

The following data will be used in the next two sections to illustrate the calculation of quantity variances in direct materials and price variances in direct materials.

Standard data:		
Standard price per pound of direct materials	$3.00	per pound
Standard quantity of direct materials per unit of product	× 2	pounds per unit of product
Standard direct materials cost	$6.00	per unit of product
Actual data:		
Pounds of direct materials purchased	7,000	pounds
Price per pound of direct materials	× $3.10	per pound
Total actual cost of purchases	$21,700	
Units of product manufactured	3,000	
Total pounds of direct materials used to produce the 3,000 units	5,800	pounds

Quantity Variances: Direct Materials An unfavorable quantity variance means that more direct materials were used than expected and that means there was abnormal spoilage or inefficient use of direct materials. A favorable quantity variance means that less direct materials were used than expected (a pleasant experience).

To calculate the quantity variance for direct materials we first want to compare the total actual quantity of direct materials used this period with the total standard quantity of direct materials allowed for this period. The total standard quantity of direct materials allowed is calculated from the standard quantity per unit of product (from the standard cost card) multiplied by the actual number of units manufactured during the accounting period.

The total standard quantity of direct materials allowed is the amount of direct materials which should have been used given the actual output.

$$\text{Total standard quantity of direct materials allowed} = \left(\text{standard quantity of direct materials per unit}\right) \times \left(\text{units of product manufactured this period}\right)$$

The total standard quantity of direct materials allowed this period answers the question, "How much direct materials should have been used given the number of units of product manufactured this period?" Notice that this may be different than the quantity of direct materials budgeted to be used this period since the budgeted quantity would be based on the planned units of product manufactured this period rather than the actual number of units of product manufactured.

For our example the total standard quantity of direct materials allowed for this period is calculated as:

$$\text{Total standard quantity of direct materials allowed} = \left(\text{2 pounds of direct materials per unit}\right) \times \left(\text{3,000 units of product manufactured}\right)$$
$$= \text{6,000 pounds of direct materials}$$

After calculating the total standard quantity of direct materials allowed, we can take the second step in calculating the quantity variance: We compare and find the difference between the total actual quantity of direct materials used and the total standard quantity of direct materials allowed. Multiplying the difference by the standard price per measure of direct materials will represent the quantity variance as a variance in dollar value.

A quantity variance is favorable when the total actual quantity of direct materials used is less than the total standard quantity allowed.

$$\text{Quantity variance: direct materials (dollar value)} = \left(\text{total actual quantity of direct materials used} - \text{total standard quantity of direct materials allowed}\right) \times \text{standard price per measure of direct materials}$$

The standard price per measure of direct materials is shown on the standard cost card and it reflects the expected price to be paid per measure of direct materials. The standard price is used to calculate the dollar value of the quantity variance rather than the actual price paid for the direct materials for this reason: consistency. Standard price is consistent over time; actual price is not. Therefore, "variations" in quantity variance over different accounting periods will reflect only changes in efficiency, not changes in actual prices—and that is the key to quantity variances. (We have price variances to reflect changes in actual price.)

For our example the dollar value of the quantity variance is:

$$\text{Quantity variance: direct materials (in dollars)} = (\text{5,800 pounds} - \text{6,000 pounds}) \times \text{\$3.00 per pound}$$
$$= \text{\$600 favorable}$$

This $600 quantity variance is labeled favorable because the total actual quantity of direct materials used was 5,800 pounds which is less than the total standard quantity of direct materials allowed, 6,000 pounds, as calculated by multiplying the number of units actually manufactured times the standard quantity of direct materials per unit of product. In other words, 200 pounds of direct materials was not needed (possibly due to some manufacturing efficiency which occurred this period) and these 200 pounds had a standard value of $600.

Price Variance: Direct Materials To calculate the price variance, we compare the actual price paid per pound of direct materials to the standard price per pound. This difference per pound is then multiplied by the actual quantity of direct materials purchased; this multiplication yields the total dollar amount saved or expended as a result of the price differential (between actual and standard). The computation for the price variance, which is sometimes referred to as the purchase price variance for direct materials, is shown as follows:

$$\textbf{Price variance: direct materials} = \left(\begin{array}{l}\textbf{actual price}\\ \textbf{paid per}\\ \textbf{pound of di-}\\ \textbf{rect materials}\end{array} - \begin{array}{l}\textbf{standard price}\\ \textbf{per pound of}\\ \textbf{direct}\\ \textbf{materials}\end{array}\right) \times \begin{array}{l}\textbf{actual}\\ \textbf{quantity}\\ \textbf{of direct}\\ \textbf{materials}\\ \textbf{purchased}\end{array}$$

Remember: The standard price per pound of direct materials is an "educated" estimate which was established much earlier and recorded on the standard cost card, and that is where it can be found. The quantity of direct materials pounds purchased is recorded on the accounting reports of direct materials purchased this period.

For our example, the price variance computation can be illustrated from the data given earlier.

A price variance is unfavorable when the actual price per measure exceeds the standard price per measure.

$$\begin{aligned}\textbf{Price variance: direct materials} &= (\$3.10 \textbf{ per pound} - \$3.00 \textbf{ per pound}) \times \begin{array}{l}\textbf{7,000}\\ \textbf{pounds}\\ \textbf{purchased}\end{array}\\ &= \underline{\underline{\$700}} \textbf{ unfavorable}\end{aligned}$$

The variance is labeled unfavorable because the actual price paid per pound of direct materials exceeds the standard price per pound.

It is important for you to note that the price variance for direct materials was calculated as the price difference multiplied by the *actual quantity purchased*—not the *actual quantity used.* The price variance for direct materials could have been calculated using *actual quantity used.* However, there are two reasons for calculating price variances for direct materials using the actual quantity *purchased* rather than actual quantity used. First, using the quantity actually purchased offers advantages in record keeping which we will illustrate later. Second, and most important, since *purchase* is an event which precedes *use,* a variance based on quantity purchased is, in essence, an "earlier report" than a variance based on quantity actually used. This is very important because variances are used to measure performance. Therefore, the earlier a variance can be reported, the earlier poor performance can be corrected or good performance expanded.

There are two reasons why a price variance is calculated on quantity purchased rather than on quantity used.

Causes of Direct Materials Variances: Quantities and Prices In general, quantity variances of direct materials may be caused by factors such as using materials

EXHIBIT 8-2
Quantity Variance and Price Variance
Direct Materials

(1)	(2)	(3)	(4)
Total actual quantity of direct material *purchased* × actual price	Total actual quantity of direct material *purchased* × standard price	Total actual quantity of direct material *used* × standard price	Total standard quantity of direct material *allowed* × standard price
7,000 pounds × \$3.10 per pound	7,000 pounds × \$3.00 per pound	5,800 pounds × \$3.00 per pound	6,000 pounds* × \$3.00 per pound
\$21,700	\$21,000	\$17,400	\$18,000
\$700 unfavorable purchase price variance		\$600 favorable quantity variance	

* 3,000 units of product manufactured × 2 pounds per unit = 6,000 pounds

having a different quality from the standard quality, or by careless use of the materials, such as improper setting of machines or handling of materials.

Price variances may be caused by factors such as purchasing materials in different bulk quantities than anticipated by the standard (resulting in different discounts), purchasing qualities of materials different from the standard qualities, or unanticipated increases in price by the supplier.

We will discuss each of these factors in more detail in Chapter 16 which is about reporting for cost control.

Summary: Variances in Direct Materials Exhibit 8-2 summarizes the computation of the price variance and quantity variance for direct materials. Column 1 is the actual cost of the 7,000 pounds of direct materials purchased. Column 2 is the actual pounds of direct materials purchased times the standard price per pound. The difference between columns 1 and 2 is the purchase price variance of \$700 unfavorable. Column 3 is the actual quantity of direct materials used multiplied times the standard price. Column 4 is the standard quantity of direct materials allowed multiplied times the standard price. The \$18,000 in column 4 is referred to as the standard direct materials cost of production. The difference between columns 3 and 4 is the quantity variance in dollars.

The price variance in direct materials is also called the purchase price variance.

The total variance for direct materials reported in the accounting period is the sum of the purchase price variance and the quantity variance. For this example, the total variance for direct materials is \$100 unfavorable computed as follows:

Direct Materials

Purchase price variance	=	**\$700**	**unfavorable**
Quantity variance, direct materials	=	**\$600**	**favorable**
Total variance, direct materials	=	**\$100**	**unfavorable**

DIRECT LABOR STANDARDS

Direct labor standards also consist of two components: a quantity standard and a price standard. The quantity standard for direct labor represents the number of direct labor hours required to produce 1 unit of the finished product. The price standard represents the labor rate the company expects to pay for 1 hour of direct labor.

Establishing the Quantity Standards for Direct Labor

A quantity standard for direct labor represents the expected number of direct labor hours it should take to produce 1 unit of the product. A quantity standard for direct labor is established for each operation necessary to produce the product. Refer back to Exhibit 8-1 and note that we established a separate quantity standard for each of the four direct labor operations necessary to produce the oak cabinet.

The quantity standard for direct labor is established in many companies through the use of an engineering analysis. The engineering analysis would take into consideration the condition and type of equipment workers must use to produce the product, the work conditions, the availability of direct materials, and any and all other factors that might influence the hours it would take an employee to perform a specific manufacturing operation. In establishing the quantity standard for direct labor, allowances must also be made for the cost of normal idle time—the cost of time during which laborers are paid but not working—that might result from fatigue or minor equipment malfunctions. (In a sense, idle time is to direct labor as shrinkage is to direct materials.)

Other methods also used to set quantity standards for direct labor include analysis of historical data as well as intuitive judgments of supervisors and anyone experienced with labor and manufacturing operations. However, the best procedure of setting quantity standards for direct labor is an engineering analysis since it represents a complete study of how labor is used in a particular manufacturing operation.

Establishing the Price Standards for Direct Labor

Labor price standards are established for each skill level with a different rate of pay.

For direct labor there is a price standard, which is actually a labor rate standard, for each level of workers' skill. And for each skill category, the labor rate standard represents the hourly rate the company expects to pay during the year. The labor rate standard is usually set by the personnel department and results from their negotiations with the union representing the factory employees. Labor rate standards are usually fairly accurate because they are based on negotiated contracts that cover specific periods of time, usually extended periods. The labor rate standards are usually revised with changes in the labor union contract.

Calculating Variances for Direct Labor

With direct labor, you can compare the total actual direct labor cost with the total standard cost of production for direct labor. Again this comparison is an essential part of the performance measurement objective and necessary to record the variances in direct labor in the general ledger.

The following data will be used in this section and the next to illustrate the calculation of **quantity variances in direct labor** and **price variances in direct labor.**

Standard data:		
Standard price of direct labor	$ 7.00	per hour
Standard quantity of direct labor per unit of product	× 3.5	hours per unit of product
Standard direct labor cost	$24.50	per unit of product
Actual data:		
Units of product manufactured	3,000	units
Total hours of direct labor worked to produce the 3,000 units	11,000	hours
Price per hour of direct labor	$ 7.10	per hour
Total actual direct labor cost	$78,100	

The total variance for direct labor is the difference between total actual cost of direct labor and total standard cost of direct labor for the units produced in the accounting period. For our example the total variance for direct labor is:

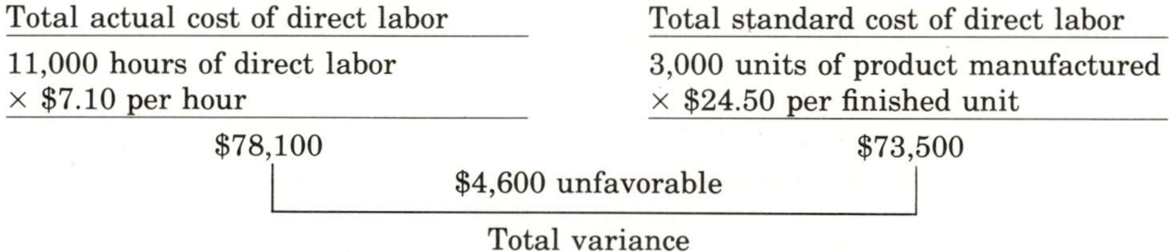

The total variance for direct labor is $4,600 unfavorable. It is unfavorable because the total actual cost of direct labor is greater than the total standard cost.

As with direct materials the total variance for direct labor can result from two sources:

Sources of direct labor variances.

1 An actual direct labor rate, that is the price actually paid for each hour of direct labor, different from the standard direct labor rate

2 Differences between the total actual quantity of direct labor used and the total standard quantity of direct labor allowed, reflecting the efficiency of direct labor use

The variance due to the effect of the price of labor can be calculated separately and isolated from the effect of the variance because of efficiency; and so can the quantity effect be calculated and isolated from the price effect. Direct labor variances are defined and calculated in much the same way as direct materials variances; the quantity measures are hours of direct labor instead of pounds of direct materials; and the prices are labor rates per hour instead of price per pound of direct materials.

Quantity Variance, Direct Labor The quantity variance for direct labor (also called efficiency variance of direct labor) is calculated in two stages. First, the total standard quantity of direct labor *allowed* for the actual number of units of product manufactured this period is calculated and then the direct labor quantity variance itself is calculated.

The direct labor quantity variance is computed in exactly the same two steps as the direct materials quantity variance.

$$\textbf{Total standard quantity of direct labor allowed} = \left(\text{standard quantity of direct labor per unit}\right) \times \left(\text{units of product manufactured this period}\right)$$

$$\textbf{Quantity variance: direct labor (dollar value)} = \left(\text{total actual quantity of direct labor used} - \text{total standard quantity of direct labor allowed}\right) \times \text{standard price per hour of direct labor}$$

The rationale for these equations is clearly the same as for the discussion of the quantity variance for direct materials. For a refresher, return to that section and reread it.

Using the data given to calculate the total direct labor variance and the equations just given we find:

$$\textbf{Total standard quantity of direct labor allowed} = \left(\text{3.5 hours of direct labor per unit}\right) \times \left(\text{3,000 units of product manufactured}\right)$$
$$= \text{10,500 hours of direct labor}$$

$$\textbf{Quantity variance: direct labor (dollar value)} = (\text{11,000 hours} - \text{10,500 hours}) \times \$7.00 \text{ per hour}$$
$$= \$3{,}500 \text{ unfavorable}$$

The quantity variance for direct labor is unfavorable because the total number of labor hours actually used exceeded the total number of hours allowed—total standard quantity of direct labor allowed—to produce the 3,000 units that were manufactured in this period. In other words, 500 more hours of direct labor were used this period than were ordinarily needed to produce the same output. At the standard price for direct labor this would cost the company an extra $3,500.

The cost data for direct materials and cost data for direct labor, as illustrated in these examples, will be brought together in a later section of this chapter which explains how standard costs are recorded in the general ledger accounts.

Price Variances: Direct Labor Price variances for direct labor are calculated in a similar manner as the price variances for direct materials: the direct labor rate—the worker's pay per hour—is the price and the quantity is the total actual number of direct labor hours worked. Because labor prices are usually referred to as labor rates, the price variance for direct labor is often referred to as a rate variance for direct labor.

The price variance for direct labor is the difference between the actual direct labor price, that is the labor rate, and the standard labor price, also expressed as a labor rate, multiplied by the actual direct labor hours worked (purchased). This computation gives the price variance for direct labor in dollars.

The direct labor price variance is computed in exactly the same manner as the direct materials price variance.

$$\textbf{Price variance: direct labor} = \left(\begin{array}{l}\textbf{actual price}\\ \textbf{per hour of}\\ \textbf{direct labor}\end{array} - \begin{array}{l}\textbf{standard price}\\ \textbf{per hour of}\\ \textbf{direct labor}\end{array}\right) \times \begin{array}{l}\textbf{actual quantity}\\ \textbf{of direct labor}\\ \textbf{hours worked}\end{array}$$

$$= (\$7.10 \text{ per hour} - \$7.00 \text{ per hour}) \times 11{,}000 \text{ hours}$$

$$= \underline{\underline{\$1{,}100}} \text{ unfavorable}$$

The standard price per hour of direct labor, in this case, $7 per hour, was predetermined; it usually represents an average wage for workers doing this kind of work and it is recorded on the standard cost card. The actual price is likewise an average wage rate determined by taking from accounting records the total wages for workers this period and dividing it by the total hours worked this period. In this case the variance is unfavorable because the actual price of direct labor per hour is greater than the standard price of direct labor per hour.

Causes of Direct Labor Variances: Quantities and Prices Reports on labor variances in the quantity of labor should be prepared on a timely basis, sometimes daily, so that corrective action can be taken in situations where the cause of the variance can be identified. Some causes of variances in the quantity of labor include: machine breakdowns, poor quality of direct materials (which might require more work than usual), use of an inexperienced employee, and changes in work conditions.

The most frequent cause of variances in the price of direct labor is assigning a worker to do a job whose rate of pay (and perhaps experience) is different from that anticipated when the standard price was established. Other causes of variances in the price of direct labor include: unanticipated changes in the cost of living index (the pay rate for direct labor is adjusted in many companies based on changes in the cost of living index), and changes in labor supply and demand conditions.

As with the direct materials variances we will discuss how to report variances in direct labor in more detail in Chapter 16 on reporting for cost control.

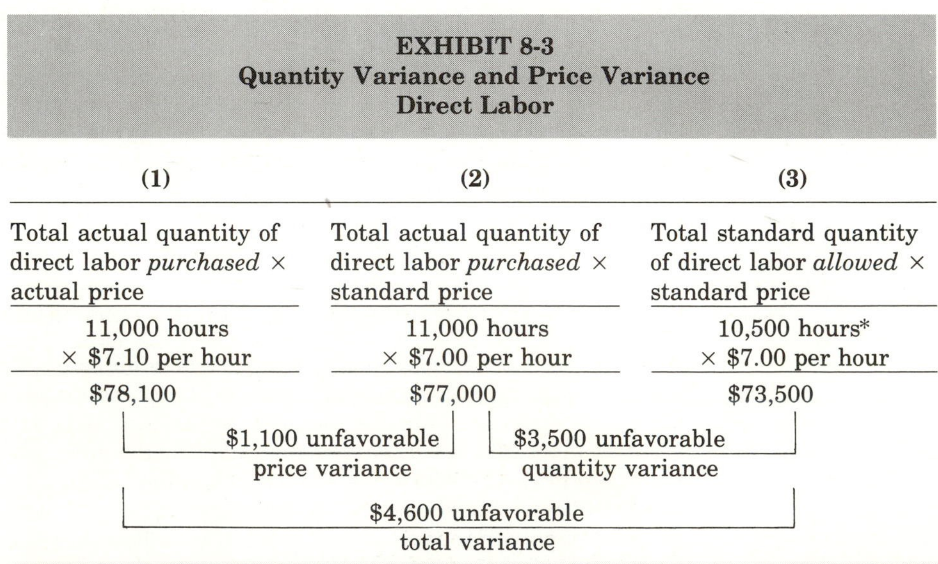

EXHIBIT 8-3
Quantity Variance and Price Variance
Direct Labor

(1)	(2)	(3)
Total actual quantity of direct labor *purchased* × actual price	Total actual quantity of direct labor *purchased* × standard price	Total standard quantity of direct labor *allowed* × standard price
11,000 hours × $7.10 per hour	11,000 hours × $7.00 per hour	10,500 hours* × $7.00 per hour
$78,100	$77,000	$73,500

$1,100 unfavorable price variance (between (1) and (2))

$3,500 unfavorable quantity variance (between (2) and (3))

$4,600 unfavorable total variance (between (1) and (3))

* 3,000 units of product manufactured × 3.5 hours per finished unit.

Summary: Variances in Direct Labor Exhibit 8-3 summarizes the computations of the price variance and quantity variance for direct labor. Column 1 is the actual cost of the direct labor purchased (and used) in the accounting period. Column 2 is the actual quantity of direct labor purchased multiplied by the standard price. The difference between the two columns is the price variance for direct labor. Column 3 is the standard cost of production. The difference between columns 2 and 3 is the quantity variance.

STANDARD COSTS IN THE GENERAL LEDGER

Journal entries in the general ledger are usually made weekly or monthly based on purchase records, direct materials requisitions, direct labor time tickets, and the units of product manufactured.

To illustrate the journal entries for standard costs, we will use the data from the example we continued through this chapter.

Usually a company calculates the price variance for direct materials at the time the direct materials are purchased and separate journal entries are made to record the price variance for direct materials and the quantity variance for direct materials.

Using the data from our previous example, at the *time of purchase* the following journal entry is made:

Materials Inventory	**$21,000**	
(7,000 pounds × $3.00 per pound)		
Price Variance—Direct Materials	**700**	
Accounts Payable		**$21,700**
(7,000 pounds × $3.10 per pound)		
(To record the purchase of 7,000 pounds of direct materials at a cost of $3.10 per pound.)		

Accounts payable is credited for the actual amount owed. Materials inventory is debited for the quantity of materials purchased times the standard price per pound of materials; and a price variance account is either debited or credited to balance the entry.

Usually direct materials price variances are recorded as the material is purchased and the direct materials quantity variance is recorded later as the material is used.

Note that when the price variance for direct materials is calculated at the time the direct materials are purchased the debit for the Materials Inventory account is calculated using the standard price per pound. This simplifies the accounting procedures for the Materials Inventory account. Since the materials are being valued at the standard price we do not have to be concerned with making cost flow assumptions such as average cost or FIFO when the materials are used to produce the product.

The quantity variance for direct materials is recorded in the general ledger on a weekly or monthly basis based on requisitions for direct materials. The journal entry to record the quantity variance for direct materials and the standard direct materials cost of production is:

Work in Process	**$18,000**	
(3,000 units × 2 pounds × $3.00 per pound)		
Quantity Variance—Direct Materials		**$ 600**
Materials Inventory		**17,400**
(5,800 pounds × $3.00 per pound)		
(To record the issue of direct materials for the production of 3,000 units of product.)		

Note in the above two journal entries that favorable variances are represented by credits and unfavorable variances are represented by debits.

The journal entry to record the standard direct labor cost, the price variance for direct labor, and quantity variance for direct labor is:

Direct labor price and quantity variances are usually recorded in the same journal entry.

Work in Process	**$73,500**	
(3,000 units × 3.5 hours × $7.00 per hour)		
Quantity Variance—Direct Labor	**3,500**	
Price Variance—Direct Labor	**1,100**	
Payroll		**$78,100**
(11,000 hours × $7.10 per hour)		
(To distribute the payroll costs to work in process and the variance accounts for direct labor.)		

Work in process is debited for the standard direct labor cost of production—3,000 units × 3.5 hours per unit × $7.00 per hour. The quantity variance and price variance for direct labor, as calculated before, are recorded, and the payroll account is closed.

The journal entry to record the completion of the 3,000 units of product is:

Completed units are transferred from work in process to finished goods using the standard cost per finished unit.

Finished Goods	**$91,500**	
Work in Process		**$91,500**
(To record the standard cost of 3,000 completed units at a standard cost per unit of $6.00 for direct materials and $24.50 for direct labor.)		

The above journal entry transfers the standard cost of the direct materials and direct labor from the Work in Process account to the Finished Goods account. These entries are summarized below in T accounts.

Materials Inventory

Debit	Credit
(1) $21,000	$17,400 (2)

Work in Process

Debit	Credit
(2) $18,000	$91,500 (4)
(3) $73,500	

Finished Goods

Debit	Credit
(4) $91,500	

Accounts Payable

Debit	Credit
	$21,700 (1)

Payroll

Debit	Credit
	$78,100 (3)

Price Variance—Direct Materials

Debit	Credit
	$700 (1)

Quality Variance—Direct Materials

Debit	Credit
	$ 600 (2)

Price Variance—Direct Labor

Debit	Credit
(3) $1,100	

Quantity Variance—Direct Labor

Debit	Credit
(3) $3,500	

GRAPHICAL ANALYSIS OF VARIANCES: DIRECT MATERIALS AND DIRECT LABOR

The variances for direct materials and direct labor discussed in our previous examples are illustrated graphically in Exhibit 8-4. The graphs in Exhibit 8-4 have quantities represented on the horizontal axis and prices on the vertical axis. Graphs *a* and *b* in Exhibit 8-4 represent the variances for direct materials. Graph *c* shows the variances associated with direct labor.

EXHIBIT 8-4
Graphic Illustration of Price and Quantity Variances

Direct Material

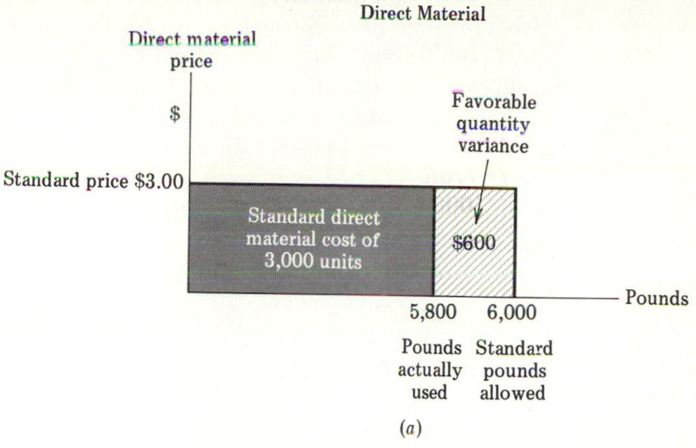

(a)

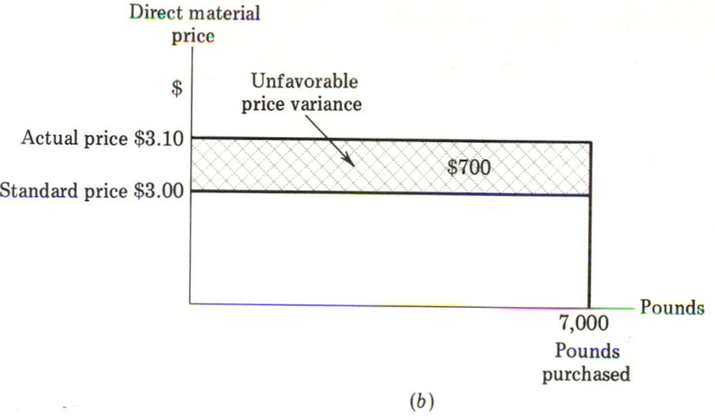

(b)

Direct Labor

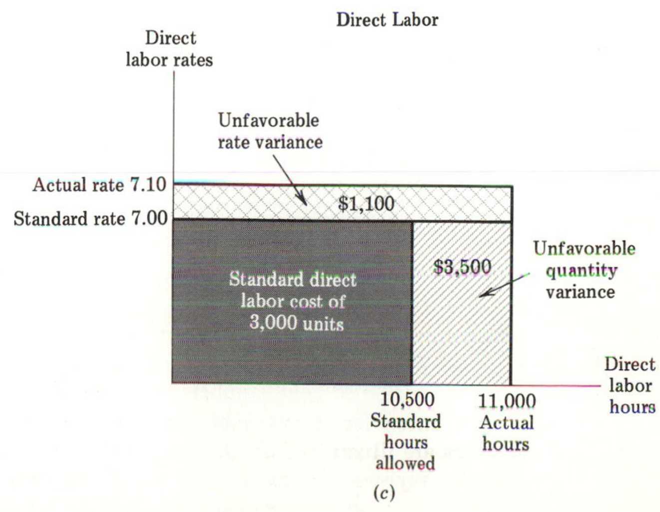

(c)

In graph *a* for direct materials the area shaded gray and bounded by the standard price per pound = \$3.00 and the standard pounds allowed = 6,000 represents the total standard direct material cost of producing 3,000 units of product.

The favorable quantity variance for direct materials is represented by the area with diagonal lines formed by the difference between the actual pounds used = 5,800 pounds, and the standard pounds allowed = 6,000 pounds, multiplied by the standard price per pound = \$3.00, thus 200 pounds × \$3.00 per pound = \$600 favorable materials quantity variance.

The price variance for direct materials shown in graph *b* is represented by the double cross-hatched area bounded by the difference between the standard price per pound = \$3.00 and the actual price per pound = \$3.10, multiplied times the actual pounds purchased, thus \$.10 per pound × 7,000 pounds = \$700 unfavorable.

The variances for direct labor are illustrated graphically in graph *c* of Exhibit 8-4. Direct labor variances can be illustrated on a single graph because the quantity of direct labor purchased and the quantity used must be the same. It is impossible to inventory unused direct labor hours. The standard cost of producing 3,000 units of product is represented by the area bounded by the standard labor rate = \$7.00 and the standard hours allowed = 10,500.

The quantity variance for direct labor is represented by the cross-hatched area formed by the difference between the standard hours allowed = 10,500 hours, and the actual hours used = 11,000 hours, the difference is multiplied by the standard direct labor rate = \$7.00, thus 500 hours × \$7.00 per hour = \$3,500 unfavorable labor quantity variance.

The rate variance for direct labor is represented by the double cross-hatched area formed by the difference between the actual direct labor rate = \$7.10 and the standard direct labor rate = \$7.00, the difference is multiplied by the actual direct labor hours purchased thus, \$.10 per hour × 11,000 hours = \$1,100 unfavorable.

SUMMARY

A standard cost consists of two components:

1 A quantity standard

2 A price standard

The **quantity standard** represents the expected amount of direct materials and the expected hours of direct labor necessary to produce 1 unit of finished product. The **price standard** represents the dollar amount management expects to pay for each measure of direct materials and the dollar amount management expects to pay for each hour of direct labor. The quantity standard and price standard are itemized on a separate standard cost card for each product the company manufactures.

Standard costs are relevant for both cost accounting and managerial accounting. In cost accounting we use standard costs to (1) simplify the collection of cost data and (2) to value inventories. In managerial accounting we use standard costs (1) to aid in the preparation of budgets, (2) to provide data for developing product strategy, and (3) to measure performance.

There are three types of standards used by manufacturing firms. Historical standards are costs which were current when the standard was developed but are updated only rarely. Theoretical standards represent the lowest cost that could be attained under perfect operating conditions. Currently attainable standards reflect the expected cost under normal operating conditions. Most companies use currently attainable standards even though they are most expensive to develop since they best satisfy the objectives of both cost and managerial accounting.

Variances for direct materials and direct labor are separated into two categories: price variance and quantity variance. The price variance for direct materials is based on the difference between the actual price of direct materials and the expected price which is the standard price. The quantity variance for direct materials is based on the difference between the actual quantity of direct materials used and the standard quantity of direct materials allowed. The price variance for direct labor, often called the rate variance, is based on the difference between the actual hourly cost of labor and the standard labor rate. The quantity variance for direct labor, which is a gauge of efficiency, arises when the actual labor hours are different from the standard direct labor hours allowed.

A standard cost bookkeeping system keeps inventories at standard cost by recording both price variances and quantity variances in separate accounts.

Review Problem

The Sanford Manufacturing Company produces a complete line of skis and ski equipment. The company recently developed standards for one particular ski, the XK10. The standard costs for one set of XK10 skis are shown below.

Standard Cost Card
One Set of XK10 Skis

8 pounds of fiberglass @ $1.50/pound	$12.00
4 direct labor hours @ $10.00/hour	40.00
Total direct materials and direct labor	$52.00

During the month of November, Sanford purchased 9,500 pounds of fiberglass for $15,200 and used 7,850 pounds in the production of 950 pairs of skis. The direct labor used during the month amounted to 3,420 hours and cost $33,516.

Required

1 Calculate the variances for direct materials and the variances for direct labor for the month of November. The price variance for direct materials is recognized at the time of purchase.

2 Prepare journal entries to record the standard costs and variances.

Solution

1 Calculation of Variances

Direct Materials

Total Actual Quantity of Direct Materials *Purchased* × Actual Price	**Total Actual Quantity of Direct Materials *Purchased* × Standard Price**	**Total Actual Quantity of Direct Materials *Used* × Standard Price**	**Total Standard Quantity of Direct Materials *Allowed* × Standard Price**
9,500 pounds @ $1.60/pound	9,500 pounds @ $1.50/pound	7,850 pounds @ $1.50/pound	*7,600 pounds @ $1.50/pound
$15,200	$14,250	$11,775	$11,400
$950 unfavorable Price variance		$375 unfavorable Quantity variance	

* Standard quantity allowed = 950 finished units × 8 pounds per unit = 7,600 pounds.

Direct Labor

Total Actual Quantity of Direct Labor *Used* × Actual Price	**Total Actual Quantity of Direct Labor *Used* × Standard Price**	**Total Standard Quantity of Direct Labor *Allowed* × Standard Price**
3,420 hours @ $9.80/hour	3,420 hours @ $10.00/hour	*3,800 hours @ $10.00/hour
$33,516	$34,200	$38,000

$684 favorable — Price variance

$3,800 favorable — Quantity variance

* Standard quantity allowed = 950 finished units × 4 hours per unit = 3,800.

2 Journal Entries

		Debit	Credit
1	**Materials Inventory**	**$14,250**	
	Price Variance—Direct Materials	**950**	
	Accounts Payable		**$15,200**
	(To record the purchase of 9,500 pounds of fiberglass.)		
2	**Work in Process**	**$11,400**	
	Quantity Variance—Direct Materials	**375**	
	Materials Inventory		**$11,775**
	(To record the issue of the direct materials to produce 950 sets of XK10 skis.)		
3	**Work in Process**	**$38,000**	
	Price Variance—Direct Labor		**$ 684**
	Quantity Variance—Direct Labor		**3,800**
	Payroll		**33,516**
	(To distribute the payroll costs to work in process and the variance accounts for direct labor.)		
4	**Finished Goods**	**$49,400**	
	Work in Process		**$49,400**
	(To record the completion of 950 sets of XK10 skis at a standard cost of $52.00 per set.)		

Glossary

Currently attainable standard cost The cost management expects to incur for efficient production operations. This level of standard includes an allowance for normal spoilage and expected idle time because of normal malfunctions in the production process.

Historical standard cost An expected cost based on historical data that once established is infrequently changed. This level of standard is primarily used to simplify the bookkeeping procedures.

Price standard The dollar amount we expect to pay for 1 hour of direct labor or one measure of direct materials.

Price variance—direct labor The difference between the actual price per hour of direct labor and the standard price per hour of direct labor multiplied by the actual quantity of direct labor hours worked (purchased).

Price variance—direct materials The difference between the actual price paid per measure of direct materials and the standard price per measure of direct materials multiplied by the actual quantity of direct materials purchased.

Quantity standard The expected amount of direct materials and the expected number of direct labor hours necessary to produce 1 unit of finished product.

Quantity variance—direct labor The difference between the total actual quantity of direct labor used and the total standard quantity of direct labor allowed multiplied by the standard price per hour of direct labor.

Quantity variance—direct materials The difference between the total quantity of direct materials used and the total standard quantity of direct materials allowed multiplied by the standard price per measure of direct materials.

Standard cost The expected cost of 1 unit of product calculated by multiplying the quantity standard times the price standard.

Standard quantity allowed The amount of direct materials or direct labor hours that should have been used to produce the actual output. It is calculated by multiplying the quantity standard times the actual number of units produced.

Theoretical standard cost An expected cost that represents the lowest possible cost under ideal operating conditions.

Questions and Problems

8-1 Define the two components of a standard cost.

8-2 List and discuss briefly five reasons a company would use standard costs.

8-3 What are the advantages of using a currently attainable standard as opposed to a theoretical standard?

8-4 How are the quantity standards established for materials and labor costs?

8-5 How are the price standards set for materials and labor costs?

8-6 List three possible causes of a materials quantity variance not mentioned in the chapter. Explain how each cause would result in either a favorable or unfavorable variance.

8-7 Why is the materials price variance generally calculated using quantities purchased rather than quantities used?

8-8 **Material Price Variance Based on Usage** Home Company manufactures tables with vinyl tops. The standard materials cost for the vinyl used per Type-R table is $7.80 based on 6 square feet of vinyl at a price of $1.30 per square foot. A production run of 1,000 tables in January resulted in usage of 6,400 square feet of vinyl at a price of $1.20 per square foot, a total cost of $7,680.

Required

Calculate the materials price variance and the materials quantity variance.

(CPA)

8-9 Variance Computation The Creebler Cookie Company produces peanut butter cookies. Standard costs for 1,000 dozen cookies are as follows:

Direct materials			
Flour	300 pounds	@ 20¢ per pound	$ 60.00
Sugar	100 pounds	@ 25¢ per pound	25.00
Peanut butter	25 pounds	@ 95¢ per pound	23.75
Eggs	1,920 eggs	@ 58¢ per dozen	92.80
			$ 201.55
Direct labor			
450 elf hours @ $1.90/elf hour			855.00
			$1,056.55

Results for the company's first month of operation showed:

1. 12,000 cookies were produced.
2. One elf quit his job after 3 days (24 hours). The remaining elves worked a total of 396 hours. Actual wages paid were $2.00/elf hour.
3. Actual purchases of direct materials during the month were:

Flour	500 pounds	@ 18¢ per pound
Sugar	100 pounds	@ 29¢ per pound
Peanut butter	30 pounds	@ 95¢ per pound
Eggs	2,400 eggs	@ 56¢ per dozen

4. Direct materials remaining in inventory at the end of the month were:

Flour	220 pounds
Sugar	None
Peanut butter	5 pounds
Eggs	420

5. There were no cookies-in-progress at the end of the month.

Required

1 Compute all direct material and direct labor variances for the first month.

2 Show that the sum of the individual direct labor variances equals the total direct labor variance (difference between total standard cost and total actual cost).

(G. Clark)

8-10 Journal Entries Sixco produces a single product for which the following standard costs have been established.

Direct materials	4 pounds @ $1.10/pound	$4.40
Direct labor	⅓ hour @ $6/hour	2.00

During a particular period the following events took place.

Purchased 4,000 pounds of direct materials paying $4,650
Used 3,800 pounds of direct materials
Purchased 320 hours of direct labor paying $1,760
Produced 900 units

Required Prepare journal entries to record the manufacturing variances for direct materials and direct labor. The direct materials price variance is recognized at the time of purchase.

8-11 Variance Computation Dr. Y. Bottoms has recently invented a revolutionary new diaper. Based on the principle of avoidance conditioning, this diaper houses a small moisture-sensitive electric current capable of producing a small shock when wet. Dr. Bottoms' theory is that this diaper will result in the rapid extinction of a form of behavior peculiar to small babies.

In anticipation of tremendous demand for his product (although field testing is still in progress), Dr. Bottoms has developed a standard cost for the production of 10,000 diapers as follows:

Direct materials:	
10,000 yards cotton cloth @ $0.30	$ 3,000
15,000 feet copper wire @ $0.27	4,050
10,000 small watch batteries @ $1.25	12,500
Direct labor:	
12,500 hours @ $3.40	42,500
Total	$62,050

During the first month of production, the Dr. Y. Bottoms Company produced 9,500 diapers.

Actual costs were as follows:

Direct materials:	
9,000 yards of cotton cloth @ $0.29	$ 2,610
14,250 feet copper wire @ $0.28	3,990
9,500 batteries @ $0.98	9,310
Direct labor:	
12,000 hours @ $3.45	41,400
Total	$57,310

Required Compute the material and labor variances.

(G. Clark)

8-12 Variance Computation and Journal Entries The Hay Company manufactures widgets and has developed the following standards for direct materials and direct labor for one widget:

Direct materials 12 pounds @ $2.50	$30.00
Direct labor 5 hours @ $3.00	$15.00
Total	$45.00

During the year 14,700 units were completed. However, 15,000 units were budgeted for production.

The actual results showed:

Direct materials: 180,000 pounds used
Direct labor: 72,000 hours used
Direct labor cost: $223,200
Purchases: 200,000 pounds of direct material @ $2.40: $480,000

Required

1 Calculate all direct materials and direct labor variances.

2 Prepare journal entries to record the above data.

8-13 Standard Cost Journal Entries The Pall Company uses a standard costing system. During the past year the following transactions occurred:

Purchases—actual cost	$ 98,750
Purchases—standard cost	$100,000
Direct materials used—standard cost	$ 90,000
Direct labor—actual cost	$182,000
Direct labor hours used—standard cost	$180,000
Standard cost of units finished	
Direct materials	$ 75,000
Direct labor	$150,000
Standard cost of goods sold	
Direct materials	$ 70,000
Direct labor	$140,000
Ending work in process—standard cost	
Direct materials	$ 10,000
Direct labor	$ 20,000

There were no beginning inventories.

Required

Calculate the price variances and quantity variances for direct materials and direct labor. (*Hint:* Use T accounts to analyze the data.)

8-14 Variance Computation Ross Shirts, Inc., manufactures short- and long-sleeve men's shirts for large stores. Ross produces a single quality shirt in lots to each customer's order and attaches the store's label to each. The standard costs for a dozen long-sleeve shirts are:

Direct materials	24 yards @ $2.20	$52.80
Direct labor	3 hours @ $9.80	29.40

During October Ross worked on three orders for long-sleeve shirts. Job cost records for the month disclose the following:

Lot	Units in Lot	Material Used	Hours Worked
30	1,000 dozen	24,100 yards	2,980
31	1,700 dozen	40,440 yards	5,130
32	1,200 dozen	28,825 yards	2,890

The following information is also available:

1 Ross purchased 95,000 yards of direct materials during the month at a cost of $212,800. The direct materials price variance is recorded when goods are purchased and all inventories are carried at standard cost.

2 Direct labor incurred amounted to $110,000 during October. According to payroll records, production employees were paid $10 per hour.

3 There was no work in process at October 1. During October lots 30 and

31 were completed, all direct material was issued for lot 32, and it was 80% completed as to direct labor.

Required

1 Prepare a schedule computing the standard direct materials and direct labor cost for October of lots 30, 31, and 32.

2 Prepare a schedule computing the direct materials price variance for October and indicate whether the variance is favorable or unfavorable.

3 Prepare schedules computing (and indicating whether the variances are favorable, or unfavorable), for each lot produced during October, the:

a direct materials quantity variance
b direct labor efficiency variance
c direct labor rate (price) variance in dollars

(CPA)

8-15 Computation of Standard and Actual Quantities from Variances On May 1, 19X5, Bovar Company began the manufacture of a new mechanical device known as "Dandy." The company installed a standard cost system in accounting for manufacturing costs. The standard costs for a unit of "Dandy" are as follows:

Direct materials	6 pounds at $1 per pound	$6.00
Direct labor	1 hour at $4 per hour	4.00

The following data were obtained from Bovar's records for the month of May:

	Units
Actual production of "Dandy"	4,000
Units sold of "Dandy"	2,500

	Debit	Credit
Sales		$50,000
Purchases (26,000 pounds)	$27,300	
Direct materials price variance	1,300	
Direct materials quantity variance	1,000	
Direct labor price variance	760	
Direct labor quantity variance		800

The amount shown above for materials price variance is applicable to raw materials purchased during May.

Required

Compute each of the following items for Bovar for the month of May. Show computations in good form.

1 Standard quantity of direct materials allowed (in pounds)

2 Actual quantity of direct materials used (in pounds)

3 Standard direct labor hours allowed

4 Actual hours worked

5 Actual direct labor rate

(CPA)

8-16 Computation of Standard Quantities from Variances The Valpo Bows & Knots Company engages in the massive production of shoelaces. The company employs four skilled laborers whose primary tasks are to cut the shoecord into appropriate lengths and apply a molten plastic coating to each end for ease in threading.

Given the following information, determine:

1 The standard quantity allowed for molten plastic for 100,000 shoelaces

2 The wage increase received by the tip-dippers

3 The standard hours allowed for cordcutters

4 The standard quantity allowed for cord for 100,000 shoelaces

Variances for the month of September were:

Materials price variance	$719.20	U
Labor price variance	26.00	U
Materials quantity variance		
Cord	100.00	F
Plastic	3.00	F
Labor quantity variance	17.51	F
Total variance	$624.69	U

1 The actual price of the shoelace cord used in September was $.025.

2 The company actually used 5,000 less feet of cord than the standard allowed.

3 Tip-dippers complained of the complexity of their task and threatened to strike. Consequently, their wages were increased as of September 1. Their production quantity did not vary from standard.

4 Cordcutters were paid at the standard rate of $3.75 per hour during September. They completed cutting the 100,000 laces in 95 hours, 20 minutes.

5 Standard hours allowed the tip-dippers were 200 at a standard rate of $5.25.

6 The standard cost for molten plastic was $30 per gallon. During September, the company used 2.9 gallons at a total actual cost of $81.20.

(G. Clark)

8-17 Variance Computation On March 1, the Aqua-Seat Company began manufacturing a unique lounge chair based on the principle of the waterbed. The company has established the following standards for direct materials and direct labor:

Direct materials:	
7 yards of floral print plastic @ $3.25	$22.75
1 2-way water-tight valve @ $1.00	1.00
6 feet metal tubing @ .75	4.50
Direct labor	
6 hours @ $4.25	25.50
Total	$53.75

During March, 1,500 chairs were produced, although the budget had provided for only 1,250.

Direct materials used in March were:	
11,000 yards of plastic @ $3.20	$35,200.00
1,499 valves @ $1.02	1,528.98
8,500 feet of metal tubing @ $.75	6,375.00
Direct labor used in March:	
6,000 hours @ $3.75	22,500.00
Total	$65,603.98

There was no work in process at the end of March.

Required

1 Compute all direct materials and direct labor variances.

2 What are the possible implications of the direct labor variance?

(G. Clark)

8-18 Variance Computation and Journal Entries Following extensive market research and feasibility of production studies, Mr. Base has founded the Edible Tableware Company of Kansas, Inc. To spare millions of housepersons from the drudgery of dishwashing and the preparation of nightly desserts, the company manufactures edible tableware in five popular flavors. Final products include plates, forks, spoons, and knives. Standard costs for each four-piece set, as determined by Mr. Base, are:

Direct materials	8 ounces @ $.04	$ .32
Direct labor	.25 hours @ $4.00	1.00

In January, the company produced 3,000 sets. This required 1,700 pounds of direct materials and 720 direct labor hours. The direct materials actually cost $.035 per ounce. Direct labor rates were actually $3.85 per hour.

Required

1 Calculate all direct materials and direct labor variances.

2 Prepare journal entries to record the above data.

(G. Clark)

8-19 Standard Costs and Job Order Costing The Jones job shop produces a wide variety of products. Many of the products are produced in sufficient quantities to justify a standard cost system. The standard cost card for one of the products is shown below:

Standard Cost
Product XLX30

Material			
Type	**Quantity**	**Price**	**Standard Cost**
A	10 pounds	$2.50	$25.00
B	8 pounds	$3.00	$24.00
C	6 pounds	$1.50	$ 9.00
Total material cost			$58.00

Labor

Operation	Hours	Price	Standard Cost
1	2.0	$12.00	$ 24.00
3	3.0	$12.60	$ 37.80
4	1.5	$18.00	$ 27.00
7	2.0	$ 9.00	$ 18.00
Total labor cost			$106.80

During the past year the company records showed raw materials purchases of:

Material	Quantity	Cost
A	100,000 pounds	$258,000
B	70,000 pounds	$205,000
C	70,000 pounds	$112,500

Jobs 108, 121, and 145 called for the production of 2,000, 3,000, and 2,500 units of product XLX30, respectively. All units were produced and the job cost sheets revealed the following information:

Actual Usage

	Material Units			Labor Hours			
Job	A	B	C	1	3	4	7
108	20,580	15,850	12,870	4,150	5,800	3,050	4,250
121	29,700	24,650	18,500	5,850	8,700	4,500	5,900
145	24,650	21,210	14,350	5,150	7,200	3,748	5,000

The actual labor rates for the operations were:

Operation	Labor Rate
1	$12.30
3	12.75
4	17.40
7	8.85

Required

Prepare journal entries for the above data assuming the materials price variance is isolated at the time of purchase and that the work in process inventories are carried at standard. For all journal entries support your answer with a detailed analysis of variances by job.

8-20 Variance Computation; Journal Entries The Smith Company uses a standard cost system. The standards are based on a budget for operations at the rate of production anticipated for the current period. The company records, in its general ledger, variations in materials prices and usage, wage rates, and labor efficiency.

Current standards are as follows:

Materials:	
Material A	$1.20 per unit
Material B	$2.60 per unit
Direct labor	$8.20 per hour

	Special Widgets	De Luxe Widgets
Finished products (content of each unit):		
Material A	12 units	12 units
Material B	6 units	8 units
Direct labor	14 hours	20 hours

The general ledger does not include a finished goods inventory account; costs are transferred directly from work in process to cost of sales at the time finished products are sold.

The budget and operating data for the month of August 19X8 are summarized below:

Budget:		
Projected direct labor hours		(hours) 9,000
Selling expenses		$4,000
Administrative expenses		$7,500
Operating data:		
Sales:		
500 special widgets		$52,700
100 deluxe widgets		$16,400
Purchases:		
Material A	8,500 units	$9,725
Material B	1,800 units	$5,635
Material requisitions:	**Material A**	**Material B**
Issued from stores:		
Standard quantity	8,400 units	3,200 units
Over standard	400 units	150 units
Returned to stores	75 units	

Direct labor hours:		
Standard		9,600 hours
Actual		10,000 hours
Wages paid:		
500 hours at	$8.40	
8,000 hours at	8.00	
1,500 hours at	7.60	
Expenses:		
Selling	$3,250	
Administrative	$6,460	

Required

Prepare journal entries to record operations for the month of August 19X8. Show computations of the amounts used in each journal entry. Materials purchases are recorded at standard.

(CPA)

STANDARD MANUFACTURING OVERHEAD COSTS

AFTER COMPLETING YOUR STUDY OF THIS CHAPTER, YOU SHOULD HAVE LEARNED:

1 What flexible budgeting is and how it differs from static budgeting.

2 How to analyze the total manufacturing overhead variance—overapplied or underapplied overhead.

3 How the concept of flexible budgeting enables us to separate the overapplied or underapplied manufacturing overhead into a volume variance and a budget variance, and that a budget variance can be further separated into a spending variance and an efficiency variance.

4 How to journalize the manufacturing overhead costs.

The three component costs of a product are direct materials cost, direct labor cost, and manufacturing overhead cost. In the preceding chapter we discussed how standard costs are established and used to assign direct materials and direct labor costs to units of production. We also illustrated how price variance and quantity variance were calculated and their role in cost accounting. This chapter focuses on the third component of the cost of a product: manufacturing overhead.

In determining standard direct materials costs and standard direct labor costs, engineering estimates are commonly used. These costs are based on estimates of the required quantities of materials and labor and the lowest available prices for the quality of materials and labor needed to do the job. We can calculate standard manufacturing overhead cost in the same way. But we do not. We do not because manufacturing overhead cost is comprised of many component costs, and to compile engineering estimates for each component cost would be very expensive. Instead, we determine standard manufacturing overhead cost by analyzing past actual output volumes and the actual manufacturing overhead cost of producing those output volumes. Using past cost-volume data to determine current manufacturing overhead costs is less costly than engineering studies, and the manufacturing overhead costs are sufficiently representative and accurate.

Standard manufacturing overhead cost per unit is determined by analysis of past costs rather than by engineering estimates.

For these reasons we determine the standard manufacturing overhead cost using **predetermined overhead rates** as discussed in Chapter 3 where we explained that a predetermined overhead rate was calculated as follows:

$$\textbf{Predetermined overhead rate} = \frac{\textbf{estimated annual overhead cost}}{\textbf{estimated annual production volume}}$$

In that chapter we did not provide any detailed discussion of how the estimated total manufacturing overhead would be derived. We now turn our attention to how these estimates are made.

We will first introduce the concept of the **flexible budget** and explain how it is used in calculating the predetermined overhead rate and how it is used to separate the **overapplied or underapplied overhead** cost into a **volume variance** and a **budget variance.** Next we will explain how the flexible budget concept is used to separate the budget variance into a **spending variance** and an **efficiency variance.**

Finally, we will illustrate how to record standard manufacturing overhead costs in the accounts.

FLEXIBLE OVERHEAD BUDGETS

A flexible overhead budget is based on an understanding of the behavior of manufacturing overhead cost as production volume changes. The cost of some components of manufacturing overhead, such as supervision salaries and depreciation, are not expected to change as production volume changes; they are *fixed* costs. The cost of other manufacturing overhead components, such as indirect materials and indirect labor, are expected to change as production volume changes; they are *variable* or mixed costs.

A flexible budget is a formula in which the expected manufacturing overhead cost is classified into fixed and variable components based on some measure of production volume. To obtain an understanding of what a flexible overhead budget is consider Exhibit 9-1. The flexible overhead budget in Exhibit 9-1 is for the assembly department of the Acme Manufacturing Company. The flexible overhead budget includes each item of manufacturing overhead for the assembly department.

EXHIBIT 9-1
ACME MANUFACTURING COMPANY
Assembly Department
Flexible Overhead Budget
For the Year Ended June 30, 19X2

Item		Fixed Cost		Variable Cost per Direct Labor Hour
Supervision		$35,000		—
Depreciation		45,000		—
Indirect labor		—		$0.75 per direct labor hour
Indirect materials		—		1.00 per direct labor hour
Lubricants		—		0.25 per direct labor hour
Total		$80,000		$2.00 per direct labor hour
		Fixed cost		Variable cost
Flexible budget formula	=	$80,000	+	$2.00 per direct labor hour

A flexible budget is summarized as a formula which shows total expected fixed cost per period and variable cost per unit of activity measure.

For each item of manufacturing overhead management has estimated the fixed cost component and variable cost component. For example, the supervision cost is estimated at a fixed cost of $35,000 for the year (with zero variable cost) and the indirect labor cost is estimated at a variable cost of $0.75 per direct labor hour (with zero fixed cost).

At the bottom of Exhibit 9-1 the data in the flexible budget are summarized into one formula called the flexible budget formula which is a summary of the individual item costs showing total expected fixed cost per period and expected variable cost per unit of activity measure.

Uses of Flexible Overhead Budgets

Flexible overhead budgets are used in both cost accounting and managerial accounting.

In cost accounting flexible overhead budgets are used to estimate the annual manufacturing overhead costs based on the expected level of production for the purpose of calculating the predetermined overhead rate.

Static budgets do not change when production volume changes.

In managerial accounting flexible budgets are used to evaluate the performance of departmental managers. Before the development of flexible overhead budgets a firm would develop a single overhead budget based on the expected level of production for both product costing and performance evaluation. The difficulty with these budgets for performance evaluation is that they were static—they were not revised when the actual production level turned out to be different than estimated. A static overhead budget is suitable for evaluating performance only in the rare situations where the actual production level turns out to be identical to the estimated production level. Since these estimates are usually made a year in advance, it is rare that actual volume equals estimated volume. The variable cost components of the overhead cost can change considerably in response to changes in production levels. What represents a good level of overhead for one volume of activity would be inappropriate for another volume of activity. For instance, the cost of electric power increases with the number of machine hours used. A flexible overhead budget automatically budgets more electricity cost as machine hours increase. A static budget does not; it provides the same budget for electricity regardless of the production level.

A flexible budget automatically adjusts the budgeted amount for changes in production level.

With a flexible budget it is possible to estimate the amount of manufacturing overhead cost that *should* be incurred at each level of production. At the end of an accounting period the actual manufacturing overhead costs incurred can be easily compared to the manufacturing overhead costs that should have been incurred given the actual production level. This after-the-fact comparison aids management in evaluating whether the manufacturing overhead costs have been controlled during the accounting period.

Departmental Flexible Budgets

Flexible budgets are usually developed for each department in a factory. There are two reasons for doing this.

First, the activity measure used for assigning manufacturing overhead to the product may be different for different departments. For example, a screw machine department might use machine hours as its activity measure to assign manufacturing overhead to the products, while an assembly department might use direct labor hours as an activity measure to assign its manufacturing overhead to the products.

Second, manufacturing overhead costs within a department are better controllable by the supervisors within that department; variances from the expected cost should be quickly brought to their attention, analyzed, and remedied. The control of manufacturing overhead costs is discussed in Chapter 17.

Selecting the Activity Base

An important part of developing a flexible overhead budget is selecting a measure of production activity. The measure of production activity is not finished units, as you might expect, but rather is direct labor hours or some other activity base.

The reason units of product are not used to measure production volume is the jointness of some manufacturing overhead costs to different products. An example of jointness is the cost of maintaining a machine. If several different products are produced on the machine, the maintenance cost benefits all products produced on the machine. But the units of product may be so different that it does not make sense to add units together. To measure the total production activity of the machine we must select a common activity measure for all products produced.

The activity base selected should be the one that best relates manufacturing overhead cost to production volume and final cost of the product. Thus, the best activity measure for manufacturing overhead cost is the one that provides the best measure of how manufacturing overhead cost varies as production volume varies. For example, if the cost of drills is dependent on the number of hours the drill presses are run, then machine hours on the drill press can be used as the activity that measures or estimates the cost of drills. In this case, the cause (machine hours) and effect (cost of drills) relationship is easily identified. However, in many situations it will not be as easy to identify the activity that provides the best measure of cause-and-effect relationships. In such situations you must have someone familiar with the process, such as the production supervisor, evaluate the potential production measure to identify whether a *logical* cause-and-effect relationship could exist between the manufacturing overhead cost and the production activity measure.

The best activity measure closely relates changes in manufacturing overhead to changes in production volume because it is based on cause and effect.

MANUFACTURING OVERHEAD STANDARDS

A manufacturing overhead standard consists of two components—a price standard and a quantity standard. The price standard is the familiar predetermined overhead rate. The quantity standard is the *standard quantity allowed* for the activity base used to compute the predetermined overhead rate.

Predetermined Overhead Rate

The predetermined overhead rate is used to assign, or to allocate, a manufacturing overhead cost to each of the jobs or products the company is producing. The manufacturing overhead cost assigned to each of the jobs or products is referred to as the applied manufacturing overhead cost.

The predetermined overhead rate is calculated by estimating the manufacturing overhead cost to be incurred during the annual accounting period and dividing it by the expected production volume for the annual accounting period.[1] A predetermined overhead rate for manufacturing overhead costs based on direct labor hours as the activity base would be calculated as follows:

$$\textbf{Predetermined overhead rate (activity base is direct labor hours)} = \frac{\textbf{estimated annual overhead costs}}{\textbf{estimated annual direct labor hours}}$$

There are two characteristics of manufacturing overhead costs which require us to use a predetermined overhead rate for an annual accounting period to assign manufacturing overhead costs to the jobs or products:

The predetermined overhead rate solves two important accounting problems, seasonality of costs and seasonality of production volume.

1 Seasonal variations in manufacturing overhead costs

2 Seasonal variations in production volume

The most striking example of seasonal variations in manufacturing overhead costs are heating and air conditioning costs. These costs are incurred only in some seasons of the year. Accountants regard it as unrealistic for the manufacturing overhead cost of a unit produced in one season to be different from the manufacturing overhead cost for a physically identical unit produced in another season. This would happen if units produced in winter included heating costs, units produced in summer included air conditioning costs, but units produced in spring and fall included neither. If the predetermined overhead rate is calculated on the basis of an annual time period, seasonal cost variations are averaged out. All unit costs have a share of factory heating and air conditioning costs.

To see how the second characteristic, periodic variations in production volume, could affect overhead rates consider what would happen if overhead rates were determined on a monthly basis. If production volume is high in one month and low during another month, while manufacturing overhead costs are fixed, the manufacturing overhead cost per unit would be drastically different for the two months.

For example, consider the following:

[1] Recall from our discussion in Chapter 3 that practical production volume or normal production volume are sometimes used to calculate the predetermined overhead rate rather than expected production volume.

Month	Fixed Manufacturing Overhead		Production Volume in Units		Fixed Manufacturing Overhead per Unit
January	$10,000	÷	2,000	=	$5.00
.	.		.		
.	.		.		
.	.		.		
.	.		.		
June	$10,000	÷	4,000	=	$2.50

(This illustration ignores variable manufacturing overhead and seasonal variations in overhead to make the point more clearly.)

In the above example the fixed manufacturing overhead cost per unit is $5.00 in January and $2.50 in June simply because production volume has changed. As you can see from the above example, the fixed manufacturing overhead costs would be constant from month to month, but the denominator of the fraction would be larger or smaller, depending on the production volume. Thus the cost per unit of physically identical units would be lower or higher, depending on the month in which they were produced.

Accountants regard this kind of variation in manufacturing overhead cost per unit as unnecessary and potentially misleading. Thus, the effects of periodic variations in production volume are averaged out by basing the predetermined overhead rate on the annual volume.

Applied Manufacturing Overhead: Standard Cost

In previous chapters we applied manufacturing overhead to the jobs or products based on the *actual* amount of some activity measure, such as actual direct labor hours or actual machine hours.

With standard overhead costs the applied overhead is based on the *standard quantity allowed* for the activity measure. For a direct labor hour activity base, the applied manufacturing overhead is calculated as follows:

In standard costing, the applied overhead depends on the standard quantity allowed rather than the actual quantity of the activity base.

Applied manufacturing overhead cost (standard cost) = predetermined overhead rate × standard direct labor hours allowed[2]

The difference between the actual manufacturing overhead cost incurred and the applied manufacturing overhead cost is referred to as *overapplied or underapplied overhead,* depending, of course, on whether applied overhead cost is greater or less than the actual overhead cost. This difference is sometimes called the *total overhead variance.*

[2] Remember from Chapter 8 that the standard direct labor hours allowed equals the standard quantity of direct labors per unit of product times the actual units of product produced during the period.

Calculating the Standard Manufacturing Overhead Cost per Unit of Product

We next illustrate how the standard manufacturing overhead cost per unit of product is calculated using the flexible budget and the direct labor standard. We will continue the Acme Manufacturing Company example with the additional data given below:

ACME MANUFACTURING COMPANY
Estimated Data
For the Year Ended June 30, 19X2

Flexible budget formula = \$80,000 + \$2.00 per direct labor hour

Estimated annual production volume	= 10,000	units
Standard quantity of direct labor per unit	= × 2.0	standard direct labor hours
Estimated standard direct labor hours to produce 10,000 units per year	= 20,000	standard direct labor hours

Based on the facts above, the predetermined overhead rate can be calculated as follows:

$$\textbf{Predetermined overhead rate (activity base is standard direct labor hours)} = \frac{\textbf{estimated annual overhead cost}}{\textbf{estimated annual standard direct labor hours}}$$

We estimate the annual manufacturing overhead cost by using the standard direct labor hours for the expected annual production volume in the flexible budget equation.

$$\begin{aligned}\textbf{Thus, estimated annual overhead cost (for the year)} &= \$80{,}000 + \left(\$2.00 \text{ per direct labor hour} \times 20{,}000 \text{ standard direct labor hours}\right)\\ &= \$80{,}000 + \$40{,}000\\ &= \$120{,}000\end{aligned}$$

We can now calculate:

$$\textbf{Predetermined overhead rate (activity base is standard direct labor hours)} = \frac{\$120{,}000}{20{,}000 \text{ standard direct labor hours}} = \$6.00 \text{ per standard direct labor hour}$$

Later in this chapter when we analyze variances for manufacturing overhead it will be useful to think of the predetermined overhead rate as consisting of two components, a fixed overhead rate and a variable overhead rate. To determine the fixed and variable components of the predetermined overhead rate:

With flexible budget information, the predetermined overhead rate can be broken into two components, a fixed overhead rate and a variable overhead rate.

Predetermined overhead rate **= fixed overhead rate + variable overhead rate**

$$= \frac{\text{\$80,000 fixed overhead}}{\text{20,000 standard direct labor hours}} + \frac{\text{\$40,000 variable overhead}}{\text{20,000 standard direct labor hours}}$$

= $4.00 per standard direct labor hour + $2.00 per standard direct labor hour

= $6 per standard direct labor hour

Using the predetermined overhead rate of $6.00 per standard direct labor hour and the standard quantity of direct labor per unit of product—2.0 hours—we can calculate the standard applied manufacturing overhead cost for one unit of Acme's products as follows:

The standard overhead cost per unit of product is the predetermined overhead rate times the standard direct labor hours per unit of product.

Applied manufacturing overhead cost (standard overhead cost per unit of product) = $6.00 per standard direct labor hour × 2.0 standard direct labor hours per unit of product

= $12.00

Notice that this standard applied manufacturing overhead cost of $12.00 per unit of product is not influenced by the number of *actual* direct labor hours used to produce the product just as the standard direct materials cost and standard direct labor cost are predetermined and not changed by month to month variations in actual cost.

Using the Predetermined Overhead Rate in Standard Product Costing

The predetermined overhead rate is used in standard product costing in the same way that the predetermined overhead rate is used in normal job order and process costing systems as described in Chapters 4 and 5. One use is to apply overhead cost to work in process. The amount of applied overhead transferred to work in process is the predetermined overhead rate times the standard direct labor hours allowed for the month's production.

A standard job order or process costing system operates the same as an actual cost system except that the standard cost per unit is substituted for the normal cost per unit.

The second use is in cost per unit calculations. We have just illustrated how the standard overhead cost per unit is calculated. The standard overhead cost per unit is added to the standard direct materials cost and standard direct labor cost per unit to obtain a total standard cost per unit. This standard cost per unit is used in accounting for the work in process inventory, the finished goods inventory, and the cost of goods sold. That is, when a unit of product is completed, its standard cost is taken out of work in process and put into finished goods. When a unit of finished product is sold, the standard cost per unit is removed from the finished goods inventory account and added to the cost of goods sold account. The process is exactly the same as when normal cost per unit was calculated, with the standard cost per unit substituted for the normal cost per unit.

Calculating Variances for Manufacturing Overhead

As you will recall from our study of job order and process costing systems, actual manufacturing overhead costs are accumulated in one account and applied manufacturing overhead is accumulated in another account. At any time, the difference in the balances of these two accounts represents the over- or underapplied overhead.

Several different factors give rise to over- or underapplied overhead. To aid in understanding the significance of over- or underapplied overhead, it is customary to calculate several variances, each of which relates to one of the factors which may have caused the over- or underapplied overhead. In the next section of this chapter we define these variances and explain how they can be used to understand and account for over- or underapplied overhead.

The following data will be used to continue the Acme Manufacturing Company example and to illustrate the calculation of variances in manufacturing overhead.

ACME MANUFACTURING COMPANY
Actual Results
For the Year Ended June 30, 19X2

Units of product manufactured	=	11,000 units
Standard quantity of direct labor per unit	=	2.00 hours
Total standard direct labor hours *allowed*	=	22,000 hours
Actual direct labor hours	=	21,000 hours

	Actual Manufacturing Overhead Cost		
Item	**Fixed Cost**	**Variable Cost**	**Total Cost**
Supervision	$37,000	—	$ 37,000
Depreciation	45,000	—	45,000
Indirect labor	—	$16,470	16,470
Indirect materials	—	22,425	22,425
Lubricants	—	4,105	4,105
Total	$82,000	$43,000	$125,000

The overapplied or underapplied overhead, that is, the total variance, is the difference between total actual manufacturing overhead cost and the total applied overhead for the total standard direct labor hours allowed. For our example the total variance for overhead is:

Total actual manufacturing overhead cost	**Total applied overhead for the 22,000 standard direct labor hours allowed***
$125,000	**$132,000 ($6.00 × 22,000 hours)**

$7,000 overapplied overhead

* 11,000 units × 2 standard hours per unit

The overhead is $7,000 overapplied since the total applied manufacturing overhead cost is more than the total actual manufacturing overhead cost.

Over- or underapplied manufacturing overhead can be divided into two components. The component variances are:

A two-way analysis of over- or underapplied overhead leads to a budget variance and a volume variance.

1 A budget variance
2 A volume variance

The *budget variance* represents the component of total variance that can be attributed to the difference between the actual overhead costs incurred and the estimated overhead costs that should have been incurred based on the standard direct labor hours allowed.

The *volume variance* represents the component of over- or underapplied overhead that can be attributed to the difference between the actual production volume and the expected production volume used in calculating the predetermined overhead rate.

Budget Variance The budget variance is calculated as the difference between the total actual manufacturing overhead cost as recorded in the accounting records and the flexible budgeted overhead cost based on the standard quantity of direct labor hours allowed. The budget variance represents the difference between the total actual manufacturing overhead cost incurred by the company and the manufacturing overhead cost that *should have been* incurred based on the standard quantity of direct labor hours allowed.

The budget variance compares the actual overhead cost to the flexible budget amount with production volume measured as standard direct labor hours allowed.

Cost Behavior Classification	Total Actual Manufacturing Overhead	Flexible Budgeted Overhead Cost for 22,000 Standard Direct Labor Hours*
Fixed		$80,000
Variable		44,000 ($2.00 × 22,000 hours)
Total	$125,000	$124,000
	$1,000 unfavorable Budget variance	

* 11,000 units × 2.0 standard direct labor hours.

The budget variance is $1,000 unfavorable. It is unfavorable because the total actual overhead cost was $1,000 greater than the flexible budget said it should have been when production volume is 22,000 standard direct labor hours.

The budget variance is primarily useful for cost control.

The budget variance provides management with information which aids in controlling costs. For example, the budget variance is usually reported on a departmental basis since many of the factors that cause the budget variance are controllable by department managers.

Exhibit 9-2 illustrates for each of the individual items the actual cost (column 1), the flexible budgeted cost, or estimated cost (column 2), and the variance between actual and budget (column 3). The flexible budgeted overhead costs for each item are calculated using 22,000 standard direct labor hours as the basic data for the

EXHIBIT 9-2
ACME MANUFACTURING COMPANY
Assembly Department
Detailed Budget Variance Computations
For the Year Ended June 30, 19X2

Item	(1) Actual Manufacturing Overhead Cost	(2) Flexible Budget Overhead Cost for 22,000 Standard Direct Labor Hours	(1 − 2) Budget Variance
Supervision	$ 37,000	$ 35,000	($2,000)
Depreciation	45,000	45,000	0
Indirect labor	16,470	16,500[a]	30
Indirect materials	22,425	22,000[b]	(425)
Lubricants	4,105	5,500[c]	1,395
Total	$125,000	$124,000	($1,000)

( ) indicates unfavorable variance.

Computations

[a] $0.75 per direct labor hour × 22,000 standard direct labor hours.
[b] $1.00 per direct labor hour × 22,000 standard direct labor hours.
[c] $0.25 per direct labor hour × 22,000 standard direct labor hours.

Acme Manufacturing Company. Note that the $1,000 unfavorable budget variance is composed of the sum of favorable (+$30 + $1,395) and unfavorable (−$2,000 − $425) variances. This analysis provides management with detailed information as to how much each of the overhead items contributed to the total budget variance. This analysis is primarily used for managerial control which we will discuss further in Chapter 17.

Exhibit 9-3 graphically illustrates the flexible budget and budget variance for Acme Manufacturing Company. As you can see from this graphical representation, actual manufacturing overhead costs above the flexible budget line represent unfavorable budget variances; actual manufacturing overhead costs below the flexible budget line represent favorable budget variances.

The volume variance reflects the difference between actual production volume and expected annual production volume.

Volume Variance for Manufacturing Overhead The volume variance represents the component of the total overhead variance that results when the actual production volume, measured by the standard quantity allowed in this example (standard direct labor hours allowed), is different from the expected annual production volume used to calculate the predetermined overhead rate. We can calculate the volume variance in either of two ways.

One way the volume variance can be calculated is to determine the difference between the total applied overhead for the standard direct labor hours allowed and the flexible budgeted overhead for the standard direct labor hours allowed. For the Acme Manufacturing Company in this example, the computation for the volume variance is shown at the bottom of page 256.

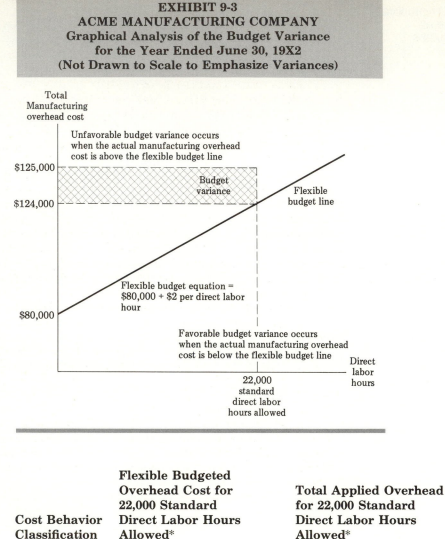

EXHIBIT 9-3
ACME MANUFACTURING COMPANY
Graphical Analysis of the Budget Variance
for the Year Ended June 30, 19X2
(Not Drawn to Scale to Emphasize Variances)

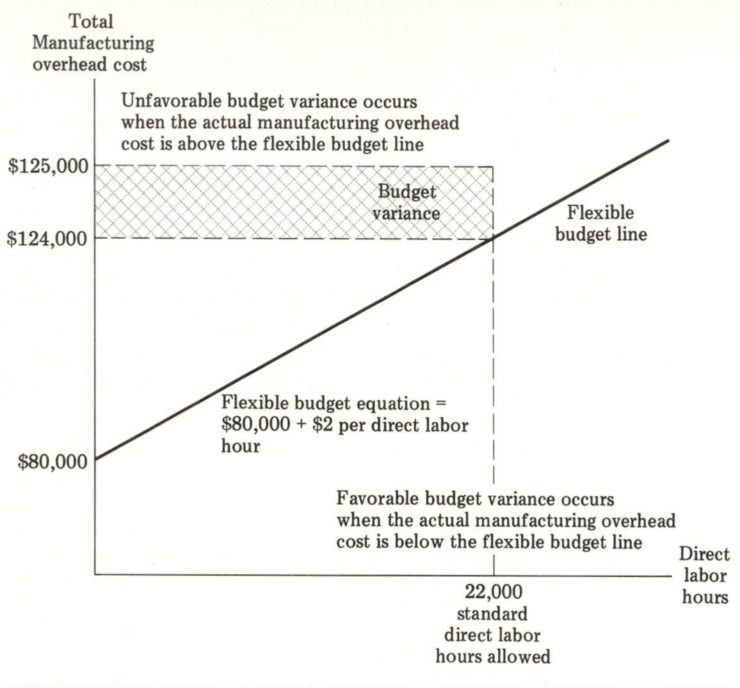

Cost Behavior Classification	Flexible Budgeted Overhead Cost for 22,000 Standard Direct Labor Hours Allowed*	Total Applied Overhead for 22,000 Standard Direct Labor Hours Allowed*
Fixed	$ 80,000	$ 88,000($4.00 × 22,000 hours)
Variable	$ 44,000(2.00 × 22,000)	44,000($2.00 × 22,000 hours)
Total	$124,000	$132,000($6.00 × 22,000 hours)

$8,000 favorable
Volume variance

* 11,000 units × 2.0 standard labor hours.

The volume variance in this example is favorable since the applied overhead for 22,000 standard direct labor hours is greater than the flexible budgeted overhead for 22,000 standard direct labor hours. This will happen when the actual production volume exceeds the expected production volume.

Why did this volume variance occur? First of all note in the above computation that the volume variance relates only to fixed overhead—the variable overhead in each column is the same. Basically the volume variance occurs only because of the way we account for fixed manufacturing overhead costs.

Budgeted fixed overhead is expected to be a constant amount for the year independent of the production volume (by definition of fixed cost). This is illustrated in part (*a*) of Exhibit 9-4. In this graph note that the fixed manufacturing overhead for the Acme Manufacturing Company is expected to be $80,000 for the year independent of the production volume. This is the way we expect budgeted fixed cost to behave with respect to production volume.

However, when we apply fixed overhead costs to the products, we multiply the fixed component of the predetermined overhead *rate* times the standard direct labor hours allowed. This means the applied fixed overhead will behave as though it were a *variable cost*. Look at part (*b*) of Exhibit 9-4 which represents the applied fixed overhead for the Acme Manufacturing Company. If no units are produced then no fixed overhead will be applied. However, we still expect to incur $80,000 of fixed overhead cost. As production volume increases fixed overhead is applied to the products at a rate of $4 per standard direct labor hour. For the 22,000 standard direct labor hours allowed, $88,000 of fixed overhead is applied.

The volume variance is the difference between the budgeted fixed overhead and the applied fixed overhead as shown in the shaded areas of part *c* of Exhibit 9-4. Note in part *c* that the volume variance is zero only at the point where the budgeted fixed overhead line crosses the applied fixed overhead line. This always occurs at the production volume where the standard direct labor hours allowed equal the standard direct labor hours used to calculate the predetermined overhead rate. For the Acme Manufacturing Company 20,000 standard direct labor hours were used to calculate the predetermined overhead rate.

This leads us to the other method of calculating the volume variance: the fixed overhead rate times the difference between the standard direct labor hours allowed for *expected* production volume and the standard direct labor hours allowed for *actual* production volume. For this example, the alternative computation for the volume variance is:

$$\textbf{Volume variance} = \begin{matrix}\textbf{fixed}\\\textbf{overhead rate}\end{matrix} \times \left(\begin{matrix}\textbf{standard}\\\textbf{direct}\\\textbf{labor hours}\\\textbf{allowed}\\\textbf{actual}\\\textbf{production}\end{matrix} - \begin{matrix}\textbf{standard}\\\textbf{direct}\\\textbf{labor hours}\\\textbf{allowed}\\\textbf{expected}\\\textbf{production}\end{matrix}\right)$$

$$= \begin{matrix}\textbf{\$4.00 per}\\\textbf{direct hour}\end{matrix} \times (\textbf{22,000 hours} - \textbf{20,000 hours})$$

$$= \textbf{\$8,000 favorable}$$

The two methods of calculating the volume variance should always give the same answer.

The volume variance does not provide management with a measure to evaluate cost control. Rather, it is a measure of whether actual production volume was above

EXHIBIT 9-4
ACME MANUFACTURING COMPANY
Graphical Analysis of the
Volume Variance
For the Year Ended June 30, 19X2

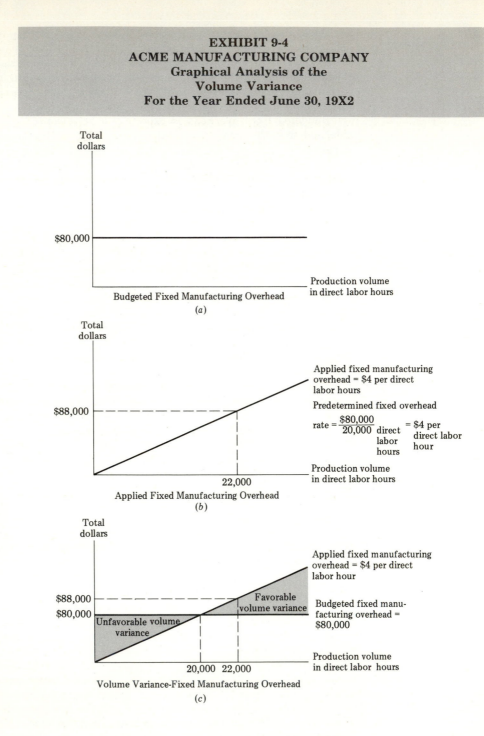

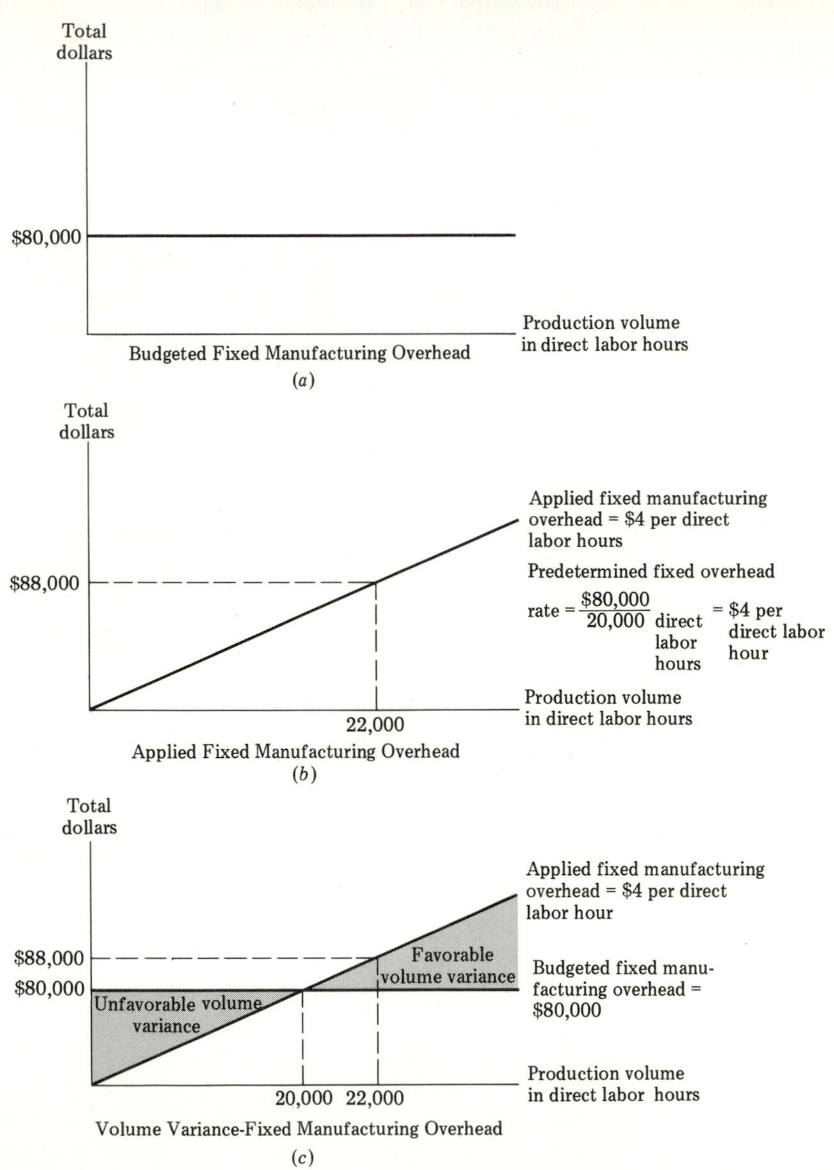

or below expected average volume. The Acme Manufacturing Company had 22,000 standard direct labor hours allowed for the year but only 20,000 direct labor hours were expected. Thus Acme produced at 2,000 direct labor hours more than expected, which resulted in an $8,000 favorable volume variance. If Acme had produced at less than 20,000 direct labor hours, the volume variance would have been unfavorable.

You may remember from Chapter 3 that expected actual, practical, or normal volume might be chosen for calculating the predetermined overhead rate. Since the choice of volume is arbitrary, the volume variance is necessarily arbitrary.

Analyzing the Budget Variance Thus far we have divided the over- or underapplied manufacturing overhead into two components as shown below:

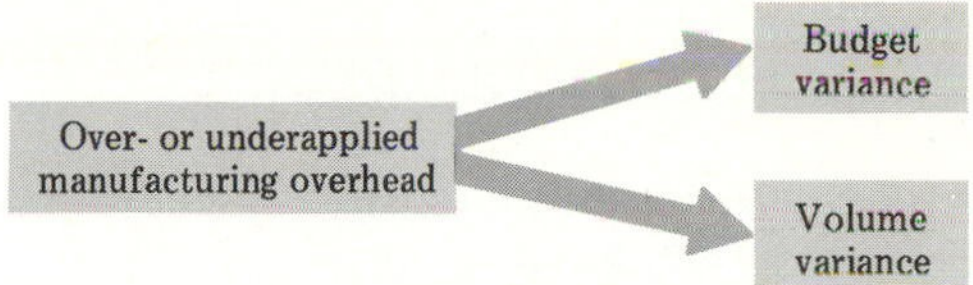

This analysis is referred to as a two-variance analysis.

Now we will show you how the budget variance can be further divided into two components: a spending variance and an efficiency variance.

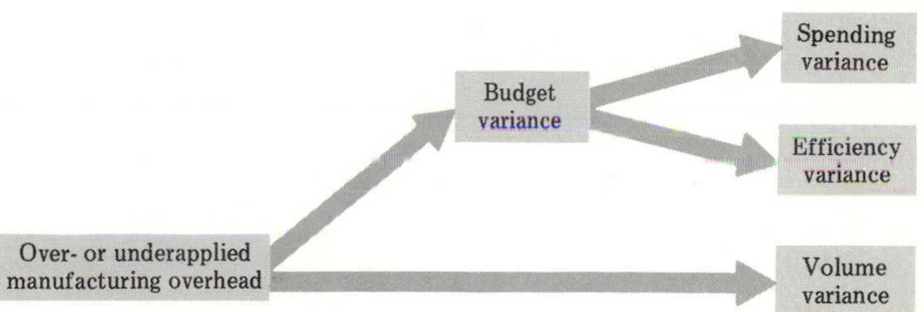

When we calculate the volume variance, efficiency variance, and spending variance we refer to this as a three-variance analysis. The spending and efficiency variances are calculated to provide management with more information to control the overhead costs. The volume variance is unchanged.

The spending variance provides information concerning whether the actual overhead cost is greater or less than the overhead cost that should have been incurred based on the *actual* direct labor hours. The spending variance assumes that the best measure of how much should be spent on overhead is the actual number of hours operated rather than the standard hours allowed. The efficiency variance provides information as to the amount of variable overhead cost that should be saved if actual direct labor hours are less than standard direct labor hours allowed.

Let us analyze these two components of the budget variance using the data given on page 253 for the Acme Manufacturing Company. We already calculated that the budget variance for the Acme Manufacturing Company is $1,000 unfavorable, which is the difference between the actual overhead cost of $125,000 and the $124,000 flexible budgeted overhead cost for 22,000 standard direct labor hours allowed. We will now show you how the budget variance is separated into a spending variance and an efficiency variance. The computations are given below:

A three-variance analysis subdivides the budget variance into a spending variance and an efficiency variance. The third variance is the volume variance which is the same as in the two-variance analysis.

Cost Behavior Classification	Total Actual Manufacturing Overhead Cost	Flexible Budgeted Overhead Cost for 21,000 Actual Direct Labor Hours	Flexible Budgeted Overhead Cost for 22,000 Standard Direct Labor Hours Allowed[a]
Fixed	———	$ 80,000	$ 80,000
Variable		42,000[b]	44,000[c]
Total	$125,000	$122,000	$124,000
	$3,000 unfavorable (Spending variance)		$2,000 favorable (Efficiency variance)

[a] 11,000 units × 2.0 standard direct labor hours.
[b] $2.00 × 21,000 actual direct labor hours.
[c] $2.00 × 22,000 standard direct labor hours.

The spending variance is $3,000 unfavorable. It is unfavorable because the actual overhead cost incurred is greater than the flexible budgeted overhead cost for the actual direct labor hours. This indicates more costs were actually incurred than should have been incurred for the actual direct labor hours worked.

The efficiency variance is $2,000 favorable; it is the difference between the flexible budgeted overhead cost for 21,000 actual direct labor hours and the flexible budgeted overhead cost for 22,000 standard direct labor hours allowed. This indicates that $2,000 of variable overhead costs should have been saved since the actual direct labor hours were less than the standard direct labor hours allowed.

The efficiency variance can also be computed as the product of the variable overhead rate multiplied by the difference between the standard direct labor hours allowed and the actual direct labor hours.

Here is an alternative way of calculating the efficiency variance which yields the same answer.

$$\text{Efficiency variance} = \text{predetermined variable overhead rate} \times \left(\text{standard direct labor hours allowed} - \text{actual direct labor hours}\right)$$
$$= \$2.00 \text{ per direct labor hour} \times (22{,}000 \text{ hours} - 21{,}000 \text{ hours})$$
$$= \$2{,}000 \text{ favorable}$$

Calculating the efficiency variance in either way yields the same results. They do for this reason: In computing the flexible budgeted overhead cost, the fixed manufacturing overhead is the same for the actual direct labor hours and the standard direct labor hours allowed. Thus we have the variable overhead rate multiplied by the difference between the standard direct labor hours allowed and the actual direct labor hours.

Notice the similarity between this variance and the direct labor quantity variance discussed in Chapter 8. The quantity in parentheses is the number of direct labor hours saved or wasted. This quantity is multiplied by the variable overhead rate to obtain the efficiency variance. The same quantity in parentheses when multiplied by the standard direct labor price yields the direct labor quantity variance.

To understand what the efficiency variance tells management, it is more helpful to calculate it using the variable overhead rate and the difference between standard and actual activity measures. In this example, the standard direct labor hours allowed represents the number of hours which should have been required to produce the goods according to the engineering estimates incorporated into the standard direct labor cost. The actual direct labor hours are taken from the payroll records in the accounting system. If actual direct labor hours used turns out to be greater than standard direct labor hours allowed, the presumption is that labor hours were wasted, sometimes for perfectly valid reasons, sometimes for not valid reasons. If the actual direct labor hours turn out to be less than the standard direct labor hours allowed, the operations were more efficient than expected, and everyone is happy.

The efficiency variance tells how much variable manufacturing overhead cost was wasted or saved as a result of wasting or saving direct labor hours. This is based on the reasonable assumption that the amount of variable manufacturing overhead which should be incurred is measurable by direct labor hours.

Remember that we showed you how to calculate a budget variance for each of the cost items that make up the total manufacturing overhead costs. Here we can do the same thing for the spending variance. This is shown in Exhibit 9-5. It tells management in which categories of overhead the spending variance occurred. Mechanically one could make the same breakdown of the efficiency variance, but doing so would provide no useful management information. Management must control the efficiency variance by controlling direct labor hours, not overhead costs.

EXHIBIT 9-5
ACME MANUFACTURING COMPANY
Detailed Analysis of Spending and Efficiency Variances
For the Year Ended June 30, 19X2

Item	(1) Actual Manufacturing Overhead Cost	(2) Flexible Budgeted Overhead Cost for 21,000 Actual Direct Labor Hours	(3) Flexible Budgeted Overhead Cost for 22,000 Standard Direct Labor Hours	(1−2) Spending Variance	(2−3) Efficiency Variance
Supervision	$ 37,000	$ 35,000	$ 35,000	($2,000)	—
Depreciation	45,000	45,000	45,000	—	—
Indirect labor	16,470	15,750	16,500	(720)	
Indirect materials	22,425	21,000	22,000	(1,425)	
Lubricants	4,105	5,250	5,500	1,145	
	$125,000	$122,000	$124,000	($3,000)	$2,000

$1,000 unfavorable budget variance

( ) indicates an unfavorable variance.

Summary: Variances in Manufacturing Overhead

Exhibit 9-6 summarizes the computation of the variances in manufacturing overhead discussed in this chapter. Column 1 is the total actual manufacturing overhead cost and column 2 is the flexible budgeted overhead for 21,000 actual direct labor hours. The difference between column 1 and column 2 is the spending variance—$3,000 unfavorable.

Column 3 is the flexible budget for 22,000 standard direct labor hours allowed. The difference between column 2 and column 3 is the efficiency variance—$2,000 favorable.

Column 4 is the total applied manufacturing overhead for 22,000 standard direct labor hours allowed. The difference between column 3 and column 4 is the volume variance—$8,000 favorable.

The budget variance is the difference between columns 1 and 2—$1,000 unfavorable.

The overapplied overhead is the difference between columns 1 and 4—$7,000 favorable.

EXHIBIT 9-6
ACME MANUFACTURING COMPANY
Variances in Manufacturing Overhead
For the Year Ended June 30, 19X2

	(1)	(2)	(3)	(4)
Cost Behavior Classification	**Actual Manufacturing Overhead Cost**	**Flexible Budgeted Overhead for 21,000 Actual Direct Labor Hours**	**Flexible Budgeted Overhead for 22,000 Standard Direct Labor Hours Allowed**	**Total Applied Manufacturing Overhead for 22,000 Standard Direct Labor Hours Allowed**
Fixed		$ 80,000	$ 80,000	$ 88,000[c]
Variable		42,000[a]	44,000[b]	44,000[b]
Total	$125,000	$122,000	$124,000	$132,000

Between (1) and (2): $3,000 unfavorable — Spending variance

Between (2) and (3): $2,000 favorable — Efficiency variance

Between (3) and (4): $8,000 favorable — Volume variance

Between (1) and (3): $1,000 unfavorable — Budget variance

Between (1) and (4): $7,000 — Overapplied overhead

[a] $2.00 per direct labor hour × 21,000 hours.
[b] $2.00 per direct labor hour × 22,000 hours.
[c] $4.00 per direct labor hour × 22,000 hours.

STANDARD MANUFACTURING OVERHEAD COSTS IN THE GENERAL LEDGER

In earlier chapters you learned that actual manufacturing overhead costs are recorded as incurred in an account called actual manufacturing overhead. As manufacturing overhead is applied it is debited to work in process and credited to an account, applied manufacturing overhead. The difference between the actual manufacturing overhead account and the applied manufacturing overhead account represents the overapplied or underapplied overhead costs. Using the data in the previous example, we will illustrate the process of entering manufacturing overhead variances in the accounts.

The journal entry to record the actual manufacturing overhead costs is:

Actual Manufacturing Overhead	**$125,000**	
Material Inventory (indirect materials)		**$22,425**
Payroll (indirect labor and supervision)		**53,470**
Accumulated Depreciation		**45,000**
Supplies (lubricants)		**4,105**
(To record the actual manufacturing overhead costs.)		

The journal entry to record the application of the manufacturing overhead is:

Work in Process	**$132,000**	
Applied Manufacturing Overhead		**$132,000**
(To record the application of the manufacturing overhead at a rate of $6 per standard direct labor hour for 22,000 standard direct labor hours.)		

Now the actual manufacturing overhead account and the applied manufacturing overhead account are closed into the variance accounts. Using the variances—spending variance, efficiency variance, and volume variance—we calculated earlier, we can make the following adjusting entry to account for the manufacturing overhead variances—overapplied or underapplied overhead costs.

Applied Manufacturing Overhead	**$132,000**	
Spending Variance Overhead	**3,000**	
Efficiency Variance Overhead		**$ 2,000**
Volume Variance Overhead		**8,000**
Actual Manufacturing Overhead		**125,000**
(To close the manufacturing overhead accounts and to record the variances in manufacturing overhead.)		

Note that in the above journal entry the unfavorable variances are represented as debit balances and favorable variances are represented as credit balances.

SUMMARY

A predetermined overhead rate is used for assigning manufacturing overhead costs to the jobs or products. With standard costs the applied manufacturing overhead is based on the standard quantity of the activity measure allowed rather than the actual quantity of the activity measure used.

Not all manufacturing overhead costs are strictly fixed and independent of production volume. Some manufacturing overhead costs are variable. Therefore, it must be expected that some part of a total manufacturing overhead cost will depend on the volume of production during the accounting period.

We can represent the fixed and variable components of manufacturing overhead cost in the formula, called the flexible budget formula, as shown below:

$$\begin{array}{l}\textbf{Budgeted}\\ \textbf{total}\\ \textbf{overhead}\end{array} = \begin{array}{l}\textbf{budgeted}\\ \textbf{fixed overhead}\\ \textbf{per period}\end{array} + \left(\begin{array}{l}\textbf{variable overhead}\\ \textbf{per measure of}\\ \textbf{activity}\end{array} \times \begin{array}{l}\textbf{total}\\ \textbf{quantity}\\ \textbf{of activity}\\ \textbf{measure}\end{array}\right)$$

or, when direct labor hours is the activity used to measure production volume, then

$$\begin{array}{l}\textbf{Budgeted}\\ \textbf{total}\\ \textbf{overhead}\end{array} = \begin{array}{l}\textbf{budgeted}\\ \textbf{fixed overhead}\\ \textbf{per period}\end{array} + \left(\begin{array}{l}\textbf{variable overhead}\\ \textbf{per direct labor}\\ \textbf{hour}\end{array} \times \begin{array}{l}\textbf{total}\\ \textbf{direct labor}\\ \textbf{hours}\end{array}\right)$$

The flexible budget formula has several functions. It is used to estimate the total annual manufacturing overhead cost for calculating the predetermined overhead rate. It is also used to resolve the total manufacturing overhead variance (overapplied or underapplied overhead) into its component variances—spending variance, efficiency variance, volume variance. The variances are used to determine if any control actions are necessary by management.

The budget variance, which comprises spending and efficiency variances, is a measure of cost control. If favorable it represents a gain, in the sense that actual costs are less than budgeted costs; if unfavorable it represents a loss, in the sense that it could have been avoided.

The spending variance reports how effectively the quantities and prices of manufacturing overhead cost items were controlled by management.

The efficiency variance is a reflection of how carefully the activity measure of production, in our example, direct labor hours, was controlled. If direct labor hours are wasted, variable manufacturing overhead cost will also be wasted. The way to control the manufacturing overhead efficiency variance is to avoid the waste of direct labor hours.

A volume variance, on the other hand, does not provide a measure of efficiency; a volume variance is a measure of whether actual production volume was above or below expected average volume.

The volume variance occurs when the standard direct labor hours allowed are different from the expected direct labor hours used to compute the predetermined overhead rate.

Review Problem

Jan Company has developed the following flexible budget formula for the year 19X5:

Flexible budgeted overhead cost = $22,000 + $1.50 per direct labor hour

Jan Company produces a single product and has established a standard quantity of 2.2 direct labor hours for each unit. The company expects to produce 5,000 units during 19X5.

During the year, the company produced 5,100 units using 11,300 direct labor hours. The manufacturing overhead costs incurred during the year amounted to $39,013.

Required

1 Calculate the predetermined overhead rate and separate it into a fixed component and a variable component.

2 Calculate the spending variance, efficiency variance, and volume variance.

3 Prepare journal entries to:
   a Record the incurrence of actual manufacturing overhead costs
   b Record the applied manufacturing overhead
   c Record the variances for manufacturing overhead

Solution

1

Predetermined overhead rate (activity base is direct labor hours)	**= Estimated annual overhead cost / Estimated standard direct labor hours**
Estimated standard direct labor hours	**= 5,000 units × 2.2 direct labor hours**
	= 11,000 hours
Estimated annual overhead cost	**= $22,000 + $1.50 × 11,000 hours**
	= $22,000 + $16,500
	= $38,500

		Total		Fixed		Variable
Predetermined overhead rate (activity base is direct labor hours)	=	**$38,500 / 11,000 hours**	=	**$22,000 / 11,000 hours**	+	**$16,500 / 11,000 hours**
	=	**$3.50 per direct labor hour**	=	**$2.00 per direct labor hour**	+	**$1.50 per direct labor hour**

2 **Standard direct labor hours allowed = 5,100 units × 2.2 hours per unit**
= 11,220 hours

Cost Behavior Classification	Actual Manufacturing Overhead Cost	Flexible Budgeted Overhead For 11,300 Actual Direct Labor Hours	Flexible Budgeted Overhead For 11,220 Standard Direct Labor Hours Allowed	Total Applied Manufacturing Overhead for 11,220 Standard Direct Labor Hours
Fixed		$22,000	$22,000	$22,440[3]
Variable		16,950[1]	16,830[2]	16,830[2]
Total	$39,013	$38,950	$38,830	$39,270

$63U Spending variance | $120U Efficiency variance | $440F Volume variance

$257F Overapplied overhead

[1] $1.50 per direct labor hour × 11,300 hours.
[2] $1.50 per direct labor hour × 11,220 hours.
[3] $2.00 per direct labor hour × 11,220 hours.

3	a **Actual Manufacturing Overhead**	**$39,013**	
	Payroll, Accumulated Depreciation, etc.		**$39,013**
	(To record the incurrence of the actual manufacturing overhead.)		
	b **Work in Process**	**$39,270**	
	Applied Manufacturing Overhead		**$39,270**
	(To record the application of manufacturing overhead to the product.)		
	c **Applied Manufacturing Overhead**	**$39,270**	
	Spending Variance Overhead	**63**	
	Efficiency Variance Overhead	**120**	
	Volume Variance Overhead		**$ 440**
	Actual Manufacturing Overhead		**39,013**
	(To close the manufacturing overhead accounts and to record the variances in manufacturing overhead.)		

Glossary

Budget variance The difference between the actual manufacturing overhead costs and the flexible budgeted overhead costs for the standard direct labor hours allowed. The budget variance can be separated into a spending variance and an efficiency variance.

Efficiency variance The difference between the flexible budgeted overhead costs for the actual direct labor hours and the flexible budgeted overhead costs for the standard direct labor hours allowed. This variance represents a measure, in dollars, of how much variable overhead can be expected to increase or decrease as direct labor is used less or more efficiently.

Flexible budget A manufacturing overhead budget that varies the amount of overhead cost allowed as production varies; the expected manufacturing overhead cost is calculated at different levels of production activity. It allows the total manufacturing overhead variance to be separated into its components—the budget variance and the volume variance.

Over- or underapplied overhead The difference between the actual manufacturing overhead cost and the applied manufacturing overhead cost. This is sometimes called the total overhead variance.

Predetermined overhead rate A ratio which shows the amount of manufacturing overhead to be assigned to jobs or products produced per unit of activity measure. A predetermined overhead rate can be separated into fixed and variable components.

Spending variance The difference between the actual manufacturing overhead cost and the flexible budgeted overhead cost for the actual direct labor hours. This variance measures both the impact of price changes for the overhead items included in the flexible budget and any savings or wastage in the usage of the items.

Volume variance The difference between the flexible budget overhead cost based on standard direct labor hours allowed and the applied manufacturing overhead. This variance is a measure of the difference between expected average production volume and actual production volume.

Questions and Problems

9-1 Why would a company use a predetermined overhead rate to assign manufacturing overhead to a product?

9-2 Distinguish between static and flexible overhead budgets.

9-3 What are the cost accounting and managerial accounting uses of a flexible budget.

9-4 Why are flexible budgets developed on departmental bases rather than one budget for the entire factory?

9-5 What information does the efficiency variance offer management?

9-6 Discuss the possible causes of the spending and efficiency variances.

9-7 What information does the volume variance offer management?

9-8 What criteria should be used to select an activity base for the flexible budget?

9-9 **Calculation of Overhead Variances** The Widget Manufacturing Co. has just adopted a standard cost system. November 19X5 is the first month of its use. The president of the company gives you the following data for November 19X5:

	Standard	Actual
Material	5 pounds per unit at $2 per pound	6 pounds per unit at $1.50 per pound
Labor	10 hours per unit at $4 per hour	8 hours per unit at $5 per hour
Variable overhead	$1 per direct labor hour	$1.10 per direct labor hour
Fixed overhead	$1 per direct labor hour	$11,500
Expected average monthly standard volume	1,000 units	
Actual volume		1,500 units

Required

Calculate the budget and volume variances for overhead.

9-10 Calculation of Overhead Variances; Finding the Variable Overhead Rate The data below relate to the month of April 19X6 for Marilyn, Inc., which uses a standard cost system:

Actual total direct labor	$43,400	
Actual hours used	14,000	hours
Standard hours allowed for good output	15,000	hours
Direct labor price variance—debit	$ 1,400	
Actual total overhead	$32,000	
Budgeted fixed costs	$ 9,000	
"Normal" activity in hours	12,000	
Predetermined overhead rate	$2.25	per direct labor hour

Required

Calculate the spending, efficiency, and volume variances for manufacturing overhead.

(CPA)

9-11 Identification of Graphical Relationships

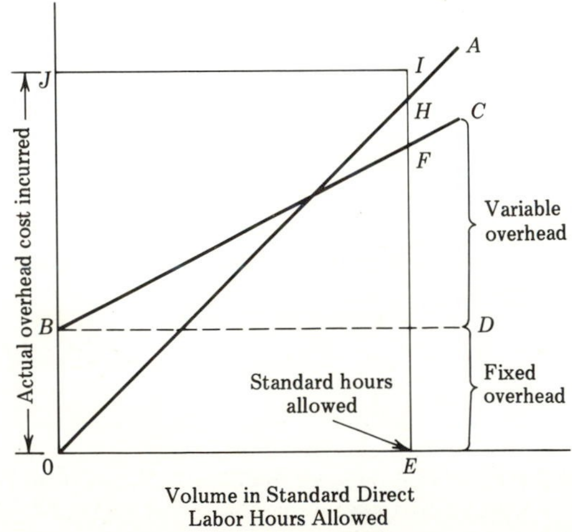

Required

Identify the following items by using two letters for each line.

1 *Amount* of overhead applied ________

2 Flexible budget line ________

3 *Amount* of budget variance ________

4 *Amount* of over- or underapplied overhead ________

5 *Amount* of volume variance ________

9-12 Computation of Overhead Variances The flexible budget shows the following monthly allowances for manufacturing overhead costs:

Percent of standard capacity	80%	100%	120%
Units produced	8,000	10,000	12,000
Manufacturing overhead costs:			
Fixed	$30,000	$30,000	$30,000
Variable	32,000	40,000	48,000
Total overhead costs	$62,000	$70,000	$78,000

The predetermined overhead rate is based on 100% of standard capacity. During the month of June, 8,000 units were completed at the following costs:

Material issued—16,200 pounds of material A @ $3.20	$51,840
Direct labor—31,800 hours @ $2.10	66,780
Manufacturing overhead costs:	$63,000

Required

Prepare a two-way variance analysis of the manufacturing overhead costs.

9-13 Calculation of Actual and Standard Hours from Overhead Variances The following information relates to a given department of Herman Company for the fourth quarter 19X4:

Actual total overhead (fixed plus variable)	$178,500
Budget formula	$110,000 plus $0.50 per hour
Predetermined overhead rate	$1.50 per hour
Spending variance	$8,000 unfavorable
Volume variance	$5,000 favorable

Required

1 Calculate the actual hours worked.

2 Calculate the standard hours allowed for good output.

(CPA)

9-14 Analysis of Overhead Relationships with Labor Hours Strayer Company had budgeted the following sales and costs for 19X3:

Unit sales	20,000
Sales	$200,000
Total production costs at standard cost	$130,000
Gross margin	$ 70,000
Beginning inventories	None
Ending inventories	None

At the end of 19X3, Strayer Company reported production and sales of 19,200 units. Actual factory overhead incurred was exactly equal to flexible budgeted factory overhead for 19X3 using actual direct labor hours and there was underapplied manufacturing overhead of $2,000 at December 31, 19X3. Factory overhead is applied to the work in process inventory on the basis of standard direct labor hours allowed for units produced. Also, there was a favorable direct labor quantity variance, but there were no direct labor price variance and no direct materials variances for 19X3.

Required

Explain why factory overhead was underapplied by $2,000, and, being as specific as the data permit, indicate which overhead variances may have been affected. Strayer uses a three-way method of analyzing the over- or underapplied overhead. The three variances are (1) spending variance, (2) efficiency variance, and (3) volume variance.

(CPA)

9-15 Three-Way Analysis of Overhead Enfin Company's annual planning anticipated producing 8,800 units of product in November. The average volume per month was anticipated to be 8,400 units per month. By the start of November, inventory reduction was a new goal of management and only 8,600 units were produced during the month.

The flexible budget formula used by management in planning overhead costs was:

Total overhead cost = $6,720 per month + $1.10 per direct labor hour

The actual overhead cost for the month was $12,300. The actual direct labor hours were 4,400. The accountant computed the direct labor efficiency variance for November to be $600 unfavorable using a standard direct labor rate of $6.00 per hour.

Required

1 Prepare a three-way analysis of manufacturing overhead.

2 How would the volume variance have been different if the company had produced 8,800 units during the month? Given the circumstances in November, would it have been more favorable for Enfin to have produced 8,800 units?

9-16 Variance Analysis Working Backwards Doreen Company produces a single product and uses a standard process cost accounting system. The standards and related data are as follows:

Direct materials 2 pounds @ $1.30 per pound	$2.60

Direct labor 1 hour @ $4 per hour	4.00
Overhead	?
"Normal" production volume	10,000 units per month
Predetermined overhead rate	$3.10 per direct labor hour
Variable overhead rate	$1.60 per direct labor hour

For May, the following data is known:

Units produced	10,600
Total direct labor cost	$43,570
Direct labor quantity (efficiency) variance	$ 400 favorable
Overhead spending variance	$ 700 unfavorable
Direct materials purchased 24,200 pounds	$31,560
Direct materials used 22,000 pounds	

Required Calculate:

1 Direct materials price variance

2 Direct materials quantity variance

3 Budgeted fixed overhead per month

4 Overhead volume variance

5 Total over- or underapplied overhead

9-17 Variance Calculation Actual Data per Unit The Jones Furniture Company uses a standard cost system in accounting for its production costs.

The standard cost of a unit of furniture follows:

Lumber, 100 feet @ $150 per 1,000 feet		$15.00
Direct labor, 4 hours @ $2.50 per hour		10.00
Manufacturing overhead:		
Fixed (30% of direct labor)	$3.00	
Variable (60% of direct labor)	6.00	9.00
Total cost per unit		34.00

The following flexible monthly overhead budget is in effect:

Direct Labor Hours	Estimated Overhead
5,200	$10,800
4,800	10,200
4,400	9,600
4,000 (normal capacity)	9,000
3,600	8,400

The actual costs per unit for the month of December were as follows:

Lumber used (110 feet @ $120 per 1,000 feet)	$13.20
Direct labor (4¼ hours @ $2.60 per hour)	11.05
Manufacturing overhead ($10,560 ÷ 1,200 units)	8.80
Total actual unit cost	$33.05

Required Prepare an analysis of the material, labor, and overhead variances.

(CPA)

9-18 Variance Calculation—Multiple Choice The Groomer Company manufactures two products used in the plastics industry, Florimene and Glyoxide. The company uses a flexible budget and a standard cost system to develop variances. Selected data follow:

	Florimene	Glyoxide
Data on standard costs:		
Direct materials per unit	3 pounds at $1.00 per pound	4 pounds at $1.10 per pound
Direct labor per unit	5 hours at $8.00 per hour	6 hours at $7.50 per hour
Variable factory overhead per unit	$3.20 per direct labor hour	$3.50 per direct labor hour
Fixed factory overhead per month	$20,700	$26,520
Normal activity per month	5,750 direct labor hours	7,800 direct labor hours
Units produced in September	1,000	1,200
Cost incurred for September:		
Direct materials	3,100 pounds at $.90 per pound	4,700 pounds at $1.15 per pound
Direct labor	4,900 hours at $7.95 per hour	7,400 hours at $7.55 per hour
Variable manufacturing overhead	$16,170	$25,234
Fixed manufacturing overhead	$20,930	$26,400

Required Select the best answer for the following questions:

1 The labor quantity variances for both products for September are:
  - **a** Florimene, $195 favorable; Glyoxide, $510 unfavorable
  - **b** Florimene, $1,700 favorable; Glyoxide, $1,000 favorable
  - **c** Florimene, $200 favorable; Glyoxide, $500 unfavorable
  - **d** Florimene, $195 favorable; Glyoxide, $510 favorable
  - **e** None of the above

2 The labor price variances for both products for September are:
  - **a** Florimene, $245 favorable; Glyoxide, $370 unfavorable
  - **b** Florimene, $200 favorable; Glyoxide, $500 unfavorable
  - **c** Florimene, $1,945 favorable; Glyoxide, $630 favorable

d Florimene, $245 unfavorable; Glyoxide, $370 favorable
e None of the above

3 The budget variances for overhead for both products for September are:

a Florimene, $720 unfavorable; Glyoxide, $786 favorable
b Florimene, $397 unfavorable; Glyoxide, $85 unfavorable
c Florimene, $400 unfavorable; Glyoxide, $86 unfavorable
d Florimene, $2,130 favorable; Glyoxide, $2,080 favorable
e None of the above

(CPA)

9-19 Variance Calculation The Bronson Company manufactures a fuel additive which has a stable selling price of $40 per drum. Since losing a government contract the company has been producing and selling 80,000 drums per month, 50% of normal capacity. Management expects to increase production to 140,000 drums per month in the coming fiscal year.

In connection with your examination of the financial statements of the Bronson Company for the year ended September 30, 19X0, you have been asked to review some computations made by Bronson's cost accountant. Your working papers disclose the following about the company's operations:

1 Standard costs per drum of product manufactured:

Materials:	
8 gallons of Miracle Mix	$16
1 empty drum	1
Direct labor—1 hour	5
Factory overhead	6

2 Costs and expenses during September 19X0:

Miracle Mix:	
500,000 gallons purchased at a cost of $950,000; 650,000 gallons used	
Empty drums:	
94,000 purchased at a cost of $94,000; 80,000 used	
Direct labor:	
82,000 hours worked at a cost of $414,100	
Factory overhead:	
Depreciation of building and machinery (fixed)	$210,000
Supervision and indirect labor (semivariable)	460,000
Other factory overhead (variable)	98,000
	$768,000

3 Other factory overhead was the only actual overhead cost which varied from the overhead budget for the September level of production; actual other factory overhead was $98,000 and the budgeted amount was $90,000.

4 At normal capacity of 160,000 drums per month, supervision and

indirect labor costs are expected to be $570,000. All cost functions are linear.

5 The company uses the two-way method for calculating overhead variances.

Required Compute the following variances for September 19X0: (*a*) materials price variance, (*b*) materials quantity variance, (*c*) labor price variance, (*d*) labor quantity variance, (*e*) overhead budget variance, and (*f*) overhead volume variance. Indicate whether each variance was favorable or unfavorable.

(CPA)

9-20 Variance Computation Material, Labor, and Overhead Roach Manufacturing Co. manufactures Knock-out, a pesticide effective in controlling pine beetles. The company uses a standard cost system and a flexible budget. Standard cost of a gallon of Knock-out is as follows:

Direct materials:	
2 quarts of Bordine	$14
4 quarts of Mapine	16
Total Direct Materials	$30
Direct labor:	
2 hours	16
Factory overhead	12
Total	58

The flexible budget system provides for $50,000 of fixed overhead at normal capacity of 10,000 direct labor hours. Variable overhead is projected at $1 per direct labor hour.

Actual results for the period indicated the following:

Production:	5,000 gallons of Knock-out	
Direct materials:		
Bordine:	12,000 quarts purchased at a cost of $7.20/quart; 10,500 quarts used	
Mapine:	20,000 quarts purchased at a cost of $3.90/quart; 19,800 quarts used	
Direct labor:	9,800 hours worked at a cost of $79,380	
Overhead:	Fixed	$48,100
	Variable	21,000
	Total overhead	$69,100

The company uses a perpetual inventory system and records purchases at standard cost.

Required Compute direct materials, direct labor, and overhead variances. The company uses a three-way analysis of overhead.

(John Moore)

10 STANDARD COST VARIANCES: WHAT TO DO WITH THEM AND HOW TO REPORT WHAT YOU DID

AFTER COMPLETING YOUR STUDY OF THIS CHAPTER, YOU SHOULD HAVE LEARNED:

1 How to calculate the standard cost of production when there are partially completed units in the ending work in process.

2 That at the end of the fiscal year standard cost variances may be (a) closed (added to) entirely to the cost of goods sold account if the amounts are small or (b) allocated between the inventory accounts on the balance sheet and the cost of goods sold account on the income statement if the amounts are so large that management does not believe standards to be attainable.

If you learned the following things from Chapters 8 and 9, then our writing and your study were successful: (1) how to calculate variances from standard costs (direct materials, direct labor, and manufacturing overhead) and (2) how to record standard costs in the general ledger. In this chapter we are going to put these concepts together into one comprehensive example to help you reinforce your understanding of standard costs, variances, and how they are recorded in the general ledger. We will discuss and illustrate two procedures to account for the standard cost variance accounts at the end of the year. We will also illustrate how equivalent units as used in process cost accounting systems are used in standard process cost accounting systems.

STANDARD COSTS AND VARIANCES: PUTTING IT ALL TOGETHER

The Beville Manufacturing Company produces a single product, a special wax used for rustproofing automobiles. Each container of wax consists of 2 pounds of a special compound produced by a manufacturing process developed by J. Beville, the founder of the company. Beville sells finished containers of wax directly to consumers for $70 each. The standard cost of producing each container of wax is:

BEVILLE MANUFACTURING COMPANY
Wax No. 1058
Standard Cost per Container
For the Year 19X3

Item	Standard Quantity	Standard Price	Standard Cost
Direct materials	2 pounds	× $4.00 per pound =	$ 8.00
Direct labor	2 hours	× $10.00 per hour =	20.00
Manufacturing overhead	2 direct labor hours	× $8.00 per direct labor hour* =	16.00
Total standard cost per container			$44.00

* The predetermined overhead rate is based on the expected annual production of 10,000 containers of wax and the following flexible budget:
Total overhead cost = $60,000 + $5.00 per direct labor hour

During the year the following actual production, costs, sales, and selling and administrative expenses occurred:

BEVILLE MANUFACTURING COMPANY
Wax No. 1058
Actual Data for the Year 19X3

Actual Production in Units (Containers)	
Beginning work in process	0
Units started	10,000
Units completed	7,000

Ending work in process (100% finished for direct materials ⅓ finished for direct labor and manufacturing overhead)	3,000

Actual Manufacturing Costs

Direct materials purchased; 24,000 pounds × $4.20 per pound	= $100,800
Direct materials used	= 22,000 pounds
Direct labor cost; 17,600 hours × $10.50 per hour	= $184,800
Manufacturing overhead cost	= $120,000

Actual Sales Revenue and Expenses

Sales, 6,000 units × $70.00 per unit	= $420,000
Selling and administrative expense	= $100,000

Given the standard costs and actual results for the Beville Manufacturing Company, we wish to:

1 Calculate the standard cost of production (we will explain what this is and how it is used in the following section)

2 Calculate standard cost variances for
   a Direct materials
   b Direct labor
   c Manufacturing overhead

3 Prepare journal entries to record
   a Standard costs
   b Manufacturing variances in the general ledger

Standard Cost of Production

In Chapters 8 and 9 our examples contained no partially completed units and we could calculate the standard cost of production by multiplying the number of units completed (total production for the period) times the standard cost per unit. However, the Beville Manufacturing Company has partially completed units in the ending work in process.

Equivalent finished units equals units completed plus equivalent finished units in ending work in process. (Beginning work in process was zero.)

To determine production for the Beville Manufacturing Company the partially completed units must be converted to equivalent finished units for direct materials, direct labor, and manufacturing overhead. Because our example contains no beginning work in process, the units completed plus the equivalent finished units in the ending work in process represent the total amount of production put forth by the Beville Company during the year.

With the basic information given for the Beville Manufacturing Company, we can prepare a standard cost summary as shown in Exhibit 10-1. Part A shows the total number of actual physical units started by the company and must be accounted for through to the end of the process. Part B shows the total number of actual physical units completed and still in work in process. The total of the completed and partially completed actual physical units must be equal to the total number of physical units in part A. Also in part B are the equivalent finished units of production for each cost category.

EXHIBIT 10-1
BEVILLE MANUFACTURING COMPANY
Standard Cost Summary
For the Year 19X3

A Units to Account for	Physical Flow
Beginning work in process	0
Units started	10,000
Total	10,000

B Units Accounted for	Physical Flow	Current Period Equivalent Finished Units: Direct Materials	Direct Labor	Manufacturing Overhead
Completed	7,000	7,000	7,000	7,000
Ending work in process	3,000	3,000	1,000*	1,000*
	10,000	10,000	8,000	8,000

C Standard Costs to Account for Cost Item	Equivalent Finished Units	Standard Cost per Unit	Total Standard Cost
Direct materials	10,000	$ 8.00	$ 80,000
Direct labor	8,000	$20.00	$160,000
Manufacturing overhead	8,000	$16.00	$128,000
		$44.00	$368,000

* 3,000 units, ⅓ finished.

In part C you see a tabulation of each of the manufacturing cost items, the equivalent finished units for each cost item from part B, the standard cost per unit for each cost item, and the total standard cost for each cost item. The total standard cost for each cost item is calculated by multiplying the equivalent finished units times the standard cost per unit. The sum of the standard costs for direct materials, direct labor, and manufacturing overhead is $368,000 which is the *total standard cost of production.* The components of this amount are used to calculate variances as well as following the flow of costs through work in process to finished goods to cost of goods sold. Its use will be illustrated in the following sections.

Computation of Standard Cost Variances

Now that we have calculated the standard cost of production for direct materials, direct labor, and manufacturing overhead we can compare the actual manufacturing costs to the standard costs to calculate variances.

Exhibit 10-2 illustrates, for our example, how we compare the actual cost data given on page 277 to the standard cost to find the cost variances for each cost item.

EXHIBIT 10-2
BEVILLE MANUFACTURING COMPANY
Computation of Manufacturing Variances
For the Year 19X3

Direct Materials

Total Actual Quantity of Direct Materials Purchased × Actual Price	Total Actual Quantity of Direct Materials Purchased × Standard Price	Total Actual Quantity of Direct Materials Used × Standard Price	Total Standard Quantity of Direct Materials Allowed × Standard Price
24,000 pounds @ $4.20 per pound	24,000 pounds @ $4.00 per pound	22,000 pounds @ $4.00 per pound	20,000 pounds* @ $4.00 per pound
$100,800 (1)	$96,000 (1)	$88,000 (2)	$80,000 (2)

$4,800 unfavorable (1) — Price variance

$8,000 unfavorable (2) — Quantity variance

* 10,000 equivalent finished units × 2 pounds per unit = 20,000 pounds allowed.

Direct Labor

Total Actual Quantity of Direct Labor Used × Actual Price	Total Actual Quantity of Direct Labor Used × Standard Price	Total Standard Quantity of Direct Labor Allowed × Standard Price
17,600 hours @ $10.50 per hour	17,600 hours @ $10.00 per hour	16,000 hours* @ 10.00 per hour
$184,800 (3)	$176,000	$160,000 (3)

$8,800 unfavorable (3) — Price variance

$16,000 unfavorable (3) — Quantity variance

* 8,000 equivalent finished units × 2 direct labor hours units = 16,000 hours allowed.

Manufacturing Overhead

Actual Manufacturing Overhead Cost	Flexible Budgeted Overhead for 17,600 Actual Direct Labor Hours	Flexible Budgeted Overhead for 16,000 Standard Direct Labor Hours Allowed	Total Applied Manufacturing Overhead for 16,000 Standard Direct Labor Hours Allowed
	$60,000 + $5 × 17,600 hours	$60,000 + $5 × 16,000 hours	16,000 hours* × $8.00 per hour
$120,000 (5) (6)	$148,000	$140,000	$128,000 (4) (6)

$28,000 Favorable (6) — Spending Variance

$8,000 Unfavorable (6) — Efficiency Variance

$12,000 Unfavorable (6) — Volume Variance

* 8,000 equivalent finished units × 2 direct labor hours per unit = 16,000 hours allowed.

The bracket numbers (1) through (6) reference the journal entries in the following section.

Equivalent finished units of output provide a meaningful measure of total production for the period.

We demonstrated the same variance calculations in Chapters 8 and 9, but here we have the additional real world complication of having to consider partially completed units in our calculations.

Note that the standard quantity allowed (amounts expected to be used) for direct materials, direct labor, and manufacturing overhead are based on the equivalent finished units of production. We do this because the equivalent finished units represent a meaningful measure of the production work that was done during the accounting period. Manufacturing variances are calculated based on the production for a period of time—a day, a week, a month, or, in our example, a year. At the end of the time period some units are complete and some units only partially completed. We cannot calculate production measures or unit costs by adding together completed units and partially completed units. Therefore, we convert the completed units and the partially completed units into equivalent finished units which can meaningfully be added together to measure total production.

Journal Entries in the General Ledger

The journal entries are given below to record for each cost item (*a*) inventories at standard cost and (*b*) variances for the Beville Manufacturing Company. All data for these journal entries are taken from Exhibit 10-2 and are keyed to Exhibit 10-2 by the journal entry number.

1	**Materials Inventory**	**$96,000**	
	Price Variance—Direct Materials	**4,800**	
	Accounts Payable		**$100,800**
	(To record the purchase of 24,000 pounds of direct materials at a cost of $4.20 per pound.)		
2	**Work in Process (Direct Materials)**	**$80,000**	
	Quantity Variance—Direct Materials	**8,000**	
	Materials Inventory		**$88,000**
	(To record the issuance of direct materials for the production of 10,000 equivalent finished units.)		
3	**Work in Process (Direct Labor)**	**$160,000**	
	Price Variance—Direct Labor	**8,800**	
	Quantity Variance—Direct Labor	**16,000**	
	Payroll		**$184,800**
	(To distribute the payroll costs to work in process and the variance accounts for direct labor.)		
4	**Work in Process (Applied Manufacturing Overhead)**	**$128,000**	
	Applied Manufacturing Overhead		**$128,000**
	(To record the application of the manufacturing overhead at a rate of $8.00 per standard direct labor hour for 16,000 standard direct labor hours.)		

5	**Actual Manufacturing Overhead**	**$120,000**	
	Miscellaneous Accounts		**$120,000**
	(To record the actual manufacturing overhead costs.)		

6	**Applied Manufacturing Overhead**	**$128,000**	
	Efficiency Variance—Overhead	**8,000**	
	Volume Variance—Overhead	**12,000**	
	Spending Variance—Overhead		**$ 28,000**
	Actual Manufacturing Overhead		**120,000**
	(To close the manufacturing overhead accounts and to record the variances in manufacturing overhead.)		

These six journal entries record the standard manufacturing costs and variances for the Beville Manufacturing Company. We must now record the standard cost of the units completed and transferred to finished goods and the revenues and costs associated with the units sold. To illustrate these journal entries we will continue the Beville Manufacturing Company example using the data given on page 277.

Seven thousand containers of wax were completed during the year and transferred to finished goods inventory. The entry to record the standard cost of the units transferred is entry 7 below:

7	**Finished Goods (Standard Cost)**	**$308,000**	
	Work in Process (Standard Cost)		**$308,000**
	(To record the standard cost of 7,000 completed containers at a standard cost per container of $44.)		

Six thousand containers of wax were sold on credit during the year at a sales price per container of $70.00. Entry 8 records the sales revenue.

8	**Accounts Receivable**	**$420,000**	
	Sales Revenue		**$420,000**
	(To record the sales revenue from the sale of 6,000 containers of wax for $70 per unit.)		

The journal entry to record the standard cost of the 6,000 containers sold is given below as entry 9.

9	**Cost of Goods Sold (Standard Cost)**	**$264,000**	
	Finished Goods (Standard Cost)		**$264,000**
	(To record the standard cost of the 6,000 containers sold at a standard cost per container of $44.)		

Based on the actual data given on page 277 for the Beville Manufacturing Company the selling and administrative expenses amounted to $100,000 for the year 19X3. The journal entry to record these expenses is given below as entry 10.

10	**Selling and Administrative Expense**	**$100,000**	
	Various Accounts		**$100,000**
	(To record actual selling and administrative expenses for the year 19X3.)		

To put the entire Beville Manufacturing Company example together, a summary of the cost flows is given in the T accounts in Exhibit 10-3. The flow of costs through the T accounts is keyed to the numbered journal entries (1–10) discussed above.

MANUFACTURING VARIANCES: WHAT TO DO WITH THEM FOR CALCULATING OPERATING INCOME

Now that we have recorded the sales revenues, actual selling and administrative expenses, standard manufacturing costs, and manufacturing variances for the Beville Manufacturing Company, the next step is to calculate operating income for 19X3. However, before we can calculate operating income we must decide how we are going to account for the manufacturing variances.

There are two ways that manufacturing variances can be accounted for:

The two methods of accounting for manufacturing variance.

1 All manufacturing variances are closed to (added to) the cost of goods sold account on the income statement.

2 All manufacturing variances are allocated between the inventory accounts on the balance sheet and the cost of goods sold account on the income statement. For example, if there was an unfavorable variance of $10,000, some of it say, $3,000, would be added to the cost of goods still in inventory and not yet sold. By this second method, inventories carry their proportional share of the variance because the actual cost turned out to be higher than expected (standard). The cost of goods sold account on the income statement would carry the remaining $7,000 of the higher actual costs. This procedure adjusts the balances of the accounts to approximately what they would have been if the company had used an actual cost system rather than a standard cost system.

The second method, in effect, converts the account balances from standard costs to actual historical costs.

Closing All Manufacturing Cost Variances to Cost of Goods Sold

If the standard costs "closely approximate" actual costs incurred, then inventories may be valued at the standard costs for purposes of external financial reporting. (Accounting Research Bulletin No. 43 allows this, as we explained in Chapter 8.) Most companies that use currently attainable cost standards will experience relatively small variances between actual costs and standard costs; therefore they report inventories at standard costs for external financial reports. In this situation, each of the manufacturing variances—for direct materials, direct labor, and manufacturing overhead—are closed to the cost of goods sold account.

The argument for **closing all the manufacturing variances to the cost of goods sold account** is that the standard cost represents the inventory costs which would have been incurred with good cost control. Any manufacturing variances from the standard cost represent either better or poorer than average cost control—a gain or loss which occurred within a particular accounting period. In the Beville Manufacturing Company example the variances occurred in the year 19X3 and should therefore affect reported income for 19X3.

The first method considers the variances as a gain or loss in the period in which they occurred.

Thus, a sound accounting treatment would be to account for manufacturing cost

EXHIBIT 10-3
BEVILLE MANUFACTURING COMPANY
T Accounts for the Year 19X3
Balance Sheet Accounts

Materials Inventory	
Balance zero (1) 96,000	38,000 (2)
Balance 8,000	

Work in Process	
Balance zero (2) 80,000 (3) 160,000 (4) 128,000	308,000 (7)
Balance 60,000	

Finished Goods	
Balance zero (7) 308,000	264,000 (9)
Balance 44,000	

Accounts Receivable	
(8) 420,000	

Payroll	
	184,800 (3)

Accounts Payable	
	100,800 (1)

Miscellaneous	
	120,000 (5) 100,000 (10)

Actual Manufacturing Overhead	
(5) 120,000	120,000 (6)
Balance 0	

Applied Manufacturing Overhead	
(6) 128,000	128,000 (4)
Balance 0	

Income Statement Accounts

Sales Revenue	
	420,000 (8)

Cost of Goods Sold	
(9) 264,000	

Selling and Administrative Expenses	
(10) 100,000	

Manufacturing Variance Accounts

Price Variance Direct Materials	
(1) 4,800	

Quantity Variance Direct Materials	
(2) 8,000	

Price Variance Direct Labor	
(3) 8,800	

Quantity Variance Direct Labor	
(3) 16,000	

Spending Variance—Overhead	
	28,000 (6)

Efficiency Variance—Overhead	
(6) 8,000	

Volume Variance—Overhead	
(6) 12,000	

1 To record the purchase of direct materials.
2 To record the issuance of direct materials for production of wax.
3 To distribute the payroll cost to work in process and the variance accounts for direct labor.
4 The application of manufacturing overhead to work in process.
5 The recording of actual manufacturing overhead costs.
6 To record the manufacturing overhead variances.
7 To transfer the standard cost of the completed containers to finished goods from work in process.
8 To record the sales revenue from the sale of 6,000 containers of wax.
9 To record the standard cost of goods sold for 6,000 containers.
10 To record the actual selling and administrative expenses for the year.

variances by closing them to the cost of goods sold account in the period in which they occurred.

For the Beville Manufacturing Company the journal entry to close the manufacturing variances to the cost of goods sold account is given below:

Cost of Goods Sold	**$29,600**	
Spending Variance—Overhead	**28,000**	
Efficiency Variance—Overhead		**$ 8,000**
Volume Variance—Overhead		**12,000**
Price Variance—Direct Materials		**4,800**
Quantity Variance—Direct Materials		**8,000**
Price Variance—Direct Labor		**8,800**
Quantity Variance—Direct Labor		**16,000**
(To close all the manufacturing variance accounts to the cost of goods sold account.)		

The data for the closing entry for the manufacturing variance accounts is obtained from the T accounts in Exhibit 10-3.

Exhibit 10-4 illustrates the income statement for the Beville Manufacturing Company for 19X3 following the first method of accounting for variances. The information for the income statement comes from the appropriate account balances in Exhibit 10-3 adjusted for the closing entry just given.

Exhibit 10-4 also contains a schedule of the manufacturing variances that were closed to the cost of goods sold account. The cost of goods sold amounts to $293,600 and consists of the standard cost of goods sold of $264,000 plus the unfavorable total manufacturing variance of $29,600. If the total manufacturing variance had been favorable then the manufacturing variance would have been deducted from the standard cost of goods sold.

Allocation of Manufacturing Variances between the Inventory Accounts on the Balance Sheet and the Cost of Goods Sold Account on the Income Statement

If the variances are large, the standards are not good measures of the cost of inventory.

If the manufacturing variances are very large, standard costs do not approximate actual costs and would not meet the requirements of Accounting Research Bulletin No. 43. Large variances probably mean that even with good cost control the product could not have been produced for its standard cost. Thus the standards are not good measures of the cost of inventory. In this situation, the manufacturing variances are allocated between the inventory accounts on the balance sheet and the cost of goods sold account on the income statement.

The purpose of **allocation of manufacturing variances** is to adjust the standard costs recorded in the inventory accounts and cost of goods sold account to the actual historical cost. Remember that manufacturing variances were calculated as the difference between actual cost and standard cost. The standard costs and manufacturing variances were then recorded in the general ledger. To follow the second method, we allocate the manufacturing variances to the inventories and cost of goods sold to convert them from standard cost to actual cost.

The allocation of each manufacturing variance is based on the standard amount of direct materials, direct labor, and manufacturing overhead in each inventory account and the cost of goods sold account. That is, the variance in direct labor is allocated based on the standard direct labor cost content of each inventory account

EXHIBIT 10-4
BEVILLE MANUFACTURING COMPANY
Income Statement
For the Year 19X3

Sales revenues		$420,000
Cost of goods sold		
Standard cost of goods sold	$264,000	
Unfavorable manufacturing variances	+ 29,600	293,600
Gross profit		$126,400
Selling and administrative expense		100,000
Operating income		$ 26,400

Manufacturing Variance Schedule

Price variance—direct materials	$ 4,800	unfavorable
Quantity variance—direct materials	8,000	unfavorable
Price variance—direct labor	8,800	unfavorable
Quantity variance—direct labor	16,000	unfavorable
Spending variance—overhead	28,000	favorable
Efficiency variance—overhead	8,000	unfavorable
Volume variance—overhead	12,000	unfavorable
Total manufacturing variance	$29,600	unfavorable

balance and of the cost of goods sold account. To illustrate the allocation procedures we will continue the Beville Manufacturing Company example.

Direct Labor The total variance in direct labor, calculated in Exhibit 10-2, is $24,800 unfavorable, as shown below:

Price variance in direct labor	= $ 8,800 unfavorable
Quantity variance in direct labor	= 16,000 unfavorable
Total variance in direct labor	= $24,800 unfavorable

The total variance in direct labor is allocated to the work in process account, finished goods account, and cost of goods sold account based on the standard direct labor cost content in the balance of each account.

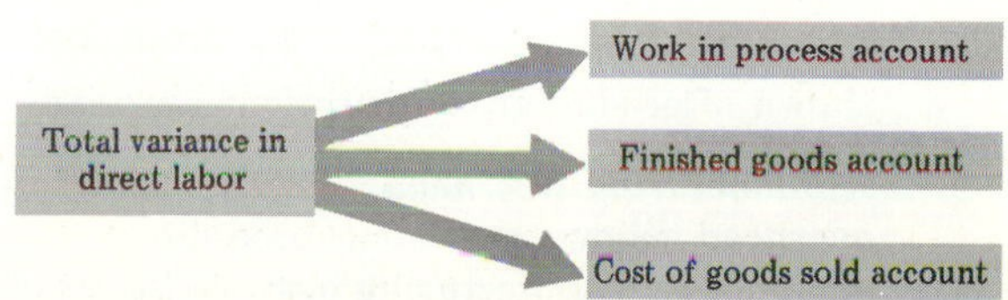

The direct labor cost variances are allocated to the accounts in proportion to their direct labor cost content.

The first step in allocating the variances in direct labor is to determine the standard cost of direct labor in the work in process account, finished goods account, and cost of goods sold account. The computations of the standard direct labor cost in each account are shown below:

Account	Explanation	Standard Direct Labor Cost
Work in process	*Equivalent* finished units in the ending work in process times the standard direct labor cost per unit, using the data from Exhibit 10-1 1,000 units × \$20.00 per unit =	\$ 20,000
Finished goods	Number of units in the ending finished goods times the standard direct labor cost per unit 1,000 units × \$20.00 per unit =	\$ 20,000
Cost of goods sold	Number of units sold times the standard direct labor cost per unit 6,000 units × \$20.00 per unit =	\$120,000
Total standard cost of direct labor		\$160,000

The allocation of the total direct labor variance is based on the proportion of the total standard direct labor cost in each account as shown below:

Account	Standard Direct Labor Cost	Proportion		Total Direct Labor Variance		Allocation of Variance in Direct Labor
Work in process	\$ 20,000	\$ 20,000 / \$160,000	×	\$24,800	=	\$ 3,100
Finished goods	\$ 20,000	\$ 20,000 / \$160,000	×	\$24,800	=	\$ 3,100
Cost of goods sold	\$120,000	\$120,000 / \$160,000	×	\$24,800	=	\$18,600
	\$160,000					\$24,800

The journal entry to record the allocation of the variance in direct labor will be shown after similar computations are made for the other variances.

Manufacturing Overhead The allocation of the total variance in manufacturing overhead follows the same procedures we illustrated for direct labor. The total variance in manufacturing overhead is \$8,000 favorable based on the computations in Exhibit 10-2.

Spending variance in overhead	$28,000	favorable
Efficiency variance in overhead	8,000	unfavorable
Volume variance in overhead	12,000	unfavorable
Total variance in overhead	$ 8,000	favorable

The total overhead variances are allocated in the same manner as the total direct labor variance was.

The total variance is allocated to the work in process account, finished goods account, and cost of goods sold account based on the standard manufacturing overhead content of each account.

Account	Explanation		Standard Manufacturing Overhead Cost
Work in process	*Equivalent* finished units in the ending work in process times the standard manufacturing overhead cost per unit, using the data from Exhibit 10-1 1,000 units × $16.00 per unit	=	$ 16,000
Finished goods	Number of units in the ending finished goods times the standard manufacturing overhead cost per unit 1,000 units × $16.00 per unit	=	$ 16,000
Cost of goods sold	Number of units sold times the standard manufacturing overhead cost per unit 6,000 units × $16.00 per unit	=	$ 96,000
Total standard cost of manufacturing overhead			$128,000

The allocation of the total variance in manufacturing overhead is shown below:

Account	Standard Manufacturing Overhead Cost	Proportion		Total Variance in Manufacturing Overhead		Allocation of Variance in Manufacturing Overhead
Work in process	$ 16,000	$\frac{\$16,000}{\$128,000}$	×	$8,000	=	$1,000
Finished goods	$ 16,000	$\frac{\$16,000}{\$128,000}$	×	$8,000	=	$1,000
Cost of goods sold	$ 96,000	$\frac{\$96,000}{\$128,000}$	×	$8,000	=	$6,000
	$128,000					$8,000

Direct Materials Now, remember, the variances associated with direct materials are: the price variance, which is based on the quantity of direct materials *purchased,* and the fact that the actual price paid for the materials is different from the price that was expected to be paid; and the quantity variance, which is based on the quantity of materials actually *used* and the price standard.

For this reason we must allocate the price variance and quantity variance in direct materials separately. Using the Beville Manufacturing Company data, we will first allocate the quantity variance in direct materials.

From Exhibit 10-2, we know for the Beville Manufacturing Company the price variance and quantity variance in direct materials are:

Price variance	$ 4,800	unfavorable
Quantity variance	8,000	unfavorable
Total variance	$12,800	unfavorable

Quantity Variance in Direct Materials Since the quantity variance in direct materials is based on the quantity of direct materials *used,* it must be allocated to the work in process account, finished goods account, and the cost of goods sold account as the direct labor and overhead variances were. A similar illustration applies.

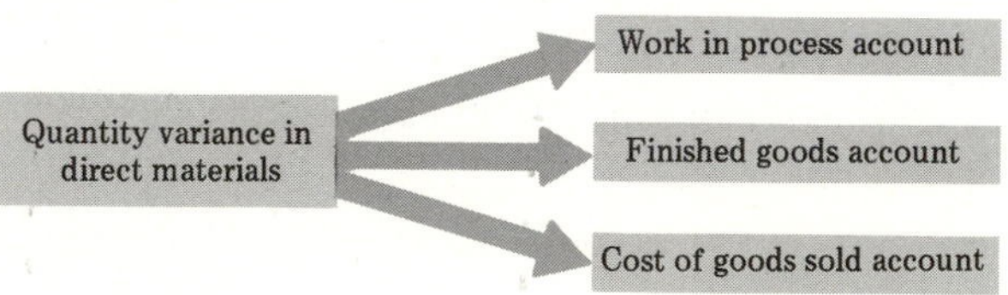

The direct materials quantity variance is allocated in the same manner as the direct labor and overhead variances.

The quantity variance in direct materials is allocated in the same manner as the variance in direct labor and manufacturing overhead. That is, the quantity variance is allocated based on the standard direct materials cost in the work in process account, finished goods account, and cost of goods sold account.

The standard direct materials balance in each account is determined as follows:

Account		Standard Direct Materials Balance
Work in process	*Equivalent* finished units in the ending work in process times the standard direct materials cost per unit, from Exhibit 10-1 3,000 units × $8.00 per unit =	$24,000
Finished goods	Number of units in the ending finished goods times the standard direct materials cost per unit 1,000 units × $8.00 per unit =	$ 8,000

Cost of goods sold	Number of units sold times the standard direct materials cost per unit 6,000 units × $8.00 per unit =	$48,000
Total standard cost of direct materials		$80,000

The allocation of the quantity variance in direct materials is based on the proportion of the total standard direct materials cost in each account as shown below:

Account	Standard Cost of Direct Materials	Proportion		Quantity Variance in Direct Materials		Allocation of the Quantity Variance in Direct Materials
Work in process	$24,000	$24,000 / $80,000	×	$8,000	=	$2,400
Finished goods	$ 8,000	$ 8,000 / $80,000	×	$8,000	=	$ 800
Cost of goods sold	$48,000	$48,000 / $80,000	×	$8,000	=	$4,800
	$80,000					$8,000

Price Variance in Direct Materials The price variance in direct materials is based on the quantity of direct materials *purchased*. Therefore, it must be allocated to the *materials inventory account*, work in process account, finished goods account, and the cost of goods sold account as shown below:

The direct materials price variance is allocated to four accounts rather than three acounts.

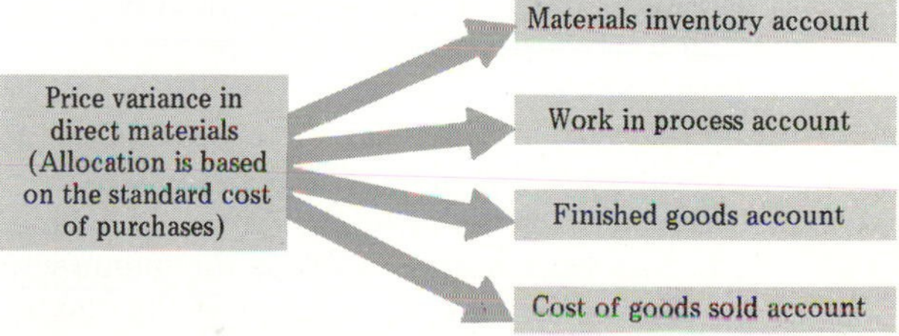

To determine the amount of direct materials price variance to allocate to each account we must first compute how much of the $96,000 standard cost of purchases (24,000 pounds × $4 per pound) is included in each account. The standard cost of purchases in the work in process, finished goods, and cost of goods sold accounts is determined by adding the quantity variance allocation in direct materials to the standard cost of direct materials in each account. The standard cost of purchases remaining in the materials inventory account is the ending balance shown in Exhibit 10-3.

The allocation of the price variance in direct materials is shown below:

Account	Standard Cost of Direct Materials	+	Quantity Variance Allocation	=	Standard Cost of Purchases	Proportion		Price Variance in Direct Materials		Price Variance Allocation
Materials inventory	$ 8,000		—		$ 8,000	$ 8,000 / $96,000	×	$4,800	=	$ 400
Work in process	$24,000	+	$2,400	=	$26,400	$26,400 / $96,000	×	$4,800	=	$1,320
Finished goods	$ 8,000	+	$ 800	=	$ 8,800	$ 8,800 / $96,000	×	$4,800	=	$ 440
Cost of goods sold	$48,000	+	$4,800	=	$52,800	$52,800 / $96,000	×	$4,800	=	$2,640
					$96,000					$4,800

Summary of Variance Allocation and Journal Entries

In the previous sections we calculated the amount of variances in the manufacturing costs to allocate to the inventory accounts and the cost of goods sold account. Now we must prepare a journal entry to close all the manufacturing variance accounts and record the allocation of the manufacturing variances in the general ledger. To illustrate the journal entry, we have summarized the allocation of the variances in Exhibit 10-5.

Part I of Exhibit 10-5 represents the standard cost balance in the inventory and cost of goods sold accounts before allocation. This information is obtained from Exhibit 10-3.

Part II of Exhibit 10-5 summarizes the allocation of the manufacturing variances. Unfavorable variances denoted by a + sign are added to the standard cost balance in the accounts. Favorable variances denoted by a − sign are subtracted from the standard cost balance. These amounts come from the computations just illustrated. The bracketed letters in the row for the total variance reference the journal entry given below.

Part III of Exhibit 10-5 represents the actual cost balance in the accounts after allocation of the variances. It is computed by adding the total unfavorable variance for each account to the standard cost balance in each account.

The journal entry to close the manufacturing variance accounts and to allocate the manufacturing variances to the inventory and cost of goods sold account is given below:

	Debit	Credit
Materials Inventory	**$ 400 (A)**	
Work in Process	**5,820 (B)**	
Finished Goods	**3,340 (C)**	
Cost of Goods Sold	**20,040 (D)**	
Spending Variance—Overhead	**28,000**	
Price Variance—Direct Materials		**$ 4,800**
Quantity Variance—Direct Materials		**8,000**
Price Variance—Direct Labor		**8,800**

EXHIBIT 10-5
Schedule to Summarize the Allocation of the Manufacturing Variances

	Accounts			
	Materials Inventory	Work in Process	Finished Goods	Cost of Good Sold
I. Standard cost balance before allocation	$8,000	$60,000	$44,000	$264,000
II Allocation of variances:				
Price variance in direct materials	+ $ 400	+ $ 1,320	+ $ 440	+ $ 2,640
Quantity variance in direct materials		+ 2,400	+ 800	+ 4,800
Total variance in direct labor		+ 3,100	+ 3,100	+ 18,600
Total variance in manufacturing overhead		− 1,000	− 1,000	− 6,000
Total variance	+ $ 400 (A)	+ $ 5,820 (B)	+ $ 3,340 (C)	+ $ 20,040 (D)
III Actual cost balance	$8,400	$65,820	$47,340	$284,040

Quantity Variance—Direct Labor	**16,000**
Efficiency Variance—Overhead	**8,000**
Volume Variance—Overhead	**12,000**

(To close the manufacturing variance accounts and to allocate the manufacturing variances to the inventory accounts and cost of goods sold.)

The debits for the inventory accounts and the cost of goods sold account represent the total variance allocated to each account in Exhibit 10-5. The debit and credits to the variance accounts represent the balance in those accounts from Exhibit 10-3.

Exhibit 10-6 illustrates the income statement for the Beville Manufacturing Company based on the allocation of the manufacturing variances. The operating income is $35,960, ($35,960 − $26,400) = $9,560 greater than the operating income when we included all the manufacturing variances in cost of goods sold as illustrated in Exhibit 10-4.

This difference is equal to the amount of the total manufacturing variance

EXHIBIT 10-6
BEVILLE MANUFACTURING COMPANY
Income Statement
For the Year 19X3

Sales revenues		$420,000
Cost of goods sold		
Standard cost of goods sold	$264,000	
Unfavorable manufacturing variances allocated to cost of goods sold	+ 20,040	284,040
Gross profit		135,960
Selling and administrative expense		100,000
Operating income		$ 35,960

allocated to the inventory accounts. From Exhibit 10-5 the amount of the total variance allocated to the inventory accounts is:

Account		
Materials inventory	$ 400	(A)
Work in process	5,820	(B)
Finished goods	3,340	(C)
Total variance allocated to the inventory accounts	$9,560	

INTERIM FINANCIAL REPORTS

In the preceding sections of this chapter we discussed the accounting for manufacturing variances at the end of the fiscal year for financial reporting. However, most companies also prepare financial reports for a quarterly or monthly time period. These quarterly or monthly financial statements are referred to as interim financial reports.

For interim financial reports, Accounting Principles Board Opinion No. 28 states that:

> Standard costs are acceptable in determining inventory valuations for interim financial reports. Unplanned or unanticipated price, quantity or volume variances should be included in the results of operations for the interim period in which they occur. Anticipated and planned price, quantity or volume variances that are expected to average out by the end of the fiscal year should be deferred at interim dates.

Variances are not allocated for interim financial statements.

This opinion states that variances should not be allocated for interim financial statements. Further, unanticipated variances should be included in the cost of goods sold section of the income statement. Anticipated variances that are expected to average out by the end of the fiscal year should be reported in the balance sheet.

The best example of an anticipated variance is the volume variance in manufacturing overhead. Recall from Chapter 9, page 257, that the volume variance in manufacturing overhead is caused by the way we account for *fixed* manufacturing overhead costs. In an actual historical costing system, the fixed manufacturing overhead cost per unit would change due to seasonal variations in production volume. Since accountants feel that changing fixed manufacturing overhead cost per unit could be misleading, they use an annual predetermined overhead rate. An annual predetermined overhead rate averages fixed manufacturing costs over the expected annual volume of production.

On interim statements the volume variance is reported on the balance sheet not on the income statement.

A predetermined annual overhead rate solves the problem of varying fixed manufacturing cost per unit. But it is one of the reasons that there is overapplied or underapplied manufacturing overhead cost at the end of each month. The portion of the overapplied or underapplied manufacturing overhead associated with seasonal fluctuations in production volume is the volume variance in overhead. Because the volume variance is (*a*) anticipated and (*b*) expected to average out over the annual accounting period, it is reported as a deferred debit or deferred credit on the balance sheet following the last sentence of Accounting Principles Board Opinion No. 28 quoted earlier.

SUMMARY

At year-end, manufacturing variances can be accounted for in either of two ways:

1 Closed directly to the cost of goods sold account

2 Allocated between the inventory accounts on the balance sheet and the cost of goods sold account on the income statement

If variances are small, they can be closed directly to cost of goods sold because currently attainable standard costs represent the manufacturing costs that management expects to incur. Many variances represent random events that are not expected to be repeated in future time periods; therefore, they should be added to the cost of goods sold in the period incurred. This is the first way of accounting for variances at year-end.

When manufacturing variances are large, the standard costs do not approximate actual costs; therefore, standard costs are not acceptable for external financial reports. In this case the manufacturing variances must be allocated between the inventory accounts on the balance sheet and the cost of goods sold account on the income statement to determine actual costs. This is the second way of accounting for variances at year-end.

For interim financial reports variances are not allocated; rather their accounting depends on whether they are unanticipated or anticipated.

Unanticipated price variances and quantity variances are closed to the cost of goods sold account.

Anticipated variances such as overhead volume variances should be deferred and reported on the balance sheet if they are expected to average out to a net variance of zero by the end of the fiscal year.

Review Problem

Kaerwer operates a machine shop on a part time basis and employs a standard cost system. In March 19X8, Kaerwer was low bidder on a contract to deliver 600 kartz by June 19X9 at a contract price of $200 each. Kaerwer's standard cost to manufacture each kartz was:

40 pounds of materials at $1.50 per pound	$ 60
4 hours of direct labor at $10 per hour	40
Manufacturing overhead (40% variable, 60% fixed)	30
Total cost	$130

During 19X8 500 kartz were started in production, 380 kartz were completed, and were transferred to finished goods. During 19X8 300 kartz were shipped to the customer. There was no beginning work in process inventory and the ending work in process inventory was one-third processed. All material was added when a kartz was started in production.

The following information is available for the year 19X8:

1 Materials purchased: 21,000 pounds at $1.52 per pound = $31,920.

2 Direct materials requisitioned and used in production totaled 21,000 pounds.

3 The direct labor payroll amounted to $10.50 per hour for 1,750 hours = $18,375.

4 Manufacturing overhead was applied on the basis of units produced. Actual manufacturing overhead incurred totaled $13,140.

Required

1 Calculate the standard cost of production for direct materials, direct labor, and manufacturing overhead.

2 Kaerwer Corporation requests that you prepare a schedule presenting a computation of the direct materials, direct labor, and manufacturing overhead variances. Overhead variances should be divided into budget and volume variances assuming a normal production volume of 400 kartz per year.

3 Allocate all manufacturing variances between the work in process, finished goods, and the cost of goods sold accounts.

(CPA)

Solution

1

KAERWER CORPORATION
Standard Cost of Production
For the Year 19X8

Units to Account for	Physical Flow
Beginning work in process	0
Units started	500
Total units	500

Units Accounted for	Physical Flow	Equivalent Finished Units for 19X8: Materials	Labor	Overhead
Units completed	380	380	380	380
Ending work in process	120*	120	40	40
Total units	500	500	420	420

Standard Costs to Account for Cost Item	Equivalent Finished Units	Standard Cost per Unit	Total Standard Cost
Direct materials	500	$ 60	$30,000
Direct labor	420	40	16,800
Manufacturing overhead	420	30	12,600
		$130	$59,400

* The ending work in process is 100% complete for materials and one-third complete for labor and overhead costs.

2 Manufacturing Variances

Direct Materials

Total Actual Quantity of Direct Materials Purchased × Actual Price	Total Actual Quantity of Direct Materials Purchased × Standard Price	Total Actual Quantity of Direct Materials Used × Standard Price	Total Standard Quantity of Direct Materials Allowed × Standard Price
21,000 pounds @ $1.52 per pound	21,000 pounds @ $1.50 per pound	21,000 pounds @ $1.50 per pound	20,000 pounds* @ $1.50 per pound
$31,920	$31,500	$31,500	$30,000

$420 unfavorable price variance

$1,500 unfavorable quantity variance

* 500 equivalent finished units × 40 pounds per unit = 20,000 pounds.

Direct Labor

Total Actual Quantity of Direct Labor Used × Actual Price	Total Actual Quantity of Direct Labor Used × Standard Price	Total Standard Quantity of Direct Labor Allowed × Standard Price
1,750 hours @ $10.50 per hour	1,750 hours @ $10.00 per hour	1,680 hours* @ $10.00 per hour
$18,375	$17,500	$16,800

$875 unfavorable price variance

$700 unfavorable quantity variance

$1,575 unfavorable total variance

* 420 equivalent finished units × 4 hours per unit = 1,680 hours.

Manufacturing Overhead

Actual Manufacturing Overhead Cost	Flexible Budgeted Overhead for 420 Equivalent Finished Units	Total Applied Manufacturing Overhead for 420 Equivalent Finished Units
	\$ 7,200[a] + 5,040[b]	420 @ \$30 per unit
\$13,140	\$12,240	\$12,600

\$900 unfavorable budget variance; \$360 favorable volume variance

\$540 unfavorable total variance

(*a*) Budgeted total fixed overhead per year = fixed overhead rate × normal production volume = 60% × \$30 × 400 units = \$7,200.

(*b*) Budgeted total variable overhead for 19X8 = 40% × \$30 × 420 units = \$5,040.

3 Allocation of manufacturing variances

Direct Materials*

Account		Standard Direct Materials Cost	Proportion		Total Direct Materials Variance		Allocation of Variance
Work in process							
120 units @ \$60.	=	\$ 7,200	\$ 7,200 / \$30,000	×	\$1,920	=	\$ 460.80
Finished goods							
80 units @ \$60.	=	\$ 4,800	\$ 4,800 / \$30,000	×	\$1,920	=	307.20
Cost of goods sold							
300 units @ \$60.	=	\$18,000	\$18,000 / \$30,000	×	\$1,920	=	1,152.00
		\$30,000					\$1,920.00

* Since the quantity purchased is equal to the quantity used, we can allocate the total direct materials variance, the price variance, and quantity variance in direct materials, rather than allocating each separately.

Direct Labor

Account		Standard Direct Labor Cost	Proportion		Total Direct Labor Variance		Allocation of Variance
Work in process							
40 units @ \$40.	=	\$ 1,600	\$ 1,600 / \$16,800	×	\$1,575	=	\$ 150.00
Finished goods							
80 units @ \$40.	=	\$ 3,200	\$ 3,200 / \$16,800	×	\$1,575	=	300.00

Cost of goods sold						
300 units @ $40.	=	$12,000	$12,000 / $16,800	×	$1,575	= 1,125.00
		$16,800				$1,575.00

Manufacturing Overhead

Account		Standard Manufacturing Overhead Cost	Proportion		Total Manufacturing Overhead Variance	Allocation of Variance
Work in process						
40 units @ $30.	=	$ 1,200	$ 1,200 / $12,600	×	$540	= $ 51.43
Finished goods						
80 units @ $30.	=	$ 2,400	$ 2,400 / $12,600	×	$540	= 102.86
Cost of goods sold						
300 units @ $30.	=	$ 9,000	$ 9,000 / $12,600	×	$540	= 385.71
		$12,600				$540.00

Glossary

Allocation of manufacturing variances At year-end, if the actual cost of production is not close to the standard cost of production, the manufacturing variances must be allocated between the inventory and cost of goods sold accounts to approximate the balances which would have been produced by an actual historical cost system. The allocation is based on the standard cost balance in the balance sheet inventory accounts and the standard cost in the cost of goods sold account.

Closing all manufacturing variances to the cost of goods sold account At year-end, if the actual cost of production is close to the standard cost of production the manufacturing variances will not be large. The total of the variance accounts can be closed to the cost of goods sold account (without allocation). This means the inventory accounts on the balance sheet are valued at the standard cost of production.

Questions and Problems

10-1 How do you calculate the standard cost of production when partially completed units exist at the end of the accounting period?

10-2 Discuss why a company would close all manufacturing variances from standard cost to the cost of goods sold account.

10-3 Discuss why a company would allocate variances from standard cost to determine actual cost for the year-end financial reports.

10-4 Why is the direct materials purchase price variance allocated differently than the direct materials quantity variance?

10-5 Distinguish between anticipated variances from standard cost and unanticipated variances from standard cost.

10-6 Discuss the criteria you should use to determine whether standard cost variances will be reported on the income statement or the balance sheet in interim financial reports.

10-7 Standard costs are being used increasingly by many manufacturing companies. Many advocates of standard costing take the position that standard costs are a proper basis for inventory valuation for external reporting purposes. Accounting Research Bulletin No. 43, however, reflects the widespread view that standard costs are not acceptable unless "adjusted at reasonable intervals to reflect current conditions so that at the balance-sheet date standard costs reasonably approximate costs computed under one of the recognized (actual cost) bases."

Required

1 Discuss the conceptual merits of using standard costs as the basis for inventory valuation for external reporting purposes.

2 Prepare general-journal entries for two alternative dispositions of a $500 unfavorable variance where *all* goods manufactured during the period are included in the ending finished goods inventory. Assume a formal standard cost system is in operation, that $300 of the variance resulted from actual costs exceeding attainable standard cost.

3 Discuss the conceptual merits of each of the two alternative methods of disposition requested in question 2.

(CPA)

10-8 Allocating Direct Labor Variances The Roy Company produces ceramic bowls. Direct labor cost is incurred uniformly throughout the production process. The standard direct labor cost per bowl is given below:

.5 hours @ $9.00 per hour = $4.50 per bowl

During 19X0 Roy Company started 8,000 bowls into production. By the end of the year 6,000 bowls were completed and 4,000 of these bowls had been sold. The ending work in process contained 2,000 bowls 50% complete. There was no beginning work in process.

The Roy Company used 3,400 direct labor hours in 19X0 at an average cost of $8.50 per hour.

Required

1 Calculate the price variance and quantity variance in direct labor.

2 Calculate the standard direct labor cost of the work in process, finished goods, and cost of goods sold.

3 Allocate the variances in direct labor to the inventory accounts and the cost of goods sold account.

10-9 Allocating Manufacturing Overhead Variances The ABC Company's inventory accounts show the standard cost of the items on hand at the end of the year. For public financial reporting the variances from standard cost are allocated between the inventory accounts and the cost of goods sold account. You are given the following information relating to manufacturing overhead.

Applied manufacturing overhead	$700,000
Actual manufacturing overhead	770,000
Applied manufacturing overhead balances at year-end:	
Work in process	$100,000
Finished goods	200,000
Cost of goods sold	400,000

Required

1 Calculate the total overhead variance.

2 Allocate the total overhead variance between the inventory accounts and the cost of goods sold account.

3 Prepare a journal entry to close the actual and applied manufacturing overhead accounts.

10-10 Allocating Direct Materials Variances The Zeon Manufacturing Company produces widgets. The direct material is added at the start of the production process. The standard direct materials cost per widget is given below:

2 pounds of plastic @ $3.00 per pound = $6.00

During 19X9 the company purchased 1,000 pounds of plastic at a cost of $3.15 per pound. In 19X9, 900 pounds of plastic were used in producing widgets.

At the end of 19X9 there were 100 widgets in work in process inventory 80% completed, 100 widgets in finished goods inventory, and 200 widgets were sold. There were no beginning inventories.

Required

1 Calculate the purchase price variance in direct materials.

2 Calculate the quantity variance in direct materials.

3 Calculate the standard direct materials cost of the materials inventory, work in process, finished goods, and cost of goods sold.

4 Allocate the quantity variance and purchase price variance in direct materials to determine the actual cost of the ending inventories and cost of goods sold.

10-11 Variance Computation and Journal Entries The Nasen Company, a producer of shirts, collects standard costs in its cost accounting system. The standard cost of producing 1 unit of product are as follows:

Direct materials:	4 yards of cloth at $1.00 per yard	$ 4.00
Direct labor:	1 hour at $8.00 per hour	8.00
Manufacturing overhead:	Applied based on direct labor hours—1 hour at $6.00 per hour*	6.00
Total standard cost per unit		$18.00

* The predetermined overhead rate is based on the expected annual production of 20,000 units and the following flexible budget:

Total overhead cost = $80,000 + $2.00 per direct labor hour

In the production process all direct materials are added at the start of the process. Direct labor and manufacturing overhead costs are incurred uniformly throughout the production process.

The actual results for the year 19X0 were as follows:

Units started	20,000
Units finished	16,000
Ending work in process (100% completed for direct materials, 80% completed for conversion costs)	4,000
Units sold	14,000
Direct materials purchased 85,000 yards at $1.05 per yard	$ 89,250
Direct materials used	75,000 yards
Direct labor 20,000 hours at $7.80 per hour	$156,000
Actual manufacturing overhead	$110,000

Required

1 Calculate the standard cost of production during 19X0.

2 Calculate the following variances:
- **a** purchase price variance in direct materials
- **b** quantity variance in direct materials
- **c** price variance in direct labor
- **d** quantity variance in direct labor
- **e** budget variance in manufacturing overhead
- **f** volume variance in manufacturing overhead

3 Prepare journal entries to record the standard costs and variances.

4 Prepare a journal entry to close the variance accounts to the cost of goods sold account.

10-12 Net Income Computations Comparing Closing All Variances to Cost of Goods Sold and Allocation of Variances The Stix Company manufactures a single product. During 19X5, the company started and completed 10,000 units. Sales units for 19X5 amounted to 6,000 units at $40 per unit. At the end of 19X5, 4,000 units were in the finished goods inventory.

Following are the costs incurred during 19X5:

Purchases of direct materials—debited to materials inventory at standard prices	$120,000	
Price variance in direct materials	$ 12,000	credit
Standard cost of direct materials	$100,000	
Quantity variance in direct materials	$ 20,000	debit
Standard cost of direct labor	$ 80,000	
Price variance in direct labor	$ 6,000	debit
Quantity variance in direct labor	$ 2,000	debit
Applied manufacturing overhead	$ 60,000	
Actual manufacturing overhead	$ 70,000	
Selling and administrative expense	$ 40,000	

Required

1 Prepare an income statement for the Stix Company assuming all manufacturing variances are closed to the cost of goods sold account.

2 Prepare an income statement for the Stix Company assuming the manufacturing variances are allocated between the inventory accounts and the cost of goods sold account.

10-13 Variance Allocation Tolbert Manufacturing Company uses a standard cost system in accounting for the cost of production of its only product, product A. The direct materials and labor standards for the production of 1 unit of product A are as follows:

- Direct materials: 10 feet of item 1 at $.75 per foot and 3 feet of item 2 at $1.00 per foot.
- Direct labor: 4 hours at $10.50 per hour.

There was no inventory on hand at July 1, 19X2. Following is a summary of costs and related data for the production of product A during the year ended June 30, 19X3.

- 100,000 feet of item 1 were purchased at $.78 per foot
- 30,000 feet of item 2 were purchased at $.90 per foot
- 8,000 units of product A were produced which required 78,000 feet of item 1, 26,000 feet of item 2, and 31,000 hours of direct labor at $10.60 per hour
- 6,000 units of product A were sold

At June 30, 19X3, there are 22,000 feet of item 1, 4,000 feet of item 2, and 2,000 completed units of product A on hand. All purchases and transfers are recorded at standard.

Required

1 Calculate for the year ended June 30, 19X3, the total debits to the materials inventory account for the purchase of item 1.

2 Calculate for the year ended June 30, 19X3, the total debits to the work in process account for direct labor.

3 Calculate the balance in the direct materials quantity variance account for item 2.

4 If all standard variances are prorated to inventories and cost of goods sold, what is the amount of direct materials quantity variance for item 2 to be prorated to materials inventory?

5 If all standard variances are prorated to inventories and cost of goods sold, calculate the amount of materials price variance for item 1 to be prorated to materials inventory.

(CPA)

10-14 Variance Allocation Calvin Corporation commenced business on December 1. The corporation uses a standard cost system in accounting for the manufacturing costs of its only product, Desex. The standard costs for 1 unit of Desex are:

Direct materials	10 pounds @ $.70 per pound	$ 7.00
Direct labor	1 hour @ $12.00 per hour	12.00

Additional information

1. The following data were extracted from the corporation's books for the month of December:

	Units	Debit	Credit
Budgeted production	3,600		
Units sold	1,500		
Sales			$45,000
Sales discounts		$ 500	
Materials price variance		$1,500	
Materials quantity variance		$ 660	
Direct labor price variance		$ 250	

2 Inventory data at December 31 indicate the following inventories were on hand:

Materials	None
Work in process	1,200 units
Finished goods	900 units

The work in process inventory was 100% complete as to materials and 50% complete as to direct labor.

Required

1 The corporation's policy is to allocate variances to the cost of goods sold and ending inventories. Prepare a schedule allocating the variances to cost of goods sold and ending inventories.

2 Prepare a schedule computing the cost of goods manufactured at standard cost and at actual cost for December. Amounts for materials and labor should be shown separately.

3 Prepare a schedule computing the actual cost of materials and labor included in the work in process inventory and in the finished goods inventory at December 31.

(CPA)

10-15 Standard Cost Flows and Allocation of Variances The records of the Beckly Company showed the following accounts at standard cost on December 31.

	December 31
Work in process—direct materials	$150,000
Finished goods—direct materials	200,000
Work in process—direct labor	300,000
Finished goods—direct labor	400,000

During the year Beckly sold 500,000 units with a standard cost of:

Direct materials	$1,000,000
Direct labor	2,000,000

The actual costs incurred for the year were:

Direct materials	$1,210,000
Direct labor	2,090,000

All materials are purchased as needed (no materials inventory is maintained). All beginning inventories were zero.

Required

1 Prepare T accounts and determine the standard cost flows in the work in process, finished goods, and variance accounts.

2 Allocate the variances to determine actual cost.

10-16 Journal Entries; Variance Allocation The materials accounts for the Butz Company are valued at standard cost throughout the year, but for public financial reporting the variances are allocated between the income statement and the balance sheet accounts. The following information is available from the company records.

Materials purchased at standard prices	$500,000
Materials purchased at actual prices	490,000
Standard production cost—direct materials	$400,000
Actual quantity of direct materials used at standard prices	446,250
Standard cost of completed units—direct materials	$300,000
Standard cost of goods sold—direct materials	200,000

Required

1 Prepare journal entries to record the data given.

2 Allocate the direct materials variances to approximate actual cost.

10-17 Process Costing: Comparison of Actual and Standard Costs Melody Corporation is a manufacturing company that produces a single product known as "Jupiter."

In analyzing production results, standard costs are used, whereas actual costs are used for financial statement reporting. The standards, which are based upon equivalent units of production, are as follows:

Direct materials per unit	1 pound at $10 per pound
Direct labor per unit	2 hours at $8 per hour

Data for the month of April 19X7 are presented below:

The beginning inventory consisted of 2,500 units which were 100% complete as to direct materials and 40% complete as to direct labor.

During the month 12,000 units were started.

The ending inventory consisted of 2,000 units which were 100% complete as to direct materials and 15% complete as to direct labor.

Costs applicable to April production are as follows:

	Actual Cost	Standard Cost*
Direct materials used (13,000 pounds)	$143,000	$120,000
Direct labor (25,000 hours actually worked)	211,150	184,800

* Standard quantities allowed times standard prices.

Required

1 For April direct materials and direct labor, compute the following:

a Equivalent units of production
b Cost per equivalent unit of production at actual and at standard cost

Show supporting computations in good form.

2 Prepare a schedule analyzing for April production the following variances as either favorable or unfavorable:
a Direct materials price
b Direct materials quantity
c Direct labor price
d Direct labor quantity

(CPA)

10-18 Variance Allocation The Butrico Manufacturing Corporation uses a standard cost system which records materials at actual cost, records materials-price variance at the time that direct materials are issued to work in process, and allocates all variances at year-end. Variances associated with direct materials are prorated based on the standard direct material cost balances in the appropriate accounts, and variances associated with direct labor and manufacturing overhead are prorated based on the standard direct labor balances in the appropriate accounts.

Materials inventory at December 31, 19X2	$ 65,000
Finished goods inventory at December 31, 19X2:	
Direct materials	87,000
Direct labor	130,500
Applied manufacturing overhead	52,200
Cost of goods sold for the year ended December 31, 19X2:	
Direct materials	348,000
Direct labor	739,500
Applied manufacturing overhead	295,800
Direct materials price variance (unfavorable)	10,000
Direct materials quantity variance (favorable)	15,000
Direct labor price variance (unfavorable)	20,000
Direct labor quantity variance (favorable)	5,000
Actual manufacturing overhead cost	340,000

There were no beginning inventories and no ending work in process inventory. Manufacturing overhead is applied at 40% of standard direct labor cost.

Required

Calculate the balances of the finished goods and cost of goods sold accounts at December 31, 19X2 after the variances have been allocated.

(CPA)

10-19 Review of Variance Computations Conti Pharmaceutical Company processes a single compound product known as Nulax and uses a standard cost accounting system. The process requires preparation and blending of three materials in large batches with a variation from the standard mixture sometimes necessary to maintain quality. Conti's cost accountant became ill at the end of October and you were engaged to determine standard costs of production and explain any differences between actual and standard costs for the month. The following information is available for the Blending Department:

1 The standard cost card for a 500-pound batch of Nulax shows the following standard costs:

	Quantity	Price		Total Cost
Materials:				
Mucilloid	250 pounds	$ .14	$35	
Dextrose	200 pounds	.09	18	
Ingredients	50 pounds	.08	4	
Total per batch	500 pounds			$ 57
Labor:				
Preparation and blending	10 hours	$9.00		90
Overhead:				
Variable	10 hours	$1.00	10	
Fixed	10 hours	.30	3	13
Total standard cost per 500-pound batch				$160

2 During October, 410 batches of 500 pounds each of the finished compound were completed and transferred to the packaging department.

3 Blending department finished goods inventory totaled 6,000 pounds at the beginning of the month and 9,000 pounds at the end of the month (assume both inventories were completely processed but not transferred and consisted of materials in their standard proportions). There were no materials or work in process inventory at the beginning or end of the month.

Inventories are carried in the accounts at standard cost.

4 During the month of October the following materials were purchased and put into production:

	Pounds	Price	Total Cost
Mucilloid	114,400	$.17	$19,448
Dextrose	85,800	.11	9,438
Ingredients	19,800	.07	1,386
Totals	220,000		$30,272

5 Wages paid for 4,212 hours of direct labor at $9.25 per hour amounted to $38,961.

6 Actual overhead costs for the month totaled $5,519.

7 The standards were established for a normal production volume of 200,000 pounds (400 batches) of Nulax per month. At this level of production variable factory overhead was budgeted at $4,000 and fixed factory overhead was budgeted at $1,200.

Required

1 Prepare a schedule presenting the computation for the blending department of:
  - **a** October production in both pounds and batches
  - **b** The standard cost of October production itemized by components of materials, labor, and overhead

2 Prepare schedules computing the differences between actual and standard costs and analyzing the differences as:
  - **a** Materials variances (for each material) caused by
    - (1) Price differences
    - (2) Quantity differences
  - **b** Labor variances caused by
    - (1) Price differences
    - (2) Quantity differences
  - **c** Overhead variances
    - (1) Budget
    - (2) Volume

(CPA)

11

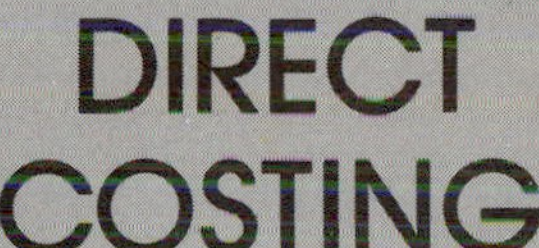

DIRECT COSTING

AFTER COMPLETING YOUR STUDY OF THIS CHAPTER, YOU SHOULD HAVE LEARNED:

1 That the costing systems you have studied so far are called absorption costing systems.

2 What direct costing is and how it differs from absorption costing.

3 That fixed manufacturing overhead is accounted for as a period cost rather than as a product cost in direct costing.

4 How to calculate net income with direct costing.

5 The different effects of direct costing and absorption costing on the amount of net income.

6 When to use direct costing and when to use absorption costing.

Before we proceed with **direct costing,** let us look back for a moment at how we have defined product costs and how we accounted for them. We have learned that product cost is defined as direct materials plus direct labor plus manufacturing overhead. We have also learned that product cost can be separated into a variable cost component and a fixed cost component. The variable product cost includes direct materials, direct labor, and the variable component of manufacturing overhead. The fixed product cost consists of the fixed component of manufacturing overhead. Direct materials, direct labor, and both fixed and variable manufacturing overhead costs are collected and allocated to various products. This type of product costing is referred to as "absorption costing." **Absorption costing** is the term cost accountants use when all costs necessary for the production of the product (the four types just listed) are assigned to the product.

In absorption costing, product cost includes direct materials, direct labor, variable overhead, and fixed overhead.

In the previous chapters we have concentrated on absorption costing because it is the generally accepted accounting procedure for determining the cost of goods sold and the ending inventory cost to be included in financial reports to individuals and groups external to the organization, such as shareholders and lenders.

What we plan to do now is show you another way of defining product costs and how to assign those costs to products. This other method of calculating product cost is called "direct costing" and it can be used with job order costing and process costing. It can also be used in either a normal cost or standard cost system. The main thing to keep in mind is that fixed manufacturing costs are excluded from product cost in direct costing systems. Only variable product costs are assigned to a product or job. Because of these definitions, what we call absorption costing is sometimes called "full" costing and what we call direct costing is called "variable" costing. These alternate terms in fact are better because they are more descriptive of each costing system. Absorption costing and direct costing are the terms most widely accepted which is why we have chosen to use them in this book.

In direct costing systems product cost includes direct materials, direct labor, and variable manufacturing overhead (fixed manufacturing overhead is excluded).

Direct costing is not considered a generally accepted accounting procedure for determining cost of goods sold and ending inventory values for external financial reports. Financial statements prepared using direct costing are restricted to use only by internal management.

Why do we have to learn another product cost concept? Absorption costing mingles variable cost and fixed cost together in calculating product cost. But to compare costs and profits of two alternatives, management must distinguish between fixed costs and variable costs. This cannot be done if management has only costs calculated in an absorption costing system. Also, net income for an accounting period, calculated using absorption costing, is affected by differences between production volume and sales volume which results in building or reducing inventory levels. Other things (such as selling prices, efficiency, etc.) equal, with direct costing net income closely follows the ups and downs of sales volume. If sales go up net income goes up and if sales are down, net income is down—net income is not directly affected by production volume. The next section will explain these differences more completely.

Direct costing supplies management with variable and fixed cost information needed for decision making. Absorption costing does not.

CALCULATING NET INCOME: DIRECT COSTING AND ABSORPTION COSTING

The difference between net income using absorption costing and direct costing results from differences in accounting for fixed manufacturing overhead. With absorption costing, the fixed manufacturing overhead is assigned to the product using a predetermined overhead rate. With direct costing, the fixed manufacturing

EXHIBIT 11-1
The Classification of Fixed Manufacturing Overhead with Direct and Absorption Costing

For any product, total cost includes only product costs. With absorption costing, fixed manufacturing overhead costs are included in product cost and are included in the cost per unit calculations. With direct costing, fixed manufacturing overhead costs are assigned to the period in which they expire; they do not become a part of the cost per unit of the products produced.

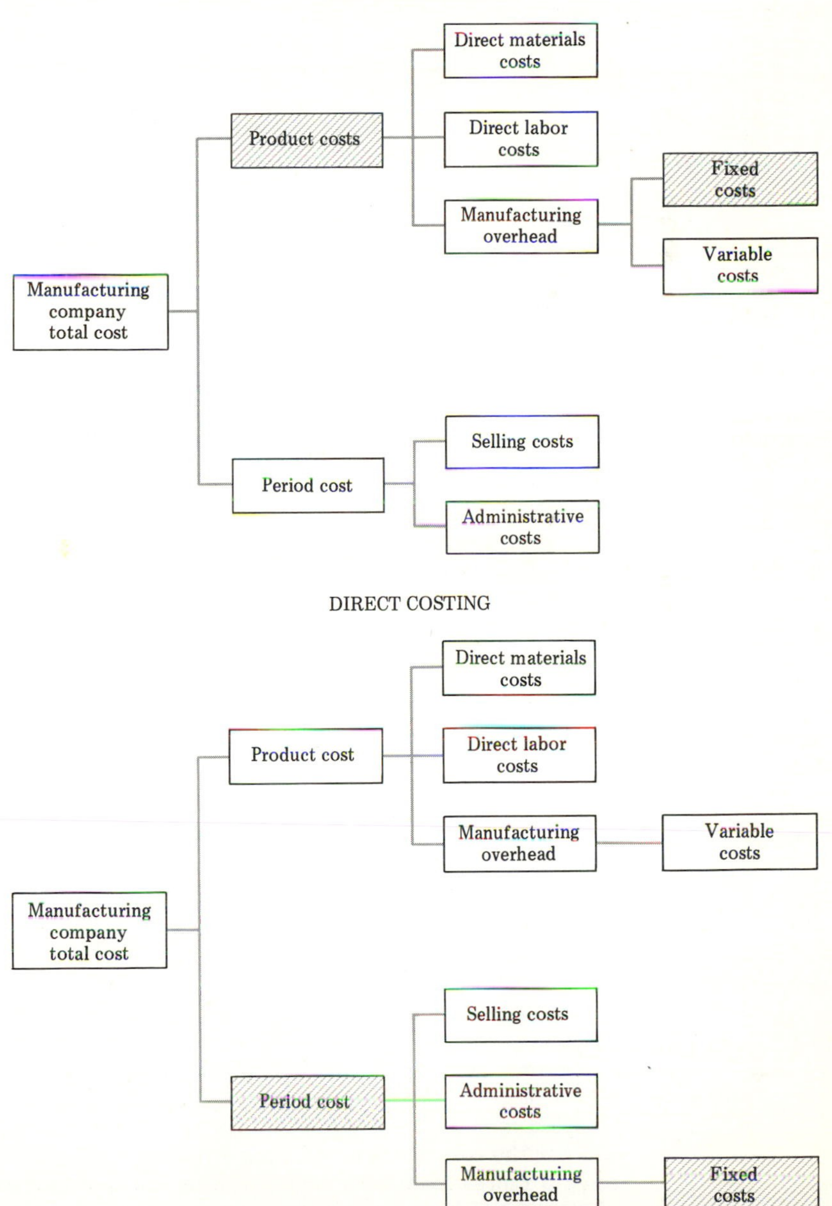

overhead is *not* assigned to the product; instead, it is treated as a period cost in the same manner as selling and administrative expenses.

Because fixed manufacturing overhead is classified differently, it is accounted for differently.

Recall from Chapter 2, page 23, how we classified the total costs of a manufacturing company into product costs and period cost. Exhibit 11-1 illustrates the costs that are classified as product costs and period cost with absorption costing and direct costing. Examine Exhibit 11-1 and note that the basic difference between absorption costing and direct costing is the classification of fixed manufacturing overhead.

Accounting for Fixed Manufacturing Costs

To see how fixed manufacturing overhead costs are accounted for under direct costing and under absorption costing, consider the data presented below for the Flores Manufacturing Company. All the calculations of cost per unit except for fixed overhead have been made.

Direct materials cost per unit		$5.00
Direct labor cost per unit		9.00
Variable manufacturing overhead cost per unit		.60
Total fixed manufacturing overhead cost per year	$92,000	
Number of units produced per year	10,000	

The product cost per unit under absorption costing is calculated as follows:

Absorption Costing

Direct materials cost	$ 5.00
Direct labor cost	9.00
Variable manufacturing cost	.60
Fixed manufacturing cost $92,000 ÷ 10,000 units	9.20
Total product cost per unit	$23.80

The product cost per unit under direct costing is calculated as follows:

With direct costing total cost per unit is lower because the fixed manufacturing overhead is not included.

Direct Costing

Direct materials	$ 5.00
Direct labor	9.00
Variable manufacturing overhead	.60
Total product cost per unit	$14.60

(With direct costing the $92,000 of fixed manufacturing overhead is treated as a period cost.)

The product cost per unit determined for absorption costing and direct costing are used to determine the cost of goods sold and the ending inventory values. For each unit of product Flores sells, $23.80 will be deducted in the income statement, as cost of goods sold, using absorption costing. Using direct costing, $14.60 will be deducted in the income statement as cost of goods sold for each unit sold. You can see that the cost of goods sold expense on the income statement will be quite a bit lower if Flores uses direct costing rather than absorption costing. But do not jump

Lower cost per unit with direct costing results in lower cost of goods sold and lower inventory values.

to the conclusion that net income will be much higher with direct costing. Direct costing will show an expense that absorption costing will not show—fixed manufacturing overhead expense. In this case, the amount of fixed overhead expense shown on the direct costing income statement will be $92,000. The complete income statements will be illustrated in a moment.

On the balance sheet each unit of product in the ending finished goods inventory is valued at $23.80 using absorption costing. Using direct costing each unit of ending finished goods inventory is valued at $14.60.

Net Income Computations

To illustrate the computation of net income under direct costing and under absorption costing, we will continue the Flores Manufacturing Company example. Assume the following additional results for the year 19X1.

Beginning finished goods in units	0
Units produced	+10,000
Units sold	− 8,000
Ending finished goods in units	2,000
Sales price per unit	$35.00
Variable selling and administrative expense	$ 1.20 per unit sold
Fixed selling and administrative expense	$58,000

Using the product cost per unit data given previously (page 310) and the above data, absorption costing and direct costing income statements are shown in Exhibit 11-2.

A direct costing income statement groups variable costs together and fixed costs together.

Direct Costing Net Income Computation In Exhibit 11-2 first look at the absorption costing income statement. It is the usual statement and should hold no surprises. Next, look at the different income statement format for direct costing as compared with absorption costing. With direct costing all variable expenses are grouped together and all fixed expenses are grouped together. The variable cost of goods sold, $116,800 in Exhibit 11-2, and the variable selling and administrative expense, $9,600 in Exhibit 11-2, are added together and deducted from sales revenues. This gives us a figure of $153,600, which is called the **contribution margin.** The contribution margin represents the total dollars available to cover the fixed manufacturing overhead costs ($92,000) and fixed selling and administrative expenses ($58,000); what remains is net income under direct costing ($3,600). We will learn in later chapters how this format for the income statement facilitates management's planning and control decisions. In this case the difference in net income between absorption costing and direct costing is dramatic. We will next examine the reasons for the difference.

Net Income Differences between Direct Costing and Absorption Costing

As you can see from Exhibit 11-2, in the top half you see that net income is $22,000, as calculated using absorption costing. In the bottom half you can see that the net income is $3,600, as calculated using direct costing. The difference between the two

The difference between direct and absorption costing net income can be dramatic.

net incomes is $18,400. This $18,400 difference is associated with the differing accounting treatment of fixed manufacturing costs under direct costing and under absorption costing.

With direct costing the fixed manufacturing costs are accounted for as a period cost and the entire fixed manufacturing overhead cost of $92,000 is deducted in calculating net income. You see the entire $92,000 on the direct costing income statement as a separate item.

With absorption costing the fixed manufacturing costs are treated as a product cost and assigned to the 10,000 units produced during 19X1. This means the ending finished goods inventory of 2,000 units will "absorb" a part of the fixed manufacturing costs. The cost of the ending finished goods inventory with absorption costing can be calculated as follows:

Cost of Ending Finished Goods Inventory:
Absorption Costing

Variable manufacturing cost	2,000 units @ $14.60 =	$29,200
Fixed manufacturing cost	2,000 units @ $ 9.20 =	18,400
Total manufacturing cost	2,000 units @ $23.80 =	$47,600

The $18,400 of fixed manufacturing cost assigned to the ending finished goods inventory is carried forward on the balance sheet until the future accounting period when these 2,000 finished units are sold. Notice that this is the difference in net income between the two methods. When the 2,000 units are sold the $18,400 fixed costs will be deducted on the income statement as a part of cost of goods sold.

With absorption costing, $18,400 of 19X1 fixed manufacturing cost remains in the balance sheet as an asset. Only $73,600 reaches the income statement as a part of cost of goods sold.

To summarize, with absorption costing the total fixed manufacturing cost of $92,000 is divided between the unsold finished units (finished goods inventory) and the finished units that are sold (cost of goods sold) as follows:

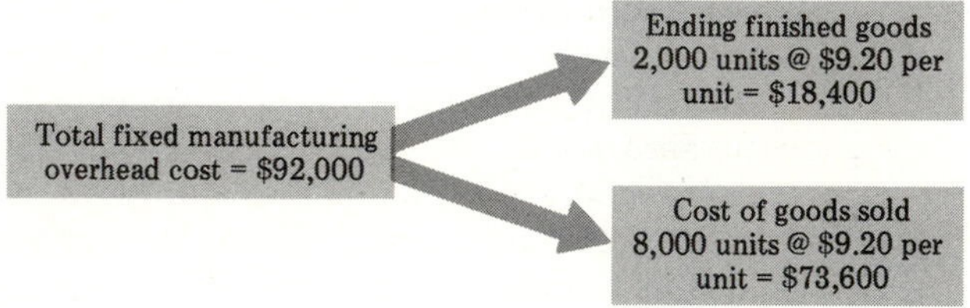

Thus, in calculating net income with absorption costing, only $73,600 of fixed manufacturing cost are included in cost of goods sold (and the income statement). Whereas, with direct costing the entire $92,000 of fixed manufacturing cost is included as part of the fixed cost deduction in the computation of net income.

Net Income Differences Extended In the example shown in Exhibit 11-2 production volume exceeded sales volume. More units were produced than were sold and inventory increased. This caused a portion of the fixed manufacturing overhead to remain in finished goods inventory, which is reported on the balance sheet using absorption costing. It also caused the net income based on absorption costing to be greater than net income based on direct costing, because less than a full year's fixed manufacturing overhead reached the income statement this year. In other situations direct costing net income will be greater than absorption costing net income. We will extend the example to illustrate the other possibilities.

In some cases absorption costing net income will exceed direct costing net income. In other circumstances the reverse will be true.

Now, we want to understand the difference in net income under absorption

EXHIBIT 11-2
FLORES MANUFACTURING COMPANY
Comparison of Direct Costing and Absorption Costing
For the Year 19X1

Absorption Costing Income Statement

Sales revenues (8,000 units @ $35.00)		$280,000
Cost of goods sold:		
Beginning finished goods	$ 0	
Cost of goods produced (10,000 units @ $23.80)	238,000	
Cost of goods available for sale	$238,000	
Ending finished goods (2,000 units @ $23.80)	47,600	
Cost of goods sold		190,400
Gross margin		$ 89,600
Selling and administrative expense		
Fixed	$ 58,000	
Variable (8,000 units @ $1.20)	9,600	67,600
Net income		$ 22,000

The difference in the cost of the ending finished goods is the fixed cost per unit of ($23.80 − $14.60) = $9.20 × 2,000 units = $18,400

Direct Costing Income Statement

Sales revenues			$280,000
Less variable costs:			
Variable cost of goods sold			
Beginning finished goods	$ 0		
Cost of goods produced (10,000 units @ $14.60)	146,000		
Cost of goods available for sale	$146,000		
Ending finished goods (2,000 units @ $14.60)	29,200		
Variable cost of goods sold		$116,800	
Variable selling and administrative expense (8,000 units @ $1.20)		9,600	$126,400
Contribution margin			$153,600
Less fixed costs:			
Manufacturing overhead		$ 92,000	
Fixed selling and administrative expense		58,000	150,000
Net income			$ 3,600

costing and under direct costing when production volume is the same as sales volume and when production volume is less than sales volume. To illustrate the net income effects we will continue the Flores Manufacturing Company example. Let us assume the same basic data given previously for 19X1 and extend it into 19X2 and 19X3 with different production volumes and sales volumes. The basic data is summarized below:

Flores Manufacturing Company
Basic Data
19X1, 19X2, 19X3

Revenue and Cost Data for 19X1, 19X2, and 19X3	
Sales price per unit	$35.00
Variable manufacturing cost (direct materials, direct labor, and variable overhead)	$14.60
Fixed manufacturing cost per year	$92,000.00
Variable selling and administrative expense per unit sold	$ 1.20
Fixed selling and administrative expense per year	$58,000.00

Production Volume and Sales Volume in Units

	19X1	19X2	19X3
Beginning finished goods	0	2,000	2,000
Units produced	10,000	10,000	8,000
Units available for sales	10,000	12,000	10,000
Ending finished goods	2,000	2,000	0
Units sold	8,000	10,000	10,000

Product Cost per Unit

		19X1		19X2		19X3
Direct costing: variable manufacturing cost		$14.60		$14.60		$14.60
Absorption costing:						
Variable manufacturing cost		$14.60		$14.60		$14.60
Fixed manufacturing cost ($92,000 fixed cost divided by the units produced)	($92,000) / (10,000)	9.20	($92,000) / (10,000)	9.20	($92,000) / (8,000)	11.50
		$23.80		$23.80		$26.10

In Exhibit 11-3 the computations for 19X1 are the same as in Exhibit 11-2. In 19X1 production exceeded sales: the net income was $22,000 using absorption costing; it was only $3,600 using variable costing.

When production volume equals sales volume, both systems report the same net income.

The calculations for 19X2 in Exhibit 11-3 show that when production volume and sales volume are equal—a company sells exactly the quantity it produces—the two product costing procedures produce the same net income (assuming efficiency is the same in the previous and current years); in this case $42,000. The reason for this is that there is no change in the amount of fixed manufacturing costs included in the finished goods inventory under absorption costing as shown below:

Change in absorption costing inventory costs.

		Beginning Finished Goods		Ending Finished Goods
Variable manufacturing cost	(2,000 units @ $14.60)	$29,200	(2,000 units @ $14.60)	$29,200
Fixed manufacturing cost	(2,000 units @ $ 9.20)	$18,400	(2,000 units @ $ 9.20)	$18,400
Cost of finished goods inventory		$47,600		$47,600

The computations for 19X3 in Exhibit 11-3 show that sales volume exceeded production volume and the net income calculated using direct costing, $42,000, exceeded absorption costing net income, $23,600, by $18,400. The absorption costing net income is lower because with absorption costing, when inventory levels are decreased, the fixed manufacturing overhead in the beginning finished goods, $18,400, is transferred from the balance sheet to the cost of goods sold account in the 19X3 income statement as shown below:

Change in absorption costing inventory costs.

		Beginning Finished Goods		Ending Finished Goods
Variable manufacturing costs	(2,000 units @ $14.60)	$29,200	(0 units @ $14.60)	$0
Fixed manufacturing costs	(2,000 units @ $ 9.20)	$18,400	(0 units @ $11.50)	$0
Cost of finished goods inventory		$47,600		$0

Therefore in 19X3 with absorption costing we have $18,400 of fixed manufacturing costs incurred in a prior year in the beginning finished goods inventory account reaching the income statement as cost of goods sold. In addition, all the fixed manufacturing costs from the year 19X3, $92,000, reach the income statement as part of the cost of the goods manufactured and sold in 19X3. On the other hand direct costing reports fixed manufacturing overhead expense for the year 19X3 of $92,000. This results in direct costing net income being $18,400 greater than absorption costing net income.

The difference between net income based on absorption costing and net income based on direct costing depends on whether there have been changes in the fixed manufacturing overhead cost in the inventory account during the accounting period. This can be calculated as the difference between the fixed manufacturing overhead cost assigned to the beginning inventory and the fixed manufacturing overhead cost assigned to the ending inventory.

For the Flores Manufacturing Company:

		19X1		19X2		19X3
Production volume in units		10,000		10,000		8,000
Sales volume in units		8,000		10,000		10,000
Direct costing net income		$ 3,600		$42,000		$42,000
Absorption costing net income		22,000		42,000		23,600
Difference in net income		−$18,400		$ 0		$18,400
Fixed manufacturing cost in beginning finished goods inventory	(0 units @ $9.20)	$ 0	(2,000 units @ $9.20)	$18,400	(2,000 units @ $9.20)	$18,400
Fixed manufacturing cost in ending finished goods inventory	(2,000 units @ $9.20)	$18,400	(2,000 units @ $9.20)	$18,400	(0 units @ $11.50)	$ 0
Change in fixed manufacturing overhead cost content of finished goods inventory		−$18,400		$ 0		$18,400

EXHIBIT 11-3
FLORES MANUFACTURING COMPANY
Net Income Differences: Direct Costing and Absorption Costing For the Years 19X1, 19X2, 19X3

	19X1	19X2	19X3	Total
Production volume in units	10,000	10,000	8,000	28,000
Sales volume in units	8,000	10,000	10,000	28,000
Absorption Costing				
Sales revenues	$280,000	$350,000	$350,000	$980,000
Cost of goods sold				
Beginning finished goods	$ 0	$ 47,600	$ 47,600	$ 0
Cost of goods produced	238,000	238,000	208,800	684,800
Cost of goods available for sale	$238,000	$285,600	$256,400	$684,800
Ending finished goods	47,600	47,600	0	0
Cost of goods sold	$190,400	$238,000	$256,400	$684,800
Gross margin	$ 89,600	$112,000	$ 93,600	$295,200
Selling and administrative expense				
Fixed	58,000	58,000	58,000	174,000
Variable	9,600	12,000	12,000	33,600
Net income	$ 22,000	$ 42,000	$ 23,600	$ 87,600
Direct Costing				
Sales revenues	$280,000	$350,000	$350,000	$980,000
Less variable costs:				
Variable cost of goods sold				
Beginning finished goods	$ 0	$ 29,200	$ 29,200	$ 0
Cost of goods produced	$146,000	146,000	116,800	408,800
Cost of goods available for sale	$146,000	$175,200	$146,000	$408,800
Ending finished goods	29,200	29,200	0	0
Variable cost of goods sold	$116,800	$146,000	$146,000	$408,800
Variable selling and administrative expense	9,600	12,000	12,000	33,600
Contribution margin	$153,600	$192,000	$192,000	$537,600
Less fixed costs:				
Manufacturing overhead	92,000	92,000	92,000	276,000
Selling and administrative expense	58,000	58,000	58,000	174,000
Net income	$ 3,600	$ 42,000	$ 42,000	$ 87,600

We can generalize from the Flores illustration that if production efficiency is equal from year to year:

1 When production volume exceeds sales volume—absorption costing net income will exceed direct costing net income.

General rules about net income differences.

2 When production volume is equal to sales volume—absorption costing net income will be equal to direct costing net income.

3 When production volume is less than sales volume—absorption costing net income will be less than direct costing net income.

The Influence of Production Volume on Net Income

To illustrate how production volume can influence net income calculated with absorption costing, let us examine the years 19X2 and 19X3 in Exhibit 11-3.

With the same sales volume, net income calculated under direct costing is the same, $42,000 in 19X2 and 19X3, even though production volume in 19X2 exceeds production volume in 19X3.

However, with the same sales volume in 19X2 and 19X3, net income calculated under absorption costing in 19X2, $42,000, is greater than net income in 19X3, $23,600. This decrease in net income in 19X3 as compared to 19X2 is caused by the fact production volume in 19X2 (10,000 units) exceeded production volume in 19X3 (8,000 units). This resulted in fixed manufacturing overhead costs incurred in a prior year and assigned to the finished goods inventory, to be matched with revenues in 19X3. Therefore, under absorption costing the year 19X3 is charged with all fixed manufacturing overhead costs incurred in 19X3 and some of the fixed manufacturing overhead costs from a prior year.

DIRECT COSTING FOR FINANCIAL REPORTING

Direct costing is not acceptable for external financial reporting.

Direct costing is widely accepted for managerial planning and control; it is not acceptable for external financial reporting. The reason it is not acceptable is explained by the accounting profession in Accounting Research Bulletin No. 43 issued by the American Institute of Certified Public Accountants (AICPA). This bulletin states that cost is the primary basis for determining the dollars assigned to inventories and that by "cost" is meant the sum of the expenditures and charges directly or indirectly incurred in producing a product or job. This has been widely interpreted as meaning all production costs including fixed manufacturing overhead must be assigned to the units produced.

The use of direct costing for financial reporting (as opposed to absorption costing) has been a controversial topic among accountants for many years. Everyone agrees that total costs should be grouped into fixed and variable categories for managerial planning and control decisions. The controversy concerns whether fixed manufacturing costs should be treated as a product cost or a period cost for external financial reporting.

Accountants who advocate the use of direct costing for external financial reporting state that the fixed manufacturing costs, such as depreciation and supervision salaries, will be incurred no matter how many units of the product are produced. These fixed manufacturing costs are viewed as the cost *to provide productive capacity* and should not be related to any specific unit of product. Rather, the fixed manufacturing costs should be expensed in the period they expire (treated as period costs).

Accountants who advocate the use of absorption costing state that to achieve the proper matching of revenues and expenses all expenses of earning the revenue should be reported in the same period in which the revenue is reported. Since fixed manufacturing costs are necessary for the production of the product they should be assigned to the product and inventoried until the product is sold. When the product is sold the cost becomes an expense and is matched with the revenue from the sale of the product.

Many companies use direct costing for internal reports and absorption costing for external reports.

Since direct costing is not acceptable for financial reporting but because it is useful for managerial planning and control decisions, many companies accumulate their cost data using direct costing for internal management. For external financial reporting they allocate the fixed manufacturing overhead costs between the inventory account and cost of goods sold account. To do this, the only change that must be made in the accounting system is to establish separate accounts for fixed and variable manufacturing overhead and to include only the variable manufacturing overhead cost in the predetermined overhead rate.

DIRECT COSTING AND MANAGERIAL ACCOUNTING

Even though direct costing is not acceptable for external financial reports, there are sufficient advantages to direct costing that many companies use it to accumulate data for planning and control decisions. The advantages of direct costing are summarized below:[1]

The advantages of direct costing in managerial accounting.

1 The net income for a period is not affected by changes in absorption of fixed expenses resulting from building or reducing inventory. Other things remaining equal (e.g., selling prices and costs) net income moves in the same direction as sales when direct costing is in use.

2 Manufacturing cost and income statements in the direct cost form follow management's thinking more closely than does the absorption cost form for these statements. For this reason, management finds it easier to understand and to use direct cost reports.

3 The impact of fixed costs on profits is emphasized because the total amount of such cost for the period appears in the income statement.

4 Contribution margin figures facilitate relative appraisal of products, territories, classes of customers, and other segments of the business without having the results obscured by allocation of fixed costs. (This will be discussed in Chapter 15.)

5 Cost-volume-profit relationship data wanted for planning purposes is readily obtained from the regular (direct costing) accounting statements. Hence management does not have to work with two separate sets of data to relate one to the other. (This will be discussed in Chapter 14.)

6 Direct costing ties in with such effective plans for cost control as standard costs and flexible budgets. In fact, the flexible budget is an aspect of direct costing and many companies thus use direct costing methods for this purpose without recognizing them as such. (Chapter 9 discussed flexible budgeting.)

SUMMARY

Direct costing is an approach to product costing in which only the variable manufacturing costs are assigned to the products. The fixed manufacturing overhead costs are assigned to the accounting period in which they expire.

[1] National Association of Accountants, *Direct Costing,* Research Series No. 23 (New York: National Association of Accountants, 1953), p. 1127.

Absorption costing is the product costing concept where both variable and fixed costs are assigned to the products. Absorption costing must be used for external financial reports.

The difference in net income between direct costing and absorption costing is the change in the fixed manufacturing overhead in the inventory accounts. In general, we can state that if production efficiency is the same in the current and previous period:

1 When production volume exceeds sales volume—absorption costing net income will exceed direct costing net income.
2 When production volume is equal to sales volume—absorption costing net income will be equal to direct costing net income.
3 When production volume is less than sales volume—absorption costing net income will be less than direct costing net income.

Direct costing is used by many companies for managerial planning and control. We will see in later chapters that direct costing provides us with the information we need for cost-volume-profit analysis and the analysis of the profitability of product lines and sales territories. It is not difficult to establish an accounting system which uses direct costing for internal management reports and absorption costing for external financial reports.

Review Problem

The S. T. Shire Company uses direct costing for internal management purposes and absorption costing for external reporting purposes.

At the end of 19X1 it was anticipated that sales would rise 20 percent the next year. Therefore, production was increased from 20,000 units to 24,000 units to meet this expected demand. However, economic conditions were not especially fruitful; only 20,000 units were sold.

The following data pertain to 19X2:

	19X2
Selling price per unit	$30
Beginning finished goods (units)	0
Sales (units)	20,000
Production (units)	24,000
Ending finished goods inventory (units)	4,000

Variable manufacturing costs per unit for 19X2:	
Direct labor	$ 7.50
Direct materials	4.50
Variable manufacturing overhead	3.00
Total variable manufacturing costs	$15.00

Annual fixed costs for 19X2:

Manufacturing	$ 96,000
Selling and administrative	100,000
Total	$196,000

There were no variable selling and administrative costs. All taxes are to be ignored. (Wouldn't that be wonderful!)

Required

1 An income statement based on direct costing for 19X2.

2 An income statement based on absorption costing for 19X2.

3 Explain the difference, if any, in the net income figures by an analysis of the inventories.

(CMA)

Solution

1

S. T. SHIRE COMPANY
Income Statement
Direct Costing
For the Year, 19X2

Sales revenue (20,000 units @ $30)		$600,000
Variable cost of goods sold:		
Cost of goods produced (24,000 units @ $15)	$360,000	
Ending finished goods (4,000 units @ $15)	60,000	300,000
Contribution margin		$300,000
Less fixed costs:		
Manufacturing	$ 96,000	
Selling and administration	100,000	196,000
Net income		$104,000

2

S. T. SHIRE COMPANY
Income Statement
Absorption Costing
For the Year, 19X2

Sales revenue (20,000 units @ $30)		$600,000
Cost of goods sold:		
Cost of goods produced (24,000 units @ $19*)	$456,000	
Ending finished goods (4,000 units @ $19*)	76,000	380,000
Gross margin		$220,000
Selling and administrative expense		100,000
Net income		$120,000

3 Net income—direct costing		$104,000
Net income—absorption costing		120,000
Difference	−	$ 16,000

Fixed manufacturing cost—beginning inventory (0 units @ $4)	=	$ 0
Fixed manufacturing cost—ending inventory (4,000 units @ $4)	=	16,000
Change in fixed cost content of inventory	−	$ 16,000

* Variable manufacturing cost	=	$15	per unit
Fixed manufacturing cost ($96,000 ÷ 24,000 units)	=	4	per unit
Total manufacturing cost		$19	per unit

Since the inventory level increased, part of 19X2 fixed manufacturing costs are retained on the balance sheet by absorption costing.

Glossary

Absorption costing A product costing procedure where all costs necessary to manufacture the product are assigned to the product. This includes fixed manufacturing overhead costs.

Contribution margin The difference between total sales and total variable costs. It represents the dollars available to cover the fixed expenses, what remains after fixed expenses represents net income.

Direct costing A product costing procedure where only the variable manufacturing costs are assigned to the product. Fixed manufacturing overhead costs are treated as period expenses.

Questions and Problems

11-1 What manufacturing costs are classified as product costs under absorption costing? Under direct costing?

11-2 How can the difference between direct costing and absorption costing net income be explained?

11-3 Discuss the income differences between direct and absorption costing when production and sales volume differ.

11-4 What are the advantages of direct costing for managerial accounting?

11-5 What are the arguments for and against the use of direct costing for financial reporting?

11-6 Fleet, Inc., manufactured 700 units of product A, a new product, in 19X5. Product A's variable and fixed manufacturing costs per unit were $6 and $2, respectively. The inventory of product A on December 31, 19X5 consisted of 100 units. There was no inventory of product A on January 1, 19X5. What would be the dollar amount of inventory on December 31, 19X5 if the direct costing method were used? If the absorption-costing method were used? (CPA)

11-7 Suppose that two companies produced and sold the same product in a very competitive market where selling prices were the same. Assume also that they had identical costs of operations. Both companies follow a policy of maintaining constant production volume from year to year even though sales fluctuate somewhat. Full Company uses absorption costing and Var Company uses direct costing.

Required

1 How would the net incomes of the companies compare from year to year? Explain briefly.

2 If you averaged the net incomes of each company over a number of years what would you expect to find? Explain briefly.

11-8 Simple Computation for Direct and Absorption Costing Gyro Gear Company produces a special gear used in automatic transmissions. Each gear sells for $28 and the company produces and sells approximately 500,000 gears each year. Cost data for 19X3 are presented below:

Direct materials	$6 per unit	
Direct labor	5 per unit	
Other costs:	**Variable**	**Fixed**
Manufacturing	$2 per unit	$3,500,000 per year
Selling and administrative	4 per unit	1,500,000 per year

Required

1 Calculate the unit cost for direct costing and absorption costing inventory valuations.

2 Assuming the company produces 500,000 gears and sells 450,000 and the selling price and cost data are as given above, calculate the net income using direct and absorption costing procedures.

(CPA)

11-9 Calculation of Inventory Values and Cost of Goods Sold with Direct Costing The following information pertains to a month's operations for the Adams Company.

Units sold	1,000
Units produced	1,100
Fixed manufacturing overhead	$2,200
Variable manufacturing overhead	$ 500
Selling and administrative expenses (all fixed)	$ 900
Direct labor	$4,000
Direct materials used	$2,100
Beginning inventories	-0-
Contribution margin	$4,000
Direct materials inventory, end	$1,000

There are no work in process inventories.

Required

1 What is the ending finished goods inventory cost and cost of goods sold under direct costing procedures?

2 Would net income be changed if absorption costing had been used? Explain your answer.

11-10 Computation of Inventory Values and Operating Profit for Direct and Absorption Costing The following information is available for Keller Corporation's new product line:

Selling price per unit	$ 15
Variable manufacturing cost per unit of production	8
Total annual fixed manufacturing costs	25,000
Variable selling and administrative costs per unit sold	3
Total annual fixed selling and administrative expenses	15,000

There was no inventory at the beginning of the year. During the year 12,500 units were produced and 10,000 units were sold.

Required

1 Calculate the value of the ending inventory assuming direct costing and absorption costing.

2 Calculate the net income under direct and absorption costing.

(CPA)

11-11 Preparation of Projected Income Statements with Direct and Absorption Costing Management of Bicent Company uses the following unit costs for the one product it manufactures:

	Cost per Unit	Cost per Month
Direct materials (all variable)	$30.00	
Direct labor (all variable)	19.00	
Manufacturing overhead:		
Variable cost	6.00	
Fixed cost per month		$45,000
Selling, general, and administrative:		
Variable cost	4.00	
Fixed cost per month		21,000

The selling price is $80 per unit. The fixed costs remain fixed within the relevant range of 4,000 to 16,000 units of production.

Management has collected the following data for the month of June 19X6:

	Units
Beginning inventory	2,000
Production	9,000
Available	11,000
Sales	7,500
Ending inventory	3,500

Required

Prepare income statements for June 19X6 under each of the following product costing methods:

1 Absorption costing

2 Direct costing

Supporting schedules calculating inventory costs per unit should be presented. Ignore income taxes.

(CPA)

11-12 Computation of Fixed Manufacturing Overhead Applied and Net Income Under Direct and Absorption Costing The following annual flexible budget has been prepared for use in making decisions relating to product X.

	100,000 Units	150,000 Units	200,000 Units
Sales volume	$800,000	$1,200,000	$1,600,000
Manufacturing costs:			
Variable	300,000	450,000	600,000
Fixed	200,000	200,000	200,000
	500,000	650,000	800,000
Selling and other expenses:			
Variable	200,000	300,000	400,000
Fixed	160,000	160,000	160,000
	360,000	460,000	560,000
Income (or loss)	$(60,000)	$ 90,000	$ 240,000

The 200,000 unit budget has been adopted and will be used for allocating fixed manufacturing costs to units of product X; at the end of the first six months the following information is available:

	Units
Production completed	120,000
Sales	60,000

All fixed costs are budgeted and incurred uniformly throughout the year and actual costs incurred have equalled the budget costs.

Over- and underapplied fixed manufacturing costs are not closed to cost of goods sold until year-end.

Required

1 Calculate the amount of fixed manufacturing cost assigned to product X during the first six months under absorption costing.

2 Calculate the reported net income (or loss) for the first six months under direct costing and under absorption costing.

3 Reconcile the difference between absorption and direct costing.

(CPA)

11-13 **Variable Costing with a Review of Standard Costing** Milner Manufacturing Company uses a job-order costing system and standard costs. It manufactures one product whose standard cost is as follows:

Materials	20 yards at $.90 per yard	$18
Direct labor	4 hours at $6 per hour	24
Total manufacturing overhead	Applied at five-sixths of direct labor cost (variable costs is 25% of manufacturing overhead)	20
Variable selling, general, and administrative expenses		12
Fixed selling, general, and administrative expenses		7
Total unit cost		$81

The standards are set based on estimated normal activity of 2,400 direct labor hours per month.

Actual activity for the month of October 19X5 was as follows:

Units of product produced	500	
Materials purchased	18,000 yards at $.92 per yard	$16,560
Materials used	9,500 yards	
Direct labor	2,100 hours at $6.10 per hour	12,810
Total manufacturing overhead		11,100

Required

1 Based on the standard costs, compute the inventory cost per unit under direct costing and absorption costing.

2 Compute the variable factory-overhead rate per direct labor hour and the total budgeted fixed manufacturing overhead per month based on estimated normal activity.

3 Prepare a schedule computing the following variances for the month of October 19X5:
a Materials price variance
b Materials quantity variance
c Labor price variance
d Labor quantity (efficiency) variance
e Overhead budget variance
f Overhead volume variance
Indicate whether each variance is favorable or unfavorable.

(CPA)

11-14 Computations for Direct and Absorption Costing The Zeta Corporation began operations in January 19X1 producing a single product. The production level for the product is estimated at 1,000 units per year. This estimate is used to assign the overhead costs to the product. Any over (under) applied overhead is closed to cost of goods sold at the end of the year. The operating results for the first two years of operations are given below:

	19X1	19X2
Sales units	700	1,100
Production units	800	1,000
Sales price per unit	$ 25.00	$ 25.00
Variable costs per unit produced		
Production	$ 8.00	$ 8.00
Selling and administrative per unit sold	$ 3.00	$ 3.00
Fixed costs per year		
Manufacturing overhead	$10,000	$10,000
Selling and administrative	$ 5,000	$ 5,000

Required

1 Prepare income statements for both years using direct and absorption costing.

2 Reconcile the differences between the net incomes for both years by analysis of inventory costs.

11-15 Direct and Absorption Costing with Differing Sales-Production Relationships The Beta Company will begin operations in 19X2 and have estimated the following manufacturing cost function for the year:

Total manufacturing costs = \$500,000 + (\$.70 × units produced)

The company plans to assign the fixed manufacturing costs to the product based on expected production of 250,000 units and any over-(under-) applied overhead is closed to cost of sales. The selling and administrative costs are estimated to be \$100,000 per year fixed plus \$.20 per unit variable. The expected selling price is \$3.70 per unit.

Required

1 Prepare income statements for the year using direct and absorption costing concepts and assuming the following estimated production and sales units:

	Production Units	Sales Units
A	250,000	200,000
B	250,000	250,000
C	300,000	250,000

You should prepare three income statements using direct costing and three income statements using absorption costing.

2 Explain the differences between the income calculated using direct costing and the income calculated using absorption costing for each year.

11-16 Income Computations—Direct and Absorption Costing The cost structure for Lindsay Manufacturing Co. appears as follows:

Total annual fixed manufacturing overhead costs	\$48,000
Total annual fixed selling and administrative costs	20,000
Variable manufacturing costs per unit of production	17.50
Variable selling and administrative costs per unit of sales	2.00

There were no beginning inventories. During the year 16,000 units were produced, and 12,000 units were sold at a sales price of \$25 per unit.

Required

For both direct and absorption costing, compute:

1 Ending inventory values

2 Net income

11-17 Income Differences between Direct and Absorption Costing You have obtained the following bits of information from the activities of DC Company for a particular year. The company uses expected annual activity for its predetermined overhead rate.

	Units
Expected annual production	8,000
Actual sales, month 1	600
Actual sales, month 2	800
Actual production, month 1	700
Actual production, month 2	750

The company estimated that the annual fixed manufacturing overhead would be $9,600 and that the variable manufacturing cost would be $.50 per unit. Through months 1 and 2, actual costs were exactly as estimated.

Required

1 For month 1, what would be the difference in net income between using absorption costing and direct costing?

2 The inventory on the balance sheet will change from the beginning to the end of the month. For month 2, will the change in inventory value be greater or less if the company uses absorption costing rather than direct costing? What will be the amount of the *difference in the inventory change* between absorption and direct costing?

11-18 Computing Absorption Costing Income from Direct Costing Income The Vice-President for Sales of Huber Corporation has received the income statement for November 19X9. The statement has been prepared on the direct cost basis and is reproduced below. The firm has just adopted a direct costing system for internal reporting purposes.

HUBER CORPORATION
Income Statement
For the Month of November 19X9
($000 Omitted)

Sales		$2,400
Less: Variable standard cost of goods sold		1,200
Manufacturing margin		$1,200
Less: Fixed manufacturing costs at budget	$600	
Fixed manufacturing cost spending variance	0	600
Gross margin		$ 600
Less: Fixed selling and administrative costs		400
Net income before taxes		$ 200

The controller attached the following notes to the statements.

- The unit sales price for November averaged $24.
- The standard unit manufacturing costs for the month were:

Variable cost	$12
Fixed cost	4
Total cost	$16

The unit rate for fixed manufacturing costs is a predetermined rate based upon a normal monthly production of 150,000 units.

- Production for November was 145,000 units.
- The inventory at November 30 consisted of 80,000 units.

Required

1 The Vice-President for Sales is not comfortable with the direct cost basis and wonders what the net income would have been under the prior absorption cost basis.
  a Present the November income statement on an absorption cost basis.
  b Reconcile and explain the difference between the direct costing and the absorption costing net income figures.

2 Explain the features associated with direct cost income measurement that should be attractive to the Vice-President for Sales.

(CPA)

11-19 Influence of Production Volume on Profits Sun Company, a wholly owned subsidiary of Guardian, Inc., produces and sells three main product lines. The company employs a standard cost accounting system for record keeping purposes.

At the beginning of 19X4, the president of Sun Company presented the budget to the parent company and accepted a commitment to contribute $15,800 to Guardian's consolidated profit in 19X4. The president has been confident that the year's profit would exceed budget target, since the monthly sales reports that he has been receiving have shown that sales for the year will exceed budget by 10%. The president is both disturbed and confused when the controller presents an adjusted forecast as of November 30, 19X4 indicating that profit will be 11% under budget. The two forecasts are presented below:

SUN COMPANY
Forecasts of Operating Results
for 19X4

	Annual Forecasts as of	
	1/1/X4	**11/30/X4**
Sales	$268,000	$294,800
Cost of sales at standard	212,000*	233,200
Gross margin at standard	$ 56,000	$ 61,600
Over- (under-) applied fixed manufacturing overhead		(6,000)
Actual gross margin	$ 56,000	$ 55,600
Selling expenses	$ 13,400	$ 14,740
Administrative expenses	26,800	26,800
Total operating expenses	$ 40,200	$ 41,540
Earnings before tax	$ 15,800	$ 14,060

* Includes fixed manufacturing overhead of $30,000.

There have been no sales price changes or product mix shifts since the 1/1/X4 forecast. The only cost variance on the income statement is the underabsorbed manufacturing overhead. This arose because the company produced only 16,000 standard machine hours (budgeted machine hours were 20,000) during 19X4 as a result of a shortage of raw materials while its principal supplier was closed by a strike. Fortunately Sun Company's finished goods inventory was large enough to fill all sales orders received.

Required

1 Analyze and explain why the profit has declined in spite of increased sales and good control over costs.

2 What plan, if any, could Sun Company adopt during December to improve their reported profit at year-end? Explain your answer.

3 Illustrate and explain how Sun Company could adopt an alternative internal cost reporting procedure which would avoid the confusing effect of the present procedure.

4 Would the alternative procedure described in part 3 be acceptable to Guardian, Inc. for external financial reporting purposes? Explain.

(CMA)

11-20 Standard Costs with Direct and Absorption Costing Norwood Corporation is considering changing its method of inventory valuation from absorption costing to direct costing and has engaged you to determine the effect of the proposed change on the 19X8 financial statements.

The corporation manufactures Gink which is sold for $20 per unit. Two pounds of direct material Marsh are added at the start of processing and labor and overhead are added evenly during the manufacturing process. Production is budgeted at 110,000 units of Gink annually. The standard costs per unit of Gink are:

Marsh	$3.00
Labor	6.00
Variable manufacturing overhead	1.00
Fixed manufacturing overhead	1.10

A process cost system is used employing standard costs. Variances from standard costs are now charged or credited to cost of goods sold. If direct costing were adopted only variances resulting from variable costs would be charged or credited to cost of goods sold.

Inventory data for 19X8 follow:

	Units	
	January 1	**December 31**
Marsh (pounds)	50,000	40,000
Work in process	0	15,000*
Finished goods	20,000	12,000

* 1/15 processed

During 19X8, 220,000 pounds of Marsh were purchased and 230,000 pounds were transferred to work in process. Also, 110,000 units of Gink were transferred to finished goods. Actual fixed manufacturing overhead during the year was $121,000. There were no variances between standard variable costs and actual variable costs during the year.

Required

1 Prepare schedules which present the computation of:
  a Equivalent units of production for material, labor, and overhead
  b Number of units sold
  c Standard unit costs under direct costing and absorption costing
  d Amount, if any, of over- or underapplied fixed manufacturing overhead

2 Prepare a comparative statement of cost of goods sold using standard direct costing and standard absorption costing.

(CPA)

PLANNING AND CONTROL: THE MASTER BUDGET

AFTER COMPLETING YOUR STUDY OF THIS CHAPTER, YOU SHOULD HAVE LEARNED:

1 Why organizations use budgets, how they are used, and how they are derived from goals, objectives, and programs.

2 That a master budget quantifies management's expectations of revenues, expenses, net income, cash flows, and financial position in two sets of budgets called operating budgets and financial budgets.

3 How to prepare a master budget through its component budgets.

Chapters 1 through 11 focused primarily on what we called cost accounting. The objective of cost accounting is to determine the average cost per unit for manufactured products so that work in process and finished goods inventory can be valued at cost on the balance sheet and subsequently transferred to cost of goods sold on the income statement when the products are sold.

The remaining chapters focus on managerial accounting—accumulating the data that management needs to make business decisions. Whereas cost accounting is governed by generally accepted accounting principles, managerial accounting is guided by relevance and cost-benefit analysis. By relevance, we simply mean that management must know what will change as a result of a decision. Managerial accountants provide information that helps management estimate expense, revenue, and profit changes. By cost-benefit analysis we mean the benefit of the information provided to management must be greater than the cost of the information. Management accounting information should help managers make more profitable decisions. The added profit (benefit) should be greater than the cost of doing the management accounting.

Managerial accounting is guided by relevance and cost-benefit analysis.

Management accounting supports two main activities: planning and control. Both planning and control are management decision-making activities. **Planning decisions** are made today about a future course for an organization to follow. **Control decisions** are necessary to keep the organization on the course selected in the plan.

In one sense, the distinction between planning and control is artificial. Control is simply evaluating the original plans in the light of current developments. Control can be thought of as replanning. If the organization finds itself deviating from the original plan, management must review the assumptions underlying that plan and either adjust it or devise a new short-run plan for getting back on the course envisioned by the original plan.

In fact, the real distinction between planning and control is the time horizon. Planning usually involves decisions about a course of action for a year or more into the future. Control involves decisions affecting activities in the next hour, day, week, month, or quarter.

Exhibit 12-1 summarizes the topics covered in this book, showing managerial accounting divided into planning topics and control topics. In this chapter we will first discuss the planning process and the role of budgets within that process. Then we will discuss and illustrate the master budget, which reflects the decisions made in the planning process.

THE PLANNING PROCESS

The planning process which leads from the goals and objectives established for the whole organization to the budgets established for the production, marketing, and financial functions of an organization consists of three major steps.

The major steps in the planning process.

1 *Goals and objectives* are established for the entire organization by top management. Relevant portions of the goals and objectives are communicated to managers throughout the organization.

2 *Programs* are formulated by managers at all levels of the organization which they believe will contribute to the accomplishment of the goals and

EXHIBIT 12-1
Topics Covered in This Book

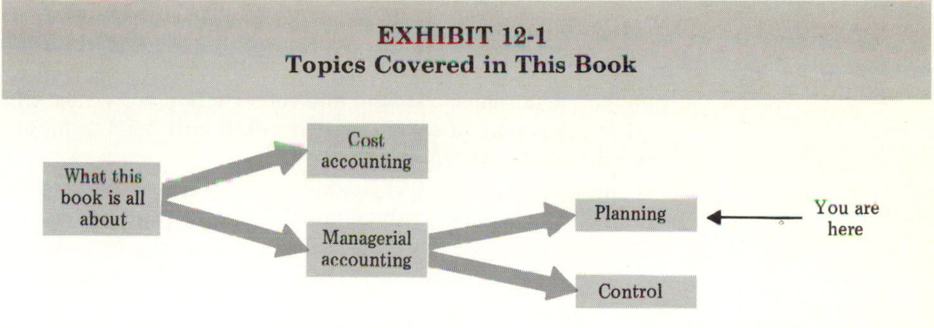

objectives and they submit the programs and their overall financial impact to top management for approval.

3 *Budgets* are formulated which reflect in detail the financial impact of the programs which have been approved by top management.

The key words in these steps are **goals, objectives, programs,** and **budgets.** The next sections of this chapter will discuss these terms.

Goals and Objectives

Goals provide long-run direction to the organization.

Goals and objectives are established as a part of the planning process of the organization. Goals are statements that define the direction of the organization over the long run. These are established by top management after reviewing the environment in which the organization operates and the skills and abilities which the organization possesses.

An organization might review the housing environment over the next five to 10 years and conclude that there is likely to be a shortage of housing which is affordable by young people who are not ready to form families. They might conclude that apartments with pleasant grounds, swimming pools, and entertainment facilities could economically be made available. The assessment of the environment leads to the conclusion that there is a need, and management believes it knows how to satisfy the need.

But even if management makes this assessment of the housing environment, they may not decide that the organization should begin to build apartments. Certain skills are required to acquire land, design apartments, coordinate construction, finance construction, and rent and manage buildings. If the organization does not have these skills nor can they acquire them, they might well conclude that serving this market opportunity should not be a part of their goals and objectives. It is the blending of the conditions in the environment with the unique abilities of the organization which leads to the establishment of goals.

Objectives establish specific targets for the next several years.

Objectives are generally more specific than goals. Goals establish the long-run directions of the organization. Objectives establish specific targets to be achieved by a certain date. If the organization just described decides that they have the internal skills and resources to serve the apartment market described earlier, they would then establish objectives for the next several years. These might state, for example, that the organization intended to acquire building sites for 1,000 units of apartments each year for the next several years. Further, they might state that an objective was to design and complete construction of a specified number of units each year for the next several years. Another objective might state that so many dollars would be borrowed per year for the next three years at specified average interest rates to finance the purchase, design, and construction activities. Objectives might also state how many people of each necessary skill will need to be hired or trained each year over the next several years.

The statements of objectives establish specific targets which management is committed to achieving and against which they are willing to have their performance measured. Further, these objectives serve as the basis for development of programs by various departments of the organization, the next step in the planning process.

Formulate Programs

Programs are specific activities to achieve objectives.

Programs are specific activities for achieving objectives. Each department of an organization develops programs that the managers of that department believe will lead to the achievement of the objectives. For example, the human resource (or personnel) department might decide that three main programs are needed as the company moves into the construction of the apartments.

The first program might be to study the labor markets carefully to determine what kinds of needed skills are available in the market and what rates of pay will be necessary to attract the required workers. This program is a research program to determine whether the organization can hire needed labor in the existing market at reasonable rates.

The second program might be to establish a system to monitor human resource needs and individual accomplishments so that people can be assigned to jobs where they are needed and promoted when their accomplishments suggest that they are ready for a new job with new responsibilities.

A third program might be a hiring and training program. It would list the planned activities for hiring necessary workers as needed, and for training existing workers so that the human resources are available as needed.

For each program developed the department manager would make an overall estimate of the expenses and revenues associated with the program. For these programs only expense is involved, and the human resources department manager might list the total estimated expense of each program, research, human resource monitoring, and hiring and training. These expense estimates would not be detailed estimates of salaries, supplies, travel, tuition, etc. This detailed level of planning occurs in the budgeting process only after the three programs have been approved.

Programs formulated by department managers are reviewed by division and corporate management to assure that they are efficient and effective means of achieving the objectives established for the organization. When approved, programs become the basis for budgets.

Establishing Budgets

Budgets quantify the financial consequence of programs.

Budgets are the financial reflection of company programs. When the programs have been approved, it is still necessary to detail their financial effects. This requires that each step of each program be reviewed to determine how many dollars will be required and how the income statement and the balance sheet will be effected if the programs are carried out. Budgets are normally done by the particular department of the organization which is responsible for implementing each program. At each higher level of management departmental budgets are reviewed and coordinated with budgets prepared in other departments so that the total budget is feasible and a satisfactory profit can be expected from doing the programs.

Since this book is an accounting book, most of the emphasis of the remainder of the chapter will be on the budgeting process. As you study this chapter, remember that behind the detail of the budgets are programs, objectives, and goals. Budgets are the financial reflections of the programs which are based on the goals and objectives and cannot exist without the earlier work being done. It is easy to lose sight of this fact when one becomes immersed in the budget process which at first glance seems very complex.

While it is true that the budget process is very complex in a large organization, it is also true that the process is a very logical process which is carried out in easily recognized steps. It is the purpose of the balance of the chapter to illustrate the logic and the steps required.

Budgeting is not difficult because of its simple logic. Your greatest difficulty in quickly understanding budgeting will be that there is so much data floating around that you must be careful not to forget (1) what step you are working on and (2) how what you are doing fits into the total budget. Before we start on the steps of the budgeting process, let's look at why organizations find budgets to be worth their cost.

Why Prepare Budgets? Organizations prepare budgets for a number of reasons including:

The reasons for preparing budgets.

1. Requiring managers to find efficient and effective ways of achieving their programs
2. Coordinating activities of different departments
3. Communicating plans throughout the organization
4. Providing a standard for performance evaluation

Required Planning Often managers feel they are so busy running the day to day operations of the company that they do not have time to plan. Managers who are required to prepare an annual budget are forced, at least once a year, to direct their attention toward the future. They must analyze their operations and determine how future events, such as changing product lines or new environmental control rules, will affect how they will achieve their own departmental objectives and contribute toward the overall organization's objectives. This analysis of the future provides a better plan of action for each manager.

Coordinate Activities To attain the organization's objectives, management must coordinate the activities of production, marketing, and finance. The budgeting process provides the basis for individuals in all parts of the organization to exchange ideas on how best to achieve objectives. For example, coordination of production and marketing helps to ensure that the production manager is aware of marketing management's anticipated demand for the products. Being aware of anticipated demand will permit the production manager to ensure that sufficient direct materials, labor, and equipment are available to produce the products marketing plans to sell. If demand cannot be satisfied with current production capacity, production capacity can be increased, the marketing manager can modify his budget, or other means of satisfying demand can be sought. The treasurer is concerned with the impact the production budget and expected sales will have on cash flow. Will there be enough cash to pay bills or must borrowing be arranged to provide for cash shortages? The budgeting process should help to point out any inconsistencies among the objectives and programs of each area and how each area contributes toward the objectives of the organization.

Communicate Plans Budgets are a form of communication that inform each manager of what other managers have agreed to do. They also inform managers of what resources will be available to carry out their programs. For example, the budget informs the marketing manager of the expected sales volume and the production manager of the expected production volume along with the resources required to achieve these expectations. In other words, the budget represents, in measurable quantities, a plan of action to achieve the organization's objectives.

Moreover, approved budgets allocate resources and authorize managers to take actions necessary to achieve their objectives.

Performance Evaluation The budget expresses the expectations of the managers in numbers. Actual performance is also measured in numbers and (compared to budget numbers) is used to evaluate current performance. It is more accurate, informative, and fair to measure current performance against a budget—a written statement of what was expected in the future, rather than against a vague expectation or against results of prior years when conditions may have been different. For example, if current production costs are lower than last year's cost, it does not necessarily mean that current performance is good. There may have been a change in the manufacturing process, in prices, in products produced, or in personnel. Thus, the lower production costs might have been expected and incorporated into the budget. Another example: If this year's sales volume is 10% above last year's, is that good or bad? If economic conditions were poor, a 10% increase might be outstanding performance, even if the prior year's increase had been 15%. Marketing management should be measured against what was reasonable to expect rather than against what was achieved in the prior year. Thus, to adequately evaluate performance, management needs to establish what can be expected. These expectations are expressed in the budget.

THE MASTER BUDGET

Master budget defined.

The master budget is a set of budgets resulting from the planning process which quantify top management's expectations of revenues, expenses, net income, cash flows, and financial position.

The master budget consists of two major parts:

Parts of the master budget.

1 An operating budget
2 A financial budget

Exhibit 12-2 shows the components of the operating budget and the components of the financial budget for a manufacturing organization. The components of the budgets would be somewhat simpler for a nonmanufacturing organization even though the concepts are the same. Studying budgeting in a manufacturing organization will give you the concepts you need to prepare and use master budgets in other types of organizations. Precise definitions and descriptions of each of the listed budgets are provided in the next section of this chapter.

The operating budget represents the expected results of operations. It contains a budget for expected sales, production and manufacturing costs, ending inventory costs, costs of goods sold, and selling and administrative expenses, all of which results in a budgeted income statement.

EXHIBIT 12-2
Master Budget
Manufacturing Organization

A. Components of the operating budget
   1. Sales budget
   2. Production budget
   3. Manufacturing cost budgets
      Direct materials budget
      Direct labor budget
      Manufacturing overhead budget
   4. Ending inventory budget
   5. Cost of goods sold budget
   6. Selling and administrative expense budget
   7. Budgeted income statement
B. Components of the financial budget
   1. Cash budget
   2. Budgeted balance sheet

The financial budget summarizes the impact of the operations on cash balances in a cash budget which shows required borrowing or excess cash and the expected financial position in a budgeted balance sheet.

Master Budget Time Periods

Most organizations prepare a master budget for a year and then break it down into monthly budgets. In this way each month's actual results can be compared to its budget shortly after the end of the month. The comparison provides managers with information indicating the likelihood of achieving the organization's objectives by the end of the year. It directs attention to potential problems, month by month, so managers can take corrective action before problems become too large.

One approach to the budget period is to prepare a budget for the organization's business year. With this approach, a budget for the next business year is completed just before the start of the business year and used for comparisons throughout the year. As the end of the business year is approached, a budget for the next year is prepared, but there may be only one or two months of the old budget left before the new budget is prepared.

A budget may cover a business year or may roll forward so that it always extends 12 months into the future.

Another approach which is used by many organizations is called a *rolling budget.* At the end of each month, the results of the previous month's operations together with any new information on changes in business conditions are used to revise the budget for the next 11 months *and* to prepare a budget for one additional month beyond so that the master budget always covers the next 12 months into the future; each month the budget "rolls" forward one month by adding one month to replace the month just past. The advantage of the rolling budget is that it makes planning a continuous activity. Also, the organization always has a master budget for 12 months into the future. Either way, the steps in preparation of the budget are the same; the only difference is the time period to which the steps are applied.

THE MASTER BUDGET ILLUSTRATED

To illustrate how to develop a master budget, we will consider the BZD Corporation. Our illustration will cover the year 19X1. Remember, though, that most companies will prepare a master budget on a monthly or quarterly basis. Nevertheless, the basic computations are the same no matter how long the time period.

The BZD Corporation manufactures two products, Zeta and Beta, in a centralized manufacturing facility. The production process requires very little time for either product so consequently work in process inventory is negligible and is not considered in the planning and budgeting process.

Based on product specifications, engineering studies, and management estimates of direct materials prices and direct labor rates, the following direct materials and direct labor costs have been estimated for products Beta and Zeta and are given in Exhibit 12-3.

EXHIBIT 12-3
BZD CORPORATION
Production Cost Data

This information would be standard cost information which is discussed in Chapters 8 and 9 if the company has a standard cost system.

Product Beta

Direct materials: 8 pounds of material No. 101 × \$1.50 per pound =	\$12.00
Direct labor: 3 hours of direct labor × \$8.00 per hour =	\$24.00
Manufacturing overhead: applied based on direct labor hours as shown in Exhibit 12-8	

Product Zeta

Direct materials: 11 pounds of material No. 102 × \$1.10 per pound =	\$12.10
Direct labor: 2 hours of direct labor × \$8.00 per hour =	\$16.00
Manufacturing overhead: applied based on direct labor hours as shown in Exhibit 12-8	

The balance sheet at the beginning of the budget period is given below:

BZD CORPORATION
Balance Sheet
January 1, 19X1

Assets

Cash		\$ 100,000
Accounts receivable		600,000
Direct materials:		
No. 101; 90,000 pounds @ \$1.50 per pound =	\$ 135,000	
No. 102; 100,000 pounds @ \$1.10 per pound =	110,000	\$ 245,000
Finished goods:		
Beta; 14,000 units @ \$57.00 per unit =	\$ 798,000	
Zeta; 20,000 units @ \$42.10 per unit =	842,000	1,640,000
Fixed assets	\$14,800,000	
Accumulated depreciation	3,700,000	11,100,000
Total assets		\$13,685,000

Liabilities and Equity	
Accounts payable—direct materials purchases	$ 400,000
Federal income taxes payable	200,000
Common stock	8,000,000
Retained earnings	5,085,000
Total liabilities and equity	$13,685,000

Additional information will be given as we describe the computation procedures for each component of the master budget for the BZD Corporation.

Sales Budget

Exhibit 12-4 shows the sales budget for the BZD Corporation. The sales budget represents the expected sales volume in both units and dollars. The budgeted sales dollars are calculated by multiplying the budgeted sales units times the budgeted sales price. We will assume that all sales for the BZD Corporation are credit sales.

The sales budget is the "cornerstone" of the master budget.

In most budgeting systems the sales budget is the starting point in preparing the master budget. The production budget and all the manufacturing cost budgets are based on estimated units to be sold. The budgeted total sales dollars is used to budget selling and administrative expenses, and in the budgeted income statement and in the cash collections section of the cash budget.

The sales budget can be developed using any one of several different methods. In some companies analysis of historical sales patterns are used to estimate trends in sales volume while other companies ask their individual sales representatives for estimated units to be sold to each customer during the budget year. These estimates are then summarized by product to determine the budgeted sales units for each product.

There are numerous methods for developing a sales budget.

With either of the above methods the budgeted sales units will be influenced by factors such as general economic conditions, industry sales patterns, pricing policies, advertising programs, and expected competitor actions.[1]

EXHIBIT 12-4
BZD CORPORATION
Sales Budget
For the Year Ended December 31, 19X1

Product	Budgeted Sales Units		Budgeted Sales Price		Budgeted Sales Dollars
Beta	70,000	×	$110	=	$ 7,700,000
Zeta	80,000	×	90	=	7,200,000
Total	150,000				$14,900,000

Notice that both unit sales and dollar sales are shown.

[1] For a description of a number of different forecasting models, see John C. Chambers, S. Mollick, and D. Smith, "How to Choose the Right Forecasting Technique," *Harvard Business Review* (July–August, 1971).

Production Budget

Once the sales budget has been prepared the production budget can be made. The production budget specifies the number of units of each product that must be produced to satisfy the sales estimates and to achieve the desired level of ending finished goods inventory.

Before illustrating the actual calculation, we should observe that there is a simple relationship which accountants use again and again in the budgeting process. It is:

The logic of budgeting is simple.

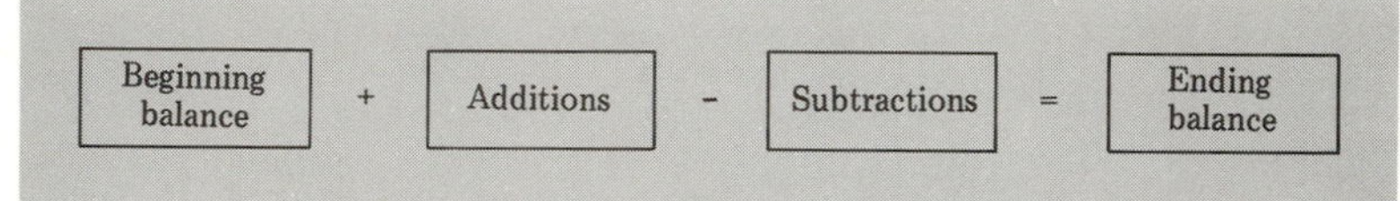

You might think that this is such an obvious relationship that it is not even worth mentioning. Yet it is the basic logic of the budgeting process. We are trying to get from starting balances to ending (budgeted) balances by estimating the additions and subtractions which will occur in a particular category during the year. In the case of accounts receivable, the additions will be sales and the subtractions will be collections from customers. In the case we are about to illustrate, the additions will be production and the subtractions will be sales, but the logic is always the same. Notice also that the order of the terms in the equation can be rearranged to simplify calculations. Instead of

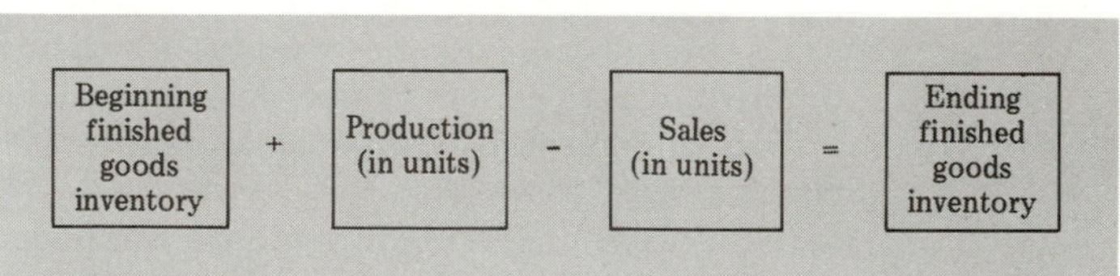

you can write the equivalent

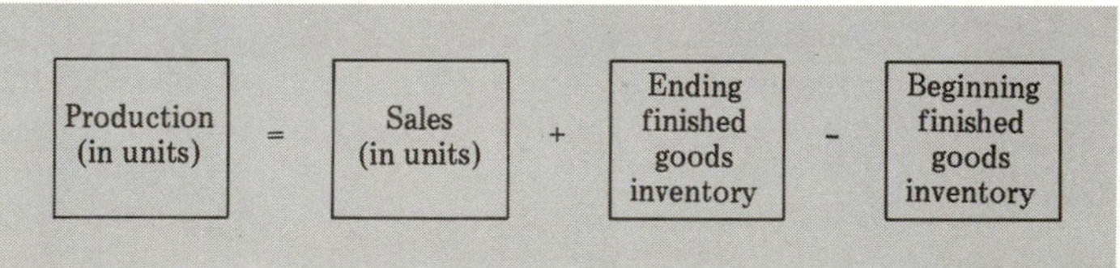

This second form is more convenient for calculating the units which must be produced, but uses the same logic.

The relationship may be used with unit data or with dollar data. In this example unit data is desired—it will be converted to dollar data using the estimated costs. In the accounts receivable example mentioned earlier, dollar data will be used rather than unit data.

The production budget for the BZD Corporation is shown in Exhibit 12-5. the budgeted sales units were obtained from the sales budget in Exhibit 12-4. The amount of desired ending finished goods inventory used in calculating the production requirements is the result of a management decision. In making this decision management generally attempts to minimize the sum of three costs: (1) the finished

EXHIBIT 12-5
BZD CORPORATION
Production Budget in Units
For the Year Ended December 31, 19X1

	Beta	Zeta	Reference
Budgeted sales units	70,000	80,000	Exhibit 12-4
plus: Estimated ending finished goods inventory	17,000	15,000	New data
Total requirements	87,000	95,000	
less: Beginning finished goods inventory	14,000	20,000	Balance sheet January 1, 19X1
Production in units	73,000	75,000	

goods inventory carrying costs, (2) the cost associated with not having finished goods inventory available when the customer requests it, and (3) the finished goods inventory ordering costs.

Manufacturing Cost Budgets

Based on the production budget, the manufacturing cost budgets for direct materials, direct labor, and manufacturing overhead can be calculated.

Direct Materials Budget The direct materials budget shows the expected amount of direct materials that will be used to produce products Beta and Zeta. The direct materials budget also shows the amount of direct materials that will have to be purchased to provide for the direct materials usage and the estimated direct materials ending inventory.

Exhibit 12-6 illustrates the computation of the direct materials budget. Part A of the budget shows the direct materials usage, which is calculated as the budgeted production in units times management's estimate of the pounds of direct materials necessary to produce 1 unit of each product. The cost of direct materials used is calculated by multiplying management's estimated cost per pound of direct materials times the direct materials usage.

The direct materials budget specifies the cost of direct materials used and the cost of direct materials purchased.

Part B of Exhibit 12-6 shows the direct materials that must be purchased to meet production requirements and the estimated direct materials ending inventory. The basic computation is shown below:

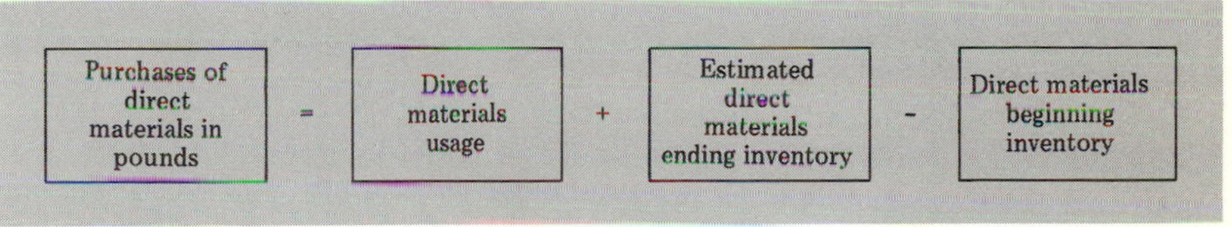

The pounds of direct materials to be purchased are translated into dollars by multiplying by management's estimated price per pound of direct materials.

EXHIBIT 12-6
BZD CORPORATION
Direct Materials Budget
For the Year Ended December 31, 19X1

A. Usage Budget

	Beta	Zeta	Total	Reference
Budgeted production in units	73,000	75,000		Exhibit 12-5
Direct materials requirements	× 8 pounds No. 101	× 11 pounds No. 102		Exhibit 12-3
Direct materials usage	584,000 pounds	825,000 pounds		
Cost per pound	× $1.50	× $1.10		Exhibit 12-3
Cost of direct materials used	$876,000	$907,500	$1,783,500	

B. Purchases Budget

	Direct Materials in Pounds			
	No. 101	No. 102	Total	Reference
Direct materials usage	584,000	825,000		Exhibit 12-6
Estimated direct materials ending inventory	+ 86,000	+ 148,000		New data
Total requirements	670,000	973,000		
Direct materials beginning inventory	− 90,000	− 100,000		Balance sheet January 1, 19X1
Purchases of direct materials	580,000	873,000		
Cost per pound	× $1.50	× $1.10		Exhibit 12-3
Cost of purchases	$870,000	$960,300	$1,830,300	

Direct Labor Budget Exhibit 12-7 illustrates the calculation of the direct labor budget for the BZD Corporation. Just like all the budgets discussed this far except the sales budget, this budget is based on the budgeted production, in units, of products Beta and Zeta. The total direct labor hours are calculated by multiplying the budgeted production in units times management's estimated direct labor hours to produce 1 unit of each of the products. The total direct labor dollars are calculated by multiplying the total hours times management's estimated labor rate. The total hours required in the direct labor budget is used to determine the number of employees necessary to produce the products and to determine the dollars the company must have available to meet their payroll costs.

Uses of the direct labor budget.

EXHIBIT 12-7
BZD CORPORATION
Direct Labor Budget
For the Year Ended December 31, 19X1

	Beta	Zeta	Total	Reference
Budgeted production requirements	73,000	75,000		Exhibit 12-5
Direct labor hours per unit	× 3 hours	× 2 hours		Exhibit 12-3
Total direct labor hours	219,000	150,000	369,000	
Direct labor cost per hour	× $8.00	× $8.00	× $8.00	Exhibit 12-3
Total direct labor cost	$1,752,000	$1,200,000	$2,952,000	

Manufacturing Overhead Budget The manufacturing overhead cost budget is shown in Exhibit 12-8. This budget is based on the classification of the manufacturing overhead cost items into variable cost and fixed cost categories.

EXHIBIT 12-8
BZD CORPORATION
Manufacturing Overhead Budget
Based on Expected Activity of 369,000 Direct Labor Hours
For the Year Ended December 31, 19X1

Budgeted variable manufacturing overhead cost.

Budgeted fixed manufacturing overhead cost estimated by management.

(1) Item	(2) (New Data) Rate per Direct Labor Hour	(3) (From Exhibit 12-7) Direct Labor Hours		(4) Total Cost	
Supplies	$1.00	× 369,000	=	$369,000	
Repairs	.80	× 369,000	=	295,200	
Indirect labor	1.00	× 369,000	=	369,000	
Other	.20	× 369,000	=	73,800	
Total variable manufacturing overhead cost					$1,107,000
Supervision				$361,000	
Depreciation				790,000	
Property tax				160,000	
Other				165,000	
Total fixed manufacturing overhead cost					$1,476,000
Total manufacturing overhead cost					$2,583,000

$$\text{Predetermined overhead rate} = \frac{\$2{,}583{,}000}{369{,}000 \text{ direct labor hours}}$$
$$= \$7.00 \text{ per direct labor hour}$$

In the BZD Corporation the variable manufacturing overhead costs are expected to change as direct labor hours change. Management has analyzed historical manufacturing overhead costs and adjusted them for any expected changes in the quantities and prices of each item. This results in the estimated variable rate per direct labor hour for each variable cost item, which is shown in column 2 of Exhibit 12-8. Each of the budgeted variable overhead costs (column 4) in Exhibit 12-8 is calculated by multiplying the variable rate (column 2) for that cost item times the budgeted direct labor hours (column 3).

The items in the manufacturing overhead budget are classified into fixed and variable categories.

The budgeted fixed manufacturing overhead costs in Exhibit 12-8 are also based on management's analysis of historical manufacturing overhead cost adjusted for expected changes in the price of each item. Since these costs are fixed, we do not expect them to change with changes in direct labor hours. Therefore, management's estimates of these costs are included directly in the manufacturing overhead budget. At the bottom line of Exhibit 12-8 is the calculation of the predetermined overhead rate to be used for product costing during the budget year 19X1.

Ending Inventory Budget

Having completed the direct materials, direct labor, and manufacturing overhead budgets, we can prepare the dollar ending inventory budget shown in Exhibit 12-9. The ending inventory for the BZD Corporation consists of direct materials and finished goods.

EXHIBIT 12-9
BZD CORPORATION
Ending Inventory Budget
December 31, 19X1

				Reference
Direct Materials Inventory				
No. 101	86,000 pounds × $1.50 per pound	=	$ 129,000	Exhibits 12-3 and 12-6
No. 102	148,000 pounds × $1.10 per pound	=	162,800	Exhibits 12-3 and 12-6
Total cost			$ 291,800	
Finished Goods Inventory				
Beta	17,000 units × $57.00 per unit*	=	$ 969,000	Exhibit 12-5
Zeta	15,000 units × $42.10 per unit*	=	631,500	Exhibit 12-5
Total cost			$1,600,500	

* Cost per unit computations

Beta				
Direct materials:	8 pounds × $1.50 per pound	=	$12.00	Exhibit 12-3
Direct labor:	3 hours × $8.00 per hour	=	24.00	Exhibit 12-3
Applied overhead:	3 hours × $7.00 per hour	=	21.00	Exhibit 12-8
Total cost per unit			$57.00	
Zeta				
Direct materials:	11 pounds × $1.10 per pound	=	$12.10	Exhibit 12-3
Direct labor:	2 hours × $8.00 per hour	=	16.00	Exhibit 12-3
Applied overhead:	2 hours × $7.00 per hour	=	14.00	Exhibit 12-8
Total cost per unit			$42.10	

The direct materials inventory is costed at the estimated cost per pound for direct materials no. 101 and no. 102. The finished goods inventory is costed at the full cost per finished unit for Beta and Zeta. The full cost per finished unit for each product is computed at the bottom of Exhibit 12-9. These costs for the ending inventories will be used to prepare the cost of goods sold budget and the budgeted balance sheet.

Cost of Goods Sold Budget

Having completed the manufacturing cost budgets and the ending inventory budget, we can now prepare the cost of goods sold budget as illustrated in Exhibit 12-10. The basic cost details of the cost of goods sold budget is obtained from four budgets: the direct materials budget, the direct labor budget, the manufacturing overhead budget, and the ending inventory budget. The cost of goods sold budget will be used in preparing the budgeted income statement for the BZD Corporation.

EXHIBIT 12-10
BZD CORPORATION
Budgeted Cost of Goods Sold
For the Year Ended December 31, 19X1

			Reference
Direct materials January 1, 19X1	$ 245,000		Balance sheet January 1, 19X1
Purchases	1,830,300		Exhibit 12-6
Cost of direct materials available	$2,075,300		
Direct materials December 31, 19X1	291,800		Exhibit 12-9
Cost of direct materials used		$1,783,500	
Direct labor		2,952,000	Exhibit 12-7
Manufacturing overhead		2,583,000	Exhibit 12-8
Total manufacturing cost		$7,318,500	
Finished goods January 1, 19X1		1,640,000	Balance sheet January 1, 19X1
Total goods available for sale		$8,958,500	
Finished goods December 31, 19X1		1,600,500	Exhibit 12-9
Cost of goods sold		$7,358,000	

Selling and Administrative Expense Budget

The selling and administrative expense budget is shown in Exhibit 12-11 for the BZD Corporation. This budget is separated into variable and fixed selling and administrative expenses based on the cost behavior patterns specified by management. The total estimated variable selling and administrative costs are calculated by multiplying the budgeted rate per sales dollar times the total estimated sales dollars. The fixed selling and administrative expenses are not expected to change; therefore, management's estimate is included as the budgeted amount.

EXHIBIT 12-11
BZD CORPORATION
Selling and Administrative Expense Budget
For the Year Ended December 31, 19X1

(1) Item	(2) Rate per Sales Dollar (New Data)		(3) Sales Dollars (from Exhibit 12-4)	(4) Total Cost	
Sales commissions	.07	×	$14,900,000	$1,043,000	
Travel	.02	×	14,900,000	298,000	
Entertainment	.01	×	14,900,000	149,000	
Total variable selling and administrative expense					$1,490,000
Salaries				$2,100,000	
Maintenance				200,000	
Supplies				200,000	
Insurance				250,000	
Property tax				400,000	
Advertising				2,210,000	
Total fixed selling and administrative expense					$5,360,000
Total selling and administrative expense					$6,850,000

Budgeted variable expense.

Budgeted fixed expense.

The selling and administrative expense budget is generally prepared simultaneously with the sales budget since many of the selling costs, such as advertising, will influence the expected volume of sales.

Budgeted Income Statement

The budgeted income statement shown in Exhibit 12-12 summarizes all the individual budgets and the budgeting work we have performed up to this point. The budgets for sales, cost of goods sold, and selling and administrative expense, are used to calculate the income before taxes. Assuming a 50% tax rate, the estimated income taxes are calculated and used to compute the net income.

EXHIBIT 12-12
BZD CORPORATION
Budgeted Income Statement
For the Year Ended December 31, 19X1

		Reference
Sales revenue	$14,900,000	Exhibit 12-4
Cost of goods sold	7,358,000	Exhibit 12-10
Gross margin	$ 7,542,000	
Selling and administrative expense	6,850,000	Exhibit 12-11
Income before taxes	$ 692,000	
Federal income taxes at 50%	346,000	New data
Net income	$ 346,000	

Cash Budget

The cash budget can reveal potential cash shortages.

The cash budget uses data from the previous budgets to budget cash receipts and disbursements of the organization. One objective of preparing a cash budget is to reveal to the manager any periods when the company might need cash. If borrowing is necessary management can take early action to obtain the necessary loans. Most companies experience seasonal peaks where merchandise must be purchased and paid for before sales are made and cash is collected from the customers. A department store preparing for the Christmas season is a good example. By preparing a cash budget, periods where the company needs cash to finance inventory can be identified early. This provides management with sufficient time to negotiate a bank loan to cover the estimated cash shortage.

Another objective of the cash budget is to point out periods where the company might have more cash than is necessary to pay bills which become due. Excess cash can be invested where it can earn an additional return for the organization.

The cash budget can reveal potential periods with excess cash.

Some firms with an active investment program for excess cash find that a cash budget on a monthly basis is not sufficient for monitoring excess cash flow. These firms prepare cash budgets on a weekly or in some cases on a daily basis. The budget period will be determined by the information management needs to effectively operate a short-term cash investment program.

The cash budget for the BZD Corporation is shown in Exhibit 12-13.

Factors that influence cash collections.

The starting point for constructing the cash budget is the beginning cash balance. Then collections from beginning accounts receivable and current sales revenue are added to the beginning cash balance to get the total cash available. Cash collections depend on many factors, such as the time lag between credit sales and collections of the accounts, the expected amount of bad debts, and the expected sale of assets, common stock, or bonds. For the BZD Corporation we will assume that (1) it expects to collect all of the beginning accounts receivable and (2) it expects to collect 91% of the credit sales made during 19X1. This means that 9% of the credit sales during 19X1 will represent the ending accounts receivable. Using this information the collections on accounts are calculated in note 1 of Exhibit 12-13.

The expected cash payments are based on the manufacturing cost budgets, the selling and administrative expense budget, and the beginning payables on the balance sheet. The cash payment for direct materials is based on the beginning accounts payable for direct materials, the purchases of direct materials, and the expected payments to be made during 19X1. We will assume the BZD Corporation expects to pay all accounts payable for direct materials existing at the beginning of 19X1 and 90% of the direct materials purchased during the year. This means the accounts payable for direct materials at December 31, 19X1 will amount to 10% of direct materials purchases. The cash payments for materials are calculated in note 2 of Exhibit 12-13.

We assumed that direct labor is paid for in the period incurred; therefore the cash payment for direct labor is the same as the expected direct labor cost computed in Exhibit 12-7.

Manufacturing overhead is also assumed to be paid for in the period incurred. The cash payment for manufacturing overhead cost is determined from Exhibit 12-8. Note that since depreciation does not require a cash payment, the expected manufacturing overhead cost is reduced by the depreciation cost to obtain the cash payments for manufacturing overhead. This is shown in note 3 of Exhibit 12-13.

The cash payments expected for selling and administrative expenses are the same as the budgeted costs since we assumed all these expenses are to be paid during 19X1.

The final item requiring a cash payment is the income tax payable. During the budget year, BZD will have to pay the $200,000 owed at the start of the year

EXHIBIT 12-13
BZD CORPORATION
Cash Budget
For the Year Ended December 31, 19X1

			Reference
Beginning cash balance		$ 100,000	Balance sheet—January 1, 19X1
Collections on accounts		14,159,000[1]	
Total cash available		$14,259,000	
Cash payments:			
Direct materials	$2,047,270[2]		
Direct labor	2,952,000		Exhibit 12-7
Manufacturing overhead	1,793,000[3]		
Selling and administrative expense	6,850,000		Exhibit 12-11
Federal income tax	459,500[4]		
Total cash payments		$14,101,770	
Ending cash balance		$ 157,230	

[1] Accounts receivable, January 1, 19X1	$ 600,000	Balance sheet—January 1, 19X1
Credit sales	14,900,000	Exhibit 12-4
Total	$15,500,000	
Accounts receivable, December 31, 19X1	1,341,000	9% of credit sales
Collections on accounts	$14,159,000	
[2] Accounts payable, January 1, 19X1	$ 400,000	Balance sheet—January 1, 19X1
Purchases of direct materials	1,830,300	Exhibit 12-6
Total	$ 2,230,000	
Accounts payment, December 31, 19X1	183,030	10% of annual purchases
Cash payments for direct materials	$ 2,047,270	
[3] Total manufacturing overhead	$ 2,583,000	Exhibit 12-8
Depreciation	790,000	Exhibit 12-8
Cash payment for manufacturing overhead	$ 1,793,000	
[4] Federal income taxes payable January 1, 19X1	$ 200,000	Balance sheet—January 1, 19X1
Federal income taxes for the year 19X1	346,000	Exhibit 12-12
Total	$ 546,000	
Federal income taxes payable December 31, 19X1	86,500	25% of budgeted taxes
Cash payment for federal income taxes	$ 459,500	

(January 1, 19X1 balance sheet) and 75% of the budget year's income tax. The total income tax to be paid is $459,500, which consists of the January 1 tax liability of $200,000 plus 75% of the budget year tax, $259,500 (Exhibit 12-12). An alternative computation of the income tax to be paid is shown in note 4 of Exhibit 12-13. Subtracting the total cash payments from the total cash available provides the estimated ending cash balance at December 31, 19X1.

Budgeted Balance Sheet

The budgeted balance sheet represents the expected financial position for the BZD Corporation on December 31, 19X1 and is illustrated in Exhibit 12-14. The budgeted balance sheet for December 31, 19X1 is constructed from the balance sheet for January 1, 19X1 and the expected changes in the accounts computed in the operating budgets and the cash budget. The source of the data to construct the budgeted balance sheet is shown in Exhibit 12-14 for each item.

The budgeted balance sheet shows the resulting account balances based on the operating budgets.

The budgeted balance sheet provides management with the expected account balances resulting from the operating budgets. If any of the accounts or relationships among the accounts are not in line with management's expectations, the operating plan might have to be changed. For example, some banks will not lend to a firm whose debt-equity ratio and/or current ratio indicate to the bank that the loan would be too risky. If the firm's budgeted balance sheet shows that these ratios are indeed too low, the operating plan would have to be changed to satisfy the loan requirement.

EXHIBIT 12-14
BZD CORPORATION
Budgeted Balance Sheet
December 31, 19X1

			Reference
Assets			
Cash		$ 157,230	Exhibit 12-13
Accounts receivable		1,341,000	Exhibit 12-13
Direct materials inventory		291,800	Exhibit 12-9
Finished goods inventory		1,600,500	Exhibit 12-9
Fixed assets	$14,800,000		Balance sheet—January 1, 19X1
Accumulated depreciation	4,490,000[1]	10,310,000	
Total assets		$13,700,530	
Liabilities and Equity			
Accounts payable—direct materials		$ 183,030	Exhibit 12-13
Federal income taxes payable		86,500	Exhibit 12-13
Common stock		8,000,000	Balance sheet—January 1, 19X1
Retained earnings		5,431,000[2]	
Total liabilities and equity		$13,700,530	

[1] $3,700,000 + $790,000 depreciation = $4,490,000 (Beginning balance sheet and Exhibit 12-8)

[2] $5,085,000 + $346,000 net income = $5,431,000 (Beginning balance sheet and Exhibit 12-12)

Master Budget Summary

To summarize the relationships between the components making up the master budget, Exhibit 12-15 has been prepared. As shown in Exhibit 12-15 the sales budget is the starting point for the budgeting process and all the other budgets are related to the sales budget.

EXHIBIT 12-15
The Interrelationships between the Component Budgets of the Master Budget

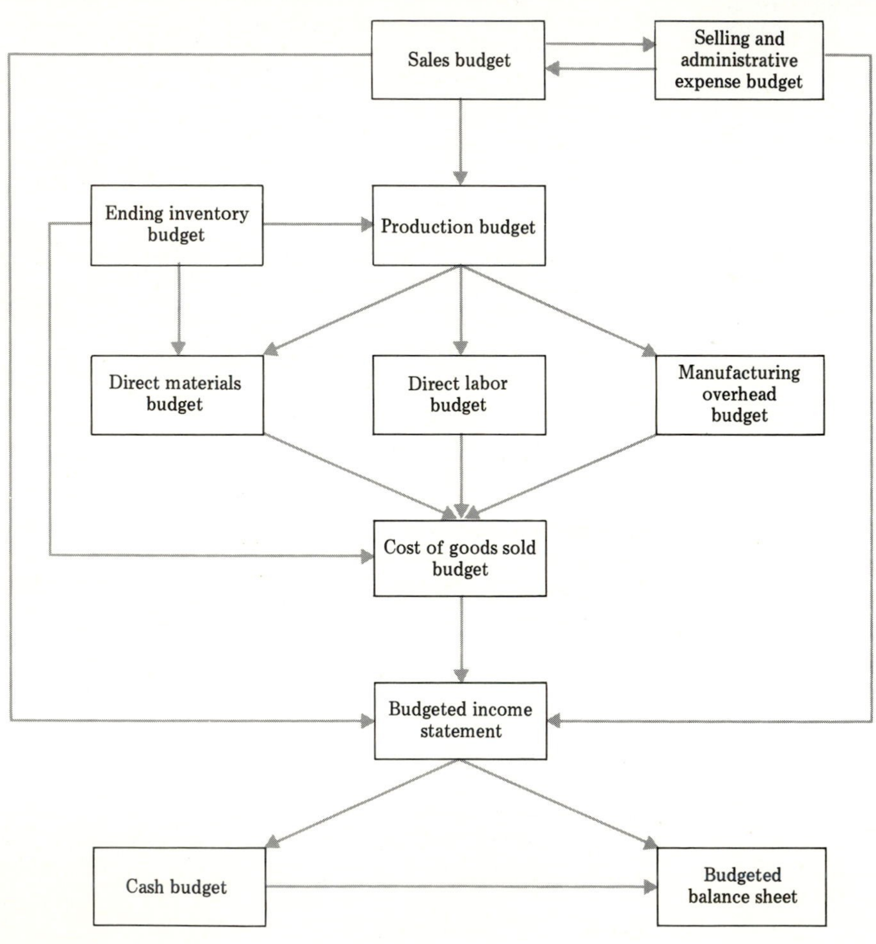

SUMMARY

Planning is establishing objectives and budgets to achieve financial goals over a specified period. Plans are determined to direct the organization to some specified future position.

Planning enables management to communicate corporate objectives to the various divisions and to coordinate the policies of the functional areas. In the process of planning, potential problems are identified and data are generated that aid in making decisions so that these anticipated problems can be avoided. The result of the planning process is a plan of action, quantified in the master budget, that can be used as a standard to evaluate the performance of the plans and the managers carrying out these plans.

Calculating the budget amounts follows a simple logical process. The process can be summarized as follows:

Beginning amount + additions − subtractions = ending amount

The appropriate additions and subtractions depend on the particular phase of the budget which is being planned.

The master budget consists of an operating budget and a financial budget.

The operating budget represents the expected results of operations. It contains a budget for expected sales, production and manufacturing costs, ending inventory costs, costs of goods sold, selling and administrative expenses, and net income.

The financial budget summarizes the operations in terms of expected cash flows and expected balances in balance sheet accounts.

Review Problem

Selected information concerning the Ace Retail Store is given below:

Account Balances as of January 1, 19X8

Cash	$ 40,000
Accounts receivable—net	53,250
Inventory	113,750
Fixed assets—net of depreciation	150,000
Total assets	$357,000
Current liabilities—inventory purchases	$ 74,750
Capital stock	100,000
Retained earnings	182,250
Total liabilities and equity	$357,000

All sales are on account and collections are 60% in the month of sale, 30% in the following month, and 9% in the second month following the month of sale; 1% are uncollectible. Recent and estimated sales are:

actual	November 19X7	$115,000
actual	December 19X7	110,000
estimated	January 19X8	120,000
	February 19X8	110,000
	March 19X8	115,000
	April 19X8	120,000
	May 19X8	130,000

Management has decided that the inventory level in units at the end of each month should be equal to the estimated sales units for the next one and one-half months. The purchase price of inventory is 65% of the sales price. All purchases are paid for in the month following the month of purchase.

All expenses are paid for in the month incurred. Variable expenses are expected to amount to 10% of sales revenues (exclusive of bad debts). Fixed expenses are expected to be $25,000 per month, including $6,000 depreciation.

Required

1 Prepare a table showing the budgeted cash collections from customers for January, February, and March.

2 Prepare a table showing the budgeted amount of inventory purchases during January, February, and March.

3 Prepare a cash budget for January, February, and March.

4 Prepare a budgeted income statement for the first quarter of 19X8.

5 Prepare a budgeted balance sheet as of March 31, 19X8.

Solution

1

ACE RETAIL STORE
Cash Collections from Customers
First Quarter, 19X8

			January		**February**		**March**
Sales made in							
November 19X7	$115,000	(9%)	$ 10,350		$		$
December 19X7	$110,000	(30%)	33,000	(9%)	9,900		
January 19X8	$120,000	(60%)	72,000	(30%)	36,000	(9%)	10,800
February 19X8	$110,000			(60%)	66,000	(30%)	33,000
March 19X8	$115,000					(60%)	69,000
Cash collections			$115,350		$111,900		$112,800

This review problem introduces the idea of bad debts. Notice that their only effect on the cash collections is that we collect 99% of total sales over the three months rather than 100%. As you will see, they also affect the income statement and balance sheet.

2

ACE RETAIL STORE
Purchases First Quarter, 19X8

	January	**February**	**March**
Estimated sales	$120,000	$110,000	$115,000
Cost of sales (65%)	$ 78,000	$ 71,500	$ 74,750
Desired ending inventory*	108,875	113,750	120,250
Total requirements	$186,875	$185,250	$195,000
Beginning inventory	113,750	108,875	113,750
Purchases	$ 73,125	$ 76,375	$ 81,250

*Desired ending inventory = 65% (next month's sales + ½ second month's sales)
January = 65% [$110,000 + ½ ($115,000)] = $108,875
February = 65% [$115,000 + ½ ($120,000)] = $113,750
March = 65% [$120,000 + ½ ($130,000)] = $120,250

In many problems it is easier to work out purchases in units and then convert to dollars. This is an example where it is easier to work directly in dollars.

3

ACE RETAIL STORES
Cash Budget
First Quarter, 19X8

	January	February	March
Beginning cash balance	$ 40,000	$ 49,600	$ 58,375
Cash receipts (from part 1)	115,350	111,900	112,800
Total cash available	$155,350	$161,500	$171,175
Cash disbursements			
Payments for purchases (from part 2)	74,750	73,125	76,375
Variable expenses (10% of sales)	12,000	11,000	11,500
Fixed expenses ($25,000–$6,000)	19,000	19,000	19,000
Total disbursements	$105,750	$103,125	$106,875
Ending cash balance	$ 49,600	$ 58,375	$ 64,300

When you compare payments for purchases here to part 2, remember that payments for purchases are made one month after the purchases. In looking at fixed expense payments remember that depreciation does not require a current cash payment.

4

ACE RETAIL STORES
Budgeted Income Statement
First Quarter, 19X8

Sales		$345,000
Cost of sales (65% of sales)		224,250
Gross profit		$120,750
Variable expenses (10% of sales)	34,500	
Fixed expenses (3 months)	75,000	
Bad debts (1% of sales)	3,450	$112,950
Profit before taxes		$ 7,800

Here is bad debts again.

5

ACE RETAIL STORES
Balance Sheet
March 31, 19X8

Cash	$ 64,300
Accounts receivable—net*	54,750
Inventory (from part 2)	120,250
Fixed assets—net	132,000
Total assets	$371,300
Current liabilities—purchases	$ 81,250
Capital stock	100,000
Retained earnings	190,050
Total liabilities and equity	$371,300

* 9% ($110,000) + (30% + 9%) ($115,000) = $54,750

Finally, bad debts shows up here since accounts receivable shows only 9% and 39% as assets rather than 10% and 40%.

The fixed asset net balance is reduced by three months' depreciation since January 1. Retained earnings is the January 1 balance plus the profit for the three months.

Glossary

Budgets Budgets reflect in detail the financial impact of programs which have been approved by management to achieve objectives and goals.

Control decisions Those decisions that are necessary to keep the organization on the course selected in the plan. Control decisions usually involve a time horizon of less than a year.

Goals Statements that provide direction to the organization over long periods of time. Goals are established by top management after reviewing the environment in which the organization operates and the skills and abilities which the organization possesses.

Objectives Objectives represent specific targets that are to be achieved by a specified date. They represent the means by which the organization will achieve its goals.

Planning decisions Those decisions that select the course of action the organization will follow in the future. Planning decisions usually involve a time horizon of a year or more.

Programs Programs represent specific activities to achieve the organization's objectives. Approved programs are the basis for the preparation of budgets.

Questions and Problems

12-1 Distinguish between planning decisions and control decisions.

12-2 Discuss the relationship between goals, objectives, programs, and budgets.

12-3 Discuss why an organization would prepare budgets.

12-4 What is a rolling budget?

12-5 Why is the sales budget the usual starting point for the budgeting process?

12-6 What are the purposes of financial budgets?

12-7 What costs are management trying to minimize when they establish the estimated ending inventory levels?

12-8 **Production Budget and Direct Materials Budget** The Monet Company has estimated sales of product W for the next four months as follows:

January	60,000 units
February	80,000 units
March	70,000 units
April	80,000 units

The inventory of product W on December 31 is 12,000 units. The management of the Monet Company has decided that at the end of each month the inventory of product W should be sufficient to satisfy 20% of the next month's estimated sales units.

The production of product W requires two different direct materials—No. 1056 and No. 1057. One unit of product W requires 2 pounds of direct materials No. 1056 and 1 pound of direct materials No. 1057. Because of the time required to obtain both direct materials, management maintains end-of-month inventories of direct materials sufficient to produce the following month's production of product W. The December 31 inventory of direct materials No. 1056 is 128,000 pounds and direct materials No. 1057 is 64,000 pounds.

Required

1 Calculate a production budget for January, February, and March.

2 Calculate a direct materials usage and purchases budget for January and February.

12-9 Computations for Cash Receipts and Disbursements Patsy Corp. has estimated its activity for December 19X6. Selected data from these estimated amounts are as follows:

Sales	$350,000
Gross profit (as a percentage of sales)	30%
Increase in accounts receivable during month	$ 10,000
Change in accounts payable during month	$ 0
Increase in inventory during month	$ 5,000

Variable selling, general and administrative expenses includes a charge for uncollectible accounts of 1% of sales.

Total selling, general and administrative expenses is $35,500 per month plus 15% of sales. Depreciation expenses of $20,000 per month is included in fixed selling, general and administrative expenses.

Required

1 Compute the estimated cash receipts for December.

2 Compute the estimated cash disbursements for December.

(CPA)

12-10 Preparation of Projected Cash, Income, and Balance Sheet Budgets The January 31, 19X6 balance sheet of Shelpat Corporation follows:

Cash	$ 8,000
Accounts receivable (net of allowance for uncollectible accounts of $2,000)	38,000
Inventory	16,000
Property, plant and equipment (net of allowance for accumulated depreciation of $60,000)	40,000
	$102,000
Accounts payable (inventory purchases)	$ 82,500
Common stock	50,000
Retained earnings (deficit)	(30,500)
	$102,000

Sales are budgeted as follows:

February	$110,000
March	$120,000

Collections are expected to be 60% in the month of sale, 38% the next month, and 2% uncollectible.

The gross margin is 25% of sales. Purchases each month are 75% of the next month's projected sales dollars. The purchases are paid in full the following month.

Other expenses for each month, paid in cash, are expected to be $16,500. Depreciation each month is $5,000.

Required

For the month of February:

1 Prepare a cash budget.

2 Prepare a projected income statement.

3 Prepare a projected balance sheet.

(CPA)

12-11 Purchases and Cash Collections Budgets with Cash Discounts The Dilly Company marks up all merchandise 25% of gross purchase price. All purchases are made on account with terms of 1/10, net 30. Purchase discounts are always taken. Normally, 60% of each month's purchases are paid for in the month of purchase while the other 40% are paid during the first 10 days of the first month after purchase. Inventories of merchandise at the end of each month are planned to be 30% of the next month's projected cost of goods sold.

Terms for sales on account are 2/10, net 30. Cash sales are not subject to discount. During the month of sale 50% of each month's sales on account are collected, 45% are collected in the succeeding month, and the remainder are usually uncollectible. In the month of sale 70% of the collections are subject to discount while 10% of the collections in the succeeding month are subject to discount.

Projected sales data for selected months follow:

	Sales on Account—Gross	Cash Sales
December	$1,900,000	$400,000
January	1,500,000	250,000
February	1,700,000	350,000
March	1,600,000	300,000
April	1,700,000	300,000

Required

For January, February, and March:

1 Prepare a purchases budget in dollars. Include the purchase discount in the budget.

2 Prepare a cash collections table.

(CPA)

12-12 Computations for Cash Budgets with Cash Discounts The Russon Corporation is a retailer whose sales are all made on credit. Sales are billed twice monthly, on the 10th of the month for the last half of the prior month's sales and on the 20th of the month for the first half of the current month's sales. The terms of all sales are 2/10, net 30. Based upon past experience, the collection experience of accounts receivable is as follows:

Within the discount period	80%
On the 30th day	18
Uncollectible	2

The sales value of shipments for May 19X0 and the forecast for the next four months are:

May (actual)	$500,000
June	600,000
July	700,000
August	700,000
September	400,000

Russon's average markup on its products is 20% of the sales price. (Cost of goods sold is 80% of selling price.)

Russon purchases merchandise for resale to meet the current month's sales demand and to maintain a desired monthly ending inventory of 25% of the next month's sales. All purchases are on credit with terms of net 30. Russon pays for one-half of a month's purchases in the month of purchase and the other half in the month following the purchase.

All sales and purchases occur uniformly throughout the month.

Required For the months of July and August calculate:

1 Collections on accounts receivable

2 Merchandise purchases

3 Payments for merchandise purchases

(CPA)

12-13 Purchases and Cash Budgets with Cash Discounts Tomlinson Retail seeks your assistance to develop cash and other budget information for May, June, and July 19X3. At April 30, 19X3, the company had cash of $5,500, accounts receivable of $437,000, inventories of $309,400, and accounts payable of $133,055.

The budget is to be based on the following assumptions:

I. *Sales*

a Each month's sales are billed on the last day of the month.

b Customers are allowed a 3% discount if payment is made within 10 days after the billing date. Receivables are booked gross.

c Within the discount period 60% of the billings are collected, 25% are collected by the end of the month, 9% are collected by the end of the second month, and 6% prove uncollectible.

II. *Purchases*

a A total of 54% of all purchases of materials and selling, general and administrative expenses are paid in the month purchased and the remainder in the following month.

b Each month's units of ending inventory is equal to 130% of the next month's units of sales.

c The cost of each unit of inventory is $20.

d Selling, general and administrative expenses, of which $2,000 is depreciation, are equal to 15% of the current month's sales.

Actual and projected sales are as follows:

19X3	Dollars	Units
March (actual)	$354,000	11,800
April (actual)	363,000	12,100
May	357,000	11,900
June	342,000	11,400
July	360,000	12,000
August	366,000	12,200

Required

1 Prepare a purchases budget for May, June, and July in units and dollars.

2 Prepare a cash budget for May, June, and July.

(CPA)

12-14 Budgeted Selling and Administrative Expense The Maxwell Company has estimated sales dollars for the first four months of 19X9 as follows:

January	$100,000
February	150,000
March	200,000
April	150,000

The selling and administrative expenses are estimated to be:

Fixed—$20,000 per month ($5,000 is depreciation on delivery trucks)
Variable—10% of sales dollars

The Maxwell Company pays 60% of the selling and administrative expenses in the month incurred and 40% the following month. Accounts payable for selling and administrative expenses at January 1 is $8,000.

Required

1 For January, February, and March:

a Calculate the estimated selling and administrative expense.

b Calculate the cash payments for selling and administrative expense.

2 Calculate the accounts payable for selling and administrative expenses at March 31.

12-15 Cash Budget and Projected Income Statement The Standard Mercantile Corporation is a wholesaler and ends its fiscal year on December

31. You have been requested in early January 19X4 to assist in the preparation of a cash budget and budgeted income statement. The following information is available regarding the company's operations:

1 Management believes the 19X3 pattern is a reasonable estimate of 19X4 sales. Sales in 19X3 were as follows:

January	$ 360,000
February	420,000
March	600,000
April	540,000
May	480,000
June	400,000
July	350,000
August	550,000
September	500,000
October	400,000
November	600,000
December	800,000
Total	$6,000,000

2 The accounts receivable at December 31 total $380,000. Sales collections are generally made as follows:

During month of sale	60%
In first subsequent month	30
In second subsequent month	9
Uncollectible	1

3 The purchase cost of inventory averages 60% of selling price. The cost of the inventory on hand at December 31 is $840,000, of which $30,000 is obsolete. Arrangements have been made to sell the obsolete inventory in January at half the normal selling price. The customer will pay cash on delivery.

The company wishes to maintain the inventory as of the first of each month at a level of three months' sales as determined by the sales forecast for the next three months. All purchases are paid for on the 10th of the following month. Accounts payable for purchases at December 31 total $370,000.

4 Recurring fixed expenses are incurred at $120,000 per month, including depreciation of $20,000. For income statement purposes the company apportions the recurring fixed expenses to the various months in the same proportion as that month's estimated total annual sales. Variable expenses amount to 10% of sales.

Payments for expenses are made as follows:

	During Month Incurred	Following Month
Fixed expenses	55%	45%
Variable expenses	70	30

5 Annual property taxes amount to $50,000 and are paid in equal installments on December 31 and March 31. The property taxes are

in addition to the expenses in item 4 above and are also apportioned to each month's income statement according to sales.

6 It is anticipated that cash dividends of $20,000 will be paid each quarter on the 15th day of the third month of the quarter.

7 During the winter unusual advertising costs will be incurred which will require cash payments of $10,000 in February and $15,000 in March. The advertising costs are in addition to the expenses in item 4 above.

8 Cash payments for equipment replacements are made at the rate of $3,000 per month. The equipment has an average estimated life of six years.

9 A $60,000 installment of the company's income tax for 19X3 is due on March 15, 19X4.

10 At December 31, 19X3 the company had a bank loan with an unpaid balance of $280,000. The loan requires a principal payment of $20,000 on the last day of each month plus interest at 2% per month on the unpaid balance at the first of the month. The entire balance is due on March 31, 19X4.

11 The cash balance at December 31, 19X3 is $100,000.

Required Prepare a cash budget and income statement budget by months for the first three months of 19X4 for the Standard Mercantile Corporation. The statement should show the amount of cash on hand (or deficiency of cash) at the end of each month.

(CPA)

12-16 Cash Budget—Nonprofit Organization United Business Education, Inc. (UBE), is a nonprofit organization which sponsors a wide variety of management seminars throughout the United States. In addition, it is heavily involved in research into improved methods of educating and motivating business executives. The seminar activity is largely supported by fees and the research program from member dues.

UBE operates on a calendar year basis and is in the process of finalizing the budget for 19X9. The following information has been taken from approved plans which are still tentative at this time.

Seminar Program

Revenue—The scheduled number of programs should produce $12,000,000 of revenue for the year. Each program is budgeted to produce the same amount of revenue. The revenue is collected during the month the program is offered. The programs are scheduled so that 12% of the revenue is collected in each of the first five months of the year. The remaining programs, accounting for the remaining 40% of the revenue, are distributed evenly through the months of September, October, and November. No programs are offered in the other four months of the year.

Direct Expenses—The seminar expenses are made up of three segments:

- Instructors' fees are paid at the rate of 70% of the seminar revenue in the month following the seminar. The instructors are considered independent contractors and are not eligible for UBE employee benefits.

- Facilities fees total $5,600,000 for the year. They are the same for each program and are paid in the month the program is given.
- Annual promotional costs of $1,000,000 are spent equally in all months except June and July when there is no promotional effort.

Research Program
Research Grants—The research program has a large number of projects nearing completion. The other main research activity this year includes the feasibility studies for new projects to be started next year. As a result, the total grant expense of $3,000,000 for 19X9 is expected to be paid out at the rate of $500,000 per month during the first six months of the year.

Salaries and Other UBE Expenses
Office Lease—Annual amount of $240,000 paid monthly at the beginning of each month. General administrative expenses (telephone, supplies, postage, etc.)—$1,500,000 annually or $125,000 a month.
Depreciation Expense—$240,000 a year.
General UBE Promotion—Annual cost of $600,000 paid monthly.
Salaries and Benefits—

Number of Employees	Annual Salary Paid Monthly	Total Annual Salaries
1	$50,000	$ 50,000
3	40,000	120,000
4	30,000	120,000
15	25,000	375,000
5	15,000	75,000
22	10,000	220,000
50		$960,000

Employee benefits amount to $240,000 or 25% of annual salaries. Except for the pension contribution, the benefits are paid as salaries are paid. The annual pension payment of $24,000 based on 2.5% of salaries (included in the total benefits and the 25% rate) is due April 15, 19X9.

Other Information
Membership Income—UBE has 100,000 members each of whom pays an annual fee of $100. The fee for the calendar year is invoiced in late June. The collection schedule is as follows:

July	60%
August	30
September	5
October	5
	100%

Capital Expenditures—The capital expenditures program calls for a total of $510,000 in cash payments to be spread evenly over the first five months of 19X9.

Cash at January 1, 19X9 is estimated at $750,000.

Required

1 Prepare a budget of the annual cash receipts and disbursements for UBE, Inc., for 19X9.

2 Prepare a cash budget for UBE, Inc., for January 19X9.

(CMA)

12-17 Budgeted Income Statement and Cash Budget with Cash Discounts Modern Products Corporation, a manufacturer of molded plastic containers, determined in October 19X8 that it might need cash to continue operations. The corporation began negotiating with a local bank for a $100,000 line of credit. In considering the credit line the bank requested a projected income statement and a cash budget for the month of November.

The following information is available:

1 Sales were budgeted at 120,000 units per month in October 19X8, December 19X8, and January 19X9 and at 90,000 units in November 19X8.

The selling price is $2 per unit. Sales are billed on the 15th and last day of each month on terms of 2/10 net 30. Past experience indicates sales are even throughout the month and 50% of the customers pay the billed amount within the discount period. The remainder pay at the end of 30 days, except for bad debts which average ½% of gross sales.

2 The inventory of finished goods on October 1 was 24,000 units. The finished goods inventory at the end of each month is to be maintained at 20% of sales anticipated for the following month. There is no work in process.

3 The inventory of materials on October 1 was 22,800 pounds. At the end of each month the raw materials inventory is to be maintained at not less than 40% of production requirements for the following month. Raw materials purchases of each month are paid in the next succeeding month on terms of net 30 days.

4 All salaries and wages are paid on the 15th and last day of each month for the period ending on the date of payment.

5 All manufacturing overhead and selling and administrative expenses are paid on the 10th of the month following the month in which incurred. Selling expenses are 10 percent of gross sales. Administrative expenses, which include depreciation of $500 per month on office furniture and fixtures, total $33,000 per month.

6 The standard cost of a molded plastic container, based on "normal" production of 100,000 units per month, is as follows:

Materials—½ pound	$ .50
Labor	.40
Variable overhead	.20
Fixed overhead	.10
Total	$1.20

Fixed overhead includes depreciation on factory equipment of $4,000 per month. Over- or underabsorbed overhead is included in cost of sales.

7 The cash balance on November 1 is expected to be $10,000.

Required

Prepare the following for Modern Products Corporation. (Do not consider income taxes.)

1 Schedules computing inventory budgets by months for
   a Finished goods production in units for October, November, and December
   b Materials purchases in pounds for October and November
2 A projected income statement for the month of November
3 A cash forecast for the month of November showing the opening balance, receipts, disbursements, and balance at end of month

(CPA)

12-18 Direct Materials Budgets The Press Company manufactures and sells industrial components. The Whitmore Plant is responsible for producing two components referred to as AD-5 and FX-3. Plastic, brass, and aluminum are used in the production of these two products.

Press Company has adopted a 13-period reporting cycle in all of its plants for budgeting purposes. Each period is four weeks long and has 20 working days. The projected inventory levels for AD-5 and FX-3 at the end of the current (seventh) period and the projected sales for these two products for the next three four-week periods are presented below.

	Projected Inventory Level (in Units) End of Seventh Period	Projected Sales (in Units)		
		Eighth Period	Ninth Period	Tenth Period
AD-5	3,000	7,500	8,750	9,500
FX-3	2,800	7,000	4,500	4,000

Past experience has shown that adequate inventory levels for AD-5 and FX-3 can be maintained if 40% of the next period's projected sales are on hand at the end of a reporting period. Based on this experience and the projected sales, the Whitmore Plant has budgeted production of 8,000 AD-5 and 6,000 of FX-3 in the eighth period. Production is assumed to be uniform for both products within each four-week period.

The direct materials specifications for AD-5 and FX-3 are as follows:

	AD-5	FX-3
Plastic	2.0 pounds	1.0 pound
Brass	0.5 pounds	—
Aluminum	—	1.5 pounds

Data relating to the purchase of direct materials follow.

	Purchase Price per Pound	Standard Purchase Lot (in Pounds)	Projected Inventory Status at the End of the Seventh Period (in Pounds)	
			On Hand	On Order
Plastic	$.40	15,000	16,000	15,000
Brass	.95	5,000	9,000	—
Aluminum	.55	10,000	14,000	10,000

The sales of AD-5 and FX-3 do not vary significantly from month to month. Payments for all direct materials orders are made in the month of delivery. Delivery occurs in the period following the placement of the order.

Required

Whitmore Plant is required to submit a report to corporate headquarters of Press Company summarizing the projected direct materials activities before each period commences. The data for the eighth period report are being assembled. Determine the following items for plastic, brass, and aluminum for inclusion in the eighth period report:

1 Projected quantities (in pounds) of each direct material to be issued to production

2 Projected quantities (in pounds) of each direct material ordered

3 The projected inventory balance (in pounds) of each direct material at the end of the period

4 The payments for purchases of each direct material

(CMA)

12-19 Making the Cash Budget Format More Useful The Pantex Corporation has gone through a period of rapid expansion to reach its present size of seven divisions. The expansion program has placed strains on its cash resources. Therefore, the need for better cash planning at the corporate level has become very important.

At the present time each division is responsible for the collection of receivables and the disbursement for all operating expenses and approved capital projects. The corporation does exercise control over division activities but has attempted to coordinate the cash needs of the divisions and the corporation. However, it has not yet developed effective division cash reports from which it can determine the needs and availability of cash in the next budgetary year. As a result of inadequate information, the corporation permitted some divisions to make expenditures for goods and services which need not have been made or which could have been postponed until a later time while other divisions had to delay expenditures which should have had a greater priority.

The 19X8 cash receipts and disbursements plan prepared by the Tapon Division for submission to the corporate office is presented on page 365.

TAPON DIVISION
Budgeted Cash Receipts and Disbursements
For the Year Ended December 31, 19X8
(000 Omitted)

Receipts	
Collection on accounts	$9,320
Miscellaneous	36
	$9,356
Disbursements	
Production	
Direct materials	2,240
Labor and fringe benefits	2,076
Overhead	2,100
Sales	
Commissions	395
Travel and entertainment	600
Other	200
Administrative	
Accounting	80
Personnel	110
General management	350
Capital expenditures	1,240
	$9,391
Excess of receipts over (under) disbursements	$ (35)

The following additional information was used by the Tapon Division to develop the cash receipts and disbursements budget.

1 Receipts—Miscellaneous receipts are estimated proceeds from the sales of unneeded equipment.

2 Sales—Travel and entertainment represents the costs required to produce the sales volume projected for the year. The other sales costs consist of $50,000 for training new sales personnel, $25,000 for attendance by sales personnel at association meetings (not sales shows), and $125,000 for sales management salaries.

3 Administration—The personnel costs include $50,000 for salary and department operating costs, $20,000 for training new personnel, and $40,000 for management training courses for current employees. The general management costs include salaries and office costs for the division management, $310,000, plus $10,000 for officials' travel to Pantex Corporation meetings and $30,000 for industry and association conferences.

4 Capital expenditures—Planned expenditures for capital items during 19X8 are as follows:

Capital programs approved by the corporation:

Items ordered for delivery in 19X8	$300,000
Items to be ordered in 19X8 for delivery in 19X8	$700,000
New programs to be submitted to corporation during 19X8	$240,000

Required Present a revised budgeted cash receipts and disbursement statement for the Tapon Division. Design the format of the revised statement to include adequate detail so as to improve the ability of the corporation to judge the urgency of the cash needs. Such a statement would be submitted by all divisions to provide the basis for overall corporation cash planning. (CMA)

12-20 Cash Budget Seasonal Cash Flows The Barker Corporation manufactures and distributes wooden baseball bats. The bats are manufactured in Georgia at its only plant. This is a seasonal business with a large portion of its sales occurring in late winter and early spring. The production schedule for the last quarter of the year is heavy in order to build up inventory to meet expected sales volume.

The company experiences a temporary cash strain during this heavy production period. Payroll costs rise during the last quarter because overtime is scheduled to meet the increased production needs. Collections from customers are low because the fall season produces only modest sales. This year the company concern is intensified because of the rapid increases in prices during the current inflationary period. In addition, the sales department forecasts sales of less than 1 million bats for the first time in three years. This decrease in sales appears to be caused by the popularity of aluminum bats.

The cash account builds up during the first and second quarters as sales exceed production. The excess cash is invested in U.S. Treasury bills and similar short-term investments. During the last half of the year the temporary investments are usually liquidated to meet the cash needs. In the early years of the company, short-term borrowing was used to supplement the funds released by selling investments, but this has not been necessary in recent years. Because costs are higher this year, the treasurer asks for a forecast for December to judge if the $90,000 in temporary investments will be adequate to carry the company through the month with a minimum balance of $10,000. Should this amount ($90,000) be insufficient, he wants to begin negotiations for a short-term loan.

The unit sales volume for the past two months and the estimate for the next four months are:

October (actual)	70,000	January (estimated)	90,000
November (actual)	50,000	February (estimated)	90,000
December (estimated)	50,000	March (estimated)	120,000

The bats are sold for $3 each. All sales are made on account. One-half of the accounts are collected in the month of the sale, 40% are collected in the month following the sale, and the remaining 10% in the second month following the sale. Customers who pay in the month of the sale receive a 2% cash discount.

The production schedule for the six-month period beginning with October reflects the company's policy of maintaining a stable year-round work force by scheduling overtime to meet production schedules:

October (actual)	90,000	January (estimated)	90,000
November (actual)	90,000	February (estimated)	100,000
December (estimated)	90,000	March (estimated)	100,000

The bats are made from wooden blocks that cost $6 each. Ten bats can be produced from each block. The blocks are acquired one year in advance so they can be properly aged. Barker pays the supplier one-twelfth of the cost of the material each month until the obligation is retired. The monthly payment is $60,000.

The plant is normally scheduled for a 40-hour, five-day work week. During the busy production season, however, the work week may be increased to six 10-hour days. Workers can produce 7.5 bats per hour. Normal monthly output is 75,000 bats. Any product above this level is done in overtime. Factory employees are paid $8 per hour (up $.50 from last year) for regular time and time and one-half for overtime.

Other manufacturing costs include variable overhead of $.30 per unit and annual fixed overhead of $280,000. Depreciation charges totaling $40,000 are included among the fixed overhead. Selling expenses include variable costs of $.20 per unit and annual fixed costs of $60,000. Fixed administrative costs are $120,000 annually. All fixed costs are incurred uniformly throughout the year.

The controller has accumulated the following additional information:

1 The balances of selected accounts, as of November 30, 19X4, are as follows:

Cash	$ 12,000
Marketable securities (cost and market are the same)	90,000
Accounts receivable	96,000
Prepaid expenses	4,800
Account payable (arising from direct materials purchase)	300,000
Accrued vacation pay	9,500
Equipment note payable	102,000
Accrued income taxes payable	50,000

2 Interest to be received from the company's temporary investments is estimated at $1,000 for December.

3 Prepaid expenses of $3,600 will expire during December, and the balance of the prepaid account is estimated at $4,200 for the end of December.

4 Barker purchased new machinery in 19X4 as part of a plant modernization program. The machinery was financed by a 24-month note of $144,000. The terms call for equal principal payments over the next 24 months with interest paid at the rate of 2% per month on the unpaid balance at the first of the month. The first payment was made May 1, 19X4.

5 Old equipment, which has a book value of $8,000, is to be sold during December for $7,500.

6 Each month the company accrues $1,700 for vacation pay by charging vacation pay expense and crediting accrued vacation pay. The plant closes for two weeks in June when all plant employees take a vacation.

7 Quarterly dividends of $.20 per share will be paid on December 15. Barker Corporation has 7,000 shares outstanding.

8 The quarterly income taxes payment of $40,000 is due on December 15, 19X4.

Required Prepare a schedule which forecasts the cash position at December 31, 19X4. What action, if any, will be required to maintain a $10,000 cash balance?

(CMA)

12-21 Cash Budget The Jafa Corporation uses direct costing for managerial purposes and prepared their December 31, 19X3 balance sheet on a direct costing basis as follows:

JAFA CORPORATION
Balance Sheet
As of December 31, 19X3

Current Assets			
Cash		$ 10,000	
Marketable securities		50,000	
Accounts receivable		80,000	
Inventories			
Finished goods	$ 67,500		
Work in process	45,000		
Direct materials	9,000	$121,500	
Total current assets			$ 261,500
Long-Term Assets			
Equipment (factory)	$ 300,000		
Less: Accumulated Depreciation	72,000	$228,000	
Plant	$1,000,000		
Less: Accumulated Depreciation	180,000	$820,000	
Property		200,000	
Total long-term assets			$1,248,000
Other Assets			
Intangibles (net)	$ 10,000		
Loan to officer of company	10,000		20,000
Total assets			$1,529,500
Current Liabilities			
Accounts payable (raw materials)		$ 25,680	
Other payables		10,000	
Notes payable (one-month note due January 15, 19X4)		50,000	
Current portion of long-term debt (due March 31, 19X4)		50,000	
Total current liabilities			$ 135,680
Long-term debt (8%, 10 years, interest payable December 31, repayment of principal at rate of $50,000 per year beginning in 19X4)			450,000
Total liabilities			$ 585,680

Owners' Equity		
Common stock (issued and outstanding, 70,000 shares, $10 per share)	$700,000	
Retained earnings	243,820	
Total owners' equity		$ 943,820
Total equities		$1,529,500

Some recent and forecast data are:

	Actual		**Forecast**			
	Nov.	**Dec.**	**Jan.**	**Feb.**	**Mar.**	**Apr.**
Cash sales (units)	1,200	1,200	1,000	1,000	1,000	2,000
Credit sales (units)	10,000	10,000	8,000	8,000	8,000	20,000
Selling and administrative expenses	$20,000	$20,000	$20,000	$20,000	$20,000	$20,000
Fixed manufacturing expenses[1]	$15,000	$15,000	$15,000	$15,000	$15,000	$15,000

[1] Excluding depreciation and amortization.

The company manufactures an automobile safety seat for children which it sells directly to a number of automobile dealers in its four-state region and to retail customers through its own outlet. The selling price through their own outlet is $30; to the dealers, the price is $20.

Since all sales through its own outlet are on a cash basis and sales to dealers, all on account, have been long established, bad debts are negligible. Terms of credit sales are net 30. In the month of the sale 60% of the credit sales are paid and the remaining 40% of the credit sales are paid in the month after the sale.

Direct materials cost $5 per unit. All purchases of direct materials are on account. Accounts payable are on terms of net 30 days; 40% are paid in the month of purchase and 60% are paid in the following month. Direct labor and variable manufacturing overhead costs are $10 per unit. Direct labor and variable manufacturing overhead costs are incurred in direct proportion to the percentage of completion and paid in cash when incurred.

At the end of each month, desired inventory levels are as follows:

Direct materials—20% of next month's requirements
Work in Process—50% of next month's requirements
Finished Goods—50% of next month's requirements

Work in process is assumed to be 50% completed at the end of the month. Direct materials are added at the beginning of production.

Depreciation on the equipment is $4,000 per month and depreciation on the plant is $5,000 per month. Amortization of intangibles is $500 per month.

Selling and administrative expenses are all fixed and half are paid in the month incurred with the balance paid in the following month.

Fixed manufacturing expenses that require cash payments are paid in the month incurred.

Long-term debt-principal is to be paid each March 31, starting in 19X4 at a rate of $50,000 per year.

The loan to the officer was made on December 31, 19X3 and is due March 31, 19X4. The loan is to be repaid on March 31, 19X4 plus interest at 16% per annum.

The firm requires a minimum cash balance of $10,000 at the end of each month. If the balance is less, marketable securities are sold in multiples of $5,000 at the end of the month. If necessary, cash is borrowed in multiples of $1,000 at the end of the month. Marketable securities earn 16% per annum and the interest is collected at the end of each month. The short-term interest rate on notes payable is 22% per annum and is paid at the time the note is repaid.

Taxes are to be ignored.

Required

Prepare a statement forecasting the cash balance at January 31, 19X4, including any necessary cash transactions to achieve company cash management objectives for January 19X4.

(CMA)

RESPONSIBILITY ACCOUNTING

AFTER COMPLETING YOUR STUDY OF THIS CHAPTER, YOU SHOULD HAVE LEARNED:

1 What responsibility accounting is and how it and management by exception guide the managerial accountant in setting up an accounting system.

2 That responsibility centers are of four types: expense centers, revenue centers, profit centers, and investment centers; and that each type of center means that a different measure of financial performance will be applied to the manager of the center.

3 How to distinguish between controllable revenues and expenses and noncontrollable revenues and expenses.

4 How budgets affect the motivation of managers in the organization.

In a small organization all important decisions can be made by one individual. However, as an organization grows and becomes more complex, it is difficult for a single individual to make all the important decisions because there are too many decisions to be made and no one can be expert in all areas of a complex organization. Consequently, decisions are delegated to managers by giving them authority over a part of the organization's operations. When decision authority is delegated to managers they, in turn, are also held responsible for the consequences of their decision making.

In this chapter we will focus on three main topics:

1 The different ways decision authority and responsibility can be delegated

2 The concept of responsibility accounting

3 The impact of budgets on human behavior

PATTERNS OF DELEGATION

Approaches to delegate decision authority and responsibility.

Decision authority and responsibility can be delegated in a number of ways. The most common approaches include delegation based on the major business functions, delegation based on product lines, and delegation based on geographical regions.

Business Functions

In some organizations decision authority and responsibility is delegated based on the *major business functions:* production, marketing, and finance. One individual is given decision authority and responsibility for all production activity, another individual for all marketing activities, and still another individual for all finance activities. This pattern of delegation is illustrated in part A of Exhibit 13-1.

Product Lines

Other organizations delegate decision authority based on *product lines,* as shown in part B of Exhibit 13-1. A single individual is responsible for the production, marketing, and financing of a product line. These individual product line managers then delegate their decision authority and responsibility to subordinate functional managers—a production manager, a marketing manager, and a financial manager.

Geographical Regions

Part C of Exhibit 13-1 illustrates a geographical delegation of decision authority and responsibility. Because business customs vary greatly from one area of the world to another, international organizations usually divide decision authority and responsibility on the basis of domestic and foreign operations. Decision authority within each of these areas may then be delegated on a geographical basis such as northern and southern regions. Finally, within a given geographic region, authority and responsibility may be divided on a functional basis.

The pattern of delegation adopted by an organization depends on the philosophy of management and the nature of the organizational activities. The philosophy of some chief executive officers is to delegate authority as little as possible and to have

EXHIBIT 13-1
Alternative Organization Forms

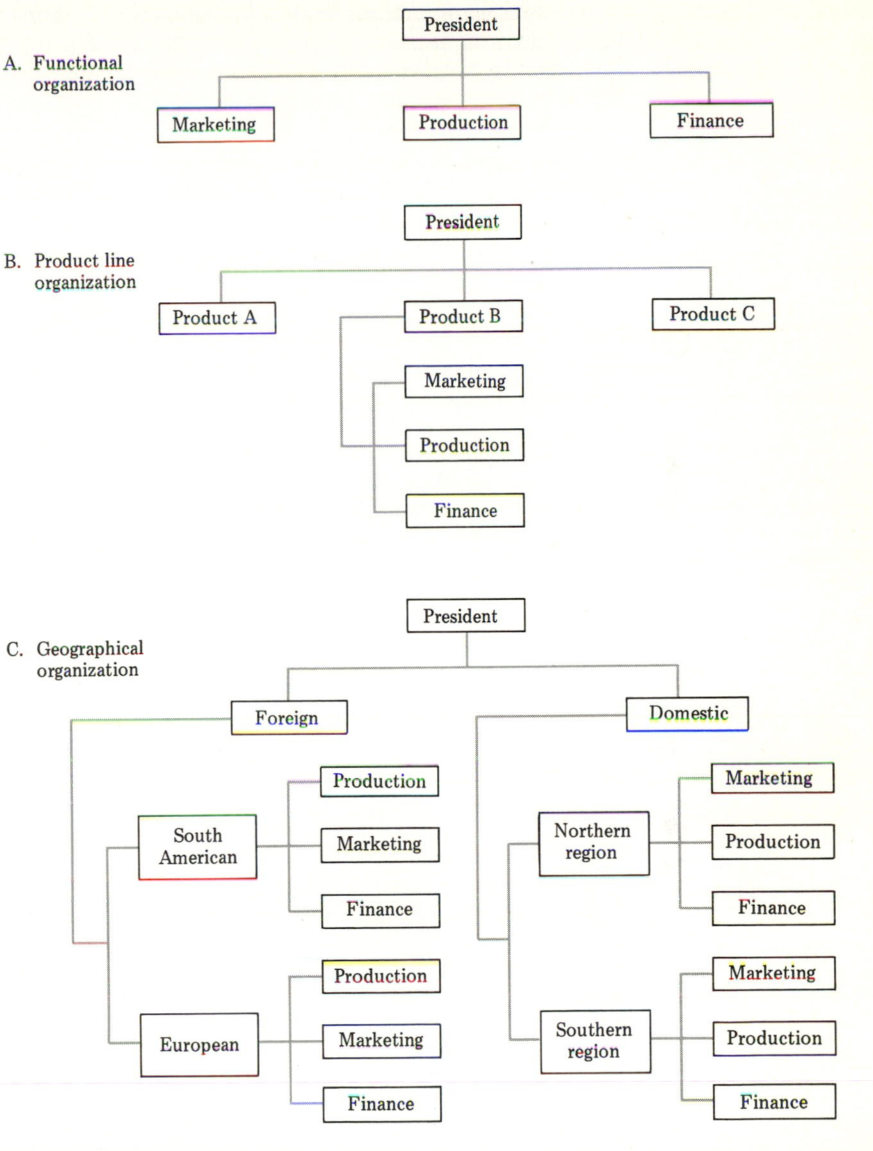

most important decisions made by specialists at corporate headquarters. Other chief executive officers adopt the philosophy that people at corporate headquarters will find it too difficult to get enough information about what is happening in a particular plant or district sales office to make good decisions promptly, and therefore more decisions will be delegated to managers at lower levels of the organization.

In addition to management philosophy, complexity of organizational activities is important. Complexity results from having different products, different production plants, and operations in different geographic regions. As mentioned earlier, large organizations are forced to delegate some decisions just because there are so many decisions to be made. In addition, complexity makes it impossible for one person or a small group of persons to be experts in all aspects of the business operation. An automobile manufacturer makes decisions which range from foundry operations to labor contracts, to the choice of which electronic equipment to put in automobiles. Few foundry experts will know much about electronics, just as few electronics experts will know much about foundry operations. The need for specialized knowledge forces delegation. Finally, business customs differ in different parts of the world. One cannot be expected to be expert in business practices everywhere. Specialists are required to operate businesses efficiently in each part of the world.

Large complex organizations delegate for the reasons just discussed. In Exhibit 13-1 we have outlined three distinct types of delegation. In fact, a large organization may use a combination of the three patterns. For example, in corporate headquarters a marketing department may make all advertising decisions for the corporation as a whole. This is functional delegation of advertising decisions by the chief executive officer. The balance of production and marketing decisions might be made by division managers for each major product line—a product line type of delegation.

One other criterion which is important in delegation is the economic impact of the decision. If a wrong decision can lead to large losses (or a correct decision lead to large gains), then the decision will probably not be delegated. For example, the purchase of $100 of office supplies is likely to be delegated to a fairly low level of the organization because even a very poor decision would probably cost no more than $100. On the other hand, the decision to sign a 20-year noncancellable lease for a major plant will cost a substantial amount. The benefit of the lease depends on future demand for the product and our ability to produce the product efficiently over a long period of time. The lease decision would likely be made at high levels in the organization.

RESPONSIBILITY ACCOUNTING SYSTEMS

The need to delegate decision authority and responsibility results from the complexity of modern organizations. The role of the managerial accountant in such an organization is to design an accounting system that provides reports that evaluate how well managers are achieving their share of the organization's goals and plans. Accounting systems specifically designed to do this are referred to as **responsibility accounting systems.**

Responsibility accounting defined.

A responsibility accounting system has been described as an accounting system which results in the preparation of accounting statements for all levels of management, designed primarily so that they can be used by managers as a tool for controlling their operations and their costs. By definition responsibility accounting systems are *tailored to the organizational structure* so that revenues and costs are accumulated and reported by centers of responsibility within the organization. Each *responsibility center* in the organization is charged *only* with the revenue and cost for which it is responsible and over which it has *control.*[1]

In the above description of a responsibility accounting system it was emphasized that to design the appropriate accounting system the accountant must understand how the organization delegates authority and assigns responsibility in order to

[1] John A. Higgins, "Responsibility Accounting," *The Arthur Andersen Chronicle,* Arthur Andersen & Company, Chicago, April 1952.

determine what kind of responsibility center, based on what revenues and expenses are controllable by each manager, is needed. The following sections discuss the different types of responsibility centers and the definition used to determine if a cost or revenue is **controllable** or **uncontrollable.**

Types of Responsibility Centers

A responsibility center tells how the financial performance of a particular manager is to be measured. Two points should be noted.

1 A manager's *total* performance depends on a variety of measures, such as quality control and morale of workforce, in addition to financial performance. The idea of a responsibility center applies to only one aspect of a manager's performance, the financial performance.

2 The financial performance of a manager should be measured by how well *controllable* factors are managed. If the manager does not have the ability to control a factor, variations in the factor should not change the measure of financial performance. For example, if the wage rate of workers employed in a department is determined by a companywide union contract, the manager of the department cannot control wage rates and should not be held responsible for them. But the manager of this department is probably responsible for avoiding unnecessary overtime work and should be held responsible for the extra amounts paid for overtime work. The responsibility accounting system should sort out these two factors and report only the effect of fluctuations in overtime payments to this department manager.

In general, there are four types of responsibility centers found in companies. They are:

Types of responsibility centers.

1 Expense centers
2 Revenue centers
3 Profit centers
4 Investment centers

All four types will exist in most large companies, although the number of each kind will depend on whether the company primarily uses a functional, a product line, or a geographic organizational structure.

An expense center manager has control over expenses.

Expense Centers An expense center manager is primarily responsible for production of a product or a service. An expense center manager decides how human resources, machinery, and materials should be combined to produce a result, for example, a unit of product. By these decisions the expense center manager controls expenses. The expense center manager has no control over revenues (the marketing activities) or investment, the decision to buy additional machinery, or the decision to carry larger inventories of materials.

The total performance of an expense center manager depends on how effectively and efficiently the expense center is operated. By effective operations we mean the nonfinancial objectives, such as maintaining quality output, meeting production schedules and deadlines, maintaining the morale of the workers, etc. Separate reporting systems are needed to report effectiveness. Efficiency means the financial performance of the manager which is measured and reported by the responsibility accounting system. The financial performance of an expense center manager is evaluated by comparing the actual expenses of operating the center to the budgeted level of expenses. Actual expenses below budgeted expenses indicate good financial performance (and good efficiency). Actual expenses above budgeted expenses reflect poor financial performance.

Expense centers are widely used forms of responsibility centers. In manufacturing organizations the production and manufacturing service departments are classified as expense centers. In retail organizations the customer complaint department and delivery department are classified as expense centers. While these departments indirectly influence revenues, the department managers have control over only the expenses of their departments; the main task of the delivery department manager is to get purchases delivered to customers on schedule while keeping actual delivery costs below budgeted delivery costs.

A revenue center manager has control over revenues and the expenses related to generating revenues.

Revenue Centers A revenue center is a part of the organization whose manager has the primary responsibility of generating sales revenues. A revenue center manager has no control over the investment in assets or the cost of producing the product, but may have control over some of the expenses of marketing the product.

Financial performance of a revenue center manager is measured by comparing the actual revenue with the budgeted revenue and comparing the actual marketing expenses with the budgeted marketing expenses. An individual sales representative is an example of a revenue center. Another example is the marketing manager of a product line division.

A profit center manager has control over revenues and expenses.

Profit Centers A profit center is an organizational unit whose manager has responsibility for both revenues and production and marketing expenses but has no control over the investment in the center's assets. Profit center managers are concerned with both production of the product and the marketing of the product. The profit center manager's concerns are broader than those of the revenue center manager because of the responsibility to manufacture the product efficiently. Financial performance of profit center managers is measured by whether the center achieves its budgeted profit.

An example of a profit center is a division of a company that produces and markets one or more of the company's products. The division manager determines the selling price, marketing strategies, and production policies. The amount of investment in division assets may be proposed by the profit center manager but the decisions are made by top management of the company.

An investment center manager has control over revenues, expenses, and the investment in assets.

Investment Centers In an investment center the manager has control over revenues, expenses, *and* the amounts invested in the center's assets. An investment center manager sets credit terms which determine the amount of accounts receivable, sets inventory policy which determines investment in inventory, and within broad limits may purchase equipment needed to produce and sell the product. Investment center managers are concerned not only with profit but with the relationship of profit to the amount invested in the center. Financial performance of investment center managers is most often measured by comparing the actual with the budgeted return on investment for the center.

Return in investment, presented in some detail in Chapter 19, is defined as investment center profit divided by investment center investment. The main problem to be discussed in Chapter 19 is how "profit" and "investment" should be defined for a particular investment center.

Controllability

A characteristic of a responsibility accounting system is that it reports to each center manager the expenses, revenue, and investment that the center manager is expected to control. In principle, if a center manager cannot control an item, it should not be included in a report to the manager of that center. An expense, revenue, or investment is considered controllable if the center manager can make decisions which will significantly change the actual amount of an item. For example, advertising expense is controllable by the marketing manager if she has the authority to decide the type and quantity of advertising the company uses to market their product. However, depreciation expense on delivery trucks is not controllable by the marketing manager if she cannot decide to buy and sell the company's delivery trucks. Notice that the advertising expense is not completely controllable by the center manager. If she buys magazine advertising she must pay the prevailing price. But she can make significant changes in advertising expense by choosing how many magazine advertisements will be run. The point is that control is never complete, and that is why the definition of control only requires that "significant" changes can be made.

Controllability does not mean 100% control.

Another example: The quantity of direct materials used in the production process is controllable by the production manager through the assignment of employees to particular machines—skillful, experienced machine operators may be able to produce more output with less waste of direct materials. However, the price of direct materials is controllable by the purchasing department through negotiation with suppliers. The responsibility accounting system therefore reports price variations to the purchasing department manager and does not report price variations to the production manager.

Two factors that determine whether a particular item is controllable or uncontrollable for a responsibility report are the time period of the report and the authority delegated to the responsibility center manager.

Economists point out that if the time period under consideration is long enough all costs can be changed and thus are controllable. However, as the time period is shortened fewer costs are controllable. For example, if management is considering the construction of a new plant, any size plant considered economical can be built; the cost of the plant is controllable. But once the plant is constructed management cannot change the cost of building the plant; the cost of the plant becomes uncontrollable. Another example is the cost of insurance. Most insurance policies are for a term of one year. The manager of the insurance department can control the cost of insurance if the time period is one year. But on a monthly or weekly basis the cost of insurance is uncontrollable. Most responsibility accounting reports concern short periods such as a week or a month.

The time period influences whether a cost is controllable or noncontrollable.

The second factor which determines whether a particular cost is controllable by a responsibility center is the decision-making authority delegated to a particular responsibility center manager. Delegation was discussed earlier in general terms where you found that management philosophy and complexity of the organization were important. These general considerations guide delegation, and it might at first seem that delegation would clearly establish responsibility and controllability. But as we observed earlier, control, even with the best delegation, is never complete. Some examples of the problem follow.

Decision-making authority influences whether a cost is controllable or noncontrollable.

We have suggested that the production manager is responsible for the quantity of direct materials used and the purchasing department is responsible for the purchase price of direct materials. On the surface this might seem like a clear division of responsibilities; however, the *quantity* of direct materials used can be considerably influenced by the *quality* of the materials purchased—more waste will likely occur if poor quality materials are purchased. And the price of the materials can be influenced by the production manager's scheduling—a rush order may force purchasing to buy materials from a more expensive than normal source. If the production manager does not have a schedule far enough in advance, the purchasing manager may not be able to obtain quantity discounts and may have to rush orders through the suppliers at premium prices. So production manager decisions have some influence on prices paid for direct materials just as purchasing quality decisions have some influence on the waste which occurs in the production process. The point is that careful delegation helps to fix responsibility, but even the best delegation cannot give complete control.

An Illustration of Responsibility Accounting

Responsibility accounting systems are based on the organization chart.

To illustrate how a responsibility accounting system operates and how information flows through the system we will use the GFC Motor Company. First, we must understand the organization. Exhibit 13-2 is an organization chart for the GFC Motor Company. The GFC Motor Company is organized functionally with a marketing vice president, a production vice president, and a financial vice president reporting to the president.

The marketing function is organized by product lines. The production function is organized according to production functions, machining, assembly, and finishing. The financial vice president is responsible for the company's finance and accounting activities.

We will illustrate how the report received by the supervisor of a production department is linked to the report received by the president of GFC Motor Company. Exhibit 13-3 illustrates the reports for three levels of responsibility in the GFC Motor Company.

Only controllable costs are included in the expense center manager's report.

Starting at the bottom of Exhibit 13-3, part C shows the responsibility report for the supervisor of the assembly department. This report contains only items that are controllable by the supervisor of the assembly department. Items such as the salary of the supervisor that are not controllable by the supervisor of the assembly

EXHIBIT 13-2
GFC MOTOR COMPANY
Organization Chart

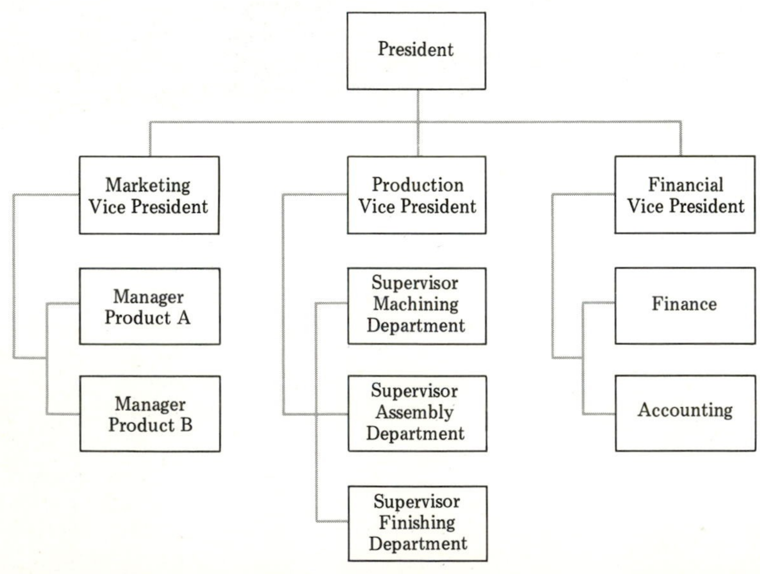

EXHIBIT 13-3
GFC MOTOR COMPANY
Responsibility Reports
Department Relationships

A. GFC MOTOR COMPANY
President's departmental cost report

	Budget		Variance Favorable (Unfavorable)	
	This Month	**Year to Date**	**This Month**	**Year to Date**
President's office	$ 3,160	$ 6,600	$ (130)	$ (190)
Marketing				
Controllable by vice president	8,420	16,900	(310)	540
Controllable by president	2,400	4,300	200	300
Production				
Controllable by vice president	→ $15,230	$27,780	$ 546	$ 867
Controllable by president	4,500	8,800	220	240
Financial				
Controllable by vice president	6,750	13,400	680	710
Controllable by president	3,000	7,100	150	250
Total	$43,460	$84,880	$1,356	$2,717

B. GFC MOTOR COMPANY
Production vice president's cost report

	Budget		Variance Favorable (Unfavorable)	
	This Month	**Year to Date**	**This Month**	**Year to Date**
Vice president's office	$ 1,050	$ 2,400	$ (102)	$ (100)
Machining				
Controllable in department	3,610	7,300	110	(20)
Controllable by vice president	2,500	3,240	70	(13)
Assembly				
Controllable in department	→ $ 2,450	$ 5,290	$ 86	$ 199
Controllable by vice president	2,000	3,190	32	128
Finishing				
Controllable in department	2,120	4,500	210	408
Controllable by vice president	1,500	1,860	140	265
Total	$15,230	$27,780	$ 546	$ 867

(continued on page 380)

C. GFC MOTOR COMPANY
Supervisor's report: Assembly department

	Budget		Variance Favorable (Unfavorable)	
	This Month	Year to Date	This Month	Year to Date
Direct materials	$ 875	$ 1,820	$ 120	$ 180
Direct labor	1,050	2,460	(70)	10
Repairs and maintenance	200	310	10	(30)
Supplies	115	260	8	15
Rework	210	440	18	24
Total	$ 2,450	$ 5,290	$ 86	$ 199

department are omitted from the department supervisor's report but are included at the higher level where they can be controlled.

The data in the total row of the supervisor's cost report are included in the production vice president's report, part B of Exhibit 13-3, along with similar data for the machining and finishing departments. Trace the data in the assembly department's cost report to the production vice president's cost report. The production vice president's report summarizes the reports for the three manufacturing departments that he or she is responsible for plus the costs of his or her department.

The president's departmental cost report, part A of Exhibit 13-3, summarizes the cost data for each functional area and includes cost data for the office. Trace the $15,230 of budgeted cost from the production vice president's cost report to the president's cost report.

Responsibility accounting reports emphasize variances from budgets.

The emphasis in responsibility accounting is on tailoring the accounting reports to the organizational structure of the company and including only the controllable costs in the reports. By doing this, managers are provided with information that can be used to facilitate their planning and control decisions.

The responsibility accounting reports in Exhibit 13-3 show only the budgeted amount and the variance. The actual costs are not shown in the report. The purpose of this is to direct management's attention to the variances so that they will focus their efforts on the important variances from budget. This is referred to as **management by exception.** Procedures for determining which variances are important are discussed in Chapter 22. For now concentrate on how the report format emphasizes the important information.

Management by Exception

A manager's time is always scarce. Management by exception is a concept which aids managers in deciding how to use their time. Managers should spend much of their time helping to solve problems. Time spent on solving problems can achieve significant improvements in performance while time spent on things that function well leads to unimportant improvements in productivity. As one individual has put it, "If it ain't broken, don't fix it."

Management by exception helps managers focus their efforts on problem areas that need fixing. In addition to reporting by responsibility, reports should highlight variances between planned results and actual results. A report which focuses on variances is called an exception report. These exceptions or variances represent potential problem areas where managers should spend their time. Chances are that activities which are proceeding according to budget provide less potential for improved performance than activities which show a variance from the budget.

All important variances should be investigated.

Some managers feel that only unfavorable variances from budget offer improvement opportunities. But favorable variances from budget also hold potential for improvements. When actual results are better than budget results (favorable variance) a better way of doing things may have been found which might be applied to other activities of the department. Of course a favorable variance might indicate that the budget for this activity was not well formulated. In either event, management attention to the variance may result in improved control or planning.

Summary: Responsibility Accounting

Decision authority is delegated and responsibility is assigned through the organization chart. Each manager's budget should reflect the revenues and expenses that are the responsibility of that particular manager. In addition, the accounting system should be organized to record actual revenues and expenses by responsibility in a manner that corresponds to the budget. In this way actual amounts can be compared to budget amounts and variances will be reported to each responsible manager. Budget variances are signals to the manager about which aspects of operations need attention. Also, a comparison of the actual with budgeted results provides the basic data for a report on the manager's performance.

An effective responsibility accounting system can exist only within the following conditions:

Conditions for an effective responsibility accounting system.

1 The area of responsibility and authority of each center should be well defined (usually by the organization chart).

2 Each responsibility center should have a clear set of goals for the manager.

3 Only the revenues, expenses, and investments that are controllable by the manager of a responsibility center should be included in the performance report for that center.

4 Performance reports for each responsibility center should be prepared highlighting variances, the items requiring management's attention. This is referred to as "management by exception."

5 The managers of each responsibility center should participate in establishing the goals that are going to be used to measure their performance. This topic is discussed further in the next section of this chapter.

BUDGETS AND HUMAN BEHAVIOR

The purpose of planning and control is to influence behavior. For example, as long as there is more than one person in an organization, it is necessary to coordinate their activities toward a common goal.

The purpose of planning is to set goals and to select methods of achieving them. Members of an organization are expected to coordinate their efforts to achieve the goals established and follow the course of action needed to achieve them. The financial results of the course of action needed to achieve the goals is expressed in the master budget for the period.

The purpose of control is to monitor results and to determine whether to alter the plan or alter the way people are doing things to achieve goals.

Both planning and control effect the way people do things, which is simply another way of saying they influence behavior.

Two aspects of behavior that are important to managerial accountants are worker **motivation** and how to get workers to direct their individual efforts toward a common company goal.

Motivation

Psychologists define motivation as an inner force that energizes, moves (hence motivates), or channels an individual's behavior toward goals. In other words:

Motivation defined.

1 Motivation is an inner force, something inside the individual.

2 Motivation directs or channels behavior toward goals.

Because motivation is internal, it can be influenced but not changed by others. A manager cannot motivate an employee. But what a manager can do is to change some rewards which will influence the strength or direction of the employee's motivation—the thing to recognize is that the change in motivation takes place within the individual.

It is the job of the manager to make sure the reward system influences the individual's motivation toward achieving the company's goals.

Goal Congruence

The importance of goal congruence.

Each member of the organization has individual goals which may or may not be consistent with the goals established by the plan of the organization. A term used to describe the relationship between an individual's goals and the goals established for the organization is **goal congruence.** If the individual by pursuing her or his internal goals is at the same time aiding in the accomplishment of goals set for the organization, then there is goal congruence between the individual and organization. If the individual pursuing her or his internal goals makes it more difficult for the organization to achieve its goals, there is no goal congruence; the individual is destructive to the organization's goals. In many cases, the lack of goal congruence is a result of the way in which the control system (budgeting and performance evaluation) is established by management and the managerial accountant. If the lack of goal congruence is a result of the control system, the control system should be changed. Since the managerial accountant has a major role in establishing the control system, he or she should be able to recognize when it isn't working, analyze why not, and recommend changes to restore goal congruence to the system.

The Role of Budgets

The budgeting process and the resulting budgets play an important role in motivating managers to achieve the company's goals. This is accomplished by using the budget as a tool to do three things:

1 To coordinate the activities of the functional areas of the business

2 To communicate the company goals to the managers

3 To establish a complete understanding as to how performance will be measured

To achieve the full benefit of the budgeting process, most companies use *participative budgeting* which means that the managers are actively involved in establishing their own budgets. This does not mean that the manager can specify the budget; rather the manager exchanges ideas with his superior as to what can be reasonably accomplished during the budget period. This approach to budgeting is necessary and important because it enables top management to identify and evaluate the goals of the individual manager; hence, through this communication during the budgeting process, goal congruence should increase. Also, participative budgeting helps to ensure that goals will be established at levels which will motivate the managers to achieve the company's goals.

Participative budgeting improves goal congruence.

SUMMARY

The need for organizations to delegate decision authority and responsibility results from the complexity of modern organizations. Managerial accountants have responded to the delegation of authority and responsibility in organizations by developing responsibility accounting systems. These systems are designed around the organization structure so that only controllable revenues and expenses are charged to a responsibility center. There are four types of responsibility centers (expense, revenue, profit, and investment), each with its own measure of financial performance.

A revenue or expense is considered controllable by a responsibility center if the center manager can make decisions which will significantly change the actual amount of an item.

The idea of management by exception helps managers allocate their time by emphasizing variances from (exceptions to) the budget. Emphasizing variances is a result of the idea that the greatest potential improvements come from spending time on those areas where the budget is not being achieved.

The purpose of planning and control is to influence behavior toward achieving organizational goals. Planning establishes goals and budgets express plans and how they are to be achieved in financial terms.

Control is monitoring the actual results of plans in progress and deciding if the plans are on target or should be altered.

The goals of individuals in the organization should be coordinated so that their collective activities will accomplish organizational goals.

It is the job of the manager to adjust the reward system so as to influence workers' motivation toward the achievement of organizational goals.

Review Problem

The Argon County Hospital is located in the county seat. Argon County is a well-known summer resort area. The county population doubles during the vacation months (May–August) and hospital activity more than doubles during these months. The hospital is organized into several departments. Although it is a relatively small hospital, its pleasant surroundings have attracted a well-trained and competent medical staff.

An administrator was hired a year ago to improve the business activities of the hospital. Among the new ideas he has introduced is responsibility accounting. This program was announced along with quarterly cost reports supplied to department heads. Previously expense data was presented to department heads infrequently. Excerpts from the announcement and the report received by the laundry supervisor are presented below.

"The hospital has adopted a '*responsibility accounting system.*' From now on you will receive quarterly reports comparing the actual expenses of operating your department with budgeted expenses. The reports will highlight the differences (variations) so you can zero in on the departure from budgeted expenses (this is called 'management by exception'). Responsibility accounting means you are accountable for keeping the expenses in your department within the budget. The variations from the budget will help you identify what expenses are out of line and the size of the variation will indicate which ones are the most important. Your first such report accompanies this announcement."

Argon County Hospital
Performance Report—Laundry Department
July–September 19X3

	Budget	Actual	(Over) Under Budget	(Over) Under Budget
Patient days	9,500	11,900	(2,400)	(25)%
Pounds processed —laundry	125,000	156,000	(31,000)	(25)
Costs:				
Laundry labor	$ 9,000	$12,500	$(3,500)	(39)
Supplies	1,100	1,875	(775)	(70)
Water, Heating and softening	1,700	2,500	(800)	(47)
Maintenance	1,400	2,200	(800)	(57)
Supervisor's salary	3,150	3,750	(600)	(19)
Allocated administration costs	4,000	5,000	(1,000)	(25)
Equipment depreciation	1,200	1,250	(50)	(4)
	$21,550	$29,075	$(7,525)	(35)%

Administrator's Comments: Expenses are significantly above budget for the quarter. Particular attention needs to be paid to labor, supplies, and maintenance.

The annual budget for 19X3 was constructed by the new administrator. Quarterly budgets were computed as one-fourth of the annual budget. The administrator compiled the budget from analysis of the prior three years' expenses. The analysis showed that all expenses increased each year with more rapid increases between the second and third year. He considered establishing the budget at an average of the prior three years' expenses hoping that the installation of the system would reduce expenses to this level. However, in view of the rapidly increasing prices he finally chose 19X2 expenses less 3% for the 19X3 budget. The activity level measured by patient days and pounds of laundry processed was set at the 19X2 volume, which was approximately equal to the volume of each of the past three years.

Required

1 Comment on the method used to construct the budget.

2 What information should be communicated by variations from budgets?

(CMA)

Solution

1 The concept of controllability is critical to designing a responsibility accounting system. The report as designed ignores two factors beyond the control of the department supervisor. First, the laundry department supervisor cannot control the volume of laundry to be done. Second, the report to the supervisor of the laundry department includes at least three items which were beyond the control of the head of the laundry department: supervisor's salary, allocated administration costs, and equipment depreciation.

The uncontrollable volume should be allowed for by use of a flexible budget. The hospital administrator constructed a fixed budget. His budget was not representative because he took one-fourth of the annual budget for the summer months. Argon Hospital experiences increased activity during the summer, and, as a result, the budget should have reflected this increased activity.

The cost figures for the budget were not developed properly. Expense estimates should be developed from the underlying volume of activities, including planned changes, and converted to dollars at current prices. The estimates in this case were based solely upon past expenses adjusted downward by a percentage apparently not related in any way to expense reduction procedures or price changes due to inflation.

The administrator also should have considered inviting the department heads to participate in the budgeting procedure. The budget figures might have been more accurate, and the participation might have motivated the department heads to cooperate in both accepting the new system and achieving budget goals.

2 Budget variations should identify expenses needing the manager's attention because they are different from the expected amounts (properly adjusted for the time period and level of activity). The causes of the variations (excess prices, excess use of resources, unexpected change in operating procedure, etc.) are not communicated directly by the variations. Analysis of the variations is necessary to determine the cause and identify possible corrective action.

The total variation from budget and the pattern of variations over time provide some of the evidence necessary to judge the effectiveness and efficiency of the manager.

Glossary

Controllable cost A cost that can be significantly changed by the decisions of a responsibility center manager.

Goal congruence The relationship between an individual's goals and the organization's goals. If the individual in pursuing his or her goals at the same time aids in the organization attaining its goals, goal congruence is said to exist.

Management by exception A concept that aids managers in focusing attention on the most important problems. Exception reports highlight the differences between actual and budgeted results and thus direct attention to potential problem areas.

Motivation An individual's inner state that energizes, activates, or moves (hence motivates), and that directs or channels behavior toward goals.

Noncontrollable cost A cost that cannot be significantly changed by the decisions of a responsibility center manager.

Responsibility accounting An accounting system resulting in the preparation of reports for all levels of management which provides information evaluating how well managers are achieving their share of organizational goals and plans.

Questions and Problems

13-1 Why do organizations delegate decision authority and assign responsibility?

13-2 What are three common organization forms? How do they differ?

13-3 Define responsibility accounting.

13-4 Distinguish between controllable and noncontrollable revenues and expenses. Give an example of an uncontrollable expense.

13-5 How is the organization chart used in responsibility accounting?

13-6 What is meant by "management by exception"?

13-7 Define motivation. What is the implication of your definition for managers?

13-8 Discuss the concept of goal congruence. Give an example of a situation where goal congruence may be lacking.

13-9 How can budgets and budgeting processes affect motivation and goal congruence?

13-10 Discuss the benefits of participative budgeting.

13-11 An important concept in management accounting is that of "responsibility accounting."

Required

1 Define the term "responsibility accounting."

2 What are the conditions that must exist for there to be effective "responsibility accounting"?

3 What benefits are said to result from "responsibility accounting"?

(CMA)

13-12 Responsibility Centers: Multiple Choice

1 A segment of an organization is referred to as a profit center if it has:

- **a** Authority to make decisions affecting the major determinants of profit including the power to choose its markets and sources of supply.
- **b** Authority to make decisions affecting the major determinants of profit including the power to choose its market and sources of supply and significant control over the amount of invested capital.
- **c** Authority to make decisions over the most significant costs of operations including the power to choose the sources of supply.
- **d** Responsibility for combining the direct materials, direct labor, and other factors of production into a final output.

2 A segment of an organization is referred to as an investment center if it has:

- **a** Authority to make decisions affecting the major determinants of profit including the power to choose its markets and sources of supply.
- **b** Authority to make decisions affecting the major determinants of profit including the power to choose its market and sources of supply and significant control over the amount of invested capital.
- **c** Authority to make decisions over the most significant costs of operations including the power to choose the sources of supply.

d Responsibility for developing markets for and selling of the output of the organization.

3 A segment of an organization is referred to as an expense center if it has:

a Responsibility for developing markets for and selling of the output of the organization.

b Authority to make decisions affecting the major determinants of profit including the power to choose its markets and sources of supply.

c Authority to make decisions over the most significant costs of operations including the power to choose the sources of supply.

d Responsibility for combining direct materials, direct labor, and other factors of production into a final output.

(CMA)

13-13 Responsibility for Variances The Fillep Co. operates a standard cost system. The variances for each department are calculated and reported to the department manager. It is expected that the manager will use the information to improve his operations and recognize that it is used by his superiors when they are evaluating his performance.

John Smith was recently appointed manager of the assembly department of the company. He has complained that the system as designed is disadvantageous to his department. Included among the variances charged to the departments is one for rejected units. The inspection occurs at the end of the assembly department. The inspectors attempt to identify the cause of the rejection so that the department where the error occurred can be charged with it. Not all errors can be easily identified with a department. These are totalled and apportioned to the departments according to the number of identified errors. The variance for rejected units in each department is a combination of the errors caused by the department plus a portion of the unidentified causes of rejects.

Required

1 Is John Smith's claim valid? Explain the reason(s) for your answer?

2 What would you recommend the company do to solve its problem with John Smith and his complaint?

(CMA)

13-14 Identifying Controllable Costs Fred Paulick is the vice president of production for the ABC Manufacturing Company. Which of the following costs would be controllable by Mr. Paulick in any given month?

1 Cost of small tools used in the assembly department

2 Janitorial labor cost for the machining department

3 Insurance cost on factory plant and equipment

4 Property taxes on manufacturing facilities

5 Factory heat, light, and power

6 Salaries of sales representatives

7 Rework cost for defective units identified in the assembly department

8 Depreciation on plant and equipment

9 Depreciation on delivery trucks

10 Lubricants for drill presses

13-15 **Profit Center Characteristics** John Knight founded the Newworld Co. over 30 years ago. Although he has relied heavily upon advice from other members of management, he has made all of the important decisions for the company. Newworld has been successful, experiencing steady growth in its early years and very rapid growth in recent years. During this period of rapid growth Knight has experienced difficulty in keeping up with the many decisions that need to be made. He feels that he is losing "control" of the company's progress.

Regular discussions regarding his concern have been held with George Armet, the company executive vice president. As a result of these discussions, Armet has studied possible alternative organizational structures to the present highly centralized functional organization.

In a carefully prepared proposal he recommends that the company reorganize according to its two product lines because the technology and marketing methods are quite different. The plastic products require different manufacturing skills and equipment from the brass products. The change could be easily accomplished because the products are manufactured in different plants. The marketing effort is also segregated along product lines within the sales function. The number of executive positions would not change, although the duties of the positions would change. There would no longer be the need for a vice president for manufacturing or a vice president for sales. Those positions would be replaced with a vice president for each of the two product lines. Armet acknowledges that there may be personnel problems at the top management level because the current vice presidents may not be competent to manage within the new structure.

The proposal also contained the recommendations that some of the decision-making power, long held by John Knight, be transferred to the new vice presidents. He argued that this would be good for the company. They would be more aware of the problems and solution alternatives of their respective product lines because they are closer to the operations. Fewer decisions will be required of each man than now are required of John Knight; this would reduce the time between problem recognition and implementation of the solution. Armet further argued that distributing the decision-making power would improve the creativity and spirit of company management.

Knight is intrigued by the proposal and the prospect that it would make the company more manageable. However, the proposal did not spell out clearly which decisions should be transferred and which should remain with the president. He requested Armet to prepare a supplemental memorandum specifying the decisions to be delegated to the vice presidents.

The memorandum presented the recommended decision areas, explaining in each case how the new vice presidents would be closer to the situation and thereby be able to make prompt, sound decisions. The following list summarizes Armet's recommendations of the decisions to be delegated to the new vice presidents.

1 Sales
   a Price policy
   b Promotional strategy
   c Credit policy

2 Operations
   1 Manufacturing procedures
   2 Labor negotiations
   3 Development of existing product lines

Required Does the company have the characteristics needed for decentralized profit centers? Briefly explain your answer.

(CMA)

13-16 Goal Congruence NEI, Inc., is a medium-sized manufacturer of precision measurement instruments which have international recognition for engineering design and quality. Tom Nash, the firm's president and founder, is concerned primarily with product reputation and with a satisfactory return.

A small technical sales force works with NEI's major customers. The salesmen are paid a salary plus commission. A limited number of manufacturers' representatives supplement the sales force and are compensated by a straight commission.

The production area is organized into profit centers, output being valued at standard cost plus 25%. Most of the production employees are skilled workers, and many of them have been with the firm since its earliest years of operation. The production employees participate in a year-end, profit-sharing bonus which is allocated on the basis of each profit center's profitability.

Tom Nash believes each production manager should have complete responsibility and control over his profit center. Therefore, they have substantial control over accepting, scheduling, and running jobs. Preference is routinely given to the most profitable jobs over the less profitable ones. Most orders are not completed by the promised delivery date, and usually expediting measures have to be taken.

Jim Case, the chief financial officer of NEI, Inc., wants the production scheduling system changed because the present system has caused several financial problems for the company. For example, the direct materials and work in process inventories are too large. Customers express their irritation over late deliveries by slow payment of their accounts. As a result of the large inventories and slow collection of accounts, the company has a severe cash flow problem. These factors have adversely affected Case's ability to arrange short-term financing through a local bank.

Case has informed Tom Nash of the difficulties in arranging a short-term loan. Again, as many times in the past, he pointed out that a major contributor to the company's financial problems is the production scheduling system. Nash replied that Case's job was to obtain the necessary financing and not to second-guess experienced production men.

Jim Case has become quite frustrated in his position as chief financial officer of NEI, Inc. He has interviewed for a similar position with several firms. However, he has experienced difficulty in changing firms because NEI has a reputation for its poor financial position.

Required

1 Discuss how the goals of the production managers and Jim Case conflict.

2 Discuss how the goals of Jim Case and Tom Nash conflict.

3 Do NEI's present management policies cause suboptimum behavior?

(CMA)

13-17 Participative Budgeting? Drake Inc., is a multiproduct firm with several manufacturing plants. Management generally has been pleased with the operation of all the plants but the Swan Plant. Swan Plant's poor operating performance has been traced to poor control over plant costs and expenses. Four plant managers have resigned or been terminated during the last three years.

David Green was appointed the new manager of the Swan Plant on February 1, 19X6. Green is a young and aggressive individual who had progressed rapidly in Drake's management development program, and he performed well in lower-level management positions.

Green had been recommended for the position by Steve Bradley, Green's immediate supervisor. Bradley was impressed by Green's technical ability and enthusiasm. Bradley explained to Green that his assignment as Swan Plant manager was approved despite the objections of some of the other members of the top management team. Bradley told Green that he had complete confidence in him and his ability and was sure that Green wanted to prove that he had made a good decision. Therefore, Bradley expected Green to have the Swan Plant on budget by June 30.

As a result of Swan Plant's past difficulties, Steve Bradley has had responsibility for formulating the last four annual budgets for the plant. The 19X6 budget was prepared during the last six months of 19X5 before Green had been appointed plant manager. The budget report covering the three-month period ending March 31 showed that Swan's costs and expenses were slightly over budget. At a meeting with Bradley, Green described the changes he had instituted the last month. Green was confident that the costs and expenses would be held in check with these changes and the situation would get no worse for the rest of the year.

Bradley repeated that he not only wanted the cost and expenses controlled but he expected Swan Plant to be on budget by June 30. Green pointed out that Swan Plant had been in poor condition for three years. He further stated that, while he appreciated the confidence Bradley had in him, he had only been in charge two months.

Steve Bradley then replied, "I am expected to meet my figures. The only way that can occur is if my subordinates exercise control over their costs and expenses and achieve their budgets. Therefore, to assure that I achieve my goals, get the Swan Plant on budget by June 30 and keep it on budget for the rest of the year."

Required

1 Present a critical evaluation of the budget practices described in the problem.

2 What are the likely immediate and long-term effects on David Green and Drake Inc., if the present method of budget administration is continued? Justify your answer.

(CMA)

14 COST-VOLUME-PROFIT ANALYSIS

AFTER COMPLETING YOUR STUDY OF THIS CHAPTER, YOU SHOULD HAVE LEARNED:

1 How the relationship between revenues, expenses, and sales volume can be expressed algebraically or graphically.

2 How to use revenue-expense-volume relationships to analyze how changes in one of these affects profit.

3 What a target profit is and how managers use cost-volume-profit analysis to find a feasible way to achieve a target profit.

4 That consideration of income tax expense merely adds one step to the analysis: converting the after-tax profit target to a before-tax profit target.

5 Why the contribution margin ratio is needed by firms with many different products and how it is used in breakeven analysis.

6 How cost-volume-profit analysis can be used to calculate a measure of risk called the margin of safety.

7 The basic assumptions underlying cost-volume-profit analysis.

It is the manager who prepares the master budget, but it is the accountant who provides much of the information the manager needs to prepare the budget. Management depends on the accountant to provide information about alternative selling prices, variable expenses, and fixed expenses. Management makes decisions about which alternatives will most likely produce the target profit. The master budget is then prepared on those decisions and aimed at the target profit. For example, some of the questions the accountant is expected to answer are:

Questions that can be answered with cost-volume-profit analysis.

- How will profit be changed by a 5% increase in the selling price of the company products?
- If variable expenses are reduced by 3%, how many units will have to be sold to generate a $500,000 profit?
- If the selling price is reduced by 2%, how many units will have to be sold to increase profit 5% above last year's profit?

To answer these questions the accountant uses a concept called **cost-volume-profit analysis**. As its name implies, cost-volume-profit analysis, of course, deals with the relationship among sales revenue, total expense[1], and sales volume.

This analysis (1) looks at how total expenses vary with changes in sales volume; (2) looks at how total revenues vary with changes in sales volume; and (3) puts together expenses and revenue variations for the various volumes sold, to see how profit varies with changes in sales volume.

To begin the analysis, the first thing you should realize is that we do not directly consider total expenses. Instead, we look at how fixed expenses vary with changes in sales volume and at how variable expenses vary with sales volume. By separating the total expenses into fixed expenses and variable expenses, formulas can be developed to estimate total expenses at various levels of sales volume. Then formulas are developed representing how revenue varies with sales volume. By combining expense formulas with revenue formulas, we can calculate estimates of profit at various sales volumes.

In this chapter we will introduce the basic concepts of cost-volume-profit analysis and illustrate how to use them, first for a firm that produces only one product. Next, the basic concepts will be extended to a multiple product firm. Finally, a graphic approach to cost-volume-profit analysis is illustrated.

BASIC CONCEPTS OF COST-VOLUME-PROFIT ANALYSIS

Methods for cost-volume-profit analysis.

Cost-volume-profit analysis is concerned with how profit is determined by sales volume, sales price, variable expenses, and fixed expenses. Accountants have developed a number of methods for cost-volume-profit analysis including (1) an equation method, (2) a contribution margin per unit method, and (3) a contribution margin ratio method. The next three sections will discuss and illustrate each of these methods.

[1] Cost-volume-profit analysis or breakeven analysis are the terms accountants use to describe the concepts in this chapter. However, since we are primarily concerned with profit computations, the term expense is used rather than cost.

Equation Method

The first thing we do in cost-volume-profit analysis is to resolve total expense into a fixed expense component and a variable expense component. Once we do this we can represent profit in terms of revenue, fixed expenses, and variable expenses, as shown by the following equation:

Basic profit equation.

Sales revenue − variable expenses − fixed expenses = profit
or
Sales revenue = variable expenses + fixed expenses + profit

To illustrate how to use this equation method of cost-volume-profit analysis, consider the data in the following example:

The Ace Company is considering the production of an industrial knife to slit open cardboard cartons. The estimated selling price is $4.00 per knife. The fixed expense of producing and distributing the knife is estimated to be $30,000 per year. The variable expense of producing and selling a knife is estimated to be $3.00 per knife.

If we let X represent the number of knives the Ace Company expects to sell, the profits can be calculated as follows:

Sales revenue − variable expenses − fixed expenses = profit
$4.00X − $3.00X − $30,000 = profit

In the equation above, we express the total sales revenue as the product of the selling price per unit times the number of units sold, $4.00X. The total variable expense is expressed as the variable expense per unit times the number of units sold, $3.00X. The total fixed expense is a constant $30,000, of course, since total fixed expenses are not expected to change with changes in sales volume.

All we need now is an estimate of the expected sales volume, and we can calculate the profit to expect at that sales volume. For example, if 10,000 knives are expected to be sold, then we can calculate the profit by substituting 10,000 for X in the equation.

$$\begin{aligned}\textbf{Profit} &= \$4.00(10{,}000) - \$3.00(10{,}000) - \$30{,}000 \\ &= \$40{,}000 - \$30{,}000 - \$30{,}000 \\ &= -\$20{,}000\end{aligned}$$

The above computations show that if 10,000 knives are sold, the Ace Company will have a loss of $20,000. It would be better to know how many knives must be sold to break even.

The **breakeven point** is the sales volume where total sales revenues are equal to total expenses and thus there is no profit or loss. To calculate the breakeven sales volume for the Ace Company, we use the profit equation, set profit at a value of zero, and solve for the sales volume X.

The breakeven point is the sales volume where total revenue is equal to total expense.

Sales revenues = variable expense + fixed expense + profit

$$\begin{aligned}\$4.00X &= \$3.00X + \$30{,}000 + 0 \\ \$1.00X &= \$30{,}000 \\ X &= \frac{\$30{,}000}{\$1.00} \\ X &= 30{,}000 \text{ units}\end{aligned}$$

Thus for the Ace Company to break even, 30,000 knives must be sold. To express the breakeven point in dollars, we multiply the breakeven sales units times the sales price per unit:

$$\textbf{Breakeven sales dollars} = \textbf{30,000 units @ \$4.00 per unit} = \textbf{\$120,000}$$

Contribution Margin per Unit Method

Another approach to cost-volume-profit analysis is the **contribution margin per unit** method. To understand what we mean by the contribution margin per unit, consider the sales price per unit and the variable expense per unit. Subtract the variable expense per unit from the sales price per unit and you get the contribution margin per unit. This is the dollar amount that the sale of 1 unit contributes toward covering the fixed expense; after the fixed expenses are covered, the contribution margin per unit represents the increase in profits for each additional unit sold.

For the Ace Company the contribution margin per unit is calculated as follows:

The contribution margin is the difference between the selling price and variable expense.

Sales price per unit	**$4.00**
(less) variable expense per unit	**−3.00**
(equals) contribution margin per unit	**$1.00**

The contribution margin per unit of $1.00 for the Ace Company is the dollar amount the sale of one knife contributes toward covering fixed expenses. To determine how many knives Ace Company will have to sell to break even we can divide the fixed expenses of the Ace Company by the contribution margin per unit.

$$\textbf{Breakeven sales volume} = \frac{\textbf{total fixed expenses}}{\textbf{contribution margin per unit}} = \frac{\$30{,}000}{\$1.00} = \textbf{30,000 units}$$

Once the breakeven point has been reached, each additional knife sold will increase profits by $1.00, which is the contribution margin per unit. If 30,001 knives are sold, total profits will be $1.00 as shown below:

Sales 30,001 units @ $4.00 per unit	=	**$120,004**
(less) variable expenses 30,001 units @ $3.00	=	**− 90,003**
(equals) total contribution margin	=	**$ 30,001**
(less) fixed expenses	=	**− 30,000**
(equals) profit	=	**$ 1**

Contribution Margin Ratio Method

Up to this point, we have measured sales volume in units of product sold. However, sales volume is not always measured in units of product. Some firms produce a service as their output, not a product. For example, CPA firms and management consulting firms produce services, and they measure their sales volume in billable hours. In other situations it might be more appropriate to measure sales volume in terms of sales dollars. This is especially true for companies producing multiple products. Consider a company such as Procter and Gamble which produces hundreds of different products. Which would make more sense, to express their overall breakeven point in units or dollars? In dollars, because they have many different units. A unit of Ivory soap is not the same as a unit of Crest toothpaste.

To illustrate the cost-volume-profit computations using dollars as the measure of sales volume, consider the Ace Company data presented below:

	Per Unit	Ratio
Sales price	**$4.00**	**100%**
(less) variable expense	**3.00**	**75%**
(equals) contribution margin	**$1.00**	**25%**
Total fixed expense, $30,000 per year		

The first column in the data above shows the contribution margin in dollars per unit. It was used to calculate the breakeven point in units in our earlier example. The second column expresses the variable expense and the contribution margin as a ratio (in percent) of the selling price. That is, variable expense as a ratio of sales price is \$3/\$4 or variable expense is 75% of sales price. Similarly, contribution margin is \$1/\$4 or 25% of sales price.

This relationship is referred to as the **contribution margin ratio** and it represents the percentage of each sales dollar that is available to cover the fixed expenses and then profits.

Letting S represent volume in sales dollars, the equation for calculating the breakeven point can be expressed as:

$$\textbf{Breakeven sales revenues} = \textbf{variable expense ratio} \times \textbf{sales revenue} + \textbf{fixed expense}$$

$$S = 75\% \times S + \$30{,}000$$

$$25\%\ S = \$30{,}000$$

$$S = \frac{\$30{,}000}{25\%}$$

$$S = \$120{,}000$$

Note the third step in the computation above. In this step we see that the fixed expense (\$30,000) is divided by the contribution margin ratio (25%) to obtain the breakeven point in dollars (\$120,000).

Thus, rather than setting up the entire equation from the beginning each time, we can simplify it as follows:

$$\textbf{Breakeven sales revenue} = \frac{\textbf{fixed expense}}{\textbf{contribution margin ratio}}$$

Which method should you use to calculate breakeven? The equation method? The contribution margin method? The contribution margin ratio method? It does not matter. It all depends on management preference and the data available. However, to determine the breakeven point for a firm that produces multiple products, the aggregate sales volume measured in dollars makes more sense to managers and the breakeven point should be expressed in sales dollars, not sales units.

MANAGERIAL USES OF COST-VOLUME-PROFIT ANALYSIS

Using these basic concepts, the accountant can provide breakeven and profit information to management to facilitate planning decisions. With cost-volume-profit analysis the accountant can determine the sales volume necessary to achieve a target profit or determine how profits will vary with changes in sales prices, variable expenses, or fixed expenses.

Target Profit

A manager invests his organization's resources in a project and expects some level of profit. The expected profit is referred to as a **target profit.** Cost-volume-profit analysis can be used to calculate the number of units that must be sold to produce the target profit. For example, assume the investment required by the Ace Company to produce the knives is \$300,000 and the manager desires an 8% return on the investment. The target profit to obtain 8% return on the investment is (.08 times \$300,000) = \$24,000. The required sales units, X, to produce a profit of \$24,000 can be calculated as follows:

$$\mathbf{X = \frac{fixed\ expenses + target\ profit}{contribution\ margin\ per\ unit}}$$

$$\mathbf{X = \frac{\$30{,}000 + \$24{,}000}{\$1.00}}$$

$$\mathbf{X = 54{,}000\ units}$$

Change in the Selling Price

A decision managers constantly face is whether to increase selling price. The main thing to consider is consumer resistance to an increased sales price, resulting in a decrease in demand for the product. Cost-volume-profit analysis can help the manager determine how much sales volume can decrease but still achieve the target profit.

To illustrate, refer to the original data for the Ace Company and assume management aims a target profit of \$24,000 and is considering a selling price increase of \$0.25 per knife. With this increase in selling price, (1) how many knives must be sold to break even and (2) how many knives must be sold to earn a \$24,000 profit?

Using cost-volume-profit analysis:

	Original Data	**\$.25 Increase in Sales Price**
Selling price per unit	**\$4.00**	**\$4.25**
Variable expense per unit	**3.00**	**3.00**
Contribution margin per unit	**\$1.00**	**\$1.25**
Total fixed expense	**\$30,000**	**\$30,000**
Target profit	**\$24,000**	**\$24,000**

Breakeven sales units	=	$\frac{30{,}000 + \$0}{\$1.00}$	$\frac{\$30{,}000 + \$0}{\$1.25}$
	=	30,000 units	24,000 units
Sales units to earn $24,000 profit	=	$\frac{\$30{,}000 + \$24{,}000}{\$1.00}$	$\frac{30{,}000 + \$24{,}000}{\$1.25}$
	=	54,000 units	43,200 units

The increase in selling price from $1.00 to $1.25 has reduced the breakeven point from 30,000 units to 24,000 units; the sales volume to earn a $24,000 profit has been reduced from 54,000 units to 43,200 units. Thus, the Ace Company could increase selling price to $1.25 per unit; if sales decreased, 10,800 units (54,000 − 43,200) due to increased selling price, the profit would be exactly $24,000. Of course, if the decrease in demand turns out to be fewer than 10,800 units, profits would be greater than $24,000.

Change in Variable Expense

Of course companies cannot always increase selling price; competitive forces in the market may make this impractical. Thus, to maintain or increase profits managers must reduce expense rather than increase selling price. Expenses might be reduced by using less expensive materials or modifying the manufacturing process to reduce the direct labor expense. Either of these changes will reduce the variable expense per unit.

To illustrate how reducing the variable expense per unit affects sales volume and profits, return again to the original data for the Ace Company. Assume that by using a less expensive material the variable expense per unit can be reduced by $.20 per unit. Also, assume the target profit remains $24,000. How many knives must be sold to (1) break even and (2) earn a $24,000 profit?

Using cost-volume-profit analysis:

		Original Data	$.20 Decrease in Variable Cost
Selling price per unit		$4.00	$4.00
Variable expense per unit		3.00	2.80
Contribution margin per unit		$1.00	$1.20
Total fixed expense		$30,000	$30,000
Target profits		$24,000	$24,000
Breakeven sales units	=	$\frac{\$30{,}000 + \$0}{\$1.00}$	$\frac{\$30{,}000 + \$0}{\$1.20}$
	=	30,000 units	25,000 units
Sales units to earn $24,000 profit	=	$\frac{\$30{,}000 + \$24{,}000}{\$1.00}$	$\frac{\$30{,}000 + \$24{,}000}{\$1.20}$
	=	54,000 units	45,000 units

The decrease in the variable expense per unit reduces the breakeven point from 30,000 units to 25,000 units. To earn a $24,000 profit the Ace Company need only sell 45,000 units rather than 54,000 units as a result of the lower variable expense.

Change in Fixed Expense

Fixed expenses may not be constant from year to year. Many times management will consider increases in a fixed expense such as advertising, expecting an increase in sales volume as a result. An increase in fixed expenses such as this in advertising expenditures will change the breakeven sales volume and the sales volume necessary to achieve target profits. Other examples of fixed expense changes are an increase in research and development, an increase in the number of salaried employees, or an increase in rent or property taxes.

By now you have been reminded that even though by definition fixed expenses do not vary with volume—that is, not over certain ranges in volume—fixed expense can change as a result of management decisions (such as the advertising change) or changes in the environment (such as the property tax change).

To illustrate how to use cost-volume-profit analysis to calculate the effect of a change in fixed expense on breakeven and target profit, refer again to the original data for the Ace Company. Assume management is considering a $3,000 increase in advertising expenditures. What impact will this increase in fixed expenses have on the breakeven sales volume and the sales volume to earn a $24,000 profit?

Using cost-volume-profit analysis we can answer the question as follows:

		Original Data	$3,000 Increase in Fixed Expense
Sales price per unit		**$4.00**	**$4.00**
Variable expense per unit		**3.00**	**3.00**
Contribution margin per unit		**$1.00**	**$1.00**
Total fixed expense		**$30,000**	**$33,000**
Target profit		**$24,000**	**$24,000**
Breakeven sales units	=	$\frac{\$30,000 + \$0}{\$1.00}$	$\frac{\$33,000 + \$0}{\$1.00}$
	=	**30,000 units**	**33,000 units**
Sales units to earn $24,000 profit	=	$\frac{\$30,000 + \$24,000}{\$1.00}$	$\frac{\$33,000 + \$24,000}{\$1.00}$
	=	**54,000 units**	**57,000 units**

The increase in fixed expenses (it is a 10% increase) increases the breakeven sales volume (by exactly 10%) and the sales volume to earn a $24,000 profit from 54,000 units to 57,000 units (about a 6% increase).

Multiple Changes

Thus far in our analysis of cost-volume-profit and our example we considered changes in only one variable. But in the real world more than one variable can change. To see what we mean, let us assume that the management of the Ace

Company is considering (1) a $3,000 increase in advertising expenditures, and (2) a $.25 increase in the sales price.

Using cost-volume-profit analysis, the impact of these two changes on the breakeven volume and the volume to achieve a $24,000 profit is computed as follows:

	Original Data	$3,000 Increase in Fixed Expense and $.25 Increase in Selling Price
Sales price per unit	**$4.00**	**$4.25**
Variable expense per unit	**3.00**	**3.00**
Contribution margin per unit	**$1.00**	**$1.25**
Total fixed expense	**$30,000**	**$33,000**
Target profit	**$24,000**	**$24,000**
Breakeven sales units =	**($30,000 + $0) / $1.00**	**($33,000 + $0) / $1.25**
=	**30,000 units**	**26,400 units**
Sales volume to earn $24,000 profit =	**($30,000 + $24,000) / $1.00**	**($33,000 + $24,000) / $1.25**
	54,000 units	**45,600 units**

Sometimes several variables change at the same time. Cost-volume-profit analysis can show the effect of changes in several variables at the same time.

The increase in the sales price of $.25 (6% price increase) more than offsets the increase in fixed expense (10% increase), thus reducing the breakeven sales volume to 26,400 units (12% decrease) and the sales volume to earn $24,000 profits to 45,600 units (15% decrease).

Let's recap the cost-volume-profit analysis we have calculated for the Ace Company thus far. The following table shows the five different strategies we have examined, each of which aims at a $24,000 target profit.

Cost-volume-profit analysis is used to evaluate different strategies to achieve the target profit.

	Original Data	**Increase in Sales Price**	**Decrease in Variable Expense**	**Increase in Fixed Expense**	**Increase in Sales Price and in Fixed Expense**
Sales price	$4.00	$4.25	$4.00	$4.00	$4.25
Variable expense	3.00	3.00	2.80	3.00	3.00
Contribution margin	$1.00	$1.25	$1.20	$1.00	$1.25
Fixed expense	$30,000	$30,000	$30,000	$33,000	$33,000
Breakeven point in units	30,000	24,000	25,000	33,000	26,400
Units to earn $24,000 profit	54,000	43,200	45,000	57,000	45,600

Which strategy the manager chooses depends on the competitive situation, estimates of whether consumers will accept the suggested increase in selling price, or whether the increase in fixed advertising expense will produce increased sales volume, or whether it is possible to lower the variable expense, or combinations of all these considerations. Furthermore, these five strategies represent only a few of the many situations that could be evaluated. A variety of other changes in controllable variables could be made and combinations of changes could be evaluated.

THE IMPACT OF TAXES ON COST-VOLUME-PROFIT ANALYSIS

Now we want to consider target profits taking into consideration the income tax expense. One step is added to the analysis: A firm aiming at certain after-tax target profit converts the after-tax target profit to an equivalent before-tax target profit, and then uses the cost-volume-profit analysis as before. To see how this is done, consider the following example:

Profit before tax	\$24,000	100%	
Income tax expense	9,600	40%	(tax rate)
Profit after tax	\$14,400	60%	

Notice that:

$$\textbf{Profit after tax} = \textbf{profit before tax} - \textbf{income tax expense}$$
$$\textbf{But income tax expense} = \textbf{profit before tax} \times \textbf{tax rate}$$

So:

$$\begin{aligned}\textbf{Profit after tax} &= \textbf{profit before tax} - (\textbf{profit before tax} \times \textbf{tax rate}).\\ &= \textbf{profit before tax } (1 - \textbf{tax rate})\end{aligned}$$

Based on the specific relationships shown above, we can generalize to:

$$\begin{aligned}\textbf{Profit after tax} &= \textbf{profit before tax} - \textbf{income tax expense}\\ &= \textbf{profit before tax} \times (1 - \textbf{tax rate})\end{aligned}$$

Solving for profit before tax:

$$\textbf{Profit before tax} = \frac{\textbf{profit after tax}}{1 - \textbf{tax rate}}$$

For this example:

$$\$24{,}000 = \frac{\$14{,}400}{60\%}$$

The following example illustrates how to include the tax rate and after-tax profits in the cost-volume-profit analysis. Refer once again to the original data for the Ace Company: Selling price is \$4.00 per unit, variable expense per unit is \$3.00, and total fixed expense is \$30,000. Suppose the tax rate is 40% and the manager of the Ace Company desires an after-tax profit of \$14,400.

The sales volume to achieve this after-tax profit is:

The effect of taxes is included in cost-volume-profit analysis by converting the after-tax profit target to a before-tax profit target.

$$X = \frac{\textbf{fixed expense} + \left(\dfrac{\textbf{profit after tax}}{(1 - \textbf{tax rate})}\right)}{\textbf{contribution margin per unit}}$$

$$X = \frac{\$30{,}000 + \left(\dfrac{\$14{,}400}{1 - .40}\right)}{\$1.00}$$

$$X = \frac{\$30{,}000 + \$24{,}000}{\$1.00}$$

$$X = 54{,}000 \text{ units}$$

To confirm the above computation examine the following income statement:

Sales 54,000 units @ $4.00	$216,000
Variable expense 54,000 units @ $3.00	162,000
Contribution margin	$ 54,000
Fixed expense	30,000
Profit before taxes	$ 24,000
Income tax expense @ 40% rate	9,600
Profit after taxes	$ 14,400

MULTIPLE PRODUCTS AND COST-VOLUME-PROFIT ANALYSIS

In multiple product firms the mix of products sold influences profit.

You have seen that the annual profit of a firm producing a single product depends on sales volume, selling price per unit, variable expense per unit, and fixed expense per year. For a firm that produces multiple products, the firm's total profit depends on (1) the total fixed expense per year of all products, (2) the sales volume, selling price, and variable expense per unit *for each* product, and (3) the mix of products sold. The mix of products sold refers to the relative quantities of each product sold.

To illustrate the impact of the **sales mix** on profits, consider the following situation for two products:

	Product	
	Y	**Z**
Sales price per unit	$10.00	$15.00
(less) variable expense per unit	8.00	12.00
(equals) contribution margin per unit	$ 2.00	$ 3.00
Total fixed expense	$120,000 per year	

If the company sold only product Y, the sales mix would consist of 1 unit of Y and 0 units of Z. It would really be a single product firm. The breakeven point would be calculated as before:

$$\text{Breakeven sales volume (1 unit of Y, 0 units of Z)} = \frac{\$120{,}000 \text{ (fixed expense)}}{\$2.00 \text{ (contribution margin per unit of Y)}}$$

$$= 60{,}000 \text{ units of Y}$$

Now suppose the company sold only product Z. The sales mix would be zero units of Y and 1 unit of Z. The breakeven point would be calculated as follows:

$$\text{Breakeven sales volume (0 units of Y, 1 unit of Z)} = \frac{\$120{,}000 \text{ (fixed expense)}}{\$3.00 \text{ (contribution margin per unit of Z)}}$$

$$= 40{,}000 \text{ units of Z}$$

Now let us assume the company sells both products in the mix of 1 unit of Y and 1 unit of Z. In other words, the company expects 50% of the sales units to be product Y and 50% of the sales units to be product Z. Because each product has a different contribution margin per unit, we cannot use either of the individual contribution margin per unit figures to calculate the breakeven point for this sales mix. What we can do is calculate the average contribution margin per unit for the sales mix as follows:

Computing the average contribution margin for the sales mix.

	Sales Mix									
	1 Unit Y		1 Unit Z		Totals		Total Units in Sales Mix		Averages for the Sales Mix	Ratio
Sales price per unit	$10	+	$15	=	$25	÷	2	=	$12.50	100%
Variable expense per unit	8	+	12	=	20	÷	2	=	10.00	80%
Contribution margin	$ 2	+	$ 3	=	$ 5	÷	2	=	$ 2.50	20%

The average sales price is $12.50 per unit; the average variable expense is $10.00 per unit, which leaves the average contribution margin per unit, $2.50. No single sale of either product Y or Z will produce these results. Rather these are averages based on the sales mix assumption that for every one unit of Y sold one unit of Z will also be sold. Using the average contribution margin per unit, the breakeven point is calculated as follows:

Sales Mix 1 Unit of Y to 1 Unit of Z

$$\text{Breakeven sales volume} = \frac{\$120{,}000 \text{ (fixed expenses)}}{\$2.50 \text{ (average contribution margin of sales mix)}}$$

$$= 48{,}000 \text{ units (total of product Y and product Z)}$$

These 48,000 sales units at the breakeven point represent the total of the sales of both product Y and product Z based on the sales mix (which is one to one). Since the sales mix represents 50% of the units Y and 50% Z, the 48,000 total units comprise:

Product	Sales Mix Ratio		Total Sales Units		Sales Units of Each Product
Y	.5	×	48,000	=	24,000
Z	.5	×	48,000	=	24,000
	1.0				48,000

The sales dollars for each product are:

Product	Sales Units		Sales Price		Sales Dollars
X	24,000	×	$10.00/unit	=	$240,000
Y	24,000	×	$15.00/unit	=	$360,000
	48,000				$600,000

As discussed earlier, the breakeven point for multiproduct firms is more meaningful to managers when stated in dollars.

The breakeven point for multiproduct firms can be calculated directly in sales dollars using the contribution margin ratio for the sales mix. For this example the computation is:

Sales Mix 1 Unit of Y to 1 Unit of X

$$\textbf{Breakeven sales dollars} = \frac{\textbf{\$120,000 (fixed expenses)}}{\textbf{20\% (sales mix contribution margin ratio)}}$$

$$= \textbf{\$600,000}$$

Because the sales price for each product is different, we cannot use the 50–50 sales mix in units ratio to resolve breakeven dollar volume for each product. For precisely the reason that their sales prices are different, we must use the ratio of the sales prices to resolve the breakeven dollar volume for each product.

The sales mix in dollars may be different than the sales mix in units.

Product	Sales Mix in Units	Sales Price	Sales Dollar Mix Ratio		Total Breakeven Sales Dollars		Individual Product Breakeven Sales Dollars
Y	1	$10	$10/$25	×	$600,000	=	$240,000
Z	1	15	$15/$25	×	$600,000	=	360,000
		$25					$600,000

Change in the Sales Mix

A change in the sales mix can influence the breakeven sales volume and the profitability of the firm. To illustrate this assume the management of the firm in the previous illustration feels that changes in customer demand may change the sales mix from 1 unit of Y and 1 unit of Z to 3 units of Y and 2 units of Z.

This means that Y will represent ($^3/_5$) = 60% of the total sales units and Z will represent ($^2/_5$) = 40%. The computation of the average contribution margin per unit is:

	Sales Mix				Total		Averages
	3 Units Y		2 Units Z	Totals	Units in Mix		for the Sales Mix
Sales price	($10×3)$30	+	($15×2)$30	= $60	÷ 5	=	$12.00
Variable expense	($8×3) 24	+	($12×2) 24	= $48	÷ 5	=	9.60
Contribution margin	$ 6	+	$ 6	= $12	÷ 5	=	$ 2.40

The breakeven point in units is:

Sales Mix 3 Units of Y, 2 Units of Z

$$\text{Breakeven sales units} = \frac{\$120{,}000 \text{ (fixed expense)}}{\$2.40 \text{ (contribution margin per unit for the sales mix)}}$$

$$= 50{,}000 \text{ units}$$

Resolving the breakeven sales units in breakeven units of product Y and breakeven units of product Z:

Product	Sales Mix Ratio		Breakeven Total Sales Units		Individual Product Breakeven Units
Y	.60	×	50,000	=	30,000
Z	.40	×	50,000	=	20,000
	1.00				50,000

Up to this point we have calculated four breakeven points in this illustration using four different sales mixes. These four sales mixes and breakeven points are summarized as follows:

Sales Mix	Prod-uct	Sales Mix in Units	Individual Product Breakeven Units
1.	Y	1	60,000
	Z	0	0
			60,000

2.	Y	0	0
	Z	1	40,000
			40,000
3.	Y	1	24,000
	Z	1	24,000
			48,000
4.	Y	3	30,000
	Z	2	20,000
			50,000

Examine the table above and note that the more units of product Z included in the sales mix the lower the breakeven sales volume. This occurs because product Z's contribution margin per unit is $3.00 and product Y's contribution margin per unit is $2.00. Hence, other things remaining equal the greater the proportion of product Z sold the greater the total contribution margin to cover fixed expenses.

MARGIN OF SAFETY

The **margin of safety** is the difference between budgeted sales and breakeven sales, expressed as a percentage of budgeted sales. In equation form:

The margin of safety is a measure of risk associated with a particular sales goal.

$$\textbf{Margin of safety} = \frac{\textbf{budgeted sales} - \textbf{breakeven sales}}{\textbf{budgeted sales}} \times 100\%$$

To illustrate how to calculate the margin of safety, consider the preceding multiproduct example. The breakeven sales volume when the sales mix is 1 unit of Y and 1 unit of Z is 48,000 units. Assume the budgeted sales volume is 60,000 units. The margin of safety is:

$$\textbf{Margin of safety} = \frac{60{,}000 - 48{,}000}{60{,}000} \times 100\%$$
$$= 20\%$$

This means that if actual sales volume is 20% less than budgeted sales volume, the firm would just break even. Managers use the margin of safety as an indication of the risk inherent in a particular sales goal. The simple presumption is that the greater the margin of safety, the lower the risk.

COST-VOLUME-PROFIT ANALYSIS: ASSUMPTIONS

The information and calculations that result from cost-volume-profit analysis are as certain as the estimates and assumptions that go into them. For cost-volume-profit analysis to be reliable, these basic assumptions must hold:

1 The total revenues of the firm change in direct proportion to changes in unit sales volume. This is the same as assuming that the average selling price is constant.

2 Total expenses can be separated into variable expenses and fixed expenses per year.

The assumptions of cost-volume-profit analysis.

3 The total variable expenses vary in direct proportion to changes in sales volume. This is the same as assuming the variable expense per unit is a constant.

4 The total fixed expenses per year, within a relevant range of volume, do not change as sales volume changes.

5 For a multiproduct firm, the sales mix remains constant for all volume levels under consideration.

6 Production volume and sales volume are equal; in other words, inventory changes do not affect profit.

As you have just seen in the preceding illustrations, management may find it useful to relax any of these assumptions, but unless explicitly changed the assumptions are as listed.

COST-VOLUME-PROFIT ANALYSIS: GRAPHIC APPROACH

The graphic approach to cost-volume-profit analysis is based on reporting total sales revenue and total expenses, both as a function of sales volume, as lines on a graph.

To illustrate the graphic approach to cost-volume-profit analysis we will use the original data for the Ace Company: selling price = \$4.00 per unit, variable expense = \$3.00 per unit, and fixed expense = \$30,000.

Exhibit 14-1 illustrates graphically a number of things:

Cost-volume-profit graphs display the basic relationships.

1 How total sales revenue varies with unit sales volume

2 How total expenses vary with unit sales volume

3 That fixed expenses do not vary with unit sales volume

4 How profits increase beyond the breakeven point with unit sales volume

Note in the graph the total fixed expense is \$30,000 and is a horizontal line. As usual, it is assumed the fixed expense per year is unchanged as sales volume changes.

To plot the total expense line, the variable expense at a rate of \$3.00 per unit is added to the fixed expense. Since the total expense line is a linear function, only two points are required to construct the line. The following table shows two points on the total expense line.

Horizontal Axis	Vertical Axis	
Unit Sales Volume	Total Expense = \$30,000 + \$3.00 (Unit Sales Volume)	Point on the Graph
0	\$30,000 + \$3.00(0 units) = \$30,000	A
30,000	\$30,000 + \$3.00(30,000 units) = \$120,000	B

Note that at zero sales volume the total expense is the fixed expense.

The total sales revenue line is constructed by multiplying the sales price of $4.00 per unit times the unit sales volume. Again, since the selling price is assumed to be constant, the total revenue line will be a straight line and only two points are needed to construct the line. The following table shows two points on the total revenue line.

Horizontal Axis Unit Sales Volume	Vertical Axis Total Revenue = $4.00 (Unit Sales Volume)	Point on the Graph
0	$4.00(0 units) = $0	C
30,000	$4.00(30,000 units) = $120,000	B

The difference between the total sales revenue line and the total expense line is the profit or loss at each level of unit sales volume. The total sales revenue line and total expense line cross at 30,000 sales units—the breakeven point. At any level of unit sales greater than the breakeven point, total sales revenue is greater than total expense; the result is profit. Also, at any unit sales less than 30,000 units, revenue is less than expenses; the result is a loss.

Profit-Volume Graph

The profit-volume graph focuses attention on profits.

Another graphical approach to cost-volume-profit analysis is shown in Exhibit 14-2. This graph is called a profit-volume graph since it focuses attention directly on how profit changes as sales volume changes. Compare the profit-volume graph to the cost-volume-profit graph in Exhibit 14-1. The cost-volume-profit graph shows the total sales revenues and total expenses on the vertical axis and the difference between them is the profit or loss at each level of sales volume (horizontal axis). The profit-volume graph shows only profit and loss on the vertical axis.

Since the relationship between profit and volume is represented by a straight line, we only need two points to plot a profit-volume line on the graph.

The total fixed expense and the breakeven point can be used to construct the profit-volume graph. The total fixed expense of $30,000 represents a $30,000 loss at zero sales volume. The breakeven point represents the unit sales volume at which there is no loss and no profit—zero profits. For the Ace Company these two points on the profit-volume graph are:

Horizontal Axis Unit Sales Volume	Vertical Axis Profit = $4.00 (Unit Sales Volume) − $3.00 (Unit Sales Volume) − $30,000	Point on the Graph
0	$4.00(0 units) − $3.00(0 units) − $30,000 = $−30,000	A
30,000	$4.00(30,000 units) − $3.00(30,000 units) − $30,000 = $0	B

EXHIBIT 14-1
ACE COMPANY
Relationships between Revenues, Expenses, Profits, and Volume
Knife Manufacturer Example

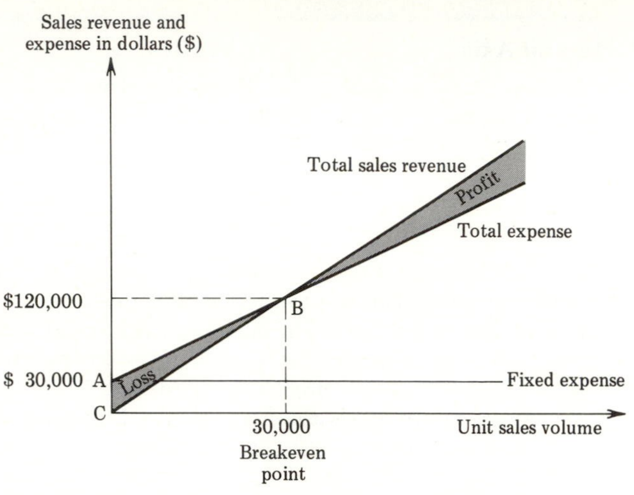

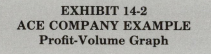

EXHIBIT 14-2
ACE COMPANY EXAMPLE
Profit-Volume Graph

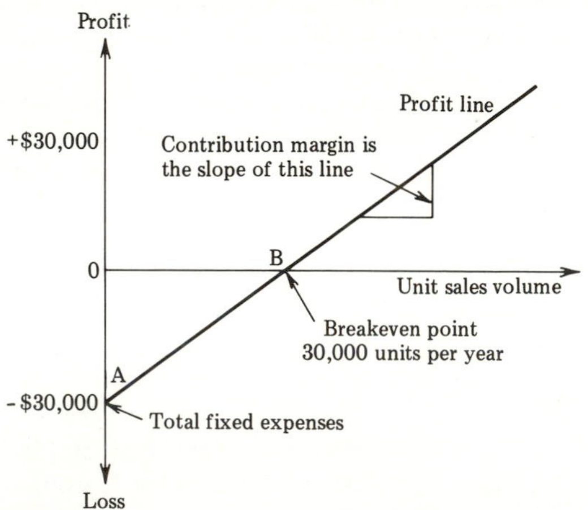

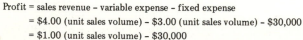

Profit = sales revenue - variable expense - fixed expense
= $4.00 (unit sales volume) - $3.00 (unit sales volume) - $30,000
= $1.00 (unit sales volume) - $30,000

As you can see the profit line begins where the fixed expense is shown as a loss on the vertical axis, and moves upward and to the right at a rate equal to the contribution margin per unit—$1.00 for the Ace Company. The contribution margin per unit is the slope of the profit line. The steeper the slope (starting at the same fixed expense) of the profit line the lower the breakeven point.

The profit-volume graph is a useful tool to visually summarize the impact of sales volume on profit.

SUMMARY

Cost-volume-profit analysis is used to determine the estimated profit resulting from a number of different budgeted sales volumes or it can be used to determine the sales volume needed to achieve a target profit.

Cost-volume-profit analysis also provides management with information about how profits are influenced by changes in the following variables: sales volume, selling price, variable expense per unit, and fixed expense per year.

For multiproduct firms a mix of products sold (sales mix) must be assumed to use cost-volume-profit analysis. With an assumed sales mix, a weighted average contribution margin per unit or per dollar of sales is calculated. Then the analysis proceeds in the usual manner.

Cost-volume-profit analysis is based on a number of assumptions. If the environment in which firms operate changes rapidly, the assumptions may be violated and this analysis may be of limited value. The accountant must be sure that the assumptions of cost-volume-profit analysis are recognized by management.

The cost-volume-profit relationships of a firm can be portrayed graphically in a cost-volume-profit graph or a profit-volume graph. Graphic portrayal of these relationships visually summarizes the impact of sales revenue, variable expenses, and fixed expenses on profits.

Review Problem

R. A. Ro and Company, maker of quality handmade pipes, has experienced a steady growth in sales for the past five years. However, increased competition has led Mr. Ro, the president, to believe that an aggressive advertising campaign will be necessary next year to maintain the company's present growth.

To prepare for next year's advertising campaign, the company's accountant has prepared and presented Mr. Ro with the following data for the current year, 19X2:

Variable expenses:	
Direct labor	$ 8.00 per pipe
Direct materials	3.25 per pipe
Variable overhead	2.50 per pipe
Total variable expenses	$13.75 per pipe
Fixed expenses:	
Manufacturing	$ 25,000
Selling	40,000
Administrative	70,000
Total fixed expenses	$135,000
Selling price per pipe	$25.00
Expected sales, 19X2 (20,000 units)	$500,000

Mr. Ro has set the sales target for 19X3 at a level of $550,000 (or 22,000 pipes).

Required

1 What is the projected profit for 19X2?

2 What is the breakeven point for 19X2 in units?

3 Mr. Ro believes additional advertising expense of $11,250 in 19X3, with all other expenses remaining constant, will be necessary to attain the 19X3 sales target. What will be the profit for 19X3 if the additional $11,250 is spent and 22,000 pipes are sold?

4 What will be the breakeven point in dollar sales for 19X3 if the additional $11,250 is spent for advertising?

5 If the additional $11,250 is spent for advertising in 19X3, what is the required sales level in dollar sales to equal 19X2's profit?

6 At a sales level of 22,000 units, what is the maximum amount which can be spent on advertising if a before-tax profit of $100,000 is desired?

(CMA)

Solution

1 Projected profit for 19X2:

Sales 20,000 units @ $25	$500,000
Variable expenses 20,000 units @ $13.75	275,000
Contribution margin	$225,000
Fixed Expenses	135,000
Profit	$ 90,000

2 Breakeven point for 19X2:

$$\textbf{Breakeven units} = \frac{\textbf{fixed expenses}}{\textbf{contribution margin per unit}}$$

$$= \frac{\$135{,}000}{\$25. - 13.75}$$

$$= \underline{\underline{12{,}000}} \text{ units for 19X2}$$

3. Projected profit for 19X3 with additional advertising expense:

Sales 22,000 units @ $25.	$550,000
Variable expenses 22,000 units @ $13.75	302,500
Contribution margin	$247,500
Fixed expenses $135,000 + $11,250	146,250
Profit	$101,250

4 Breakeven point for 19X3 with increased fixed expense:

$$\textbf{Breakeven dollars} = \frac{\textbf{fixed expense}}{\textbf{contribution margin ratio}}$$

$$= \frac{\$146{,}250}{1 - \left(\frac{\$13.75}{\$25.00}\right)} = \frac{\$146{,}250}{45\%}$$

$$= \underline{\underline{\$325{,}000}} \text{ for 19X3}$$

5 19X3 sales dollars to achieve 19X2's profit:

$$\textbf{Sales dollars} = \frac{\textbf{fixed expense + target profit}}{\textbf{contribution margin ratio}}$$

$$= \frac{\$146{,}250 + \$90{,}000}{45\%}$$

$$= \underline{\underline{\$525{,}000}} \text{ for 19X3}$$

6 Maximum advertising expense for a profit of $100,000:

$$\textbf{Profit} = \text{sales} - \text{variable expense} - \text{fixed expense} - \text{advertising}$$
$$\$100{,}000 = (22{,}000 \times \$25) - (22{,}000 \times \$13.75) - \$135{,}000 - \text{advertising}$$
$$\$100{,}000 = \$550{,}000 - \$302{,}500 - \$135{,}000 - \text{advertising}$$
$$\text{advertising} = \underline{\underline{\$12{,}500}}$$

Glossary

Breakeven point The volume of sales where total revenue is equal to total expense and profit is therefore zero. Sales volume may be measured in units or dollars.

Contribution margin per unit The difference between the selling price per unit and the total variable expense per unit. It represents the amount from the sale of each unit available to cover fixed expense and then profits.

Contribution margin ratio The ratio of the contribution margin to the sales revenue. It represents the percentage of each sales dollar that is available to cover fixed expenses and then profits.

Cost-volume-profit analysis The analysis of the relationship between selling price, variable expense, fixed expense, volume, and profits. The relationship may be expressed mathematically or graphically.

Margin of safety The difference between the budgeted sales volume and the breakeven sales volume divided by the budgeted sales volume. It is used by managers as a measure of risk.

Sales mix The relative proportion of the total sales volume from each product. A sales mix only exists in multiproduct situations. A change in the sales mix can affect the breakeven point and the volume of sales to achieve a given profit.

Target profits The level of profits desired by management for a given time period. Target profits is expressed as an absolute amount but may be calculated as a percentage of sales, or a percentage of investment.

Questions and Problems

14-1. What is the objective of cost-volume-profit analysis?

14-2. Define contribution margin per unit and contribution margin ratio.

14-3 How can the cost-volume-profit formula be used to evaluate alternative profit plans?

14-4 What are the assumptions underlying cost-volume-profit analysis?

14-5 How is income tax expense brought into cost-volume-profit analysis?

14-6 Certain terms are fundamental to cost-volume-profit analysis. Explain the meaning of each of the following terms.

a Fixed expenses
b Variable expenses
c Relevant range
d Breakeven point
e Margin of safety
f Sales mix

(CPA)

14-7 The Oliver Company plans to market a new product. Based on its market studies, Oliver estimates that it can sell 5,500 units in 19X6. The selling price will be $2.00 per unit. Variable expenses are estimated to be 40% of the selling price. Fixed expenses are estimated to be $6,000.

What is the breakeven point in units and dollars?

(CPA)

14-8 Breakeven, Target Profit, and Expense Changes In a recent period Zero Company has the following experience:

Sales (10,000 units @ $200)			$2,000,000
	Fixed	**Variable**	
Direct materials	$ —	$ 200,000	
Direct labor	—	400,000	
Factory overhead	160,000	600,000	
Administrative expenses	180,000	80,000	
Other expenses	200,000	120,000	
Total	$540,000	$1,400,000	1,940,000
Net income			$ 60,000

Required

1 Calculate the breakeven point for Zero Company in terms of units and sales dollars.

2 What sales volume would be required to generate a net income of $96,000?

3 What is the new breakeven point in units if management makes a decision which increases fixed expenses by $18,000?

(CPA)

14-9 Multiple Choice

1 An accountant would typically have the following in mind when referring to the "margin of safety":
a the excess of budgeted or actual sales over the variable expenses and the fixed expenses at breakeven
b the excess of budgeted or actual sales revenue over the fixed expenses
c the excess of actual sales over budgeted sales
d the excess of sales revenue over the variable expenses
e none of the above

2 Which of these alternatives would generally decrease contribution margin per unit the most?

a a 15% decrease in selling price
b a 15% increase in variable expense
c a 15% increase in selling price
d a 15% decrease in variable expense
e a 15% decrease in fixed expense

3 If fixed expenses decrease while variable expense per unit remains constant, the new contribution margin in relation to the old will be
a unchanged
b higher
c lower
d indeterminate
e none of the above

The graph below applies to items 4 and 5 only.

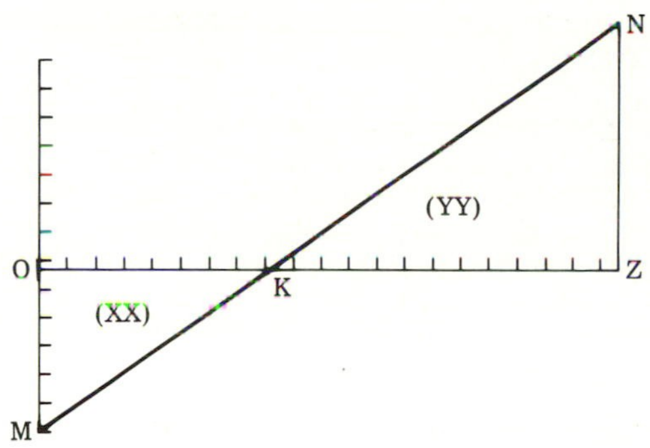

4 On the profit/volume chart above, which of the following are true?
a the areas XX and YY and the point K represent profit, loss, and volume of sales at breakeven point, respectively
b the line O–Z represents the volumes of sales
c the two lines O–M and N–Z represent fixed expenses
d the line M–N represents total expenses
e none of the above is true

5 The vertical scale represents
a volume of sales
b units produced
c profit above O and loss below O
d contribution margin
e none of the above

(CMA)

14-10 Breakeven and Analysis of Changes Pawnee Company operated at normal capacity during the current year producing 40,000 units of its single product. Sales totaled 40,000 units at an average price of $20 per unit. Variable manufacturing expenses were $8 per unit, and variable marketing expenses were $4 per unit sold. Fixed expenses were incurred uniformly throughout the year and amounted to $188,000 for manufacturing and $64,000 for marketing. There was no year-end work in process inventory.

Required

1 What is Pawnee's breakeven point in sales dollars for the current year?

2 If Pawnee is subject to an income tax rate of 30%, what is the number

of units required to be sold in the current year to earn an after-tax profit of $126,000?

3 Pawnee's variable manufacturing expenses are expected to increase 10% in the coming year. What will be Pawnee's breakeven point in sales dollars for the coming year?

4 If Pawnee's variable manufacturing expenses do increase 10%, what selling price will yield Pawnee the same contribution margin per unit in the coming year?

(CMA)

14-11 Breakeven and Analysis of Changes The Statement of Income for Davann Co. presented below represents the operating results for the fiscal year just ended. Davann had sales of 1,800 tons of product during the current year. The manufacturing capacity of Davann's facilities is 3,000 tons of product.

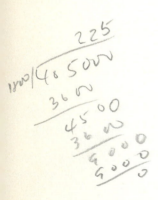

DAVANN CO.
Statement of Income
For the Year Ended December 31, 19X0

Sales		$900,000
Variable expenses		
Manufacturing	$315,000	
Selling	180,000	
Total variable expenses		$495,000
Contribution margin		$405,000
Fixed expenses		
Manufacturing	$ 90,000	
Selling	112,500	
Administration	45,000	
Total fixed expenses		$247,500
Net income before income taxes		$157,500
Income taxes (40%)		63,000
Net income after income taxes		$ 94,500

Required

Each of the following questions is independent.

1 Calculate the breakeven volume in tons of product for 19X0.

2 If the sales volume is estimated to be 2,100 tons in the next year, and if the prices and expenses stay at the same levels and amounts next year, what is the after-tax net income that Davann can expect for 19X1?

3 Davann has a potential foreign customer that has offered to buy 1,500 tons at $450 per ton. Assume that all of Davann's expenses would be at the same levels and rates as in 19X0. What net income after taxes would Davann make if it took this order and accepted only 1,500 tons of business from regular customers so as not to exceed capacity?

4 Davann plans to market its product in a new territory. Davann estimates that an advertising and promotion program costing $61,500 annually would need to be undertaken for the next two or three years.

In addition, a $25 per ton sales commission over and above the current commission to the sales force in the new territory would be required. How many tons would have to be sold in the new territory to maintain Davann's current after-tax income of $94,500?

5 Davann is considering replacing a highly labor intensive process with an automatic machine. This would result in an increase of $58,500 annually in manufacturing fixed expense. The variable manufacturing expenses would decrease $25 per ton. What is the new breakeven volume in tons?

(CMA)

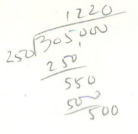

14-12 Profit-Volume Graph: Multiple Choice The SAB Company uses a profit-volume graph similar to the one shown below to represent the profit/volume relationships of its operations. The vertical (y axis) is the profit in dollars and the horizontal (x axis) is the volume in units. The diagonal line is the contribution margin line.

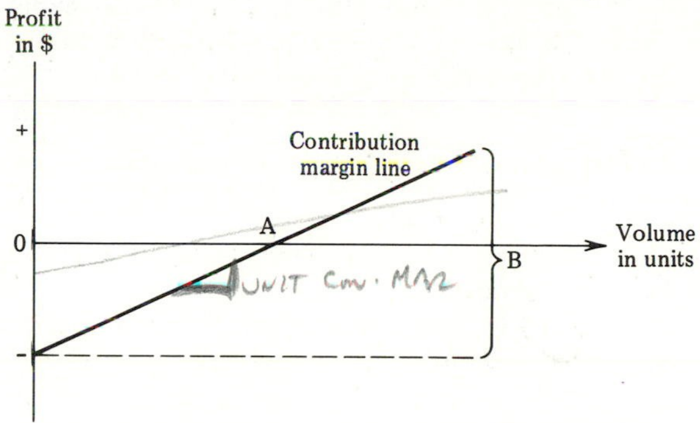

Required

1 Point A on the profit-volume graph represents
   a the point where fixed expenses equal sales.
   b the point where fixed expenses equal variable expenses.
   c a volume level of zero units.
   d the point where total expenses equal total sales.
   e the point where the rate of contribution margin increases.

2 The vertical distance from the dotted line to the contribution margin line denoted as B on the profit-volume graph represents
   a the total contribution margin.
   b the contribution margin per unit.
   c the contribution margin rate.
   d total sales.
   e the sum of the variable and fixed expenses.

3 If SAB Company's fixed expenses were to increase,
   a the contribution margin line would shift upward parallel to the present line.
   b the contribution margin line would shift downward parallel to the present line.
   c the slope of the contribution margin line would be more pronounced (steeper).

d the slope of the contribution margin line would be less pronounced (flatter).
e the contribution margin line would coincide with the present contribution margin line.

4 If SAB Company's variable expenses per unit were to increase but its unit selling price stays constant,
a the contribution margin line would shift upward parallel to the present line.
b the contribution margin line would shift downward parallel to the present line.
c the slope of the contribution margin line would be more pronounced (steeper).
d the slope of the contribution margin line would be less pronounced (flatter).
e the slope of the contribution margin line probably would change but how it would change is not determinable.

5 If SAB Company decided to increase its unit selling price to offset exactly the increase in the variable expense per unit,
a the contribution margin line would shift upward parallel to the present line.
b the contribution margin line would shift downward parallel to the present line.
c the slope of the contribution margin line would be more pronounced (steeper).
d the slope of the contribution margin line would be less pronounced (flatter).
e the contribution margin line would coincide with the present contribution margin line.

(CMA)

14-13 The Impact of the Product Mix The Anzo Company produces two products, X and Y, whose selling price and expenses are given below:

	X	Y
Sales price	$10	$14
Variable expense per unit	6	8
Contribution margin	$ 4	$ 6
Fixed expense	$70,000 per year	

Unit sales of the two products historically have been almost identical. Management is considering the possibility of increasing its advertising budget for product Y by $10,000 in hopes of changing the product mix to 1.5 units of Y sold for each unit of X sold.

Required

1 Assuming unit sales are divided evenly between the two products, calculate the breakeven point in sales dollars.
2 Assuming the additional $10,000 is spent on advertising product Y and the product mix is 1.5 units of Y for each unit of X sold, calculate the breakeven point.
3 Prepare a profit-volume graph to illustrate the change in the product mix.

14-14 Breakeven with Multiple Products The Dooley Co. manufactures two products, baubles and trinkets. The following are projections for the coming year.

	Baubles		Trinkets		
	Units	Amount	Units	Amount	Totals
Sales	10,000	$10,000	7,500	$10,000	$20,000
Expenses					
Fixed		2,000		5,600	7,600
Variable		6,000		3,000	9,000
		8,000		8,600	16,600
Profit before taxes		$ 2,000		$ 1,400	$ 3,400

1 Assuming that the facilities are not jointly used, the breakeven output (in units) for baubles would be
a 8,000 b 7,000 c 6,000 d 5,000

2 The breakeven volume (dollars) for trinkets would be
a $8,000 b $7,000 c $6,000 d $5,000

3 Assuming that consumers purchase a sales mix of four baubles and three trinkets, the sales mix unit contribution margin would be
a $4.40 b $4.00 c $1.33 d $1.10

4 If consumers purchase a sales mix of four baubles and three trinkets, the breakeven output for the two products would be
a 6,909 baubles; 6,909 trinkets
b 6,909 baubles; 5,182 trinkets
c 5,000 baubles; 8,000 trinkets
d 5,000 baubles; 6,000 trinkets

5 If baubles and trinkets are sold at a one-to-one sales mix and there is no change in the Dooley Co.'s expense-volume structures, the breakeven volume would be
a $22,500 b $15,750 c $13,300 d $10,858

6 If the sales mix is defined as one bauble and one trinket, the weighted average contribution margin ratio would be
a 7/10 b 4/7 c 2/5 d 19/50

(CPA)

14-15. Breakeven, Sales Price, and Target Profit All-Day Candy Company is a wholesale distributor of candy. The company services grocery, convenience, and drug stores in a large metropolitan area.

Small but steady growth in sales has been achieved by the All-Day Candy Company over the past few years while candy prices have been increasing. The company is formulating its plans for the coming fiscal year. Presented below are the data used to project the current year's after-tax profit of $110,400.

Average selling price		$4.00 per box	
Average variable expenses			
Cost of candy		$2.00 per box	
Selling expenses		.40 per box	
Total		$2.40 per box	
Annual fixed expenses			
Selling	$160,000		
Administrative	280,000		
Total	$440,000		
Expected annual sales volume (390,000 boxes)			$1,560,000
Tax rate			40%

Manufacturers of candy have announced that they will increase prices of their products an average of 15% in the coming year due to increases in materials (sugar, cocoa, peanuts, etc.) and labor expenses. All-Day Candy Company expects that all other expenses will remain at the same rates or levels as the current year.

Required

1 What is All-Day Candy Company's breakeven point in boxes of candy for the current year?

2 What selling price per box must All-Day Candy Company charge to cover the 15% increase in the cost of candy and still maintain the current average contribution margin per box?

3 What volume of sales in dollars must the All-Day Candy Company achieve in the coming year to maintain the same net income after taxes as projected for the current year if the selling price of candy remains at $4.00 per box and the cost of candy increases 15%?

(CMA)

14-16 Breakeven Analysis—Hospital The Columbus Hospital operates a general hospital but rents space and beds to separate entities for specialized areas such as pediatrics, maternity, psychiatric, etc. Columbus charges each separate entity for common services to its patients such as meals and laundry and for administrative services such as billings, collections, etc. All uncollectible accounts are charged directly to the entity. Space and bed rentals are fixed for the year.

For the entire year ended June 30, 19X3, the pediatrics department at Columbus Hospital charged each patient an average of $65 per day, had a capacity of 60 beds, operated 24 hours per day for 365 days, and had revenue of $1,138,800.

Expenses charged by the hospital to the pediatrics department for the year ended June 30, 19X3, were as follows:

	Basis of Allocation	
	Patient Days	Bed Capacity
Dietary	$ 42,952	
Janitorial		$ 12,800
Laundry	28,000	

Laboratory, other than direct charges to patients	47,800	
Pharmacy	33,800	
Repairs and maintenance	5,200	7,140
General administrative services		131,760
Rent		275,320
Billings and collections	40,000	
Bad debt expense	47,000	
Other	18,048	25,980
	$262,800	$453,000

The only personnel directly employed by the pediatrics department are supervising nurses, nurses, and aides. The hospital has minimum personnel requirements based on total annual patient days. Hospital requirements beginning at the minimum, expected level of operation follow:

Annual Patient Days	Aides	Nurses	Supervising Nurses
10,000–14,000	21	11	4
14,001–17,000	22	12	4
17,001–23,725	22	13	4
23,726–25,550	25	14	5
25,551–27,375	26	14	5
27,376–29,200	29	16	6

The staffing levels above represent full-time equivalents, and it should be assumed that the pediatrics department always employs only the minimum number of required full-time equivalent personnel.

Annual salaries for each class of employee follow: supervising nurses, $18,000; nurses, $13,000; and aides, $5,000. Salary expense for the year ended June 30, 19X3, for supervising nurses, nurses, and aides was $72,000, $169,000, and $110,000, respectively.

The pediatrics department operated at 100% capacity during 111 days for the past year. It is estimated that during 90 of these capacity days, the demand averaged 17 patients more than capacity and even went as high as 20 patients more on some days. The hospital has an additional 20 beds available for rent for the year ending June 30, 19X4.

Required

1 Calculate the minimum number of patient days required for the pediatrics department to break even for the year ending June 30, 19X4, if the additional 20 beds are not rented. Patient demand is unknown, but assume that revenue per patient day, expense per patient day, expense per bed, and employee salary rates will remain the same as for the year ended June 30, 19X3.

2 Assuming for purposes of this problem that patient demand, revenue per patient day, expense per patient day, expense per bed, and employee

salary rates for the year ending June 30, 19X4 remain the same as for the year ended June 30, 19X3, should the pediatrics department rent the additional 20 beds? Show the annual gain or loss from the additional beds.

(CPA)

14-17 Breakeven Target Profit Mr. Calderone started a pizza restaurant in 19X0. For this purpose a building was rented for $400 per month. Two people were hired to work full time at the restaurant and six college students were hired to work 30 hours per week delivering pizza. An outside accountant was hired to provide tax and bookkeeping services for $300 per month. The necessary restaurant equipment and delivery cars were purchased with cash. Mr. Calderone has noticed that expenses for utilities and supplies have been rather constant.

Mr. Calderone increased his business between 19X0 and 19X3. Profits have more than doubled since 19X0. Mr. Calderone does not understand why his profits have increased faster than his volume.

A projected income statement for 19X4 has been prepared by the accountant and is shown below:

CALDERONE COMPANY
Projected Income Statement
For the Year Ended December 31, 19X4

Sales		$95,000
Cost of food sold	$28,500	
Wages and fringe benefits of restaurant help	8,150	
Wages and fringe benefits of delivery people	17,300	
Rent	4,800	
Accounting services	3,600	
Depreciation of delivery equipment	5,000	
Depreciation of restaurant equipment	3,000	
Utilities	2,325	
Supplies (soap, floor wax, etc.)	1,200	73,875
Net income before taxes		21,125
Income taxes		6,338
Net income		$14,787

Note: The average pizza sells for $5.00. Assume that Mr. Calderone pays 30% of his income in income taxes.

Required

1 What is the breakeven point in number of pizzas that must be sold?

2 Mr. Calderone would like an after-tax net income of $20,000. What volume must be reached in number of pizzas in order to obtain the desired income?

3 Briefly explain to Mr. Calderone why his profits have increased at a faster rate than his sales.

(CMA)

14-18 Cost-Volume-Profit Analysis with Multiple Products Hewtex Electronics manufactures two products—tape recorders and electronic calculators—and sells them nationally to wholesalers and retailers. The Hewtex management is very pleased with the company's performance for the current fiscal year. Projected sales through December 31, 19X7, indicate that 70,000 tape recorders and 140,000 electronic calculators will be sold this year. The projected earnings statement, which appears below, shows that Hewtex will exceed its earnings goal of 9% on sales after taxes.

The tape recorder business has been fairly stable the last few years, and the company does not intend to change the price of this product. However, the competition among manufacturers of electronic calculators has been increasing. Hewtex's calculators have been very popular with consumers. In order to sustain this interest in their calculators and to meet the price reductions expected from competitors, management has decided to reduce the wholesale price of its calculator from $22.50 to $20.00 per unit effective January 1, 19X8. At the time the company plans to spend an additional $57,000 on advertising during fiscal year 19X8. As a consequence of these actions, management estimates that 80% of its total revenue will be derived from calculator sales as compared to 75% in 19X7. As in prior years, the sales mix is assumed to be the same at all volume levels.

The total fixed overhead will not change in 19X8, nor will the variable overhead rates (applied on a direct labor hour base). However, the cost of materials and direct labor is expected to change.

Hewtex estimates that material costs will drop 10% for the tape recorders and 20% for the calculators in 19X8. However, direct labor rates for both products will increase 10% in the coming year.

HEWTEX ELECTRONICS
Projected Earnings Statement
For the Year Ended December 31, 19X7

	Tape Recorders		Electronic Calculators		
	Total Amount (000 Omitted)	Per Unit	Total Amount (000 Omitted)	Per Unit	Total (000 Omitted)
Sales	$1,050	$15.00	$3,150	$22.50	$4,200.0
Production costs					
Materials	$ 280	$ 4.00	$ 630	$ 4.50	$ 910.0
Direct labor	140	2.00	420	3.00	560.0
Variable overhead	140	2.00	280	2.00	420.0
Fixed overhead	70	1.00	210	1.50	280.0
Total production costs	$ 630	$ 9.00	$1,540	$11.00	$2,170.0
Gross margin	$ 420	$ 6.00	$1,610	$11.50	$2,030.0
Fixed selling and administrative expense					1,040.0
Net income before income taxes					$ 990.0
Income taxes (55%)					544.5
Net income					$ 445.5

Required

1 How many tape recorder and electronic calculator units did Hewtex Electronics have to sell in 19X7 to break even?

2 What volume of sales is required if Hewtex Electronics is to earn a net income after taxes in 19X8 which is 15% higher than the 19X7 profit after taxes?

3. How many tape recorder and electronic calculator units will Hewtex have to sell in 19X8 to break even?

(CMA)

14-19 Contribution Margin Calculation for Multiple Products Pralina Products Company is a regional firm which has three major product lines—cereals, breakfast bars, and dog food. The income statement was prepared by product line using full costing.

PRALINA PRODUCTS COMPANY
Income Statement
For the Year Ended April 30, 19X8
(000 omitted)

	Cereals	Breakfast Bars	Dog Food	Total
Sales in pounds	2,000	500	500	3,000
Revenue from sales	$1,000	$400	$200	$1,600
Cost of goods sold				
Direct materials	$ 330	$160	$100	$ 590
Direct labor	90	40	20	150
Factory overhead	108	48	24	180
Total cost of goods sold	$ 528	$248	$144	$ 920
Gross margin	$ 472	$152	$ 56	$ 680
Operating expenses				
Selling expenses				
Advertising	$ 50	$ 30	$ 20	$ 100
Commissions	50	40	20	110
Salaries and related benefits	30	20	10	60
Total selling expenses	$ 130	$ 90	$ 50	$ 270
General and administrative expenses				
Licenses	$ 50	$ 20	$ 15	$ 85
Salaries and related benefits	60	25	15	100
Total general and administrative expenses	$ 110	$ 45	$ 30	$ 185
Total operating expenses	$ 240	$135	$ 80	$ 455
Operating income before taxes	$ 232	$ 17	$ (24)	$ 225

Other Data

1 *Cost of goods sold* The company's inventories of direct materials and finished products do not vary significantly from year to year. The

inventories at April 30, 19X8 were essentially identical to those at April 30, 19X7.

Factory overhead was applied to products at 120% of direct labor dollars. The actual factory overhead costs for the 19X7–X8 fiscal year were as follows:

Variable indirect labor and supplies	$15,000
Variable employee benefits on factory labor	30,000
Supervisory salaries and related benefits	35,000
Plant occupancy costs	100,000
	$180,000

There was no overapplied or underapplied overhead at year-end.

2 *Advertising* The company has been unable to determine any direct causal relationship between the level of sales volume and the level of advertising expenditures. However, because management believes advertising is necessary, an annual advertising program is implemented for each product line. Each product line is advertised independently of the others.

3 *Commissions* Sales commissions are paid to the salesforce at the rates of 5% on the cereals and 10% on the breakfast bars and dog food.

4 *Licenses* Various licenses are required for each product line. These are renewed annually for each product line.

5 *Salaries and related benefits* Sales and general and administrative personnel devote time and effort to all product lines. Their salaries and wages are allocated on the basis of management's estimates of time spent on each product line.

Required

1 The controller of Pralina Products Company has recommended that the company do a cost-volume-profit analysis of its operations. As a first step the controller has requested that you prepare a revised income statement for Pralina Products Company that employs product contribution margin format which will be useful in cost-volume-profit analysis. The statement should show the profit contribution for each product line and the operating income before taxes for the company as a whole.

2 Calculate the breakeven in sales dollars for 19X8.

3 What volume of sales dollars is necessary to achieve a 19X9 operating income before taxes 20% higher than in 19X8 assuming the revenue, cost and product mix patterns as in 19X8?

(CMA)

14-20 Unit Cost Computation and Breakeven Metal Industries, Inc., operates its production department only when orders are received for one or both of its two products, two sizes of metal discs. The manufacturing process begins with the cutting of doughnut-shaped rings from rectangular strips of sheet metal; these rings are then pressed into discs. The sheets of metal, each 4 feet long and weighing 32 ounces, are purchased at $1.36 per running foot. The department has been operating at a loss for the past year as shown below.

Sales for the year	$172,000
Expenses	177,200
Net loss for the department	$ 5,200

The following information is available.

1 Ten thousand 4-foot pieces of metal yielded 40,000 large discs, each weighing 4 ounces and selling for $2.90, and 40,000 small discs, each weighing 2.4 ounces and selling for $1.40.

2 The corporation has been producing at less than "normal capacity" and has had no spoilage in the cutting step of the process. The skeletons remaining after the rings have been cut are sold for scrap at $.80 per pound.

3 The variable conversion cost of each large disc is 80% of the disc's direct materials cost and variable conversion cost of each small disc is 75% of the disc's direct materials cost. Variable conversion costs are the sum of direct labor and variable overhead.

4 Fixed costs were $86,000.

Required

1 For each of the parts manufactured, prepare a schedule computing:
  a Material cost per unit after deducting the value of salvage
  b Variable conversion cost per unit
  c Contribution margin per unit
  d Total contribution margin for all units sold

2 Compute the number of units the corporation must sell to break even. Assume no spoiled units and a product mix of one large disc to each small disc.

(CPA)

15 RELEVANT COSTS AND NONRECURRING DECISIONS

AFTER COMPLETING YOUR STUDY OF THIS CHAPTER, YOU SHOULD HAVE LEARNED:

1 The management accountant's role in nonrecurring decisions.

2 What we mean by "special order," and how managers use relevant cost concepts to calculate the change in profits which result from accepting a special order.

3 How to calculate and use relevant costs in the make or buy decision.

4 How relevant cost concepts are used to analyze data to decide whether to add or drop a product line.

5 How to analyze whether multiple products should be sold at the split-off point or processed further to increase total income.

Managerial accountants assemble the relevant information to aid management in decision making.

Managers need information to make decisions, or more specifically to determine the change in profit which will result from each of several alternative courses of action. If the decision will change both revenues and expenses, managers must estimate the changes in each to estimate the change in profit. In many decisions only expenses will change. In this case the most profitable decision will be the one with the lowest expense. Managers compare the expenses of one alternative against the expenses of another. The managerial accountant provides the revenue and expense information. The obvious question at this point is: How does the managerial accountant know what information a manager will need to make decisions? The answer is *relevance*. The managerial accountant reports information based on its relevance to the particular management decision. We will discuss relevance in more detail soon. But remember that in Chapter 1 relevance emphasized the *changes* in revenue or expense resulting from a particular decision because the only way profit can be changed is by changing revenue or expense. This chapter will apply the concept of relevance to the kinds of decisions which are called nonrecurring decisions.

Routine planning and control decisions recur with a regular frequency. Nonrecurring decisions do not recur in any systematic time sequence. An example of a recurring decision is when management has to determine each month the quantity of each product to produce based on expected demand and desired finished goods inventory levels. Some examples of decisions that are nonrecurring are:

1 We have been presented with a special large order for our product below our normal selling price. Should we accept or reject the order?
2 We are currently buying a part from an outside supplier. Some of our facilities are idle. Should we make the part ourselves?
3 Should we sell a multiple product at the split-off point? Or process it further?
4 Should we discontinue one of several product lines?
5 Should we add a new product line?

Decisions like these generally do not occur regularly. Rather they are opportunities presented to management as they arise throughout the year. The managerial accountant plays a vital role in these decisions because he assembles the relevant information management will use to make each decision.

We will first review the concept of relevant "costs" and then illustrate it in some practical examples. Finally, we will illustrate the use of relevant costs in analyzing several important nonrecurring decisions.

RELEVANT COSTS

In Chapter 1 we discussed how reporting issues of information for managerial decision making were resolved. **Relevant costs** were defined in Chapter 1 as information that will affect the accomplishment of the objectives of the decision maker and will change as a result of the decision. (Of course, the concept of relevance applies not only to costs but to revenue as well. So, whatever we say about how costs are relevant to a particular decision, we are also concerned about revenues relevant to that decision.) In the discussion that follows we shall use the term cost in the broad relevant cost sense of any revenues and expenses which will change as a result of a current decision.

The definition of relevant costs implies two important characteristics:

Characteristics of relevant costs.

1 Relevant costs are costs *not* yet incurred.

2 Relevant costs change as a result of a particular current *decision* (made before the costs are incurred).

Relevant costs are future costs.

The first characteristic of a relevant cost: The cost is related to a decision which will change something which will occur in the future. Decisions are based on what management expects to occur in the future, not what has occurred in the past. *Therefore,* relevant costs for decision-making can be considered as future costs. For example, a marketing manager is considering eliminating a product line. The marketing manager's decision will be based on the *future* demand, *future* selling price, *future* manufacturing costs, and *future* marketing expenses of the product line. The historical product costs are not relevant to this decision—those costs occurred in the past. However, historical costs can be and are used to make estimates of the future costs.

Relevant costs differ depending on the circumstances.

The second characteristic of a relevant cost: The cost can be affected by the result of a particular decision. If management is considering the purchase of materials from two different suppliers and the price is $3.50 per pound from both suppliers, then the price of the materials is not relevant. Because the price is the same from each supplier, the purchase decision most likely would be based on such nonprice considerations as the reliability of the supplier in meeting delivery dates and the financial stability of the supplier. However, if the price is $3.40 per pound from one supplier and $3.50 per pound from the other supplier, the materials price is relevant to the purchase decision. The important point here is that if the price is *different* between alternatives, it is relevant to management's decision. If the price is not different between alternatives, it is not relevant.

In the following sections of this chapter we discuss how the concept of relevant costs is used by the managerial accountant to analyze several nonrecurring decisions.

SPECIAL ORDERS AND CAPACITY UTILIZATION

Often a company has idle productive capacity. When a plant is built or equipment purchased, it usually has the capacity to meet peak demands for several years into the future. To build only for current needs would require continuous expansion. In such cases management may be asked to consider producing a special order of a product to be sold at a price below the normal selling price for that product. Given these idle facilities, management in many companies might be willing to consider producing a special order of product to be sold below the normal selling price—provided that such a special order will not affect the regular sales of the same product.

To illustrate the cost analysis for such a special order, consider the following facts:

> The Blair Company has capacity to manufacture 200,000 CB radios per year. Based on evaluations of past sales and future trends, during the coming year, 19X1, they expect to manufacture 140,000 radios and sell them for $100 each through their regular marketing channels. The manufacturing costs for the year are expected to be $3,000,000 fixed and $40 per unit variable. The marketing expenses are expected to be $2,000,000 fixed plus $12 per unit variable.

EXHIBIT 15-1
BLAIR COMPANY
Budgeted Income Statement
For the Year 19X1

	Per Unit	Total
Sales 140,000 units	$100.00	$14,000,000
Variable expenses		
Manufacturing	40.00	5,600,000
Marketing	12.00	1,680,000
Contribution margin	$ 48.00	$ 6,720,000
Fixed expenses		
Manufacturing	21.43	3,000,000
Marketing	14.29	2,000,000
Net income	$ 12.28	$ 1,720,000

A lower than normal price may be attractive if the company has idle capacity.

As you can see, the Blair Company will have an excess productive capacity of 60,000 radios. Along comes a discount chain which offers to purchase from the Blair Company 30,000 radios at a price of $70 each. The discount chain expects to pay all shipping expenses. Now one of the important things to consider about this special offer is that there will be no regular marketing expenses. That is, there will be no variable marketing expenses. After all, the discount chain has approached the Blair Company and offered to purchase 30,000 radios. The Blair Company does not have to spend any money to sell these radios.

Blair management believes that this order will have no adverse effect on the sales made through regular marketing channels—Blair will sell the 140,000 radios whether or not it accepts this special order to produce an additional 30,000 radios. However, if the order is not accepted, there will be 60,000 units of idle capacity.

Without the special order the Blair Company expects to earn a profit of $12.28 per unit or a net income of $1,720,000 as shown in Exhibit 15-1.

On the surface it appears that management will be reluctant to accept this special order. As you can calculate from the exhibit, the total cost per unit to manufacture and market the CB radios is ($40.00 + $12.00 + $21.43 + $14.29) or $83.72. This total cost per unit is greater than the purchase offer of $70 per unit.

Is the decision as simple as it seems here? Or is there something else the Blair Company should evaluate to determine whether to accept the special order?

For the Blair Company to make an informed decision whether to accept or reject the special order, the accountant must determine the relevant costs, that is, the revenues and expenses that will change as a result of this special order. How will the expenses, revenues, and profit shown in Exhibit 15-1 change as a result of accepting the special order?

Exhibit 15-2 shows how. In this case, the relevant costs are the revenue and variable manufacturing expenses. They result in a $900,000 increase in net income. The variable marketing expenses are irrelevant because they will be the same

EXHIBIT 15-2
BLAIR COMPANY
Comparative Income Statements
For Special Order of CB Radios
($000)

		140,000 Units without Special Order		170,000 Units with Special Order	Difference
Revenues	(140 @ $100)	$14,000	(140 @ $100 + 30 @ $70)	$16,100	$2,100
Variable expenses					
Manufacturing	(140 @ $40)	5,600	(170 @ $40)	6,800	1,200
Marketing	(140 @ $12)	1,680	(140 @ $12)	1,680	0
Contribution margin		$ 6,720		$ 7,620	$ 900
Fixed expenses					
Manufacturing		3,000		3,000	0
Marketing		2,000		2,000	0
Net income		$ 1,720		$ 2,620	$ 900

whether management accepts or rejects the special order since the discount chain is willing to pay all shipping expenses and Blair Company will not incur any variable marketing expenses on the special order. Both the fixed manufacturing and marketing expenses are irrelevant to the decision. These expenses are irrelevant because they also will not change with management's decision.

Alternative Reporting Format

Exhibit 15-2 illustrated the profit impact of the special order by comparing income statements with and without the special order. Depending on management's preference, the accountant will sometimes prepare an analysis showing only the relevant costs as illustrated in Exhibit 15-3. Only the revenue and expense changes

EXHIBIT 15-3
BLAIR COMPANY
Relevant Revenue and Expense
For Special Order of CB Radios

Revenues 30,000 units @ $70	$2,100,000
Variable manufacturing expense 30,000 units @ $40	1,200,000
Differential income	$ 900,000

which will result from accepting the special order appear in the exhibit. Whether the data are presented as comparative income statements or as only relevant costs will depend on management's preference.

Beware of Unit Fixed Expense

In analyzing these decisions we must be careful how we handle fixed expenses. We noted above that the fixed expenses were irrelevant because they did not change as a result of the decision. Note that it was the *total* fixed expenses that did not change. We have to keep this in mind, because the per unit fixed expense does change and this should not be misinterpreted in making a decision.

For nonrecurring decisions, it is best to analyze total fixed costs to determine their relevance to the decision.

Without the special order the per unit manufacturing fixed expense is $21.43 ($3,000,000/140,000).

With the special order the per unit fixed manufacturing expense is $17.65 ($3,000,000/170,000).

However, this change in the per unit fixed manufacturing expense is irrelevant because the Blair Company will incur the same amount of *total* fixed expense regardless of the decision. The total fixed expense is used to determine the change in net income. Thus, in analyzing nonrecurring decisions like this special order, it is important to compare total fixed expense rather than unit fixed expenses in order to determine relevance.

Other Factors in the Decision

In determining whether Blair Company should accept or reject the special order, management must consider factors other than just the immediate impact on income. Blair management believed that the special order would not have any effect on Blair Company's sales to their regular customers. However, if any of the regular customers discover the terms of the special order, they might demand a price reduction or seek another source of supply. Some customers who would have bought from the usual retailers may buy from the discount chain, and sales which would have brought in $100 revenue will bring only $70 per unit.

Other factors that can influence the special-order decision.

The Robinson-Patman Act forbids the quotation of different prices to competing customers unless the price difference can be justified by reduced manufacturing and/or marketing costs related to the specific customer. This act relates to *competing* customers for the *same* product. This act does not apply to situations where idle capacity is used to produce for a noncompeting market or where idle capacity is used to produce other than regular products.

Both of these considerations may lead Blair to reject the special order even though it would add to profit. Perhaps some modification of the product and sale under the discounter's own brand name would help meet both problems.

MAKE OR BUY DECISIONS

Quite frequently when manufacturing companies find that a portion of their production facilities is expected to be idle, they will consider manufacturing a part or subassembly they are currently purchasing from an outside supplier. For example, should Ford Motor Company use idle capacity to manufacture their own bumper shocks or should they buy them from General Motors? Should a watch manufacturer use idle capacity to produce its own watch bands or buy them from an outside supplier?

When situations like these arise, the accountant is often asked to provide an analysis comparing the cost of making the part "in house" with the cost of purchasing the part. To do this analysis the accountant identifies the relevant costs: the costs that would change as a result of the decision to make the part rather than buy it from an outside supplier.

To illustrate the analysis for a make or buy decision, assume a company is currently purchasing 20,000 parts from an outside contractor at $34 per part. If the company manufactures the part the inventory cost will be the following.

	Cost/Part	Total Cost 20,000 Parts
Direct materials	$12	$240,000
Direct labor	10	200,000
Variable overhead	6	120,000
Fixed overhead	8	160,000
	$36	$720,000

Comparing the total "in house" manufacturing cost of $720,000 with the $680,000 (20,000 parts @ $34) purchase cost, it appears on the surface that the company should purchase the part.

However, before presenting the data to management the managerial accountant should examine the facts underlying the $160,000 of fixed overhead charged to the 20,000 parts. Suppose that $60,000 of the $160,000 fixed overhead cost represents existing costs such as depreciation on the building, property taxes, and insurance that the company will incur regardless of whether the company makes or buys the part. These fixed costs are **unavoidable expenses,** independent of management's decision in this particular matter. The other $100,000 of fixed overhead costs represents **avoidable expenses;** if the company buys the part, they will not be incurred (management does not make the part). These might be costs such as supervision salaries, indirect labor costs, and the costs of special dies and jigs necessary to produce this particular part. Because these fixed costs are avoidable (they will change) if the company buys the part, they are relevant costs. Assuming the company's only alternatives for the idle facilities are either to make the part or leave the facilities idle, the analysis of the relevant costs are as follows:

Analysis of the relevant costs for the make or buy decision.

	Make		Buy		Difference
	Cost/ Part	Total Cost 20,000 Parts	Cost/ Part	Total Cost 20,000 Parts	Make Minus Buy
Direct materials	$12	$240,000	—	—	$240,000
Direct labor	10	200,000	—	—	200,000
Variable overhead	6	120,000	—	—	120,000
Fixed overhead	5	100,000	—	—	100,000
Purchase price	—	—	$34	$680,000	−680,000
Total costs	$33	$660,000	$34	$680,000	−$ 20,000

Comparing the total manufacturing cost of the $660,000 with the $680,000 purchase cost, the company should use its idle facilities to manufacture the part.

Let us take this analysis of relevant costs one step further. What would the decision be if the volume were reduced to 15,000 parts? The total manufacturing cost would be:

Volume can be an important factor in the make or buy decision.

	Make		Buy		Difference
	Cost/ Part	Total Cost 15,000 Parts	Cost/ Part	Total Cost 15,000 Parts	Make Minus Buy
Direct materials	$12	$180,000	—	—	$180,000
Direct labor	10	150,000	—	—	150,000
Variable overhead	6	90,000	—	—	90,000
Fixed overhead	6.67	100,000	—	—	100,000
Purchase price	—	—	$34	$510,000	−510,000
Total costs	$34.67	$520,000	$34	$510,000	+$ 10,000

Comparing the total manufacturing cost of $520,000 with the purchase cost of $510,000 (15,000 × $34), the company should purchase the part. What happened here is that the reduction in the number of parts produced did not decrease the total fixed cost. Hence, when fixed costs are relevant, volume is a relevant factor to be considered in make or buy cost analysis.

Through the use of *cost-volume* analysis, we can determine the number of parts the company must produce to be indifferent between buying the part and making the part. In other words, we can calculate a kind of "breakeven" volume where the total cost of buying is equal to the total cost of making the parts. We will refer to this level of volume as the **indifference cost volume.** To calculate the indifference cost volume, we set the mathematical representation of the total cost of making the part equal to the mathematical representation of the total cost of buying the part.

At the indifference cost volume, management is indifferent between buying and making the part.

To illustrate, let X represent volume, and the per part purchase cost is $34, from our example. If the company buys the part from the outside supplier, the total purchase cost will be:

Total buy cost = $34X

This mathematical representation for buying the part contains no fixed costs, only variable costs—the purchase price per part.

If the company decides to manufacture the part, the total manufacturing cost will be:

Total make cost = $100,000 + $28X

The total manufactured cost depends on the relevant fixed overhead of $100,000 as well as these per part costs: variable direct materials ($12), variable direct labor ($10), and variable overhead ($6) which together amount to $28 per part.

To determine the volume where the company would be indifferent to making

Computing the indifference cost volume.

versus buying the part, the two cost functions are set equal to each other and solved for X. For this example:

$$\begin{aligned} \text{Total make cost} &= \text{total buy cost} \\ \$100{,}000 + \$28X &= \$34X \\ \$100{,}000 &= \$\ 6X \\ 16{,}667 \text{ parts} &= X \end{aligned}$$

The indifference cost volume is 16,667 parts, which tells us that if the expected volume is higher, the company should make the part; if expected volume is lower, the company should buy it.

Exhibit 15-4 graphically illustrates the indifference cost volume for this make or buy decision. The cost function for buying the part, $34X, starts at zero cost and increases at a rate of $34 per part purchased. The cost function for making the part, $100,000 + $28X, starts at a fixed cost of $100,000 and increases at a rate of $28 per part. The two cost functions cross at 16,667 parts. If the expected volume is below 16,667 parts, buying the part would be the alternative with the least total costs. If the expected volume is above 16,667 parts, making the part would incur the least total costs.

Qualitative Factors

The above analysis only considered the quantitative factors of the make or buy decision. That is, we only analyzed the monetary amounts involved in the decision. As in the special-order decision, qualitative factors—nonmonetary factors—sometimes dominate management's make or buy decision. For example, a management

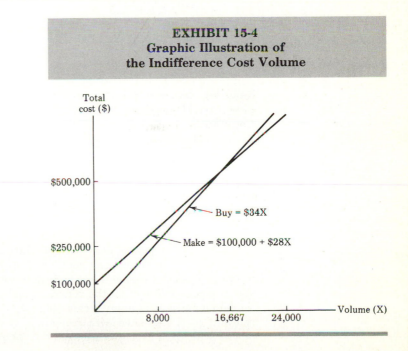

EXHIBIT 15-4
Graphic Illustration of the Indifference Cost Volume

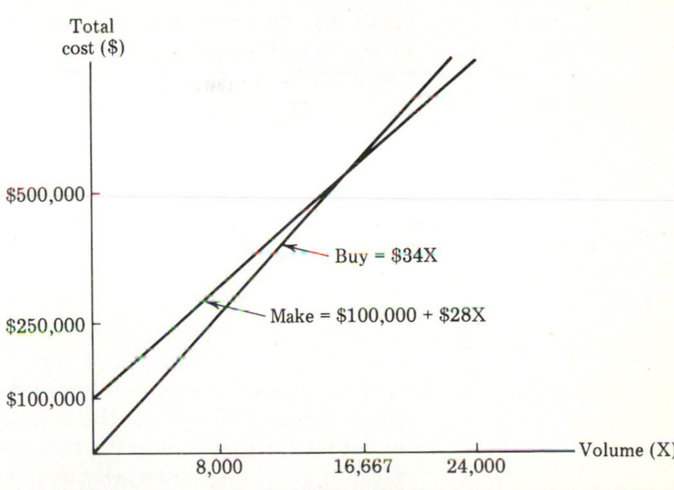

may have established a good relationship with a particular supplier and will want to maintain that relationship. Thus, management may prefer to buy, even if buying is a bit more costly. Furthermore, most suppliers prefer to be able to fill a regular pattern of orders from buyers. That is, suppliers will be more responsive to companies that buy regular amounts on a regular basis rather than companies that buy unusual amounts, either very large or very small amounts, sporadically. Customers who order parts from suppliers when business is good and make their own parts when business is slack may have a difficult time obtaining their required parts when they need them most. In some situations, having a reliable outside supplier when business is good is worth the additional costs the company will incur buying the parts during slack business periods.

Nonmonetary factors that influence the make or buy decision.

On the other hand, managements who want to exert better control over the quality of parts might manufacture them rather than buy even if the cost to buy them from a supplier is lower.

ADDING OR DROPPING PRODUCTS

As consumers' preferences change, products can become obsolete and have to be dropped from the company's product line. At the same time new products are developed and added to the company's product line. An important factor in the decision to add or drop a product is whether it will increase or decrease the future income of the company. To assess the change in income, the managerial accountant must determine the relevant costs.

The change in future income is an important factor in management's decision to add or drop a product line.

To illustrate the analysis for the addition or deletion of a product, consider the income statement for the Super Y Drugstore given below:

	Super Y Drugstore: Product Lines			
	Drugs	Cosmetics	General Merchandise	Total
Sales revenue	$50,000	$25,000	$25,000	$100,000
Less: variable expenses	25,000	10,000	12,000	47,000
Contribution margin	$25,000	$15,000	$13,000	$ 53,000
Less: fixed expenses				
Avoidable	$10,000	$ 8,000	$11,000	$ 29,000
Unavoidable	3,000	3,000	3,000	9,000
Total fixed expenses	$13,000	$11,000	$14,000	$ 38,000
Net income (loss)	$12,000	$ 4,000	($ 1,000)	$ 15,000

Super Y Drugstore has three product lines: drugs, cosmetics, and general merchandise. The income statement for Super Y Drugstore shows total net income of $15,000, which includes a loss of $1,000 from the sale of general merchandise. On the surface it appears that the general merchandise product line should be dropped. To help management analyze this issue, the managerial accountant determines the relevant costs associated with dropping general merchandise. In making decisions of this type, fixed expenses are classified as avoidable or unavoidable.

Avoidable expenses are those expenses that will not be incurred if one alternative is chosen, in this case if the product line is eliminated. For the general merchandise product line of Super Y Drugstore, avoidable fixed expenses include salaries of employees assigned entirely to the general merchandise department and advertising expenses incurred solely for the benefit of general merchandise.

Unavoidable fixed expenses are those expenses that are independent of the decision and will continue to be incurred if the product line is eliminated. For Super Y Drugstore this would include expenses such as the salary of the store general manager, rent expense, and utilities expense allocated to this product line.

Now, back to the question: Should Super Y Drugstore drop the general merchandise product line? In answering this question, let us assume that if the general merchandise product line is dropped the store space will be idle.

If the general merchandise product line is dropped, net income will decrease by $2,000 as shown below:

Analysis of relevant costs to evaluate whether to drop a product line.

	Super Y Drugstore in Total		
	(1) Keep General Merchandise	(2) Drop General Merchandise	(1 − 2) Difference
Sales revenue	$100,000	$75,000	$25,000
Less: variable expenses	47,000	35,000	12,000
Contribution margin	$ 53,000	$40,000	$13,000
Less: fixed expenses			
Avoidable	29,000	18,000	11,000
Unavoidable	9,000	9,000	-0-
Total fixed expenses	$ 38,000	$27,000	$11,000
Net income	$ 15,000	$13,000	$ 2,000

The above analysis shows that the general merchandise product line contributes $13,000 toward covering its avoidable fixed expenses. The $13,000 of contribution margin more than covers the $11,000 of avoidable fixed expenses associated with general merchandise.

This analysis shows that Super Y Drugstore should not drop the general merchandise product line unless a more profitable use could be found for the space that general merchandise occupied in the store.

MULTIPLE PRODUCT DECISIONS

The manufacturing process in some firms is such that multiple products are produced from a single set of inputs. The multiple products are classified as either joint products or by-products. In Chapter 7, we discussed how joint costs and separable costs are assigned to each multiple product. Joint costs are the manufacturing costs incurred prior to the separation of the multiple products and benefit all products. Separable costs are the manufacturing costs incurred after the multiple products are separated and benefit only one of the products.

Types of multiple product decisions.

In this chapter, we are interested in the relevance of joint costs and separable costs for multiple product decisions. Basically, we are interested in two types of multiple product decisions: those affecting all the products and those affecting the further processing of a single product.

Sell at Split-Off Point? Or Process Further?

The decision as to whether a product should be sold at the split-off point or processed further (with the incurrence of further costs) is faced by many manufacturers. For example, in the meat-packing industry cowhides can be sold at the split-off point as unprocessed animal hide or the cowhides can be processed for the removal of undesirable constituents, treated with tannin, and finished into leather for sale to shoe manufacturers. Whether the cowhides are sold at the split-off point or after further processing depends on the profitability of the additional processing.

Sometimes manufacturers producing multiple products are selling them at the split-off point and a change in market conditions will cause the manufacturer to evaluate whether it might be more profitable to process the products beyond the split-off point. To make this kind of decision the relevant costs are only those related to the additional processing of each product beyond the split-off point. The joint costs are not relevant to the further processing decision.

To illustrate the relevant costs for the sell at the split-off point or process further decision, consider the following situation:

Assume a joint cost of $5,000 is incurred in processing 1,500 gallons of materials that yields at split-off 900 gallons of product X and 600 gallons of product Y.

For product X: further processing at a cost of $1.50 per gallon is necessary to prepare it for shipment to customers. After this additional processing, X is sold for $6.00 per gallon.

For product Y: no additional processing is required; it is sold at the split-off point for $3.00 per gallon. This situation can be represented in a diagram as follows:

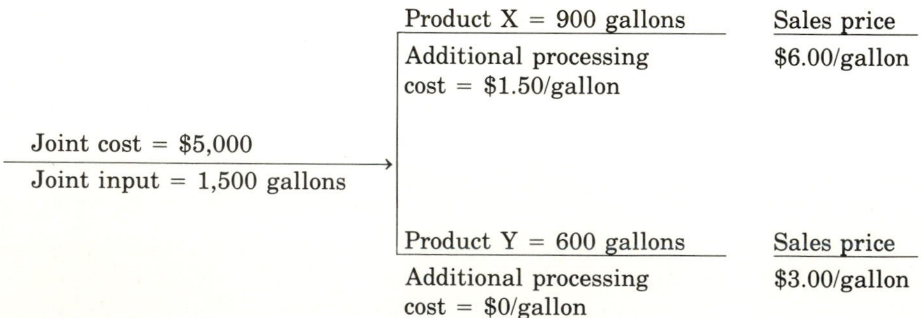

The profit from the multiple products sold as described above is $850 as shown on the following page.

	Product X	Product Y	Total
Sales	(900 × $6.00) = $5,400	(600 × $3) $1,800	$7,200
Additional processing cost	(900 × $1.50) = 1,350	0	1,350
Profit before joint cost	$4,050	$1,800	$5,850
Joint cost			$5,000
Profit			$ 850

Now assume that a new market has been identified for product Y. The selling price in this new market is $4.00 per gallon. To prepare product Y for the new market, additional processing costs of $.50 per gallon will have to be incurred. If the company enters the new market, profit will increase over the $850 by $300 as shown below:

Joint costs are not relevant to decisions affecting a single product.

Product Y: Additional Profit

	Per Unit	Total
Additional revenue ($4.00 − $3.00) per unit	$1.00 × 600 gallons =	$600
(less) Additional cost	.50 × 600 gallons =	300
(equals) Additional profit	$ .50 × 600 gallons =	$300
Decision: Process Y for the new market.		

Note that the joint costs are irrelevant to the decision about what to do with product Y after separation. The joint costs do not change whether product Y is sold at the split-off point or processed further. An extended comparison of profit from selling product Y after additional processing with the profit from selling it at the split-off point is shown below:

	Sell Y After Additional Processing			Sell Y at Split-Off	
	Product X	Product Y	Total	Total*	Difference
Sales	(900 × $6) $5,400	(600 × $4) $2,400	$7,800	$7,200	$600
Additional processing costs	(900 × $1.50) 1,350	(600 × $.50) 300	1,650	1,350	300
Profit before joint costs	$4,050	$2,100	$6,150	$5,850	$300
Joint costs			5,000	5,000	0
Profit			$1,150	$ 850	$300

* From first calculation for this example.

Note that to analyze the relevant costs for this decision, it was not necessary to consider joint costs. The two relevant costs are the increase in revenue and the increased cost to process product Y for the new market.

Decisions Affecting All Multiple Products

To illustrate the relevant costs when all multiple products are being evaluated consider the following situation.[1]

> Assume the Jopo Company's manufacturing process is such that 1 unit of input X processed in department I will yield 3 units of product A and 2 units of product B. Also assume that only 40,000 units of material X can be acquired per month.
>
> The fixed costs of department I total \$500,000 per month and the variable operation cost in department I is \$2.00 per unit of X processed.
>
> Product A can either be sold at the point of split-off for \$8.00 per unit or processed further in department II at a cost of \$6.00 per unit and then sold at a price of \$15.00 per unit.
>
> Product B can be sold for \$7.00 at the split-off point or processed further in department III at a cost of \$4.00 per unit and then sold for \$10.00 per unit.
>
> These facts are summarized in Exhibit 15-5 in the form of a diagram.

EXHIBIT 15-5
Diagram for the Products of Jopo Company

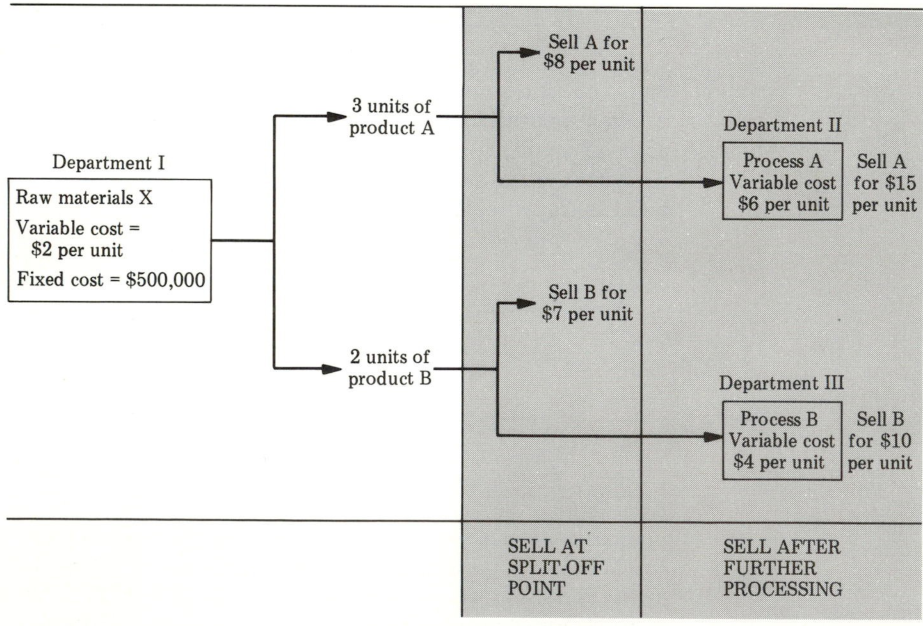

[1] The following example is based on R. Hartley, "Decision Making with Joint Products," *Accounting Review* (October 1971), pp. 746–755.

To decide whether all the products or none of the products should be produced, management compares *total* revenues with *total* costs for each of the possible alternatives represented in the diagram in Exhibit 15-5.

First, management must decide whether each of the products should be sold at the split-off point or processed further. The calculations for this decision (as shown below) require only the additional revenues and additional costs associated with processing products A and B beyond the split-off point.

Product A

Additional revenue per unit ($15 − $8)	$7.00
(less) Additional cost per unit in department II	6.00
(equals) Additional profit per unit	$1.00

Decision: Product A is most profitable if processed further and sold for $15.

Product B

Additional revenue per unit ($10 − $7)	$3.00
(less) Additional cost per unit in department III	4.00
(equals) Additional loss per unit	($1.00)

Decision: Product B is most profitable if sold at the split-off point.

After determining the most profitable point to sell each of the two products, the profit before joint costs is calculated and compared with the joint costs incurred in department I. Since only 40,000 units of X are available, the maximum yield of department I will be 120,000 units of A (40,000 × 3) and 80,000 units of B (40,000 × 2). The calculations are as follows:

Analysis of whether to produce all of the multiple products.

		Product A		Product B	Total
Sales	(120,000 × $15)	$1,800,000	(80,000 × $7)	$560,000	$2,360,000
Additional processing costs	(120,000 × $6)	720,000		0	720,000
Profit before joint costs		$1,080,000		$560,000	$1,640,000
Joint costs			($500,000 + $2 × 40,000)		580,000
Profit					$1,060,000

Decision: Produce products A and B.

Notice that nowhere in the analysis was the allocation of joint costs to products A and B necessary. The decision whether to sell the products at the split-off point or to process them further considers only the additional revenues and additional costs. The decision to produce the multiple products considers the total revenues and total costs of the products as a group including the joint costs since they are affected by the decision.

SUMMARY

Nonrecurring decisions do not occur on a regular basis; rather they are alternatives presented to management as they arise throughout the year.

Nonrecurring decisions (like all decisions) are evaluated using the concept of relevant costs. Relevant costs (including revenues) are *future* costs that affect the accomplishment of the objectives of the decision maker and will *change* as a result of management's decision.

Most nonrecurring decisions have to do with unused or idle plant capacity. Decisions to accept a special order at a price below the normal selling price should be based only on relevant costs. Make or buy decisions involve choosing between purchasing a part or producing the part with unused or idle capacity.

The change in the future income of the company is an important factor in management's decision to add or drop a product line. In analyzing the data for this decision the managerial accountant classifies expenses as avoidable or unavoidable. Avoidable expenses are those expenses that will not be incurred if the product line is eliminated. Unavoidable expenses are those that are independent of the decision and will continue to be incurred whether or not the product line is eliminated.

Decisions relating to multiple products include (1) should the product be sold at the split-off point or processed further, and (2) should the multiple products be produced? Neither decision requires the allocation of the joint costs.

The relevant costs for the sell at the split-off point or process further decision include the added revenue and added cost of further processing. The joint processing costs are not relevant.

The relevant costs when management is considering production of all or none of the multiple products include the total revenues and total costs for all of the multiple products, including the costs of further processing when analysis shows it to be profitable.

Review Problem

Nubo Manufacturing, Inc., is presently operating at 50% of capacity producing about 50,000 units annually of a patented electronic component. Nubo recently received an offer from a company in Yokohama, Japan, to purchase 30,000 components at $6.00 per unit. The buyer would pay all shipping costs of the finished product. Nubo has not previously sold components in Japan. Budgeted production costs for 50,000 and 80,000 units of output follow:

Units	50,000	80,000
Costs		
Direct materials	$ 75,000	$120,000
Direct labor	75,000	120,000
Factory overhead	200,000	260,000
Total costs	$350,000	$500,000
Cost per unit	$7.00	$6.25

The sales manager thinks the order should be accepted, even if it results in a loss of $1.00 per unit, because he feels the sales may build future markets. The production manager does not wish to have the order accepted primarily because the order would show a loss of $.25 per unit when computed on the new average unit cost. The treasurer has made a quick computation indicating that accepting the order will actually increase profits.

Required

1 Explain what apparently caused the drop in cost from $7.00 per unit to $6.25 per unit when budgeted production increased from 50,000 to 80,000 units. Show supporting computations.

2 a Explain whether (either or both) the production manager or the treasurer is correct in his reasoning.

b Explain why the conclusions of the production manager and the treasurer differ.

3 Explain why each of the following may affect the decision to accept or reject the special order.

a The likelihood of repeat special sales and/or all sales to be made at $6.00 per unit.

b Whether the sales are made to customers operating in two separate, isolated markets or whether the sales are made to customers competing in the same market.

(CPA)

Solution

1 The drop in cost per unit results from the fixed portion of factory overhead. If no costs were fixed, the cost per unit would remain at $7.00 with the increase in the number of units.

Units	50,000	80,000
Variable costs		
Direct materials ($1.50)	$ 75,000	$120,000
Direct labor ($1.50)	75,000	120,000
Variable factory overhead ($2)*	100,000	160,000
Total ($5)	$250,000	$400,000
Fixed costs		
Factory overhead	100,000	100,000
Total cost	$350,000	$500,000

$$\text{Fixed cost per unit } \frac{\$100{,}000}{50{,}000} = \$2 \quad \frac{\$100{,}000}{80{,}000} = 1.25$$

$$\text{* Variable factory overhead} = \frac{\$260{,}000 - \$200{,}000}{80{,}000 - 50{,}000} = \$2 \text{ per unit}$$

Fixed factory overhead = $260,000 − ($2 × 80,000 units) = $100,000

2 a The treasurer is correct since the selling price, $6, exceeds the relevant cost per unit, $5. The fixed overhead costs do not change.

b The production manager erroneously considers the fixed overhead costs a relevant cost, when, in fact, they will not change. The company has excess capacity and the fixed overhead costs will remain the same with the acceptance of the order. The treasurer realizes the relevant costs are $5 with the selling price of $6.

3 a With 50,000 units of excess capacity, the likelihood of repeat special sales orders is quite attractive and may influence Nubo to accept the order.

b If the sales are made to customers operating in isolated markets, the company has more of a tendency to accept the special order. If the special order is to customers in the same market, the special order may affect the current sales and, therefore, would have a tendency to be rejected.

Review Problem

Yardley Corporation uses a joint process to produce products A, B, and C. Each product may be sold at its split-off point or processed further. Additional processing costs are entirely variable and are traceable to the respective products produced. Joint production costs for 19X5 were $50,000. Relevant data follows:

			Sales Values and Additional Costs If Processed Further	
Product	**Units Produced**	**Sales Value at Split-Off**	**Sales Value**	**Additional Costs**
A	20,000	$ 45,000	$60,000	$20,000
B	15,000	75,000	98,000	20,000
C	15,000	30,000	62,000	18,000
		$150,000		

Required To maximize profits, which products should Yardley subject to further processing? Why?

(CPA)

Solution

Product	Additional Revenue	Additional Costs	Additional Income
A	$15,000	$20,000	($ 5,000)
B	23,000	20,000	3,000
C	32,000	18,000	14,000

Answer: Process products B and C further, since the additional processing will result in an increase in profits, as shown above.

Glossary

Avoidable expense Those expenses that will not be incurred if one alternative is chosen. These expenses are relevant to the decision.

Indifference cost volume In a make or buy decision, the volume of parts where the total cost of making is equal to the total cost of buying.

Relevant cost Any cost or revenue that affects the accomplishment of the objectives of the decision maker and will change as a result of a decision.

Unavoidable expense Those expenses that are independent of the decision and will continue to be incurred regardless of management's choice. These expenses are not relevant to the decision.

Questions and Problems

15-1 What is a nonrecurring decision?

15-2 Define avoidable cost.

15-3 Discuss the relevant cost concept.

15-4 Distinguish between a fixed expense and an unavoidable expense.

15-5 What impact does volume of production have on make or buy decisions?

15-6 What qualitative factors might influence a decision maker in deciding whether to make or buy a part?

15-7 Discuss the relevant costs associated with the decisions to sell products at the split-off point or process them further.

15-8 Make or Buy Decision The Harry Bonzale Company is trying to decide whether they should make or buy subassembly XZ101. Currently they have idle capacity that could be used to produce up to 15,000 units of the subassembly. However, their current needs are 10,000 units. A cost analyst has prepared the following estimates for producing the subassembly:

Annual additional set-up and maintenance costs	$15,000 per year
Allocated general factory overhead	10,000 per year
Depreciation on current equipment	20,000 per year
Total fixed costs	$45,000 per year
Direct materials costs	$2.00 per unit
Direct labor	3.00 per unit
Variable overhead	3.00 per unit
Total variable costs	$8.00 per unit

The Specialty Manufacturing Company has offered to sell the subassembly to the Harry Bonzale Company for $10.00 per unit.

Required

1 Should the Harry Bonzale Company make or buy the subassembly?

2 At what volume would Bonzale be indifferent between making or buying the subassembly?

15-9 Sell at Split-Off? Or Process Further? The Cum-Clean Corporation produces a variety of cleaning compounds and solutions for both industrial and household use. While most of its products are processed independently, a few are related.

"Grit 337" is a coarse cleaning powder with many industrial uses. It costs $1.60 a pound to make and has a selling price of $2.00 a pound.

A small portion of the annual production of this product is retained for further processing in the mixing department where it is combined with several other ingredients to form a paste which is marketed as a silver polish selling for $4.00 per jar. This further processing requires ¼ pound of Grit 337 per jar. Other ingredients, labor, and variable overhead associated with this further processing cost $2.50 per jar. Variable selling costs amount to $.30 per jar. If the decision were made to cease production of the silver polish, $5,600 of fixed mixing department costs could be avoided.

Required

Calculate the minimum number of jars of silver polish that would have to be sold to justify further processing of Grit 337.

(CMA)

15-10 Pricing with Idle Capacity E. Berg and Sons build custom-made pleasure boats which range in price from $10,000 to $250,000. For the past 30 years, Mr. Berg, Sr. has determined the selling price of each boat by estimating the costs of materials and labor, allocating a portion of overhead, and adding 20% to these estimated costs.

For example, a recent price quotation was determined as follows:

Direct materials	$ 5,000
Direct labor	8,000
Overhead	2,000
	$15,000
Plus 20%	3,000
Selling price	$18,000

.60 FIXED
.40 VARIABLE

The overhead figure was determined by estimating total overhead costs for the year and allocating them at 25% of direct labor.

If a customer rejected the price and business was slack, Mr. Berg, Sr. would often be willing to reduce his markup to as little as 5% over estimated costs. Thus, average markup for the year is estimated at 15%.

Total overhead which includes selling and administrative expenses for the year has been estimated at $150,000 of which $90,000 is fixed and the remainder is variable in direct proportion to direct labor.

Required

Assume the customer in the example rejected the $18,000 quotation and also rejected a $15,750 quotation (5% markup) during a slack period. The customer countered with a $15,000 offer.

1 What is the difference in net income for the year between accepting or rejecting the customer's offer?

2 What is the minimum selling price Mr. Berg, Sr. could have quoted without reducing or increasing net income?

(CMA)

15-11 Special Order Requiring Reduction of Existing Sales George Jackson operates a small machine shop. He manufactures one standard product available from many other similar businesses and he also manufactures products to customer order. His accountant prepared the annual income statement shown below:

	Custom Sales	Standard Sales	Total
Sales	$50,000	$25,000	$75,000
Materials	$10,000	$ 8,000	$18,000
Labor	20,000	9,000	29,000
Depreciation	6,300	3,600	9,900
Rent	6,000	1,000	7,000
Heat and light	600	100	700
Other overhead	1,800	300	2,100
Total expense	$44,700	$22,000	$66,700
Net income	$ 5,300	$ 3,000	$ 8,300

The depreciation charges are for machines used exclusively in the respective product lines. The rent is for the building space which has been leased for 10 years at $7,000 per year. The rent, heat and light, and other overhead are apportioned to the product lines based on amount of floor space occupied.

A valued custom parts customer has asked Jackson if he would manufacture 5,000 special units for him. Jackson is working at capacity and would have to give up some other business in order to take this business. He cannot refuse to produce custom orders already agreed to but he could reduce the output of his standard product by about one-half for one year while producing the specially requested custom part. The customer is willing to pay $7.00 for each part. The material cost will be about $2.00 per unit and the labor will be $3.60 per unit. Jackson will have to spend $2,000 for a special device which will be discarded when the job is done.

Required Should Jackson take the order? Explain your answer.

(CMA)

15-12 Sell or Process Further Decision From a particular joint process, Watkins Company produces three products, X, Y, and Z. Each product may be sold at the point of split-off or processed further. Additional processing requires no special facilities, and production costs of further processing are entirely variable and traceable to the products involved.

In 19X3, all three products were processed beyond split-off. Joint production costs for the year were $60,000. Sales values and costs needed to evaluate Watkins' 19X3 production policy follow:

	Product		
	X	Y	Z
Units produced	6,000	4,000	2,000
Sales values at split-off	$25,000	$41,000	$24,000
Additional costs and sales values if processed further			
Sales value	$42,000	$45,000	$32,000
Added costs	$ 9,000	$ 7,000	$ 8,000

Joint costs are allocated to the products in proportion to the output of each product.

Required

Which products should be subjected to additional processing to maximize profits?

(CPA)

15-13 Temporary Plant Closing Stac Industries is a multiproduct company with several manufacturing plants. The Clinton Plant manufactures and distributes two household cleaning and polishing compounds, Regular Cleen-Brite and Heavy-Duty Cleen Brite. The forecasted operating results for the first six months of 19X2, when 100,000 cases of each compound are expected to be manufactured and sold, are presented in the following statement.

Cleen-Brite Compounds—Clinton Plant
Results of Operations for the
Six-Month Period Ending June 30, 19X2
($000 Omitted)

	Regular	Heavy-Duty	Total
Sales	$2,000	$3,000	$5,000
Cost of sales	1,600	1,900	3,500
Gross profit	$ 400	$1,100	$1,500
Selling and administrative expenses			
Variable	$ 400	$ 700	$1,100
Fixed*	240	360	600
Total selling and administrative expenses	$ 640	$1,060	$1,700
Income (loss) before taxes	$ (240)	$ 40	$ (200)

* The fixed selling and administrative expenses are allocated between the two products on the basis of dollar sales volume.

The regular compound sells for $20 a case and the heavy-duty sells for $30 a case. The manufacturing costs by case of product are presented in the schedule below. Each product is manufactured on a separate production line. Annual normal manufacturing capacity is 200,000 cases of each product. However, the plant is capable of producing 250,000 cases of regular compound and 350,000 cases of heavy-duty compound annually.

	Cost per Case	
	Regular	Heavy-Duty
Direct materials	$ 7.00	$ 8.00
Direct labor	4.00	4.00
Variable manufacturing overhead	1.00	2.00
Fixed manufacturing overhead*	4.00	5.00
Total manufacturing cost	$16.00	$19.00
Variable selling and administrative expenses	$ 4.00	$ 7.00

* Depreciation charges are 50% of the fixed manufacturing overhead of each line.

Top management believes the loss for the first six months reflects a light profit margin caused by intense competition. Management also believes that many companies will be forced out of this market by next year and profits should improve.

Required

Assume that for the last six months of 19X2 a selling price of $23 and volume level of 50,000 cases for the regular compound and a selling price of $35 and volume of 35,000 cases for the heavy-duty compound can be expected.

1 Should Stac Industries consider closing down its operations until 19X3 in order to minimize its losses? Support your answer with appropriate calculations.

2 Identify and discuss the qualitative factors which should be considered in deciding whether the Clinton plant should be closed down during the last six months of 19X2.

(CMA)

15-14 Product Line Decisions—Multiple Choice The officers of Bradshaw Company are reviewing the profitability of the company's four products and the potential effect of several proposals for varying the product mix. An excerpt from the income statement and other data follow:

	Total	Product P	Product Q	Product R	Product S
Sales	$62,600	$10,000	$18,000	$12,600	$22,000
Cost of goods sold	44,274	4,750	7,056	13,968	18,500
Gross profit	$18,326	$ 5,250	$10,944	$(1,368)	$ 3,500
Operating expenses	12,012	1,990	2,976	2,826	4,220
Income before income taxes	$ 6,314	$ 3,260	$ 7,968	$(4,194)	$ (720)
Units sold		1,000	1,200	1,800	2,000
Sales price per unit		$ 10.00	$ 15.00	$ 7.00	$ 11.00
Variable cost of goods sold per unit		$ 2.50	$ 3.00	$ 6.50	$ 6.00
Variable operating expenses per unit		$ 1.17	$ 1.25	$ 1.00	$ 1.20

Each of the following proposals is to be considered independently of the other proposals. Consider only the product changes stated in each proposal; the activity of other products remains stable. Ignore income taxes.

1 If product R is discontinued, the effect on income will be a
- **a** $900 increase
- **b** $4,194 increase
- **c** $12,600 decrease
- **d** $1,368 increase
- **e** None of the above

2 If product R is discontinued and a consequent loss of customers causes a decrease of 200 units in sales of Q, the total effect on income will be
- **a** $15,600 decrease
- **b** $2,866 increase
- **c** $2,044 increase
- **d** $1,250 decrease
- **e** None of the above

3 If the sales price of R is increased to $8 with a decrease in the number of units sold to 1,500, the effect on income will be a
- **a** $2,199 decrease
- **b** $600 decrease
- **c** $750 increase
- **d** $2,199 increase
- **e** None of the above

4 The plant in which R is produced can be utilized to produce a new product, T. The total variable costs and expenses per unit of T are $8.05, and 1,600 units can be sold at $9.50 each. If T is introduced and R is discontinued, the total effect on income will be a
- **a** $2,600 increase
- **b** $2,320 increase
- **c** $3,220 increase
- **d** $1,420 increase
- **e** None of the above

(CPA)

15-15 Profitability Analysis for Products and Territories Justa Corporation produces and sells three products. The products, A, B, and C, are sold in a local market and in a regional market. At the end of the first quarter of the current year, the following income statement has been prepared:

	Total	Local	Regional
Sales	$1,300,000	$1,000,000	$300,000
Cost of goods sold	1,010,000	775,000	235,000
Gross margin	$ 290,000	$ 225,000	$ 65,000
Selling expenses	$ 105,000	$ 60,000	$ 45,000
Administrative expenses	52,000	40,000	12,000
Total	$ 157,000	$ 100,000	$ 57,000
Net income	$ 133,000	$ 125,000	$ 8,000

Management has expressed special concern with the regional market because of its poor net income. This market was entered a year ago because of excess capacity. It was originally believed that the net income would improve with time, but after a year no noticeable improvement can be seen from the results as reported in the quarterly statement above.

In attempting to decide whether to eliminate the regional market, the following information has been gathered:

	Products		
	A	B	C
Sales	$500,000	$400,000	$400,000
Variable manufacturing expenses as a percentage of sales	60%	70%	60%
Variable selling expenses as a percentage of sales	3%	2%	2%

Product	Sales by Markets Local	Regional
A	$400,000	$100,000
B	300,000	100,000
C	300,000	100,000

All administrative expenses are fixed. Both the fixed administrative and fixed manufacturing expenses are unavoidable to the three products and the two markets. Remaining selling expenses are fixed for the period and avoidable by market. All fixed expenses are based upon a prorated yearly amount.

Required

1 Prepare the quarterly income statement showing contribution margins by markets.

2 Assuming there are no alternative uses for Justa Corporation's present capacity, would you recommend dropping the regional market? Why or why not?

3 Prepare the quarterly income statement showing contribution margins by products.

4 It is believed that a new product can be ready for sale next year if Justa Corporation decides to continue research. The new product can be produced by converting equipment presently used in producing product C. This conversion will increase fixed expenses by $10,000 per quarter. What must the minimum contribution margin be per quarter for the new product to make the changeover financially feasible?

(CMA)

15-16 Special Order Anchor Company manufactures several different styles of jewelry cases. Management estimates that during the third quarter of 19X6 the company will be operating at 80% of normal capacity. Because the company desires a higher utilization of plant capacity, the company will consider a special order.

Anchor has received special-order inquiries from two companies. The first order is from JCP Inc., which would like to market a jewelry case similar to one of Anchor's cases. The JCP jewelry case would be marketed under JCP's own label. JCP Inc., has offered Anchor $5.75 per jewelry case for 20,000 cases to be shipped by October 1, 19X6. The cost data for the Anchor jewelry case which is similar to the specifications of the JCP special order are as follows:

Regular selling price per unit	$9.00
Costs per unit	
Direct materials	$2.50
Direct labor .5 hours @ $6.00	3.00
Total overhead .25 machine hours @ $4.00	1.00
Total costs	$6.50

According to the specifications provided by JCP Inc., the special-order case requires less expensive direct materials. Consequently, the direct materials will only cost $2.25 per case. Management has estimated that the remaining costs, labor time, and machine time will be the same as the Anchor jewelry case.

The second special order was submitted by the Krage Co. for 7,500 jewelry cases at $7.50 per case. These jewelry cases, as with the JCP cases, would be marketed under the Krage label and have to be shipped by October 1, 19X6. However, the Krage jewelry case is different from any jewelry case in the Anchor line. The estimated per unit costs of this case are as follows:

Direct materials	$3.25
Direct labor .5 hours @ $6.00	3.00
Total overhead .5 machine hours @ $4.00	2.00
Total costs	$8.25

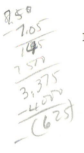

In addition, for the Krage order Anchor will incur $1,500 in additional set-up costs and will have to purchase a $2,500 special device to manufacture these cases. This device will be discarded once the special order is completed.

The Anchor manufacturing capabilities are limited to the total machine hours available. The plant capacity under normal operations is 7,500 machine hours per month. The budgeted fixed overhead per month amounts to $18,000. All manufacturing overhead costs are applied to production on the basis of machine hours at $4.00 per hour, calculated using 7,500 monthly machine hours.

Anchor will have the entire third quarter to work on the special orders. Management does not expect any repeat sales to be generated from either special order. Company practice precludes Anchor from subcontracting any portion of an order when special orders are not expected to generate repeat sales.

Required

Should Anchor Company accept either special order? Justify your answer and show your calculations.

(CMA)

15-17 Make or Buy Decision The Vernom Corporation, which produces and sells to wholesalers a highly successful line of summer lotions and insect repellents, has decided to diversify in order to stabilize sales throughout the year. A natural area for the company to consider is the production of winter lotions and creams to prevent dry and chapped skin.

After considerable research, a winter products line has been developed. However, because of the conservative nature of the company management, Vernom's president has decided to introduce only one of the new products for this coming winter. If the product is a success, further expansion in future years will be initiated.

The product selected (called Chap-off) is a lip balm that will be sold in a lipstick-type tube. The product will be sold to wholesalers in boxes of 24 tubes for $8.00 per box. Because of available capacity, no additional fixed charges will be incurred to produce the product. However, $100,000 of the company's present fixed costs will be allocated to the new product.

Using the estimated sales and production of 100,000 boxes of Chap-off as the standard volume, the accounting department has developed the following costs:

Direct labor	$2.00 per box
Direct materials	$3.00 per box
Overhead (fixed and variable)	$1.50 per box
Total	$6.50 per box

Vernom has approached a cosmetics manufacturer to discuss the possibility of purchasing the tubes for Chap-off rather than manufacture their own. The purchase price of the empty tubes from the cosmetics manufacturer would be $.90 per 24 tubes. If the Vernom Corporation accepts the purchase proposal, it is estimated that per unit direct labor and variable overhead costs would be reduced by 10% and direct materials costs would be reduced by 20%.

Required

1 Should the Vernom Corporation make or buy the tubes? Show calculations to support your answer.

2 What would be the maximum purchase price acceptable to the Vernom Corporation for the tubes? Support your answer with an appropriate explanation.

3 Instead of sales of 100,000 boxes, revised estimates show sales volume at 125,000 boxes. At this new volume additional equipment, at an annual rental of $10,000, must be acquired to manufacture the tubes. However, this incremental cost would be the only additional fixed cost required even if sales increased to 300,000 boxes. (The 300,000 level is the goal for the third year of production.) Under these circumstances should the Vernom Corporation make or buy the tubes? Show calculations to support your answer.

4 The company has the option of making and buying at the same time. What would be your answer to 3 if this alternative were considered? Show calculations to support your answer.

5 What nonquantifiable factors should the Vernom Corporation consider in determining whether they should make or buy the lipstick tubes?

(CMA)

16 COST CONTROL: ANALYSIS AND REPORTING

AFTER COMPLETING YOUR STUDY OF THIS CHAPTER, YOU SHOULD HAVE LEARNED:

1 A new cost classification scheme: engineered costs, managed costs, and capacity costs; and how this classification is useful in reporting for cost control.

2 That the relationship (or lack of a clear relationship) between inputs and outputs of a process determines whether a cost is an engineered cost, managed cost, or capacity cost.

3 How to prepare monthly reports for the control of engineered costs. Reporting for control of managed and capacity costs will be discussed in the next chapter.

4 The sources of information and analysis for the day-to-day control of engineered costs.

The previous chapters in the managerial accounting section of this book have been primarily concerned with planning decisions. We now begin the study of the other components of managerial accounting—control decisions. In simplest terms, a control

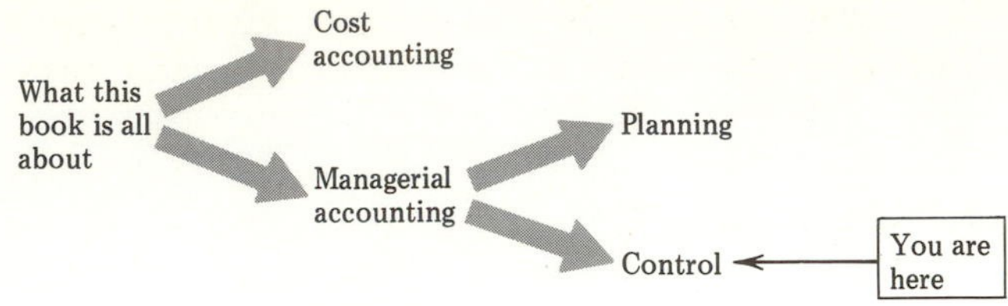

decision begins when the accountant reports that the actual costs differ from the planned (budgeted) costs. The focus of the accountant is comparing planned and actual financial results and reporting the differences to managers who make the control decisions. You should notice two things. First, the accountant's role is *reporting* and that the emphasis is on *financial results*. By reporting differences between planned and actual financial results the accountant is signalling that some management action may be needed to keep the organization on plan. Second, the task of the manager is broader than control of financial results. The manager is probably also responsible for control of product quality, meeting delivery schedules, maintaining a quality work force, and a number of other responsibilities. While recognizing that these other responsibilities exist, the accountant's reporting focuses on the manager's financial responsibilities. Other reporting systems may be necessary to report how well the manager is accomplishing nonfinancial responsibilities.

Accounting reports emphasize financial results.

In earlier chapters we saw that cost classifications such as fixed versus variable, product versus period, etc., were important to planning and cost accounting. These classifications are also used in reporting for control, but two other sets of classifications are also important for control reporting. These other cost classifications are:

New cost classifications.

1 Controllable versus noncontrollable
2 Engineered versus managed versus capacity

Controllable versus noncontrollable relates to the responsibility accounting system. The difference between planned and actual financial results is reported to managers who have authority to control the actual results. By controlling the actual results, we mean that the manager can make decisions which will significantly change the actual amount of the result. If we are talking about costs, the manager must be able to make decisions which will significantly change the quantity of the item used or be able to make decisions that will significantly change the price paid for the item. If the decisions of the manager can significantly change the quantity used or the price, the cost would be classified as *controllable*. If the manager cannot make decisions which will significantly change the quantity used or price of the item, then the cost is *not controllable* by that particular manager. Of course, all costs are controllable by some manager in the organization. In principle, a cost should not be reported to a manager unless the manager can control the cost (which is really the basis of responsibility accounting discussed in Chapter 31). You will see occasional violations of this principle, but these violations should not be frequent.

To summarize, a financial result is controllable if a manager can significantly change the amount of the item. It is important to distinguish between which items are controllable by a particular manager because a principle of responsibility accounting (and reporting for control) is that only items which are controllable by a manager should be included in the control report prepared for that manager.

We next turn to a discussion of the engineered versus managed versus capacity classification. Once this new classification system has been discussed we will illustrate reporting for control of direct materials and direct labor costs. Reporting for control of some additional engineered costs, for managed costs, and for capacity costs will be discussed in Chapter 17.

ENGINEERED, MANAGED, AND CAPACITY COSTS

The classification of engineered, managed, and capacity costs is based on:

1 How accurately we can determine the relationship between the outputs from a process and the inputs to that process

2 The length of time between when the input is made and when the output is completed

All processes involve an **input-output relationship.** Outputs are the results of the process. For example, if the process is a production process, the outputs would be units of product—perhaps measured as the number of cans of beans produced. If the process is a service process, the output would be the amount of service provided—perhaps measured by the number of inquiries answered or number of people served. If the process is learning, the output would be knowledge gained—perhaps measured by the grade you receive in the course. As you realize, the process of measuring output is never perfect. It is easier to measure the output of some processes than of other processes.

Inputs are the things that must be put in to the process to make it operate. If the process is canning beans, the inputs include beans, cans, labor, water, electricity, equipment, and so on. If the process is learning, the inputs are the time of the student, time of the instructor, books, and so forth. The type of inputs required depends on the process.

Some input output relationships are easy to measure.

For some processes, the relationship between the input and the output is quite easy to determine and the output follows the input after a very short time period. In the production of a can of beans, it takes the input of one can (and some other inputs) to produce one unit of output. The relationship between input and output is very definite. This is important to reporting for control because if two cans are used but only one unit of output is produced, there is a presumption that one of the cans has been wasted (or was defective), that something has gone wrong.

Also in the canning example, the output occurs very soon after the input. The beans, cans, and other inputs are used and a few minutes later the output occurs. The time period between input and output is very short in canning beans. In contrast, consider again the learning process. We said that the inputs included student time, teacher time, books, etc. But we all know that with the same book and the same amount of student and teacher time that some students will learn more than other students. The relationship between input and output cannot be measured nearly as accurately as in the case of bean canning. Further, the learning process takes longer than canning beans. Your learning of cost and managerial accounting may spread over 10, 15, or more weeks. There are inputs to the process all along, but the output occurs when you can put the knowledge together and use it on an examination. The long time of the learning process creates difficulties in relating inputs and outputs because a number of conditions could have changed during the

For some process the relationship between inputs and outputs is not easily measured.

period of learning. For example, if you have a part-time job in the spring, your concentration on learning may be less than during the winter when going to school may be your full-time job. If the learning process extends from the winter into the spring, other factors will affect the output of the process. In canning beans, very little is changed from the time you start a can of beans to the time the can of beans is completed. So the learning process is different from the canning process in that it is more difficult to relate inputs and outputs and the time required by the learning process is much longer than in producing beans. This means that it is much more difficult to prepare control reports for learning than it is to prepare control reports for canning beans.

In reporting for cost control, cost is a measure of input while the output may be measured in units of product produced, hours of service performed, sales made, etc.

Engineered Costs

Engineered cost defined.

An **engineered cost** item is a type of input that has an explicit *physical* relationship with output. It is often physically necessary to use one unit of the input to produce one unit of output. For example, each automobile produced (the output) requires a certain amount of sheet metal, a battery, a set of tires, an engine, etc. (the inputs).

For an engineered cost, there are two ways of determining the relationship between cost and output:

1 By engineering analysis (thus the name engineered cost)

2 By analysis of historical cost

Engineering analysis is used to determine input-output relationships.

In designing a product, engineers determine what materials will be needed to build the product. The materials needed depend on the characteristics of the end product—does it need to be strong, light, is appearance important, etc? Based on their analysis, the engineers develop a materials list which shows the type and quantity of materials needed to build the product. Engineers also study the types of production machinery which are available for building the product. With the choice of equipment made, the various types and amounts of labor required can also be estimated. Engineers will develop a list of the steps in the production process, with the amounts of labor required for each step.

As you can see from the description, direct materials and direct labor represent important examples of engineered cost inputs which are needed to produce an output of product. You saw in our discussion of standard cost systems that standard costs are developed for both direct materials and direct labor. These standards reflect the engineering relationship between input and output. Through daily operating decisions such as scheduling production volume, assignment of employees to various jobs, and care in keeping machines properly adjusted, management exercises control over the amount of actual direct labor and direct materials cost. We will discuss how reporting can assist managers in controlling these costs.

Analysis of historical costs is used to determine input-output relationships.

Analysis of historical costs means finding a statistical relationship between cost (input) and output. The graphic method of finding the relationship was illustrated in Chapter 2. You will remember that data from the accounting records was grouped in pairs, each pair consisting of the cost for a month and the output for that same month. The pairs of data were plotted on a graph which shows output on the horizontal scale and the amount of cost on the vertical scale. After the data is plotted on the graph, a straight line is drawn. This line is used to represent the relationship. Exhibit 2-9 summarizes the analysis of historical costs method. You might like to look back at it now. This method is used where engineering estimates have not been made because the engineering time to do it would be too expensive.

Variable manufacturing overhead is considered an engineered cost since the analysis of historical cost can be used to relate the amount of variable overhead (input) to the output of the manufacturing process. Also, some selling and administrative expenses are engineered. For many repetitive clerical activities we can find a close relationship between the cost of the activity (input) and the output. Consider a key punch operation where holes are punched into data processing cards to represent data. A key punch machine which is operated much like a typewriter makes the holes in the cards as the key punch operator types the data into the keyboard. Here the labor cost of the key punch operator is the input and the output could be measured as the number of cards punched or the number of data items entered on the cards. The relationship between the number of data items entered and the cost of the operator's time can be determined by an engineering analysis or by analysis of historical data. Standards can be developed to relate the inputs (actual cost of labor and number of cards used) to the output.

A complete discussion of reporting for control of manufacturing overhead costs and administrative costs is deferred to Chapter 17. The idea is introduced here to give you a more complete understanding of what is included in the definition of engineered costs.

Managed Costs

Managed costs defined.

When no accurate relationship between input and output can be established either by engineering analysis or analysis of historical costs the costs are called **managed costs.** Managed costs are expected to produce an output which benefits the organization, just as engineered costs are expected to produce an output. But it is difficult to find the precise relationship between the amount spent on a managed cost (input) and the output. A managed cost is the opposite of an engineered cost. Often it is difficult to measure the output of a managed cost. Also, frequently there is a significant time lag between the input and the output or benefit resulting from incurring the managed cost. Two good examples of managed costs are advertising and research and development expenditures. In the case of advertising, it is difficult to measure the output produced solely by the advertising expenditure because other sales promotion efforts are happening at the same time. The final output of advertising should be increased sales, but increased sales may be the result of sales representatives' efforts, changes in competitive conditions, changes in the price of the product, and many other factors, all of which are happening at the same time.

It is difficult to measure the output of a managed cost.

Managers try to measure the increase in sales resulting from advertising from careful statistical studies and from test market studies and similar means, but the results are generally not conclusive. Research and development is a different kind of example. The output of research and development is usually fairly definite—new products, improvements in existing products, or improved methods of producing products. Even with a definite measurable output, research and development costs are a managed cost because there is usually a considerable time lag between the time the cost is incurred and the time the new product is developed. Often the time lag on new products is three to five years. This makes it difficult to find a close relationship between particular research and development expenditures and the output of new products or new production methods.

Usually, once managed costs are budgeted, they tend to be fixed for the budget year, although the costs are not incurred in one lump sum but rather incurred regularly throughout the year. This provides the possibility of reviewing these expenditures on a monthly or quarterly basis. Even though the outputs are hard to measure, management should at least ask itself on some regular schedule whether they believe that they are getting the anticipated benefit from the amounts spent on managed costs. The inclusion of managed costs in control reports reminds management to be asking these questions. The term managed cost comes from management's regular review of the amounts being spent on these costs. Even though the managed costs are generally fixed costs, management can manage them by deciding to decrease or increase the amounts spent on the costs at the time of the monthly reviews. Reporting for control of managed costs is discussed in more detail in Chapter 17.

Capacity Costs

Capacity costs defined.

Capacity costs are those costs a company incurs to provide production, distribution, and administrative capabilities. They are the costs of having production facilities (plant and equipment), distribution facilities (warehouses and delivery trucks), and an administrative organization (key personnel) available and ready to operate. Capacity costs include such things as depreciation of buildings and equipment, property taxes and insurance, and salaries of key personnel.

Capacity costs originate with the purchase of buildings and equipment and employment of key personnel and last for extended periods of time. Because capacity costs have already been incurred and are fixed in the short run, management lacks ability to make significant changes in capacity costs during the budget year. However, in long-range planning, management allocates resources for the expansion of facilities. These planning decisions determine the amount of capacity costs that the firm will incur over a number of years.

In the long run, capacity costs exhibit a clear and definite relationship between input costs and output product. For example, a plant to produce 100,000 units of output annually might cost $10 million to build. The $10 million cost represents the input and the output is 100,000 units of product per year. Had the company decided to build a plant with capacity of 130,000 units of product per year its cost would have been greater than $10 million. A smaller plant would have cost less. However, once the decision is made and the plant is built the capacity cost is committed and cannot easily be changed. The control of capacity cost is discussed in Chapter 17.

Capacity costs originate from the capital budgeting decisions.

With any cost classification, the boundaries that define each class are not completely distinct or clear. As a result, engineered costs, managed costs, and capacity costs sometimes tend to blur into one another. How accurately do you need to be able to determine the relationship between input and output for a cost to be an engineered cost rather than a managed cost? For most costs the proper classification will be clear, but for some costs different reasonable accountants might reach different conclusions. We remind you of the two criteria for classifying costs.

1 How accurately can the relationship between input (cost) and output (product) be determined?

2 Over what time horizon can management significantly change the cost? Can they make control decisions daily, monthly, or must they wait a period of years?

The following table summarizes the characteristics of engineered, managed, and capacity costs.

Summary of cost characteristics.

Type of Cost	Decision Time Horizon	Input-Output Relationship
Engineered	Short—daily	Strong
Managed	Moderate—monthly or quarterly	Weak
Capacity	Long—1–20 years or longer	Strong

As there are differences among engineered, managed, and capacity costs, so also are there differences in how they are reported and controlled. The balance of this chapter will be devoted to a discussion of control reporting for direct materials and direct labor costs. Since a standard cost system is used, it should be a familiar subject.

ENGINEERED COSTS: DIRECT MATERIALS AND DIRECT LABOR

A standard cost applies to engineered cost items. As we saw in Chapter 8, a standard cost is a predetermined cost which the organization's engineers have calculated from the cost of the required input materials to produce a unit of output (product). An accountant's report for control of direct materials or direct labor simply compares the *actual total cost* of producing the *actual quantity of output* to the *total standard cost* of producing that *actual quantity of output.*

Efficiency versus Effectiveness

Engineered cost analysis is concerned with how efficiently the output was produced.

The analysis of engineered costs is concerned with measuring how efficiently the output quantity was produced. Remember that by efficiency we mean producing a given quantity of output with the minimum possible cost. In calculating standard cost variances (in Chapter 8) we realized that the actual units produced would probably not be equal to the budgeted quantity of units. The budget was probably prepared some months earlier. The actual production level will probably not equal the budgeted production level for a number of reasons, such as production responding to changes in demand or a machine breakdown resulting in less production time than planned.

In contrast to efficiency, effectiveness is defined as whether or not the organization met its objectives (setting aside cost considerations). To measure how *effectively* a part of a manufacturing activity has operated, we simply compare the budgeted output with the actual output for that activity. For example, if 10,000 units are budgeted to be produced during the month of June and only 9,000 units are actually produced, did the activity operate effectively? The answer is no. In many manufacturing companies the various production activities are "sequential"—the output from department A is one of the inputs for department B, B's output is C's input, etc. If one production department fails to meet its budgeted production volume, the subsequent departments will experience idle time. Also many companies have manufacturing facilities in different parts of the country, each contributing

Effectiveness is concerned with meeting the organization's objectives.

subassemblies or parts to a main assembly operation in a still different location. If one of the manufacturing operations fails to meet its budgeted production volume, the assembly operation will become idle and customer orders may be delayed. Because a certain amount of variation in production volume is expected, inventories of parts are maintained at various plants. The assembly plant would have enough subassemblies and parts on hand to operate with short delays from the other plants, but an important delay could lead to the problems just mentioned.

In any case, failure to meet budgeted production volume is unfavorable: Not only will actual production be less than budgeted, potentially resulting in lost sales, but the company will also incur cost for idle labor in departments beyond the one which failed to meet its budget. The department which failed to meet its budget has been ineffective (not necessarily inefficient) because it failed to meet its production objective as expressed in its production budget.

Comparing budgeted and actual output volumes provides an indication of how *effective* management was in meeting a budget objective. But it does not tell us how *efficiently* the objective was achieved. That is, it does not provide a measure of efficiency.

To measure efficiency, we must compare the *actual cost* of the *actual outputs* with the *standard cost* of the *actual outputs*. By this means, we obtain a separate measure of efficiency. Note that we are comparing the actual costs with the standard costs, each for the same volume—the actual ouput volume. The difference in costs represents the total variance which we can resolve into component price and quantity variances for direct materials and direct labor. To calculate these component variances, we simply use the variance computation procedures learned in Chapter 8.

Reporting for Control of Engineered Costs

To illustrate how to prepare reports for direct materials and direct labor control, consider the UCA Manufacturing Company. The company has two manufacturing departments, fabricating and assembly. A single product, identified by the code name XY1056, is produced by processing it through the fabricating and the assembly departments. Two operations are performed in the fabricating department and three operations in the assembly department. You can see what the operations are by examining the standard cost card shown in Exhibit 16-1.

Assume that prior to the month of June the company has budgeted for that month production of 10,000 units of product XY1056 to satisfy the anticipated demand. The actual results for the month of June reveal that both departments produced 9,500 units of product XY1056 and recorded the following transactions:

1 Purchased 40,000 square feet of sheet metal at a cost of $1.10 per square foot.

2 Purchased 15,000 units of part 1056 at a cost of $9.80 per unit.

3 Issued 36,500 square feet of sheet metal to the fabricating department.

4 Issued 9,800 units of part 1056 to the assembly department.

5 Actual direct labor hours worked in fabricating were 4,850 hours consisting of 1,800 hours for punch press and 3,050 hours for folding. Actual direct labor hours worked in assembly were 9,750 hours consisting of 1,850 hours for deburring, 6,200 hours for assembly, and 1,700 hours for painting. The direct labor cost was $39,285 in fabricating and $63,375 in assembly.

EXHIBIT 16-1
UCA MANUFACTURING COMPANY
Standard Cost Card
Product XY1056

	Direct Materials		
Department-Item	**Standard Quantity**	**Standard Price per Unit**	**Standard Cost**
Fabricating—Sheet Metal	4 square feet	$ 1.00	$ 4.00
Assembly—part #1056	1 unit	10.00	10.00
Total direct materials			$14.00

		Direct Labor		
Department	**Operation**	**Standard Hours**	**Standard Rate per Hour**	**Standard Cost**
Fabricating	Punch press	.2	$8.00	$ 1.60
Fabricating	Folding	.3	8.00	2.40
Assembly	Deburring	.2	7.00	1.40
Assembly	Assembly	.6	7.00	4.20
Assembly	Painting	.2	7.00	1.40
Total direct labor				$11.00

Using the above information, we will illustrate reporting for control of direct materials cost and direct labor cost.

Material Price Variances Exhibit 16-2 illustrates a report showing the material price variance for each direct materials item. The report includes for each item:

The materials price variance report contains information to help management identify the cause of the variance.

1 A description of the direct materials
2 The supplier of each material
3 The quantity purchased
4 The actual price per unit
5 The standard price per unit
6 The resulting purchase price variance

The material price variance report is prepared for the employee in charge of purchasing. Depending on the size of the organization, this employee could be a purchasing manager with a staff of buyers; in a small organization all the purchasing might be done by the production manager.

EXHIBIT 16-2
UCA MANUFACTURING COMPANY
Report of Material Price Variance
For the Month of June 19X8

Item	Supplier	Quantity Purchased	Actual Price per Unit	Standard Price per Unit	Price Difference per Unit	Materials Price Variance
Sheet metal	Xomac Co.	40,000 square feet	$1.10	$ 1.00	($.10)	$4,000 unfavorable
Part #1056	Poncho Parts Co.	15,000 units	$9.80	$10.00	$.20	$3,000 favorable
Total material price variance						$1,000 unfavorable

The material price variance report is based on historical data (probably last month) and shows the effects of actual events measured in dollars. Management uses this information to correct any inefficiencies as well as to detect and maintain efficiencies. The signal of purchasing efficiencies is the price variance.

Material price variances can be caused by a number of factors including:

Causes of materials price variances.

- The wrong supplier
- Incorrect size of purchase affecting the quantity discount
- Incorrect quality
- Rush orders that increase the shipping costs
- Incorrect standard prices
- Changes in supply and demand

In most companies the responsibility for the material price variance rests with the purchasing department, and it is the purchasing department manager who is responsible for the follow-up necessary to identify the cause of the variance.

Direct Materials Quantity Variances Exhibit 16-3 illustrates the analysis of direct materials and direct labor cost controllable by the supervisor of the fabricating department. This report shows for each item the direct materials quantity variance, the direct labor quantity variance by operation, and the direct labor price variance. The usefulness of the report depends on the follow-up procedures for identifying the variances and determining whether or not they are *significant.* Such follow-up procedures should be sufficient to identify the cause of the variance to enable management to decide what to do about it.

The first part of Exhibit 16-3 reports the total direct materials quantity variance. For the most effective quantity and cost control, the material standard quantity and costs should be based on the amount of materials that should have been used for the actual units produced. This means that allowances for normal spoilage will be incorporated in the standard quantity. This report of direct materials costs is usually prepared on a monthly basis and provides a summary of how efficiently direct materials were used during the period.

EXHIBIT 16-3
UCA MANUFACTURING COMPANY
Fabricating Department
Analysis of Direct Materials and Direct Labor
For the Month of June 19X8

Direct Materials—Quantity Variance

Item	Actual Quantity Used	Standard Quantity Allowed	Difference	Standard Price	Quantity Variance
Sheet metal	36,500 sq. ft.	38,000[1] sq. ft.	1,500 sq. ft.	$1.00 per sq. ft.	$1,500 favorable

[1] 9,500 finished units of product × 4 sq. ft. per unit = 38,000 sq. ft.

Direct Labor—Quantity Variance

Operation	Actual Hours Worked	Standard Hours Allowed	Difference	Standard Labor Rate	Quantity Variance
Punch Press	1,800	1,900[2]	100	$8.00 per hour	$ 800 favorable
Folding	3,050	2,850[3]	(200)	$8.00 per hour	$1,600 unfavorable
Total	4,850	4,750	(100)		$ 800 unfavorable

[2] 9,500 finished units of product × .2 hours per unit = 1,900 hours
[3] 9,500 finished units of product × .3 hours per unit = 2,850 hours

Direct Labor—Price Variance

Actual cost of direct labor	$39,285
Standard cost of actual direct labor hours:	
4,850 hours × $8.00 per hour =	38,800
Direct labor price variance	$ 485 unfavorable

For day-to-day control of direct materials usage, the supervisor generally relies on:

Sources of information for day-to-day control of direct materials quantity variance.

1 Excess materials requisitions

2 The amount of scrap and spoilage that is occurring on a daily basis

The spoiled units are identified at inspection points strategically located throughout the manufacturing process. If the spoilage at a point in the process begins to exceed normal, the supervisor in charge of that process is notified and an investigation is initiated to identify the cause of the spoilage. In a similar fashion scrap tickets prepared by machine operators or materials handling personnel are collected daily by the supervisor in charge of the operation. Scrap tickets indicate the quantity of scrap produced by a particular process. If the scrap quantity exceeds normal amounts the supervisor would investigate the process even before the direct materials quantity variance is reported.

Direct materials quantity variances can be caused by any number of factors depending on the nature of the manufacturing process. Many times the variance can be traced to factors such as:

Causes of direct materials quantity variance.

- Inferior materials causing excess spoilage or scrap
- Incorrect machine settings
- Inexperienced personnel working the machines
- Incorrect standards
- Changes in the production process

You should be aware that all materials quantity variances are not the fault of the production supervisor. For instance, if the purchasing department acquires some direct materials at a "bargain price" and accepts lower quality than the standard, the result might be a favorable material price variance but an unfavorable materials quantity variance because of excess spoilage. Likewise, if the supervisor of manufacturing constantly requests rush orders of materials, the purchasing department may have to pay additional freight charges and premium prices to obtain the materials when needed. The important point here is that only through an investigation can we determine the *cause* of a variance. The accounting analysis simply signals the need for an investigation and provides a starting point.

The cause of a variance is determined through management's investigation.

Direct Labor Quantity Variances The second part of Exhibit 16-3 shows the direct labor quantity variance by operation for the fabricating department. The direct labor quantity standards represent the currently attainable level of performance under normal operating conditions. The most widely used basis for setting labor quantity standards is engineering time studies. These studies consider factors affecting employee performance—the plant layout, condition of equipment—as well as the level of employee experience and training required for the operation.

The report of the direct labor quantity variance in Exhibit 16-3 shows the quantity variance for each operation—punch press and folding—in the fabricating department. This breakdown of the total direct labor quantity variance provides the supervisor of the fabricating department with information as to how much each operation contributed to the total direct labor quantity variance. As you can see the total direct labor quantity variance is $800 unfavorable and consists of the following components:

Direct labor quantity variances can be analyzed by operation.

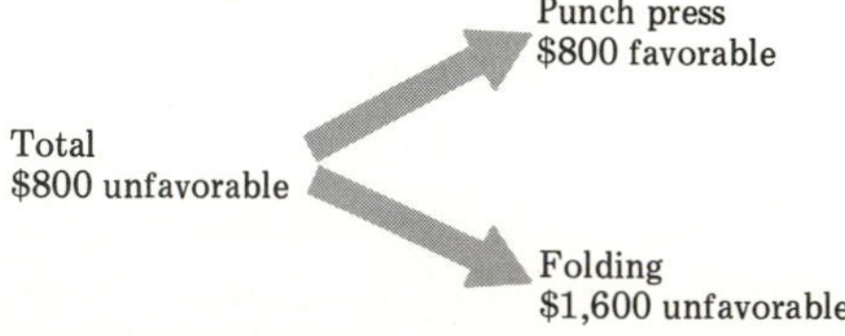

The analysis in Exhibit 16-3 indicates the efficiency of the direct labor operations, measured as the quantity variance in direct labor, for the month of June. For day-to-day control, the department supervisor relies on employee time tickets which indicate the number of hours spent daily on each operation and the number of units completed during that day. At the end of each work shift, the employee time tickets are collected and the standard direct labor hours allowed are computed for the units completed during that shift and compared to the actual hours worked.

EXHIBIT 16-4
UCA MANUFACTURING COMPANY
Daily Direct Labor Efficiency Report
Fabricating Department
For Wednesday June 20, 19X8

Employee Number	Operation	Units Completed	Standard Hours Allowed	Actual Hours Worked	Difference	Difference as a Percent of Standard
7654	Punch Press	35	(35 × .2 hours) 7 hours	8 hours	1 hour	(1 ÷ 7) = 14%
⋮						
7843	Punch Press	30	(30 × .2 hours) 6 hours	8 hours	2 hours	(2 ÷ 6) = 33%

Direct labor costs are analyzed on a daily basis.

Exhibit 16-4 illustrates a daily direct labor report for the UCA Manufacturing Company. The report in Exhibit 16-4 summarizes the information on the employee time tickets and is prepared at the end of each work shift. This information is reported to the department supervisor and any significant variance is investigated immediately rather than waiting for the report illustrated in Exhibit 16-3.

Actual direct labor quantity variances can be caused by a number of factors including:

Causes of direct labor quantity variances.

- Use of nonstandard equipment
- Use of inexperienced employees
- Lost time because of unexpected machine breakdowns or lack of materials
- Materials of lower quality than standard
- Failure to revise the standard when the production operation changes

Labor variances are reported to the department supervisor who conducts an investigation to identify the cause of variances determined to be significant. Once the cause is identified and corrected, the supervisor prepares a report specifying the cause and how it was corrected.

Direct Labor Price Variances The direct labor price variance is reported to the production supervisor because such a variance generally results from the way the workers are assigned to tasks rather than from a difference in labor rates. Most often labor rates are set by union contracts and change infrequently at known dates. It is relatively easy to bring standards up to date when labor rates change.

Suppose that a particular task or production operation calls for unskilled workers but the production supervisor assigns a semiskilled worker to the task. The semiskilled worker would likely be paid a higher wage than an unskilled worker. Since the task calls for an unskilled worker, the standard rate will be based on the unskilled worker's wage rate. When the semiskilled worker is assigned the task, an unfavorable direct labor price variance will result. If the semiskilled worker performs the task more efficiently, the unfavorable direct labor price variance could be offset to some extent by a favorable direct labor quantity variance. The combination of skilled, semiskilled, and unskilled workers is sometimes called the labor mix. Thus, it is sometimes said that a direct labor price variance is caused by the labor mix.

Of course there may be good reasons why a production supervisor assigns a semiskilled worker to a task which is normally done by an unskilled worker. It may be that at the particular moment there is an excess of semiskilled workers and a shortage of unskilled workers. In that case, departing from the standard direct labor mix may be the only way to meet production objectives. As noted earlier, the direct labor quantity variances may also be affected by the labor mix. For these reasons, the direct labor price variance is reported as the responsibility of the production supervisor, a signal that if a significant direct labor price variance occurs the investigation should probably begin in the production department.

Other ways to analyze direct materials and direct labor.

In Exhibit 16-3 we illustrated direct materials variances by item and direct labor variances by operations within a department. There are some manufacturing situations where the material quantity variance might also be reported by job order. This type of analysis provides the supervisor with additional information to begin the search for the cause of the variance. Also, direct labor quantity variances can be analyzed for each operation within a department as we illustrated in Exhibit 16-3 as well as by job. Generally, reporting follows job responsibilities. If a supervisor is responsible for a particular job, reporting by job order is useful because we know that the manager of the job should be involved in the investigation of any significant variance which occurs on that job.

SUMMARY

For control reporting, costs are classified as engineered costs, managed costs, and capacity costs.

Engineered costs are costs that have an explicit physical relationship with outputs. The relationship between inputs (costs) and outputs can be accurately determined from the technical specifications of the product or from an analysis of historical costs. Engineered costs can be changed by daily operating decisions of management.

Managed costs originate during the annual budgeting and resource allocation process. We cannot accurately find a clear and definite relationship between the cost of the inputs and the resulting output. Throughout the year managed costs are reviewed and the amount of the expenditure can be changed.

Capacity costs represent the costs of productive and distributive capabilities and administrative organization. These costs originate with decisions to add to plant and equipment and to administrative capability. They represent cost commitments for extended periods of time which cannot be easily changed.

Direct materials and direct labor are engineered costs for which standard costs are developed. Control information is developed by comparing the actual cost of the actual output quantity with the standard cost of the actual output quantity.

Price variances in direct materials are reported at the time of purchase to the individual responsible for the purchasing activity.

Direct materials quantity variances are reported on a monthly basis. Day-to-day control of direct materials quantities relies on excess materials requisitions and monitoring the volume of scrap and spoilage.

Direct labor quantity variances are reported by operation on a monthly basis. For day-to-day control direct labor quantity variances are calculated for each employee.

Direct labor price variances are reported to department supervisors since the most likely cause of the variance is assigning an employee to a task that specifies a standard labor rate different than the employee's actual labor rate. This is called the labor mix cause of a direct labor price variance.

Review Problem

Using the data in the chapter prepare an analysis of the direct materials quantity variance, direct labor quantity variance, and direct labor price variance for the assembly department.

Solution

UCA MANUFACTURING COMPANY
Assembly Department
Analysis of Direct Materials and Direct Labor
For the Month of June 19X8

Direct Materials—Quantity Variance

Item	Actual Quantity Used	Standard Quantity Allowed	Difference	Standard Price	Quantity Variance
Part No. 1056	9,800 parts	9,500[1] parts	(300)	$10.00	$3,000 unfavorable

[1] 9,500 finished units of product × 1 part per unit = 9,500 parts

Direct Labor—Quantity Variance

Operation	Actual Hours Worked	Standard Hours Allowed	Difference	Standard Labor Rate	Quantity Variance
Deburring	1,850	1,900[2]	50	$7.00 per hour	$ 350 favorable
Assembly	6,200	5,700[3]	(500)	$7.00 per hour	$3,500 unfavorable
Painting	1,700	1,900[4]	200	$7.00 per hour	$1,400 favorable
Total	9,750	9,500	(250)		$1,750 unfavorable

[2] 9,500 finished units of product × .2 hours per unit = 1,900 hours
[3] 9,500 finished units of product × .6 hours per unit = 5,700 hours
[4] 9,500 finished units of product × .2 hours per unit = 1,900 hours

Direct Labor—Price Variance

Actual cost of direct labor	$63,375
Standard cost of actual direct labor hours:	
9,750 hours × $7.00 per hour =	68,250
Direct labor price variance	$ 4,875 favorable

Glossary

Capacity cost A cost which is incurred to provide production, distribution, and administrative capabilities. It originates from the firm's purchase of buildings and equipment and the employment of key personnel. It represents a commitment for an extended period of time. For the annual planning period capacity costs tend to be fixed.

Engineered cost A cost that has an explicit physical relationship with output and tends to fluctuate with day-to-day changes in production volume or sales volume. Direct materials and direct labor costs are examples of an engineered cost.

Input-output relationship The relationship between the amount of cost incurred and the outputs of a process. Some costs exhibit a strong input-output relationship such as direct materials. With direct materials for each unit of output the direct materials input can be physically identified.

Managed cost A cost where no accurate relationship between input and output can be established by engineering analysis or by analysis of historical data. Once budgeted these costs tend to be fixed for the annual planning period.

Questions and Problems

16-1 Explain the difference between effectiveness and efficiency.

16-2 Define and discuss the differences between an engineered, managed, and capacity cost.

16-3 Explain briefly the two criteria used to classify costs as engineered, managed, or capacity.

16-4 All managed costs are fixed costs. Do you agree?

16-5 How would management's approach to controlling engineered costs differ from the approach to controlling managed costs?

16-6 How would management's approach to controlling engineered costs differ from the approach to controlling capacity costs?

16-7 What documents are used for the day-to-day control of the direct materials quantity variance?

16-8 What documents are used for the day-to-day control of the direct labor quantity variance?

16-9 Can the responsibility for the direct materials price variance and direct materials quantity variance be completely separated? Explain briefly.

16-10 Discuss the possible causes of the two direct materials variances.

16-11 Discuss the possible causes of the two direct labor variances.

16-12 Analysis of Labor Quantity Variance by Employee The following information concerning direct labor was collected for the assembly department during the first shift of operations on July 9.

Employee No.	Operation No.	Units Completed	Hours Worked
1057	A-108	51	8
1081	A-108	69	8
1093	A-109	41	8
1112	A-109	35	8
1114	A-109	44	8

The standard direct labor time for the assembly operations are:

Operation No. A-108	.15 hours per unit
Operation No. A-109	.20 hours per unit

Required

1 Prepare an analysis of the labor quantity variance by operation.

2 Prepare an analysis of the labor quantity variance by employee.

16-13 Calculating Variances by Product Mill Company manufactures and sells two similar types of industrial components which are substitutes for each other. One component is manufactured from plastic, while the other uses metal. Both components are manufactured in the same plant but in separate production departments.

The 19X4 sales mix was different from that which was budgeted. More metal components were sold than planned because of reduced availability of plastic components. Some increase in the volume of metal components was also due to the lower than budgeted price. The sales volume of plastic components was down because of lost production.

A general shortage of plastic required Mill Company to use an inferior grade. This plastic cost $0.05 more per pound than the standard plastic, and 10% of the materials used in production was not suitable. The plastic shortage is expected to ease in 19X5, and the regular plastic will be available in adequate quantities at $0.45 per pound.

Manufacturing Operation The company coordinates its direct materials purchases and production schedules with sales so that changes in inventory levels are insignificant and inventories of direct materials and finished goods are very low. Production equaled 260,000 plastic units and 260,000 metal units during 19X4. The purchases and use of direct materials in 19X4 were as follows:

Plastic	
Purchases (at actual price)	620,000 lbs. @ $0.45 = $279,000
Used in production (at standard price)	600,000 lbs. @ $0.40 = $240,000
Metal	
Purchases (at actual price)	550,000 lbs. @ $1.40 = $770,000
Used in production (at standard price)	525,000 lbs. @ $1.40 = $735,000

The production required the following amounts of direct labor hours and total direct labor wages in 19X4.

	Direct Labor Hours	Actual Average Wage Rate	Total Wage
Plastic department	72,000	$5.75	$414,000
Metal department	125,000	$6.20	$775,000

A large proportion of the workers in the plastics department were inexperienced and average wages were therefore lower than standard. However, the inexperience resulted in nonproductive time equal to 10% of standard hours of production and in material scrap equal to 3% of the standard material quantities.

The company uses a standard cost system to aid in controlling costs and preparing timely reports. The standard costs for 19X4 were:

	Plastic	Metal
Direct materials	2 lbs. @ $0.40 = $0.80	2 lbs. @ $1.40 = $2.80
Direct labor	.25 hrs. @ $6.00 = 1.50	.5 hrs. @ $6.00 = 3.00

Required

Management is concerned about the large manufacturing cost variances which occurred in the production of the plastic component. Determine for the plastics department and metal department the cost variances for direct materials and direct labor. Present a detailed analysis which associates a dollar amount with probable causes of the variances.

(CMA)

16-14 Calculation of Variances by Job The Justin Company has recently installed a standard cost accounting system to simplify its factory bookkeeping and to aid in cost control. The company makes standard items for inventory, but because of the many products in its line, each is manufactured periodically under a production order. Prior to the installation of the system, job order cost sheets were maintained for each production order. Since the introduction of the standard cost system, however, they have not been kept.

The fabricating department is managed by a general supervisor who has overall responsibility for scheduling, performance, and cost control. The department consists of four work centers. Each work center is manned by a four-person work group or team and the centers are aided by a 12-person support group. Departmental practice is to assign a job to one team and expect the team to perform most of the work necessary to complete the job, including acquisition of materials and supplies from the stores department and machining and assembling. This has been practical and satisfactory in the past and is readily accepted by the employees.

Information regarding production cost standards, products produced, and actual cost for the fabricating department in March is presented below:

Unit Standard Costs

	Part		
	A7A	C6D	C7A
Direct materials	$2.00	$3.00	$1.50
Direct labor	1.50	2.00	1.00

Analysis of the Fabricating Department Account for March

Charges		
Direct materials		
Job no. 307-11	$ 5,200	
Job no. 307-12	2,900	
Job no. 307-14	9,400	$17,500
Direct labor charges		
Job no. 307-11	$ 4,000	
Job no. 307-12	2,100	
Job no. 307-14	6,200	12,300
Total charges to department for March		$29,800
Credits for direct materials and direct labor		
Completed jobs		
Job no. 307-11		
2,000 units part A7A @ $3.50	$ 7,000	
Job no. 307-12		
1,000 units part C6D @ $5.00	5,000	
Job no. 307-14		
6,000 units part C7A @ $2.50	15,000	$27,000
Variances transferred to the factory variance account		
Materials[1]	$ 1,500	
Direct labor[2]	1,300	2,800
Total credits		$29,800

[1] Materials price variances are isolated at acquisition and charged to the stores department.
[2] All direct labor was paid at the standard wage rate during March.

Required

1 Justin Company assumes that its efforts to control costs in the fabricating department would be aided if variances were calculated by jobs. Management intends to add this analysis next month. Calculate all the variances by job that might contribute to cost control under this assumption.

2 Do you agree with the company's plan to initiate the calculation of job variances in addition to the currently calculated departmental variances? Explain your answer.

(CMA)

16-15 **Identifying the Cause of Labor Variances** The Felton Company manufactures a complete line of radios. Because a large number of models have plastic cases, the company has its own molding department for producing the cases. The month of April was devoted to the production of the plastic case for one of the portable radios—Model SX76.

The molding department has two operations—molding and trimming. The standard labor cost for producing 10 plastic cases for Model SX76 is as follows:

Molders	.50 hrs. @ $6.00 =	$3.00
Trimmers	.25 hrs. @ $4.00 =	1.00
		$4.00

During April, 70,000 plastic cases were produced in the molding department. However, 10% of these cases (7,000) had to be discarded because they were found to be defective at final inspection. The purchasing department had changed to a new plastic supplier to take advantage of a lower price for comparable plastic. The new plastic turned out to be of a lower quality and resulted in the rejection of completed cases.

The actual direct labor hours worked and direct labor costs charged to the molding department are shown below.

Direct Labor Charged to the Molding Department

Molders	3,800 hrs. @ $6.25 =	$23,750
Trimmers	1,600 hrs. @ $4.15 =	6,640
Total labor charges		$30,390

As a result of poor scheduling by the production scheduling department, the supervisor of the molding department had to shift molders to the trimmer operation for 200 hours during April. The company paid the molding workers their regular hourly rate even though they were performing a lower rated task. There was no significant loss of efficiency caused by the shift. In addition, the supervisor of the department indicated that 75 hours and 35 hours of idle time occurred in the molding and trimming operations respectively as a result of unexpected machinery repairs required during the month.

Required

1 The monthly report which compares actual costs with standard cost of output for the month of April shows the following labor variance for the molding department:

Actual labor costs for April	$30,390
Standard labor cost of output (63,000 × $4.00/10)	25,200
Unfavorable labor variance	$ 5,190

This variance is significantly higher than normal and management would like an explanation. Prepare a detailed analysis of the unfavorable labor variance for the molding department which shows the variance resulting from (*a*) labor rates, (*b*) labor substitution, (*c*) materials substitution, (*d*) operating efficiency, and (*e*) idle time.

2 The supervisor of the molding department is concerned with the large variances charged to the department and feels that the variances because of labor substitution and the change in direct materials should not be charged to the department. Does the supervisor have a valid argument? Briefly justify your position.

(CMA)

16-16 Revision of Direct Labor Rates Landeau Manufacturing Company has a process cost accounting system. A report which compares the actual results with both a monthly plan and a flexible budget is prepared monthly. The standard direct labor rates used in the flexible budget are established each year at the time the annual plan is formulated and held constant for the entire year.

The standard direct labor rates in effect for the fiscal year ending June 30, 19X8 and the standard hours allowed for the output for the month of April are shown in the schedule below:

	Standard Direct Labor Rate per Hour	Standard Direct Labor Hours Allowed for Output
Labor class III	$8.00	500
Labor class II	$7.00	500
Labor class I	$5.00	500

The wage rates for each labor class increased on January 1, 19X8 under the terms of a new union contract negotiated in December 19X7. The standard wage rates were not revised to reflect the new contract.

The actual direct labor hours (DLH) worked and the actual direct labor rates per hour experienced for the month of April were as follows:

	Actual Direct Labor Rate per Hour	Actual Direct Labor Hours
Labor class III	$8.50	550
Labor class II	$7.50	650
Labor class I	$5.40	375

Required

1 Calculate the direct labor price variance and the direct labor quantity variance by labor class.

2 Discuss the advantages and disadvantages of a standard cost system in which the standard direct labor rates per hour are not changed during the year to reflect such events as a new labor contract.

(CMA)

16-17 Interpretation of Labor Variances The Clark Company has a contract with a labor union that guarantees a minimum wage of $500 per month to each direct labor employee having at least 12 years of service. One hundred employees currently qualify for coverage. All direct labor employees are paid $5.00 per hour.

The direct labor budget for 19X0 was based on the annual usage of 400,000 hours of direct labor × $5, or a total of $2,000,000. Of this amount, $50,000 (100 employees × $500) per month (or $600,000 for the year) was regarded as fixed. Thus, the budget for any given month was determined by the formula, $50,000 + ($3.50 × direct labor hours worked).

Data on performance for the first three months of 19X0 follow:

	January	February	March
Direct labor hours worked	22,000	32,000	42,000
Direct labor cost budgeted	$127,000	$162,000	$197,000
Direct labor costs incurred	$110,000	$160,000	$210,000
Variance (U-unfavorable; F-favorable)	$ 17,000F	$ 2,000F	$ 13,000U

The factory manager was perplexed by the results, which showed favorable variances when production was low and unfavorable variances when production was high, because he believed his control over labor cost was consistently good.

Required

1 Why did the variances arise? Explain and illustrate using amounts and diagrams as necessary.

2 Does this direct labor budget provide a basis for controlling direct labor cost? Explain, indicating changes that might be made to improve control over direct labor cost and to facilitate performance evaluation of direct labor employees.

(CPA)

16-18 Establishing Output Standards The Alton Company is going to expand its punch press department. It is about to purchase three new punch presses from Equipment Manufacturers, Inc. Equipment Manufacturers' engineers report that their mechanical studies indicate that for Alton's intended use the output rate for one press should be 1,000 pieces per hour. Alton has very similar presses now in operation. At the present time, production from these presses averages 600 pieces per hour.

A study of the Alton experience shows the average is derived from the following individual outputs.

Worker	Daily Output
L. Jones	750
J. Green	750
R. Smith	600
H. Brown	500
R. Alters	550
G. Hoag	450
Total	3,600
Average	600

Alton management plans to institute a standard cost accounting system in the very near future. The company engineers favor a standard based upon 1,000 pieces per hour, the accounting department favors a standard for 750 pieces per hour, and the department supervisor is arguing for 600 pieces per hour.

Required

1 What arguments would each proponent be likely to use to support his case?

2 Which alternative best reconciles the needs of cost control and the motivation of improved performance? Explain why you made that choice.

(CMA)

17 COST CONTROL: ANALYSIS AND REPORTING CONCLUDED

AFTER COMPLETING YOUR STUDY OF THIS CHAPTER, YOU SHOULD HAVE LEARNED:

1 That flexible budgets are used to control engineered costs whose cost behavior is partially fixed.

2 To interpret the budget variance, and to divide it into spending and efficiency variances.

3 That managed costs can be controlled either by breaking them into small components and using engineered cost control techniques or by rigorous analysis in the budgeting process.

4 How capacity costs are controlled through long-range planning and by follow-up audits.

In Chapter 16 you learned how to use a standard cost system to report for control of variable engineered costs such as direct materials and direct labor. For direct materials and direct labor you can establish a physical relationship between the inputs (and their cost) and the outputs (the units of product produced). Through this physical relationship we can determine what the outputs *should have* cost.

We now turn our attention to the use of flexible budgets to prepare reports for control of engineered costs which are partly fixed and partly variable. Overhead costs are the most prominent example of costs which are partly fixed and partly variable. For example, the electricity used in a factory is partly fixed and partly variable. The cost of electricity used to light the factory is the same amount whether the plant is operated at 50% of capacity or at 80% of capacity. The electricity used to operate the machines is variable, depending on how much the machines are used. But when the electric bill arrives it shows the total electricity used, both for lighting and operating machines. Thus, the total electricity bill will be partly fixed and partly variable.

Flexible budgets were introduced in Chapter 9 where they were used to divide over- or underapplied overhead (the difference between actual manufacturing overhead cost and applied manufacturing overhead costs) into three parts: (1) the spending variance, (2) the efficiency variance, and (3) the production volume variance. Chapter 9 concentrated on how to calculate the variances and how they were recorded in the accounting records. In this chapter we are interested in the meaning of the variances for control of engineered costs. After completing the discussion of flexible budget variances, we will turn to reporting for control of managed and capacity costs.

FLEXIBLE BUDGETS

In a standard cost system we used a concept called "standard quantity allowed" to represent the amount of direct materials or direct labor which should have been used *given the actual output* for the period. The standard quantity allowed is calculated by multiplying the standard quantity per unit of output times the actual units of output. This simple calculation works because the cost is variable; if 10% more units of output are produced, 10% more input should be required. The **flexible budget** is a way of determining what a mixed cost (part fixed and part variable) should be for a particular level of output. Of course, the volume of output must be within the relevant range of the flexible budget.

Flexible budgets are used to control mixed costs.

A flexible budget recognizes that as output volume increases the total cost will increase, but not in the same proportion as volume increases. That is, with a mixed cost a 10% increase in volume of output may lead to a 6% increase in total cost. This happens because as output volume increases the variable part of the cost does increase, but the fixed cost remains constant. With part of the cost increasing and the other part remaining constant, the total cost increases, but not by the same percentage that volume increases.

Flexible budgets are prepared on a departmental basis.

Another difference between a standard cost and a flexible budget system is that in the standard cost system output can be measured in units of production, while in a flexible budget system output is generally measured using direct labor hours for an assembly department or machine hours for a machining operation. This is done because a separate standard is developed for each product and a flexible budget generally is developed for a department. The overhead costs of the department benefit all products produced in the department and the flexible budget provides no way of dividing the overhead cost by product. Direct labor hours or machine hours are used as a *substitute* measure of output. Because all products in an assembly department contain direct labor hours, it can be used as a measure of output even when products are different. A large unit will contain more direct labor hours than a small product. So even though it would not be sensible to add one large product to one small product and say that there were 2 units of output, it is sensible to add the direct labor hours because the larger number of direct labor hours contained in the larger unit will show that more productive effort (and more overhead cost) was required to produce the larger unit.

As discussed on page 248 of Chapter 9, the best measure of output volume is the one that most closely reflects the kinds of overhead cost and relates best the variations in overhead cost to the variations in output volume. We suggested that direct labor hours might be used in an assembly operation because often assembly operations use a large amount of direct labor and many of the overhead costs of an assembly operation are fringe benefits, supervision, timekeeping, and other direct labor related costs. Further, in an assembly operation, the amount of output is generally related to the amount of direct labor used. In contrast, in a machining department the largest overhead cost items are likely to be depreciation, taxes, insurance on the machinery, machine maintenance, power used to operate the machines, and other machine related costs. Further, the amount of output often depends on how many hours the machines are operated. These considerations lead to selection of machine hours as the best measure of output in a machining department.

Flexible Budgets Illustrated

To illustrate the use of flexible budgets for cost control, consider the flexible budget in Exhibit 17-1 for the machining department of the Dade Corporation.

The flexible budget for the machining department shows the estimated fixed cost and variable cost per machine hour for each cost item. The column labeled total cost represents the costs the company expects to incur based on the production of 3,000 large size units of product and 4,000 small size units of product. Each large size unit requires 1 machine hour to complete. Each small size unit requires one-half hour of machine time to complete.

The cost items included in the flexible budget for the machining department are separated into three different categories: controllable, allocated, and noncontrollable.

The **controllable costs,** part A of Exhibit 17-1, represent those cost items that are the responsibility of the department supervisor. Controllable costs typically include items such as indirect labor, cutting tools, lubricants for machining, and power costs which are incurred in the machining department.

The **allocated costs,** part B of Exhibit 17-1, represent costs incurred in manufacturing service departments and allocated to the machining department. The fixed maintenance cost of $2,000 included in the machining department's flexible budget is the expected cost of routine maintenance such as cleaning and adjusting the machinery. This cost occurs regardless of the level of activity in the department. The variable maintenance cost of $.50 per machine hour represents the expected cost of maintenance that results from running the machinery. This would include things such as repair or replacement of moving parts, lubrication, and similar costs. The maintenance costs are included in the report because the department manager can reduce the amount of maintenance needed by careful use of the machinery.

EXHIBIT 17-1
DADE CORPORATION
Machining Department
Flexible Budget
For June 19X8

Cost Item	Fixed Cost	Variable Cost (Per Machine Hour)	Total Cost (For 5,000 Machine Hours)*
A. Controllable			
Indirect labor	$ —	$1.70	$ 8,500
Cutting tools	—	.20	1,000
Lubricants	—	.10	500
Power	500	.20	1,500
B. Allocated			
Maintenance	2,000	.50	4,500
C. Noncontrollable			
Manager and assistant manager's salary	5,000	—	5,000
Depreciation	15,000	—	15,000
Total	$22,500	$2.70	$36,000

* 3,000 large units of product @ 1.0 standard machine hours per unit = 3,000
4,000 small units of product @ 0.5 standard machine hours per unit = 2,000
Total planned machine hours = 5,000

The **noncontrollable costs,** part C of Exhibit 17-1, represent the costs that are assigned to the machining department because that is where they are incurred. The department supervisor has no control over them because they are capacity costs.

Why are noncontrollable costs included in a flexible budget report? They could be excluded since the purpose of the report is cost control. However, there are two reasons why many companies include the noncontrollable costs in the flexible budget. First, the same flexible budget which is used for control may also be used for product costing. Second, some companies argue that the noncontrollable costs should be included in the flexible budget so the department supervisor is aware of the total cost of operating the department. Neither of these reasons is very persuasive and it would be best to exclude noncontrollable costs from the control report. But you should not be surprised if you see flexible budget control reports that contain noncontrollable items.

Variance Computation

Now, let us jump ahead in time and assume the actual results of operations for the machining department for the month of June are as follows:

Production output: 3,000 large units of product	
3,500 small units of product	
Actual machine hours operated:	4,850
Actual costs:	
Indirect labor	$ 9,010
Cutting tools	1,100
Lubricants	500
Power	1,600
Maintenance	4,210
Supervision	5,000
Depreciation	15,000
Total actual cost	$36,420

Based on the flexible budget in Exhibit 17-1 and the actual results we next compute the budget variance and the spending and efficiency variance.

Budget Variance The original budget for the machining department in Exhibit 17-1 was for the production of 3,000 large and 4,000 small units of product.

To evaluate efficiency a revised budget based on actual output is calculated and compared to the actual cost.

The actual results, given above, show that 3,000 large and 3,500 small units of product were produced. To compare the actual overhead cost for the actual level of production with the overhead budget for the planned units of production would not provide a measure of the performance of the supervisor in controlling costs. Such a comparison fails because we would expect total costs to be lower with a lower level of production since part of the overhead cost is variable. For this reason a revised overhead budget for the actual output is calculated using the flexible budget formulas in Exhibit 17-1.

The revised overhead budget for the actual level of output is shown in Exhibit 17-2 and compared with the actual overhead costs; the result of the comparison is a variance for each overhead item charged to the machining department. Each variance calculated is termed a **budget variance** and is the same as the computation of the budget variance in Chapter 9.

As in Chapter 9, it is necessary to first calculate the standard quantity of machine hours allowed for June's actual output. It is shown below:

$$\textbf{Standard quantity allowed} = \textbf{units of output} \times \textbf{standard machine hours per unit of output}$$

large size = 3,000 units × 1 hour per unit	=	**3,000 hours**
small size = 3,500 units × ½ hour per unit	=	**1,750 hours**
Total standard quantity allowed	=	**4,750 hours**

The budget variance is the difference between the actual cost and the flexible budgeted cost for the actual output.

The budget variance, computed for each individual item in the overhead budget, shows management how much each overhead item contributed to the total budget variance. If management decided that the total variance for the department is significant enough to justify an investigation of the cause of the variance, the item by item variance would help management decide where to start the investigation. In this case, the investigation would probably center on what caused the excess use of indirect labor.

Spending and Efficiency Variances The manufacturing overhead budget variance can be divided into a spending and an efficiency variance. The budget variance assumes that the best measure of the amount that should be spent on overhead costs

EXHIBIT 17-2
DADE CORPORATION
Machining Department
Budget Variance Report
For June 19X8

Cost Item	Actual Overhead Cost	Flexible Budget Overhead Cost for 4,750 Standard Machine Hours	Budget Variance
A. Controllable			
Indirect labor	$ 9,010	$ 8,075 (1)	$ 935 unfavorable
Cutting tools	1,100	950 (2)	150 unfavorable
Lubricants	500	475 (3)	25 unfavorable
Power	1,600	1,450 (4)	150 unfavorable
B. Allocated			
Maintenance	4,210	4,375 (5)	165 favorable
C. Noncontrollable			
Supervision	5,000	5,000	0
Depreciation	15,000	15,000	0
Total	$36,420	$35,325	$1,095 unfavorable

(1) $1.70 per machine hour × 4,750 standard machine hours
(2) .20 per machine hour × 4,750 standard machine hours
(3) .10 per machine hour × 4,750 standard machine hours
(4) $500 plus .20 per machine hour × 4,750 standard machine hours
(5) $2,000 plus .50 per machine hour × 4,750 standard machine hours

is the standard hours allowed. This is the same as assuming that the best measure is units produced, since the standard hours allowed is simply a constant amount (the standard hours for one unit of output) times the number of units produced.

The **spending variance** assumes the best measure of the amount of overhead cost that *should* be spent is based on the *actual* machine hours worked rather than the *standard* machine hours allowed. The spending variance for the machining department is calculated for each cost item in Exhibit 17-3. This provides the supervisor of the machining department with information as to how much each cost item contributed to the total spending variance.

Exhibit 17-3 also shows the efficiency variance which we shall discuss next. The **efficiency variance** is the difference between the flexible budgeted overhead costs using actual machine hours and the flexible budgeted overhead costs using the standard machine hours allowed. Since the budgeted fixed overhead is constant the efficiency variance is associated only with the variable component of manufacturing overhead and can be calculated as follows:

Computation of the efficiency variance.

$$\text{Efficiency variance in overhead} = \left[\text{standard machine hours allowed} - \text{actual machine hours}\right] \times \text{variable overhead rate per machine hour}$$

EXHIBIT 17-3
DADE CORPORATION
Machining Department
Spending and Efficiency Variance Computations
For June 19X8

Cost Item	(1) **Actual Overhead Cost**	(2) **Flexible Budget Overhead Cost for 4,850 Actual Machine Hours**	(3) **Flexible Budget Overhead Cost for 4,750 Standard Machine Hours**	(1 – 2) **Spending Variance**	(2 – 3) **Efficiency Variance**
A. Controllable					
Indirect labor	$ 9,010	$ 8,245	$ 8,075	$765 unfavorable	
Cutting tools	1,100	970	950	130 unfavorable	Not calculated
Lubricants	500	485	475	15 unfavorable	for individual
Power	1,600	1,470	1,450	130 unfavorable	items
B. Allocated					
Maintenance	4,210	4,425	4,375	215 favorable	
C. Noncontrollable					
Supervision	5,000	5,000	5,000	0	
Depreciation	15,000	15,000	15,000	0	
Total	$36,420	$35,595	$35,325	$825 unfavorable	$270 unfavorable

The efficiency variance is a measure of the amount of variable overhead cost that was wasted or saved as a result of the inefficiency or efficiency in the use of machine hours. If actual machine hours are less than standard machine hours allowed then less variable overhead cost should be incurred. For the machining department, illustrated in Exhibit 17-3, the actual machine hours were 100 hours greater than the standard machine hours allowed (4,850 hours versus 4,750 hours) resulting in an increase in variable overhead costs of ($2.70 × 100 machine hours) = $270. The efficiency variance in overhead assumes that additional machine hours cause increased variable overhead cost; more indirect labor, cutting tools, lubricants, power, and maintenance were used as a result of the extra machine hours.

The efficiency variance is controlled by controlling the volume measure.

Note that in Exhibit 17-3 we did not calculate the efficiency variance on an item by item basis. The reason for this is that the efficiency variance is controlled by controlling the use of machine hours, not the use of the individual items that make up overhead.

We noted earlier that the budget variance is the sum of the spending variance and the efficiency variance. We have just seen that the efficiency variance is controlled by controlling the use of machine hours rather than the actual overhead cost items. But the spending variance is controlled by controlling the individual overhead cost items. This difference in the needed control makes it difficult for management to know what action may be needed in response to a budget variance.

For this reason, we believe that reporting for overhead cost control should be based on the spending and efficiency variances as shown in Exhibit 17-3 rather than on the budget variance as shown in Exhibit 17-2.

Causes of Overhead Variances

In order to investigate a variance or to choose an appropriate corrective action the department manager must understand the causes of overhead variances. In the following sections we discuss the causes of the controllable and allocated overhead costs. There is no discussion of the cause of variances in capacity costs since these variances are beyond the control of the department manager.

Controllable Costs The spending variance is the difference between the actual overhead cost as recorded in the accounting records and the flexible budgeted overhead costs using the actual hours of activity. To properly interpret a spending variance you should be aware that both price and quantity differences can cause a spending variance. One cause of a spending variance is the difference between the actual price paid for an item and the expected price for that item used in establishing the flexible budget. For example, if you expect to buy oil at $1 per quart and the actual price turns out to be $1.40 per quart, a spending variance will result. Another factor affecting the spending variance is quantity; the quantity of an overhead cost item actually used may be different from the quantity specified in the flexible budget. For example, the budget might call for the use of 10 gallons of tool coolant for each 1,000 units produced. If 11 gallons of coolant per 1,000 units produced were actually used, this would create a spending variance in overhead.

Both price and quantity factors can cause a spending variance.

As with direct materials and direct labor variances, management must first decide whether the variance is large enough to be significant. If significant, an investigation finds the cause of the variance. Finally, with the cause of the variance discovered, management can decide what corrective action, if any, is needed. The performance report such as the one in Exhibit 17-3 provides the starting point for the investigation.

Allocated Costs The allocated costs, part B of Exhibit 17-3, represent the actual maintenance cost of $4,210 charged to the machining department during the month of June. Allocated costs are somewhat different than controllable costs because two managers in the organization share responsibility for control of the allocated cost. The manager of the machining department is responsible for controlling the amount of maintenance services used. The manager of the maintenance services department is responsible for the cost of providing the required amount of maintenance service. In the case of maintenance, the manager of the machining department can minimize the quantity of maintenance service used by ensuring that workers are using machinery carefully. For example, the machining manager can be sure that the machines are not run at higher than normal speeds to make up for lost production time. However, the cost of providing the maintenance service is controlled by the manager of the maintenance department, who tries to assure that the needed maintenance work is done as efficiently as possible.

Control of allocated costs is divided among managers.

In the case of maintenance, the responsibility for control of allocated costs is more or less evenly divided. Other service department costs may be allocated where the manager of the machining department would be able to exercise little significant control over the amount of the service used. An example of this would be the cost of a company cafeteria serving meals to workers. The cost might be allocated to the machining department, even though the machining manager can do nothing to change the number of meals eaten by the machining department workers. In this case, the allocated cost is more like an uncontrollable capacity cost than a controllable cost. You can make a rather strong argument for not allocating uncontrollable costs, but it is sometimes done for the same two reasons mentioned earlier for including noncontrollable costs in the flexible budget of a department.

Allocated costs are controlled by developing flexible budgets for the service departments.

A practical way to control service department costs that many organizations follow is to prepare flexible budgets and performance reports for the service departments using the format of the overhead report in Exhibit 17-2. This service department report compares the actual service department cost with the estimated cost based on the flexible budget amount for the actual outputs. The key to implementing the flexible budget concept in the service departments is to identify a measure of service department output that causes the service department costs to fluctuate. Some common output measures used are shown in the following table.

Measures of service department output volume.

Service Department	**Output Measure**
Repairs and maintenance	Repair hours
Cafeteria	Number of employees served
Power plant	Kilowatt hours generated
Material handling	Pounds of material moved
Production scheduling	Orders processed
Personnel	Number of employees served

Once a flexible budget has been established for the service department, the actual cost and output data can be collected and a flexible budget prepared for the actual level of output.

APPLICATION OF FLEXIBLE BUDGETS TO NONMANUFACTURING ACTIVITIES

Flexible budgets have been used to plan and control manufacturing costs for many years. Lately, management has been relying more and more on using flexible budgets to control nonmanufacturing activities as well. Nonmanufacturing activities include selling, administrative, and distribution functions. Flexible budgets can be developed for any activity that is repetitive and exhibits a measurable output volume. These criteria fit many nonmanufacturing activities.

The first step in establishing flexible budgets for nonmanufacturing activities is to identify the activity and decide how the output volume will be measured. The criterion for selecting the measure of the output volume for the activity is the same as for manufacturing cost centers. That is, the measure of output volume should be the one that is most closely related to fluctuations in the activity's costs. Some nonmanufacturing activities and possible measures of output volume are shown below.

Measures of nonmanufacturing activity output volume.

Activity	Measure of Output Volume
Warehousing operations	Pounds or crates handled
Packing of finished goods	Units processed
Delivery of products	Miles driven
Motor pool	Miles driven, number of trucks or automobiles
Order entry	Orders processed
Billing	Lines typed
Key punching	Cards processed

Flexible budgets are established for nonmanufacturing cost centers using the same procedures applied to manufacturing cost centers. A measure is chosen that reflects the most direct relationship between the cost incurred and the output measure of the cost center. Exhibit 17-4 illustrates a flexible budget for a warehousing and shipping operation. The flexible budget is separated into controllable and noncontrollable costs and the fixed and variable components are identified. In this particular example there are no allocated costs but they could exist as they do for manufacturing departments.

The actual costs are collected for each item in the flexible budget and compared with a budget based on actual activity. A performance report is shown in Exhibit 17-5 for 9,700 units shipped.

EXHIBIT 17-4
UCA MANUFACTURING COMPANY
Flexible Budget
Warehouse and Shipping Department
For June 19X8

Item	Fixed Cost	Variable Cost (Per Unit Handled)	Budget at Expected Volume (10,000 Units)
Controllable			
Product handling labor	$ 1,500	$ .10	$ 2,500
Packing labor	1,000	.50	6,000
Shipping clerks	3,000	.05	3,500
Packing materials		1.00	10,000
Miscellaneous supplies		.20	2,000
Total controllable	$ 5,500	$1.85	$24,000
Noncontrollable			
Supervision	$ 8,000	$ —	$ 8,000
Depreciation	10,000	—	10,000
Insurance	2,000	—	2,000
Total noncontrollable	$20,000	$ —	$20,000
Total costs	$25,500	$1.85	$44,000

EXHIBIT 17-5
UCA MANUFACTURING COMPANY
Performance Report
Warehouse and Shipping Department
For the Month of June 19X8

Item	(1) Actual	(2) Flexible Budget 9,700 Units	(1–2) Budget Variance
Controllable			
Product handling labor	$ 3,120	$ 2,470 (1)	$650 unfavorable
Packing labor	5,900	5,850 (2)	50 unfavorable
Shipping clerks	3,650	3,485 (3)	165 unfavorable
Packing materials	9,200	9,700 (4)	500 favorable
Miscellaneous supplies	1,980	1,940 (5)	40 unfavorable
Total controllable	$23,850	$23,445	$405 unfavorable
Noncontrollable			
Supervision	$ 7,500	$ 8,000	$500 favorable
Depreciation	10,000	10,000	—
Insurance	2,000	2,000	—
Total noncontrollable	$19,500	$20,000	$500 favorable
Total costs	$43,350	$43,445	$ 95 favorable

(1) ($1,500 + $.10 × 9,700)
(2) ($1,000 + $.50 × 9,700)
(3) ($3,000 + $.05 × 9,700)
(4) ($1.00 × 9,700)
(5) ($.20 × 9,700)

MANAGED COSTS

Resources that management commits to projects with a duration of a year or longer are considered *managed costs*. Managed costs include expenditures on research and development, advertising, and training and development of employees. At the beginning of the annual budgeting process management decides on objectives which it wishes to attain for research and development, advertising, and employee training and development. A dollar amount is then budgeted to attain these objectives. For example, $10 million might be budgeted to develop a new product of a certain type, $2 million for a national advertising campaign to introduce another product, and $3 million for improvement of employee skills through continuing education programs.

Input-output relationships are not easily measured for managed costs.

The main problem in controlling managed costs is the lack of an easily measurable relationship between the cost (input) and the output. Research and development costs incurred in the current year may not provide any revenue producing results for a number of years, whereas advertising costs incurred in one year may generate revenue for a number of years following. In either case, it is not easy to determine the relationship between the costs incurred (input) and the resulting revenue (the output). Another problem in controlling managed costs is the measure of output. As just suggested, the ultimate output of research and development is added revenue, but can it be measured earlier by the number of patents obtained? The number of new products developed? Or both?

Because of these problems management usually chooses one of the following strategies to control managed costs:

Strategies for controlling managed costs.

1 Some managed costs can be broken into small components so that output measures can be developed and engineered cost control concepts can be used.

2 When no formal output measure can be developed, managed costs are controlled through the budgeting process and regular monitoring of amounts spent and progress to the extent it can be measured.

Developing Output Measures for Components of a Managed Cost

Some managed costs can be controlled in much the same way as engineered costs are controlled. If, for example, the cost of a data processing operation is considered in total, it might be considered a managed cost, because it would be difficult to specify the measure of output for the entire operation. A data processing department is responsible for producing a variety of reports, payroll checks, invoices for customers, keeping track of inventories, developing programs for new applications, and modifying programs for existing applications. Taken as a whole, it is hard to specify what could be used as a measure of output. But the various tasks just described provide a set of measures of output for various subactivities of the data processing activity. In fact, for most repetitive activities, standards can be developed for performance of the activity. For example, standards have been developed for key punching data into cards for entry into the computer system, for customer orders processed, and for processing of payroll checks. A standard cost can be developed for the payroll processing operation where the measure of output is the number of checks prepared, and the input costs are labor for entering data into the system, labor for running the payroll on the computer, and labor for putting checks into envelopes, cost of the computer time used, etc. The accounting system records the amount of labor, computer time, supplies, etc., used in processing the payroll, and this actual cost can be compared with the standard cost and analyzed as discussed earlier in this chapter.

To illustrate how managed costs can be controlled in much the same way as engineered costs, assume that UCA Manufacturing Company employs five keypunch operators, each at a salary of $1,000 per month. Each operator should be able to process 8,000 computer cards per month, indicating that five employees should process 40,000 (8,000 × 5) computer cards each month. Assume that during the month of June 19X8, 37,500 computer cards were processed and the actual salary cost amounted to $5,000.

If the salary cost of the keypunch operators is treated as a managed cost, the performance report would show the following:

Actual Cost	Budgeted Cost	Variance
	5 employees @ $1,000 each	
$5,000	$5,000	$0

The engineered cost control approach treats the cost of the keypunch operators as a variable cost even though it actually is a fixed salary cost. To analyze the salary as a variable cost the unit cost of each computer card processed is calculated as follows:

$$\textbf{Cost of processing each card} = \frac{\$5{,}000}{40{,}000 \text{ cards}} = \$.125 \text{ per card}$$

Thus, if 37,500 computer cards are processed the expected cost is:

Expected cost to process 37,500 computer cards = 37,500 × $.125 = $4,687.50

Given that the actual cost is $5,000 the performance report would show the following:

Using engineered cost control concepts to evaluate a managed cost.

Actual Cost	Budgeted Cost	Variance
	37,500 × $.125	
$5,000	$4,687.50	$312.50 unfavorable

The analysis of the salary cost using an engineering cost approach shows a variance of $312.50 unfavorable. This indicates to management that the hours available for keypunching computer cards were not fully used during the budget period.

What does this variance tell management? First that the keypunch operators have idle time. Management can then consider how better to use the time of the operators. They might, for instance, train them to do other jobs so that when they are not needed as keypunch operators they can be assigned to other jobs. Or, they could ask whether it would be better to have four full-time keypunch operators and then use overtime or part-time workers as needed. According to the standard, four full-time keypunch operators can process 32,000 cards per month (4 workers × 8,000 cards per worker). If during June, there had been four full-time operators, there would have been 5,500 (37,500 − 32,000) cards to be processed on overtime or by part-time people. If we assume that there are approximately 160 working hours per month, the standard says that an operator should be able to process 50 cards per hour, 8,000 cards per month divided by 160 hours per month. We can use this number to calculate that it would require almost 110 overtime or part-time hours to process the extra cards if the company had only four full-time operators (5,500 cards divided by 50 cards per hour). This number of hours would be difficult to obtain on an overtime basis with only four workers. It might be possible to hire an operator who was willing to work part time as needed. If so, the workload could be handled with four full-time people and a part-time person. However, since the extra workload is relatively heavy, it is probably better for management to keep five full-time people and try to use the excess hours in other jobs.

The point is that using an engineered cost control approach in this situation results in raising questions about the idle time and whether there are better ways to handle the workload. If the costs are treated as a managed cost, some of these questions might never be raised.

Control of Managed Costs through the Budgeting Process

For managed costs which cannot be subdivided into parts with measurable output, that is, costs which cannot be controlled as engineered costs, control is exercised through the budgeting process and through monitoring operations. The two most important approaches are the following:

1 Require managers to break their total operations into activities. For each activity, the manager must budget the cost and state explicitly what can be accomplished for the budgeted amount. Finally, the manager ranks the various activities showing which activities should be eliminated if the full proposed budget cannot be approved.

2 Require managers to select milestones in each project. Each milestone must be a definite event so that one knows when the milestone has been accomplished. The budget is then divided by milestone so that it shows how much should have been spent to reach the milestone. At each milestone management can compare actual expenditures to budgeted expenditures to see if any cost variance has occurred.

This part of the chapter discusses these two approaches.

Zero-Base Budgeting Zero-base budgeting is an example of the first approach. We shall discuss zero-base budgeting because it is a popular example of the first approach. The initial step is for managers to divide the operations of the department into groups of related activities called "decision units." Decision units in the loan division of a bank might include reviewing existing loans monthly, calling on prospective business loan customers at least once every three months, providing monthly statements of loan balances to loan customers, and many other similar activities. The decision units are of varying importance. You would almost say that some are mandatory if the bank is to stay in the lending business. Others would involve improvements beyond the minimum level of the activity. For example, along with the decision units mentioned above, there might be another decision package calling for weekly review of existing loans rather than monthly. When both decision units are presented as a part of the zero-base budgeting process, management sees the cost of reviewing loans monthly, and then in the other decision unit, management would see the additional cost of reviewing loans weekly rather than monthly. With this information, management can decide if the benefit of reviewing loans weekly rather than monthly is worth the extra cost which is budgeted for the weekly review decision package.

For the system to work, there should be a decision unit for each activity which represents the cost of doing the minimum level of activity. The minimum level of activity represents the level below which the decision unit should be entirely eliminated. After the decision unit for the minimum level of activity has been determined and a budget prepared for that unit, management may add additional decision units, with appropriate budgets, for increasing the level of the activity above the minimum as just illustrated with the loan review example. In this way, the benefit of each activity is identified along with its cost so that management can make the best possible budgeting decisions.

After each decision unit has been described and its budget developed, the second step in the zero based budgeting process is for the department manager to give each decision unit a priority and to rank all decision units proposed by the department. The third step in the process is for top management to review the decision units proposed by all departments. Top management must decide if they agree with the priorities assigned by the department managers. If some decision units proposed by the department manager cannot be funded, the priorities and ranking of decision units help top management decide which decision units should be eliminated. If top management finds it necessary to cut budgets, they know which activities they are cutting by cutting budgets. This should lead to better budgeting decisions for managed costs. The final step in the process is to transform the budgets for the approved decision units in each department into a departmental budget which is used to compare actual costs with budgeted costs and to report variances.

To illustrate, consider the budget report for a research and development department shown in Exhibit 17-6. The budget report reveals that the department is working on three projects which were proposed as decision units in the approved budget. For each project the financial performance is reported to the research and development manager in terms of the monthly budgeted costs, actual costs and variance, and year to date financial information in terms of actual costs and variance. The financial report would be accompanied by a narrative report for each decision unit which shows the progress toward the decision unit objectives.

The information in the financial and narrative reports is used by the manager of the research and development department to determine whether the costs of each project are being incurred as planned. Significant variances would be investigated by the manager and if necessary corrective action would be taken.

EXHIBIT 17-6
Budget Report
Research and Development
June 19X8

	June			Year to Date	
Decision Unit	**Budget**	**Actual**	**Variance**	**Actual**	**Variance**
Develop product X-10	$ 8,000	$ 9,000	$1,000 unfavorable	$ 40,000	$ 500 unfavorable
Improve product X-20	15,000	14,500	500 favorable	85,000	2,000 unfavorable
Modify chemical content of product X-40	6,000	5,000	1,000 favorable	40,000	3,000 favorable
Total	$29,000	$28,500	$ 500 favorable	$165,000	$ 500 favorable

Project Time Budgets The second approach to control of managed costs which cannot be subdivided into engineered costs is to develop milestones for the various managed cost projects, with budgets showing the costs necessary to accomplish each milestone. This approach works well with any project and could be illustrated with many projects. But let us consider a construction project. Suppose that we are planning to build a sun deck adjoining the bedroom of our house. We have decided that the following major steps will be required. The completion of each step becomes a milestone we will use for control. The steps are:

1 Purchase the lumber, cement, nails, and other materials.

2 Dig foundation holes for each of the posts which will be needed to support the deck.

3 Install the supporting posts and floor joists to support the floor.

4 Install the trim and railings.

5 Install a superinsulated sliding glass door between the bedroom and the deck.

Having identified the milestones, it is necessary to budget the cost required to complete each of them. The first is expensive because it includes the cost of acquiring all of the needed materials. The second step includes labor and the cost of a rented post hole digger (phd). The final three steps include primarily labor because you have all the needed tools. In practice, budgets for each step would list cost by category such as labor, materials, rental costs, etc. For our purposes, the illustration will show only the total costs by milestone. They are as follows:

Step Number	Cost
1	$1,200
2	400
3	200
4	200
5	400
Total Cost	$2,400

Control reports are prepared when milestones are completed.

A control report would be prepared when each milestone was completed. Notice that this would lead to reporting on an irregular time schedule. For example, if the purchase of materials was spread over two days, the first control report would be prepared at the end of two days. Suppose that it was three days later that the second milestone was reached, the post holes were dug, and the concrete footings were poured and hardened. The next report would occur at the fifth day after the project was started. To illustrate, suppose that the third step was completed at the end of the sixth day; the budget report at that point would appear as illustrated in Exhibit 17-7.

Of course the time period of this project is very short. In most managed cost situations, the time required for completion would be much longer. With this type of reporting, management will receive five budget reports during the project. Without this kind of reporting, management would have no real idea of whether the project

EXHIBIT 17-7
Budget Report
Deck Construction Project

Step	Budgeted Cost	Actual Cost	Variance	Date Completed
1	$1,200	$1,300	$100 unfavorable	August 2, 19X1
2	400	350	50 favorable	August 5, 19X1
3	200	210	10 unfavorable	August 6, 19X1
Totals	$1,800	$1,860	$ 60 unfavorable	

was likely to be above or below budget until it was completed. The only milestone would be completion of the total project. In fact on a small project like this, management might not like to receive reports every few days. But in larger projects, such as the construction of a house, apartment building, a bridge, or a road, it might be vital to receive budget reports while the project is still in progress, so that if problems were developing, management would have time to take corrective action.

In summary, we have discussed three ways of reporting for managed costs. The first is to divide the managed cost activity into smaller parts where the activity is like an engineered cost and can be controlled by engineered cost reporting methods described earlier in this chapter. The second method is to break the total activity into decision units and prepare descriptions of the output of each decision unit and a budget for the unit. Having the benefit of the decision unit described along with its budgeted cost, management should be able to make sound budgeting decisions. The third approach is to develop milestones for the activity with budgets prepared showing the expected cost for completing each milestone. With this kind of budgeting, a control report can be prepared at the completion of each milestone showing how the actual cost of reaching the milestone compares with the budget cost for reaching the same milestone. If significant variances have occurred, management can investigate them and take corrective action as needed.

In the final section of this chapter, we take a brief look at reporting for control of capacity costs.

CAPACITY COSTS

Capacity costs as the name implies represents costs incurred to provide or increase productive, distributive, or administrative capacity of an organization. Examples of capacity costs are depreciation charges for the manufacturing plant and equipment, depreciation on the warehouse for finished goods, depreciation on delivery trucks, property taxes on buildings and grounds, salaries of some employees such as the key administrative staff and rent payments on long-term rental agreements. These costs are incurred because of previous commitments made by management. They cannot be changed significantly in the short run without major modification in the organization's objective.

Capacity costs are controlled through careful evaluation and follow up audits.

The magnitude of most capacity costs is first considered in budgeting equipment purchases for the organization. Decisions dealing with the size of new manufacturing facilities are based on estimates of future demand and the most economical means of satisfying the demand. Once the size of facilities to be acquired is decided and a depreciation method is selected and contracts signed, little can be done to modify the annual depreciation charge. Also, property taxes and insurance costs will be committed once the facilities have been acquired.

Capacity costs are not so much controlled as they are carefully evaluated and decided upon. Nevertheless, they are controlled to the extent of careful evaluation of alternatives before long-term commitments are made and through follow-up audits of the implementation of the long-term commitments to see if actual results correspond to planned results. Capital budgeting is discussed in Chapters 25 and 26.

SUMMARY

Flexible budgets are used to control engineered costs that contain both fixed and variable costs. Since the engineered costs included in a flexible budget are usually joint to many products, output volume is measured using factors such as direct labor hours or machine hours.

Costs included in a flexible budget are categorized as controllable, allocated, and noncontrollable.

Controllable costs are those costs that are the primary responsibility of the department supervisor.

Allocated costs represent those costs incurred in manufacturing service departments and allocated to the departments producing the product based on the amount of service used.

Producing department supervisors can control the quantity of each service used so they are included in the producing department's flexible budget. Since the cost of the service is controlled by the service department manager, a flexible budget is also prepared for each service department.

Noncontrollable costs are those costs assigned to a department that the department supervisor cannot influence. Whether they should be included in performance reports is based on management's judgment.

Flexible budgets are used to evaluate the efficiency of actual operations through the computation of a revised budgeted cost based on the actual results of operations. The revised budgeted cost is compared with the actual cost to compute a budget variance which can be further divided into a spending and an efficiency variance. The cause of the budget variance, which includes the spending and the efficiency variance, is determined from careful analysis of the department operations.

Some managed costs are controlled by breaking them into smaller components and using engineered cost control analysis. This requires the development of output measures to calculate an after the fact budgeted cost to compare with the actual cost.

Other managed costs are controlled through the budgeting process. During the budgeting process, department supervisors are required to critically evaluate and establish priorities for all activities in their department. Based on the priorities top management determines which activities to fund. The funded activities are the basis for the preparation of budgets which are compared to the actual results of operations.

Another approach is to establish milestones for each project and prepare the budget to show the planned cost of achieving each milestone. Then at the completion of each milestone a control report can be prepared comparing budgeted and actual cost.

Capacity costs represent costs the organization has committed to incur to provide productive, distributive, and administrative capacity. These costs originate in the decision to make long-term commitments. The control of capacity costs is in the careful evaluation of alternatives in planning long-term commitments and through follow-up audits of the implementation of the long-term commitment decisions.

Review Problem

The Xexon Corporation expects to produce 10,000 units of product during June 19X8. It takes 2 standard direct labor hours to produce 1 unit of product. The manufacturing overhead budget based on direct labor hours is given below:

Cost Item	Fixed Cost	Variable Cost (Per Direct Labor Hour)	Total Cost (For 20,000 Direct Labor Hours)
Controllable			
Set-up	$ 500	$ .50	$10,500
Rework	—	.20	4,000
Maintenance	300	.10	2,300
Repairs	—	.15	3,000
Power	400	.05	1,400
Noncontrollable			
Supervision	3,000	—	3,000
Depreciation	10,000	—	10,000
Insurance	1,000	—	1,000
Total	$15,200	$1.00	$35,200

The actual results for the month of June were as follows:

Units of product produced	9,400
Actual direct labor hours	20,000
Actual costs	
Set-up	$11,000
Rework	5,000
Maintenance	2,100
Repairs	2,800
Power	1,500
Supervision	3,100
Depreciation	10,000
Insurance	1,000
Total	$36,500

Required Calculate the spending variance for each cost item and the efficiency variance in total.

Solution

XEXON CORPORATION
Spending and Efficiency Variance Computation
For June 19X8

Cost Item	Actual Overhead Cost	Flexible Budget Overhead Cost for 20,000 Actual Direct Labor Hours	Flexible Budget Overhead Cost for 18,800* Standard Direct Labor Hours	Spending Variance	Efficiency Variance
Controllable					
Set-up	$11,000	$10,500	$ 9,900	$ 500 unfavorable	
Rework	5,000	4,000	3,760	1,000 unfavorable	
Maintenance	2,100	2,300	2,180	200 favorable	
Repairs	2,800	3,000	2,820	200 favorable	
Power	1,500	1,400	1,340	100 unfavorable	
Noncontrollable					
Supervision	3,100	3,000	3,000	100 unfavorable	
Depreciation	10,000	10,000	10,000	0	
Insurance	1,000	1,000	1,000	0	
Total	$36,500	$35,200	$34,000	$1,300 unfavorable	$1,200 unfavorable

* 9,400 units of product × 2 direct labor hours per unit = 18,800 standard direct labor hours.

Glossary

Allocated cost A departmental cost that results from the distribution of another department's cost.

Budget variance The difference between the actual overhead cost incurred and the budgeted overhead cost based on actual output.

Controllable cost A cost that can be significantly influenced by the actions of the departmental manager.

Efficiency variance The difference between the overhead cost based on actual level of activity and the overhead cost based on the allowable level of activity. The variance assumes that if the actual activity level is smaller (larger) than the allowable level less (more) variable overhead will be incurred.

Flexible budget A budget that relates total mixed cost to an activity base and provides the way of calculating a budgeted cost for different levels of activity within a relevant range.

Noncontrollable cost A cost that cannot be influenced by the actions of the departmental manager.

Spending variance The difference between the actual overhead cost and the budgeted cost based on actual activity. This variance may be caused by both price and quantity factors.

Questions and Problems

17-1 Why are different control techniques applied to engineered costs than are applied to managed costs?

17-2 Why do the control techniques differ for direct labor and manufacturing overhead?

17-3 What is the difference between a controllable cost and an allocated cost?

17-4 What are the benefits of separating the budget variance into spending and efficiency components?

17-5 What approaches does management use for controlling managed costs?

17-6 All selling and administrative costs are either managed or capacity. Do you agree? Explain briefly.

17-7 **Using Flexible Budgets to Evaluate Performance** The University of Boyne offers an extensive continuing education program in many cities throughout the state. For the convenience of its faculty and administrative staff and also to save costs, the university operates a motor pool. Until February the motor pool operated with 20 vehicles. However, an additional automobile was acquired in February this year, increasing the total to 21 vehicles. The motor pool furnishes gasoline, oil, and other supplies for the cars, and hires one mechanic who does routine maintenance and minor repairs. Major repairs are done at a nearby commercial garage. A supervisor manages the operations.

Each year the supervisor prepares an operating budget for the motor pool. The budget informs university management of the funds needed to operate the pool. Depreciation on the automobiles is recorded in the budget in order to determine the cost per mile.

The schedule below presents the annual budget approved by the university. The actual costs for March are compared to one-twelfth of the annual budget.

University Motor Pool
Budget Report
For March 19X6

	Annual Budget	One Month Budget	March Actual	Over* Under
Gasoline	$24,000	$2,000	$2,800	$800*
Oil, minor repairs, parts, and supplies	3,600	300	380	80*
Outside repairs	2,700	225	50	175
Insurance	6,000	500	525	25*
Salaries and benefits	30,000	2,500	2,500	—
Depreciation	26,400	2,200	2,310	110*
Total	$92,700	$7,725	$8,565	$840*
Total miles	600,000	50,000	63,000	
Cost per mile	$0.1545	$0.1545	$0.1359	
Number of automobiles	20	20	21	

(CMA)

The annual budget was constructed upon the following assumptions:

a 20 automobiles in the pool
b 30,000 miles per year per automobile
c 15 miles per gallon per automobile
d $.60 per gallon of gas
e $.006 per mile for oil, minor repairs, parts, and supplies
f $135 per automobile in outside repairs

The supervisor is unhappy with the monthly report comparing budget and actual costs for March. He claims it presents unfairly his performance for March. His previous employer used flexible budgeting to compare actual costs to budgeted amounts.

Required

1 Employing flexible budgeting techniques, prepare a report which shows budgeted amounts, actual costs, and monthly variation for March.

2 Explain briefly the basis of your budget figure for outside repairs.

17-8 Flexible Budgets for a Restaurant Pearsons, a successful regional chain of moderately priced menu restaurants with a carryout delicatessen department, is planning to expand to a nationwide operation. As the chain gets larger and the territory covered becomes wider, managerial control and reporting techniques become more important.

The company management believes that a budget program for the entire company as well as each restaurant-deli unit is needed. The budget presented below has been prepared for the typical unit in the chain. A new unit once it is in operation is expected to perform in accordance with the budget.

Typical Pearsons Restaurant-Deli
Budgeted Income Statement for the Year Ended December 31
(000 Omitted)

	Delicatessen	Restaurant	Total
Gross sales	$1,000	$2,500	$3,500
Purchases	$ 600	$1,000	$1,600
Hourly wages	50	875	925
Franchise fee	30	75	105
Advertising	100	200	300
Utilities	70	125	195
Depreciation	50	75	125
Lease expense	30	50	80
Salaries	30	50	80
Total	$ 960	$2,450	$3,410
Net income before income taxes	$ 40	$ 50	$ 90

All units are of approximately the same size with the amount of space devoted to the carryout delicatessen similar in each unit. The style of the facilities and the equipment used are uniform in all units. The unit operators are expected to carry out the advertising program recommended by the corporation. The corporation charges a franchise fee which is a percentage of gross sales for the use of the company name, the building and facilities design, and the advertising advice. The Akron, Ohio unit was selected to test the budget program. The Akron, Ohio restaurant-deli performance for the year ended December 31, 19X8 compared to the typical budget is presented below:

Pearsons Restaurant-Deli
Akron, Ohio
Net Income for the Year Ended
December 31, 19X8

	Actual Results				Over
	Delicatessen	Restaurant	Total	Budget	(Under) Budget
Gross sales	$1,200	$2,000	$3,200	$3,500	$(300)
Purchases	$ 780	$ 800	$1,580	$1,600	$(20)
Hourly wages	60	700	760	925	(165)
Franchise fee	36	60	96	105	(9)
Advertising	100	200	300	300	—
Utilities	76	100	176	195	(19)
Depreciation	50	75	125	125	—
Lease expense	30	50	80	80	—
Salaries	30	50	80	80	—
Total	$1,162	$2,035	$3,197	$3,410	$(213)
Net income before income taxes	$ 38	$ (35)	$ 3	$ 90	$(87)

A careful review of the report and a discussion of its meaning was carried out by the company management. One conclusion was that a more meaningful comparison would result if a flexible budget analysis for each of the two lines were performed rather than just the single budget comparison as in the test case.

Required

1 Prepare a schedule which compares a flexible budget for the deli line of the Akron restaurant-deli to its actual performance.

2 Would a complete report, comparing a flexible budget to the performance of each of the two operations, make the problems of the Akron operation easier to identify? Explain, using an example from the problem and your answer to requirement 1.

3 Should a flexible budget comparison to actual performance become part of the regular reporting system

a For the annual review?

b For a monthly review?

Explain your answer.

(CMA)

17-9 Flexible Budget with Explanations The Jason Plant of Cast Corporation has been in operation for 15 months. Jason employs a standard cost system for its manufacturing operations. The first six-month performance was affected by the usual problems associated with a new operation. Since that time the operations have been running smoothly. Unfortunately, however, the plant has not been able to produce profits on a consistent basis. As the product requirements to meet sales demand have increased, the profit performance has deteriorated.

The plant production manager commented at a staff meeting in which the plant general manager, the corporate controller, and the corporate budget director were in attendance that the changing production requirements make it more difficult to control manufacturing expenses. He further noted that the budget for the plant, included in the company's annual profit plan, was not useful for judging the plant's performance because of the changes in the operating levels. The meeting resulted in a decision to prepare a report which would compare the plant's actual manufacturing expense performance with a budget of manufacturing expense based on actual direct labor hours in the plant.

The plant production manager and the plant accountant studied the cost patterns for recent months, and volume and cost data from other Cast plants. Then they prepared the following flexible budget schedule for a month with 200,000 planned production hours which at standard would result in 50,000 units of output. The corporate controller reviewed and approved the flexible budget.

	Amount	Per Direct Labor Hour
Manufacturing Expenses		
Variable		
Indirect labor	$160,000	$ .80
Supplies	26,000	.13
Power	14,000	.07
		$1.00
Fixed		
Supervisory	$ 64,000	
Heat and light	15,000	
Property taxes	5,000	
	$284,000	

The manufacturing expense reports prepared for the first three months after the flexible budget program was approved were pleasing to the plant production manager. They showed that manufacturing expenses were in line with the flexible budget allowance. This was also reflected by the report prepared for November, which is presented below, when 50,500 units were manufactured. However, the plant was still not producing an adequate profit because the variances from standard costs were quite large.

Jason Plant
Manufacturing Expenses
November 19X9
220,000 Actual Direct Labor Production Hours

	Actual Costs	Allowed Costs	(Over) Under Budget
Variable			
Indirect labor	$177,000	$176,000	$(1,000)
Supplies	27,400	28,600	1,200
Power	16,000	15,400	(600)
Fixed			
Supervisory labor	65,000	64,000	(1,000)
Heat and light	15,500	15,000	(500)
Property taxes	5,000	5,000	0
	$305,900	$304,000	$(1,900)

Required

1 Explain the advantages of flexible budgeting over fixed budgeting for cost control purposes.

2 Calculate the excess amount over standard spent on manufacturing expense items during November 19X9. Analyze this excess amount into those variances due to:
 a Efficiency
 b Spending

3 Explain what the management of Jason Plant should do to reduce:
 a The efficiency variance
 b The spending variance

(CMA)

17-10 Flexible Cost Budget The Melcher Company produces farm equipment at several plants. The business is seasonal. The company has attempted to use budgeting for planning and controlling activities, but the variable nature of the business has caused some company officials to be skeptical about the usefulness of budgeting to the company. The accountant for the Adrian plant has been using a system he calls "flexible budgeting" to help his plant management control operations.

The company president has asked the Adrian plant accountant to explain what the term means, how he applies the system at the Adrian plant, and how it could be applied to the company as a whole. The accountant presents the following data as part of his explanation.

Budget data for 19X3	
Normal monthly volume of the plant in direct labor hours	10,000 hours
Normal monthly volume of the plant in units	5,000 units
Estimated overhead at normal monthly volume	
Variable (controllable):	
Indirect labor	$ 6,650
Indirect materials	600
Repairs	750
Total variable	$ 8,000
Fixed (noncontrollable)	
Depreciation	$ 3,250
Supervision	3,000
Total fixed	$ 6,250
Total fixed and variable	$14,250
Planned units for January 19X3	4,000
Actual data for January 19X3	
Direct labor hours worked	8,400
Units produced	3,800
Cost incurred	
Indirect labor	$ 6,000
Indirect materials	600
Repairs	1,800
Depreciation	3,250
Supervision	3,000
Total	$14,650

Required

1 Prepare a budget for January.

2 Prepare a report for January comparing actual and budgeted costs for the actual activity for the month showing spending and efficiency variances.

(CMA)

17-11 Analysis of Warehousing Operations The Boxwidth Company has decided to use a flexible budget to develop control information for its warehousing operation. Based on an analysis of historical data the following controllable and noncontrollable costs have been identified for a normal month of operations.

Controllable Cost	Fixed	Variable
Indirect product handling labor	$ 5,000	1.00 per 100 units
Storage and shipping pallets	—	2.00 per pallet
Utilities	500	1.00 per 100 units
Shipping clerks	500	.50 per shipment
Miscellaneous supplies		.25 per shipment
Total	$ 6,000	

Noncontrollable	
Supervision salaries	$ 2,500
Depreciation	20,000
Property taxes	4,000
Total	$26,500

During the month the warehousing operation processed 50,000 units using 450 pallets. This activity was associated with 300 shipments to customers. The actual cost of this activity by item is shown below:

Item	
Indirect product handling labor	$ 5,450
Storage and shipping pallets	930
Utilities	1,010
Shipping clerks	700
Miscellaneous supplies	85
Supervision salaries	2,500
Depreciation	20,000
Property taxes	4,000
Total cost	$34,675

Required Prepare an analysis of the warehousing operation to measure the performance of the warehouse manager.

17-12 Preparation and Use of Flexible Budgets Department A is one of 15 departments in a manufacturing plant and is involved in the production of all of the six products manufactured. The department is highly mechanized and as a result its output is measured in machine hours. Flexible budgets are utilized throughout the factory in planning and controlling costs, but here the focus is upon the application of flexible budgets only in department A. The following data covering a time span of approximately six months were taken from the various budgets, accounting records, and performance reports (only representative items and amounts are utilized here):

On March 15, 19X1 the following flexible budget was approved for the department; it will be used throughout the 19X2 fiscal year which begins July 1, 19X1. This flexible budget was developed through the cooperative efforts of the department manager, his supervisor, and certain staff members from the budget department.

19X2 Flexible Budget—Department A

Controllable Costs	Fixed Amount per Month	Variable Rate per Machine Hour
Employee salaries	$ 9,000	—
Indirect wages	18,000	$.07
Indirect materials	—	.09
Other costs	6,000	.03
Total	$33,000	$.19

On May 5, 19X1 the annual sales plan and the production budget were completed. In order to continue preparation of the annual profit plan (which was detailed by month), the production budget was translated to planned activity for each of the factory departments. The planned activity for department A was:

	For the 12 Months Ending June 30, 19X2				
	Year	July	Aug.	Sept.	Remaining nine months
Planned output in machine hours	325,000	22,000	25,000	29,000	249,000

On August 31, 19X1 the manager of department A was informed that his planned output for September had been revised to 34,000 machine hours. He expressed some doubt as to whether this volume could be attained.

At the end of September 19X1 the accounting records provided the following actual data for the month for the department:

Actual output in machine hours	33,000
Actual controllable costs incurred	
Employee salaries	$ 9,300
Indirect wages	20,500
Indirect materials	2,850
Other costs	7,510
Total	$40,160

Required

Explain and illustrate how the flexible budget should be utilized:

1 In budgeting costs when the annual sales plan and production budget are completed (about May 5, 19X1 or shortly thereafter)

2 In budgeting a cost revision based upon a revised production budget (August 31, 19X1 or shortly thereafter)

3 In preparing a cost performance report for September 19X1

(CPA)

17-13 Equivalent Production; Variance Calculation; Performance Reports The Dopern Company employs departmental budgets and performance reports in planning and controlling its process costing operations. Department A's budget for January was for the production of 1,000 units of equivalent production, a normal month's volume.

The following performance report was prepared for January by the company's accountant:

Variable Costs	**Budget**	**Actual**	**Variance**
Direct materials	$20,000	$23,100	$3,100 unfavorable
Direct labor	10,000	10,500	500 unfavorable
Indirect labor	1,650	1,776	126 unfavorable
Power	210	220	10 unfavorable
Supplies	320	330	10 unfavorable
Total	$32,180	$35,926	$3,746 unfavorable
Fixed Costs			
Rent	400	400	—
Supervision	1,000	1,000	—
Depreciation	500	500	—
Other	100	100	—
Total	$ 2,000	$ 2,000	—
Grand total	$34,180	$37,926	$3,746

Direct materials are introduced at various stages of the process. All conversion costs are incurred uniformly throughout the process. Because production fluctuates from month to month, the fixed overhead is applied at the rate of $2 per equivalent unit of direct labor.

All variable costs are applied monthly as incurred.

There was no opening inventory at January 1. Of the 1,100 new units started during January, 900 were completed and shipped. There was no finished goods inventory. The units in process at January 31 were estimated to be 75% complete as to direct materials and 80% complete as to conversion costs. There is no shrinkage, spoilage, or waste of materials.

Required

1 Calculate the equivalent units for January production.

2 Calculate the under- or overapplied overhead for January.

3 Calculate the cost of goods sold and the cost of the work in process inventory at January 31 at actual cost.

4 Comment on the performance report in 150 words or less. What specific conclusions, if any, can be drawn from the report?

(CPA)

17-14 Variance Calculation and Identification of Sources The Carberg Corporation manufactures and sells a single product. The cost system used by the company is a standard cost system. The standard cost per unit of product is shown below:

Materials—1 pound plastic @ $2.00	$ 2.00
Direct labor 1.6 hours @ $4.00	6.40
Variable overhead cost	3.00
Fixed overhead cost	1.45
Total	$12.85

The overhead cost per unit was calculated from the following annual overhead cost budget for a 60,000 unit volume.

Variable overhead cost	
Indirect labor 30,000 hours @ $4.00	$120,000
Supplies—oil 60,000 gallons @ $.50	30,000
Allocated variable service department costs	30,000
Total variable overhead cost	$180,000
Fixed overhead cost	
Supervision	$ 27,000
Depreciation	45,000
Other fixed costs	15,000
Total fixed overhead cost	$ 87,000
Total budgeted annual overhead cost at 60,000 units	$267,000

The charges to the manufacturing department for November, when 5,000 units were produced, are given below:

Materials 5,300 pounds @ $2.00	$ 10,600
Direct labor 8,200 hours @ $4.10	33,620
Indirect labor 2,400 hours @ $4.10	9,840
Supplies—oil 6,000 gallons @ $0.55	3,300
Allocated variable service department costs	3,200
Supervision	2,475
Depreciation	3,750
Other	1,250
Total	$ 68,035

The purchasing department normally buys about the same quantity as is used in production during a month. In November, 5,300 pounds were purchased at a price of $2.10 per pound.

Required

1 Calculate the following variances from standard costs for the data given:

a Materials price
b Materials efficiency
c Direct labor price
d Direct labor efficiency
e Overhead budget

2 The company has divided its responsibilities such that the purchasing department is responsible for the price at which materials and supplies are purchased. The manufacturing department is responsible for the quantities of materials used. Does this division of responsibilities solve the conflict between price and quantity variances? Explain your answer.

3 Prepare a report which details the overhead budget variance. The report, which will be given to the manufacturing department manager, should display only that part of the variance that is the responsibility of the manager and should highlight the information in ways that would be useful to that manager in evaluating departmental performance and when considering corrective action.

4 Assume that the department manager performs the timekeeping function for this manufacturing department. From time to time analysis of overhead and direct labor variances has shown that the department manager has deliberately misclassified labor hours (e.g., listed direct labor hours as indirect labor hours and vice versa) so that only one of the two labor variances is unfavorable. It is not feasible economically to hire a separate timekeeper. What should the company do, if anything, to resolve this problem?

(CMA)

17-15 Control of Managed Costs The supervisor of an order entry system has recently attempted to measure the workload of the three employees who process sales orders. Salary is budgeted at $400 per week per employee. By observing the work of the employees the supervisor estimates each employee can process ten sales orders per hour during a seven-hour workday.

At the end of a recent four-week period the budget report showed the following:

Actual Salary	Budgeted Salary	Variance
$5,700	$4,800	$900 unfavorable

During this period of time the employees processed 5,000 sales orders.

Required

1 Analyze the cost of processing the sales orders as though it were an engineered cost.

2 What do you think caused the $900 unfavorable variance?

17-16 Control of Manufacturing Service Department Costs The Stevenson Works is a medium-sized manufacturing plant in a capital intensive industry. The corporation's profitability is very low at the moment. As a result, investment funds are limited and hiring is restricted. These consequences of the corporation's problems have placed a strain on the plant's repair and maintenance program. The result has been a reduction in work efficiency and cost control effectiveness in the repair and maintenance area.

The assistant controller proposes the installation of a maintenance work order system to overcome these problems. This system would require a work order to be prepared for each repair request and for each regular maintenance activity. The maintenance superintendent would record the estimated time to complete a job and send one copy of the work order to the department in which the work was to be done. The work order would also serve as a cost sheet for a job. The actual cost of the parts and supplies used on the job as well as the actual labor costs incurred in completing the job would be recorded directly on the work order. A copy of the completed work order with the actual costs would be the basis of the charge to the department in which the repair or maintenance activity occurred.

The maintenance superintendent opposes the program on the grounds that the added paperwork will be costly and nonproductive. The superintendent states that the departmental clerk who now schedules repair and maintenance activities is doing a good job without all the extra forms the new system would require. The real problem, in the superintendent's opinion, is that the department is understaffed.

Required Discuss how much a maintenance work order system would aid in cost control. (CMA)

17-17 Control of Capacity Costs Dickson, Inc., has formal policies and procedures to screen and ultimately approve capital projects. Proposed capital projects are classified as one of the following types:

- Expansion requiring new plant and equipment
- Expansion by replacement of present equipment with more productive equipment
- Replacement of old equipment with new equipment of similar quality

All expansion projects and replacement projects which will cost more than $50,000 must be submitted to the top management capital investment committee for approval. The investment committee evaluates proposed projects considering the costs and benefits outlined in the supporting proposal and the long-range effects on the company. The projected revenue and/or expense effects of the projects, once operational, are included in the proposal. Once a project is accepted, the committee approves an expenditure budget for the project from its inception until it becomes operational. The expenditures required each year for the expansions or replacements are also incorporated into Dickson's annual budget procedure. The budgeted revenue and/or cost effects of the projects, for the periods in whch they become operational, are incorporated into the five-year forecast.

Dickson, Inc., does not have a procedure for evaluating projects once they have been implemented and become operational. The vice-president of finance has recommended that Dickson establish a post-completion audit program to evaluate its capital expenditure projects.

Required Discuss the benefits a company could derive from a post-completion audit program for capital expenditure projects.

(CMA)

REVENUE VARIANCES AND INCOME ANALYSIS

AFTER COMPLETING YOUR STUDY OF THIS CHAPTER, YOU SHOULD HAVE LEARNED:

1 How information is provided to profit center managers to help them better manage their departments.

2 That there are four main causes for differences between budgeted net income before taxes as shown on the master budget and actual net income before taxes as shown on the monthly income statements.

3 That each of the four causes gives rise to a separate variance. The four variances are a sales volume variance, a sales price variance, a sales mix variance, and an expense variance.

4 That the concept of standard costs and flexible budgets can be applied to separate the expense variance further, if added detail is needed by managers.

5 That variance computations are the same for analysis of income by territory and by product as for analysis of a profit center.

In July, Michael Elia had been manager of a new branch store of the Paint and Paper Corporation for a little over six months. He had just received the June income statement for his store, its sixth month of operations. Each store of the Paint and Paper chain is a profit center. Before the opening of the store, Michael had participated in the development of an income budget for the store. On the basis of his experience as assistant manager of another branch store, he felt confident that the budget for his branch was realistic and attainable.

The branch income statement for June showed that actual income was below budgeted income for the month. The difference between actual and budgeted income was not great, but Michael was anxious to make sure that no unfavorable trends were developing. He had been promoted into this job, and he felt that future promotions were possible if he did well as manager of this branch store. Further, if the actual income of his store exceeded budgeted income at year-end, he would be entitled to a bonus in addition to his regular salary. If there was a problem, he wanted to discover it now and take corrective action immediately.

He had learned in his earlier jobs that accounting reports could help pinpoint problems and opportunities for income improvement. With that idea in mind, he sat down to analyze the June income statement.

The June income statement is shown below. Some additional data to be used in the example are included below the statement.

PAINT AND PAPER CORPORATION
Seward Branch Store
Income Statement
Month of June

	Budget	Actual	Variance
Sales			
Paint	$ 6,000	$ 4,480	$1,520 U
Wallpaper	6,400	6,480	80 F
Total sales	$12,400	$10,960	$1,440 U
Cost of goods sold			
Paint	$ 3,600	$ 2,880	$ 720 F
Wallpaper	4,000	4,050	50 U
Other variable store expense	1,240	1,050	190 F
Fixed store expense	2,300	2,150	150 F
Share of corporate expense	600	600	—
Total expense	$11,740	$10,730	$1,010 F
Store income before taxes	$ 660	$ 230	$ 430 U

Budget Data
Seward Branch Store

	Wallpaper	Paint
Sales in units	800 rolls	400 gallons
Average selling price	$8 per roll	$15 per gallon
Average cost of goods sold	$5 per roll	$ 9 per gallon
Other variable store expense	10% of sales	
Fixed store expense	$2,300 per month	
Share of corporate expense	$ 600 per month	

During the month of June, 810 rolls of wallpaper and 320 gallons of paint were actually sold. The main reason that actual paint sales were below budget was that a nearby discount store had held a paint sale during the month. Even Michael had to agree that the discount store paint was a good buy at that price. His store had sold some paint that week for people who wanted advice on special colors, services which the discount store did not provide. During the balance of the month, sales had been close to budgeted levels.

Michael first looked at the sales part of the income statement. He saw that the variance column showed the difference between the budgeted amount and the actual amount. The letter F or U behind the variance indicated whether the variance had a favorable or unfavorable impact on store profit. The wallpaper variance was favorable, but too small to be concerned with. The paint variance was fairly large and unfavorable. Michael knew that the bulk of the variance was due to sales lost when the discount store had its sale, but he also thought he had better determine how his actual price compared to the budgeted average price of $15 per gallon. He found the actual average price by dividing the total paint sales by the 320 gallons actually sold during the month. The actual average selling price was $14 per gallon ($4,480/320 gallons). This confirmed his suspicion that his average selling price was low. The discount store's sale had not only caused some lost sales units, but he had also offered discounts to some regular customers rather than lose them to the discount store.

The cost of goods sold and the variable store expense variances were potentially misleading. For instance, the paint variance showed favorable, but it mainly reflected the fact that he sold 320 gallons not the 400 gallons budgeted. The wallpaper variance showed unfavorable, but in fact it reflected the fact that he had sold more rolls than budgeted. He felt that he could get a better idea if he calculated the cost of goods sold per unit and compared that with the budgeted amount. The actual cost of goods sold per gallon of paint was $9 and per roll of paper was $5. These figures exactly matched the budgeted amounts, indicating that in both cases the variance shown was totally a result of the differences in sales volume; the cost per unit was not creating any of the variance.

The variance in the other variable and the fixed store expenses reflected the fact that Michael had been training his clerks to be careful in their use of supplies. They were small in amount, but since the actual and budgeted profits were low, they had a significant effect on the profit for the month. Michael felt that this was an area in which he could demonstrate that he was an above average store manager.

The kind of analysis which Michael did is an illustration of the kind of analysis which is done by profit center managers. In a larger, more complex operation, a more organized and complex approach is required. The topic of this chapter is a discussion of profit analysis in a more complex operation. Michael's interest in showing good performance and the effect of store results on his bonus are typical concerns of a profit center manager.

PROFIT ANALYSIS PROCEDURE

As you can see from the illustration just completed, analysis of profit center results seeks to answer the question: Why is actual income different from budgeted income? Many factors can cause such a difference. Demand for the products may have increased or decreased, competition may have been more or less severe than anticipated, or employees may have been more or less efficient than planned. As you saw in Chapter 13 in the discussion of responsibility accounting, management must investigate significant variances to find their cause. By itself the variance does not show the cause, but it is a signal for management to investigate to find the cause of the variance. Once the cause is found, management can then choose what corrective action may be appropriate.

But before management decides on the appropriate investigations, the income variance can be broken down into some more specific variances to give management a better idea of what deserves investigation and where the investigation should start. The more specific variances follow the format of an income statement. Revenue variances are calculated to answer three questions.

Questions revenue variances are calculated to answer.

1 Was the actual sales volume different from the planned sales volume?

2 Were actual sales prices different from planned sales prices?

3 Was the mix of products sold (in the illustration wallpaper versus paint) different than anticipated?

Since we have not yet discussed revenue variances, this chapter will introduce the idea of revenue variances, how they are calculated, and how they are used.

Although the simple illustration did not require it, the analysis of expense variances often makes use of standard cost and flexible budget analysis discussed in earlier chapters. In this chapter, we shall discuss how the variances listed below can be applied to help a profit center manager discover opportunities for improving operations. In order to illustrate these ideas, we shall introduce a slightly more complex example as the discussion progresses.

In summary, the balance of the chapter will be devoted to calculating and using the following variances in profit center analysis.

- Sales volume variance
- Sales price variance
- Sales mix variance
- Expense variances

For ease of understanding, we shall discuss the sales mix variance after the expense variances. Each variance will be illustrated and then the possible causes and managerial use of each variance will be considered.

COMPUTING THE VARIANCES

To illustrate the computation of three of the four variances listed above, we will assume a single product company that uses direct costing (rather than absorption costing) to calculate budgeted and actual net income. For purposes of illustration assume the following budgeted data for the month of January 19X9.

Budgeted production	20,000 units
Budgeted sales	20,000 units
Budgeted sales price	$6.00 per unit
Budgeted variable expense	
Manufacturing	$2.00 per unit
Selling and administration	$1.00 per unit
Budgeted fixed expense	
Manufacturing	$30,000 per month
Selling and administration	$20,000 per month

Based on these data, a budgeted income statement can be prepared as follows.

Budgeted Income Statement
Single Product Firm
For the Month of January, 19X9

	Per Unit	Master Budget
Sales in units		20,000
Sales revenue	$6.00	$120,000
Variable expenses		
Manufacturing (variable cost of goods sold)	2.00	40,000
Selling and administration	1.00	20,000
Total variable expense	$3.00	$ 60,000
Contribution margin	$3.00	$ 60,000
Fixed expense		
Manufacturing		30,000
Selling and administration		20,000
Total fixed expense		$ 50,000
Net income before taxes		$ 10,000

The sales revenue is simply 20,000 units sold times the selling price of $6 per unit. The variable expenses are the variable amounts per unit times the 20,000 units sold. The fixed expenses are the budgeted amounts per month.

With these facts as our base, we need only the actual results for January operations to illustrate the computation of the first two sales variances of interest to a profit center manager.

Sales Volume Variance

The sales volume variance occurs when actual unit sales are different from master budget unit sales. To illustrate the computation of the variance, assume that during January 19X9 the Single Product Company actually sold 19,000 units at $6 per unit. Also, actual manufacturing, selling, and administration expense-volume relations for January were identical to the master budget expense-volume relations. That is, the actual variable amounts per unit and the total fixed amounts per month were equal to the master budget amounts. This results in a difference between master budget and actual income before taxes of $3,000 as shown below:

Comparison of Master Budget and Actual Income
For Computing the Sales Volume Variance
Single Product Company
For the Month of January, 19X9

	Master Budget		Actual		
	Per Unit	Total	Per Unit	Total	Variance
Sales in units		20,000		19,000	1,000 U
Sales revenues	$6.00	$120,000	$6.00	$114,000	$6,000 U
Variable expenses					
Manufacturing	$2.00	40,000	$2.00	38,000	2,000 F
Selling and administration	1.00	20,000	1.00	19,000	1,000 F
Total variable expenses	$3.00	$ 60,000	$3.00	$ 57,000	$3,000 F
Contribution margin	$3.00	$ 60,000	$3.00	$ 57,000	$3,000 U
Fixed expenses					
Manufacturing		30,000		30,000	—
Selling and administration		20,000		20,000	—
Total fixed expense		$ 50,000		$ 50,000	—
Net income before taxes		$ 10,000		$ 7,000	$3,000 U

U indicates an unfavorable variance

The variance in net income before taxes of $3,000 unfavorable results from the fact that actual sales volume is 1,000 units (19,000 units − 20,000 units) less than master budget sales volume. The reduced unit sales volume reduces sales revenues by $6,000 (1,000 units × $6 per unit) and reduces variable expenses by $3,000 (1,000 units × $3 per unit). The change in sales volume has no impact on the fixed expenses because fixed expenses are defined as those expenses whose amount is independent of fluctuations in volume within the relevant range. The volume change results in decreases in two categories, total revenue and total variable expense, which combine to reduce income before taxes by $3,000. This result can be summarized by the sales volume variance. The sales volume variance is defined as the master budget contribution margin per unit times the difference between actual and master budget sales volume in units. For this example,

Sales volume variance computations.

Sales volume variance = master budget contribution margin per unit × (actual sales units − master budget sales units)
Sales volume variance = ($6 − $2 − $1) × (19,000 units − 20,000 units)
= $3,000 unfavorable

The variance is unfavorable since actual sales volume is less than master budget sales volume. Other things equal, smaller sales volume will result in smaller income before taxes.

Causes of sales volume variance.

The sales volume variance can be caused by many factors such as unanticipated changes in general economic conditions, differences in effectiveness of sales representatives, or differences in the effectiveness of the advertising program. As with all variances, if the size of the variance is significant, management will want to identify its cause.

In large organizations, the sales volume variance is calculated separately for each distribution channel (such as wholesale versus retail), for each geographic region, and possibly for each product line. There are two reasons for separating the sales volume variance into these categories:

Sales volume variances are calculated by distribution channel, geographic region, and product lines.

1 If management is to investigate the variance, it provides a more precise starting point for the investigation.

2 It permits reporting to follow the principle of responsibility accounting.

Reporting by channel of distribution shows management whether the variance occurred in the wholesale or retail divisions. A geographic division might direct the investigation to activities in Africa rather than in Europe, if the separate variance occurred in African sales. A separation according to product line would direct the investigation to the product lines which were causing the sales volume variance.

The second reason for separating the sales volume variance is so that reporting can follow the principle of responsibility accounting. As discussed in Chapter 13, responsibility accounting suggests that variances should be reported to each manager according to their responsibility and authority.

Sales Price Variance

To illustrate the calculation of the sales price variance we will change our assumptions about the actual events of the month of January. Assume now that the actual unit sales for January were equal to master budget unit sales. Also assume as before that the actual expense-volume relations are the same as master budget expense-volume relations. Finally, assume that the only difference between actual and master budget is that actual selling price was $5.90 per unit rather than the master budget amount of $6 per unit. The reduced sales price results in a reduction of income before taxes of $2,000 as can be seen in the budget report below:

Comparison of Master Budget and Actual Income
For Computing the Sales Price Variance
Single Product Company
For the Month of January 19X9

	Master Budget		Actual		
	Per Unit	Total	Per Unit	Total	Variance
Sales in units		20,000		20,000	—
Sales revenues	$6.00	$120,000	$5.90	$118,000	$2,000 U
Variable expenses					
Manufacturing	2.00	40,000	2.00	40,000	—
Selling and administration	1.00	20,000	1.00	20,000	—
Total variable expense	$3.00	$ 60,000	$3.00	$ 60,000	—
Contribution margin	$3.00	$ 60,000	$2.90	$ 58,000	$2,000 U

Comparison of Master Budget and Actual Income
For Computing the Sales Price Variance
Single Product Company
For the Month of January 19X9

	Master Budget		Actual		
	Per Unit	Total	Per Unit	Total	Variance
Fixed expenses					
Manufacturing		30,000		30,000	—
Selling and administration		20,000		20,000	—
Total fixed expense		$ 50,000		$ 50,000	—
Income before taxes		$ 10,000		$ 8,000	$2,000 U

The variance in income before taxes of $2,000 unfavorable results from the reduction in the selling price of the product. The sales price variance is calculated as the difference between the actual selling price per unit and the master budget selling price per unit times the actual sales volume in units. For this example,

Sales price variance.

Sales price variance = (actual selling price − master budget selling price) × actual sales volume in units
Sales price variance = ($5.90 − $6.00) × 20,000 units
= $2,000 unfavorable

The variance is unfavorable since the actual price is less than the master budget price, and thus has an unfavorable effect on income before taxes.

Causes of sales price variance.

The sales price variance may be caused by market conditions, unusual discounts allowed by sales representatives, or by a new pricing policy by sales management. The actual cause of the variance can only be determined by investigation. If management investigated and found that the sales representatives were allowing unjustified sales discounts in order to make sales more easily, management would probably ask the sales manager to work with the sales representatives to make sure that they were getting a fair market price for the product. If top management found that the cause of the variance was a new pricing policy by the sales manager, top management would want to evaluate the new policy. If they thought it was justified, they should probably revise the master budget price and the master budget. Sometimes, however, organizations do not like to revise budgets during the year. If so, they would reflect the new pricing policy in the next year's budget and expect to have price variances for the remaining months of the current year.

If management decides not to investigate the variances because the variances are too small to be significant, the variance will be a monthly reminder of the income impact of the changes in prices.

Expense Variances

Expense variances result from differences between master budget expense-volume relations and actual expense-volume relations. The variable expense per unit may be higher or lower than budgeted or the fixed expense per month may be higher or lower than budgeted. To illustrate the calculation of total expense variances, assume that actual production and sales equal their budgeted amounts, that no sales price variance exists, and that the actual expense-volume relations are as follows:

Variable expenses	
Manufacturing	$1.90 per unit
Selling and administration	1.15 per unit
Fixed expenses	
Manufacturing	$31,000 for January
Selling and administration	20,500 for January

The total variance in income before taxes is unfavorable by $2,500, as illustrated in the following budget report.

Comparison of Budget and Actual Income
For Computing the Expense Variances
Single Product Company
For the Month of January 19X9

	Master Budget		Actual		
	Per Unit	Total	Per Unit	Total	Variance
Sales in units		20,000		20,000	—
Sales revenues	$6.00	$120,000	$6.00	$120,000	—
Variable expenses					
Manufacturing	2.00	40,000	1.90	38,000	2,000 F
Selling and administration	1.00	20,000	1.15	23,000	3,000 U
Total variable expense	$3.00	$ 60,000	$3.05	$ 61,000	$1,000 U
Contribution margin	$3.00	$ 60,000	$2.95	$ 59,000	$1,000 U
Fixed expenses					
Manufacturing		30,000		31,000	1,000 U
Selling and administration		20,000		20,500	500 U
Total fixed expense		$ 50,000		$ 51,500	$1,500 U
Net income before taxes		$ 10,000		$ 7,500	$2,500 U

The total expense variance is separated into manufacturing and selling and administration.

The total expense variance of $2,500 is a combination of variances which occurred in manufacturing and in selling and administration. It is common practice to separate and report separate expense variances for each function. In this case, the variance would be separated into a manufacturing portion and a selling and administration portion. In an actual situation, there would likely be separate variances reported for research and development and personnel; selling and administration variances would also be separated. To avoid having to repeat the same analysis for many different functions, the data given for the Single Product Company only permit a two-part separation.

The expense variance for selling and administration is $3,500 computed as follows:

	Actual	Budget	Variance
Variable selling and administration	$23,000	$20,000	$3,000 unfavorable
Fixed selling and administration	20,500	20,000	500 unfavorable
Total	$43,500	$40,000	$3,500 unfavorable

The expense variance for manufacturing activities is $1,000 favorable and is computed in a similar manner.

Manufacturing variances are analyzed by direct materials, direct labor, and manufacturing overhead.

	Actual	Budget	Variance
Variable manufacturing	$38,000	$40,000	$2,000 favorable
Fixed manufacturing	31,000	30,000	1,000 unfavorable
Total	$69,000	$70,000	$1,000 favorable

Using standard costs and flexible budgets as presented in Chapters 8 and 9, the manufacturing variances are usually broken into price and quantity variances for direct materials and direct labor and into spending and efficiency variances for manufacturing overhead. This further division of variances helps management pin down the starting point for the investigation of significant variances and permits reporting that follows the principles of responsibility accounting.

Sales Mix Variance

Sales mix refers to the proportions in which the various products are sold.

The sales mix variance can only occur in a company which is selling more than one product. Sales mix is the proportion in which the various products are sold. For example, if a firm has two products, Uno and Duo, and in the month of June sells 200 units of Uno and 300 units of Duo, the sales mix for June can be described in two ways. The first way is simply to say that the company sold 200 units of Uno and 300 units of Duo. The second way of describing the sales mix is to say that (200/500) or 40% of the units sold were Uno and (300/500) or 60% were Duo.

The mix of products sold can influence net income.

The sales mix is important because some products contribute more to profit than others; that is, they have a greater contribution margin per unit or a greater contribution margin expressed as a percentage of sales. To continue the example, suppose that the contribution margin on Uno is $4 per unit and the contribution margin on Duo is $6 per unit. The total contribution margin for June sales is $2,600, the contribution margin from Uno totals $800, $4 per unit times 200 units, and the contribution margin from Duo totals $1,800, $6 per unit times 300 units. Suppose that in July costs and selling prices remain the same and that the total number of units sold is still 500, except that in July 250 units of Uno and 250 units of Duo are sold. What is the contribution margin in July? It will be $2,500, down $300 from the previous month. Why? Because the sales mix has shifted toward the less profitable product. During July, the sales mix was 250 units of each product or 50% of each product. You saw earlier that the sales mix in June was 40% Uno and 60% Duo.

Because changes in sales mix change total contribution margin and total profit, managers need to know when changes in sales mix have occurred and also how much the changes in sales mix have changed profit. The function of the sales mix variance is to report the impact of changed sales mix on income before taxes to profit center managers and other interested managers. Now we shall describe how the sales mix variance is calculated and used.

In developing the original master budget, a specific sales mix of products is assumed. If the actual sales mix differs from the mix used in preparing the master budget, the actual income before tax will differ from the master budget income before tax even though total sales volume may equal master budget sales volume. To illustrate the calculation of the sales mix variance, consider a company which budgeted the following sales and expenses for its two products, Alpha and Beta:

Master Budget Contribution for Products Alpha and Beta

	Alpha	Beta	Total
Sales in units	1,000	1,000	2,000
Sales revenue	$10,000	$10,000	$20,000
Variable expense	6,000	4,000	10,000
Contribution margin	$ 4,000	$ 6,000	$10,000
Contribution margin/unit	$4.00	$6.00	$5.00
Mix = 50% Alpha; 50% Beta			

The budgeted data shown above result in a sales mix of 50% Alpha and 50% Beta. This mix produces an average contribution margin per unit of $5. (Actually it is a weighted average which is weighted in proportion to the number of units of each product sold, but we shall use the simpler term average to mean weighted average in the discussion which follows.) Notice that neither product has a contribution margin per unit of $5; the $5 per unit is an average based on the budgeted sales mix.

Sales volume can be measured in units or dollars.

It is also possible to measure total sales volume in dollars of sales rather than in units. If there were many different products, it would in fact be easier to measure volume in dollars. If sales volume is measured in dollars, then contribution margin is expressed as a percentage of sales dollars rather than on a per unit basis. In this illustration, the total volume measured in dollars is $20,000, the sales revenue given in the data. The contribution margin percentage is 50%, the $10,000 total contribution margin divided by the $20,000 total sales revenue. The fact that the contribution margin percentage in this example is the same as the percentage sales mix is strictly a coincidence. Usually the contribution margin percentage would be different from the sales mix percentage.

Assume the actual results show no variance for sales prices, expense-volume relations, or total sales volume measured in units or dollars. The only difference between the budgeted results and the actual results is that the mix of products sold is 40% Alpha and 60% Beta. The actual results reveal an average contribution margin of $5.20 per unit calculated as shown below. More important, it results in a variance in net income before taxes even though there is no sales price, sales volume, or expense variance.

Actual Contribution for Products Alpha and Beta

	Alpha	Beta	Total
Sales in units	800	1,200	2,000
Sales revenues	$8,000	$12,000	$20,000
Variable expense	4,800	4,800	9,600
Contribution margin	$3,200	$ 7,200	$10,400
Contribution margin/unit	$4.00	$6.00	$5.20
Mix = 40% Alpha; 60% Beta			

Again, neither product has a contribution margin per unit of $5.20; the $5.20 is an average based on the proportion of each product actually sold.

The change in sales mix, in this case toward the more profitable product, Beta, increases the average contribution margin from the budget $5 per unit to $5.20 per unit and results in a favorable sales mix variance of $400. The steps in the computation of the sales mix variance are the following:

Steps in the calculation of the sales mix variance.

1 Calculate the actual average contribution margin per unit by dividing the total actual contribution margin by the total actual number of units sold. In this case the $5.20 is found by dividing $10,400 total contribution margin by 2,000 total actual units sold.

2 Next, subtract the master budget contribution margin per unit from the actual contribution margin per unit found in the first step. In this example, $5 is subtracted from $5.20.

3 Multiply the difference between actual and master budget contribution margin per unit times the actual total units sold. For the illustration we multiply the 20-cent difference in contribution margin per unit times the 2,000 total units sold.

4 Decide if the variance is favorable or unfavorable by seeing whether the actual contribution margin per unit is greater or less than the budgeted contribution margin per unit. Other things equal, the higher the average contribution margin per unit, the higher the total profit will be.

This can be summarized as follows.

Sales mix variance computations.

Sales mix variance = (actual average contribution margin per unit − master budget average contribution margin per unit) × actual sales in units

Sales mix variance = ($5.20 per unit − $5 per unit) × 2,000 units
= $400 favorable

What does this variance tell the profit center manager and other interested managers? In this example, since the sales mix variance is favorable, managers

The importance of the sales mix variance.

know that net income before tax was increased because a higher proportion of the more profitable product was sold. If relatively more of the less profitable product had been sold, the result would have been less net income before taxes. This conclusion may seem obvious in the illustrations we have been considering because each stage of the illustration assumed that only one thing was different from budget. In this illustration, we assumed a difference in sales mix but no difference in sales volume, sales prices, or expense-volume relations. The more normal situation is that all these may be different than budgeted. Then being able to compute the variances we have illustrated is very useful in sorting out what has happened. The variances help managers decide what action, if any, is called for. In the next section of this chapter we shall consider a final example where all the variances discussed in this chapter occur at the same time.

ANALYSIS OF PROFIT CENTER RESULTS IN A MULTIPRODUCT FIRM

To illustrate the calculation of the variances in net income before tax for a profit center when all variances occur at the same time, we shall use the BOD Corporation. The needed budget data are presented as Exhibit 18-1 and the actual data are

EXHIBIT 18-1
BOD CORPORATION
Master Budget Sales and Cost Data
For the Year Ended December 31, 19X2
($000 Omitted Except in per Unit Columns)

	Products				
	Beta		Zeta		
	Per Unit	Total	Per Unit	Total	Master Budget
Sales in units		70,000		80,000	150,000
Sales revenues	$100	$7,000	$150	$12,000	$19,000
Variable expense					
Manufacturing	$ 37	$2,590	$ 64	$ 5,120	$ 7,710
Marketing	10	700	15	1,200	1,900
Total variable expense	$ 47	$3,290	$ 79	$ 6,320	$ 9,610
Contribution margin	$ 53	$3,710	$ 71	$ 5,680	$ 9,390
Fixed expense					
Manufacturing					$ 1,301
Marketing					1,950
Administration					1,500
Total					$ 4,751
Net income before taxes					$ 4,639

EXHIBIT 18-2
BOD CORPORATION
Actual Sales and Cost Data
For the Year Ended December 31, 19X2
($000 Omitted Except in per Unit Columns)

	Products				
	Beta		Zeta		
	Per Unit	Total	Per Unit	Total	Actual Total
Sales in units		75,000		70,000	145,000
Sales revenues	$98	$7,350	$160	$11,200	$18,550
Variable expense					
Manufacturing	$40	$3,000	$ 66	$ 4,620	$ 7,620
Marketing	10	750	17	1,190	1,940
Total variable expense	$50	$3,750	$ 83	$ 5,810	$ 9,560
Contribution margin	$48	$3,600	$ 77	$ 5,390	$ 8,990
Fixed expense					
Manufacturing					$ 1,380
Marketing					1,900
Administration					1,600
Total					$ 4,880
Net income before taxes					$ 4,110

presented as Exhibit 18-2. Using the budgeted and actual data we will calculate the total difference between master budget net income before taxes and actual net income before taxes and then separate the total difference into sales volume, sales mix, sales price, and expense variances.

This situation differs from the previous illustrations because sales volume, sales mix, sales price, and expense variances exist simultaneously, the situation usually encountered in practice. Previously, by comparing the actual net income before taxes to the master budget net income before taxes, we found a single variance. With the variances existing simultaneously, we need to prepare a flexible budget to separate the individual variances.

The first step in separating the variances is to calculate the flexible budget for the actual sales volume (and sales mix). Then use the equations from this chapter to compute the sales volume, sales mix, expense, and sales price variances.

Exhibit 18-3 illustrates how the master budget, the flexible budget, and the actual income statement are used to produce the required variances. The last two columns contain the four variances themselves.

The flexible budget in column 2 of Exhibit 18-3 is calculated as follows.

BOD CORPORATION
Calculation of Flexible Budget
For the Year Ended December 31, 19X2
($000 Omitted)

Flexible budgets are used to calculate sales volume, sales mix, sales price, and expense variances.

Sales revenue (actual units sold × budgeted selling price)

Beta 75,000 units @ $100	$ 7,500
Zeta 70,000 units @ $150	10,500
	$18,000

Variable expenses − manufacturing (actual units sold × budgeted variable expense per unit)

Beta 75,000 units @ $37	$ 2,775
Zeta 70,000 units @ $64	4,480
	$ 7,255

Variable expenses − marketing (actual units sold × budgeted variable expense per unit)

Beta 75,000 units @ $10	$ 750
Zeta 70,000 units @ $15	1,050
	$ 1,800

It is not necessary to show calculation of the fixed expenses for the flexible budget because budgeted fixed expenses are not expected to change as long as the volume is within the relevant range. The amounts of variable expense do need to be recalculated when the volume has changed because budgeted variable expenses do change with volume changes.

With the flexible budget calculated, each line is deducted from the corresponding line in the master budget column to obtain two of our four variances, the sales volume variance and the sales mix variance. What appears is the total of the sales volume and sales mix variances at the contribution margin line and also at the net income before taxes line. The computations at the bottom of the exhibit show how the sales volume variance is separated from the sales mix variance. These computations are explained more completely in the next section of the chapter.

To obtain the sales price variance and the expense variances, we compare, from Exhibit 18-3, the flexible budget column and the actual column. The differences between these two columns are due to changes in the selling price per unit or to changes in expenses. When comparing the flexible budget with the actual results, note that the sales volume and sales mix are not different because the actual sales volume and sales mix were used in calculating the flexible budget column. Thus, the differences between the second and third columns must result only from price and expense differences.

Sales Volume and Sales Mix Variances

The total variance in Exhibit 18-3 due to sales volume and sales mix is $445 unfavorable. This total variance can be separated into sales volume and sales mix components using sales units to measure volume.[1]

[1] For a discussion of the alternative methods, see Nikolai G. Chumachenko, "Once Again: The Volume-Mix-Price/Cost Budget Variance Analysis," *The Accounting Review* (October 1968), pp. 753–762.

EXHIBIT 18-3
BOD CORPORATION
Calculation of Volume-Mix and Expense-Price Variances
For the Year Ended December 31, 19X2
($000 Omitted)

	(1) Master Budget	(2) Flexible Budget	(3) Actual	(1−2) Volume and Mix	(2−3) Expense and Price
Sales in units	150,000	145,000	145,000	5,000 U	N/A
Sales revenues	$19,000	$18,000	$18,550	$1,000 U	$550 F
Variable expenses					
Manufacturing	$ 7,710	$ 7,255	$ 7,620	$ 455 F	$365 U
Marketing	1,900	1,800	1,940	100 F	140 U
Total variable expense	$ 9,610	$ 9,055	$ 9,560	$ 555 F	$505 U
Contribution margin	$ 9,390	$ 8,945	$ 8,990	$ 445 U	$ 45 F
Fixed expenses					
Manufacturing	$ 1,301	$ 1,301	$ 1,380	0	$ 79 U
Marketing	1,950	1,950	1,900	0	50 F
Administration	1,500	1,500	1,600	0	100 U
Total fixed expense	$ 4,751	$ 4,751	$ 4,880	0	$129 U
Net income before taxes	$ 4,639	$ 4,194	$ 4,110	$ 445 U	$ 84 U

$$\text{Sales volume variance} = \text{master budget average contribution margin per unit} \times \left[\text{actual sales units} - \text{master budget sales units}\right]$$

$$= \frac{\$9{,}390}{150{,}000} \times (145{,}000 - 150{,}000) \qquad = \$313 \text{ U}$$

$$\text{Sales mix variance} = \left[\text{flexible budget average contribution margin per unit} - \text{master budget average contribution margin per unit}\right] \times \text{actual sales units}$$

$$= \left[\frac{\$8{,}945}{145{,}000} - \frac{\$9{,}390}{150{,}000}\right] \times 145{,}000 \qquad = \$132 \text{ U}$$

Total sales volume and sales mix variance = $445 U

The volume variance can be calculated by determining the difference in units and multiplying it by the master budget average contribution per unit. In equation form:

Sales volume variance.

$$\textbf{Sales volume variance} = \textbf{master budget average contribution per unit} \times \left[\textbf{actual sales units} - \textbf{master budget sales units}\right]$$

$$\text{Sales volume variance} = \frac{\$9{,}390}{150{,}000} \times (145{,}000 - 150{,}000) = \$313\ \text{U}$$

This indicates that at the budgeted mix a 5,000 unit decrease in sales volume reduced income by $313. Notice the calculation provides no information concerning the cause of the variance; it shows the dollar impact of a sales volume change at the budgeted mix.

The sales mix variance is calculated by subtracting the master budget and flexible budget average contribution per unit and multiplying the difference times the actual sales volume, measured in units. In equation form:

Sales mix variance.

$$\text{Sales mix variance} = \left[\text{flexible budget average contribution per unit} - \text{master budget average contribution per unit}\right] \times \text{actual sales units}$$

$$\text{Sales mix variance} = \left[\frac{\$8{,}945}{145{,}000} - \frac{\$9{,}390}{150{,}000}\right] \times 145{,}000 = \$132\ \text{U}$$

This indicates the actual mix of products sold differed from the master budget mix resulting in a lower average contribution margin per unit. This resulted from the increase in the percentage of Beta sold since Beta has the *lower* contribution per unit; as indicated below:

	Master Budget Contribution Margin per Unit	Budgeted Sales Units	Sales Mix %	Actual Sales Units	Sales Mix %
Beta	$53	70,000	47	75,000	52
Zeta	$71	80,000	53	70,000	48
Total		150,000	100	145,000	100

Price and Expense Variances

The $550 favorable price variance in Exhibit 18-3 results from the fact the average actual sales price exceeded the average flexible budget sales price. This can be broken down by product as follows:

Beta ($ 98.00 − $100.00) × 75,000 =	**$150**	**U**
Zeta ($160.00 − $150.00) × 70,000 =	**700**	**F**
	$550	**F**

The total expense variance is $634 unfavorable which can be summarized by function as shown on page 525.

BOD CORPORATION
Expense Variances by Function

Manufacturing		
Variable	$365 U	
Fixed	79 U	$444 U
Marketing		
Variable	$140 U	
Fixed	50 F	90 U
Administration		100 U
Total		$634 U

Again these variances provide indications as to what each segment of the business is contributing to the total difference between the master budget income and the actual income. They provide management with information that can be used to decide whether it is worth spending the time needed to investigate the cause of the variances.

ANALYSIS OF PRODUCTS AND SALES TERRITORIES

In the next two sections of this chapter we will illustrate how the variances studied in this chapter can be used to analyze individual products and sales territories. If there is a manager responsible for a product or territory, that manager would probably be designated a profit center or revenue center manager and would use the variances as we have described earlier. If there is no manager responsible for the product or territory, the analysis might produce information which managers would use to decide if a given territory or product can be made more profitable. If the profitability is not satisfactory and management can find no way of improving it, the product or territory might be abandoned.

A direct cost is physically traceable to a cost object.

Before we begin the topic of analysis by product or territory, two terms need to be defined. They will be applied to divide some of the fixed expenses between products and territories. The two terms are **direct** and **common.** In its accounting meaning, the term direct means that there is a physical link between a cost or expense and some object. We have frequently used the terms direct materials and direct labor. Direct means that these materials and labor costs are physically related to the units of product. Because of the physical link, the amount of direct materials or direct labor used in a product may be measured.

Costs and expenses may be direct to objects other than products. For example, a cost may be direct to a department because it is physically used in that department and nowhere else. The salary of the manager of a department represents a *direct* cost of the department. If there are several products produced in the department, the salary of the department manager is not direct to the products because he or she does not physically work on the products and the amount of time spent on each product cannot be measured. The department manager's salary can be *allocated* to the products but not measured to them.

A common cost is not physically traceable to a cost object.

Since the department manager's salary is not direct to the products it is a *common* cost. That is, the cost benefits, or is common to, all the products. If the department manager's salary is to be divided among each product, allocation rather than measurement is required.

The important point to note is that if a cost or expense is direct to some object, the amount of the cost or expense applicable to that object can be measured. If a cost or expense is common, the only way the cost can be assigned to the object is by allocation. In management accounting such as profit center accounting, costs are usually not allocated. If a cost is not direct, it is simply not divided at all. Recall that cost accounting does divide common costs by allocation to products.

A cost is direct or common depending on the cost object.

One final point to be mentioned. A particular cost may be direct to one object and common as far as other objects are concerned. We have already illustrated this idea by saying that the department manager's salary is direct to the department but not to the product. The department manager's salary would also be direct to the plant in which the department is located. The expenses of a sales office are direct to the sales territory in which it is located and direct to the marketing activity, but probably not direct to each individual product sold.

In the illustrations that follow, some expenses will be direct and others common. The direct expenses will be identified with each product or territory.

Product Analysis

Based on the classification of fixed expenses as direct and common with respect to product, Exhibit 18-4 shows the product contribution for Beta. The analysis in Exhibit 18-4 compares the master budget **product contribution** with the actual product contribution. This difference has been separated into sales volume and expense and sales price components by calculating a flexible budget in column 2. The sales volume variance is $265 favorable and results from the sale of 5,000 units in excess of the master budget volume. Since only one product is being analyzed there is no sales mix variance.

The expense-sales price variance of $378 unfavorable can be separated into a sales price variance of $150 unfavorable and an expense variance of $228 unfavorable. If needed, the expense variance can be further separated by functional category as follows:

Manufacturing		
Variable	$225 U	
Fixed	23 U	$248 U
Marketing		
Variable	$ 0	
Fixed	20 F	20 F
Total		$228 U

Profitability analysis of product lines.

This analysis provides management with an indication of the factors that caused the difference between the master budget and actual product contribution for product Beta. The same type of analysis would be appropriate for product Zeta.

EXHIBIT 18-4
BOD CORPORATION
Contribution Analysis of
Product Beta
For the Year Ended December 31, 19X1
($000 Omitted)

	(1) Master Budget	(2) Flexible Budget	(3) Actual	(1−2) Sales Volume	(2−3) Expense and Price
Sales in units	70,000	75,000	75,000	5,000 F	N/A
Sales revenue	$7,000	$7,500	$7,350	$500 F	$150 U
Variable expense					
Manufacturing	$2,590	$2,775	$3,000	$185 U	$225 U
Marketing	700	750	750	50 U	0
Total variable expense	$3,290	$3,525	$3,750	$235 U	$225 U
Contribution margin	$3,710	$3,975	$3,600	$265 F	$375 U
Direct fixed expenses					
Manufacturing	292	292	315	0	23 U
Marketing	400	400	380	0	20 F
Total direct fixed expenses	$ 692	$ 692	$ 695	0	$ 3 U
Product contribution	$3,018	$3,283	$2,905	$265 F	$378 U

Territory Analysis

Individual sales territories can be analyzed in a manner analogous to the procedures illustrated in Exhibit 18-3. In many organizations the marketing function is divided into geographical sales territories and master budgets are developed for each territory showing the expected territory contribution to corporate income. The **territory contribution** is the difference between the contribution margin and the direct fixed costs for the territory.

At the end of the accounting period, when the actual data are collected, top management desires to evaluate the performance of the territory managers. The cost accountant can aid in this evaluation by preparing a report that details the sales volume, expense, sales price, and sales mix variances for each sales territory. To accomplish this the actual sales and expense data must be collected by territory. With this data the procedures to compute sales volume, expense, sales price, and sales mix variances can be applied to the territories.

To illustrate the computations we will use the unit sales price and unit variable expense data for products Beta and Zeta given in Exhibits 18-1 and 18-2. Assume the following master budget and actual data for the northern sales territory:

BOD CORPORATION
Budgeted and Actual Sales and Expense Data
Northern Sales Territory
For the Year Ended December 31, 19X1
($000 Omitted)

	Master Budget			Actual		
	Beta	**Zeta**	**Total**	**Beta**	**Zeta**	**Total**
Sales in units	40,000	20,000	60,000	45,000	25,000	70,000
Sales revenues	$4,000	$3,000	$7,000	$4,410	$4,000	$8,410
Variable manufacturing expenses	$1,480	$1,280	$2,760	$1,665	$1,600	$3,265
Variable marketing expenses	400	300	700	450	425	875
Total variable expenses	$1,880	$1,580	$3,460	$2,115	$2,025	$4,140
Contribution margin	$2,120	$1,420	$3,540	$2,295	$1,975	$4,270
Direct fixed expenses			850			875
Territory contribution			$2,690			$3,395

Note that in calculating the actual territory contribution the variable manufacturing costs are at budgeted unit costs. The budgeted unit cost is used rather than the actual unit cost, since the territory managers are not responsible for manufacturing variances.

The direct fixed expenses would include items such as the territory manager's salary and advertising expenses incurred entirely for the benefit of the northern sales territory.

Profitability analysis of sales territories.

Exhibit 18-5 illustrates the computation of the sales volume, sales mix, sales price, and expense variances for the northern sales territory. These computations are identical to the analysis of the BOD Company in Exhibit 18-3.

INTERPRETING THE VARIANCES

The rationale for computing variances is that their values will provide information to management as to whether corrective action should be taken. The analysis of variances can indicate the location of potential problem areas such as manufacturing, marketing, or administration or the product or sales territory whose actual results are below budget but the analysis reveals no information concerning the cause of the variance. The underlying cause of a particular variance can only be determined by investigating the product, process, or functional area of concern to management.

EXHIBIT 18-5
BOD CORPORATION
Contribution Analysis of Northern Territory
($000 Omitted)

	Master Budget	Flexible Budget	Actual	Volume and Mix	Expense and Price
Sales in units	60,000	70,000	70,000	10,000 F	N/A
Sales revenues	$7,000	$8,250	$8,410	$1,250 F	$160 F
Variable manufacturing expenses	$2,760	$3,265	$3,265	$ 505 U	$ 0
Variable marketing expenses	700	825	875	125 U	50 U
Total variable expenses	$3,460	$4,090	$4,140	$ 630 U	$ 50 U
Contribution margin	$3,540	$4,160	$4,270	$ 620 F	$110 F
Direct fixed expenses	850	850	875	0	25 U
Territory contribution	$2,690	$3,310	$3,395	$ 620 F	$ 85 F

$$\text{Sales volume variance} = \text{master budget average contribution margin per unit} \times \left[\text{actual sales units} - \text{master budget sales units}\right]$$

$$= \frac{\$3{,}540}{60{,}000} \times (70{,}000 - 60{,}000) \qquad = \$590 \text{ F}$$

$$\text{Sales mix variance} = \left[\text{flexible budget average contribution margin per unit} - \text{master budget average contribution margin per unit}\right] \times \text{actual sales units}$$

$$= \left[\frac{\$4{,}160}{70{,}000} - \frac{\$3{,}540}{60{,}000}\right] \times 70{,}000 \qquad = \$\ 30 \text{ F}$$

Total sales volume and sales mix variance = $620 F

SUMMARY

As actual data are collected they are compared to the budgeted data to provide management with an indication of potential problem areas that might require an investigation.

The variances calculated can be classified as due to changes in sales volume, sales mix, expense, or sales price.

These variances can be computed at the company level, for each profit center by product or territory, depending on the needs of management.

The expense variances are generally summarized by functional area with the manufacturing variances further analyzed through the use of standard costs and flexible budgets as discussed in Chapters 8 and 9.

Review Problem

The SVI Company has developed the following budgeted information for the year 19X2.

SVI COMPANY
Budgeted Income Statement
For Year Ended December 31, 19X2

	Product A	Product B	Total
Sales in units	2,000	2,500	4,500
Sales revenue	$30,000	$25,000	$55,000
Variable expenses			
Manufacturing	12,000	10,000	22,000
Selling	4,000	2,500	6,500
Total variable expense	$16,000	$12,500	$28,500
Contribution margin	$14,000	$12,500	$26,500
Fixed expenses			
Manufacturing			7,000
Selling			4,500
Administrative			1,900
Total fixed expenses			$13,400
Net income before taxes			$13,100

At the end of the year the following actual data had been collected.

SVI COMPANY
Income Statement
For Year Ended December 31, 19X2

	Product A	Product B	Total
Sales in units	1,875	2,900	4,775
Sales revenue	$26,250	$26,100	$52,350
Variable expenses			
Manufacturing	13,125	8,700	21,825
Selling	3,750	4,350	8,100
Total variable, expense	$16,875	$13,050	$29,925
Contribution margin	$ 9,375	$13,050	$22,425

Fixed expenses	
Manufacturing	6,775
Selling	4,800
Administration	1,970
Total fixed expenses	$13,545
Net income before taxes	$ 8,880

Required Calculate the sales price, expense, sales volume, and sales mix variances for the SVI Company. In computing the sales volume and sales mix variances use units sold as the measure of volume.

Solution

The first step in computing the variances is the construction of a flexible budget for 19X2 using the actual volume and the budgeted prices and expenses.

SVI COMPANY
Flexible Budgeted Income Statement
For the Year Ended December 31, 19X2

	Product A	Product B	Total
Sales in units	1,875	2,900	4,775
Sales revenues	$28,125	$29,000	$57,125
Variable expenses			
Manufacturing	11,250	11,600	22,850
Selling	3,750	2,900	6,650
Total variable expenses	$15,000	$14,500	$29,500
Contribution margin	$13,125	$14,500	$27,625
Fixed expenses			
Manufacturing			7,000
Selling			4,500
Administration			1,900
Total fixed expenses			$13,400
Net income before taxes			$14,225

The second step is to compare the master budget, flexible budget, and actual data to isolate the variances as shown on page 532.

SVI COMPANY
Comparative Income Statements
For the Year Ended December 31, 19X2

	Master Budget	Flexible Budget	Actual	Volume and Mix		Expense and Price	
Sales in units	4,500	4,775	4,775	275	F	N/A	
Sales revenues	$55,000	$57,125	$52,350	$2,125	F	$4,775	U

(continued)

Variable expenses							
Manufacturing	22,000	22,850	21,825	850	U	1,025	F
Selling	6,500	6,650	8,100	150	U	1,450	U
Total variable expenses	$28,500	$29,500	$29,925	$1,000	U	$ 425	U
Contribution margin	$26,500	$27,625	$22,425	$1,125	F	$5,250	U
Fixed expenses							
Manufacturing	$ 7,000	$ 7,000	$ 6,775	—		$ 225	F
Selling	4,500	4,500	4,800	—		300	U
Administration	1,900	1,900	1,970	—		70	U
Total fixed expenses	$13,400	$13,400	$13,545	—		$ 145	U
Net income before taxes	$13,100	$14,225	$ 8,880	$1,125	F	$5,345	U

Variance Computation

$$\text{Sales volume variance} = \frac{\$26{,}500}{4{,}500} \times [4{,}775 - 4{,}500] = \$1{,}619.44\ \text{F}$$

$$\text{Sales mix variance} = \left[\frac{\$27{,}625}{4{,}775} - \frac{\$26{,}500}{4{,}500}\right] \times 4{,}775 = \$494.44\ \text{U}$$

Total volume and mix	$1,125.00	F
Expense variance:		
Variable		
Manufacturing	$1,025	F
Selling	1,450	U
Fixed		
Manufacturing	225	F
Selling	300	U
Administration	70	U
Total	$ 570	U
Sales price variance:	4,775	U
Total expense and sales price variances	$5,345	U

Glossary

Common expense An expense that is incurred for the benefit of more than one product, territory, or other cost object. An expense may be common to products and direct to the territories.

Direct expense An expense that is incurred solely for the benefit of one product or territory. An expense may be common to products and direct to a territory.

Expense variance The difference between the budgeted and actual income associated with changes in manufacturing, selling, or administrative expenses.

Product contribution The total dollars each product contributes toward covering the common product expenses and, thereafter, income.

Sales mix variance The difference between the master budget and actual income associated with a change in the relative proportions of the products sold.

Sales price variance The difference between the master budget and actual income associated with a change in the average selling price of the products.

Sales volume variance The difference between the master budget and actual income associated with a difference between actual sales volume and master budget sales volume.

Territory contribution The total dollars each territory contributes toward covering the common territory expenses and, thereafter, income.

Questions and Problems

18-1 What is the purpose of comparing actual net income with budgeted net income?

18-2 What information should the managerial accountant provide to profit center managers to help them manage their operations?

18-3 What questions are revenue variances calculated to answer?

18-4 Define the four categories that are used to classify variances.

18-5 Why is the sales volume variance sometimes calculated by geographic region?

18-6 "By providing timely variance computations the accountant can aid management in identifying the cause of the variance." Comment on this statement.

18-7 Compare a master budget with a flexible budget.

18-8 Distinguish between common and direct costs.

18-9 **Computation of Variances** The Acme Company produces two products, A and B. The budgeted contribution margins for the current year are shown below:

	A	B	Total
Sales in units	500	300	800
Sales in dollars	$5,000	$4,500	$9,500
Variable cost	3,500	3,000	6,500
Contribution margin	$1,500	$1,500	$3,000

The actual results showed a total contribution of $4,200. The product contributions are as follows:

	A	B	Total
Sales in units	400	400	800
Sales in dollars	$4,800	$5,600	$10,400
Variable costs	3,000	3,200	6,200
Contribution margin	$1,800	$2,400	$ 4,200

Required Compute the sales volume, sales mix, sales price, and expense variances.

18-10 Computation of Variances Following are budgeted and actual income statements for Duo, Inc., for the year ended December 31, 19X7.

DUO, INC.
Income Statement
For the Year Ended
December 31, 19X7
(000 Omitted)

	Product AR-10		Product ZR-7		Total	
	Budget	Actual	Budget	Actual	Budget	Actual
Unit sales	2,000	2,800	6,000	5,600	8,000	8,400
Sales	$6,000	$7,560	$12,000	$11,760	$18,000	$19,320
Cost of goods sold	$2,400	$2,800	$ 6,000	$ 5,880	$ 8,400	$ 8,680
Fixed costs	1,800	1,900	2,400	2,400	4,200	4,300
Total costs	$4,200	$4,700	$ 8,400	$ 8,280	$12,600	$12,980
Net profit	$1,800	$2,860	$ 3,600	$ 3,480	$ 5,400	$ 6,340

Required

Calculate the difference between actual and budgeted net profit associated with volume, mix, sales price, and expense factors.

(CMA)

18-11 Computation of Variances for Sales Territories The Ajax Company would like to analyze the profitability of their sales territories. Based on a preliminary analysis, they have identified territory 15 as currently the most profitable territory and plan to use it as a standard for evaluating the other territories. The sales people in each territory have some discretion in setting the product sales price and in incurring the variable selling expenses, such as travel and entertainment expenses.

Last month's results for territories 15 and 20 are given below:

Territory 15

Product	Sales Units	Sales Dollars	Standard Variable Manufacturing Cost	Variable Sales Expense	Contribution Margin
A	500	$ 5,000	$ 3,000	$1,000	$1,000
B	300	4,500	3,600	600	300
C	400	4,800	2,400	800	1,600
D	800	7,200	2,000	1,200	4,000
Total	2,000	$21,500	$11,000	$3,600	$6,900

Territory 20

Product	Sales Units	Sales Dollars	Standard Variable Manufacturing Cost	Variable Sales Expense	Contribution Margin
A	600	$ 5,400	$ 3,600	$1,200	$ 600
B	400	6,400	4,800	1,200	400
C	300	3,900	1,800	450	1,650
D	600	6,000	1,500	1,500	3,000
Total	1,900	$21,700	$11,700	$4,350	$5,650

Required

Using territory 15 as the master budget calculate the sales volume, sales mix, expense, and sales price variances for territory 20 using units as the measure of volume.

18-12 Computation of Variances The following budget and actual data are from the XYZ Company for the past year.

Budget

Product	Sales Units	Sales Dollars	Variable Costs	Contribution Margin
Alpha	2,000	$ 50,000	$30,000	$20,000
Beta	1,500	60,000	52,500	7,500
Total	3,500	$110,000	$82,500	$27,500

Actual

Product	Sales Units	Sales Dollars	Variable Costs	Contribution Margin
Alpha	1,800	$ 48,600	$29,700	$18,900
Beta	1,700	61,200	56,100	5,100
Total	3,500	$109,800	$85,800	$24,000

Required

Calculate the sales volume, sales mix, expense, and sales price variances.

18-13 Variance Computation The Dallas Manufacturing Company produces novelty items for sale to commercial and industrial customers. For the year 19X1 a budgeted profit of $28,000 was estimated based on sales of $200,000. The budget by type of customer is given on page 536.

	Industrial	Commercial	Total
Sales in units	28,000	48,000	76,000
Sales revenues	$80,000	$120,000	$200,000
Variable cost	56,000	96,000	152,000
Contribution margin	$24,000	$ 24,000	$ 48,000
Fixed cost			20,000
Net income			$ 28,000

Actual sales amounted to $190,000, however; profits were only $22,800. The breakdown by type of customer is given below:

	Industrial	Commercial	Total
Sales	$60,000	$130,000	$190,000
Variable cost	39,600	106,600	146,200
Contribution margin	$20,400	$ 23,400	$ 43,800
Fixed cost			21,000
Net income			$ 22,800

Required Analyze the difference between actual and budgeted results indicating the areas where actual and budgeted results differ. Use sales dollars to measure volume.

18-14 Variance Computation The Bonzat Company is a wholesale organization dealing in two products, Bots and Wets. For 19X1 the estimated sales are 50,000 units for Bots and 30,000 units for Wets. The anticipated sales price and cost are shown below:

	Bots	Wets
Sales price per unit	$24	$30
Purchase price per unit	12	20
Variable selling costs per unit	3	5

The fixed selling and administrative expense is estimated at $500,000 for 19X1.

During 19X1 the actual sales volume amounted to 40,000 units for Bots and 27,000 units for Wets. The actual sales price, purchase price, variable selling cost per unit, and fixed selling expense were exactly as budgeted yet the company showed a loss for the year of $5,000.

Required Prepare an analysis comparing the actual results with the budget indicating the factors that created the difference.

18-15 Volume and Mix Variances The Arsco Company makes three grades of indoor-outdoor carpets. The sales volume for the annual budget is determined by estimating the total market volume for indoor-outdoor carpet, and then applying the company's prior-year market share, adjusted for planned changes due to company programs for the coming year. The volume is apportioned between the three grades based upon the prior year's sales mix, again adjusted for planned changes due to company programs for the coming year.

Given below are the company budget for 19X3 and the results of operations for 19X3.

Budget

	Grade 1	Grade 2	Grade 3	Total
Sales in units	1,000 rolls	1,000 rolls	2,000 rolls	4,000 rolls
Sales in dollars	$1,000	$2,000	$3,000	$6,000
Variable expense	700	1,600	2,300	4,600
Contribution margin	$ 300	$ 400	$ 700	$1,400
Direct fixed expense	200	200	300	700
Direct margin	$ 100	$ 200	$ 400	$ 700
Selling and administrative expense				$ 250
Net income				$ 450

($000 omitted)

Actual

	Grade 1	Grade 2	Grade 3	Total
Sales in units	800 rolls	1,000 rolls	2,100 rolls	3,900 rolls
Sales in dollars	$810	$2,000	$3,000	$5,810
Variable expense	560	1,610	2,320	4,490
Contribution margin	$250	$ 390	$ 680	$1,320
Direct fixed expense	210	220	315	745
Direct margin	$ 40	$ 170	$ 365	$ 575
Selling and administrative expense				275
Net income				$ 300

($000 omitted)

Industry volume was estimated at 40,000 rolls for budgeting purposes. Actual industry volume for 19X3 was 38,000 rolls.

Required

1 Calculate the profit impact of the unit sales volume variance for 19X3 using budgeted contribution margins.

2 What portion of the variance, if any, can be attributed to the state of the carpet market?

3 What is the dollar impact on profits (using budgeted contribution margins) of the shift in sales mix from the budgeted mix?

(CMA)

18-16 Gross Margin Analysis Mill Company manufactures and sells two similar types of industrial components which are substitutes for each other. One component is manufactured from plastic, while the other uses metal. Both components are manufactured in the same plant but in separate production departments. The budgeted and actual income statements for Mill Company for the 19X4 fiscal year are presented below.

MILL COMPANY
Budgeted and Actual Income Statements
For the Fiscal Year Ending December 31, 19X4
(000 Omitted)

	Budget			Actual Results			Over (Under) Budget
	Plastic	Metal	Total	Plastic	Metal	Total	
Net sales in units	300	200	500	260	260	520	20
Revenue from net sales	$1,800	$2,000	$3,800	$1,560	$2,470	$4,030	$ 230
Cost of sales at standard	900	1,500	2,400	780	1,950	2,730	330
Gross margin before manufacturing variances	$ 900	$ 500	$1,400	$ 780	$ 520	$1,300	$(100)

The 19X4 sales mix was different from that which was budgeted. More metal components were sold than planned because of reduced availability of plastic components. Some increase in the volume of metal components was also due to the lower than budgeted price. The sales volume of plastic components was down because of lost production.

Required

The management of Mill Company would like a detailed explanation of why gross margin before manufacturing variances was $100,000 less than originally budgeted for 19X4. Calculate a sales price variance, a sales volume variance, and a sales mix variance to explain the $100,000.

(CMA)

18-17 Salesman Performance Mill Company prepares monthly and annual "Salesman Performance Reports" on each of the territorial salesmen. Copies of the annual report for two salesmen—John Fowler and James Barnes—are shown on pages 539 and 540.

SALESMAN PERFORMANCE REPORT
Salesman: John Fowler
For the Fiscal Year Ended December 31, 19X4

	Territory Budget			Actual Results		
	Plastic	**Metal**	**Total**	**Plastic**	**Metal**	**Total**
Sales in units	24,000	16,000	40,000	24,000	17,000	41,000
Sales in dollars	$144,000	$160,000	$304,000	$144,000	$161,500	$305,500
Cost of sales at standard	72,000	120,000	192,000	72,000	127,500	199,500
Gross profit at standard	$ 72,000	$ 40,000	$112,000	$ 72,000	$ 34,000	$106,000
Operating expenses						
Salary			$ 4,000			$ 4,000
Commissions			9,120			9,165
Employee benefits			1,968			1,975
Sales administration and promotion[1]						
Regular orders			11,400			10,000
Special handling orders			1,200			800
Travel and entertainment			6,250			6,000
Shipping and packing			12,000			12,300
Total operating expenses			$ 45,938			$ 44,240
Salesman profit contribution			$ 66,062			$ 61,760
Other data						
Salesman miles traveled						32,000
Salesman calls						1,200
Number of regular orders						1,250
Number of special handling orders						50
Average size of order						$ 235

[1] Sales administration and promotion costs plus sales administration salaries are charged to the salesmen at the rate of $8 per regular order and $16 per special handling order.

Mill Company has classified the 12 territories into three types, according to characteristics such as travel required, customer demographics, and product prices. A territory budget is formulated for each of the three classifications to be used for comparison purposes. Fowler and Barnes are assigned to territories which are similar and have the same territorial classification.

The purpose of the Salesman Performance Report is to compare the salesman's performance with the planned activity and to show the salesman's contribution toward company profits.

The company has divided its market area into 12 territories. The 12 territorial salesmen are paid a salary of $4,000 plus a 3% commission on net sales. Salesmen are reimbursed for the allowable travel and enter-

SALESMAN PERFORMANCE REPORT
Salesman: James Barnes
For the Fiscal Year Ended December 31, 19X4

	Territory Budget			Actual Results		
	Plastic	Metal	Total	Plastic	Metal	Total
Sales in units	24,000	16,000	40,000	20,000	20,000	40,000
Sales in dollars	$144,000	$160,000	$304,000	$120,000	$190,000	$310,000
Cost of sales at standard	72,000	120,000	192,000	60,000	150,000	210,000
Gross profit at standard	$ 72,000	$ 40,000	$112,000	$ 60,000	$ 40,000	$100,000
Operating expenses						
Salary			$ 4,000			$ 4,000
Commissions			9,120			9,300
Employee benefits			1,968			1,995
Sales administration and promotion[1]						
Regular orders			11,400			11,600
Special handling orders			1,200			2,400
Travel and entertainment			6,250			7,500
Shipping and packing			12,000			12,000
Total operating expenses			$ 45,938			$ 48,795
Salesman profit contribution			$ 66,062			$ 51,205
Other data						
Salesman miles traveled						28,000
Salesman calls						1,000
Number of regular orders						1,450
Number of special handling orders						150
Average size of order						$ 194

[1] Sales administration and promotion costs plus sales administration salaries are charged to the salesmen at the rate of $8 per regular order and $16 per special handling order.

tainment costs they incur. The company's experience with uncollectible accounts justifies a bad-debt estimate of 1/10 of 1% of net sales. The sales administration and promotion account includes all costs to administer, process, and promote sales, except salaries. Warehouse employees are paid on an hourly basis. Shipping and packing costs average $.30 per component sold (for both plastic and metal). The warehouse operating costs include such items as depreciation, utilities, insurance, and property taxes. General administrative expenses include all costs incurred for the overall administration of the company.

All expenses which can be identified with the salesman's effort to generate and produce sales are included on the report. Sales administration and promotion costs (including salaries) are charged to the salesman according to the number of regular and special handling orders the salesmen write. Special handling orders require approximately twice as much administrative effort as regular orders; consequently, the charge for special handling orders is double the charge for regular orders ($16 versus $8). The 19X4 rate was determined by dividing the amount budgeted for sales administration salaries and sales administration and promotion costs ($160,000) by the estimated total orders (regular, 18,000; special handling, 1,000) weighted by the amount of administrative effort. Special handling orders comprise approximately 5% of the total orders handled.

Required

1 Evaluate, from the company's point of view, the performance of the two salesmen whose reports are presented. Use the appropriate numerical data to support your answer.

2 What changes, if any, would you make in the Salesman Performance Report presently employed by Mill Company to make it more useful for evaluating salesmen? Explain your answer.

18-18 Computation of Budgeted Income Statement and Comparison with Actual and a Product Analysis The Bartlett Company produces two products, A and B, in two separate facilities specifically designed for each product. For the year 19X1 the estimated sales price and standard costs are given below:

Product A

Sales price per unit		$ 90.00
Variable cost per unit:		
Material	3 pounds @ $1.00/pound	$ 3.00
Labor—direct	6 hours @ $3.00/hour	18.00
Variable overhead	$4.00/direct labor hour	24.00
Total standard variable cost		$ 45.00
Total annual fixed manufacturing cost		$1,200,000

Product B

Sales price per unit		$ 94.00
Variable cost per unit:		
Material	4 pounds @ $1.50/pound	$ 6.00
Labor—direct	5 hours @ $3.00/hour	15.00
Variable overhead	$4.00/direct labor hour	20.00
Total standard variable cost		$ 41.00
Total annual fixed manufacturing overhead		$ 960,000

All selling and administrative expenses are fixed and are estimated at $1,500,000 for 19X1. The selling and administrative expenses are common to products A and B. The sales budget for 19X1 estimated that sales would be 50,000 units of A and 40,000 units of B.

During 19X1 production and sales were 52,000 units for A and 41,000 for B. The income statement for 19X1 follows:

BARTLETT COMPANY
Income Statement
For Year Ended December 31, 19X1

	Product A	Product B	Total
Sales	$4,600,000	$3,895,000	$8,495,000
Cost of goods sold			
Material	$ 170,000	$ 260,000	$ 430,000
Labor	875,000	635,000	1,510,000
Variable overhead	1,220,000	800,000	2,020,000
Fixed overhead	1,080,000	970,000	2,050,000
Total cost of goods sold	$3,345,000	$2,665,000	$6,010,000
Gross profit	$1,255,000	$1,230,000	$2,485,000
Selling and administrative expense			$1,400,000
Profit before taxes			$1,085,000

Required

1 Compute a budgeted income statement for 19X1.

2 Compute the sales volume, sales mix, sales price, and expense variances.

3 Prepare a contribution analysis for products A and B.

18-19 Comprehensive Problem on Chapters 16, 17, and 18 The Markley Division of Rosette Industries manufactures and sells patio chairs. The chairs are manufactured in two versions—a metal model and a plastic model of a lesser quality. The company uses its own sales force to sell the chairs to retail stores and to catalog outlets. Generally, customers purchase both the metal and the plastic versions.

The chairs are manufactured on two different assembly lines located in adjoining buildings. The division management and sales department occupy the third building on the property. The division management includes a division controller responsible for the divisional financial activities and the preparation of reports explaining the differences between actual and budgeted performance. The controller structures these reports so that the sales activities are distinguished from cost factors and can be analyzed separately.

The operating results for the first three months of the fiscal year as compared to the budget follow. The budget for the current year was based upon the assumption that Markley Division would maintain its present market share of the estimated total patio chair market (plastic and metal combined). A status report had been sent to corporate management toward the end of the second month indicating that divisional operating income for the first quarter would probably be about 45% below budget; this estimate was just about on target. The division's operating income was below budget even though industry volume for patio chairs increased by 10% more than was expected at the time the budget was developed.

The manufacturing activities for the quarter resulted in the production of 55,000 plastic chairs and 22,500 metal chairs. The actual costs incurred by each manufacturing unit are presented on the following pages.

			Plastic Model	Metal Model
Direct materials (stated in equivalent finished chairs)				
	Quantity	**Price**		
Purchases				
Plastic	60,000	$5.66	$339,000	
Metal	30,000	$6.00		$180,000
Usage				
Plastic	56,000	$5.00	280,000	
Metal	23,000	$6.00		138,000
Direct labor				
9,300 hours @ $6.00 per hour			55,800	
5,600 hours @ $8.00 per hour				44,800
Manufacturing overhead				
Variable				
Supplies			43,000	18,000
Power			50,000	15,000
Employee benefits			19,000	12,000
Fixed				
Supervision			14,000	11,000
Depreciation			12,000	9,000
Property taxes and other items			1,900	1,300

MARKLEY DIVISION
Operating Results for the First Quarter

	Actual	Budget	Favorable (Unfavorable) Relative to the Budget
Sales in units			
Plastic model	60,000	50,000	10,000
Metal model	20,000	25,000	(5,000)
Sales revenue			
Plastic model	$630,000	$500,000	$130,000
Metal model	300,000	375,000	(75,000)
Total sales	$930,000	$875,000	$ 55,000
Less variable manufacturing costs (at standard)			
Plastic model	$480,000	$400,000	($80,000)
Metal model	200,000	250,000	50,000
Selling			
Commissions	46,500	43,750	(2,750)
Bad debt allowance	9,300	8,750	(550)
Total variable costs (except variable manufacturing variances)	$735,800	$702,500	($33,300)

Contribution margin (except variable manufacturing variances)	$194,200	$172,500	$ 21,700
Less other costs			
Variable manufacturing cost variances from standards	$ 49,600	$ —	$(49,600)
Fixed manufacturing costs	49,200	48,000	(1,200)
Fixed selling and administrative costs	38,500	36,000	(2,500)
Corporation offices allocation	18,500	17,500	(1,000)
Total other costs	$155,800	$101,500	($54,300)
Divisional operational income	$ 38,400	$ 71,000	($32,600)

The standard variable manufacturing costs per unit and the budgeted monthly fixed manufacturing costs established for the current year are presented below.

	Plastic Model	Metal Model
Direct material	$ 5.00	$ 6.00
Direct labor		
1/6 hour @ $6.00 per DLH	1.00	
1/4 hour @ $8.00 per DLH		2.00
Variable overhead		
1/6 hour @ $12.00 per DLH	2.00	
1/4 hour @ $8.00 per DLH		2.00
Standard variable manufacturing cost per unit	$ 8.00	$10.00
Budgeted fixed costs per month		
Supervision	$4,500	$3,500
Depreciation	4,000	3,000
Property taxes and other items	600	400
Total budgeted fixed costs for month	$9,100	$6,900

Required

1 Explain the variance in Markley Division's contribution margin attributable to sales activities by calculating the:
  a Sales price and variable sales expense variances
  b Sales mix variance
  c Sales volume variance

2 What portion of sales volume variance, if any, can be attributed to a change in Markley Division's market share?

3 Analyze the variance in Markley Division's variable manufacturing costs ($49,600) in as much detail as the data permit.

4 Based upon your analyses prepared for requirements 1, 2, and 3:

a Identify the major cause of Markley Division's unfavorable profit performance.

b Did Markley's management attempt to correct this problem? Explain your answer.

c What other steps, if any, could Markley's management have taken to improve the division's operating income? Explain your answer.

(CMA)

DIVISIONAL PERFORMANCE ANALYSIS

AFTER COMPLETING YOUR STUDY OF THIS CHAPTER, YOU SHOULD HAVE LEARNED:

1 Why managers are concerned about asset management as well as profitability.

2 Two measures of investment center financial performance: return on investment and residual income.

3 The advantages of return on investment and residual income for measuring investment center performance.

4 The problems associated with measuring investment center profits and investments.

5 That other aspects of divisional performance analysis such as new product development and personnel development should be measured along with the measure of financial performance.

In Chapter 18, we discussed situations in which the financial performance of a manager might be measured as a profit center. In a profit center, a manager's financial performance is satisfactory if the actual profit of the unit is equal to or exceeds budgeted profit. That measure of financial performance works well in many units of an organization, but not for all units. What follows is an illustration of a situation where an investment center measure would be better than a profit center measure. We will define the investment center measure carefully after the illustration. For now all you need to know is that in an investment center the manager has incentive to meet profit objectives while at the same time minimizing the investment in assets used to meet the profit objective.

Ile-de-France operates 10 bicycle rental shops in the Paris area. Bicycles are normally rented on an hourly or daily basis to tourists. Each shop is responsible for renting, repairing, and keeping records for its own operations. The manager of each shop is evaluated on a profit center basis. A budgeted profit is established for each shop considering the demand, competition, and other conditions in each shop's territory.

The operator of the Left Bank shop has a relatively high budgeted profit reflecting the density of the tourist population in the area. The shop manager has gradually increased its stock of repair parts until it has a much higher inventory than any other shop even allowing for their high level of rental activity. The controller of Ile-de-France was surprised when the shop manager recently requested the purchase of 10 more bikes even though there are frequently unrented bikes in the shop. When asked to justify the request for 10 more bikes, the manager replied that the way to maximize profits was to have bikes available whenever people want to rent them. "If you do not have a bike when the customer wants it, that rental is lost forever," said the shop manager.

While recognizing the truth of the shop manager's statement, the Ile-de-France controller realized that if all shops followed this strategy capital would have to be raised from borrowing or added owner investment to finance a large number of new bike purchases. Regardless of which source of capital was used, the added capital could be obtained only if Ile-de-France could promise a reasonable return on the investment. But the controller had calculated that a new bike will yield a reasonable rate of return only if it is rented at least 50 days per year. The manager of the Left Bank shop did not seem to be concerned about the number of days per year that each bike could be rented. As long as it could be rented for just a few days a year it would bring in more revenue than its expenses and would increase shop profits.

Was the manager of the Left Bank shop a poor manager? No. Since financial performance was measured by comparing actual to budgeted profit, she was doing all possible to increase actual profits. The high investment in repair parts assured speedy repairs as needed. Having many bikes would mean no lost sales due to lack of bikes. The results were not necessarily in the best interest of Ile-de-France (the total organization) because the system provided the shop manager no incentive to keep the investment in each shop low. The problem was the system of measuring financial performance, not poor management.

Ile-de-France can correct the problem in their system in either of two ways.

1 Corporate management can control the investment in each shop centrally. This means that the shop managers will have no authority to decide how many bikes they will have or how large a parts inventory to keep.

2 Ile-de-France can choose to measure the financial performance of shop managers by the investment center approach.

Using the first approach, the president of Ile-de-France would make (or delegate to someone at corporate headquarters) the decision of how many bikes would be allowed at each shop. They might follow a rule such as providing one bike for every 50 rental days budgeted for each shop each year. If the shop did not generate the number of rental days budgeted, bikes would be taken from that shop and given to other shops which were generating more than their budgeted rental days. Corporate officers would also decide what inventory of repair parts each shop could maintain. They might be permitted to maintain a 30-day supply of frequently used parts but be required to order less frequently used parts from a central corporate inventory. This would likely lead to a reduction in the parts inventory at the Left Bank shop since their inventory was highest in the company, even when compared to their high level of bicycle rentals. With investment controlled by corporate headquarters, the profit center measure of financial performance might work well and solve the problems we saw in the illustration.

The second way of correcting the problem is to consider each shop an investment center and measure financial performance in a way that provides the manager of each shop with incentive to balance added investment in assets against added profits. A responsibility accounting system which provides this incentive includes investment in measuring financial performance. The measure of financial performance calculated is either the return on investment (ROI) or the residual income (RI) for each investment center. The financial performance of the investment center is evaluated by comparing *actual* return on investment to *budgeted* return on investment *or* by comparing *actual* residual income to *budgeted* residual income.

Return on investment is defined as you might expect:

Return on investment defined.

$$\textbf{Return on investment} = \frac{\textbf{profit}}{\textbf{investment}}$$

There are some problems in defining what is meant by profit and investment for a unit or subdivision of an organization. These problems are discussed later in this chapter.

Residual income is defined as follows:

Residual income defined.

$$\textbf{Residual income} = \textbf{profit} - \textbf{capital charge}$$

Residual income is positive only when the profit of the investment center is greater than a **capital charge.** In effect, the manager of an investment center has something similar to an additional expense, the capital charge. The capital charge is calculated by multiplying the investment in the investment center times a required minimum rate of return. The higher the investment, the higher the capital charge which the investment center must cover with profit. We mentioned that there are some problems in defining profit and investment when calculating ROI. Those same problems exist in using RI.

The Ile-de-France example illustrates the main reason why corporations use investment centers and ROI or RI to measure financial performance of managers. The manager of an investment center has incentive to increase investment *only* when the expected added profit is great enough to provide a satisfactory return on the added investment. In addition to this main reason, there are two other reasons for using investment centers.

To summarize this section, a list of the three reasons for using investment centers (either ROI or RI) is given below:

Reasons for using ROI or RI to evaluate the financial performance of investment centers.

1 To provide incentives for unit managers to balance profit and investment in decision making.

2 To guide corporate management in making more capital available to units of the organization which will use it most effectively to generate profits.

3 To provide corporate management a basis of measuring the relative profitability of units of different size. The ROI does this directly; the RI can be used to make this judgment.

Before we go on to examine ROI and RI in detail, you should remember that the relationship between profit and investment is important to management since a primary objective of most profit-seeking organizations is to earn a satisfactory rate of return on the capital invested in the organization. This is a necessary objective since management can obtain needed capital only if investors believe that they will receive a satisfactory return on their investment.

Many organizations are divided by product lines or geographically and top management generally desires a measure of relative profitability of each unit. To simply compare profits of units is inadequate since one unit may have more assets at its disposal than other units. Generally, the greater the assets invested in a unit, the higher the profit which is expected from that unit. Just because a unit's profits increase from year to year does not indicate that it is operating more efficiently. If total assets have also increased, then increased profits should be expected. To alleviate these problems, management of most profit-seeking organizations uses some measure which relates profit to investment, ROI or RI.

The balance of this chapter will more completely define return on investment and residual income and compare these two approaches to investment center analysis. The chapter will conclude with a discussion of a problem which is common to both ROI and RI, how to measure the investment in a subdivision of the organization.

RETURN ON INVESTMENT AND RESIDUAL INCOME

Earlier in the chapter we listed three reasons why management might choose to use an investment center measure of financial performance rather than a profit center measure. We also noted that if management chooses the investment center for a particular unit they may implement it by either the return on investment or the residual income technique. How does management decide to use either ROI or RI when they have chosen to use an investment center? Each has advantages. This section of the chapter discusses the advantages of each.

Return on Investment

Recall that return on investment is the ratio of profits to the amount invested.

$$\textbf{ROI} = \frac{\textbf{profit}}{\textbf{investment}}$$

There are two major advantages of using return on investment to measure investment center performance.

Advantages of return on investment.

1 Most managers have an intuitive understanding of return on investment.

2 Return on investment is directly related to two other measures of efficiency which managers are accustomed to using, **profit as a percentage of sales** and **asset turnover**.

Many things in ordinary life are expressed as a return on investment. If we deposit money in a savings account the interest we can expect to earn on the account is expressed as a percentage, as ROI. Return on investment is one of the common characteristics used to describe other types of investments. Because we see return on investment every day, it is well understood.

Return on Investment and the Dupont Formula The relationship of ROI to two other ratios, profit as a percentage of sales and asset turnover, is important because it provides management with a means of analyzing the ROI and finding ways of improving the ROI by an investment center. The method of analysis is often referred to as the Dupont formula after the giant chemical company of the same name. Dupont was one of the early companies to make use of this type of analysis.

Profit as a percentage of sales allows comparison of two divisions of different size.

Profit as a percentage of sales is defined as follows:

$$\textbf{Profit as a percentage of sales} = \frac{\textbf{profit}}{\textbf{total sales}} \times 100\%$$

Profit as a percentage of sales is a useful measure of efficiency in expense control. It can be thought of as the percentage of each sales dollar left as profit, after all expenses are covered. It is convenient for comparing companies of different size in the same industry because stating it as a percentage removes the size effect. For example, suppose that the bottling division of Fizzie Corporation reports profits of \$300,000 and the bottling division of Growler Company reports profits of \$400,000. With just this limited information it might appear that Growler was doing better. But suppose that Fizzie's sales are \$1,500,000 while Growler's are \$2,500,000. Profit as a percentage of sales shows that Fizzie is able to keep more of each sales dollar as profit. The profit as a percentage of sales for each of them is as follows:

$$\textbf{Fizzie} = \frac{\$300{,}000}{\$1{,}500{,}000} \times 100\% = 20\%$$

$$\textbf{Growler} = \frac{\$400{,}000}{\$2{,}500{,}000} \times 100\% = 16\%$$

The use of a percentage permits direct comparison of these two divisions of different size. Of course, if everything else were equal, it would be better to have \$400,000 profit than \$300,000 profit. But it is unlikely that other things are equal. Growler Company is likely to have more assets invested in its bottling division to support its higher level of sales.

Asset turnover measures how efficiently management is using the assets to generate sales dollars.

Asset turnover is a convenient measure of the total amount of assets invested compared to the sales generated by those assets. It is defined as follows:

$$\textbf{Asset turnover} = \frac{\textbf{sales}}{\textbf{investment}}$$

Asset turnover measures efficiency in the use of assets by showing how many dollars of sales are generated from each dollar invested in assets. If the profit as a percentage of sales is constant, the more sales dollars generated from a dollar invested in assets the better.

The way in which these two measures of efficiency are related to ROI can be shown algebraically. It is this algebraic expression which Dupont and others have found so useful and which is called the Dupont formula. The Dupont formula shows that ROI can be expanded into the algebraic product of profit as a percentage of sales times asset turnover.

Relationship between ROI, profit as a percentage of sales, and asset turnover.

Dupont Formula

$$\textbf{ROI} = \frac{\textbf{profit}}{\textbf{investment}} = \frac{\textbf{profit}}{\textbf{sales}} \times \frac{\textbf{sales}}{\textbf{investment}} \times \textbf{100\%}$$

This formula indicates that ROI can be affected by changing either (1) the profit as a percentage of sales or (2) the asset turnover. Profit as a percentage of sales can be changed by either increasing the average selling price or by decreasing expenses while holding sales constant. Asset turnover can be changed by increasing sales with constant assets or by decreasing assets while maintaining the sales level.

To illustrate the ROI calculation consider the balance sheet and the income statement of the Parts Division of Zomack Corporation shown in Exhibit 19-1. Using total assets less current liabilities to measure investment the ROI of the Parts Division is 20% computed as follows.

$$\textbf{ROI} = \frac{\textbf{profit}}{\textbf{investment}} = \frac{\textbf{\$200}}{\textbf{\$1,000}} \times \textbf{100\%} = \textbf{20\%}$$

or

$$\textbf{Profit as a percentage of sales} = \frac{\textbf{\$200}}{\textbf{\$1,600}} \times \textbf{100\%} = \textbf{12.5\%}$$

$$\textbf{Asset turnover} = \frac{\textbf{\$1,600}}{\textbf{\$1,000}} = \textbf{1.6 times}$$

$$\textbf{ROI} = \textbf{12.5\%} \times \textbf{1.6} = \textbf{20\%}$$

We noted earlier that in calculating ROI, decisions must be made about the definition of both profit and investment. Zomack follows fairly common definitions using profit before taxes but after corporate allocations and defining investment as the total assets minus current liabilities. The point to be aware of is that different definitions are possible. We shall discuss alternative definitions of investment later in this chapter.

When using balance sheet ratios, it is usually desirable to use monthly averages rather than values at a particular moment such as the end of the year. This is particularly important when the balance sheet values fluctuate during the year. But for the purpose of our illustrations we will generally use beginning or ending balance sheet values to simplify the calculations and make the points more clear.

ROI as a Planning Tool ROI can be used to evaluate alternative strategies for improving profitability of a division. To illustrate, assume that Zomack Corporation's management has observed that competitors of the Parts Division are earning more than a 20% return on investment and that Zomack corporate management desires to increase the ROI from the current 20% to 25%. Initially, management would want to know the approximate amount of changes that would have to be made to

EXHIBIT 19-1
ZOMACK CORPORATION
Division Financial Statements
Parts Division
Balance Sheet
As of December 31, 19X0
($000)

Assets		**Liabilities & Equities**	
Cash	$ 100	Accounts payable	$ 400
Accounts receivable—net	300	Other payables	200
Inventory	400		
Total current assets	$ 800	Total current liabilities	$ 600
Net plant and equipment	800	Total equity	1,000
Total assets	$1,600	Total liabilities and equity	$1,600

Parts Division
Income Statement
For the Year Ended December 31, 19X0
($000)

Sales		$1,600
Variable expenses		
Manufacturing	$800	
Operating	200	
Total variable expenses		1,000
Contribution margin		$ 600
Direct fixed expenses		
Manufacturing depreciation	$100	
Operating expenses	200	
Total direct fixed expenses		300
Profit before corporation allocations		$ 300
Corporate allocations		100
Profit before taxes		$ 200

meet the new target. Using data from Exhibit 19-1, they compute the current position and consider three types of alternatives.

Present Situation

$$\text{ROI} = \frac{\text{profit}}{\text{sales}} \times \frac{\text{sales}}{\text{investment}} \times 100\%$$

$$\text{ROI} = \frac{\$200}{\$1{,}600} \times \frac{\$1{,}600}{\$1{,}000} \times 100\%$$

$$= .125 \times 1.6 \times 100\%$$

$$= 20\%$$

By setting the ROI to the desired 25% level and then treating one of the other three variables (profit, sales, investment) as an unknown, the changes which would be required to achieve the higher ROI can be calculated. Let us do this for several alternatives.

Relationship between investment and ROI.

Alternative 1: How much must investment be decreased with other variables constant to achieve a 25% ROI?

$$25\% = \frac{\$200}{\$1{,}600} \times \frac{\$1{,}600}{\text{investment}} \times 100\%$$

$$.25 \times \text{investment} = \$200$$

$$\text{investment} = \underline{\underline{\$800}}$$

To achieve a 25% ROI investment must decrease from its present $1,000 to $800 while sales and profits remain constant.

The feasibility of reducing investment by this amount must then be considered. Perhaps it can be accomplished fairly quickly by reducing the level of accounts receivable, inventory, or cash. In the longer run, plant and equipment might be reduced. Management must decide on whether it would be possible to maintain sales or profits with such reductions in these assets.

But certainly management would want to explore other alternatives before deciding. Since profit is part of the equation, one could ask whether profit can be increased to improve the ROI. Two distinct types of changes are possible. First, profit could be increased by decreasing expenses. The important question is how much must expenses be reduced (and therefore profits increased) in order to achieve the 25% ROI? The other type of change could be to increase profit by increasing sales. These two types of change become alternatives 2 and 3 which are illustrated below.

Alternative 2: How much must expenses be decreased (and profits increased) with sales and investment constant to achieve a 25% ROI?

$$25\% = \frac{\text{profit}}{\$1{,}600} \times \frac{\$1{,}600}{\$1{,}000} \times 100\%$$

$$.25 \times \$1{,}000 = \text{profit}$$

$$\text{profit} = \underline{\underline{\$250}}$$

Relationship between expenses and ROI.

In order to achieve a 25% ROI profit must rise from $200 to $250—sales and investment constant. This implies that expenses must be reduced by $50.

Again management must decide which expenses, if any, can be reduced without losing sales. Comparing the Parts Division's expenses expressed as a percentage of sales to industry averages for expenses as a percentage of sales might provide some clues. If, for example, the travel expense of the Parts Division's sales representatives is 3% of sales while the average for the industry is 2.1%, there may be a possibility of saving in this expense category by scheduling sales visits more efficiently.

But consider the third alternative. We want to know how much sales must be increased to achieve the 25% ROI, given that profit as a percentage of sales remains a constant 12.5% and investment is unchanged. Like alternative 2, this alternative assumes profits can be increased, but in this case by generating more sales rather than reducing expenses. The calculations are slightly different since 12.5% must be substituted for $\frac{\text{Profits}}{\text{Sales}}$, the first term in the equation.

Relationship between sales and ROI.

Alternative 3: How much must sales be increased with return on sales and investment constant to achieve a 25% ROI?

$$25\% = 12.5\% \times \frac{\text{sales}}{\$1{,}000}$$

$$\frac{25\%}{12.5\%} \times \$1{,}000 = \text{sales}$$

$$\text{Sales} = \underline{\underline{\$2{,}000}}$$

In order to achieve a 25% ROI sales must rise $400 from $1,600 with investment and return on sales constant.

You might object to sales rising with profit as a percentage of sales constant. Constant profit as a percentage of sales could imply all variable expenses, but total expenses are usually semivariable. But with rising sales, management might allow some discretionary fixed costs such as advertising or research to increase, resulting in an unchanged return on sales as total sales rise.

Residual Income

Residual income provides incentive to investment center managers to consider the size of the investment by a capital charge which depends on the amount invested in the center. The capital charge increases as the amount of assets is increased. The capital charge thus becomes similar to an expense which management tries to minimize by minimizing investment.

Suppose that management of Zomack Corporation wishes to compute residual income for its Parts Division, described earlier in this chapter. Suppose further that they have decided to use a capital charge rate (minimum required rate of return) of 18%. The 18% rate provides incentive to the Parts Division to make no additions to investment which did not promise a return on investment of at least 18%. If investment is again defined as total assets minus current liabilities, the capital charge will be $180,000 = ($1,600,000 − $600,000) × 18%. The residual income would be $20,000, the profit before taxes less the capital charge as shown below:

The capital charge is the expense division management must cover for the use of the assets.

Profit before taxes from Exhibit 19-1	=	**$200,000**
(less) Capital charge .18 × $1,000,000	=	**180,000**
(equals) Residual income		**$ 20,000**

Since the residual income is positive, management of the Parts Division is earning more than the 18% capital charge rate on investment, generally a favorable sign.

To summarize, residual income is profit before taxes minus the capital charge. The capital charge is computed by taking a charge rate times the investment. Algebraically:

Residual income = profit before taxes − (investment × charge rate)

A positive RI indicates a return greater than the organization's target return and a negative RI indicates a return less than the organization's target return.

The rate used in most organizations to compute the capital charge is generally based on the organization's cost of capital.[1] Some organizations will use different rates for different assets. For example, current assets might be charged a lower rate than fixed assets since the resources in current assets are more liquid and more easily shifted to other uses. Different rates may also be used for different divisions reflecting the risk of the industry with which the division is associated.

Advantages of Residual Income In our discussion of ROI we said it had two major advantages: it was easily understood and it was directly related to other important ratios through the Dupont formula. What are the advantages of residual income? Again there are two that we shall discuss in this section.

Both ROI and RI direct management's attention to profitability and asset management. Both measures of divisional performance are used in practice. However, there are differences between them. The ROI measure is a *ratio* and directs management's attention to the rate of return on each dollar in the investment base. The RI measure is an amount of dollars returned on the investment base. To see how this can affect division management's decisions, consider an organization that has specified a minimum ROI of 20%. Assume that a division has a current ROI of 25% and has a proposal for an investment of $50,000 that is expected to yield 23% or add $11,500 to divisional profit before taxes. Since the ROI on the proposed investment is less than the current ROI, division management might well reject the proposal even though the ROI is greater than the organization's minimum. Managers do not like to make investments which will reduce their division's ROI.

If the RI measure is used and the division is charged 20% on the added investment, divisional management would be inclined to accept the proposal since the division's RI will increase by $1,500 as shown below:

Increase in profit before taxes	**$11,500**
Increase in capital charge .20 × $50,000	**10,000**
Increase in residual income	**$ 1,500**

ROI and RI can lead division management to different decisions.

When ROI is used to measure divisional performance, management is told to maximize a ratio. When RI is used, management is told to maximize a dollar amount. As the above illustration points out this can influence a manager's decision. The advantage of RI is that it encourages the investment center manager to make all investments that promise a return greater than the capital charge.

Different capital charge rates can be used for different assets.

The second advantage of the RI measure is that different capital charge rates can be used to charge the divisions for different types of assets. For example, the organization might want to charge a lower rate for current assets than fixed assets to reflect a perceived lower risk of investing in current assets. Also the fixed assets might be separated into different categories according to risk and different rates used to charge the interest to the divisions. Special-purpose equipment might be charged a higher rate than general-purpose equipment to reflect the higher risk of investing in specialized equipment.

[1] One method that organizations use to estimate cost of capital involves weighted average cost of debt and equity capital. See H. Bierman, Jr. and S. Smidt, *The Capital Budgeting Decision*, 5th ed. (New York: The Macmillan Company, 1980).

MEASURING PROFIT

Both the ROI and RI measures of division performance require some measure of profit. Responsibility accounting requires that all revenues and expenses controllable by the division manager should be included in the profit computation. However, there is no definitive answer as to whether corporate expenses should be allocated to the divisions and included in computing divisional income.

The argument for allocating corporate expenses to the divisions is that they represent the cost of services provided to the division by corporate offices. However, the cost of many corporate services are not controllable by the divisional managers. At a minimum, arbitrary allocations of corporate expenses should be avoided. If corporate expenses are to be allocated to the divisions, the allocated expenses should be based on the *actual* services provided to each division. The divisional income statement should show all allocated corporate expenses separate from the controllable expenses.

Allocated corporate expenses should be reported separately.

MEASURING THE INVESTMENT BASE

Two commonly used measures of the **investment base** are total assets and total assets less current liabilities. In general, the items included in the investment base should only include those resources that are used to produce the profit for the division. This implies that assets under construction or idle assets should not be included since they do not contribute to the profit of the division. Care should be taken though in deciding to exclude idle assets since a division manager might decide to cease production of a product if the return on the assets involved is not satisfactory. As discussed in Chapter 15, *any* positive contribution margin from idle assets will usually improve the total organization's income.

The investment base should include only productive assets.

Total assets includes cash, receivables, inventory, and fixed assets. In many organizations cash is controlled centrally in order to minimize the amount of idle cash on hand for the organization as a whole. This means that only a small cash balance is held by the divisions. In these situations the cash balance that would be required by the division if it were an independent company would be greater than its actual cash balance. Many companies will include in the investment base an amount of cash that approximates the amount the division would have to carry if it were an independent company. The amount is sometimes estimated as a standard percentage of annual sales.

Accounts receivable are generally included at their net amount, after deduction of the allowance for doubtful accounts. In most situations the division management can influence the amount of accounts receivable through the volume of sales generated, the credit terms extended to customers, and the collection policies implemented for overdue accounts.

Inventories are generally included since the division must carry inventory to absorb fluctuations in demand to avoid stockout and backorder costs. However, it should be noted that if the organization uses LIFO to value inventories the ending inventories will be undervalued during periods of inflation. Many organizations will use standard or average costs to calculate the inventory values and profit before taxes to avoid the valuation problems created using LIFO.

Fixed assets can be included at cost or at cost minus accumulated depreciation.

Either measure presents problems—discussed in the next part of this chapter—in using ROI or RI as a measure of financial performance. The use of total assets to measure the investment base tends to overstate the amount of resources invested in the division by the organization, since suppliers normally supply some of the division resources by extending credit to the division. By deducting the current liabilities from the total assets to compute the investment base a better measure of the resources supplied by the organization to generate the profit is achieved. If management has very little control over the current liabilities, some organizations will not deduct the current liabilities from total assets. In some organizations all payables are handled centrally and division management has little control over the payment of the liabilities. From a motivational point of view, using total assets as the investment base would be acceptable but it would overstate the resources supplied to the division by the organization.

Current liabilities measure the division resources financed by suppliers.

Valuing Fixed Assets for Investment Center Reporting

The measure of fixed assets to include in the investment base presents some serious problems in investment center reporting. To illustrate one potential problem, assume the Parts Division of the Zomack Corporation, introduced in Exhibit 19-1, is considering the purchase of a new piece of equipment that will cost $150,000. The equipment has a five-year life, no salvage value, and it is anticipated that annual cash operating savings will amount to $52,000. Assume Zomack has a minimum rate of return of 20%. Even though this book has not yet shown you how to make the computation, this investment promises a return in excess of the 20% minimum rate of return. This indicates that the investment is desirable for the organization and should be undertaken by the division.

Net Book Value Assuming ROI and RI are calculated using **net book value** of the fixed assets, what impact will this investment have on the ROI and RI for the Parts Division? Exhibit 19-2 illustrates the impact of this investment on ROI and RI. The first part of Exhibit 19-2 shows the ROI computations for each year based on the net book value of the asset at the beginning of the year. As you can see, in the first year the ROI is 14.7% and in the second year is 18.3%. Both of these ROI figures are less than the Zomack's minimum return on investment of 20%. This fact might cause the divisional manager to reject the investment.

ROI increases over the life of an investment because of the decrease in net book value.

In future years ROI will increase because of the decreasing investment base caused by the annual increase in accumulated depreciation. Exhibit 19-2 illustrates how the ROI increases from 14.7% to 73.3% over the five-year life of the investment. Calculating ROI using average book value or accelerated depreciation methods would not change the increasing pattern of ROI.

RI increases over the life of the investment because of the decrease in net book value.

The same profitability pattern appears when RI is used to measure divisional performance. The second part of Exhibit 19-2 illustrates how RI increases from a negative $8,000 in year 1 to a positive $16,000 in year 5. Again, division management might reject the investment because of the negative RI in years 1 and 2.

Gross Book Value To avoid this illusion of an increasing ROI and RI when profit before taxes is constant, some organizations use **gross book value** to compute the fixed asset portion of the investment base. For this example the ROI on the investment using gross book value is:

EXHIBIT 19-2
The Impact on ROI and RI of a New Asset Over Time
ROI Computations for an Asset with a Five-Year Life Using Net Book Value

Year	Net Book Value at Beginning of Year	Cost Savings		Depreciation		Profit Before Taxes	ROI
1	$150,000	$52,000	−	$30,000	=	$22,000	14.7%
2	120,000	52,000	−	30,000	=	22,000	18.3
3	90,000	52,000	−	30,000	=	22,000	24.4
4	60,000	52,000	−	30,000	=	22,000	36.6
5	30,000	52,000	−	30,000	=	22,000	73.3

RI Computations for an Asset with a Five-Year Life Using Net Book Value

Year	Net Book Value at Beginning of Year	Profit Before Taxes		Capital Charge 20% of Investment Base		RI
1	$150,000	$22,000	−	$30,000	=	($8,000)
2	120,000	22,000	−	24,000	=	(2,000)
3	90,000	22,000	−	18,000	=	4,000
4	60,000	22,000	−	12,000	=	10,000
5	30,000	22,000	−	6,000	=	16,000

$$\text{ROI} = \frac{\text{profit before taxes}}{\text{gross book value}} \times 100\%$$

$$14.7\% = \frac{\$\ 22{,}000}{\$150{,}000} \times 100\%$$

Since the profit before taxes is assumed constant over the five-year life of the investment, the ROI will be 14.7% in each year using gross book value as the measure of the investment base.

Gross book value of fixed assets creates a constant ROI and RI over the assets' life.

The same situation arises with RI computed using gross book value. For the proposed investment the RI is a constant −$8,000 for the five-year life of the investment. This results from the cost savings of $52,000 less depreciation of $30,000 and a capital charge of $30,000 (.20 × $150,000). Again the investment appears not to be desirable to division management since the RI has decreased.

To summarize, both the ROI and RI measures of performance can lead divisional management to decisions that may not be in the best interests of the organization. The problems arise because of the reliance on historical cost and traditional depreciation procedures to calculate both the income and the value of the investment base. An approach to resolving some of the problems encountered with gross and net book values in measuring the investment base is to assign replacement cost values to the fixed assets. If the replacement cost of the fixed assets can be adequately determined for all divisions, then the comparison of ROI or RI across divisions would be more consistent than with historical cost, since all investment bases would be expressed in terms of the same economic concepts and values.

OTHER PERFORMANCE MEASURES

ROI and RI provide measures of the profitability of a division given some investment base. In addition to these measures most organizations will use performance factors, such as market penetration, sales growth, and profit growth, and compare the actual results to budgeted amounts and prior-year results. This provides top management with additional information to evaluate the performance of the division even though these factors are implicitly included in the ROI and RI computations.

Other factors important to a division's performance are new product development and personnel development. For the continuing existence and growth of most organizations they must funnel some of their financial resources in the research and development of new products but most of the costs expended on new product development will not generate revenues for a number of years into the future. The organization's management needs to monitor the programs operated at the divisional level to ensure a proper amount of consideration is given to the long-term prospects of the division.

Personnel development is important at the divisional level since organizations require a training ground to develop experienced divisional and organizational managers. A divisional manager should ensure that the employees receive the appropriate experience and education to prepare them for future positions in the organization.

SUMMARY

The financial performance of an investment center can be measured using return on investment or residual income.

Return on investment is defined as the ratio of profits to the dollars invested in the division. The advantages of return on investment are that most managers have an intuitive understanding of return on investment and it is related to two other measures of efficiency which managers are accustomed to using, profit as a percentage of sales and asset turnover.

Residual income is defined as profit before taxes less a capital charge. The capital charge is the investment in the division times the charge rate. The advantages of residual income are that it encourages investment in assets that promise a return greater than the capital charge and different capital charge rates can be used to charge divisions for different types of assets.

In measuring profit and investment divisional managers should be held responsible for revenues, expenses, and investments which they can control. If corporate expenses are allocated to the divisions they should be shown separately on the division income statement.

In measuring division investment fixed assets can be valued at net book value or gross book value. Both valuations can cause division managers to make investment decisions not in the organization's best interests. This problem arises because of the reliance on historical costs and traditional depreciation procedures. An approach to resolving this problem is to value fixed assets at replacement cost.

Other divisional performance measures include market penetration, sales growth, profit growth, new product development, and personnel development.

Review Problem

The ABC division's average asset balances for 19X3 are as follows:

Cash		$ 10,000
Accounts receivable		15,000
Inventory		25,000
Fixed assets—cost	$100,000	
Accumulated depreciation	40,000	60,000
Total assets		$110,000
Current liabilities		$ 30,000
Equity		80,000
Total liabilities and equity		$100,000

During 19X3 the division's profit before taxes was $12,000 on sales revenues of $160,000.

Required

1 Compute the ROI using total assets less current liabilities to measure the investment base.

2 Compute the RI using a capital charge of 10%.

3 Top management would like the division to increase its ROI by 5% during 19X4. What change in the profit to sales percentage or asset turnover ratio would increase the ROI by 5%?

Solution

1 Computation of ROI:

$$\textbf{ROI} = \frac{\textbf{profit}}{\textbf{investment base}} \times 100\%$$

$$\textbf{ROI} = \frac{\$12{,}000}{\$80{,}000} \times 100\% = 15\%$$

2 Computation of RI:

Profit before taxes	**$12,000**
Capital charge (.10 × $80,000)	**8,000**
Residual income	**$ 4,000**

3 Alternatives to increase ROI by 5%:

$$\text{ROI} = \frac{\text{profit}}{\text{sales}} \times \frac{\text{sales}}{\text{investment base}} \times 100\%$$

$$\text{Current ROI} = \frac{\$12{,}000}{\$160{,}000} \times \frac{\$160{,}000}{\$80{,}000} \times 100\%$$

$$.075 \times 2.0 \times 100\% = 15\%$$

$$\text{Desired ROI} = 20\% \; (15\% + 5\% \text{ increase})$$

Increase in profit percentage:

$$20\% = \frac{\text{profit}}{\text{sales}} \times 2.0$$

$$\frac{\text{profit}}{\text{sales}} = \frac{20\%}{2.0} = 10\%$$

Increase in investment turnover:

$$20\% = 7.5\% \times \frac{\text{sales}}{\text{investment}}$$

$$\frac{\text{sales}}{\text{investment}} = \frac{20\%}{7.5\%} = 2.67 \text{ times}$$

Glossary

Asset turnover The ratio of sales to the investment base. It represents the sales dollars generated for each dollar of investment and is one component in computing ROI.

Capital charge The charge to divisions for the use of assets supplied by the organization. It is used in calculating residual income.

Dupont formula A formula that relates ROI to profit as a percentage of sales and asset turnover.

Gross book value The historical cost of fixed assets used by some organizations as part of the investment base.

Investment base The denominator in the ROI calculation and the base for computing the capital charge with RI.

Net book value The historical cost of fixed assets less accumulated depreciation. It is used by some organizations as a part of the investment base.

Profit as a percentage of sales The ratio of profit to sales. It represents the percentage of each sales dollar that flows into profit and is one component in computing ROI.

Residual income A measure of divisional performance calculated as the profit before taxes less a capital charge.

Return on investment A measure of divisional performance calculated as the ratio of profit to investment.

Questions and Problems

19-1 Why do managers include a measure of the investment base in evaluating the financial performance of divisions?

19-2 Should corporate expenses be allocated to the divisions for the purpose of calculating divisional profit?

19-3 Discuss two alternatives for measuring the investment base.

19-4 Compare the use of gross book value and net book value as measures of fixed assets to be included in the investment base.

19-5 What are the advantages of using ROI to measure divisional performance?

19-6 What are the advantages of using RI to measure divisional performance?

19-7 For measuring divisional performance, which do you prefer, ROI or RI? Why?

19-8 What other performance measures can be used to evaluate divisional performance?

19-9 **ROI Computations** The following data were selected from the financial statements of three divisions.

	Division		
	1	**2**	**3**
Sales	$100,000	?	?
Income	?	?	$15,000
Investment base	?	$90,000	$25,000
Return on sales	1%	10%	3%
Asset turnover	?	3	?
Return on investment	2%	?	?

Required

Calculate the missing figures using ROI concepts.

19-10 **ROI as a Planning Tool** A division of a large manufacturing company produces electrical generators for an industrial market. In recent years the division has been producing a ROI of 20%. The management would like the ROI to increase to 25% in the next year. The company uses direct costing to calculate division income. The following data have been taken from the preliminary forecasts for the next year.

Investment base	$10,000,000
Sales price per unit	$ 1,200
Variable cost per unit	$ 800
Annual fixed costs	$ 2,000,000

Required

1 Calculate the income the division will need to achieve a 25% ROI.

2 Calculate the sales volume in units and dollars necessary to generate the 25% ROI.

3 Compute the ROI using return on sales and investment turnover to verify the computations in 1 and 2 above.

19-11 **Comparison of ROI and RI as Performance Measures** The ABC Company is segmented into two divisions, Big and Small. Selected data from the division financial statements are given below:

	Division	
	Big	**Small**
Investment base	$10,000,000	$6,000,000
Income before taxes	$ 1,800,000	$1,320,000

Required

1 Calculate the ROI for the two divisions and the RI using a charge rate of 15%. Which is the most profitable?

2 Repeat 1 using a capital charge rate of 10%.

19-12 **Ranking of Divisions Using ROI and RI** The ABC company is segmented into three divisions A, B, and C. All divisions were formed in the same year and now all assets have left exactly one-half of their expected life. Top management is attempting to determine which of the divisions is the most profitable. The following data have been prepared for your analysis:

		Division	
	A	**B**	**C**
Net income before taxes	$ 78,000	$ 90,000	$ 96,000
Investment base-gross book value	$390,000	$500,000	$600,000
Investment base-net book value	$195,000	$250,000	$300,000

Required

Prepare rankings of the three divisions using ROI or RI with a capital charge rate of 10% that each division manager might use to assert that hers is the most profitable division.

19-13 **Performance Analysis of Divisional Managers** The Texon Company is organized into autonomous divisions along regional market lines. Each division manager is responsible for sales, cost of operations, acquisition and financing of divisional assets, and working capital management.

The vice president of general operations for the company will retire in September 19X5. A review of the performance, attitudes, and skills of several management employees has been undertaken. Interviews with qualified outside candidates also have been held. The selection committee has narrowed the choice to the managers of divisions A and F.

Both candidates were appointed division managers in late 19X1. The manager of division A had been the assistant manager of the division for the prior five years. The manager of division F had served as assistant division manager of division B before being appointed to his present post. He took over division F, a division newly formed in 19X0, when its first manager left to join a competitor. The financial results of their performance in the past three years is reported on the following page:

	Division A			Division F		
	19X2	19X3	19X4	19X2	19X3	19X4
			($000 omitted)			
Estimated industry sales —market area	$10,000	$12,000	$13,000	$5,000	$6,000	$6,500
Division sales	$ 1,000	$ 1,100	$ 1,210	$ 450	$ 600	$ 750
Variable expense	$ 300	$ 320	$ 345	$ 135	$ 175	$ 210
Managed expense	400	405	420	170	200	230
Committed expense	275	325	350	140	200	250
Total expense	$ 975	$ 1,050	$ 1,115	$ 445	$ 575	$ 690
Net income	$ 25	$ 50	$ 95	$ 5	$ 25	$ 60
Assets employed	$ 330	$ 340	$ 360	$ 170	$ 240	$ 300
Liabilities incurred	103	105	115	47	100	130
Net investment	227	235	245	123	140	170
Return on investment	11%	21%	39%	4%	18%	35%

Required

1 Texon Co. measures the performance of the divisions and the division managers on the basis of their return on investment (ROI). Is this an appropriate measurement for the division managers? Explain.

2 Many believe that a single measure, such as ROI, is inadequate to fully evaluate performance. What additional measure(s) could be used for performance evaluation? Give reasons for each measure listed.

3 On the basis of the information given, which manager would you recommend for vice president of general operations? Present reasons to support your answer.

(CMA)

19-14 Divisional Performance Evaluation George Johnson was hired on July 1, 19X0 as assistant general manager of the Botel Division of Staple, Inc. It was understood that he would be elevated to general manager of the division on January 1, 19X2 when the then current general manager retired and this was duly done. In addition to becoming acquainted with the division and the general manager's duties, Mr. Johnson was specifically charged with the responsibility for development of the 19X1 and 19X2 budgets. As general manager in 19X2, he was also responsible for the 19X3 budget.

Staple Inc., is a multiproduct company which is highly decentralized. Each division is quite autonomous. The corporation staff approves division prepared operating budgets but seldom makes major changes in them. The corporate staff actively participates in decisions requiring capital investment (for expansion or replacement) and makes the final decisions. The division management is responsible for implementing the capital program. The major method used by Staple to measure division performance is contribution return on division net investment. The budgets presented below were approved by the corporation. Revision of the 19X3 budget is not considered necessary even though 19X2 actually departed from the approved 19X2 budget.

BOTEL DIVISION
($000 Omitted)

Accounts	Actual 19X0	Actual 19X1	Actual 19X2	Budget 19X2	Budget 19X3
Sales	$1,000	$1,500	$1,800	$2,000	$2,400
Less division variable costs					
Material and labor	250	375	450	500	600
Repairs	50	75	50	100	120
Supplies	20	30	36	40	48
Less division managed costs					
Employee training	30	35	25	40	45
Maintenance	50	55	40	60	70
Less division committed costs					
Depreciation	120	160	160	200	200
Rent	80	100	110	140	140
Total	$ 600	$ 830	$ 871	$1,080	$1,223
Division net contribution	$ 400	$ 670	$ 929	$ 920	$1,177
Division investment					
Accounts receivable	$ 100	$ 150	$ 180	$ 200	$ 240
Inventory	200	300	270	400	480
Fixed assets	1,590	2,565	2,800	3,380	4,000
Less: Accounts and wages payable	(150)	(225)	(350)	(300)	(360)
Net investment	$1,740	$2,790	$2,900	$3,680	$4,360
Contribution return on net investment	23%	24%	32%	25%	27%

Required

1 Identify Johnson's responsibilities under the management and measurement program described above.

2 Appraise the performance of Johnson in 19X2.

3 Recommend to the president any changes in the responsibilities assigned to managers or in the measurement methods used to evaluate division management based upon your analysis.

(CMA)

19-15 Dysfunctional Aspects of ROI The Notewon Corporation is a highly diversified company which grants its divisional executives a significant amount of authority in operating the divisions. Each division is responsible for its own sales, pricing, production, costs of operations, and the management of accounts receivable, inventories, accounts payable, and use of existing facilities. Cash is managed by corporate headquarters; all cash in excess of normal operating needs of the divisions is transferred periodically to corporate headquarters for redistribution or investment.

The divisional executives are responsible for presenting requests to corporate management for investment projects. The proposals are analyzed and documented at corporate headquarters. The final decision to commit funds to acquire equipment, to expand existing facilities, or for other investment purposes rests with corporate management. This procedure for investment projects is necessitated by Notewon's capital allocation policy.

The corporation evaluates the performance of division executives by the return on investment (ROI) measure. The asset base is composed of net fixed assets employed plus working capital exclusive of cash.

The ROI performance of a divisional executive is the most important appraisal factor for salary changes. In addition, the annual performance bonus is based on the ROI results with increases in ROI having a significant impact on the amount of the bonus.

The Notewon Corporation adopted the ROI performance measure and related compensation procedures about 10 years ago. The corporation did so to increase the awareness of divisional management of the importance of the profit/asset relationship and to provide additional incentive to the divisional executives to seek investment opportunities.

The corporation seems to have benefited from the program. The ROI for the corporation as a whole increased during the first years of the program. Although the ROI has continued to grow in each division, the corporate ROI has declined in recent years. The corporation has accumulated a sizable amount of cash and short-term marketable securities in the past three years.

The corporation management is concerned about the increase in the short-term marketable securities. A recent article in a financial publication suggested that the use of ROI was overemphasized by some companies with results similar to those experienced by Notewon.

Required

1 Explain, using the concepts of goal congruence and motivation of divisional executives, how Notewon Corporation's overemphasis on the use of the ROI measure might result in the recent decline in the corporation's return on investment and the increase in cash and short-term marketable securities.

2 What changes could be made in Notewon Corporation's compensation policy to avoid this problem? Explain your answer.

(CMA)

19-16 **Investment Center?** The ATCO Co. purchased the Dexter Co. three years ago. Prior to the acquisition Dexter manufactured and sold plastic products to a wide variety of customers. Dexter has since become a division of ATCO and now only manufactures plastic components for products made by ATCO's Macon Division. Macon sells its products to hardware wholesalers.

ATCO's corporate management gives the Dexter Division management a considerable amount of authority in running the division's operations. However, corporate management retains authority for decisions regarding capital investments, price setting of all products, and the quantity of each product to be produced by the Dexter Division.

ATCO has a formal performance evaluation program for the management of all its divisions. The performance evaluation program relies heavily on each division's return on investment. The income statement of Dexter Division presented below provides the basis for the evaluation of Dexter's divisional management.

The financial statements for the divisions are prepared by the corporate accounting staff. The corporate general services costs are allocated on the basis of sales dollars and the computer department's actual costs are apportioned among the divisions on the basis of use. The net division investment includes division fixed assets at net book value (cost less depreciation), division inventory, and corporate working capital apportioned to the divisions on the basis of sales dollars.

DEXTER DIVISION OF ATCO CO.
Income Statement
For the Year Ended October 31, 19X0
($000 Omitted)

Sales		$4,000
Cost and expenses		
Product costs		
Direct materials	$ 500	
Direct labor	1,100	
Factory overhead	1,300	
Total	$2,900	
Less: Increase in inventory	350	$2,550
Engineering and research		120
Shipping and receiving		240
Division administration		
Manager's office	$ 210	
Cost accounting	40	
Personnel	82	332
Corporate costs		
Computer	$ 48	
General services	230	278
Total costs and expenses		$3,520
Divisional operating income		$ 480
Net plant investment		$1,600
Return on investment		30%

Required

1 Discuss the financial reporting and performance evaluation program of ATCO Co. as it relates to the responsibilities of the Dexter Division.

2 Based upon your response to 1, recommend appropriate revisions of the financial information and reports used to evaluate the performance of Dexter's divisional management. If revisions are not necessary, explain why they are not needed.

(CMA)

19-17 Performance Evaluation Using RI Bio-grade Products is a multiproduct company manufacturing animal feeds and feed supplements. The need for a widely based manufacturing and distribution system has led to a highly decentralized management structure. Each divisional manager is responsible for production and distribution of corporate products in one of eight geographical areas of the country.

Residual income is used to evaluate divisional managers. The residual income for each division equals each division's contribution to corporate profits before taxes less a 20% capital charge on a division's investment base. The investment base for each division is the sum of its year-end balances of accounts receivable, inventories, and net plant fixed assets (cost less accumulated depreciation). Corporate policies dictate that divisions minimize their investments in receivables and inventories. Investments in plant fixed assets are a joint division/corporate decision based on proposals made by divisional plant managers, available corporate funds, and general corporate policy.

Alex Williams, divisional manager for the southeastern sector, prepared the 19X7 and preliminary 19X8 budgets in late 19X6 for his division. Final approval of the 19X8 budget took place in late 19X7 after adjustments for trends and other information developed during 19X7. Preliminary work on the 19X9 budget also took place at that time. In early October 19X8, Williams asked the divisional controller to prepare a report which presents performance for the first nine months of 19X8. The report is reproduced below:

Bio-Grade Products—Southeastern Sector
($000 Omitted)

	19X8			19X7	
	Annual Budget	Nine-Month Budget[1]	Nine-Month Actual	Annual Budget	Actual Results
Sales	$2,800	$2,100	$2,200	$2,500	$2,430
Divisional costs and expenses					
Direct materials and labor	$1,064	$ 798	$ 995	$ 900	$ 890
Supplies	44	33	35	35	43
Maintenance and repairs	200	150	60	175	160
Plant depreciation	120	90	90	110	110
Administration	120	90	90	90	100
Total divisional costs and expenses	$1,548	$1,161	$1,270	$1,310	$1,303
Divisional margin	$1,252	$ 939	$ 930	$1,190	$1,127
Allocated corporate fixed costs	360	270	240	340	320
Divisional contribution to corporate profits	$ 892	$ 669	$ 690	$ 850	$ 807
Capital charge on divisional investment (20%)	420	321[2]	300[2]	370	365
Divisional residual income	$ 472	$ 348	$ 390	$ 480	$ 442

	19X8			19X7	
	Budgeted Balances December 31	Budgeted Balances September 30	Actual Balances September 30	Budgeted Balances December 31	Actual Balances December 31
Division investment:					
Accounts receivable	$ 280	$ 290	$ 250	$ 250	$ 250
Inventories	500	500	650	450	475
Plant fixed assets (net)	1,320	1,350	1,100	1,150	1,100
Total	$2,100	$2,140	$2,000	$1,850	$1,825
Capital charge (20%)	$ 420	$ 321[2]	$ 300[2]	$ 370	$ 365

[1] Bio-grade's sales occur uniformly throughout the year.

[2] Capital charge is calculated at only 15% to reflect that only nine months or three-fourths of the fiscal year has passed.

Required

1 Evaluate the performance of Alex Williams for the nine months ending September 19X8. Support your evaluation with pertinent facts from the problem.

2 Identify the features of Bio-grade Products divisional performance measurement reporting and evaluating system which need to be revised if it is to reflect effectively the responsibilities of the divisional managers.

(CMA)

20 TRANSFER PRICING

AFTER COMPLETING YOUR STUDY OF THIS CHAPTER, YOU SHOULD HAVE LEARNED:

1 How the need for transfer prices arises when two or more divisions of an organization exchange products or services.

2 That transfer prices may be based on either market prices or cost of manufacturing.

3 How cost based transfer prices are of four types based either on full or variable costs and either actual costs or standard costs.

4 How improper transfer prices may lead to poor production and selling decisions by division managers.

You have probably had the experience of buying hot dogs for a picnic. You may have even decided to buy that pound of hot dogs from one particular store because its price was lower. Selling prices are generally established by competition. The competition is quite open in groceries where the price of many items is advertised in newspapers. Competition exists in other products as well, but the prices may not be advertised. The customer seeks the best price by shopping from one dealer to another. Most people buy automobiles by visiting several dealers to get the best price for the sports car of their dreams.

In business purchases the process is similar. A buyer will usually obtain several price quotations from manufacturers who can produce the needed quality and deliver the quantities needed on time. The buyer will usually select the supplier with the lowest price. The buyer's willingness to shop for the lowest price provides incentive for sellers to keep prices as low as possible. But if the price is too low, the seller will often stop selling that product. Costs establish a lower limit for prices because in the long run sellers will not be willing to sell a product at a loss.

When one division of a large company buys a product or service from another division of the same company, a special kind of a selling price called a transfer price is established. Sometimes it is established by competition as other selling prices are, but often other considerations suggest alternative methods to establish a transfer price.

Transfer price defined.

A **transfer price** is a selling price established for goods or services sold by one division of a single organization to another division of the same organization. The special name, transfer price, is used because the method of establishing the transfer price is sometimes different from the method used to establish regular selling prices that you see in a store.

Before considering the various methods of establishing transfer prices, we will look at an illustration which describes how managers think when they establish a transfer price. Read the description with the idea of understanding how you would feel if you were one of the managers in the illustration.

THE NEED FOR A TRANSFER PRICE

Darwin Morris manages the United States toy division of Multiproducts Corporation. Multiproducts' German subsidiary had developed a new child's bicycle which Darwin thought would sell well in the United States. The key to simplifying the bicycle was high-quality bearings which permitted most of the bicycle to be made from plastic parts which the toy division could produce at a low cost. There would be a royalty to the German subsidiary, but the product should still be quite profitable.

While the bearings could be purchased from several suppliers, Darwin thought naturally of Multiproducts' bearings division. The bearings division had just completed a highly automated plant which could produce the bearings required for the new product. Darwin was aware of unused capacity in the new bearing plant and thought that would mean the bearings division would be willing to quote a very low price for the bearings. With unused capacity, any price which exceeds variable costs would provide a positive contribution margin and add to the bearings division's profits, and variable costs should be very low in the new plant.

Darwin arranged to have lunch with Nick Muller, the manager of the bearings division. Darwin was soon explaining the new product and its importance for the bearings division as well as for the toy division. Nick's immediate thought was that he would welcome the new business. Even though sales would have a distinct seasonal pattern, he needed a relatively high volume of sales to make the new bearing plant profitable. Further, he reflected that if the sale were arranged between Darwin and himself, he would not have to pay any sales commissions. There certainly would be no credit problems or investment in accounts receivable because "payment" would be made by a simple bookkeeping entry. So the expense of selling to the toy division would actually be less than the expense of selling to customers outside of the organization. Nick felt that the toy division should be prepared to pay at least the outside market price for this type of bearing because the bearings division could assure high quality and more reliable deliveries than outside suppliers.

Lunch ended without a discussion of prices. Darwin agreed to send Nick the specifications for the bearings along with an estimate of the quantity to be purchased in the first year of production. Nick agreed to respond with a firm price quotation for the first year's production.

Transfer prices influence the profits of two divisions.

Multiproducts Corporation needs a transfer price for the bearings. If the bearings division is to supply the toy division, a transfer price will be needed to record sales revenue for the bearings division and the cost of the bearings for the toy division. Naturally, the toy division wants the lowest possible transfer price (cost) to reduce its expenses and increase divisional profits. Similarly, the bearings division wants the highest possible transfer price to increase its revenue and divisional profits.

If bearings and toys were independent companies rather than divisions of Multiproducts Corporation, toy would have solicited bids from several suppliers and have chosen the lowest price offered by a bidder who could meet quality and delivery standards.

Participants in Establishing Transfer Prices

The managers of the two divisions realize that it is in the best interest of Multiproducts Corporation (because of savings of sales commissions, lack of credit losses, utilization of spare capacity, etc.) to have the bearings manufactured by the bearings division. It is also in the best interests of each division manager. But this does not mean that the two division managers will agree on the transfer price.

Corporate management would normally prefer not to interfere in the price setting process. An important reason for organizing the corporation into divisions is to give responsibility for decisions to division managers who are close to the problems and who can make informed decisions more quickly than can corporate level management. But corporate management does want the division managers to agree on the terms of the sale, and to not waste too much time on reaching agreement. The division managers' time should be spent on improving marketing, production, or other aspects of their divisions.

Corporate managers evaluate divisional performance as profit centers or investment centers in order to encourage each division manager to act as an independent manager, but in a manner which furthers corporatewide profitability and return on investment.

Three different sets of managers are concerned with establishing a transfer price, each with somewhat different objectives.

The manager of the "buying" division is concerned with the price.

1 The manager of the toy division wants to maximize the profit of his division by minimizing the cost of the bearings and thereby minimizing his expense. He could purchase the bearings from an "outside" supplier (a supplier who is not a division of Multiproducts Corporation) but he expects that he might have to pay a higher price and perhaps receive poorer quality and delivery schedules.

The manager of the "selling" division is concerned with the price.

2 The manager of the bearings division wants to maximize the profit of this division by maximizing the contribution margin he can generate from his plant. Since the new plant has idle capacity, he will not have to give up sales to other customers in order to sell bearings to the toy division. He can therefore maximize his profits by maximizing his contribution margin. He will do this by selling as many bearings as possible at the highest possible selling price.

Corporate management is concerned with the price.

3 Corporate management wishes to have the toy division sell as many bicycles as possible (assuming that it is a profitable product) and to have the bearings division make the bearings, because the relevant costs of producing them in the bearings division's new plant is undoubtedly lower than buying them from an outside supplier. They recognize that if the bearings division quotes too high a price the toy division might find an outside supplier (also with idle capacity) who would quote a fairly low price.

Transfer Pricing Policies

To achieve the benefits of divisional organization and to encourage quick transfer pricing decisions which are in the best interests of the total company, most large companies establish a transfer pricing policy which outlines the method division managers should use to make transfer price decisions.

Transfer price methods are of two general types:

Types of transfer prices.

1 Market based transfer prices

2 Cost based transfer prices

Market based transfer prices are often considered ideal because the situation is similar to what division managers would face if they were managing independent companies. The external market price provides management with an indication of the profitability of the divisions as though they were independent companies. This facilitates comparing the division's profitability with similar organizations in the same line of business.

But sometimes no outside market exists so market prices cannot be used; and even if an outside market exists it may not be competitive. Hence the market based price might not produce results which are in the best interest of the company as a whole.

Cost based prices have at least four variations which depend on the type of product cost accounting system employed. The four variations can be illustrated as follows:

Costs that can be used to set transfer prices.

	Actual Cost	Standard Cost
Full Cost	1	2
Variable Cost	3	4

The balance of this chapter will be devoted to a discussion of the advantages and disadvantages of the various methods of establishing a transfer pricing policy. Transfer prices are needed in any company in which products or services are transferred from one division to another division within the company.

To summarize, there are five methods of transfer pricing we will consider, one market based method and four cost based methods. We will discuss market based prices first followed by a discussion of the cost based prices.

MARKET BASED TRANSFER PRICES

Adjustments are usually made to market prices.

If a competitive market external to the organization exists for the product being exchanged by the divisions, the external market price is the most desirable transfer price. Adjustments to the external market price might be made for any reduction in selling expenses, shipping expense, or credit investigation costs since these costs are generally going to be lower on a sale to another division rather than to an outside customer.

To make the market based transfer price work both the selling and buying divisions should have roughly equal bargaining power. This is done by permitting the selling division to refuse to supply the buying division if the price is too low and permitting the buying division to buy from an outside supplier if the selling division's price is too high. Thus each division will have the freedom to select products, prices, suppliers, and customers as if they were independent organizations. Both buyer and seller will have the same bargaining power as if they were independent. Just as important, corporate managers will be able to hold the division managers accountable for their results because they make decisions as independently as possible.

By establishing a transfer price that simulates the results of a transaction between independent managers, the division managers are supplied with accurate cost data which they need to make the most profitable decisions, for their divisions and for the company as a whole. If the selling division can sell its products both externally and internally, it should select the alternative which produces the highest profit for the division. Sometimes this will mean temporarily selling products below their full cost. Likewise, the purchasing division should acquire its inputs from the source which provides the lowest cost, whether inside or outside.

Consider the following example. A division manufactures a metal ring which is needed by another division of the same company. The cost of manufacturing the ring is estimated as follows.

Variable cost	4¢
Fixed cost	2¢
Total cost	6¢

Suppose that at the moment demand is low for this type of product and an outside supplier has offered to sell the rings to the buying division for 5 cents per ring. The division which manufactures the ring would like to sell as many rings as possible at as high a price as possible. But if the manufacturing facilities will be idle (if not used to produce the ring), the selling division will earn a greater profit by selling the rings at 5 cents than by leaving the facilities idle. At 5 cents per ring, the rings produce a contribution margin of 1 cent each (5 cents selling price minus 4 cents variable expense). If the selling division refuses to sell at 5 cents per ring, it will have zero variable expense, but also zero revenue and the fixed costs will continue. If they sell 100,000 rings at 5 cents each, they will generate $1,000 additional contribution margin (1 cent × 100,000 units) from the idle facilities, which will add a corresponding amount to profits.

Change the example a bit. Suppose that the manufacturing division uses all its capacity to manufacture rings under a long-term contract to sell them for 7 cents per ring. The manufacturing division has no idle capacity. The only way they could manufacture the rings for the buying division would be to give up some of their profitable outside business. In this case it is in the interest of the company as a whole and in the interest of the buying division to buy them from the outside supplier at 5 cents per unit. The company should not give up sales at 7 cents per unit to save spending 5 cents per unit for the rings from the outside supplier. In this case the manufacturing division would refuse to sell to the buying division and the buying division would therefore purchase the needed rings from the outside supplier.

The point is that when a competitive outside market exists and the divisions are free to buy or sell outside as they wish, each division manager acting in his own best interest will also achieve the best interest of the total organization. In times when the selling division has idle capacity it should be willing to lower prices as long as the sale generates the most contribution margin possible from the idle facilities. This maximizes the selling division's profit. When demand is high relative to supply, both the selling and buying divisions should expect higher prices. When the supplying division is at full capacity and the buying division can buy the product outside at a lower price than the supplying division is selling to outside customers, it is best for the corporation to have the buying division buy from the outside supplier. Otherwise the selling division would have to turn down sales at a good price in order to use the production facilities to produce products the buying division could buy more cheaply outside.

Arbitration is used to settle transfer price disputes.

But what happens when the buying division is not free to purchase parts from outside suppliers? Often arbitration by top management is required to settle differences between division managers. Top management would usually like to avoid the need for arbitration because having decisions made by top management defeats some of the purpose of establishing independent divisions. Let us look at a few situations which often lead to arbitration where top management makes the transfer pricing decision.

Arbitrated Transfer Prices

Conditions not favorable to market prices.

Market prices cannot always be used for transfer prices because of the lack of a competitive market. Often there is no competitive market because the product transferred is different than other products on the market in terms of quality, transportation costs, special design modifications, or credit terms. In these circumstances, division managers will attempt to agree to a transfer price by negotiation, but since there is no market price to serve as reference point, they may not be able to reach agreement between themselves and arbitration may be necessary.

Another circumstance which may lead to arbitration is when management does not wish to buy from an outside supplier because they do not wish to disclose a secret ingredient or a secret process. In these circumstances the manager of the buying division lacks the negotiating power that comes from the ability to go outside to buy the product and the two division managers may not be able to negotiate a transfer price. Again arbitration by top management will be required.

Some organizations adopt the policy that the buying and selling divisions are required to transact their business internally if the conditions of sale are similar to outside conditions. But agreeing on what is "similar" may create conflicts between the division managers and require arbitration by top management.

Problems with using market prices.

Another problem occasionally encountered with a market price is that suppliers outside the organization might quote a temporarily lower price to dump excess inventory or to use idle capacity. The temporary loss of sales may have a disruptive effect on the selling division. Normally the supplying division would lower their price to meet the competition if the idle capacity exists in the entire industry. But the potential disruption from renegotiating prices frequently may cause corporate management to adopt a policy which requires divisions to focus on long-run market prices ignoring temporary fluctuations in market price.

If arbitration is used frequently, the divisional managers will lose some independence and perhaps some of the motivation that results from managing an independent division.

COST BASED TRANSFER PRICES

Cost based transfer prices are used in three circumstances:

1 No market price exists. This occurs when the product is partially completed and not usually sold at this stage of production.

2 Difficulties in determining market prices cause disputes among division managers.

3 Where the product contains a secret ingredient or requires a secret production process that management does not wish to disclose to outsiders.

In these situations organizations rely on cost figures to establish the transfer price. But what costs should be used?

Standard Versus Actual Costs

Standard costs aid in controlling the cost of the selling division.

In order to keep the selling division from passing costs resulting from inefficient operations to the buying division, the selling division should base their cost calculations on standard costs rather than actual cost. The use of standard costs will tend to provide an incentive to the selling division management to control their operating cost as a way of improving profitability.

The use of standard costs is feasible only if the selling divisions have standard cost systems. It would usually be too expensive to have engineers develop standard costs just for transfer pricing purposes. If standards are not available, actual costs will be used as the only available alternative.

Once the cost (standard or actual) has been determined, a profit margin is usually added to the cost to determine the transfer price. If the selling division sells some of its product to companies outside the organization the outside profit margin is often used in computing the transfer price. If the selling division does not sell to outside customers, profit margin may be based on averages for either the industry or the organization.

Full Cost Versus Variable Costs

A major problem with using a cost based transfer price is that the entire transfer price appears to be a variable cost to the buying division. Each unit costs the buying division its transfer price. But the transfer price represents both fixed and variable costs and a profit margin. The treatment of the transfer price as a completely variable cost by the buying division may lead the buying division to make decisions that are not in the best interests of the organization as a whole. To illustrate, assume that division S supplies subassemblies to division B at a transfer price of $50. The transfer price consists of the following:

Standard Variable Cost	$30	
Standard Fixed Cost	10	(Based on normal capacity)
Profit	10	
Transfer Price	$50	

Further assume the buying division incurs additional variable costs of $20 per unit prior to the sale of the final product and that idle production capacity exists for both divisions. If B has an opportunity for a special order of the final product for $60 per unit it will probably reject the opportunity since its profits would decrease by $10 per unit with a transfer price of $50 as shown below:

Division B Profits

Sales price	$60
Variable cost	−20
Transfer price	−50
Contribution per unit	($10)

Problems with using full cost.

However, for the organization as a whole the short-run profits would increase $10 per unit as shown below:

Organization Profits

Sales price	$60
Variable cost—B	−20
Variable cost—S	−30
Contribution per unit	$10

This example illustrates a situation where the organization's total profits are decreased because of the buying division treating the entire transfer price as a variable cost. This situation must be carefully monitored in organizations that have divisions which are primarily manufacturing and others that primarily market the products.

One solution to this problem would be to require the selling division to sell its product to the buying division at variable cost rather than full cost plus a profit margin. Then the buying division would know the real variable costs to the organization because the transfer price would be equal to the variable cost and the error would be avoided. To illustrate, if the transfer price between division S and division B were division S's variable cost, division B's analysis of the situation would be as follows.

Division B Profits

Sales price	$60
Variable cost in division B	−20
Transfer price	−30
Contribution per unit	$10

Knowing the real variable costs, division B would make the decision that we earlier found was in the best interest of the total organization.

Problems with using variable costs.

The main problem with requiring division S to always make inside sales at a transfer price equal to the variable cost is that inside sales would never generate a profit. Since the selling price will always equal the variable costs, the contribution margin would be zero, and the selling division would have no incentive to make these kinds of sales. In fact, if most of the selling division's sales were inside, the division would continually operate at a loss and the motivation of the manager would likely be quite low.

Still market prices remain the best choice if they exist. To illustrate how it

Market based prices are preferred over cost based prices.

would work in this case suppose that division S could sell all of its output for $50 per unit, the contribution to organization profits would be $20 per unit as computed below even if division B sells nothing.

Organization Profits	
Sales price (division S)	$50
Variable costs	30
Contribution per unit	$20

In this case the organization would be better off if S sold to external parties rather than selling to B and then having B sell their final product for $60 where the organizational contribution is only $10 per unit.

As you should have learned from the above discussion, there is probably no transfer price that does not create some potential problem for organization management. Transfer prices are required in situations where intracompany sales exist and management evaluates performance using either profits, return on investment, or residual income. Management must decide if the advantages of divisional organization, primarily the opportunity given to division managers to operate almost as though they were managing independent businesses, is worth the risk of decisions being made which are not always in the best interests of the total organization. As our discussion has pointed out, the danger of poor decisions arises most frequently where market prices *cannot* be used to determine transfer prices.

Transfer prices should be evaluated based on the benefits and costs of using them.

SUMMARY

Transfer prices are used in situations where two or more divisions of one organization exchange products or services. The objectives of a transfer price system are to allow each division manager to operate in an independent manner and to provide division managers with data that will lead to correct decisions.

Transfer prices are based either on outside market prices or cost of production. When a competitive external market exists a market based price determined through negotiation is the best procedure for establishing the transfer price in most situations. Problems arise when there is no comparable outside market or when division managers are not free to buy and sell outside as they wish.

When transfer prices are cost based they should be established using standard costs so that the selling division cannot pass costs of inefficient operations to the buying division.

Problems arise in the use of a cost based transfer price since the buying division treats the entire transfer price as a variable cost when it includes some fixed costs and a profit margin for the organization. Top management must decide if the costs of using a transfer pricing mechanism are less than the benefits of creating profit or investment centers.

Review Problem

The Ajax division of Gumco Corporation, which is operating at full capacity, has been asked by the Defco division of Gumco to supply it with an electrical fitting number 1726. Ajax sells this part to its regular (outside) customers for $7.50 each. Defco has offered to pay $5 each for the fitting. Defco will put the fitting into a brake unit which it is manufacturing for a commercial airplane manufacturer.

Ajax has a variable cost of producing fitting number 1726 of $4.25. The cost of the brake unit being built by Defco is estimated as follows:

Purchased Parts—outside vendors	$22.50
Ajax fitting—1726	5.00
Other variable costs	14.00
Fixed overhead and administration	8.00
	$49.50

Defco is anxious to sell to the airplane manufacturer because Defco is currently operating at 50% capacity. Because other manufacturers of brakes also have excess capacity Defco believes a price of $50 per unit is necessary to get the job. That is why they have proposed a lower than normal price to the Ajax division, even though Ajax is operating at full capacity.

The company uses return on investment to measure the financial performance of division managers.

Required

1 Assume that you are the division controller of Ajax. Would you recommend that Ajax supply fitting 1726 to Defco? (Ignore any income tax issues.) Why or why not?

2 Would it be to the short-run economic advantage of the Gumco Corporation for the Ajax division to supply Defco division with fitting 1726 at $5 each? (Ignore any income tax issues.) Explain your answer.

3 Discuss the organizational and manager behavior difficulties, if any, inherent in this situation. As the Gumco controller what would you advise the Gumco Corporation president do in this situation?

(CMA)

Solution

1 Ajax should not supply Defco with fitting 1726 for the $5 per unit price. Ajax is operating at capacity and would lose $2.50 ($7.50 − $5.00) for each fitting sold to Defco. The management performance of Ajax is measured by return on investment; selling to Defco at $5 per unit would adversely affect this performance measure.

2 The nature of the $8 per unit fixed overhead and administration is critical to deciding what is best for Gumco. It seems likely that these are fixed costs which will continue whether or not the brake units are sold. Given this assumption, Defco should sell the brake units at $50 per unit even if they have to pay $7.50 per unit for the electrical fitting from an outside supplier. At $7.50 per unit, the brake unit sales will generate a positive contribution margin of $6 per unit as shown below.

Selling price	$50.00
Less: variable expenses	
Purchased parts	−22.50
Fitting 1726	− 7.50
Other variable	−14.00
Contribution margin per unit	$ 6.00

If the Defco Division makes the correct analysis of their situation, they will realize that they do not need to obtain the part from Ajax at $5 per unit to make the order better than leaving the facilities idle.

As long as Defco can buy the fittings from an outside supplier for less than $7.50 per unit, there is no economic advantage to the Gumco Corporation in having Ajax Division supply Defco.

3 As noted in part 2, the best interests of Gumco are served if Defco accepts the brake unit order rather than leaving their facilities idle. Therefore, Gumco should assure that Defco makes the proper analysis of the situation and does not refuse the order because the total cost (including the fixed overhead and administration) is close to the selling price of $50 which is required to get the order.

Defco might appeal to Gumco for arbitration in the hope that Gumco would force Ajax to sell to Defco at a price lower than $7.50 per fitting. This appeal should be rejected since it is not in Gumco's interest to have Ajax lose sales at $7.50 per unit just to make sales to Defco at $5 per unit.

The appeal for arbitration should also be rejected for a second reason. If Gumco forces Ajax to take less profitable sales, Gumco will find it difficult to hold Ajax to its profit target at year-end. The purpose of the divisional organization is to make managers operate as though they were independent businesses. To order them to do something which reduces their profit undermines the motivation of the division managers to act independently.

Therefore, the Gumco controller should recommend that each division should be free to act in accordance with its best interests. The company is better served in the long run if Ajax is permitted to continue dealing with its regular customers at the market price. If Defco is having difficulties, the solution does not lie with temporary help at the expense of another division but with a more substantive course of action.

Glossary

Cost based transfer price A transfer price determined by adding a profit margin to the costs of the selling division. While costs can be calculated on either full or variable costing systems using either actual or standard cost, a full standard cost is most often used.

Market based transfer price A transfer price based on the market prices of outside sellers and buyers. Generally, the price is negotiated between the division managers because of imperfect markets and a desire to share cost savings on sales commissions, credit costs, etc., between the selling and buying divisions.

Transfer price The selling price established for goods or services exchanged between two divisions of a single organization.

Questions and Problems

20-1 What conditions make transfer prices necessary?

20-2 What are the objectives of a transfer price system?

20-3 What conditions must exist for a market based transfer price to work in achieving the objectives of the transfer pricing system?

20-4 Why is there a need for division managers to negotiate when transfer prices are market based?

20-5 What type of cost should be used in establishing a cost based transfer price? Why?

20-6 What problems can arise from using a cost based transfer price?

20-7 Special Orders and Transfer Prices The Barnhart Division of the Simon Corporation produces an electrical component that is used by the Sweeney Division in producing their finished product. The Barnhart Division is operating at full capacity producing the electrical component for an active external market in addition to supplying the Sweeney Division. The transfer price currently in use is the market price of the electrical component which is $10 per unit. The Barnhart Division's variable costs are $6 per unit for this component.

The Sweeney Division is operating at 60% capacity and has a chance to sell a special order if the selling price can be reduced. The cost analyst prepared the following analysis of the costs in the Sweeney Division:

Variable costs	
Manufacturing	$10
Administrative	2
Electrical component purchased from Barnhart	10
Total variable cost	$22
Fixed costs*	7
Total cost	$29

* Based on normal capacity.

The $29 cost is considered too high to obtain the special order and Sweeney Division's manager would like the Barnhart Division to reduce the transfer price to $6 so they can quote a price of $25 for the special order. They feel quite sure the order can be obtained for a price of $25 per unit.

Required

1 As the manager of the Barnhart Division, how would you respond to the Sweeney Division's proposal?

2 From the corporate point of view, should the transfers be made at the $6 price?

3 If the Barnhart Division could sell all their output for $13 per unit, what would be the appropriate transfer price?

20-8 Transfer Price and Choice of Supplier The parts division of Specialty Manufacturing Company has been supplying parts to the Nomake Division using 20% of its productive capacity. The current transfer price is $250 per unit.

During the past year the parts division remodeled its manufacturing operations and the fixed costs were increased. Because of the increased fixed cost the parts division proposed raising the transfer price to the Nomake Division to $275 per unit. When the new price was transmitted to the Nomake Division, they decided to obtain outside quotes for the parts. One supplier quoted a price of $240 and the Nomake Division was planning to order the parts from the outside supplier.

When the manager of the parts division learned the Nomake Division was planning to purchase the parts from an outside supplier she had the following analysis prepared detailing the unit cost of producing the part.

Variable cost	$225
Fixed cost	40
Total cost	$265

Using the analysis, the parts division manager argued that the outside supplier's quoted price should be ignored since it was less than her unit cost and probably could not be maintained in the long run.

Nomake Division argued that even if the parts division facilities used to produce the part would be idle if Nomake purchased from the outside supplier, the quoted price was also being offered by other outside suppliers and Nomake should pay no more than $240 per unit.

Required

1 Should the parts division be willing to meet the outside price? Even if an outside supplier quotes a price of $215 per unit?

2 Should top management arbitrate?

20-9 **Transfer Prices and Divisional Profitability** A. R. Oma, Inc., manufactures a line of men's perfumes and after-shaving lotions. The manufacturing process is basically a series of mixing operations with the addition of certain aromatic and coloring ingredients; the finished product is packaged in a company-produced glass bottle and packed in cases containing six bottles.

A. R. Oma feels that the sale of its product is heavily influenced by the appearance and appeal of the bottle and has, therefore, devoted considerable managerial effort to the bottle production process. This has resulted in the development of certain unique bottle production processes in which management takes considerable pride.

The two areas (i.e., perfume production and bottle manufacture) have evolved over the years in an almost independent manner; in fact, a rivalry has developed between management personnel as to "which division is the more important" to A. R. Oma. This attitude is probably intensified because the bottle manufacturing plant was purchased intact 10 years ago and no real interchange of management personnel or ideas (except at the top corporate level) has taken place.

Since the acquisition, all bottle production has been sold to the perfume division. Each division is considered a separate profit center and evaluated as such. As the new corporate controller you are responsible for the definition of a proper transfer value to use in crediting the bottle production profit center and in debiting the packaging profit center.

At your request, the perfume division general manager has asked certain other bottle manufacturers to quote a price for the quantity and sizes demanded by the perfume division. These competitive prices are:

Volume in Cases	Total Price	Price per Case
2,000,000	$ 4,000,000	$2.00
4,000,000	$ 7,000,000	$1.75
6,000,000	$10,000,000	$1.67

A cost analysis of the internal bottle plant indicates that they can produce bottles at these costs.

Volume in Cases	Total Price	Price per Case
2,000,000	$3,200,000	$1.60
4,000,000	$5,200,000	$1.30
6,000,000	$7,200,000	$1.20

(Your cost analysts point out that these costs represent fixed costs of $1,200,000 per year and variable costs of $1 per case.)

These figures have given rise to considerable corporate discussion as to the proper transfer price for perfume bottles. This interest is heightened because a significant portion of each division manager's income is a bonus based on profit results.

The perfume division has the following costs in addition to the bottle costs:

Volume in Cases	Total Cost	Cost per Case
2,000,000	$16,400,000	$8.20
4,000,000	$32,400,000	$8.10
6,000,000	$48,400,000	$8.07

After considerable analysis, the marketing research department has furnished you with the following price-demand relationship for the finished product:

Sales Volume in Cases	Total Sales Revenue	Sales Price per Case
2,000,000	$25,000,000	$12.50
4,000,000	$45,600,000	$11.40
6,000,000	$63,900,000	$10.65

Required

1 The A.R. Oma Company has used market price transfer prices in the past. Using the current market prices and costs, and assuming a volume of 6,000,000 cases, calculate the income for:
   a The bottle division
   b The perfume division
   c The corporation

2 Redo 1 assuming a transfer price of $1.50 per case for the bottles.

3 Ignore 2. Is this production and sales level the most profitable volume for:
   a The bottle division
   b The perfume division
   c The corporation

   Explain your answer.

(CMA)

20-10 Evaluating Alternative Transfer Prices MBR, Inc., consists of three divisions which formerly were three independent manufacturing companies. Bader Corporation and Roach Company merged in 19X5 and the merged corporation acquired Mitchell Company in 19X6. The name of the corporation was subsequently changed to MBR, Inc., and each company became a separate division retaining the name of its former company.

The three divisions have operated as if they were still independent companies. Each division has its own sales force and production facilities. Each division management is responsible for sales, cost of operations, acquisition and financing of divisional assets, and working capital management. The corporate management of MBR evaluates the performance of the divisions and division managements on the basis of return on investment.

Mitchell Division has just been awarded a contract for a product which uses a component that is manufactured by the Roach Division as well as by outside suppliers. Mitchell used a cost figure of $3.80 for the component manufactured by Roach in preparing its bid for the new product. This cost figure was supplied by Roach in response to Mitchell's request for the average variable cost of the component and represents the standard variable manufacturing cost and variable selling and distribution expense.

Roach has an active sales force that is continually soliciting new prospects. Roach's regular selling price for the component Mitchell needs for the new product is $6.50. Sales of this component are expected to increase. However, the Roach management has indicated that it could supply Mitchell with the required quantities of the component at the regular selling price less variable selling and distribution expenses. Mitchell's management has responded by offering to pay standard variable manufacturing cost plus 20%.

The two divisions have been unable to agree on a transfer price. Corporate management has never established a transfer price policy because interdivisional transactions have never occurred. As a compromise, the corporate vice president of finance has suggested a price equal to the standard full manufacturing cost (i.e., no selling and distribution expenses) plus a 15% markup. This price has also been rejected by the two division managers because each considered it grossly unfair.

The unit cost structure for the Roach component and the three suggested prices are shown below:

Regular selling price	$6.50
Standard variable manufacturing cost	$3.20
Standard fixed manufacturing cost	1.20
Variable selling and distribution expenses	.60
	$5.00
Regular selling price less variable selling and distribution expenses ($6.50 − .60)	$5.90
Variable manufacturing plus 20% ($3.20 × 1.20)	$3.84
Standard full manufacturing cost plus 15% ($4.40 × 1.15)	$5.06

Required

1 Discuss the effect each of the three proposed prices might have on the Roach division management's attitude toward intracompany business.

2 Is the negotiation of a price between the Mitchell and Roach Divisions a satisfactory method to solve the transfer price problem? Explain your answer.

3 Should the corporate management of MBR, Inc., become involved in this transfer price controversy? Explain your answer.

(CMA)

20-11 Evaluating Transfer Prices The Lorax Electric Company manufactures a large variety of systems and individual components for the electronics industry. The firm is organized into several divisions with division managers given the authority to make virtually all operating decisions. Management control over divisional operations is maintained by a system of divisional profit and return on investment measures which are reviewed regularly by top management. The top management of Lorax has been quite pleased with the effectiveness of the system they have been using and believe that it is responsible for the company's improved profitability over the last few years.

The devices division manufactures solid-state devices and is operating at capacity. The systems division has asked the devices division to supply a large quantity of integrated circuit IC378. The devices division currently is selling this component to its regular customers at $40 per hundred.

The systems division, which is operating at about 60% capacity, wants this particular component for a digital clock system. It has an opportunity to supply large quantities of these digital clock systems to Centonic Electric, a major producer of clock radios and other popular electronic home entertainment equipment. This is the first opportunity any of the Lorax divisions has had to do business with Centonic Electric. Centonic Electric has offered to pay $7.50 per clock system.

The systems division prepared an analysis of the probable costs to produce the clock systems. The amount that could be paid to the devices division for the integrated circuits was determined by working backward from the selling price. The cost estimates employed by the division reflected the highest per unit cost the systems division could incur for each cost component and still leave a sufficient margin so that the division's income statement could show reasonable improvement. The cost estimates are summarized below.

Proposed selling price		$7.50
Costs excluding required integrated circuits (IC378)		
Components purchased from outside suppliers	$2.75	
Circuit board etching—labor and variable overhead	.40	
Assembly, testing, packaging—labor and variable overhead	1.35	
Fixed overhead allocations	1.50	
Profit margin	.50	6.50
Amount which can be paid for integrated circuits IC378 (5 @ $20 per hundred)		$1.00

As a result of this analysis, the systems division offered the devices division a price of $20 per hundred for the integrated circuit. This bid was refused by the manager of the devices division because he felt the systems division should at least meet the price of $40 per hundred which regular customers pay. When the systems division found that it could not obtain a comparable integrated circuit from outside vendors, the situation was brought to an arbitration committee which had been set up to review such problems.

The arbitration committee prepared an analysis which showed that $.15 would cover variable costs of producing the integrated circuit, $.28 would cover the full cost including fixed overhead, and $.35 would provide a gross margin equal to the average gross margin on all the products sold by the devices division. The manager of the systems division reacted by stating, "They could sell us that integrated circuit for $.20 and still earn a positive contribution toward profit. In fact, they should be required to sell at their variable cost—$.15 and not be allowed to take advantage of us."

Lou Belcher, manager of devices, countered by arguing that, "It doesn't make sense to sell to the systems division at $20 per hundred when we can get $40 per hundred outside on all we can produce. In fact, systems could pay us up to almost $60 per hundred and they would still have a positive contribution to profit."

The recommendation of the committee, to set the price at $.35 per unit ($35 per hundred), so that devices could earn a "fair" gross margin, was rejected by both division managers. Consequently, the problem was brought to the attention of the vice president of operations and his staff.

Required

1 What is the immediate economic effect on the Lorax Company as a whole if the devices division were required to supply IC378 to the systems division at $.35 per unit—the price recommended by the arbitration committee. Explain your answer.

2 Discuss the advisability of intervention by top management as a solution to transfer pricing disputes between division managers such as the one experienced by Lorax Electric Company.

3 Suppose that Lorax adopted a policy of requiring that the price to be paid in all internal transfers by the buying division would be equal to the variable costs per unit of the selling division for that product and that the supplying division would be required to sell if the buying division decided to buy the item. Discuss the consequences of adopting such a policy as a way of avoiding the need for the arbitration committee or for intervention by the vice president.

(CMA)

21 DECISION MAKING AND MANAGERIAL ACCOUNTING

AFTER COMPLETING YOUR STUDY OF THIS CHAPTER, YOU SHOULD HAVE LEARNED:

1 The four basic characteristics needed to understand decision situations.

2 That decisions with certainty become complex because of the variety of possible actions.

3 What it means to make a decision with uncertainty and various criteria used in making these decisions.

4 What is meant by "perfect" information, how its value is calculated, and how it is used in deciding whether to obtain more information.

5 How the value of imperfect information is calculated and used in deciding whether to buy additional information.

6 How measures of risk can be calculated and how they can improve decision making.

Managerial accounting is concerned with aiding managers in making decisions. Managerial accountants do this by:

How managerial accountants aid managers in decision making.

1 Designing and operating accounting systems to provide information needed for decisions

2 Helping managers analyze information so they can predict how their decisions will affect the profits of the organization

Decision situations can be understood and analyzed by knowing the following four characteristics:

There are four important characteristics of each decision.

1 **Actions** represent the alternatives available to the decision maker. For example, a product line manager could request the production of 100,000 units or 200,000 units of product. Each production level would be a different action. They are called actions because each one reflects an act which the manager may choose.

2 **Events** represent the various states of nature that can occur and influence the payoff of a specific action. For example, demand could be 100,000 units, or 200,000 units. Neither of these events is directly within the control of the manager but the level of demand that occurs affects the profitability of each action. In contrast to actions which managers can choose, the manager has no choice about which event will occur.

3 **Payoffs** represent the monetary consequences of each individual action given a specific event. Usually it is the profit which will be earned. For example, what will the profit be if management requests production of 200,000 units but demand is only 100,000 units? The profit will probably be lower than if management requested production of 100,000 units and demand was 100,000 units or if management requested 200,000 units of production and demand was for 200,000 units. The point is, the profitability of each action is affected not only by the action chosen but also by the event which occurs. The payoffs are a list of all the different profits which will occur with each combination of a particular action and a particular event. As you can imagine, there are a variety of payoffs connected with each decision situation. We will discuss later in the chapter how a payoff table is used to organize all of these combinations.

Of course, payoffs for some decisions might be expressed in terms of revenues or expenses if only revenues or only expenses were affected by the decision.[1]

4 **Probabilities** represent the likelihood of each specific event occurring. For example, the probability of demand being 100,000 units might be 40% and the probability of demand being 200,000 units might be 60%. The important thing to notice is that the probabilities are associated with events, not actions. You may have noticed one important fact from the example; the probabilities must always add to 100%.

[1] Theoretically payoffs should be expressed in terms of utilities which reflect the decision maker's personal preferences in a particular decision situation rather than as monetary payoffs. But the idea can be understood by working with monetary payoffs. For a discussion of utility theory, see R. D. Luce, and H. Raiffa, *Games and Decisions,* New York: Wiley, 1957 or Ira Horowitz, *An Introduction to Quantitative Analysis,* 2d ed., New York: McGraw-Hill, 1972 (chap. 3).

It is useful to classify decisions based on the probabilities of the specific events. If the probability of a specific event occurring is equal to 1 and the probability of all other events occurring is equal to 0 then the decision maker knows precisely which event is going to occur. This type of decision is said to be made with certainty, because the decision maker is certain about what event will occur. This simplifies decision making.

If the probability of each specific event occurring is between 0 and 1 (but not exactly 0 or 1) then the decision maker is not sure which event is going to occur. There is some possibility (or probability) that each event will occur. This type of decision is said to be made with uncertainty, because the decision maker is uncertain about which event will occur. This decision situation is more difficult because often the best action depends on which event occurs. Which event will occur is uncertain so the decision maker is also uncertain about which action is best.

In the following sections of this chapter we will discuss these two decision situations: decisions with certainty and decisions with uncertainty.

DECISIONS WITH CERTAINTY

In decision making with certainty it is assumed that the decision maker knows exactly what event is going to occur. The task of the decision maker is to select the action that provides the highest payoff.

This situation rarely, if ever, exists if one is strict about the definition. After all, who knows the future with certainty? But there are some decisions which we make over and over again, every day or week, where the decision is stable so that we assume certainty. We go to the bus stop at the same time each day, assuming that the bus will arrive approximately on time. We do not bother to calculate every day what we will do if the bus is early or late. If the bus is early or late, then we may start considering alternate means of transportation or the consequences of being early or late, but we do not do it in advance because the bus is usually on time. We make our decision with certainty.

Decisions with certainty can be complex.

If there are a large number of alternative actions to consider, the decision can become quite complex even though certainty is assumed. For example, oil companies generally have a variety of crude oils from which they can make products ranging from gasoline to heating oil to plastics. They may feel certain about how much crude oil they will have next week and how much of the various products could be sold, but the number of alternate actions can be well over 100. They make this decision using a mathematical technique called linear programming. The problem is difficult not because of uncertainty but because of the large number of alternative courses of action, each with a different profit payoff.

DECISIONS WITH UNCERTAINTY

Decisions with uncertainty arise when the decision maker does not know which future event will occur. For example, manufacturers of fashion clothing must make production volume decisions before they know whether consumer acceptance of their clothing line will be high, moderate, or low. The Christmas tree salesman must decide how many trees to order knowing that if too many are ordered they will have to be thrown away and if too few are ordered sales will be lost.

There are two basic approaches to decision making under uncertainty. One approach assumes no probabilities can be estimated for the future events and the

There are two distinct approaches to decision making with uncertainty.

second approach assumes probabilities can be estimated for the future events. We will use a common illustration in the following sections to discuss both approaches to decision making with uncertainty.

To illustrate decisions with uncertainty, consider the Kindem Construction Company. Kindem has recently purchased a parcel of land in Miami and has decided to develop a condominium apartment project. Two sizes of developments are being considered: large and small. However, the current state of the economy is making it difficult for Kindem to estimate the demand for condominium apartments. Kindem realizes that if they build a large development (action) and demand is low (event) the company could have sizable losses. On the other hand, if a small development is built (action) and demand is high (event) the company will not earn as much profit as it could have earned from a large development.

Exhibit 21-1 is a payoff table showing the profit associated with each action and each event. We noted earlier that the payoff of each management action could differ depending on which event occurred. We also observed that if we had many possible actions and events there could be many different payoffs. A *payoff table* is an organized way of listing the different payoffs which will occur with each combination of action and an event.

Each row of the payoff table represents an action management is considering. In the example, management is considering only two actions, a small development or a large development, so there are only two rows. Kindem could have considered other alternatives, such as a 50 apartment condominium, a 100 apartment condominium, a 150 apartment condominium, or a 200 apartment condominium. If so, the payoff table would have four rows, one for each possible size of the development. The columns of the payoff table represent the possible events. Again in this case there are only two columns, representing the two possible demands which Kindem management believes may occur. If other events were likely, the number of columns could be expanded to accommodate the other events. Finally, the boxes formed by the intersection of each column and row contain the payoff which will occur *if* management chooses the action represented by this row and *if* the particular event represented by the column occurs.

If Kindem builds a small development and demand is low, the profit is $200,000. However, if a large development is built and demand is low, Kindem will lose $100,000. But if demand is high, profits will be $500,000 if a large development is built but only $250,000 if a small development is built.

EXHIBIT 21-1
KINDEM CONSTRUCTION COMPANY
Payoff Table (Profits)
Condominium Development Project

A payoff table organizes the possibilities when uncertainty exists.

		Events	
		Low Demand	**High Demand**
Actions	**Small development**	$200,000	$250,000
	Large development	−$100,000	$500,000

The various profit and loss estimates appearing in the payoff table are made by the accountant using marketing estimates of number of apartments and their selling prices and using engineering estimates of types of materials required and their costs. The managerial accountant in fact prepared a budgeted income statement for each box of the payoff table, but only the final profit needed to be entered in the table.

Now the question is: Should Kindem build a small or large development? There are several ways this question could be answered.

Decision Making with Uncertainty without Probabilities

Maximin and maximax are two ways of choosing an action when probabilities are unknown.

In some situations the decision maker may have little basis for estimating the probability of each possible event. In these situations the decision maker might use a decision criterion that does not require an estimate of the probabilities of the future events. Two of the most popular criteria available are called "maximin" and "maximax."

These criteria might lead to different decisions so it is important that the managerial accountant and the decision maker understand the basic concepts underlying each criterion.

Maximin The maximin decision criterion is a conservative approach to decision making. The objective of the maximin criterion is to *maxi*mize the *min*imum profit. There are two steps involved. (1) The decision maker will list the smallest profit which will occur for each action. For each action all other profits will be ignored. (2) The decision maker will then choose from the *new* list the alternative with the greatest profit. In other words, the decision maker will choose the action that produces the largest of the smallest profits. It sounds terribly complicated when you say it, but it really is not, as our illustration will show.

To illustrate the maximin criterion, consider the Kindem example summarized in Exhibit 21-1. If Kindem chooses to build a small development the *minimum* profit is $200,000. If Kindem chooses to build a large development the *minimum* profit is actually a loss of −$100,000.

Using this information we can prepare the new list of payoffs shown in Exhibit 21-2. The list in Exhibit 21-2 shows the minimum profit for each action available to Kindem. Using the maximin criterion Kindem would select the action that yields the maximum of the minimum profits. In this case Kindem would build the small development. If demand turns out to be high, Kindem can still make a $250,000 profit but they give up the possibility of a $500,000 profit in order to avoid the possibility of a $100,000 loss. This action should produce a minimum profit of $200,000 which is the best of the minimum payoffs.

The maximin decision criterion is considered to be conservative since it only considers the lowest profit possibilities and then avoids the worst possibilities—but at the same time may give up the possibility of the highest profits.

Maximax While the maximin criterion takes the pessimistic view of the world, the maximax criterion takes the optimistic view. With the maximax criterion the decision maker bases his choice of action on the *largest* profit associated with each action. Thus the maximax criterion *maxi*mizes the *max*imum payoff (and ignores the minimum profits). Again there are two steps: (1) List the highest profit expected with each action, ignoring all profits from an action except the highest, and (2) choose from the new list the alternative promising the highest possible profit. This

EXHIBIT 21-2
KINDEM CONSTRUCTION COMPANY
List of Payoffs—Maximin Criterion

Maximin illustrated.

		Minimum Profit
Actions	Small development	$200,000
	Large development	−$100,000

criterion is easier to put into words because you simply choose the action that promises the highest possible return.

To illustrate the maximax criterion, again consider the Kindem Company data in Exhibit 21-1. Selecting the maximum profit for each alternative action we have constructed a new list of payoffs in Exhibit 21-3. If Kindem chooses to build a small development the *maximum* profit is $250,000. If Kindem chooses to build a large development, the *maximum* profit is $500,000. Using the maximax criterion Kindem would choose to build the large development since this action provides the opportunity to obtain the largest of all profits. Note that while this choice provides the opportunity of the largest profit it also provides for the possibility of a $100,000 loss. Unfortunately, if management does not know the probabilities of the two events, low or high demand, they are left in the uncomfortable position of not knowing the chance of a $100,000 loss.

These two decision criteria led to different decisions by management. This should not bother you. It simply shows that there is more than one philosophy toward how decisions should be made. The major problem with these decision criteria is that they do not incorporate any information about the probabilities of the various events occurring. In the next section we will discuss a criterion that does use probability information. Most people believe it is a better criterion.

EXHIBIT 21-3
KINDEM CONSTRUCTION COMPANY
List of Payoffs—Maximax Criterion

Maximax illustrated.

		Maximum Profit
Actions	Small development	$250,000
	Large development	$500,000

Decision Making with Uncertainty with Probabilities

In many situations the decision maker can make meaningful probability estimates for each event. When this can be done, the **expected value** criterion can be used to select the best alternative.

There is some disagreement about how estimates of probabilities should be made. We will not get heavily into the arguments but just explain what they are. Some statisticians argue that the only meaningful probabilities are probabilities that can be arrived at objectively. For instance, if we were rolling a fair die (with six sides) most people would agree that the probability of rolling the number 5 is 1/6 or 16.67%. If there were doubt we could roll the die a large number of times and would find that the side numbered 5 would be on top 16.67% of the time. That is why these types of probabilities are called objective probabilities. They can be determined without judgment. If, however, we are estimating the probability of selling 100,000 automobiles, different people would make different estimates. These latter probabilities are called subjective probabilities. They rely on the judgment of experienced individuals but there is no way of verifying the estimates by repeated tests as in the case of the die. To reject these probabilities as not being meaningful would be similar to rejecting experienced judgment. If the subjectively determined probabilities are meaningful to the decision maker, they should be used in the analysis of the decision problem.

Our main concern is, given the probabilities, how they can help in making decisions. The *expected value criterion* requires that probabilities have been estimated for each possible event. Then the expected value of each action is calculated and the action producing the best expected value is selected. We will define expected value mathematically and then go on to explain in words.

$$\textbf{Expected value} = E(a) = \sum_{i=1}^{n} X_i P(X_i)$$

Expected value uses estimates of the probability of various events.

where a **= the action being considered**
n **= the number of events being considered**
X_i **= the payoff for action** a **if event** i **occurs**
$P(X_i)$ **= the probability of event** i **occurring**

Σ means adding together each X_i **times each** $P(X_i)$

Expected value is the weighted average payoff.

In words, an expected value is calculated for each action. The expected value is simply the weighted average payoff for the action. The weights are probabilities of each event. Calculating the weighted average when the weights are the probabilities is easy. Because the probabilities add to 1, all that is necessary is to multiply each payoff times the probability and add all of the products together. We will illustrate the computation of the expected values (weighted averages) by returning to the Kindem Company example.

Suppose that the management of the Kindem Company believes that the probability of low demand for the condominiums is 50% and the probability of high demand is 50%. This information along with the other basic data for the Kindem Company is shown in Exhibit 21-4. Also shown in Exhibit 21-4 is the computation of the expected value for the two actions available to Kindem Company. If Kindem Company chooses to build the small development the expected profits are $225,000 and if they choose to build the large development the expected profits are $200,000. Based on the expected value criterion Kindem would choose to build the small development, because the expected value of this action is higher.

EXHIBIT 21-4
KINDEM CONSTRUCTION COMPANY
Payoff Table and
Expected Value Computation

		Events	
		Low Demand	**High Demand**
Probability of event		**50%**	**50%**
Actions	**Small development**	$200,000	$250,000
	Large development	−$100,000	$500,000

Expected value (small development) = 50%($200,000) + 50%($250,000) = $225,000
Expected value (large development) = 50%(−$100,000) + 50%($500,000) = $200,000

You should notice that the probabilities are quite important when using the expected value criterion. With probabilities of 50% and 50% the decision is to build the small development. But if management believed the probability of high demand was 60%, the large development would be chosen. If the probability of high demand is 60%, the probability of low demand must be 40% since the probabilities must add to 100%. The expected values are then:

The decision may differ depending on the probabilities of the events.

Expected value (small development)
= 40% ($200,000) + 60% ($250,000) = $230,000
Expected value (large development)
= 40% (−$100,000) + 60% ($500,000) = $260,000

But if high demand is more likely, it is not surprising that the larger development would be built.

The Value of Perfect Information In most decision situations, it is possible to obtain some additional information. The previous illustration showed that the estimated probabilities were important to Kindem Company's decision in the sense that a different estimate of the probabilities would change the decision. Improved information may result in a better estimate of the probabilities. Kindem might hire a market research company to study the potential demand for condominiums in Miami. Such a study could possibly improve the estimate of probabilities for the two events: high demand and low demand. With **perfect information** about the future Kindem would know precisely which of the two events will occur and the proper decision would be clear.

Perfect information means never having to apologize for the estimate of probabilities.

While some form of additional information is generally obtainable at a cost, perfect information concerning future events is usually not available. However, if the value of perfect information could be calculated, it would provide the decision maker with an upper limit on the amount which should be paid for additional information concerning the probability of the various future events.

When people are introduced to the idea of perfect information, they sometimes make the mistake of assuming that perfect information will assure making the highest profit in the payoff table, in the Kindem example, \$500,000. This is not correct. Perfect information cannot change the actual demand from low to high—it would be nice if it could. Perfect information will only assure that management makes the correct decision, since the decision is now made with certainty.

Return to the Kindem example. If perfect information reveals that demand is low, the correct decision is what? Build the small development and earn a profit of \$250,000. However, if perfect information reveals that demand is high, the best decision is to build the large development and earn a profit of \$500,000.

If Kindem buys perfect information, there is a 50% chance that the perfect information will reveal low demand and Kindem will build the small development and earn \$250,000 of income. There is also 50% chance that perfect information will reveal high demand and Kindem will build the large development and earn \$500,000 of income. The expected value *with* perfect information is:

Expected value (with perfect information)
= 50% (\$250,000) + 50% (\$500,000)
= \$375,000

The above calculation of the expected value with perfect information takes the optimum payoff associated with each event and multiplies it by the probability of the event occurring. These calculations are totaled for all events and the result is the expected value with perfect information.

The expected value with perfect information represents the long-run average profits Kindem would earn if they made a number of decisions like this and had perfect information. The value of perfect information is the difference between the expected value with the current information and the expected value with perfect information. For the Kindem Company:

The value of perfect information.

Expected value (with perfect information)	**= \$375,000**
Expected value (no additional information)	**= \$225,000**
Value of perfect information	**= \$150,000**

The \$150,000 value of perfect information represents the most Kindem would be willing to pay for perfect knowledge of the probability of each level of demand. Since perfect information is generally not available, the basic question Kindem has to answer is whether to purchase imperfect information (the market research). If the cost of the market research information is \$150,000 or greater, the decision is easy—Kindem should not buy the market research. If the cost is less than \$150,000, the value of the research information has to be determined. We will discuss this determination next.

The Value of Imperfect Information We just suggested that perfect information is usually not available but **imperfect information** can be obtained. Suppose that Kindem Company can hire a market research firm to study the demand for condominiums in the Miami area. The market research firm may report either an optimistic or pessimistic outlook for demand for condominiums. They will not estimate the probability of high demand but will provide a report with more information. Either of these reports from the market research firm will change Kindem's assessment of the probabilities of high or low demand.

Exhibit 21-5 shows the potential impact of the marketing research studies on Kindem's decision. Part A of Exhibit 21-5 is the payoff table assuming no additional information. Part B represents the revised payoff table assuming the market

EXHIBIT 21-5
KINDEM CONSTRUCTION COMPANY
Payoff Table
Effects of Imperfect Information

A. NO REPORT

		Events		
	Probability of Events	Low Demand 50%	High Demand 50%	Expected Value
Actions	Small development	$200,000	$250,000	$225,000
	Large development	−$100,000	$500,000	$200,000

B. PESSIMISTIC REPORT

		Events		
	Probability of Events	Low Demand 75%	High Demand 25%	Expected Value
Actions	Small development	$200,000	$250,000	$212,500
	Large development	−$100,000	$500,000	$ 50,000

C. OPTIMISTIC REPORT

		Events		
	Probability of Events	Low Demand 25%	High Demand 75%	Expected Value
Actions	Small development	$200,000	$250,000	$237,500
	Large development	−$100,000	$500,000	$350,000

Added information may lead management to revise its estimate of probabilities of events.

research report is pessimistic. With a pessimistic report, Kindem will change the probabilities of the events and Kindem would choose to build the small development since this action has the highest expected profits. Part C of Exhibit 21-5 represents the revised payoff table assuming the market research report is optimistic. With an optimistic report Kindem would revise the probabilities and choose to build a large development.

Should Kindem hire the market research firm? To answer this question Kindem must assess the probability of receiving a pessimistic report or an optimistic report from the market research firm. Assume that Kindem assesses a 50% chance of receiving an optimistic report and a 50% chance of receiving a pessimistic report.

Based on these probabilities of receiving an optimistic or pessimistic report we can calculate the expected value with the marketing study as follows:

Expected value with marketing study = probability of pessimistic report times (highest expected value with pessimistic report) + probability of optimistic report times (highest expected value with optimistic report) =

	50%($212,500)
+	**50%($350,000)**
	$281,250

The most Kindem would be willing to pay for the marketing study is the difference between the expected value with the marketing study and the expected value without the marketing study.

The value of imperfect information illustrated.

Expected value with marketing study	=	**$281,250**
Expected value without marketing study	=	**225,000**
Maximum value of marketing study		**$ 56,250**

DECISION ALTERNATIVES WITH DIFFERENT PROBABILITIES

In the Kindem Company example, we considered two events (low demand and high demand) whose probabilities of occurring affected both actions Kindem was considering. In other decision situations the accountant may have to deal with a different probability distribution for each action available to management. To further illustrate the computation of expected values and to introduce other statistical measures consider the following decision situation.

The Spray Company is considering the introduction of a new product. Management has two products to choose from but only sufficient resources to introduce one of the products. The anticipated demand, probability of demand, and profits for each product are given below:

Product X			**Product Y**		
Product Demand (Units)	**Probability of Demand**	**Profit**	**Product Demand (Units)**	**Probability of Demand**	**Profit**
50,000	20%	$−8,000	30,000	15%	$−12,000
60,000	10	−5,000	40,000	15	−10,000
70,000	30	11,000	50,000	40	14,000
80,000	20	14,000	60,000	20	16,000
90,000	20	17,000	70,000	10	18,000
	100%			100%	

The accountant could present management with the above data describing each product. However, if management were considering a large number of alternatives, this form of data presentation might be more confusing than helpful. For this reason, the accountant usually calculates some summary statistics to describe the alternatives.

We shall discuss two statistics which are often useful in describing alternative actions.

The accountant uses statistics to summarize important characteristics of actions.

1 The expected value (which was previously introduced).
2 The coefficient of variation of the possible values. In order to calculate the coefficient of variation it is useful to first calculate the standard deviation.

Expected Value

A summary statistic discussed in the previous section was the expected value. For the two alternatives, the expected profits are:

Expected profits
Product X
= .20(−8,000) + .10(−5,000) + .30(11,000) + .20(14,000) + .20(17,000)
= $7,400

Expected profits
Product Y
= .15(−12,000) + .15(−10,000) + .40(14,000) + .20(16,000) + .10(18,000)
= $7,300

Based strictly on the expected values, the manager would choose product X. However, it must be recognized that the expected value represents the weighted average return from many observations and that any one observation could range from a loss of $8,000 to a profit of $17,000 for product X. The *range* for product Y is from a loss of $12,000 to a profit of $18,000. The range is a measure of the dispersion of the possible profits for the products but it only considers the extreme (low and high) profit possibilities.

Coefficient of Variation

To provide more information about the dispersion of the profits for the two alternatives, the accountant can calculate the standard deviation. The **standard deviation** is the square root of the average squared differences between the expected value and the observations, calculated as follows:

$$\sigma_x = \left[\sum_{i=1}^{n} P(X_i)(X_i - E(X))^2\right]^{1/2}$$

If you are not used to working with mathematical symbols, the formula makes it look pretty complicated. But it is not that difficult if you take it in steps.

1 Subtract the weighted average payoff (the expected value) from each payoff and square the difference by multiplying the difference by itself.
2 Take the weighted average of the squared differences (from step 1) using the probabilities as the weights.
3 Find the square root of the weighted average found in step 2.

For the two alternatives, the standard deviations are calculated as follows:

$$\sigma_x = (.20\,(-8{,}000 - 7{,}400)^2 + .10(-5{,}000 - 7{,}400)^2 + .30\,(11{,}000-7{,}400)^2$$
$$+ .20\,(14{,}000 - 7{,}400)^2 + .20\,(17{,}000 - 7{,}400)^2)^{1/2}$$
$$\sigma_x = \$9{,}687$$
$$\sigma_y = (.15\,(-12{,}000 - 7{,}300)^2 + .15\,(-10{,}000 - 7{,}300)^2 + .40\,(14{,}000 - 7{,}300)^2$$
$$+ .20\,(16{,}000 - 7{,}300)^2 + .10\,(18{,}000 - 7{,}300)^2)^{1/2}$$
$$\sigma_y = \$12{,}054$$

The amount of the standard deviation depends on the scale of measurement. To compare the dispersion of the two alternatives, a measure of *relative* dispersion is needed. The statistic used to measure relative dispersion is the coefficient of variation, which is computed as follows:

$$V_x = \left[\frac{\sigma_x}{E(X)}\right] \cdot 100\%$$

The **coefficient of variation** measures the standard deviation as a percentage of the expected value. The closer the coefficient of variation is to 0 the less the amount of dispersion in the data and the less risky the alternative. For the two alternatives:

$$V_x = \left[\frac{9{,}687}{7{,}400}\right] \cdot 100$$
$$= 130.90\%$$
$$V_y = \left[\frac{12{,}054}{7{,}300}\right] \cdot 100$$
$$= 165.12\%$$

Since product X has a smaller coefficient of variation than product Y, we can say that product X has a smaller relative dispersion of possible payoffs. The expected value and coefficient of variation are used by the decision maker to select the alternative. In this example product X has the highest expected value and lowest coefficient of variation so it would probably be selected.

SUMMARY

Decision making is the process of choosing between alternative courses of actions. The managerial accountant is involved in identifying different alternatives and calculating the outcomes or payoffs of the alternatives. A useful tool for summarizing a decision situation is a payoff table. A payoff table shows the actions, events, and monetary consequences that result from each combination of an action and an event.

Decision situations can be classified based on the probabilities of the various events occurring. Decisions with certainty means that only one event can occur and the action that maximizes the payoff is chosen. This may be a complex problem because many actions may be possible. Quantitative techniques, such as linear programming, have been developed to aid the decision maker in choosing actions with certainty. Decisions with uncertainty are situations where the decision maker does not know which specific event will occur.

If the decision maker has little confidence in assigning probabilities to the future events, the maximin and maximax criteria can be used to select an action. The maximin strategy maximizes the minimum profit; the maximax strategy maximizes the maximum profit.

If the decision maker can assign meaningful probabilities to the future events the expected value criterion can be used to select an action.

The value of perfect information and the value of imperfect information provide the decision maker with an upper limit to the dollars that should be paid for additional information, by calculating how much additional profit can be earned by having improved estimates of the probabilities of events.

Review Problem

Vendo, Inc., operates the concession stands at the university football stadium. The university has had successful football teams for many years; the result is a stadium always full. The university is located in an area which suffers no rain during the football season. From time to time, Vendo has found itself very short of donuts and at other times it has had many left over. A review of the records of sales of the past five seasons revealed the following frequency of donuts sold.

10,000 donuts		5 games
20,000 donuts		10 games
30,000 donuts		20 games
40,000 donuts		15 games
	Total	50 games

Donuts sell for 50 cents each and cost Vendo 30 cents each. Unsold donuts are given to a local orphanage. The only relevant expense is the cost of the donuts.

Required

1 Assuming that only the four quantities listed were ever sold and that the differences were caused by random events, prepare a payoff table (ignore income taxes) to represent the four possible strategies of ordering 10,000, 20,000, 30,000, or 40,000 donuts.

2 Using the expected value decision rule determine the best strategy.

3 What is the dollar value of perfect information in this problem?

(CMA)

Solution

1 and 2

		Events (Demand)				
Probability of Events		**10%**	**20%**	**40%**	**30%**	**Expected Value**
		10,000	**20,000**	**30,000**	**40,000**	
Actions (Order)	**10,000**	$2,000	$2,000	$2,000	$2,000	$2,000
	20,000	−$1,000	$4,000	$4,000	$4,000	$3,500
	30,000	−$4,000	$1,000	$6,000	$6,000	$4,000
	40,000	−$7,000	−$2,000	$3,000	$8,000	$2,500

The calculation of the payoff for ordering 30,000 and selling only 20,000 donuts is as follows:

Sales 20,000 @ \$.50	\$10,000
Cost of donuts 30,000 @ \$.30	9,000
Payoff	\$ 1,000

All other payoffs are calculated the same way.

The calculation of the expected value for ordering 30,000 donuts is:

$$10\%(-4{,}000) + 20\%(1{,}000) + 40\%(6{,}000) + 30\%(6{,}000) = \underline{\underline{\$4{,}000}}$$

Expected values of other actions are calculated the same way.

The best strategy, using the expected value decision rule, is to order 30,000 donuts because on the average Vendo will earn \$4,000 per game.

3 The value of perfect information is the difference between the average profit using the best strategy with existing probabilities and the average profit if Vendo knew in advance what the sales level would be each Saturday.

Average profit if Vendo knew sales level:

10%(2,000) + 20%(4,000) + 40%(6,000) + 30%(8,000)	=	\$5,800
Average profit from expected value strategy	=	4,000
Dollar value of perfect information		\$1,800

Glossary

Actions Alternative acts which a decision maker may choose. Actions are controlled by the decision maker.

Coefficient of variation A measure of relative dispersion used to compare the variability of two different alternatives.

Events The states of nature that can occur and influence the payoff associated with a particular action. The decision maker cannot control events.

Expected value The weighted average payoff a decision maker would receive from the selection of a particular action.

Payoff The monetary consequences of a particular action given that a particular event occurs.

Probability A number between zero and one representing the likelihood of a specific event occurring.

Standard deviation A measure of the dispersion of the data around the mean. It can be interpreted as a measure of the inherent uncertainty in a decision situation.

Value of perfect information The maximum amount a decision maker would be willing to pay for exact knowledge of which event will occur.

Value of imperfect information The maximum amount a decision maker would be willing to pay for a particular set of additional information. It is the amount by which the expected profit will be improved by having the additional information.

Questions and Problems

21-1 Distinguish between decision making with certainty and uncertainty.

21-2 What makes some decisions with certainty complex?

21-3 Distinguish between objective and subjective probabilities.

21-4 What is the expected value?

21-5 Of what use is the value of perfect information to the decision maker?

21-6 For the comparison of two alternatives, what statistical measures are usually useful?

21-7 What criteria are available to a decision maker making choices with uncertainty?

21-8 **Payoff Table, Expected Values, and Value of Perfect Information** The XOX Company produces a single perishable product that is manufactured in batches of 100 units. The maximum production is 500 units per month. The variable production costs average $5 per unit and the sales price is $15 per unit. Any unsold units are disposed of at the end of the month at no cost. Based on historical data, management has estimated the following demands and probabilities for a normal month:

Unit Demand	Probability
100	10%
200	25
300	25
400	30
500	10

Required

1 Prepare a payoff table showing the actions available to management and the potential outcomes.

2 Determine the production strategy that will maximize the expected profits.

3 What is the maximum amount management would be willing to pay for perfect knowledge of the monthly demand?

21-9 **Computation of Summary Statistics for Comparison of Alternatives** The P. O. Box Company is considering purchasing a new folding machine to replace the one they are currently using. After reviewing several proposals they have narrowed their choice to either alternative A or B. The only difference between the two alternatives is the distributions of their per unit costs. The distributions of the per unit costs for 1,000 units for the two alternatives are as follows:

Alternative A		Alternative B	
Unit Cost	Probability	Unit Cost	Probability
$100	20%	$115	20%
115	30	120	40
120	40	125	20
130	10	135	20
	100%		100%

Required

1 Calculate the expected per unit cost, standard deviation, and coefficient of variation for each alternative.

2 Write a brief comparison of the two alternatives to be presented to the board of directors.

21-10 Computation of Summary Statistics for Comparison of Alternatives The ABC Company is considering introducing either product W or Z. Current resources are only sufficient to introduce one product so management must choose which of the two products to introduce. To aid management in their decision process the marketing department has prepared the following sales estimates for the products.

Product W		Product Z	
Sales Units	Probability	Sales Units	Probability
100,000	10%	200,000	10%
150,000	30	300,000	20
200,000	50	400,000	40
250,000	10	500,000	30

The total fixed expense and contribution margin per unit for the products are estimated to be the following:

	Product	
	W	Z
Fixed expense per year	$150,000	$200,000
Contribution margin per unit	$1.00	$.60

Required

1 Calculate the profit associated with each estimated sales volume for both products.

2 Calculate summary statistics to aid management in their choice between products W and Z.

3 Assuming the investment for the development, production, and marketing of both products is the same, which would you recommend to management?

21-11 Decision Making with Uncertainty The marketing manager of the ZOX Corporation is attempting to choose between three distribution alternatives for marketing a new product. The profit associated with each alternative is dependent on the events that occur in the marketplace. The profit associated with each alternative and event is given below:

		Events		
		E1	**E2**	**E3**
	A1	$30,000	$40,000	$10,000
Actions	**A2**	40,000	8,000	20,000
	A3	9,000	20,000	50,000

Required

Assuming the marketing manager has no knowledge concerning the likelihood of the various events occurring, which action would be chosen if the maximin strategy is followed? The maximax strategy?

21-12 Calculating the Value of Imperfect Information* An oil well wildcatter, J. Anderson, is considering investing $50,000 in oil well drilling. He has estimated that the probability of finding oil on this piece of property is 40%. If oil is found, it will generate revenues of $150,000 resulting in a profit of $100,000.

Required

1 Calculate the expected value of making and not making the oil well investment.

2 How much would Mr. Anderson pay for perfect information concerning whether oil is present in this piece of property?

Having consulted with his accountant (Charles Cautions), Mr. Anderson feels he needs more information before proceeding with this investment. Stochastic Geological Testing Company performs geological tests of the subsurface of the land.

The testing company has informed Mr. Anderson that a favorable result will indicate there is a 60% chance of oil and a 40% chance of no oil. Similarly, an unfavorable test result will indicate a 20% chance of oil and an 80% chance of no oil. Mr. Anderson estimates there is a 50% chance of an unfavorable test and a 50% chance of a favorable test.

3 Calculate the expected value of the investment if the report is favorable. Is unfavorable.

4 What is the maximum amount Mr. Anderson would be willing to pay for the geological test?

* Adapted from "Report of Committee on Managerial Decision Models," *Accounting Review Supplement* (1969), pp. 61–64.

21-13 Expected Value Computations The marketing manager has estimated the probabilities of various demands occurring given different sales prices as presented in the following table:

Sales Price	Demand (Units)			
	8,000	9,000	10,000	11,000
$40	40%	40%	20%	0%
35	20	45	25	10
30	20	20	30	30
25	0	20	40	40

Required

1 Calculate the expected total sales revenue for each sales price.

2 Which sales price should be selected to maximize the expected total revenue?

21-14 Calculation of Probabilities and Expected Costs You are taking your annual ski trip to Colorado. In most years the weather is warm and sunny. But last year it was cold and windy and there were a number of days on which it was too cold to ski.

You potentially have five days to ski this year, but you have decided that you will ski only if the weather is pleasant (better than Minnesota). After checking with weather service records, you conclude that there is virtually no chance of having three or more bad days out of five. But there seems to be a 25% chance that you might encounter one bad day and four good days. You also estimate that there is a 15% chance that you would encounter two bad days and three good days.

On arriving at the ski area, you find that lift ticket rates have gone up again, but they are still reasonable compared to other areas. You may buy a lift ticket each day you ski for $15 per day or you may buy a lift ticket for five consecutive days, not-transferable, nonrefundable, not replaceable if lost or stolen, for $65.

Required

Which type of lift ticket should you buy given the data above? Give your reasons.

21-15 Using Expected Value in Product Purchases The Jessica Co. has been searching for more formal ways to analyze its alternative courses of action. The expected value decision approach is among those considered. In order to test the effectiveness of the expected value approach, a one-year trial in a small department was authorized.

This department buys and resells a perishable product. A large purchase at the beginning of each month provides a lower cost than more frequent purchases and also assures that Jessica Co. can buy all of the item it wants. Unfortunately, if too much is purchased the product unsold at the end of the month is worthless and must be discarded.

If an inadequate quantity is purchased, additional quantities would not be purchased because they would probably be of poor quality and be overpriced. Jessica chooses to lose the potential sales rather than furnish a poor quality product. The standard purchase arrangement is $50,000 plus $.50 for each unit purchased for orders of 100,000 units or more. Jessica sells the product for $1.25 per unit to its customers.

The needs of Jessica's customers limit the possible sales volumes to only four quantities per month—100,000, 120,000, 140,000 or 180,000 units. However, the total quantity demanded for a given month cannot be determined prior to the date Jessica must make its purchases. The sales managers are willing to place a probability estimate on each of the four possible sales volumes each month. They noted that the probabilities for the four sales volumes change from month to month because of the seasonal nature of their customers' businesses. Their probability estimates for December 19X8 sales units are 10% for 100,000, 30% for 120,000, 40% for 140,000, and 20% for 180,000.

The following schedule shows the quantity purchased each month based upon the expected value decision model. The actual units sold and products discarded or sales lost are shown also.

	Quantity (in Units)			Sales Units Lost
	Purchased	**Sold**	**Discarded**	
January	100,000	100,000	—	20,000
February	120,000	100,000	20,000	—
March	180,000	140,000	40,000	—
April	100,000	100,000	—	80,000
May	100,000	100,000	—	—
June	140,000	140,000	—	—
July	140,000	100,000	40,000	—
August	140,000	120,000	20,000	—
September	120,000	100,000	20,000	—
October	120,000	120,000	—	20,000
November	180,000	140,000	40,000	—

Required

1 What quantity should be ordered for December 19X8 if the expected value decision approach is used?

2 Suppose Jessica could ascertain its customers' needs prior to making its purchases. What is the maximum amount Jessica would pay to obtain this information for December?

3 The approach did not result in purchases equal to potential sales except during two months. Is the approach unsuitable in this case or is this a characteristic of the approach? Explain your answer.

(CMA)

21-16 Calculation of Expected Sales and Net Income Vernon Enterprises designs and manufactures toys. Past experience indicates that the product life cycle of a toy is three years. Promotional advertising produces large sales in the early years, but there is a substantial sales decline in the final year of a toy's life.

Consumer demand for new toys placed on the market tends to fall into three classes. About 30% of the new toys sell well above expectations, 60% percent sell as anticipated, and 10% have poor consumer acceptance.

A new toy has been developed. The following sales projections were made by carefully evaluating consumer demand for the new toy:

Consumer Demand for New Toy	Chance of Occurring	Estimated Sales in Year 1	Year 2	Year 3
Above average	30%	$1,200,000	$2,500,000	$600,000
Average	60	700,000	1.700,000	400,000
Below average	10	200,000	900,000	150,000

Variable costs are estimated at 30% of the selling price. Special machinery must be purchased at a cost of $860,000 and will be installed in an unused portion of the factory which Vernon has unsuccessfully been trying to rent to someone for several years and has no prospects for future utilization. Fixed expenses (excluding depreciation) of a cash-flow nature are estimated at $50,000 per year on the new toy. The new machinery will be depreciated by the sum-of-the-years'-digits method with an estimated salvage value of $110,000 and will be sold at the beginning of the fourth year. Advertising and promotional expenses will be incurred uniformly and will total $100,000 the first year, $150,000 the second year, and $50,000 the third year. These expenses will be deducted as incurred for income tax reporting.

Vernon believes that state and federal income taxes will total 60% of income in the foreseeable future and may be assumed to be paid uniformly over the year income is earned.

Required

1 Prepare a schedule computing the probable sales of this new toy in each of the three years, taking into account the probability of above average, average, and below average sales occurring.

2 Prepare a schedule computing the probable net income for the new toy in each of the three years of its life.

(CPA)

21-17 Calculation of Expected Contribution with Different Sales Prices The president of Benjamin Industries has requested your assistance in the evaluation of a financial management problem in the home appliances division.

Management wants to determine the best sales price for a new appliance which has a variable expense of $4 per unit. The sales manager has estimated probabilities of achieving annual sales levels for various selling prices as shown in the following chart:

Sales Level (Units)	Selling Price			
	$4	$5	$6	$7
20,000	—	—	20%	80%
30,000	—	10%	40	20
40,000	50%	50	20	—
50,000	50	40	20	—

Required

Prepare a schedule computing the expected value of the total contribution margin for each of the sales prices proposed for the new product. The schedule should include the expected sales levels in units (weighted according to the sales manager's estimated probabilities), the expected total monetary sales, expected variable expenses, and the expected contribution margin.

(CPA)

21-18 Calculation of Probabilities and Expected Profits Commercial Products Corporation has requested your assistance in determining the potential loss on a binding purchase contract which will be in effect at the end of the corporation's fiscal year. The corporation produces a chemical compound which deteriorates and must be discarded if it is not sold by the end of the month during which it is produced.

The total variable cost of the manufactured compound is $25 per unit and it is sold for $40 per unit. The compound can be purchased from a competitor for $40 per unit plus $5 freight per unit. It is estimated that failure to fill orders would result in the complete loss of 8 out of 10 customers placing orders for the compound.

The corporation has sold the compound for the past 30 months. Demand has been irregular and there is no sales trend. During this period sales per month have been:

Units Sold per Month	Number of Months*
4,000	6
5,000	15
6,000	9

Required

1 For each of the following, prepare a schedule of the
   a Probability of sales of 4,000, 5,000, or 6,000 units in any month.
   b Expected contribution margin if sales of 4,000, 5,000, or 6,000 units are made in one month and 4,000, 5,000, or 6,000 units are manufactured for sales in the same month. Assume all sales orders are filled.

2 The cost of the primary ingredient used to manufacture the compound is $12 per unit of compound. It is estimated that there is a 60% chance that the primary ingredient supplier's plant may be shut down by a strike for an indefinite period. A substitute ingredient is available at $18 per unit of compound but the corporation must contract immediately to purchase the substitute or it will be unavailable when needed. A firm purchase contract for either the primary or the substitute ingredient must now be made with one of the suppliers for production next month. If an order were placed for the primary ingredient and a

* Occurred in random sequence.

strike should occur, the corporation would be released from the contract and management would purchase the compound from the competitor. Assume that 5,000 units are to be manufactured and all sales orders are to be filled.

a Compute the expected monthly contribution margin from sales of 4,000, 5,000, and 6,000 units if the substitute ingredient is ordered.

b Prepare a schedule computing the average monthly contribution margin the corporation should expect if the primary ingredient is ordered with the existing probability of a strike at the supplier's plant. Assume the corporation plans to produce 5,000 units.

c Should management order the primary or substitute ingredient during the anticipated strike period? Why?

d Should management purchase the compound from the competitor to fill sales orders when the orders cannot be otherwise filled? Why?

(CPA)

21-19 Computing Expected Profit When Aplet, Inc., purchased Avcont Company in 19X0, Aplet's was expanding and profitable. The subsidiary has been quite profitable until recently. Beginning in 19X3 the market share dropped, costs increased primarily due to increased prices of inputs, and the profits turned into losses. The income statements for 19X3 and 19X4 are presented along with an estimate of the 19X5 income made in October 19X5.

AVCONT COMPANY
Income Statement for Years Ending December 31
(000 Omitted)

	19X3	19X4	19X5 (Est.)
Industry unit sales	1,300	1,200	1,200
Avcont unit sales	120	110	110
Sales	$1,200	$1,100	$1,100
Less: Variable expenses			
Materials	$ 175	$ 170	$ 175
Labor	210	215	225
Manufacturing overhead	100	99	100
Selling	125	115	120
Administration	50	50	60
	$ 660	$ 649	$ 680
Contribution margin	$ 540	$ 451	$ 420
Less: Fixed expenses			
Manufacturing[1]	$ 200	$ 210	$ 230
Selling[1]	125	140	145
Administration[1]	135	145	145
	$ 460	$ 495	$ 520
Net income (loss)	$ 80	$ (44)	$ (100)

[1] Depreciation included in fixed expenses.

Manufacturing	$ 60	$ 70	$ 70
Selling	5	6	6
Administration	8	8	9
	$ 73	$ 84	$ 85

The subsidiary management is optimistic about the volume of sales for 19X6. Recent sales promotion efforts seem to be beneficial, and Avcont expects to increase unit sales 10% during 19X6 even though industry volume is expected to decline to 1,100,000 units. However, Avcont management also knows its variable cost rates will increase 10% in 19X6 over 19X5 levels.

Avcont management wants to take action to reverse the unsatisfactory results the company has been experiencing. One proposal under consideration is to increase the price of Avcont's product. Some members of management believe that the market might accept an 8% increase in prices at this time without effecting the expected 10% increase in unit sales volume because no price increases have taken place in this market since 19X2. Several competitors are also considering price increases for 19X6.

Other members of Aplet management question the feasibility of a price increase because Avcont is operating in an industry that is experiencing declining sales. The marketing department believes a price increase will make the expected increase in unit sales volume less likely during 19X6. Its estimate of the possible effect of the 8% price increase on unit sales are as follows:

Increase (Decrease) in 19X6 Unit Sales Volume	Probability
10%	40%
5	30
0	20
(5)	10
	100%

Required

1 Calculate Avcont Company's profits for 19X6 if the 8% price increase takes place and unit sales volume increases 10%.

2 What are Avcont Company's expected profits for 19X6 if the probabilistic sales data assembled by the marketing department are used?

(CMA)

21-20 Calculation of Probabilities and Expected Contribution Food Products, Inc.; posed the following problem to your management consulting firm and requested guidelines which can be applied in the future to obtain the largest net income.

A Food Products plant on the coast produces a food product and ships its production of 10,000 units per day by air in an airplane owned by Food Products. The area is sometimes fogbound and shipment can then be made only by rail. The plant does not operate unless shipments are made. Extra costs of preparation for rail shipment reduce the contribution margin of this product from \$.40 per unit to \$.18 per unit and there is an additional fixed cost of \$3,100 for modification of packaging facilities to convert to rail shipment (incurred only once per conversion).

The fog may last for several days and Food Products normally starts shipping by rail only after rail shipments become necessary to meet commitments to customers.

A meteorological report reveals that during the past 10 years the area has been fogbound 250 times for one day and that fog continued 100 times for a second consecutive day, 40 times for a third consecutive day, 20 times for a fourth consecutive day, and 10 times for a fifth consecutive day. Occasions and length of fog were both random. Fog never continued more than five days and there were never two separate occurrences of fog in any six-day period.

Required

1 Prepare a schedule presenting the computation of the daily contribution margin (ignore fixed conversion cost)
 a When there is no fog and shipment is made by air.
 b When there is fog and shipment is made by rail.

2 Prepare a schedule presenting the computation of the probabilities of the possible combinations of foggy and clear weather on the days following a fogbound day. Your schedule should show the probability that, if fog first occurs on a particular day:
 a The next four days will be foggy.
 b The next three days will be foggy and the fifth day will be clear.
 c The next two days will be foggy and the fourth and fifth days will be clear.
 d The next day will be foggy and the third, fourth, and fifth days will be clear.
 e The next four days will be clear.

3 Assume you determine it is probable that it would be unprofitable to start shipping by rail on either the fourth or fifth consecutive foggy day. Prepare a schedule presenting the computation of the expected value marginal income or loss that should be expected from rail shipments if rail shipments were started on the third consecutive foggy day and the probability that the next two days will be foggy is .25, the probability that the next day will be foggy and the fifth day will be clear is .25, and the probability that the next two days will be clear is .50.

(CPA)

22 MEASURING THE SIGNIFICANCE OF VARIANCES

AFTER COMPLETING YOUR STUDY OF THIS CHAPTER, YOU SHOULD HAVE LEARNED:

1 That a variance should be investigated only if the benefits of the investigation exceed the cost of investigation.

2 How to structure the variance investigation problem using the concept of expected value.

3 How to use statistical quality control concepts to determine whether a process is operating in a state of "statistical control."

4 How to develop and use variance investigation rules.

A **variance** is the difference between a budgeted result and an actual result. If a variance is "big enough" to be significant it signals management that:

One of two actions may result from an investigation of significant variances.

1 The cause of the variance should be determined and corrected so the budget will be achieved or
2 The budget is no longer feasible and should be revised

Should all variances be investigated? Why does a variance have to be big enough before it is investigated? The reason is that an organization incurs a cost (1) to investigate a variance and (2) to take one of the corrective actions listed above. The cost of investigating a variance and taking corrective action should be incurred only when there is a reasonable chance that the benefits of investigation and correction will be greater than the cost of investigation and correction. The major topic of this chapter is deciding when to investigate a variance and when not to investigate a variance.

The idea of variances was introduced in Chapters 8 and 9 in the discussion of standard cost systems. In later chapters we introduced additional variances which concern managers of profit centers and investment centers. But the idea of interpreting the significance of a variance is general and applies to all variances. This is why we study it at this point of the book.

Variances caused by random fluctuations should not be investigated.

Once variances have been calculated and reported to management, how does management determine the course of action to follow? We suggested above that not all variances should be investigated. Variances representing minor deviations from budgeted amounts caused only by random fluctuations in the operations of the business should not be investigated. For example, if a quantity standard stipulates that one pint of paint should be used in finishing a window frame it can be expected that some frames might take more than one pint and other frames might require less than one pint. This variation in paint quantity can occur because of fluctuations in the air pressure that runs the paint gun or fluctuations in the thickness of the paint applied to the frame. These deviations are part of the normal operations and probably cannot be changed without a costly change in the painting process, such as purchasing a higher quality painting system. Variances of this type are referred to as random fluctuations, or chance variations, and should not be investigated since they lead to no corrective action. As long as the variances are small we do not try to retrain the workers nor do we change the painting process. The potential benefit is not worth the cost.

A common misconception held by some individuals is that only unfavorable variances should be investigated. This is definitely not true. Investigation of favorable variances might reveal improvements in operating procedures that can be applied in other parts of the organization to reduce costs. Also, a favorable variance might suggest a change in the standard and often standard costs are used to estimate variable costs and contribution margins. A standard cost is a valid input to the decision process only when it is up to date.

Variances should be investigated when the benefits resulting from the investigation exceed the costs incurred to conduct the investigation and correct the cause of the variance. Variances that are the result of random fluctuations (chance variations) should not be investigated. The benefits of the investigation will not exceed the costs.

In this chapter we consider three different approaches to deciding whether to investigate a variance.

Three approaches for deciding whether to investigate a variance.

1 The expected value approach
2 The statistical quality control approach
3 The managerial judgment approach

EXPECTED VALUE APPROACH

The **expected value approach to variance investigation** is based on the concept of minimizing the expected value of the costs associated with either (1) investigating the process or (2) not investigating the process. If the expected cost of investigating is less than the expected cost of not investigating, the variance should be investigated. This approach to the variance investigation decision requires the manager to estimate the following costs:

To use the expected value approach managers must estimate three types of cost and the probability of being out of control.

1 The cost of investigating the process.

2 The cost of correcting the process when the investigation reveals it is out of control.

3 The cost of allowing the process to operate in an **out-of-control state.** This represents the benefits associated with investigating and correcting an out-of-control process.

In addition to these cost estimates the manager must estimate the probability that the process is in an **in-control state** or an out-of-control state. (Remember, the probability that the process is in control plus the probability the process is out of control must add to 100% as all well-behaved probabilities do.)

While the expected value approach is not used extensively in practice, it is useful because the ideas discussed are the basis of the statistical quality control and the managerial judgment approaches as well as for the expected value approach.

In the following section we present some statistical background of the variance investigation decision. This will be followed by the formulation of the expected value approach. The section will finish with a numerical example.

Probability Estimates

The decision to investigate a variance requires careful analysis using probabilities because when a variance occurs, management does not know (1) whether the variance means a significant change has occurred in the production process or (2) whether the variance is a result of the random fluctuations that occur in every production process. As we saw earlier, a variance which is the result of random factors can be ignored (it is small and should average out), while a variance which signals a significant change is generally worth investigating and taking corrective action. The fact that we are not certain about the cause of a variance suggests using probabilities in the decision process.

To put it a bit more formally, the actual cost recorded for a production process is governed in part by some probability distribution. That is, we expect the actual cost of the production process to follow some pattern that can be described by a probability distribution. For example, in a particular department we might expect the labor cost per unit to follow a normal distribution with a mean of \$10 per unit and a standard deviation of \$4 when the process is in control. If the process is out of control we would still expect the cost to follow a normal distribution, but perhaps now with a mean of \$14 per unit and standard deviation of \$4. Typically, the in control and out of control cost distributions will overlap, as shown in Exhibit 22-1, so that when an observation is reported management will not know for sure whether

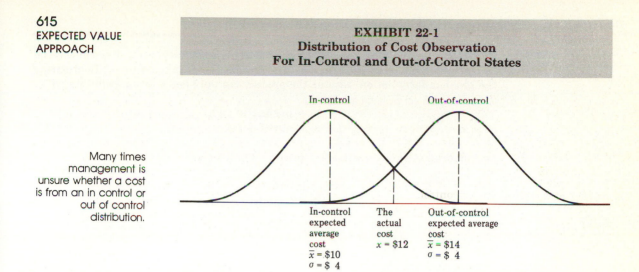

EXHIBIT 22-1
Distribution of Cost Observation
For In-Control and Out-of-Control States

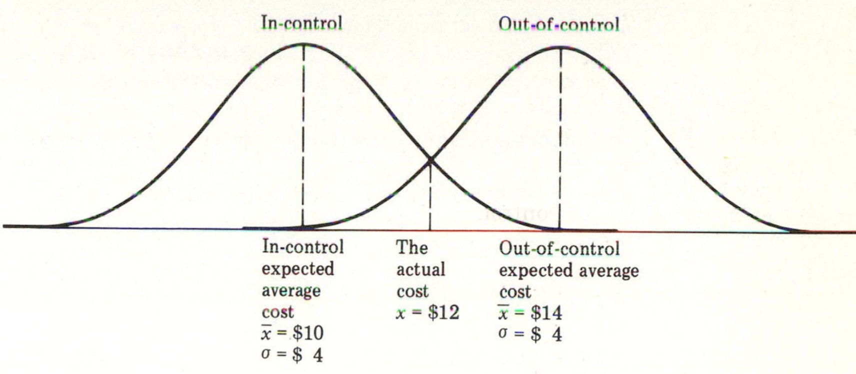

Many times management is unsure whether a cost is from an in control or out of control distribution.

the observation resulted from an in-control distribution (because of a random factor and no action required) or an out-of-control distribution (action required). Exhibit 22-1 illustrates this point.

Suppose that the actual average labor cost per unit for this week is $12 per unit. You can see that $12 per unit could have occurred from either the in-control or out-of-control distributions. How likely it is depends on the portion of the distribution outside the value which occurred. In this case it appears that $12 per unit is about equally likely to have come from either distribution. In contrast, a value of $9 per unit would be quite likely to have come from the in-control distribution and quite unlikely to have come from the out-of-control distribution because $9 per unit is at the extreme end of the out-of-control distribution.

The point of all of this is that management has to start the variance evaluation analysis with a judgment of whether the process is in control or out of control. For some amounts, managers will have a pretty good idea (for example, the $9 per unit) about the state of the process. However, for a wide variety of amounts, management will have to rely on their knowledge of whether there were problems in operations this week or whether things went smoothly. If there were problems, management might feel that the chance of being out of control is relatively high. If things went smoothly, management might feel that the chance of being out of control is low.

Managerial judgment is used to estimate the probability of the process being in control and out of control.

Based on experience and observations, management's judgment as to the chance of the process being in control or out of control is expressed as probabilities. Since we are assuming the process can only be in one of two states, the probability of the process being in control plus the probability of the process being out of control must add to one. These probability estimates are used in formulating the expected value approach to the variance investigation decision, as discussed in the following section.

Expected Value Formulation

With some simplifying assumptions the variance investigation decision can be formulated to minimize the expected costs associated with the decision.[1] To illustrate the problem formulation, assume the process can only be in two possible states:

$$S_1 = \textbf{in control}$$
$$S_2 = \textbf{out of control}$$

and that only two actions are available to management:

$$a_1 = \textbf{investigate}$$
$$a_2 = \textbf{do not investigate}$$

With two states and two alternatives, the investigation problem can be formulated as a payoff table. Exhibit 22-2 shows the two actions available to management and the possible results of these actions. The process is either in control or out of control and the manager can either investigate or not investigate. The payoffs in the table are symbols for costs which we will discuss next.

Determining the cost of an investigation.

The cost C is the cost of investigating the cause of the variance. It is incurred when management chooses to investigate whether or not the process turns out to be in control or out of control. Note that if management decides to investigate a process and the investigation shows the process to be in control, management made the wrong decision in investigating. It is good that the process is in control, but it would have been in control without the investigation. Thus, the cost spent on investigation produced no benefit. The amount of this cost will be dependent on the type of process being evaluated. If a labor quantity variance associated with a simple assembly operation is being evaluated, the investigation might consist of the supervisor discussing the problem with the individuals involved and observing the assembly of the product in order to identify the cause of the variance. If the variance is a material quantity variance associated with a complex chemical operation, the investigation might require a team of chemical engineers to perform tests at various points in the operation to identify the cause of the variance. These tests might require substantial time delays and perhaps even shutdown of the manufacturing process. The investigation cost could be quite large in this case.

Determining the cost of correcting an out-of-control process.

The cost M represents the cost of correcting the process and is incurred when management investigates an out-of-control process and therefore takes corrective action. It is assumed that when the process is out of control an investigation will always reveal the cause of the variance. As with the cost of investigation this cost will depend on the specific circumstances causing the variance. The cost may be the cost of replacing a piece of equipment or it might be the cost of changing a standard cost if investigation shows that the standard is out of date.

Determining the cost of letting the process operate out of control.

The cost of not investigating is zero when the process is in control (right investigation decision). The cost of not investigating is L when the process is out of control (wrong investigation decision). L represents the incremental costs the company will incur from the process continuing to operate in the out-of-control state. Going back to the illustration in Exhibit 22-1, the average labor cost per unit

[1] It is assumed that if the process is out of control an investigation will always reveal the cause of the variance; if the process is not investigated it will continue; the decision maker is willing to make the decision based on expected values. See H. Bierman Jr., and T. Dyckman, *Managerial Cost Accounting,* 2d ed. (New York: The Macmillan Company, 1976), p. 504.

EXHIBIT 22-2
Payoff Table
Two State-Two Alternatives
Investigation Problem

		States	
		In-Control S_1	**Out-of-Control** S_2
Actions	**Investigate** a_1	C	$C + M$
	Do not investigate a_2	Zero	L

C is the cost of an investigation.
M is the cost of correcting an out-of-control process.
L is the cost of allowing the process to operate out of control.

will be $14, as long as the process continues out of control, $4 per unit more than the average labor cost per unit if the process is in control. This incremental $4 per unit times the number of units produced until the out-of-control state is corrected is cost L. Avoiding cost L is the benefit of investigating an out-of-control process.

If we call the probabilities associated with S_1 and S_2, p_1 and p_2 respectively, the expected value of the cost associated with each action can be calculated as follows:

Calculation of the expected value of management's alternatives.

$$E(a_1) = p_1C + p_2(C + M)$$
$$E(a_2) = p_1(\text{zero}) + p_2L$$

Notice that this calculation gives a weighted average cost of investigating or not investigating the variance—the two choices available to management. The weights are the probabilities of each state and the costs are simply those shown in the payoff table of Exhibit 22-2. If the expected cost of a_1 is less than a_2 the process would be investigated, because this action has the lowest expected cost and management maximizes profit in this case by minimizing cost. If you are not too comfortable with the equations. the numerical example in the next section should help you.

To avoid calculating the expected costs each time a variance is reported, a **breakeven probability** can be calculated using the expected value formulas above. It is found by setting the expected cost of investigating, a_1, equal to the expected cost of not investigating, a_2.

Computing the "breakeven" probability.

$$E(a_1) = E(a_2)$$
$$p_1C + p_2(C + M) = p_1(\text{zero}) + p_2L$$
$$\text{since } p_1 = 1 - p_2$$

(because the probability of all events must total one)

$$(1-p_2)C + p_2(C+M) = (1-p_2)(\text{zero}) + p_2L$$
$$C - (C\,p_2) + (C\,p_2) + (p_2M) = p_2L$$
$$C + p_2M = p_2L$$
$$C = p_2L - p_2M$$
$$C = p_2(L - M)$$
$$\frac{C}{L-M} = p_2$$

The ratio $C/(L-M)$ is the probability of being in the out-of-control state that would cause the manager to be indifferent between investigating and not investigating the process because the expected cost of the two actions is equal. If the probability of being out of control (p_2) is greater than $C/(L-M)$, the process should be investigated since the expected cost of not investigating is greater than the expected cost of investigating.

Also, by calculating the breakeven probability management only has to estimate when the probability of an out-of-control state is greater than the breakeven probability. This avoids having the manager estimate an exact probability of being out of control. Many managers are more confident in estimating whether a probability is greater than a given number rather than estimating an exact probability.

An Example of the Expected Value Approach

To illustrate the expected value approach to variance investigation assume the following facts:

Cost of investigation	$C =$ **\$ 800**
Cost of correcting the out of control process	$M =$ **\$ 2,000**
Cost of allowing the process to operate out of control	$L =$ **\$10,000**
Probability of being in control	$p_1 =$ **.95**
Probability of being out of control	$p_2 =$ **.05**
	1.00

We will reverse the order of computation by calculating first the breakeven probability.

$$\frac{C}{L-M} = \frac{\$800}{\$10{,}000 - \$2{,}000} = .10$$

Thus, if the probability of the process being out of control is greater than 10%, the expected cost of an investigation is less than the expected cost of not investigating. However, because the estimate of p_2 is only 5%, management would not investigate since the expected cost of not investigating is less than the expected cost of investigation.

This conclusion can be confirmed by computing the expected value (weighted average cost) of each alternative.

$$E(a_1) = .95(\$800) + .05(\$2{,}000 + \$800) = \$900$$
$$E(a_2) = .95\ (0) + .05\ (\$10{,}000) = \$500$$

Since a_2—do not investigate—is the lowest cost alternative (\$500 versus \$900) management would not investigate. As it always should, this approach to the problem gives the same answer as the approach using the breakeven probability.

The expected value formulation for the variance investigation problem (either breakeven probability or lowest expected cost) is intuitively appealing because it is logical and it forces the manager to estimate the costs associated with the decision. But the development of the estimates is difficult enough that it is not widely used in practice. Estimating the values of the probability distribution for the out-of-control state is difficult since the cost records would contain only a few, if any, of these observations that occurred when the process is out of control. Processes are most often in control.

Problems in estimating the cost of letting the process operate out of control.

The most difficult dollar amount to estimate is the cost of allowing an out-of-control process to continue out of control (L). As in our illustration, it might be possible to identify the cost per unit difference from allowing the process to operate out of control. But how many units will be involved? Over what time period will the process remain out of control? Some suggest that the time from now until some other problem develops or until standards are expected to be revised is the appropriate time period. But how do you predict when the next problem might arise? And would management decide to investigate the new problem?

The cost of correcting an out-of-control situation (M) is also difficult to estimate until you know what the problem is. But you will not know that until you have investigated.

Because of these complications management generally simplifies the variance investigation decision by using statistical quality control techniques or managerial judgment. We discuss these two approaches next.

STATISTICAL QUALITY CONTROL APPROACH

Statistical quality control assumes the outputs from a process are subject to chance variation.

The objective of **statistical quality control** is to determine whether a process is operating in a state of *statistical control*. A process is considered to be in a state of statistical control when the variability of the process outputs is confined to chance variation. For example, we might have a quantity standard that specifies an average labor time of 0.5 hours per unit of product. This does not mean that each unit of product will require exactly 0.5 hours or that a sample of 4 units will always average 0.5 hours. If accounting records show employees averaging either 0.55 hours per unit or 0.45 hours per unit, the variance from the average time of 0.5 hours would probably be considered chance variation. Generally, it is not anticipated that employees will always produce at the average rate per hour but sometimes they will be below average and other times above average. When the observed variation from the expected average is large enough, the variation would be considered abnormal and the process would be investigated to see if there is a controllable cause. For example, if the accounting records in our example showed the employees averaging 0.75 hours to produce a unit, the process might be investigated. Statistical quality control procedures can be applied to variances to indicate what size variance should be considered normal (and not investigated) and what size variance should be considered abnormal (and investigated).

The basic concept behind statistical quality control is that manufacturing and other repetitive processes are subject to a certain amount of variability because of chance. And there is some stable pattern of variability in the measurements taken from a repetitive process. So long as the measurements of the process are within this pattern of variability the process is considered to be in a state of statistical control. A measurement outside the acceptable pattern of variability is considered a signal that the process is out of control, the cause of which should be investigated and corrected.

A control chart, illustrated in Exhibit 22-3, is a graphical presentation of the range of chance variation that management can expect from an in-control process. The upper and the lower **control limits** establish boundaries of in-control operation. Exhibit 22-3 shows that for our assumed assembly operation management can expect average assembly times ranging from 0.3 hours per unit to 0.7 hours per unit. Any observed average labor times outside of this range suggests abnormal performance and the process should be investigated.

A control chart shows the expected range of chance variation.

EXHIBIT 22-3
Control Chart
Assembly Operation

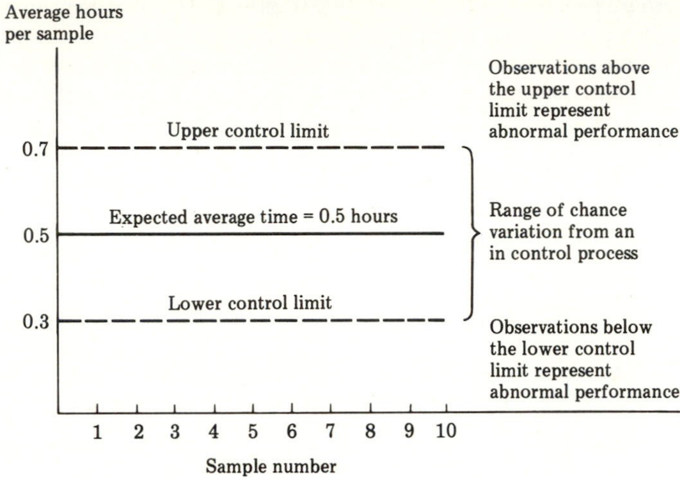

The sample number at the bottom of the control chart might represent various weeks or days for which the average time per unit was calculated. This will be illustrated in the next section of this chapter with a new example.

Control Chart Computations

The upper and lower control limits on a control chart are calculated using sample observations from the process. For example, consider an assembly process where over a 10-day period management has each day taken a sample of the time required to assemble a unit. Each sample consisted of 4 units. The time required to assemble each unit in each sample is given in Exhibit 22-4.

Once the data have been collected the next step in constructing a control chart is to calculate for each sample the average time to assemble the units in the sample and the range of times within each sample. The computations for sample 1 in Exhibit 22-4 are given below:

Control charts are constructed using data obtained from sampling the process.

$$\textbf{Sample average} = \bar{x} = (5 + 6 + 4 + 6) \div 4$$
$$\bar{x} = 21 \div 4$$
$$\bar{x} = 5.25 \textbf{ hours}$$

$$\textbf{Sample range} = R = \textbf{largest time minus smallest time}$$
$$R = 6 - 4$$
$$R = 2 \textbf{ hours}$$

EXHIBIT 22-4
Basic Data for Calculating Control Chart Parameters

Sample Number	Hours to Assemble Each Unit 1	2	3	4	Sample Average	Sample Range
1	5	6	4	6	5.25	2
2	4	3	5	6	4.50	3
3	7	4	5	3	4.75	4
4	6	8	6	5	6.25	3
5	4	6	5	4	4.75	2
6	5	5	4	6	5.00	2
7	4	6	5	5	5.00	2
8	6	5	7	5	5.75	2
9	5	6	6	4	5.25	2
10	7	5	5	4	5.25	3
Total					51.75	25

$$\text{Average of sample averages, } \bar{\bar{x}} = \frac{51.75}{10} = 5.175 \text{ hours}$$

$$\text{Average of sample ranges, } \bar{R} = \frac{25}{10} = 2.5 \text{ hours}$$

Having calculated the averages for each sample the next step is to calculate the average of the sample averages (labeled $\bar{\bar{x}}$) and the average of the sample ranges (labeled $\bar{R}$). These computations are shown below. The total of the averages and the ranges are simply divided by the numbers of samples.

$$\textbf{Average of sample averages} = \bar{\bar{x}} = 51.75 \div 10$$
$$\bar{\bar{x}} = 5.175 \text{ hours}$$
$$\textbf{Average of sample ranges} = \bar{R} = 25 \div 10$$
$$\bar{R} = 2.5 \text{ hours}$$

Width of Control Limits With this information we are now ready to draw the control chart. The value for $\bar{\bar{x}}$ represents the center line of the control chart. The control limits are calculated using the average of the sample ranges, $\bar{R}$. However, before illustrating the mechanics of calculating the control limits let us discuss how the control limits are used and how wide they should be.

The control limits are used to differentiate the normal observations with no controllable cause (random fluctuations) from the abnormal observations that might have controllable causes. Observations that fall within the control limits are assumed to be from an in-control process while observations falling outside the control limits are assumed to be from an out-of-control process which should be investigated. However, patterns of observations might also cause the manager to investigate the process even if the observations all fall within the control limits. If a number of observations appear close to one of the control limits, management might investigate to see if the mean of the process has changed even though the observations are not yet outside the control limits. Also, if there appears to be a

Observations that indicate an out-of-control process.

EXHIBIT 22-5
Sample Observations
For Four Different Situations

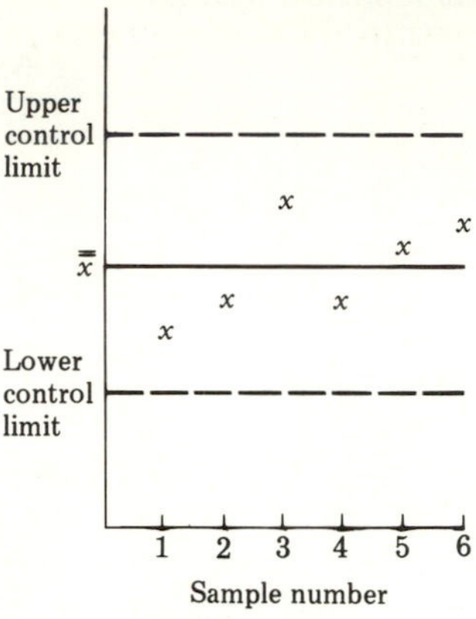

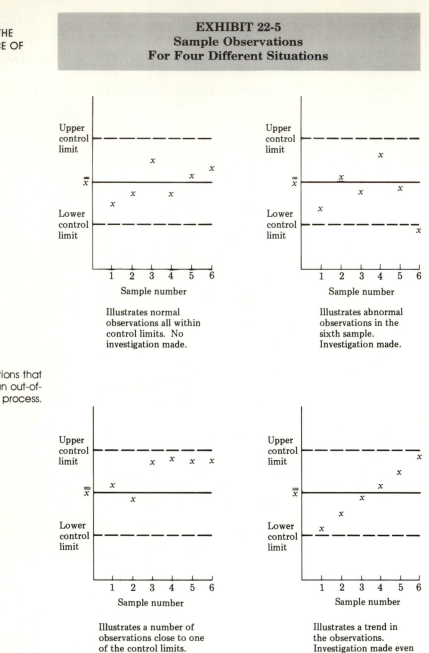

Illustrates normal observations all within control limits. No investigation made.

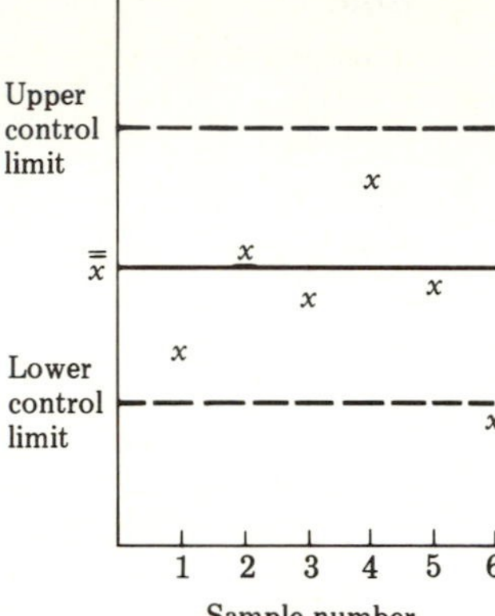

Illustrates abnormal observations in the sixth sample. Investigation made.

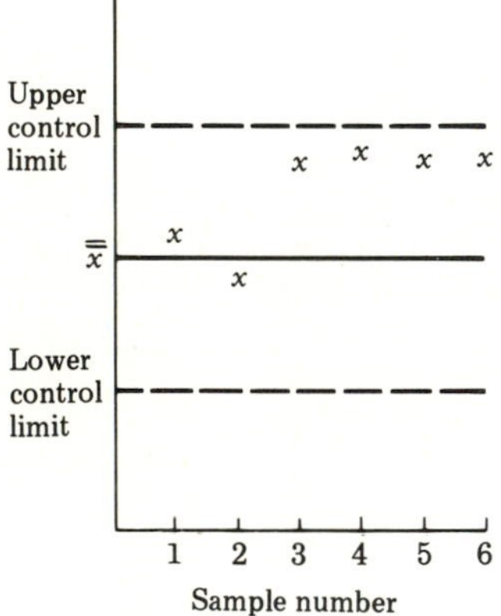

Illustrates a number of observations close to one of the control limits. Investigation made even though no observations are outside the control limits.

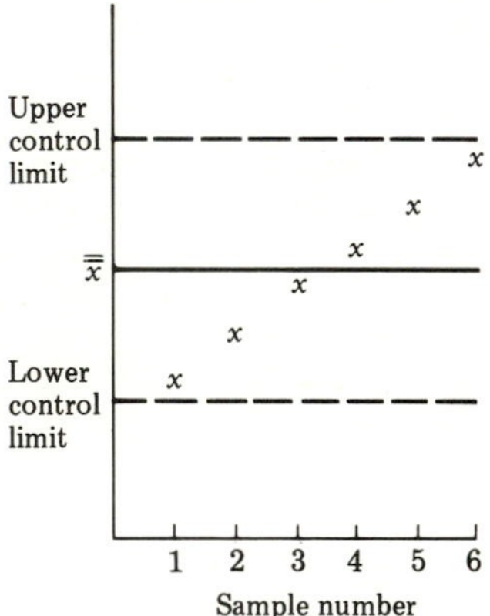

Illustrates a trend in the observations. Investigation made even though no observations are outside the control limits.

trend associated with the observations an investigation might be initiated. The trend could indicate the process is moving to an out-of-control state. These possibilities are illustrated in Exhibit 22-5.

The width of the control limits is expressed in terms of the number of standard deviations (σ) between the average, $\bar{\bar{x}}$, and the limit. The sample averages can be assumed to be normally distributed. This means that for a process which is in control 68.3% of the observations will fall within $\bar{\bar{x}} \pm 1\sigma$, 95.5% within $\bar{\bar{x}} \pm 2\sigma$, and 99.7% within $\bar{\bar{x}} \pm 3\sigma$.

Determining the width of the control limits.

How does management decide to use 3σ limits rather than 2σ limits? In setting the limits for control charts management is attempting to minimize the costs associated with what are called **Type I** and **Type II errors.** A Type I error results when an in-control process is investigated. It is similar to the cost we labeled C in the expected value approach. The cost of this error is the investigation cost which is wasted because the process would have been in control with no investigation. A Type II error results when an out-of-control process is not investigated. The cost of a Type II error is the incremental cost of allowing the system to continue to operate in an out-of-control condition. It is similar to the cost we labeled L in the expected value approach. Assuming the process is investigated only when observations fall outside the control limits, the wider the control limits the lower the probability of a Type I error and the higher the probability of a Type II error.

In practice control limits of plus and minus three standard deviations are the most popular. These limits may be appropriate, but they have been chosen based on management's intuition rather than careful analysis of costs. To carry the example a step further, if control limits of three standard deviations are desired, statistical tables such as the one in Exhibit 22-6 make it easy to construct the limits using the average of the sample averages, $\bar{\bar{x}}$, and the average range, $\bar{R}$.

EXHIBIT 22-6
Factors for Calculating Three-Sigma Control Limits Using the Average Range, $\bar{R}$

Sample Size	Factor A_2
2	1.88
3	1.02
4	0.73
5	0.58
6	0.48
7	0.42
8	0.37
9	0.34
10	0.31

From Eugene L. Grant and Richard L. Leavenworth, *Statistical Quality Control*, 5th ed. (New York: McGraw-Hill Book Company, 1980), p 631. Used with the permission of McGraw-Hill Book Company.

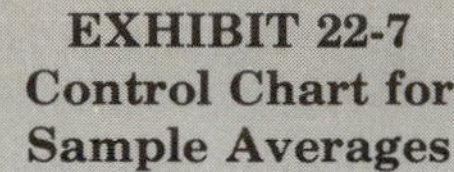

EXHIBIT 22-7
Control Chart for Sample Averages

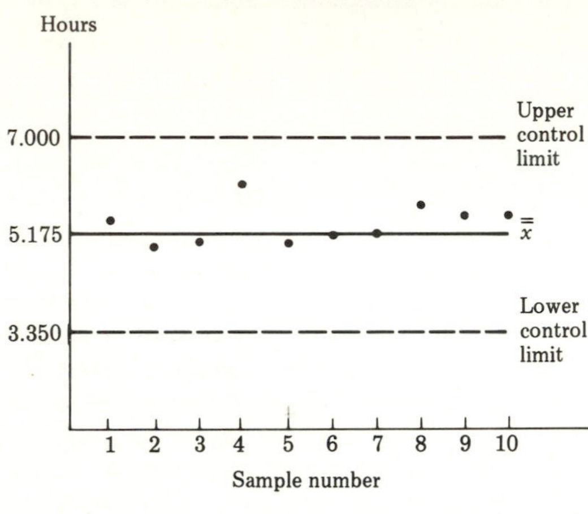

Calculating the Control Limits Now, returning to data in Exhibit 22-4, the upper and lower control limits are calculated as follows:

Calculation of upper and lower control limits.

$$\begin{aligned}\textbf{Upper control limit} &= \bar{\bar{x}} + A_2\bar{R} \\ &= 5.175 + .73(2.5) \\ &= 7.000 \text{ hours} \\ \textbf{Lower control limit} &= \bar{\bar{x}} - A_2\bar{R} \\ &= 5.175 - .73(2.5) \\ &= 3.350 \text{ hours}\end{aligned}$$

Exhibit 22-7 is the control chart for the data given in Exhibit 22-4. None of the observations is outside the control limits indicating the process is in a state of statistical control. If any of the sample means were outside of the control limits, they would indicate a need for an investigation. As future samples are collected, their mean will be plotted on the control chart to evaluate whether the process should be investigated or not.

Control charts are applicable to activities where the process is repetitive and stationary (not changing) over time. This would include some administrative activities such as keypunch operations and preparation of invoices in addition to many manufacturing activities.

MANAGERIAL JUDGMENT APPROACH

Over the years managerial personnel have developed general guidelines that are used to determine whether a variance should be investigated and is referred to as the **managerial judgment approach.** These guidelines look at the variance:

Variance investigation guidelines based on managerial judgment.

1 As an absolute dollar amount

2 As a percentage of the budget amount

To illustrate the first approach, management might feel, based on historical experience, that any variance greater than $500 should be investigated. The $500 absolute dollar amount is established by comparing the cost of investigating the variance with the potential savings resulting from bringing the process back into control and eliminating future variances from the same cause. As with the previous decision rules, management does not want to investigate variances where the investigation costs exceed the potential cost savings. The absolute dollar amount avoids investigating small variances where the cost savings would almost always be less than the investigation cost.

Problems with using an absolute dollar amount rule.

The problem with an absolute amount rule is that the probability that the process is out of control might be fairly high in some situations and fairly low in others. For example, if the budgeted amount is $1,000 and the variance is $500 intuition indicates a high probability that something has gone wrong, the process is out of control, to generate a variance which is 50% of the budgeted amount. On the other hand, if the budgeted amount is $10,000 and the variance is $500, intuition indicates a low probability of something gone wrong; a variance of only 5% of the budgeted amount ($500) $10,000 is fairly common in some processes.

To overcome this difficulty of the absolute dollar amount rule, investigation rules look at the variance as a percentage of budget. For example, based on historical experience management might feel that any variance greater than 10% of budget should be investigated. That is, a 10% variance means the process is likely to be out of control. But even if the process is out of control, for some small budget items a 10% variance may not be significant when the absolute dollar amount is examined. To illustrate, a 10% deviation for an expense item of $1 million would certainly be worth investigating: the variance is $100,000. But a 10% deviation for a budget item of $100 means a variance of only $10. The cost of investigating a $10 variance would almost always be greater than the potential cost savings from correcting the out-of-control situation.

Problems with using a percentage rule.

For this reason many companies establish a combined rule that requires a certain percentage amount *as well as* a minimum absolute amount. Some companies determine significance based on the item in question. For example, one company reported in a Conference Board survey that investigations were performed if any of the following conditions held:[2]

- Variances exceeding 1% of budget for direct labor
- Variances exceeding $500 or 10% of budget for overhead
- Variances exceeding 10% of budget for profits
- Variances exceeding 5% of budget for revenues

While these rules can be criticized for lack of statistical justification, they are simple and inexpensive to apply. The incremental benefits of using the expected value approach or the control chart approach may not be high enough to justify their development and implementation costs.

You should notice that even the managerial judgment approaches are consistent

[2] Jeremy Bacon, *Managing the Budget Function*, National Industrial Conference Board (New York, 1970), p. 42.

with the ideas of expected value and statistical control charts. The absolute dollar amount is set by intuitively comparing the cost of investigation and correction against the savings in cost resulting from correcting the out-of-control condition. The percentage amount is looking at the variance to judge whether it is likely to be caused by random factors or by an out-of-control situation. A small percentage amount is likely to have random causes; a large percentage amount is likely to have a controllable cause. This is the same kind of thinking used more formally in the expected value approach.

SUMMARY

A variance is the difference between a budgeted result and an actual result. If the variance is significant it should be investigated.

There are three approaches to the variance investigation problem: the expected value approach, the statistical quality control approach, and the managerial judgment approach.

The expected value approach is based on minimizing the expected costs associated with either investigating or not investigating the process. It requires the manager to estimate the probability of the process being in control and out of control.

The statistical quality control approach attempts to determine whether a process is operating in a state of statistical control. This is done by estimating upper and lower control limits to establish the range of chance variation management can expect from an in-control process. Observations outside of the control limits indicate an out-of-control process.

The managerial judgment approach is based on management experience and intuition. While these managerial rules lack statistical justification, from a cost-benefit viewpoint they may be the most logical strategy in many situations and they rely on the same kind of thinking which is used more formally by the earlier two approaches.

Review Problem

The Stat Company has been operating a new manufacturing process for about five months and the supervisor estimates that there is a 90% chance the process is currently operating in an in-control state. The process is such that if it is in an in-control or an out-of-control state it will not change without some form of intervention.

If the process is investigated the cost of the investigation is estimated to be $2,000 and if a correction is necessary the cost of correction will be an additional $1,000. If the process is allowed to operate in an out-of-control state the incremental cost is expected to be $11,000 over the planning horizon.

Required

1 Prepare a payoff table showing the decision situation faced by management.

2 Calculate the probability of the process being out of control that would make management indifferent between investigating and not investigating the process.

3 Calculate the expected cost of each action.

Solution

1 Payoff table

		States	
		.90 In-Control	.10 Out-of-Control
Actions	**Investigate**	\$2,000	\$2,000 + \$1,000
	Do not investigate	\$0	\$11,000

2 Breakeven probability $= \dfrac{C}{L\text{-}M}$

$$= \frac{\$2{,}000}{\$11{,}000 - \$1{,}000} = \frac{\$2{,}000}{\$10{,}000} = 20\%$$

3 $E(a_1) = .9\ (\$2{,}000) + .1\ (\$3{,}000) = \$2{,}100$
$E(a_2) = .9\ (\$0) + .1\ (\$11{,}000) = \$1{,}100$

Glossary

Breakeven probability The probability of the process being out of control that causes the manager to be indifferent about investigating and not investigating the process, because the expected cost of not investigating equals the expected cost of investigating.

Control limits The upper and lower bounds of a statistical control chart that are used to differentiate whether a particular observation indicates that the process is in or out of control.

Expected value approach to variance investigation A procedure for making the investigation decision based on minimizing the expected costs associated with the alternatives available to the manager.

In-control state A situation where the process is operating in a manner acceptable to management.

Managerial judgment approach to variance investigation A procedure for making the variance investigation decision based on management's experience and intuition.

Out-of-control state A situation where the process is operating in a manner unacceptable to management.

Statistical quality control approach to variance investigation A procedure for making the variance investigation decision based on the use of a control chart showing the expected cost and the upper and lower control limits.

Type I error An error resulting from investigating a process when it is in control. The cost of the error is the wasted investigation cost.

Type II error An error resulting from not investigating a process when it is out of control. The cost of this error is the incremental cost of letting the system continue to operate out of control.

Variance The difference between a budgeted result and an actual result.

Questions and Problems

22-1 Should all variances be investigated? Explain why or why not.

22-2 What are the factors that should be considered in making the variance investigation decision?

22-3 What are the problems of estimating the costs to use the expected value approach to the variance investigation problem?

22-4 Define a Type I error and a Type II error.

22-5 What costs are management attempting to minimize in selecting the upper and the lower control limits on a statistical control chart? Explain briefly.

22-6 In what situations is it appropriate to use a statistical control chart?

22-7 Discuss the types of observations that would lead to an investigation when a statistical control chart is used in making variance investigation decisions.

22-8 What is the advantage of using rules based on managerial judgment to make the variance investigation decision?

22-9 **Variance Investigation Decision** Given for a manufacturing process:

Cost of investigation	= $ 400
Cost of correction	= $ 300
Incremental cost of process running out of control	= $2,000

Required

1 Calculate the probability of being out of control that would make management indifferent toward investigating or not investigating.

2 If the probability of being out of control is .10 should the process be investigated?

22-10 **Computation of Cost Savings to Warrant an Investigation** The supervisor of a manufacturing process has estimated that the probability of the process being out of control is 8%. The investigation cost is $600 and the correction cost is $200.

Required

What do the incremental cost savings have to be to warrant an investigation?

22-11 **Variance Investigation Decision** A partially automated process is used to produce ceramic ashtrays.

The cost associated with investigating the process is $300 and the correction cost if a problem is found is $200. If the process is allowed to run out of control the incremental cost is $1,200. Currently the supervisor feels there is a 95% chance the process is in control.

Required

1 Calculate the "breakeven" probability.

2 Should the process be investigated?

22-12 **Variance Investigation Decision** The manager of a manufacturing process has asked you to provide some analytical help in deciding whether the process he is in charge of should be investigated. The estimated cost of investigating the process is $250 and the correction cost is $150. The incremental cost of letting the process run out of control over the planning horizon is $1,150. The manager estimates there is a 90% chance the process is currently in control.

Required

1 Prepare a payoff table to represent the manager's decision problem.

2 Calculate the expected cost of his two actions.

3 Should the process be investigated?

22-13 Variance Investigation Decision The fabricating department has been operating smoothly for the past month and the supervisor feels there is a 95% chance the costs are in control. The investigation and correction costs are estimated at $500 and $300, respectively. The cost savings if the process is out of control and corrected are estimated at $8,300.

Required

1 Calculate the expected cost associated with investigating and not investigating the process.

2 Should the process be investigated?

22-14 Variance Investigation Decision The ABC Company manufactures and assembles a line of infant toys for distribution to wholesalers.

Currently the supervisor of the assembly process feels there is about a 95% chance the process is in control. When the process is investigated the cost amounts to $400 and if a problem is found the correction cost is $200. The incremental cost of the assembly running out of control over the planning horizon is $10,200.

Required

1 Calculate the "breakeven" probability for the variance investigation decision.

2 Should the process be investigated? Verify your answer by calculating the expected cost of each of the manager's alternatives.

22-15 Control Chart Computations Over the past 10-day period a time study engineer has observed the following times to assemble each unit of product.

	Hours to Assemble Each Unit			
Day	**1**	**2**	**3**	**4**
1	2	3	2	4
2	3	2	3	3
3	4	3	5	2
4	3	2	5	3
5	5	4	3	4
6	2	4	3	4
7	4	6	3	4
8	5	4	2	3
9	6	3	5	4
10	3	2	4	4

Required

1 Calculate the value of the center line ($\bar{\bar{x}}$) and the average range ($\bar{R}$) for the data collected by the time study engineer.

2 Draw a control chart using three sigma control limits and plot the average times for the 10 observations.

3 Should the assembly operation be investigated?

22-16 **Control Chart Computations** The Ace Manufacturing Company produces industrial gears from powdered metals. The following five samples of pounds to produce one gear were taken over a five-day period. Each sample consisted of six gears.

	Pounds of Input for Each Gear					
Sample	**1**	**2**	**3**	**4**	**5**	**6**
1	3	4	6	5	3	4
2	6	5	3	6	4	5
3	7	4	6	3	4	5
4	4	6	5	6	3	5
5	3	5	7	6	4	5

Required

1 Prepare a control chart using three sigma control limits and plot the data.

2 Is the process out of control?

22-17 **Control Chart Computations** Management is concerned about the number of machine hours to produce 1 unit of part no. 1087. An industrial engineer has collected information about the number of machine hours to produce part no. 1087. Sample averages and ranges for 10 samples of four units each are given below:

Sample No.	Sample Average ($\bar{x}$)	Sample Range (R)
1	10.6 hours	3.2 hours
2	11.7	2.8
3	12.8	3.4
4	9.4	4.0
5	10.3	3.6
6	9.2	3.8
7	12.4	2.9
8	11.8	3.9
9	12.2	2.8
10	9.8	3.8

Required

1 Construct a control chart using three sigma control limits.

2 Is the process out of control?

3 Assume the following samples of four units each are collected by the industrial engineering department:

	Machine Hours per Unit			
Sample No.	**1**	**2**	**3**	**4**
11	12.2	9.8	10.0	12.2
12	12.4	8.4	12.9	9.2
13	8.6	13.2	9.3	12.8
14	8.2	8.8	11.9	9.8

Based on these last four samples, should the process be investigated?

COST ESTIMATION

AFTER COMPLETING YOUR STUDY OF THIS CHAPTER, YOU SHOULD HAVE LEARNED:

1 How accountants determine the fixed and variable cost amounts required for many cost accounting procedures and management decisions discussed earlier in the book.

2 How the engineering approach to cost estimation works and why it is used for some estimates even though it is expensive.

3 To identify the advantages and disadvantages of the relatively simple high-low and graphic methods of estimating cost functions.

4 How regression analysis is an objective method which makes use of all acceptable data and also provides additional useful statistics.

5 What the assumptions of regression analysis are and how to determine whether the assumptions are met in a particular case.

6 How learning occurs in manufacturing processes and how it should be used in cost estimation.

In Chapter 2 various cost behavior patterns were discussed. Costs were classified as variable, fixed, semivariable, or step depending on how they changed in amount as production volume or sales volume changed. Cost-volume classifications are important in estimating future costs needed for product costing, managerial decision making, and management control.

We illustrated in Chapter 3 how estimated overhead costs were used to calculate predetermined overhead rates. Chapters 8 and 9 illustrated the use of standard costs (estimated costs) for assigning direct materials, direct labor, and applied manufacturing overhead to the product. In the chapters dealing with managerial planning and control decisions, cost estimates were important inputs into the decision process. This chapter will concentrate on how cost estimates are made based on either an analysis of operations or by analyzing historical data.

Some costs in a manufacturing process are relatively simple to estimate. For instance, the depreciation cost on buildings and equipment can be estimated from the cost of the assets and the depreciation methods. In this situation, the depreciation cost is determined by a specific calculation, and except for the units of production depreciation method, the amount does not vary depending on volume. Most costs, however, are caused by some activity. For example, direct labor cost results from the activity of employees producing products, electricity cost results from the activity of running machinery and lighting to produce products, the cost of grinding wheels results from the activity of producing products. Even though we know that volume of activity affects the amount of cost, the cost cannot be estimated precisely for each level of volume. If volume remained constant for several days, management would still expect the actual cost to vary from day to day but only within some usual range. Some days the employees might average 30 minutes per unit of production and other days 28 minutes simply because of changes in things like the weather or the feelings of the workers. Because of this, costs associated with any particular volume level can be represented by a probability distribution. For example, if 5,000 units are to be produced, the actual labor cost observed is from a probability distribution like the following:

Probability distribution of costs.

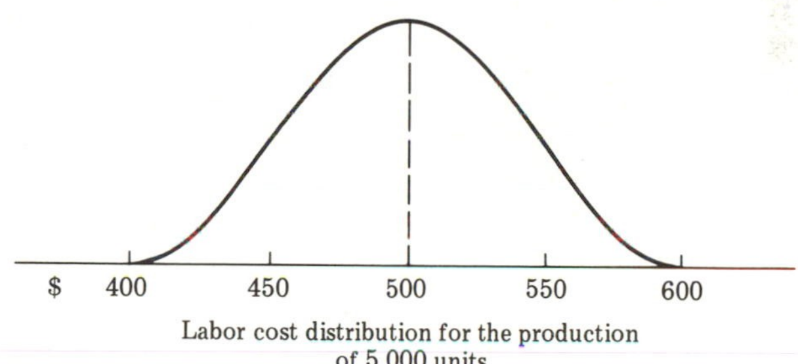

Labor cost distribution for the production of 5,000 units

The expected cost of the 5,000 units is $500, however; the cost could range from $400 to $600 simply because of the random behavior of the manufacturing process. We will use this information about the distribution of the cost data to develop interval estimates of the costs. For example, we might state that the expected cost is $500 plus or minus $100.

In this chapter we concentrate on two approaches to cost estimation:

1 An engineering approach

2 An analysis of historical data approach

AN ENGINEERING APPROACH TO COST ESTIMATES

Time and motion studies are used to estimate direct labor costs.

The approach to **engineering cost estimates** identifies a physical relationship between the manufacturing activity and the cost. For direct labor cost, time and motion studies are used to determine the hours necessary to perform each activity. In time and motion studies, industrial engineers, with stop watches, observe the production of a product to (1) measure the amount of time it takes employees to perform a specific task, and (2) determine if there is a more efficient way of doing the work. Based on these observations, the industrial engineers determine the standard amount of time required to perform the task. The standard direct labor rate is determined from the company's contract with the labor union. The estimated direct labor cost per unit of product is calculated by multiplying the standard labor time by the standard labor rate.

Product specifications determine direct materials costs.

The engineering approach to estimating direct materials cost identifies the specific quantities and quality of direct materials required to produce a product by studying the characteristics of the materials and specifications of the machines used to produce the product. In preparing these direct materials cost estimates, allowances are made for spoilage and scrap based on the efficiency of the manufacturing process. Prices of the direct materials are estimated from quotes by suppliers.

The engineering approach generally produces good cost estimates. Also, since a complete analysis is performed for the direct labor operations and direct materials requirements, alternative manufacturing procedures can be identified which may lead to cost reductions. The approach is normative in that it attempts to determine what costs *should be* rather than what they will be.

Since the engineering approach to cost estimation relies on identifying physical relationships, it is not easily applied to the indirect costs of producing a product such as supplies costs and factory office costs. Due to the expense of performing an engineering analysis, it is generally only used for large cost elements such as direct labor and direct materials.

COST ESTIMATION FROM HISTORICAL DATA

When the engineering approach to cost estimation is too expensive, cost accountants analyze historical costs to estimate future costs. The basic assumption is that future costs will behave in the same manner as historical costs. If the production process for which the cost is incurred has changed, the historical cost observations as recorded in the accounting records will not be useful in estimating the future cost. For example, if there has been a recent change in machinery or materials, cost data prior to the change should not be used to estimate future costs. Changes in the skills of the employees or changes in compensation methods can cause historical costs to be inappropriate for estimating future costs.

Changes in the production process can make historical costs inappropriate for estimating future costs.

When changes in the production process have occurred we must either omit the cost data from our analysis or adjust the historical cost data to reflect the change. For example, if we are estimating the cost of electricity and the utility company has recently raised the electric rate, we could take the quantity of electricity used from the old electric bills and calculate electricity costs using the new rate. Or, we could base the estimated electricity cost on the actual electricity cost recorded since the rate change if we have enough data since the rate change.

As discussed in Chapter 2, page 35, pairs of historical data are obtained from the accounting records. For each accounting period the pair consists of (1) the cost

Data for cost estimation are collected in pairs.

incurred and (2) the measure of activity. For electricity cost we might use machine hours to measure activity. Thus, for each month we would collect the cost of electricity and the number of machine hours worked. An important part of using historical cost data to estimate future costs is the selection of an appropriate activity measure that relates to the cost. The activity measure selected should be one which causes the cost to change. Since electricity use is caused by operating machines, machine hours is an appropriate measure of activity for electricity cost.

Identification of Causal Factors

Cause and effect relationships are based on knowledge of the process.

To develop an estimate of a cost function, a relationship must be identified or hypothesized between the cost and the activity measure. As noted above, the engineering approach for direct labor and direct materials uses physical observations to identify the activity that causes costs to fluctuate. This observation of the physical relationship between cost and activity is the best procedure for identifying the causal activity. Unfortunately for many costs, this is not possible since the relationship is indirect and thus not readily observable. The cause-effect relationship must be inferred based on an understanding of why the cost is incurred. The accountant relies heavily on the experience and knowledge of the engineers and managers who daily observe the process to select the activity measure. These individuals can provide a logical basis for explaining why a particular activity causes a cost to vary. The activity measure (cause) chosen can be supported or rejected through the use of statistical analysis which is discussed latter in this chapter.

Some widely used activity bases which have been found to be causes of certain types of manufacturing overhead costs include: direct labor hours, direct labor

EXHIBIT 23-1
Assembly Department
Indirect Labor Costs

Month	*X* Direct Labor Hours	*Y* Indirect Labor Cost
1. January	5,320	$ 1,560
2. February	6,230	1,780
3. March	4,800	1,305
4. April	5,600	1,420
5. May	3,780	1,160
6. June	4,000	1,410
7. July	4,280	1,380
8. August	6,170	1,480
9. September	3,750	1,140
10. October	5,860	1,550
11. November	4,300	1,200
12. December	6,100	1,510
Totals	60,190	$16,895

dollars, machine hours, and units of production. For selling and administrative expenses, sales units and sales dollars are often appropriate activity measures.

The objective of analyzing historical cost data is to determine the average amount of change in the cost (the dependent variable) associated with a unit of change in an activity measure (the independent variable). The statistical analysis does not establish a cause and effect relationship, rather it aids in estimation of the value of the dependent variable given a value for the independent variable. The cause and effect relationship must be determined in advance from our knowledge of the process.

The following sections will discuss three approaches for cost estimation from historical data, graphic, high-low, and regression. Exhibit 23-1 contains 12 months of data from the accounting records of an assembly operation that will be used to illustrate the three alternative approaches to cost estimation for indirect labor cost. The approaches can be applied to a wide variety of other costs.

Graphic Approach

The graphic approach is based on visually fitting a line to the data.

The **graphic analysis of cost** was discussed in Chapter 2, so an extended discussion will not be repeated. This method requires the historical costs and related activity measures be plotted on a graph. Next, a straight line is drawn on the graph which comes close to as many of the points as possible. After the line is drawn the points can be ignored since the estimated fixed cost and estimated variable cost are determined from the line.

Exhibit 23-2 illustrates the graphic approach for the data given in Exhibit 23-1. The fixed cost and variable cost are estimated using the total costs associated with 4,000 and 6,000 direct labor hours. The calculations are shown below:

$$\textbf{Variable cost per direct labor hour} = \frac{\textbf{change in total cost}}{\textbf{change in volume}}$$

$$\frac{\$1{,}570 - \$1{,}250}{6{,}000 - 4{,}000}$$

$$= \underline{\underline{\$.16}} \text{ per direct labor hour}$$

Total cost at 6,000 direct labor hours	= **$1,570**
Variable cost at 6,000 direct labor hours ($.16 × 6,000)	= **$ 960**
Total fixed cost	**$ 610 per month**

Any two volumes could be chosen to estimate the variable cost per direct labor hour, although errors in reading the graph are generally minimized by choosing points near the ends of the line. Any point on the line can be used to estimate total fixed cost.

To estimate the total indirect labor cost for a month the following formula is used:

Total indirect labor cost per month = $610 + ($.16 × direct labor hours)

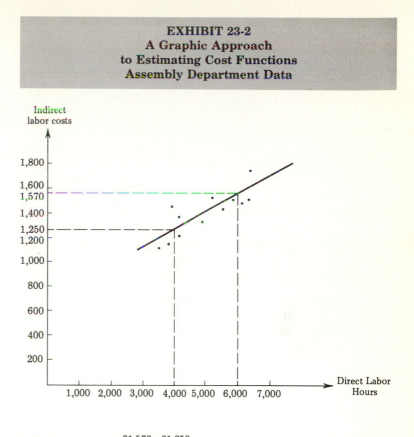

EXHIBIT 23-2
A Graphic Approach
to Estimating Cost Functions
Assembly Department Data

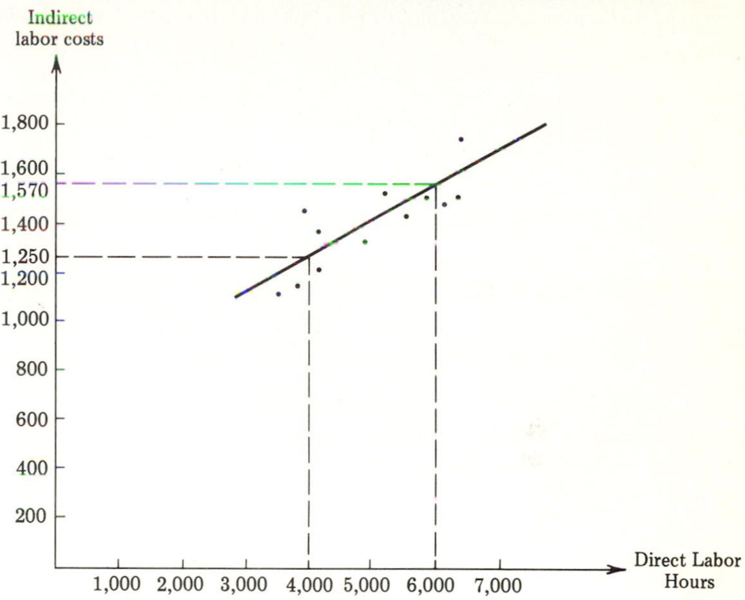

$$\text{Variable cost per DLH} = \frac{\$1{,}570 - \$1{,}250}{6{,}000 - 4{,}000} = \$.16$$

Fixed cost per month = \$1,570 − \$.16(6,000) = \$610

Total indirect labor cost = \$610 + (\$.16 × direct labor hours)

High-Low Approach

The high-low approach is based on fitting a line to two points.

The **high-low analysis of cost** estimation is a relatively crude approximation of the graphic approach. The high-low approach requires the selection of two points from the historical data set; one representing a high cost and one representing a low cost. Sometimes a fixed rule is established such as selecting the highest and lowest amount of the independent variable (thus the name). In the assembly department example the independent variable is direct labor hours. This rule has the advantage of picking two definite points which makes the process one which is easily done by a clerk; it requires no judgment as to which two points to select. It is unsatisfactory, however, if a point is selected which is not representative of all the costs.

To see how the high-low method works, let us apply it to the data in Exhibit 23-1. The extreme observations for the assembly center data are \$1,140 at 3,750 direct labor hours and \$1,780 at 6,230 direct labor hours.

Using these two observations the variable cost and fixed cost are calculated in the same manner as with the graphic approach:

$$\textbf{Variable cost per direct labor hour} = \frac{\textbf{change in total cost}}{\textbf{change in volume}}$$

$$= \frac{\$1{,}780 - \$1{,}140}{6{,}230 - 3{,}750}$$

$$= \$.258 \textbf{ per direct labor hour}$$

Total cost at 6,230 direct labor hours	**= $1,780**
Variable cost at 6,230 direct labor hours ($.258 × 6,230)	**= 1,607**
Total fixed cost	**= $ 173 per month**

To estimate the total indirect labor cost for a month the following formula is used:

Total indirect labor cost per month = $173 + ($.258 × direct labor hours)

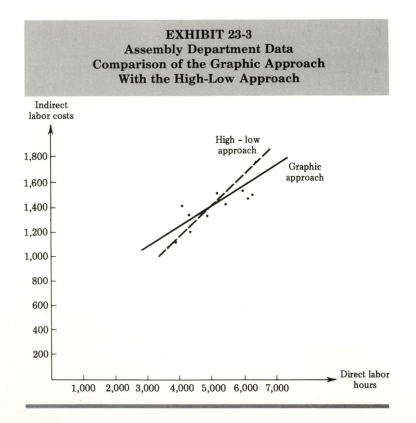

EXHIBIT 23-3
Assembly Department Data
Comparison of the Graphic Approach With the High-Low Approach

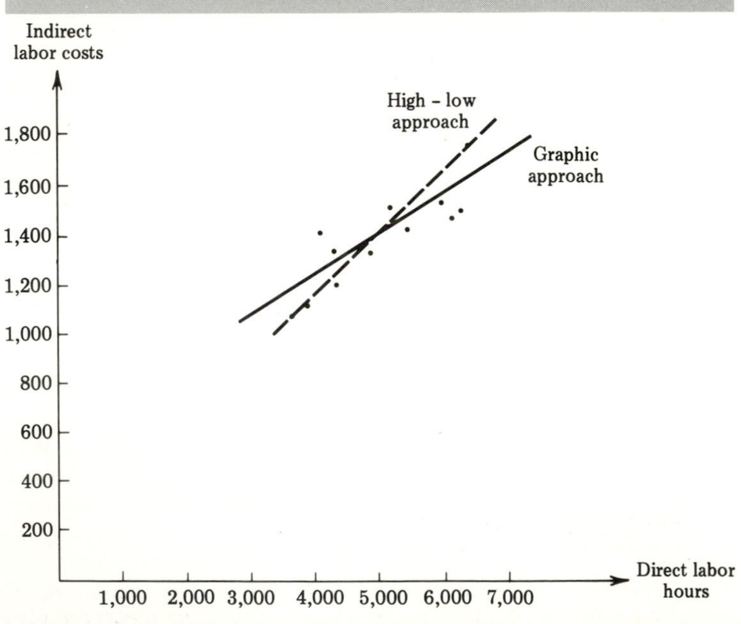

A comparison of the graphic and high-low approaches to cost estimation.

The cost formula we arrived at using the high-low approach is different than the cost formula using the graphic approach as shown below:

High-Low Approach

Total indirect labor cost = \$173 + (\$.258 × direct labor hours)

Graphic Approach

Total indirect labor cost = \$610 + (\$.16 × direct labor hours)

The difference exists because we only used two observations to compute the total cost formula with the high-low approach and we used all 12 observations in selecting the total cost formula with the graphic approach.

Exhibit 23-3 shows the total cost lines for both the high-low approach and the graphic approach. The total cost line for the graphic approach was drawn as close to all the observations as possible. The total cost line for the high-low approach was drawn to connect two observations (the high cost and low cost). The total cost line for the graphic method provides better cost estimates since more observations are used to calculate the total cost line.

The advantage of the high-low method is that it is simple and inexpensive. But it does not use all the data available to estimate the cost and if either of the two points selected represents unusual events (called an outlier) the high-low approach can provide very inaccurate estimates of the cost. Consider the following graph where the two data points selected are both outliers. The broken line is fitted by the high-low approach. The solid line represents a line that might be drawn using the graphic approach.

The high-low approach can provide misleading results.

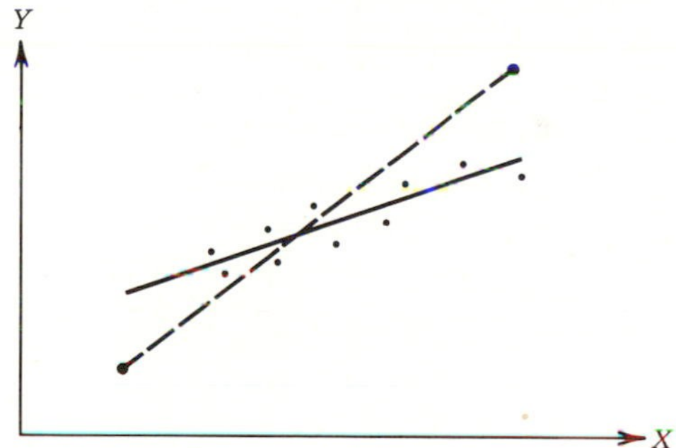

In this situation the high-low method uses the outliers to estimate a cost function that has little association with the data. This is why a rule that required use of the highest and the lowest cost would not be appropriate. Some flexibility in choice of points must be allowed. The graphic approach avoids this problem since all data is plotted and the outliers can be ignored when drawing the line.

Regression Approach

Regression is the term used for the process of fitting a "least-squares" line to a set of data to find the relationship between the dependent variable (indirect labor cost) and the independent variable (indirect labor hours). Regression analysis has the advantages of (1) being an objective procedure, (2) using all the data, and (3) providing some supplemental statistical information which is useful in evaluating how good an estimator the selected line is. If only two variables (one dependent and one independent) are used, the analysis is called "simple regression"; with more than two variables (more independent variables) the analysis is called "multiple regression." The objective of the procedure is to find the line such that the sum of the squared deviations between the regression line and the observations is minimized. Thus, the line is known as the "least-squares" line.

The general idea of least squares is as shown below:[1]

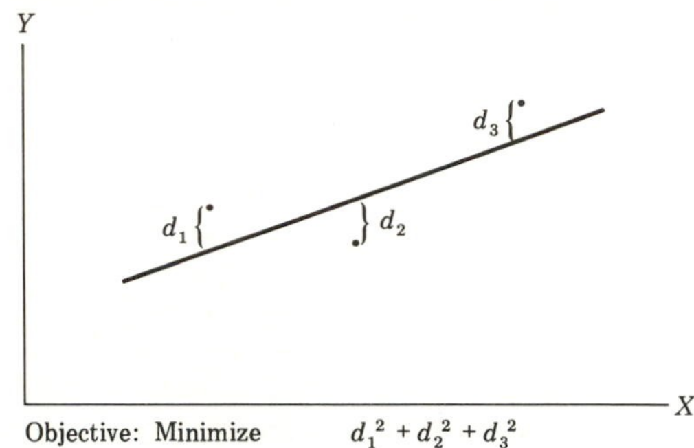

Of course a line based on only three observations would not be very reliable.

There are many computer programs available to compute the values of the regression line as well as some of its related statistics. For simple regression many of the computer programs make use of the following "normal equations" to solve for the parameters a (fixed cost) and b (variable cost per unit):

The normal equations.

$$\Sigma y = aN \times b\Sigma x$$
$$\Sigma xy = a\Sigma x + b\Sigma x^2$$

where N = number of observations
Σy = sum of the values of the dependent variable
Σx = sum of the values of the independent variable
Σx^2 = sum of the squared values of the independent variable
Σxy = sum of the product of x times y

The normal equations represent two simultaneous equations in two unknowns. Solving the equations for a and b, respectively, yields:

$$a = \frac{\Sigma y - b\Sigma x}{N}$$

$$b = \frac{N\,\Sigma(xy) - \Sigma x \Sigma y}{N\Sigma x^2 - (\Sigma x)^2}$$

Calculations for the assembly center cost data using the above equations are shown in Exhibit 23-4. The resulting equation, $\hat{y} = \$609 + \$.159X$, can be used to estimate the total indirect labor cost (dependent variable) for given values of direct labor hours (independent variable).

[1] If we tried to minimize the sum of the d_i's, many choices of totally unsuitable lines would be available where the sum of the d_i's equals zero; hence, regression minimizes the sum of the squares of the d_i's.

EXHIBIT 23-4
Assembly Center
Indirect Labor
Regression Analysis

Month	Direct Labor Hours x	Indirect Labor Cost y	x^2	xy
January	5,320	$ 1,560	28,302,400	8,299,200
February	6,230	1,780	38,812,900	11,089,400
March	4,800	1,305	23,040,000	6,264,000
April	5,600	1,420	31,360,000	7,952,000
May	3,780	1,160	14,288,400	4,384,800
June	4,000	1,410	16,000,000	5,640,000
July	4,280	1,380	18,318,400	5,906,400
August	6,170	1,480	38,068,900	9,131,600
September	3,750	1,140	14,062,500	4,275,000
October	5,860	1,550	34,339,600	9,083,000
November	4,300	1,200	18,490,000	5,160,000
December	6,100	1,510	37,210,000	9,211,000
Total	60,190	$16,895	312,293,100	86,396,400

$$N = 12$$
$$\Sigma x = 60{,}190 \qquad \Sigma x^2 = 312{,}294{,}100$$
$$\Sigma y = 16{,}895 \qquad \Sigma(xy) = 86{,}396{,}400$$

$$b = \frac{N\,\Sigma(xy) - \Sigma x\,\Sigma y}{N\,\Sigma x^2 - (\Sigma x)^2} = \frac{12 \times 86{,}396{,}400 - 60{,}190 \times 16{,}895}{12 \times 312{,}293{,}100 - (60{,}190)^2}$$

$$= \frac{1{,}036{,}756{,}800 - 1{,}016{,}910{,}050}{3{,}747{,}517{,}200 - 3{,}622{,}836{,}100} = \frac{19{,}846{,}750}{124{,}681{,}100} = \underline{\underline{.159}}$$

$$a = \frac{\Sigma y - b\,\Sigma x}{N} = \frac{16{,}895 - .159\,(60{,}190)}{12} = \underline{\underline{609}}$$

Thus,

$\hat{y} = \$609 + .159x$ ← The resulting equation

The cost functions resulting from the three techniques used in this chapter are summarized below:

In selecting an approach to cost estimation the costs and benefits need to be evaluated.

Technique	Resulting Equation
High-low	$\hat{y} = \$173 + \$.258X$
Graphic method	$\hat{y} = \$610 + \$.16X$
Regression analysis	$\hat{y} = \$609 + \$.159X$

The high-low method uses two extreme observations in estimating the cost function, the graphic method uses all observations and visually fits a line to the data, while the regression analysis minimizes the squared differences of all the points to estimate the cost function. Of the three techniques regression analysis provides the most reliable results; however, it requires a computer for all but the simplest problems. In selecting a technique, costs and benefits should be weighed. If a manager's decision can be changed by small errors in estimated cost, then regression analysis is probably justified. If the decision is not sensitive to the estimated cost function and a computer is not available, the graphic method might be appropriate.

ADDITIONAL USEFUL STATISTICS FROM REGRESSION ANALYSIS

As noted earlier, regression analysis provides an objective method of estimating fixed and variable costs which uses all available data and provides other useful statistics concerning the data. We shall study three additional statistics.

1 Standard error of the estimate
2 Coefficient of determination
3 Standard error of the regression coefficient and its t value

Standard Error of the Estimate

The method of least squares provides an estimate of the fixed indirect labor cost of \$609 and an estimate of the variable indirect labor cost of \$.159 per direct labor hour. Using these estimates of the fixed and variable indirect labor cost, the total indirect labor cost for 5,000 direct labor hours can be estimated as follows:

Estimated total indirect labor cost (for 5,000 direct labor hours) **= \$609 + (\$.159 × 5,000)**

= \$1,404

The estimated indirect labor cost of \$1,404 for 5,000 direct labor hours represents the *average* cost management can expect to incur based on the least-squares line. The actual cost might be greater or less than this average cost. The interval within which the actual cost might fluctuate can be determined using the standard error of the estimate. Recall the distribution of costs we discussed in the first section of this chapter.

The **standard error of the estimate** is the standard deviation about the least-squares line. The standard error of the estimate for simple regression is calculated as follows:

$$S_e = \sqrt{\frac{\Sigma(y - \hat{y})^2}{N - 2}}$$

Equation for computing the standard error of the estimate.

where S_e = standard error of the estimate
y = the actual cost observations
$\hat{y}$ = the estimated cost from the least-squares line; $\hat{y} = a + bx$
N = number of observations[2]

[2] The standard error of the estimate is computed using $N - 2$ rather than N since two values, a and b, are computed from the same observations used to compute S_e. $N - 2$ represents the degrees of freedom about the least-squares line.

EXHIBIT 23-5
Assembly Center Data
Standard Error of the Estimate

x Actual	y Actual	$\hat{y}$ Estimate*	$y - \hat{y}$ Error	$(y - \hat{y})^2$ Squared Error
5,320	$ 1,560	$1,454	$ 106	11,236
6,230	1,780	1,600	180	32,400
4,800	1,305	1,372	− 67	4,489
5,600	1,420	1,499	− 79	6,241
3,780	1,160	1,210	− 50	2,500
4,000	1,410	1,245	165	27,225
4,280	1,380	1,289	91	8,281
6,170	1,480	1,590	− 110	12,100
3,750	1,140	1,205	− 65	4,255
5,860	1,550	1,540	10	100
4,300	1,200	1,292	− 92	8,464
6,100	1,510	1,578	− 68	4,624
60,190	$16,895			121,915

$$\text{Standard error of the estimate} = \sqrt{\frac{121{,}915}{(12 - 2)}} = \$110$$

* From $\hat{y} = \$609 + \$.159x$

Exhibit 23-5 illustrates the calculation of the standard error of the estimate for the assembly center data. The standard error of the estimate for the assembly center data computed in Exhibit 23-5 is $110. This value can be used to compute confidence intervals around the expected indirect labor cost. Using the cost estimate for 5,000 indirect labor hours, the 95% confidence limits are computed as follows:[3]

Confidence intervals based on the standard error of the estimate.

$$\hat{y} = (\$609 + \$.159 \times 5{,}000 \text{ direct labor hours}) \pm t_{.025}(\$110)$$
$$\hat{y} = \$1{,}404 \pm 2.228\,(\$110)$$
$$\hat{y} = \$1{,}404 \pm \$245$$

The above computation tells management they can be 95% confident the actual indirect labor cost for 5,000 direct labor hours will be between $1,649 ($1,404 + $245) and $1,159 ($1,404 − $245).

[3] The t value for calculating the 95% confidence limits is obtained from the table given in Exhibit 23-6. The t value is based on the number of degrees of freedom. For simple regression the degrees of freedom are the number of observations minus two. In this example the degrees of freedom are 12 − 2 = 10.

EXHIBIT 23-6
***t* Values**

Degrees of Freedom	95% Confidence Interval t .025	90% Confidence Interval t .05
1	12.706	6.314
2	4.303	2.920
3	3.182	2.353
4	2.776	2.132
5	2.571	2.015
6	2.447	1.943
7	2.365	1.895
8	2.306	1.860
9	2.262	1.833
10	2.228	1.812
11	2.201	1.796
12	2.179	1.782
13	2.160	1.771
14	2.145	1.761
15	2.131	1.753
16	2.120	1.746
17	2.110	1.740
18	2.101	1.734
19	2.093	1.729
20	2.086	1.725
21	2.080	1.721
22	2.074	1.717
23	2.069	1.714
24	2.064	1.711
25	2.060	1.708
26	2.056	1.706
27	2.052	1.703
28	2.048	1.701
29	2.045	1.699
inf.	1.960	1.645

From E. S. Pearson and H. O. Hartley, *Biometrika Tables for Statisticians,* Vol. I, 3d ed., 1966 published by the Cambridge University Press. Reprinted with the permission of the Biometrika Trustees.

Coefficient of Determination

The **coefficient of determination,** abbreviated as r^2, is a measure of the percentage of the variation in the y's that can be attributed to the linear relationship with x. We know that the amount of a cost in a particular month depends on things other than volume of activity. We are developing a statistic which explains how much of the variation in cost is explained by variation in volume of activity.

In order to understand the meaning of r^2 it is necessary to step back and ask ourselves the question, "If we had only a set of historical cost data but no associated activity level, how would we estimate the amount of cost to be incurred in future periods?" To be more specific, suppose that you have the data in the "indirect labor cost" column of Exhibit 23-1 but no other information. You know that the data is monthly, but not which data goes with which month. More importantly, you do not know how many direct labor hours of activity were associated with each cost. How would you estimate the cost for next month? You might examine the data and look at the range, but that would not give you a single estimated amount. You might look to see if some amount had recurred a number of times, but in this case the amount has been different each month, so no one observation was any more frequent than any other. Probably you would decide to calculate the average cost and use that as the best estimator available given your limited information. You might feel uncomfortable making an estimate with such limited information, but the average would probably be the best estimate you could make.

Now consider the situation in which you have the results of a regression analysis. You can estimate the amount of indirect labor cost using the regression formula given a specific number of direct labor hours. You feel much more confident about the estimate because you had some logical basis for your prediction—that a higher volume of activity (as measured by direct labor hours) probably requires a higher indirect labor cost to serve the direct laborers.

With these ideas, we can examine the potential improvement of our estimate provided by the use of regression analysis. However, we need some definitions to express the idea.

let y = the actual cost observations (the indirect labor costs for each month)
$\bar{y}$ = the average of all the cost observations (simply add all the observations together and divide by the number of observations)
$\hat{y}$ = the predicted indirect labor cost using the regression equation

Now, we ask ourselves, what would be the errors in our estimate if we had predicted the actual indirect labor cost (the y's) using the average value ($\bar{y}$). For each month, the errors would be $(y - \bar{y})$. For statistical reasons the error measure we use is the squared error. So the total of the squares of the errors resulting from the cost estimates without regression is $\Sigma(y - \bar{y})^2$. This is the measure of the amount of error resulting from using the average value to estimate the total indirect labor cost. The estimate using regression analysis should be better than using the average as the estimate, but it will not be perfect. We measure the errors in the regression estimate in the same way by subtracting the predicted amount $\hat{y}$ at each level of activity from the actual amount, y at that activity level. Again for statistical reasons, we square the differences so the measure of error using the regression is $\Sigma(y - \hat{y})^2$. The final step is to calculate a ratio (you can think of it as a percentage) that shows how much we have improved the estimate. This is done by taking the difference between the error resulting from using the average and the error resulting from using the regression and dividing the difference by the error resulting from using the average. Algebraically, this is:[4]

Calculation of the coefficient of determination.

$$r^2 = \frac{\Sigma(y - \bar{y})^2 - \Sigma(y - \hat{y})^2}{\Sigma(y - \bar{y})^2}$$

[4] An alternative formulation is:

$$r^2 = 1 - \frac{\Sigma(y - \bar{y})^2}{\Sigma(y - \bar{y})^2} = 1 - \frac{\text{variance not related to regression line}}{\text{total variance}}$$

Thus, the coefficient of determination is an important statistic because it represents a measure of the percentage of the variation in the y's that can be attributed to the linear relationship with x.

The coefficient of determination can range between zero and one. If it is zero it means that we have made no improvement in the prediction, which is often expressed by saying that there is no linear relationship between indirect labor cost and direct labor hours. If it were equal to one, it would mean that there was a perfect linear relationship between the two variables, that all predictions using the regression formula had been exactly the same as the actual data. If the coefficient of determination were one, all historical costs would fall into a straight line when graphed. Exhibit 23-7 illustrates these concepts graphically. We would not expect to find this perfect association in practice, but we would hope to find r^2 as high as possible.

EXHIBIT 23-7
Graphs Illustrating
The Coefficient of Determination

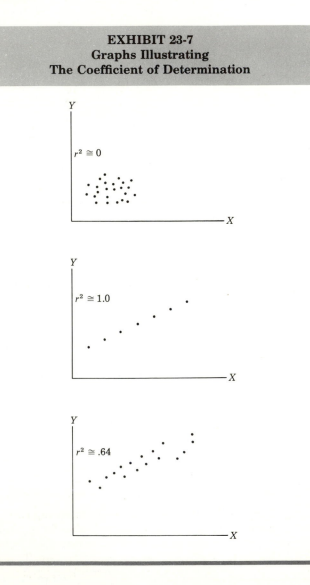

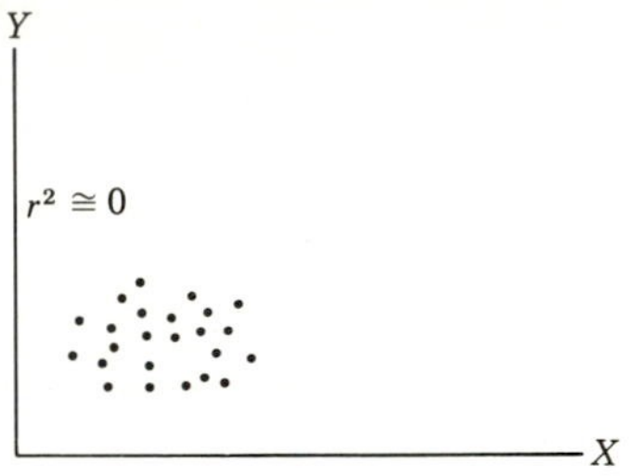

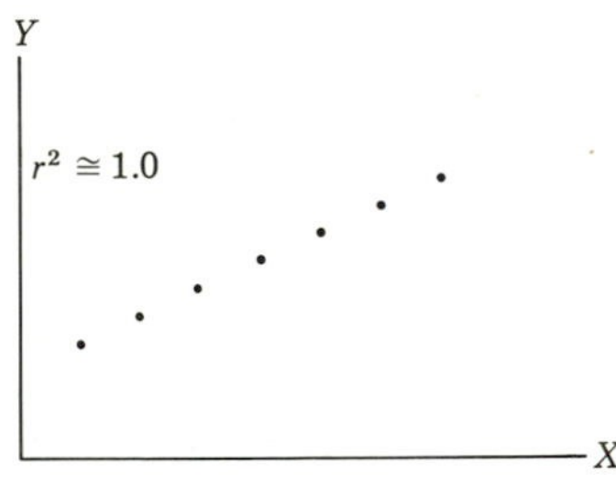

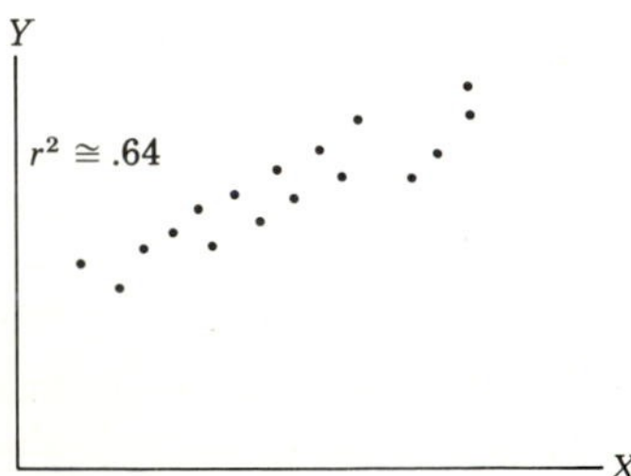

EXHIBIT 23-8
Assembly Center Data
Coefficient of Determination

x Actual	y Actual	$\hat{y}$ Estimate*	$y - \hat{y}$ Error	$(y - \hat{y})^2$ Squared Error	$y - \bar{y}$ Error	$(y - \bar{y})^2$ Squared Error
5,320	$ 1,560	$1,454	$ 106	11,236	$ 152	23,104
6,230	1,780	1,600	180	32,400	372	138,384
4,800	1,305	1,372	− 67	4,489	− 103	10,609
5,600	1,420	1,499	− 79	6,241	12	144
3,780	1,160	1,210	− 50	2,500	− 248	61,504
4,000	1,410	1,245	165	27,225	2	4
4,280	1,380	1,289	91	8,281	− 28	784
6,170	1,480	1,590	− 110	12,100	72	5,184
3,750	1,140	1,205	− 65	4,255	− 268	71,824
5,860	1,550	1,540	10	100	142	20,164
4,300	1,200	1,292	− 92	8,464	− 208	43,264
6,100	1,510	1,578	− 68	4,624	102	10,404
60,190	$16,895			121,915		385,373

$$\bar{y} = \frac{\$16,895}{12} = 1,408$$

$$r^2 = \frac{385,373 - 121,915}{385,373} = .68$$

* From $\hat{y} = \$609 + \$.159X$

For the asssembly center data, the coefficient of determination is .68 which means that 68% of the variation in the indirect labor cost can be attributed to the linear relationship with direct labor hours. The calculations are illustrated in Exhibit 23-8. Keep in mind that a high value of r^2 does not establish a cause-and-effect relationship. It merely provides an estimate of the strength of the linear relationship between the dependent and independent variables. Both variables might be a function of another variable and no cause-and-effect relationship may exist. For instance, the sales of refrigerators and dishwashers might be highly associated; however, we could not say that the sale of a refrigerator causes the sale of a dishwasher. Both variables have been found to be a function of housing starts.

High values of r^2 do not imply a cause-and-effect relationship.

Standard Error of the Regression Coefficient and Its t Value

Regression analysis assumes a linear relationship between y and x. The equation calculated for the assembly center implied that for each unit change in direct labor hours the indirect labor costs would increase by $.159. If there were no linear relationship between x and y, then b would be zero. To evaluate the significance of the association, a null hypothesis that $b = 0$ is evaluated. (The alternate hypothesis

Computation of the standard error of the regression coefficient.

is that $b \neq 0$.) To accomplish this, the standard error of the regression coefficient is needed and this statistic is calculated as follows:

$$S_b = \frac{S_e}{\sqrt{\Sigma(x - \bar{x})^2}}$$

Remember that S_e is the standard error of the estimate, the statistic we discussed a few pages ago and which we use to establish a confidence interval around the estimate of total cost.

To test the null hypothesis that $b = 0$, we need to calculate a t value which represents the number of standard errors the computed value of b lies away from zero. Such a statistic, called a ***t* value,** is calculated as follows:

$$t \text{ value} = \frac{b}{S_b}$$

EXHIBIT 23-9
Assembly Center Data
Standard Error of the Regression Coefficient and Its *t* Value

Month	x	$x - \bar{x}$	$(x - \bar{x})^2$
January	5,320	304	92,416
February	6,230	1,214	1,473,796
March	4,800	− 216	46,656
April	5,600	584	341,056
May	3,780	− 1,236	1,527,696
June	4,000	− 1,016	1,032,256
July	4,280	− 736	541,696
August	6,170	1,154	1,331,716
September	3,750	− 1,266	1,602,756
October	5,860	844	712,336
November	4,300	− 716	512,656
December	6,100	1,084	1,175,056
Totals	60,190		10,390,092

$$\bar{x} = \frac{60{,}190}{12} = 5{,}016$$

$$S_b = \frac{S_e^*}{\sqrt{\Sigma(x - \bar{x})^2}}$$

$$S_b = \frac{110}{\sqrt{10{,}390{,}092}} = \frac{110}{3{,}223} = .034$$

$$t = \frac{.159}{.034} = 4.676$$

* Calculated in Exhibit 23-5.

High t values indicate a linear relationship.

The higher the t value the more confidence we can have in accepting that a linear relationship exists between x and y. That is, the regression line does in fact have the slope b and not the slope zero. As a rule of thumb t values greater than 2.0 are indicators of acceptable reliability.

The calculations of the t value for the assembly center data are illustrated in Exhibit 23-9. The t value for the assembly center data is 4.676. The t value for the 95% confidence interval obtained from Exhibit 23-6 for 10 degrees of freedom is 2.228. Since the t value for the assembly center data is greater than the t value for the 95% confidence interval, management can be more than 95% confident that the true value of b is different from zero. Therefore, the hypothesis that $b = 0$ is rejected. It is highly likely that there is a linear relationship between x and y or in the example between direct labor hours and indirect labor cost.

MULTIPLE REGRESSION

In simple regression only one independent variable was used. In some cases it might be desirable to incorporate more than one independent variable in the analysis for greater accuracy in the estimate. Generally, this is expressed as a linear equation such as:

Multiple regression uses more than one independent variable.

$$y = a + b_1x_1 + b_2x_2 + b_3x_3 + \cdots + b_nx_n$$

where y is the dependent variable and the x_n's are the independent variables. The values of the b_n's represent the change in the value of y with each unit of change in the x_n's. To estimate the coefficients of the multiple regression equation (the b_n's), the least-squares technique is utilized in a procedure which basically is the same as with simple regression. That is, the objective is to minimize the sum of the squared differences. The calculations for multiple regression can become very complex and computer routines are used to find the coefficients.

As with simple regression, confidence intervals can be calculated using the standard error of the estimate. The coefficient of determination can be calculated to determine the percentage of change in y that is related to a change in all the x_i's. In multiple regression the value of r^2 is referred to as the "coefficient of multiple determination." Multiple since more than one independent variable is used.

t values can also be calculated for *each* of the coefficients in the multiple regression equation in order to determine if each coefficient's value is significantly different from zero. As in simple regression, the t values provide a measure of the confidence we can have that a linear relationship exists between each independent variable and the dependent variable.

To illustrate the application of multiple regression, assume the following data have been obtained from the accounting records concerning the sales of three products and the associated selling and administrative expenses.[5]

[5] Adapted from *The Accounting Review Supplement to Vol. XLVI* (American Accounting Association, 1971) pp. 229–231.

Periods	Sales ($000) Product A	Product B	Product C	Selling and Administrative Expense ($000)
1	$2,000	$400	$600	$450
2	1,940	430	610	445
3	1,950	380	630	445
4	1,860	460	620	438
5	1,820	390	640	433
6	1,860	440	580	437
7	1,880	420	570	438
8	1,850	380	580	434
9	1,810	390	580	430
10	1,770	290	610	425

Using a computerized regression routine with selling and administrative expenses being the dependent variable and the sales of each product being the independent variables, the following results were obtained:

Selling and administrative expense	**= $228. +**	**$.098** S_A **+**	**$.025** S_B **+**	**$.024** S_C
Standard error of the regression coefficients	**(3.45)**	**(.002)**	**(.002)**	**(.004)**
***t* values**	**66.0**	**49.0**	**12.5**	**6.0**
Standard error of the estimate	**.29**			
Coefficient of multiple determination	**= .98**			

With multiple regression, the coefficients in the regression formula represent the amount of change in the dependent variable with a one unit change in the independent variable. However, for this association to hold, the independent variables must not be highly correlated with each other. To evaluate this, the coefficients of determination can be calculated relating the independent variables. For the sales data, the coefficients of determination are:

Product A versus product B $r^2 = 0.17$
Product A versus product C $r^2 = 0.01$
Product B versus product C $r^2 = 0.02$

The low r^2's show that correlation among the independent variables will not present a problem. As a rule of thumb, if the r^2 between two independent variables exceeds .50, management should consider dropping one of the independent variables from the analysis.

THE ASSUMPTIONS OF REGRESSION ANALYSIS

There are a number of assumptions which are made in using regression to estimate costs. Some we have already mentioned. This section summarizes the five most important assumptions or conditions which should be met to make the regression reliable. They are:

1 Linearity
2 Constant variance
3 Normality
4 Autocorrelation
5 Multicollinearity

These problems can be identified by various plots of **residuals** which are produced by the computer programs used to do the regression. We will not teach you how to do the plots. But you should be able to recognize a problem that is shown by a plot and understand why it represents a problem for the managerial accountant.

Linearity

A linear relationship is assumed between y and x.

When regression analysis is used to develop an estimated cost function, a linear relationship between the dependent and independent variables is assumed. To examine the data for the appropriateness of a linear model a plot of standardized residuals versus the variable x can be used. Residuals are the differences between the actual data and the forecast data using the regression formula $(y - \hat{y})$. The residuals are standardized by dividing each residual by the standard error of the estimate (S_e).

If the linear model is appropriate, the plot will show the standardized residuals randomly distributed around zero. If the linear model is not appropriate, the residuals will show some systematic pattern. In Exhibit 23-10 we shall use a shaded area rather than the actual plots of the standardized residuals to represent the pattern formed by standardized residuals when plotted. The use of a shaded area makes the contrasts clearer. Exhibit 23-10*a* illustrates a residual plot where a linear model is appropriate. Exhibit 23-10*b* illustrates a plot where a curvilinear model would be appropriate.

Constant Variance

The variance in the y's is assumed to be the same for each value of x.

In using either simple or multiple regression analysis, the assumption is made that the residuals are from a normal probability distribution having a mean of zero and a variance that is constant for each value of the independent variable. When the variance is constant, the condition is referred to as homoscedasticity. If the variance is nonconstant (heteroscedasticity), the the t tests of the coefficients are incorrect and the reliability of the coefficients cannot be determined. This situation is likely to be encountered when the observations cover a wide range of activity since the variance of the cost observation is likely to be larger at higher levels of activity. For instance, the variability of the costs associated with the production of 100,000 autos is likely to be greater than the variability associated with 30,000 autos.

To examine the data for nonconstant error variance (heteroscedasticity) the plot of the standardized residuals versus x can be used. If the variance is constant for all values of x, the plot will appear as Exhibit 23-10*a*. If the variance is increasing with larger values of x, then the plot will appear as Exhibit 23-10*d* which illustrates the auto example discussed above where the variability of the cost is increasing as production volume increases. Another check for nonconstant error variance is to plot the residuals against the predicted values $\hat{y}$. If the variance is increasing as $\hat{y}$ increases, the plot will appear as in Exhibit 23-10*e*. This approach is particularly helpful when multiple regression is being used.

Normality

The residuals are assumed to be normally distributed.

Small deviations from normality among the residuals will not create any major problems. However, when considering the use of coefficients estimated by multiple regression, it is desirable to check the normality of the residuals. This can be accomplished by preparing a probability plot of the standardized residuals. A probability plot of the standardized residuals is in Exhibit 23-10*c*. The vertical axis represents the standardized residuals from the least-squares line. The horizontal axis represents the standardized residuals expected from a normal distribution. If the residuals from the least-squares line are normally distributed, they should appear as illustrated in Exhibit 23-10*c*.

Autocorrelation

The residuals are assumed to be independent.

Regression analysis assumes that the residuals are not autocorrelated. Autocorrelation in the residuals means the value of the residual in period t is partially determined by the residuals in periods $t - 1, t - 2, \ldots t - n$. The consequences of autocorrelated residuals has been summarized by Benston[6] as follows: (1) the standard errors of the regression coefficients will be seriously underestimated, (2) the sampling variances of the coefficients will be very large, and (3) predictions of cost made from the regression equation will be more variable than is ordinarily expected from least-squares estimators.

Autocorrelation is sometimes found in cost data because of the stickiness of costs when activity decreases. For instance, when production activity is increasing, overtime is utilized or additional employees are hired and the labor costs are behaving as a strictly variable cost. However, when the activity level starts to decrease the employees tend to spread the work out and the costs do not decrease in the same proportions as they increased. Managers do not lay off unneeded workers as quickly as the drop in workload would indicate. This makes costs "sticky" as volume declines. The cost tends to stick at its higher level rather than fall.

To check for autocorrelation the residuals can be plotted against time. Exhibit 23-10*f* illustrates the residual plot when no autocorrelation exists. Learning how to do the job better will also result in autocorrelations. Exhibit 23-10*g* represents a situation where some learning has taken place over time. This is illustrated by the positive residuals at the start of the process and negative residuals as the employees become more adept at performing their tasks.

[6] George Benston, "Multiple Regression Analysis of Cost Behavior," *Accounting Review* (October 1966) pp. 657–672.

EXHIBIT 23-10
Residual Plots for Evaluating The Assumptions of Regression Analysis

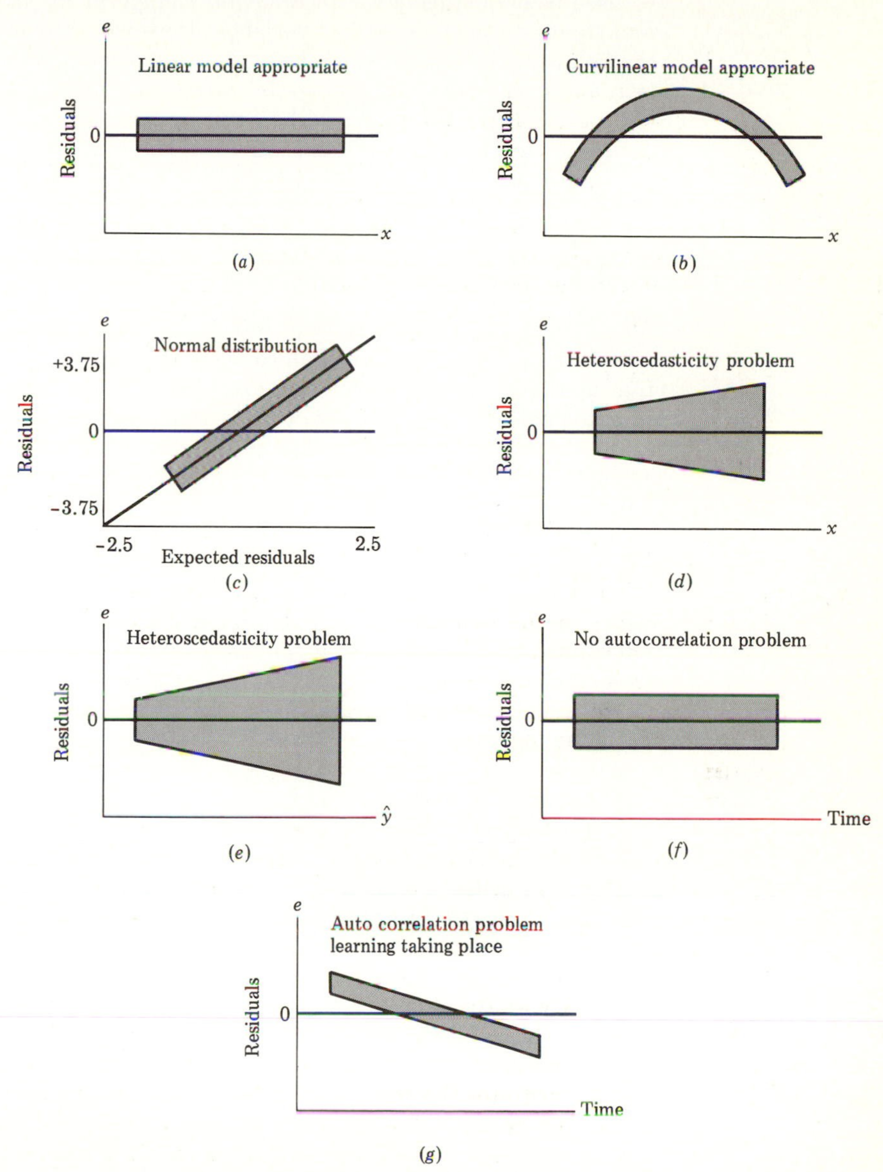

For a discussion of residual analysis see N. R. Draper and H. Smith, *Applied Regression Analysis,* 2d ed. (New York: John Wiley and Sons, Inc., 1981), p. 141.

Multicollinearity

No correlation is assumed between the independent variables with multiple regression.

When multiple regression is used, it is assumed that the independent variables are not correlated. If they are correlated, the condition is referred to as multicollinearity. Correlation between the independent variables means that the coefficients cannot be used as estimates of the incremental change in the dependent variable with a unit change in the independent variables. However, the complete regression function can be used to estimate the total costs so long as the independent variables continue to remain correlated. In managerial accounting terms, if multicollinearity exists, the total cost prediction would be accurate as long as the independent variables remained correlated in the same way. But the individual coefficients would not be good estimates of the variable cost per unit of the independent variable.

LEARNING CURVES

Many times when a process is started it will take the employees longer to perform a task than after they have gained some experience. And studies have confirmed that up to a certain point the more experience the employee has the less time it will take to perform the task. Exhibit 23-11 is a graph of how the average time per unit decreases as more units are produced. The line graphed in Exhibit 23-11 is referred to as a **learning curve** since it represents the improvement in the employees' abilities as a result of experience in performing a task (learning). The steady state

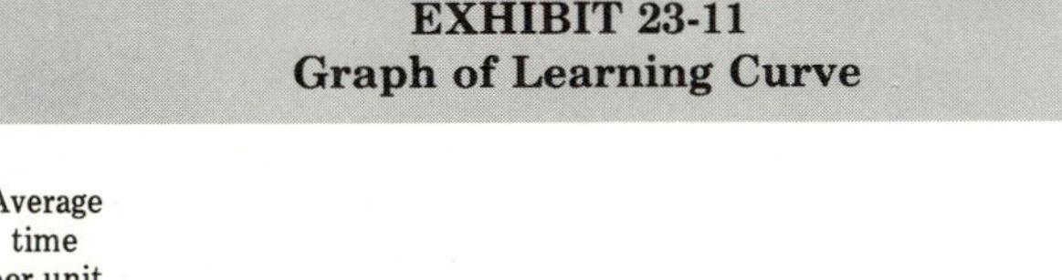

EXHIBIT 23-11
Graph of Learning Curve

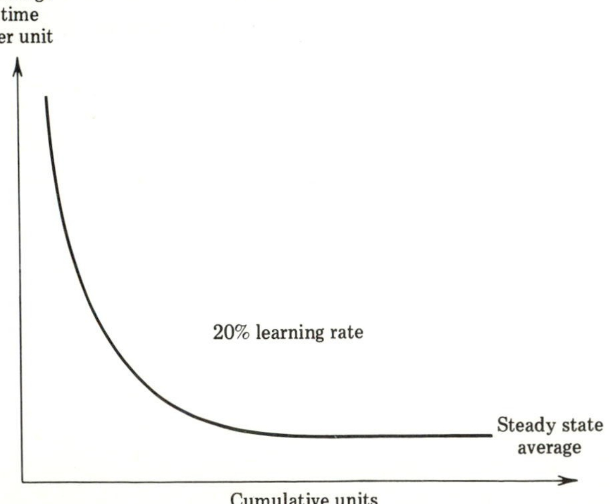

The line shows the relationship between the average time per unit and the total number of units of the same kind produced. The line slopes downward to the right to show that as the total number of units increases learning should be expected to reduce the average time per unit.

average represents the point where learning no longer has an impact on the average time to complete a unit; that is, the average time (and cost) per unit becomes a straight horizontal line.

To illustrate the learning curve concept, assume a company is starting the production of a new product and the first batch of 40 units requires an average of 20 hours per unit for a total 800 hours. When the cumulative units produced doubles, the average time for all units produced will be 80% of the average of the first batch if we also assume a 20% **learning rate.** Assuming the second batch contains 40 units, the cumulative average time for producing each of the 80 units now produced is .8 × 20 hours or 16 hours. The total time for the production of the 80 units is thus 1,280 hours (16 × 80). Since the first 40 units required 800 hours, the second batch of 40 units required only an additional 480 hours (1,280 − 800). The calculation for 320 units is illustrated below:[7]

Experience reduces the amount of time it takes an employee to perform a task.

Cumulative Units	Average Time per Unit	Total Time for Cumulative Units
40	20	800
80	16(.8 × 20)	1,280
160	12.8(.8 × 16)	2,048
320	10.24(.8 × 12.8)	3,276.8

The key to understanding the table is to notice that the amount in the cumulative units column is doubling each time. And each time the number of cumulative units doubles, the average time per unit for the total number of units drops by 20% with a 20% learning rate. Rather than taking the old average time and subtracting 20%, we multiply the old average time by 0.8 or (1.0 − 20%) because the arithmetic is simpler.

Whether the learning rate is 10%, 20%, 30%, or some other percentage depends on the complexity of the process and how workers learn. Each company has to estimate the learning rate for a process based on its past experience with similar production situations.

Learning curves can be very important in budgeting costs for products where only a few relatively costly products are being produced. The airplane manufacturing industry is one which has made extensive use of the concept. The company may produce 300 planes of a certain model. Since the cost of producing the first plane may exceed $50 million, it is important for management to predict what will happen to the cost per plane as learning occurs over the time the 300 planes are built.

The learning curve applies to the amount of time required to produce a unit. Since costs like direct labor, indirect labor, power, and similar costs depend on the amount of time required, we would expect these costs per unit to decline as learning takes place. Other costs, however, do not depend on the length of production time and we would not expect these costs to decline. Examples of costs which are not affected by the learning curve are direct materials and fixed costs such as supervisory salaries.

[7] This learning process can be described mathematically by an exponential function of the following form:

$$Y = a X^b$$

where Y = *cumulative average* amount of time to complete X units
a = amount of time to complete the first unit or batch
X = total number of units or batches completed
b = an index based on the learning rate

SUMMARY

The actual costs observed from a production process form a probability distribution due to the random nature of the production process. The cost estimation process can be based on an engineering analysis of the production operations or an analysis of the historical data.

The engineering analysis is a normative approach and attempts to determine what the costs should be. This approach generally produces good estimates and is usually only applied to direct labor and direct materials costs.

In developing cost estimates from historical data, the accounting and production records should be thoroughly analyzed prior to any computations to either eliminate or adjust any unrepresentative data. Two simple approaches to cost estimation are the high-low and graphic methods. Both of these methods can produce reasonable estimates in some situations. However, there is no way to evaluate the quality of the estimate produced by these methods.

Regression analysis generally requires a computer to use, but it is an objective method which uses all available data and also provides additional important pieces of information, the percentage of the total variation in cost linearly related to the activity measure, the standard error of the estimate, and the significance of the relationship through the t value. Regression analysis is based on several assumptions and the validity of each assumption should be evaluated prior to using the cost function resulting from regression.

During the start-up phase of many projects, employees improve their skills as they produce more and more units. Improvement continues until a steady state is reached and the average production time per unit levels off. In these situations, learning curve concepts should be used to estimate the costs of production.

Review Problem

Computations for Simple Regression* The ABC Company has obtained the following data concerning sales and selling and administration expenses from the accounting records.

Year	Sales ($000)	Selling and Administrative Expenses ($000)
19X1	$3,000	$450
19X2	2,980	445
19X3	2,960	445
19X4	2,940	438
19X5	2,850	433
19X6	2,880	437
19X7	2,870	438
19X8	2,810	434
19X9	2,780	430
19X0	2,670	425

* Adapted from *The Accounting Review Supplement to Vol. XLVI* (American Accounting Association, 1971), pp. 229–231.

The company would like you to calculate a regression equation that could be used to determine the selling and administrative expense given an estimate of total sales. An analysis of the useability of the regression equation is also requested. To aid you in the computations the following data have been prepared.

Year	x Sales	y S&A Expenses	x^2	xy	$(y-\hat{y})^2$	$(y-\bar{y})^2$	$(x-\bar{x})^2$
19X1	$ 3,000	$ 450	9,000,000	1,350,000	12.96	144	15,876
19X2	2,980	445	8,880,400	1,326,100	.00	49	11,236
19X3	2,960	445	8,761,600	1,317,200	1.96	49	7,396
19X4	2,940	438	8,643,600	1,287,720	16.81	0	4,356
19X5	2,850	433	8,122,500	1,234,050	7.84	25	576
19X6	2,880	437	8,294,400	1,258,560	.85	1	36
19X7	2,870	438	8,236,900	1,257,060	.61	0	16
19X8	2,810	434	7,896,100	1,219,540	1.00	16	4,096
19X9	2,780	430	7,728,400	1,195,400	.76	64	8,836
19X0	2,670	425	7,128,900	1,134,750	3.53	169	41,616
	$28,740	$4,375	82,692,800	12,580,380	46.32	517	94,040

Residual graphs and a probability plot are presented on pages 658 and 659.

Solution

The computations of the regression coefficients and statistics to analyze the useability of the regression equation are as follows:

$$b = \frac{N\Sigma(xy) - \Sigma x \Sigma y}{N\Sigma x^2 - (\Sigma x)^2} = \frac{10(12{,}580{,}380) - 28{,}740(4{,}375)}{10(82{,}692{,}800) - (28{,}740)^2}$$

$$= \$.071 \text{ per dollar of sales}$$

$$a = \frac{\Sigma y - b\Sigma x}{N} = \frac{4{,}375 - .071(28{,}740)}{10}$$

$$= \$233 \text{ per year (\$000 omitted)}$$

$$r^2 = \frac{\Sigma(y-\bar{y})^2 - \Sigma(y-\hat{y})^2}{\Sigma(y-\bar{y})^2} = \frac{517 - 46.32}{517}$$

$$= .91$$

$$S_e = \sqrt{\frac{\Sigma(y-\hat{y})^2}{N-2}} = \sqrt{\frac{46.32}{10-2}}$$

$$= \$2.41 \text{ (\$000 omitted)}$$

$$S_b = \frac{S_e}{\sqrt{\Sigma(x-\bar{x})^2}} = \frac{2.41}{\sqrt{94{,}040}}$$

$$= .008$$

$$t = \frac{b}{S_b} = \frac{.071}{.008}$$

$$= 8.88$$

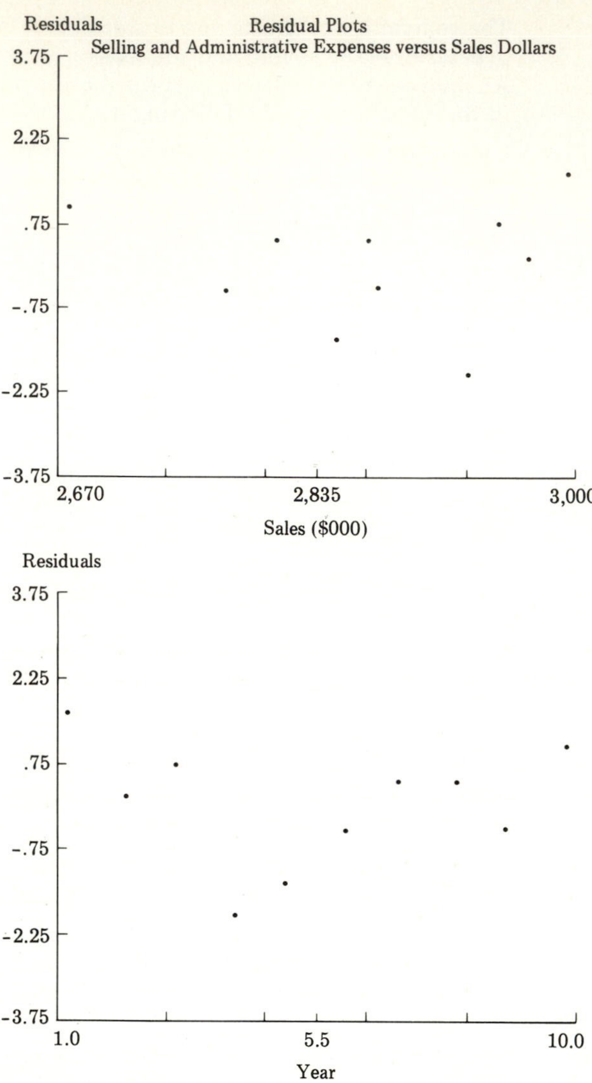

The data for selling and administrative expenses produced a high value for r^2 indicating that 91% of the variability in selling and administrative expenses is associated with the variability in sales volume. The t value of 8.88 indicates the value of b is a good estimate of the association between the two variables.

An examination of the residual plots indicates that the assumptions underlying regression analysis are satisfied by the data except for the common problem of heteroscedasticity. The second plot shows a random scatter, indicating no autocorrelation. (See Exhibit 23-10*f*.) The first plot appears to show a widening trend as the X values increase indicating a possible heteroscedasticity problem. (See Exhibit 23-10*d*.) The final plot shows the residuals forming close to a straight line, the hoped-for pattern. (See Exhibit 23-10*c*.)

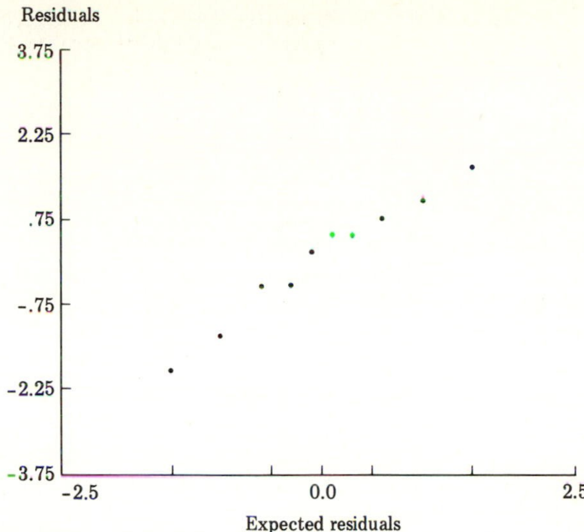

While the heteroscedasticity raises questions, it frequently appears in cost data. The other indications are quite favorable and the regression is probably the best that can be found.

Glossary

Coefficient of determination A measure of the percentage of the total variation in the dependent variable that is associated with the variation in the independent variable.

Engineering cost estimates Cost estimates that result from an engineering analysis of the manufacturing process. These analyses are usually performed only for direct materials and direct labor.

Graphic analysis of cost A procedure for developing a cost estimate where the historical data are plotted and a straight estimating line is drawn to come as close to as many of the data points as possible.

High-low analysis of cost A procedure for developing a cost estimate where the straight estimating line is drawn on a graph connecting two widely separated cost observations (often the highest and lowest cost).

Learning curve An exponential function that describes the decrease in the average production time per unit as the cumulative production volume increases.

Learning rate The rate of change in the cumulative average time per unit as the number of units produced doubles.

Regression analysis The process of fitting a line to a set of historical data to minimize the sum of the squared differences between the line and the data.

Residuals The vertical differences between the regression line and the actual historical data. A graphical analysis of the residuals can be used to evaluate the assumptions of regression analysis.

Standard error of the estimate A dispersion measure of the actual observations around the regression line. It can be used to calculate confidence intervals for the estimated data.

***t* value** The number of standardized standard errors the computed value of the regression coefficients lie away from zero. It is used to test the null hypothesis that $b = 0$.

Questions and Problems

23-1 If production is held constant at 10,000 units per month, what factors might cause the labor cost to range between $70,000 and $80,000?

23-2 The engineering approach to cost estimation generally produces an excellent cost estimate. What other benefits accrue to the organization from the use of the engineering approach?

23-3 Why is the engineering approach only applied to the major cost elements?

23-4 Discuss three factors that can render historical cost observations useless for cost estimating.

23-5 The coefficient of determination indicates the amount of variation in the dependent variable that is associated with variation in the independent variable. Provide a brief explanation of why the coefficient of determination is calculated as it is.

23-6 Identify and discuss the assumptions of regression analysis.

23-7 Describe two situations where the learning curve would be the appropriate cost function for estimating the direct labor cost of producing a product.

23-8 Would the learning curve concept be applicable to the estimation of direct materials cost? Explain.

23-9 **High-Low Method** The Nolan Company has experienced the following sales volume and expenses for the last six months.

	Selling Expense	Sales Dollars
January	$ 876	$4,400
February	1,112	6,123
March	1,100	5,284
April	1,200	6,500
May	1,300	6,700
June	870	4,300

Ms. Nolan is concerned as to what the selling expenses will be for the next six months.

Required

1 Use the high-low method to determine the formula of a line for forecasting selling expenses.

2 Use the formula to forecast selling expense for each of the following six months assuming sales are forecasted as follows:

July	$7,200	October	$6,300
August	6,500	November	7,500
September	8,100	December	7,300

3 What would be your main concern about your forecast for the month of September? Would you have similar concerns for other months?

23-10 Interpreting Residual Plots The Saw Company used simple regression analysis to estimate the cost function for a process started six months ago. The residuals from the analysis (which was based on weekly data) are presented below:

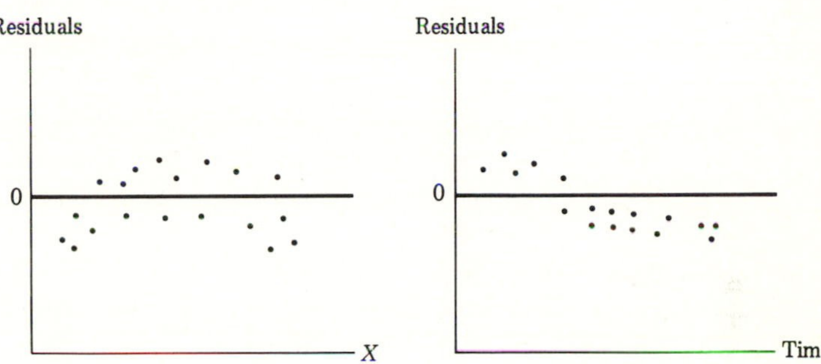

Required

What do the two plots of the residuals tell you about the cost function. *Hint:* Refer to Exhibit 23-10.

23-11 Comparing the High-Low and Graphic Methods The Ann Company has selected the following information from their accounting records:

	Labor Hours	Overhead Cost
January	6,000	$1,800
February	4,800	1,630
March	7,080	1,750
April	8,000	1,900
May	4,000	1,400
June	6,070	1,690
July	6,050	1,710
August	6,200	1,740
September	8,100	1,960
October	10,100	2,200
November	13,000	3,200
December	12,900	2,800

Required

1 Using the high-low method, estimate a cost function for the overhead cost.

2 Plot the data and visually fit a line to the data. Calculate the cost function for the overhead cost.

3 Evaluate the function computed in part 1 compared with the results of part 2.

23-12 Multiple Choice—High-Low Approach Maintenance expenses of a company are to be analyzed for the purpose of constructing a flexible budget. Examination of past records disclosed the following costs and volume measures:

	Highest	Lowest
Cost per month	$39,200	$32,000
Machine hours	24,000	15,000

1 Using the high-low point method of analysis, the estimated variable cost per machine hour is
  a $1.25 **c** $0.80
  b $12.50 **d** $0.08

2 Using the high-low technique the estimated annual fixed cost for maintenance expenditures is
  a $35,600 **c** $30,800
  b $13,250 **d** $20,000

3 Adams Corporation has developed the following flexible budget formula for annual indirect labor cost:

Total cost = $4,800 + $0.50 per machine hour

Operating budgets for the current month are based upon 20,000 hours of planned machine time. Indirect labor costs included in this planning budget are
  a $14,800 **c** $14,400
  b $10,000 **d** $10,400

23-13 Multiple Choice—Regression Approach Labor hours and production costs for the last four months of 19X9, which you believe are representative for the year, were as follows:

Month	Labor Hours	Total Production Costs
September	2,500	$ 20,000
October	3,500	25,000
November	4,500	30,000
December	3,500	25,000
Total	14,000	$100,000

Based upon the above information and using the least-squares method of computation with the letters listed below, select the best answer for each of questions 1 through 5.

Let a = fixed production costs per month
b = variable production costs per labor hour
n = number of months
x = labor hours per month
y = total monthly production costs
Σ = summation

1 The equation(s) required for applying the least-squares method of computation of fixed and variable production costs could be expressed

a $\Sigma xy = a\Sigma x + b\Sigma x^2$
b $\Sigma y = na + b\Sigma x$
c $y = a + bx^2$
$\Sigma y = na + b\Sigma x$
d $\Sigma xy = a\Sigma x + b\Sigma x^2$
$\Sigma y = na + b\Sigma x$

2 The cost function derived by the least-squares method

a would be linear
b must be tested for minima and maxima
c would be parabolic
d would indicate maximum costs at the point of the function's point of inflection

3 Monthly production costs could be expressed

a $y = ax + b$ **c** $y = b + ax$
b $y = a + bx$ **d** $y = \Sigma a + bx$

4 Using the least-squares method of computation, the fixed monthly production cost is

a \$10,000 **c** \$7,500
b \$9,500 **d** \$5,000

5 Using the least-squares method of computation, the variable production cost per labor hour is

a \$6.00 **c** \$3.00
b \$5.00 **d** \$2.00

(CPA)

23-14 Comparison of High-Low and Regression Approaches The Ramon Co. manufactures a wide range of products at several different plant locations. The Franklin plant, which manufactures electrical components, has been experiencing some difficulties with fluctuating monthly overhead costs. The fluctuations have made it difficult to estimate the level of overhead that will be incurred for any one month.

Management wants to be able to estimate overhead costs accurately in order to plan its operation and financial needs better. A trade association publication to which Ramon Co. subscribes indicates that, for companies manufacturing electrical components, overhead tends to vary with direct labor hours.

Another member of the accounting staff suggested that a good starting place for determining the cost behavior pattern of overhead costs would be an analysis of historical data. The historical cost behavior pattern would provide a basis for estimating future overhead costs. The methods proposed for determining the cost behavior pattern included the high-low method, the graphic method, simple linear regression, and multiple regression. Of these methods Ramon Co. decided to employ the high-low method and the simple linear regression. Data on direct labor hours and the respective overhead costs incurred were collected for the past two years. The raw data are as follows:

19X3	**Direct Labor Hours**	**Overhead Costs**
January	20,000	$84,000
February	25,000	99,000
March	22,000	89,500
April	23,000	90,000
May	20,000	81,500
June	19,000	75,500
July	14,000	70,500
August	10,000	64,500
September	12,000	69,000
October	17,000	75,000
November	16,000	71,500
December	19,000	78,000
19X4		
January	21,000	$86,000
February	24,000	93,000
March	23,000	93,000
April	22,000	87,000
May	20,000	80,000
June	18,000	76,500
July	12,000	67,500
August	13,000	71,000
September	15,000	73,500
October	17,000	72,500
November	15,000	71,000
December	18,000	75,000

Using linear regression, the following data were obtained:

Coefficient of determination	.9109
Coefficients of regression equation	
Constant	39,859
Independent variable	2.1549
Standard error of the estimate	2,840
Standard error of the regression coefficient for the independent variable	.1437

t statistic for a 95% confidence interval (22 degrees of freedom) from the table	2.074

Required

1 Using the high-low method, determine the cost function for overhead costs for the Franklin plant.

2 Using the results of the regression analysis, calculate the estimate of overhead costs for 22,500 direct labor hours.

3 Calculate a 95% confidence interval for the estimate of the overhead cost for 22,500 direct labor hours.

4 Of the two proposed methods (high-low, linear regression), which one should Ramon Co. employ to determine the historical cost behavior pattern of Franklin plant's overhead costs? Explain your answer completely, indicating the reason why the other method should not be used.

(CMA)

23-15 Multiple Choice—Using Regression Results The Alpha Company which produces several different products is making plans for the introduction of a new product which it will sell for $6 a unit. The following estimates have been made for manufacturing costs of 100,000 units to be produced the first year:

Direct materials	$50,000	
Direct labor	$40,000	(the labor rate is $4 an hour)

Overhead costs have not yet been estimated for the new product but monthly data on total production and overhead cost for the past 24 months have been analyzed using simple linear regression. The following results were derived from the simple regression and will provide the basis for overhead cost estimates for the new product.

Simple Regression Analysis Results ($y = a + bx$)
Dependent variable (y)—Factory overhead costs
Independent variable (x)—Direct labor hours

Computed values	
y-intercept	$40,000
Coefficient of independent variable	$2.10
Coefficient of determination	.908
Standard error of estimate	$ 2,840
Standard error of regression coefficient	.42
Mean value of independent variable	$18,000

1 What percentage of the variation in overhead costs is explained by the independent variable?
- a 90.8%
- b 42%
- c 48.8%
- d 95.3%
- e Some other amount than those shown above

2 To determine a confidence interval for the parameter estimated by b in the regression computation, an appropriate t value would be selected from a table of values from Student's t distribution corresponding to the desired level of confidence and having

a 0 degrees of freedom
b 2 degrees of freedom
c 10 degrees of freedom
d 22 degrees of freedom
e 24 degrees of freedom

3 Assuming that the appropriate t value is 2.07, a 95% confidence interval for the b values would be

a (1.23, 2.97)
b (.10, 4.10)
c (2.1, 2.97)
d (.22, 3.97)
e Some amount other than those shown above

4 The total overhead cost for an estimated activity level of 20,000 direct labor hours would be

a $42,000
b $82,000
c $122,000
d $222,000
e Some other amount than those shown above

5 The expected contribution margin per unit to be earned during the first year on 100,000 units of the new product would be

a $4.49
b $4.89
c $0.30
d $5.10
e Some amount other than those shown above

(CMA)

23-16 Evaluating the Results of Regression Analysis The controller of the Connecticut Electronics Company believes that the identification of the variable and fixed components of the firm's costs will enable the firm to make better planning and control decisions. Among the costs the controller is concerned about is the behavior of indirect supplies expense. He believes there is some correlation between the machine hours worked and the amount of indirect supplies used.

A member of the controller's staff has suggested that a simple linear regression model be used to determine the cost behavior of the indirect supplies. The regression equation shown below was developed from 40 pairs of observations using the least-squares method of regression. The regression function and related measures are as follows:

$$S = \$200 + \$4H$$

where S = total monthly costs of indirect supplies
H = machine hours per month

Standard error of estimate: $S_e = 100$
Coefficient of determination: $r^2 = .76$

Required

1 When a simple linear regression model is used to make inferences about a population relationship from sample data, what assumptions must be made before the inferences can be accepted as valid?

2 Assume the assumptions identified in requirement 1 are satisfied for the indirect supplies expense of Connecticut Electronics Company.

a Explain the meaning of "200" and "4" in the regression function $S = \$200 + \$4H$.

b Calculate the estimated cost of indirect supplies if 900 machine hours are to be used during a month.

c In addition to the estimate for the cost of indirect supplies, the controller would like the range of values for the estimate if a 95% confidence interval is specified. He would use this range to judge whether the estimated costs indicated by the regression analysis were good enough for planning purposes. Calculate, for 900 machine hours, the range of the estimate for the cost of indirect supplies with a 95% confidence interval.
Hint: You need to use data from Exhibit 23-6.

3 Explain briefly

a What the coefficient of determination measures.

b What the value of the coefficient of determination ($r^2 = .76$) indicates in this case if Connecticut Electronics Company wishes to predict the total cost of indirect supplies on the basis of estimated machine hours.

(CMA)

23-17 Selecting a Regression Equation The Alma Plant manufactures the industrial product line of CJS Industries. Plant management wants to be able to get a good, yet quick, estimate of the manufacturing overhead costs which can be expected to be incurred each month. The easiest and simplest method to accomplish this task appears to be to develop a flexible budget formula for the manufacturing overhead costs.

The plant's accounting staff suggested that simple linear regression be used to determine the cost behavior pattern of the overhead costs. The regression data can provide the basis for the flexible budget formula. Sufficient evidence is available to conclude that manufacturing overhead costs vary with direct labor hours. The actual direct labor hours and the corresponding manufacturing overhead costs for each month of the last three years were used in the linear regression analysis.

The three-year period contained various occurrences not uncommon to many businesses. During the first year production was severely curtailed during two months because of wildcat strikes. In the second year production was reduced in one month because of material shortages and increased (overtime scheduled) during two months to meet the units required for a one-time sales order. At the end of the second year, employee benefits were raised significantly as the result of a labor agreement. Production during the third year was not affected by any special circumstances.

Various members of Alma's accounting staff raised some issues regarding the historical data collected for the regression analysis. These issues were as follows:

1 Some members of the accounting staff believed that the use of data from all 36 months would provide a more accurate portrayal of the cost behavior. While they recognized that any of the monthly data could include efficiencies and inefficiencies, they believed these efficiencies/inefficiencies would tend to balance out over a longer period of time.

2 Other members of the accounting staff suggested that only those months which were considered normal should be used so that the regression would not be distorted.

3 Still other members felt that only the most recent 12 months should be used because they were the most current.

4 Some members questioned whether historical data should be used at all to form the basis for a flexible budget formula.

The accounting department ran two regression analyses of the data—one using the data from all 36 months and the other using only the data from the last 12 months. The information derived from the two linear regressions is shown below.

Least-Squares Regression Analyses

	Data from All 36 Months	Data from Most Recent 12 Months
Coefficients of the regression equation:		
Constant	\$123,810	\$109,020
Independent variable (DLH)	\$1.6003	\$4.1977
Coefficient of determination	.2218	.4748
Standard error of the estimate	13,003	7,473
Standard error of the regression coefficient for the independent variable	.9744	1.3959
Calculated *t* statistic for the regression coefficient	1.6423	3.0072
t statistic required for a 95% confidence interval with		
34 degrees of freedom (36 − 2)		
10 degrees of freedom (12 − 2)	1.960	2.228

Required

1 From the results of Alma plant's regression analysis which used the data from the last 12 months:

a Formulate the flexible budget formula to estimate monthly manufacturing overhead costs.

b Calculate the estimate of overhead costs for a month when 25,000 direct labor hours are worked.

2 Using *only* the results of the two regression analyses, explain which of the two results (12 months versus 36 months) you would use as a basis for the flexible budget formula.

3 How would the four specific issues raised by the members of Alma's accounting staff influence your willingness to use the results of the statistical analyses as the basis for the flexible budget formula? Explain your answer.

(CMA)

23-18 Interpreting and Using the Results of Regression Analysis The Johnstar Co. makes a very expensive chemical product. The production costs average about $1,000 per pound and the product sells for $2,500 per pound. The material is very dangerous. Therefore, it is made each day to fill the customer orders for the day. Failure to deliver the quantity required results in a shutdown for the customers and high-cost penalty for Johnstar (plus customer ill will).

Predicting the final weight of a batch of the chemical being processed has been a serious problem. This is critical because of the serious cost of failure to meet customer needs.

A consultant recommended that the batches be weighed one-half way through the six-hour processing period. He proposed that linear regression be used to predict the final weight from the midpoint weight. If the prediction indicated that too little of the chemical would be available, then a new batch could be started and still delivered in time to satisfy customers' needs for the day.

Included in the report of a study made by the consultant during a one-week period were the following items:

Observation No.	Weight in Pounds at 3 Hours	Final Weight in Pounds	Observation No.	Weight in Pounds at 3 Hours	Final Weight in Pounds
1	55	90	11	60	80
2	45	75	12	35	60
3	40	80	13	35	80
4	60	80	14	55	60
5	40	45	15	35	75
6	60	80	16	50	90
7	50	80	17	30	60
8	55	95	18	60	105
9	50	100	19	50	60
10	35	75	20	20	30

Data from the regression analysis:

Coefficient of determination	0.4126
Coefficient of the regression equation	
Constant	28.6
Independent variable	1.008
Standard error of the estimate	14.2
Standard error of the regression coefficient for the independent variable	0.2796
The t statistic for a 95% confidence interval (18 degrees of freedom)	2.101

Required

1 Using the results of the regression analysis by the consultant, calculate the estimated weight of today's first batch which weighs 42 pounds at the end of three hours processing time.

2 Customer orders for today total 68 pounds. The nature of the process is such that the smallest batch that can be started will weigh at least 20 pounds at the end of six hours. Using only the data from the regression analysis, would you start another batch? (Remember that today's first batch weighed 42 pounds at the end of three hours.)

3 Is the relationship between the variables such that this regression analysis provides an adequate prediction model for the Johnstar Co.? Explain your answer.

(CMA)

23-19 Computations for Regression Analysis The Barrett Company is attempting to estimate the cost of producing a new machine part. Based on an engineering analysis the estimated material and labor costs are as follows:

Material	3 pounds @ $2.00/pound	$6.00
Labor	2 hours @ $6.00/hour	$12.00

They are having difficulty, though, with estimating the amount of variable overhead that will be incurred in the production of the machine part. From the historical records the accountant has provided you with the following data for the past 10 months:

Month	Machine Hours	Factory Overhead Cost
1	890	$4,800
2	950	5,020
3	1,080	5,500
4	1,170	6,000
5	1,210	5,800
6	1,300	6,090
7	1,350	6,010
8	1,380	7,020
9	1,450	6,500
10	1,490	6,600

Required

1 Using the machine hours and factory overhead cost data:
 a Prepare a graph.
 b Estimate the cost using the graphic method.
 c Use least-squares analysis to estimate the cost.
 d Compare the two cost estimates.

2 Assuming that it will take four machine hours to produce one part, how much variable overhead should be assigned to each part?

3 What is the estimated total variable cost for the production of 300 machine parts?

23-20 Computations for Regression Analysis: Computer Program Required The XYZ Company wishes to estimate a cost function for their selling and administrative expenses. During the past two years they have been recording their expenses and sales figures on a monthly basis. From the accounting records the following data have been provided.

Month	Sales Dollars	Selling and Administrative Expenses
1	$ 450,000	$ 40,500
2	480,700	46,000
3	510,000	51,000
4	590,000	58,050
5	600,000	69,000
6	625,000	69,010
7	650,000	72,000
8	720,000	77,050
9	750,000	79,010
10	780,000	80,020
11	790,125	81,080
12	780,130	82,090
13	801,250	83,078
14	811,350	84,040
15	820,900	88,017
16	810,250	92,525
17	845,500	93,050
18	875,400	98,060
19	890,150	102,000
20	1,000,000	107,000
21	1,100,000	112,000
22	1,200,000	115,000
23	1,500,000	120,000
24	1,600,000	135,000

Required

1 Using the least-squares analysis estimate a cost function for the selling and administrative expense data.

2 Calculate the
a Coefficient of determination
b t value for the b coefficient

3 If the estimated annual sales are $1,550,000, what would be the estimated selling and administrative expense?

23-21 Calculations for Multiple Regression Analysis: Computer Program Required The MRP Company produces and sells two products. They have been collecting sales data by product but the selling and administrative expenses have only been collected in total. For pricing purposes the company would like to know the variable selling and administrative expenses associated with each product. From the accounting records you are provided with the following data:

Month	Sales Units: Product 1	Sales Units: Product 2	Selling and Administrative Expenses
1	2,250	6,000	$50,125
2	2,380	7,500	55,500
3	2,500	7,800	58,125
4	2,700	8,300	62,155
5	3,450	8,450	63,175
6	3,780	9,625	65,000
7	3,920	9,875	72,130
8	4,300	10,000	73,125
9	4,650	12,000	80,000
10	4,800	13,500	82,000

Required

1 Using multiple regression estimate a cost function for the selling and administrative expenses.

2 What is the variable selling and administrative expense for each product?

23-22 Learning Curve Computations The Leach Company is starting the production of a new product. They plan on producing the product in batches of 100 units. The first run of 100 units required 200 labor hours of production time. Based on historical experience, the company expects to have a learning curve with a 20% learning rate for labor hours.

Required

Prepare a schedule showing the average time per unit and total time for cumulative units for the production of 200, 400, and 800 cumulative units.

23-23 Learning Curve Computations for Bid Preparation The Burns Company is manufacturing a special part for the Raleigh Corporation. The first batch of 500 parts produced resulted in the following costs:

Direct materials 1,000 pounds @ $2.00/pound	$ 2,000
Direct labor 2,000 hours @ $5.00/hour	10,000
Variable overhead 160% of direct labor cost	16,000
Fixed manufacturing expenses (special dies)	10,000
Total cost	$38,000

The Raleigh Corporation would like the Burns Company to produce an additional 1,500 units in batches of 500 each and has asked them to prepare a bid for the additional units. In analyzing the situation, Burns would like to prepare a bid that would ensure a $20,000 contribution margin on the new order. Burns feels that the special dies used for the first 500 units will be usable for the additional 1,500 units. Based on previous experience, Burns estimates that the employees should experience a 20% learning rate for this job.

Required

Prepare an estimate of the bid that Burns should submit to the Raleigh Corporation.

23-24 Choosing the Independent Variables* The ABC Company produces three products in two departments. The direct labor hours required for production of the products are given below:

	Product		
	A	B	C
Department 1	.500	.250	.333
Department 2	.250	.125	.750

The accounting records have provided the following information concerning direct labor cost and overhead cost.

	Direct Labor Cost ($000)			Overhead Cost ($000)		
Year	Department 1	Department 2	Total	Department 1	Department 2	Total
19X1	$140	$170	$310	$341	$434	$775
19X2	135	150	285	340	421	761
19X3	140	160	300	342	428	770
19X4	130	150	280	339	422	761
19X5	130	155	285	338	425	763
19X6	125	140	265	337	414	751
19X7	120	150	270	335	420	755
19X8	115	140	255	334	413	747
19X9	120	140	260	336	414	750
19X0	115	135	250	335	410	745

Using the above data two different regressions have been made to estimate the overhead expense. First, total overhead cost had been found as a function of total direct labor dollars.

Overhead cost	=	$617	+ $.51 DL$
Standard error		(4,100)	(.01)
t values		150	51
Standard error of the estimate		.71	
Coefficient of determination		.98	

Second, overhead for each department has been found as a function of the direct labor dollars in each department.

	Department 1		Department 2	
Overhead expense	= $301.4	+ .29 DL$$_1$	$316.1	+ $.70 DL$$_2$
Standard error	(2.35)	(.02)	(3.31)	(.02)
t values	128.3	14.5	95.5	35

* Adapted from *The Accounting Review Supplement to Vol. XLVI* (American Accounting Association, 1971) pp. 229–231.

	Department 1	Department 2
Standard error of the estimate	.53	.72
Coefficient of determination	.96	.98

Residual plots for the three equations are shown below:

Residual Plots
Total Overhead Cost versus Total Direct Labor Cost

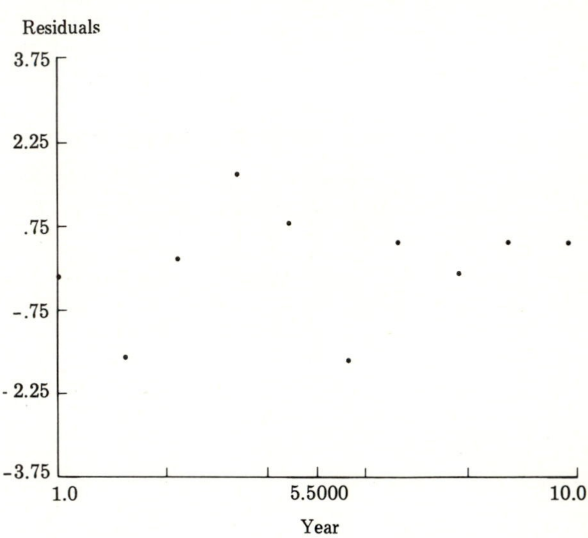

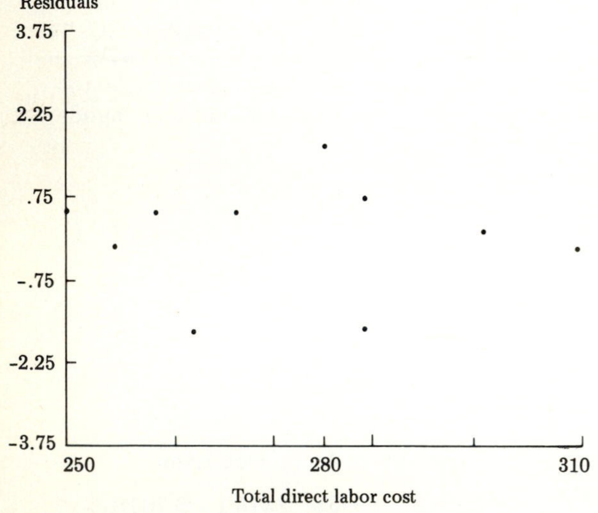

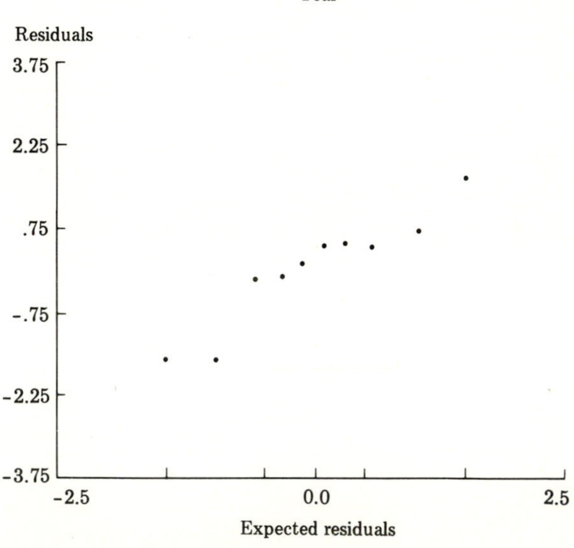

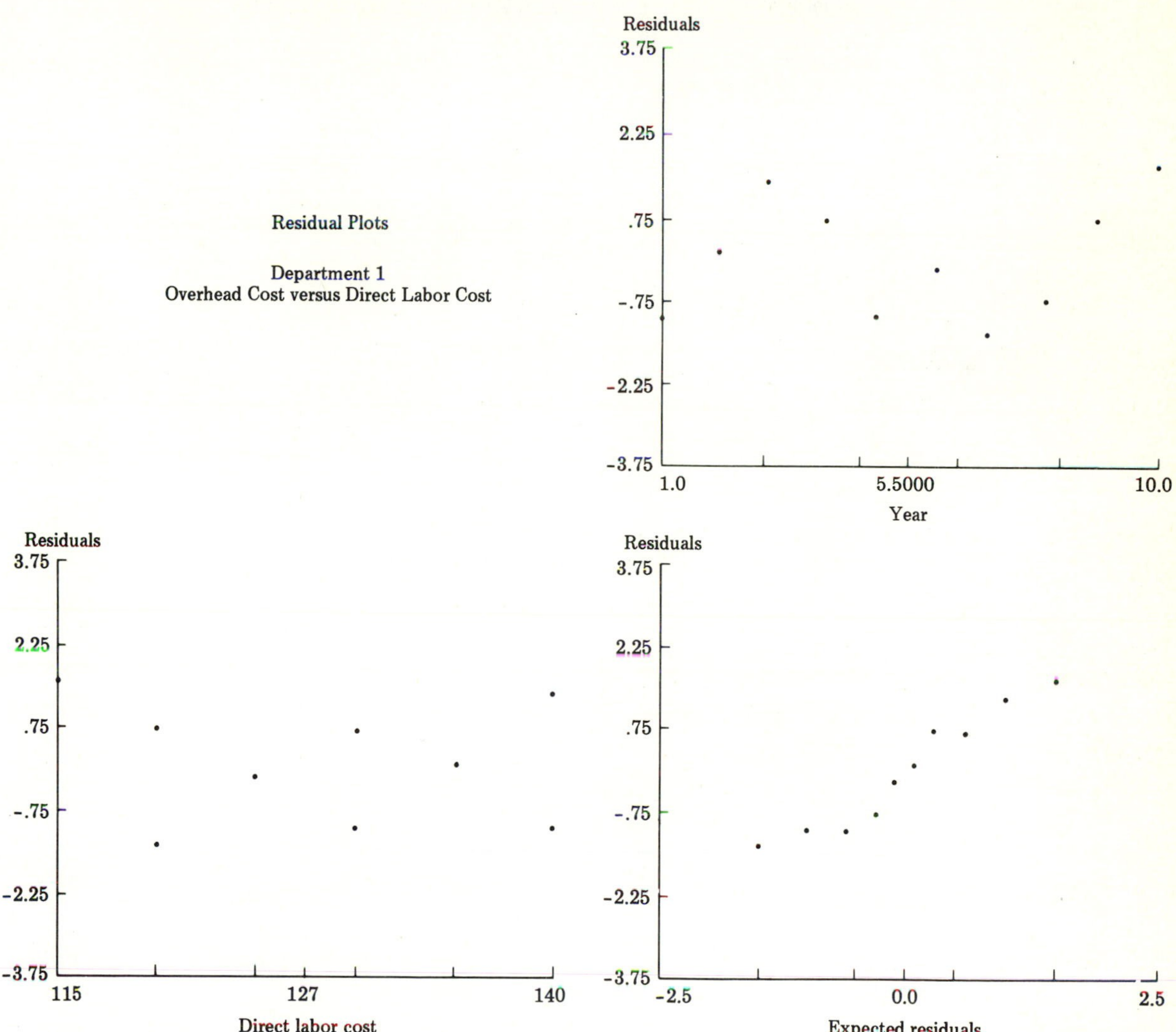

Residual Plots
Department 1
Overhead Cost versus Direct Labor Cost
Residuals
3.75
2.25
.75
-.75
-2.25
-3.75
1.0
5.5000
10.0
Year
Residuals
3.75
2.25
.75
-.75
-2.25
-3.75
115
127
140
Direct labor cost
Residuals
3.75
2.25
.75
-.75
-2.25
-3.75
-2.5
0.0
2.5
Expected residuals

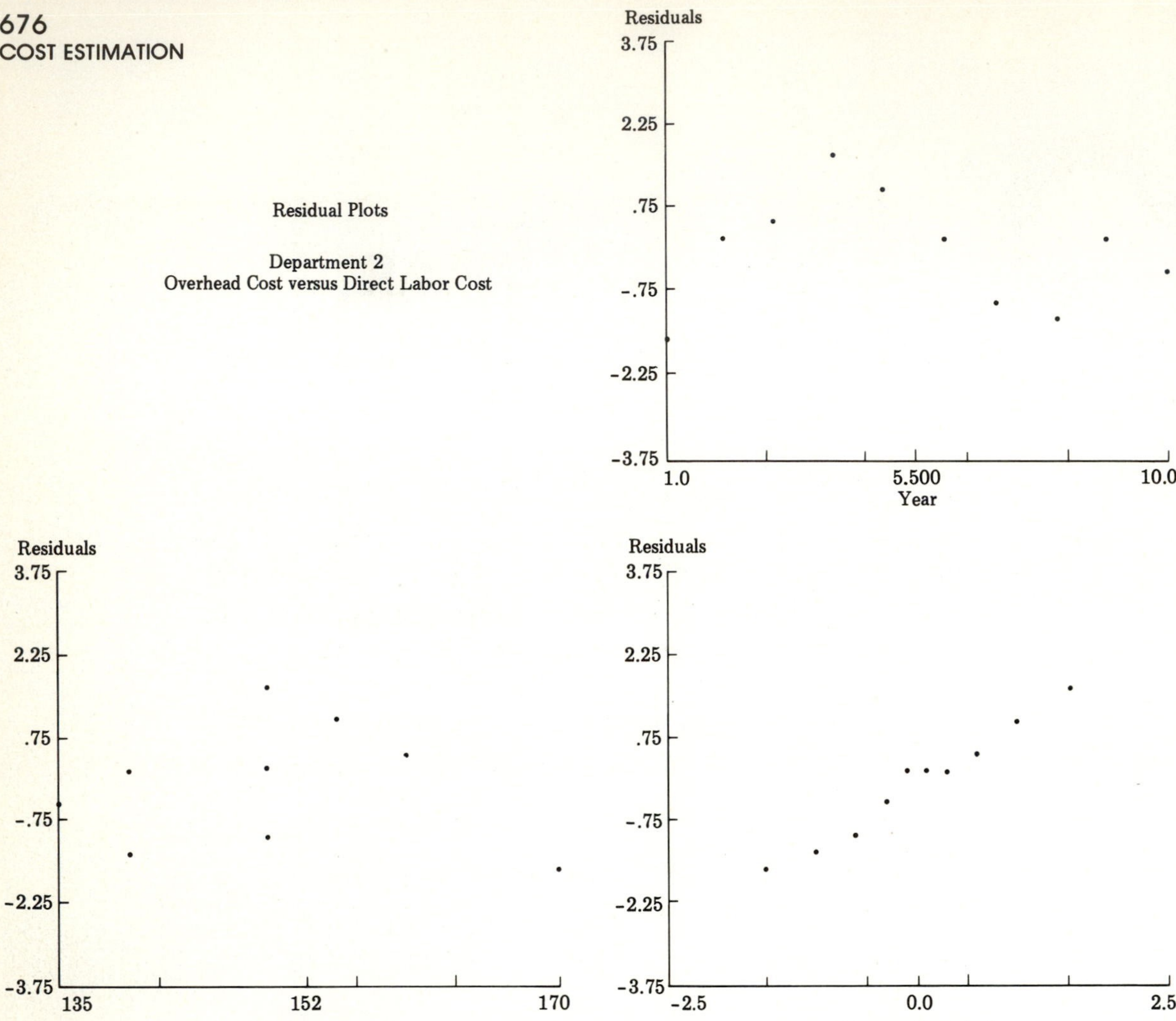

Required Which of the above regression equations should be used to forecast the total overhead cost? Explain your answer. Which equation(s) should be used for calculating overhead rates? Explain your answer.

24 LINEAR PROGRAMMING

AFTER COMPLETING YOUR STUDY OF THIS CHAPTER, YOU SHOULD HAVE LEARNED:

1 How mathematical models are helpful to managers in making planning decisions.

2 How linear programming models have been successfully applied to problems such as production scheduling, product mix, advertising policy, and planning shipping routes.

3 How to formulate problems into linear programs.

4 How a linear programming model can be solved by graphic means.

5 How information from the output of a simplex solution to a linear programming problem is used by managers and accountants.

In the chapters dealing with short-term planning and control decisions the examples assumed no restrictions on production or sales. The discussion and analysis in these decision situations concentrated on determining the relevant costs for a particular decision and summarizing these costs in a meaningful manner for management's consideration. However, in practice managers are often faced with situations which have multiple restrictions and many different alternatives. As an aid to management a number of mathematical techniques have been developed that are capable of providing information to help management select the best alternative.

Some of the problems where mathematical techniques have been used to help managers evaluate alternatives include:

Some managerial problems are solvable by math models.

1 A company manufactures two products in a single manufacturing plant. Production volume is limited to a total of 10,000 units per year. Management wants to know what mix of products should be produced and sold to *maximize* the company's total contribution margin.

2 A company's production manager is concerned about the total production costs and inventory costs. The production manager wants to determine a production schedule and inventory policy that will satisfy product demand and *minimize* the total production costs plus the inventory costs.

3 An advertising manager has a budget of $10 million to spend on advertising for the year 19X4. The advertising manager wants to know how the budget should be allocated between television, radio, and magazine ads to *maximize* the total sales revenue.

4 A company has two production plants and several warehouses located throughout the country. Given the customers' demands for the product, the vice president of manufacturing would like to determine which production plant should supply each warehouse to *minimize* the total shipping costs.

In all the above problems a single mathematical technique, **linear programming,** has been used to provide the managers with a suggested solution. Even though the problems are quite different, linear programming has been used to solve each problem because of two common characteristics:

Common characteristics of linear programs.

1 Each problem has a specific *objective.*

2 Each problem has restrictions or *constraints.*[1]

In linear programming the objective is to *maximize* or *minimize* something. In problem 1, the objective is to *maximize* total contribution margin; in problem 2, the objective is to *minimize* the total of the production cost plus the cost of carrying (or owning) inventory; in problem 3, the objective is to *maximize* total sales revenue; and in problem 4, the objective is to *minimize* total shipping costs.

The second common characteristic is that each problem has some restrictions that limit how the objective is achieved. In problem 1, the restriction is that total production volume is limited to 10,000 units per year; in problem 2, the restriction is that product demand must be satisfied; in problem 3, the restriction is the $10 million fixed advertising budget; in problem 4, the restriction is satisfying the customers' demand for the product at each warehouse.

[1] Linear programming assumes that the objective function and constraint equations are linear and that solutions in fractional units are acceptable to the decision maker. If a problem violates these assumptions nonlinear programming or integer programming would be used.

Because of these two common characteristics we can formulate and solve each problem in a similar fashion. In this chapter we will first illustrate how linear programs are formulated and solved. Next, we will discuss how management uses the solution to the linear program.

LINEAR PROGRAMMING EXAMPLE

To illustrate the use of linear programming let us consider the Acme Company, a manufacturer who produces industrial knives and wire cutters. In the production process a single piece of equipment is used to fabricate the knives and has the capacity to produce 80,000 knives per year. Another piece of equipment is used to produce the wire cutters and has the capacity to produce 40,000 wire cutters per year. Once the knives and wire cutters are fabricated they are assembled and sharpened by a common work force. There are currently 100,000 labor hours available without hiring new employees, and Acme's management is unwilling to hire employees unless they are confident that continuing employment can be provided. For the current planning period Acme does not plan to hire additional employees. A further fact, important in the analysis which follows, is that each knife and each wire cutter requires 1 labor hour to assemble and sharpen. Acme's management estimates that knives will sell for $4.75 each and that wire cutters will sell for $10 each. The variable costs are estimated to be $4 per unit for the knives and $9 per unit for the wire cutters. Thus, the contribution margin is $.75 per unit for knives and $1 per unit for the wire cutters as shown below:

	Knife	Wire Cutter
Sales price per unit	$4.75	$10.00
Variable cost per unit	4.00	9.00
Contribution margin per unit	$ .75	$ 1.00

Acme's problem is to determine how many knives and wire cutters should be produced and sold to maximize the total contribution. In the following sections we will illustrate how to formulate and solve this problem.

Problem Formulation

As discussed previously each linear program has an objective and constraints (the restraints mentioned earlier). Acme's objective is to maximize the total contribution margin from the production and sales of knives and wire cutters. To illustrate the formulation of the objective, let us define two variables:

$$X_1 = \text{the number of knives produced and sold}$$
$$X_2 = \text{the number of wire cutters produced and sold}$$

We have already shown that the contribution margin for each knife is $.75. Since X_1 represents the number of knives to be produced and sold, $.75 times X_1 represents the contribution margin from selling X_1 knives. Similarly, the contribution margin from selling wire cutters is \$1 times X_2, and the total contribution margin from the sale of both products is represented by the following equation:

$$\textbf{Total contribution margin} = \$.75X_1 + \$1X_2$$

The above equation is used to calculate the total contribution margin from selling X_1 knives and X_2 wire cutters. Acme's objective, though, is to *maximize* the total contribution margin. Including the maximization in the equation results in the following objective function:

Objective function.

$$\textbf{Maximize total contribution margin} = \$.75X_1 + \$1X_2$$

This is the formal statement of the objective function for the linear programming problem.

If only the contribution per unit is considered, Acme's management might conclude that they should produce and sell as many wire cutters as possible since the wire cutters have the higher contribution per unit. However, before the decision is made the constraints on production should be considered.

We know the maximum number of wire cutters that can be produced is 40,000 because that is the maximum capacity of the equipment used to produce wire cutters. This **constraint equation** is written as follows:

Constraint equation.

$$1X_2 \leq 40{,}000$$

where $\leq$ means *less than or equal to.* This relationship is referred to as an inequality since it says that the number of wire cutters produced must be less than or equal to 40,000, the wire cutter equipment capacity.

Similarly, the equipment capacity for knives is 80,000 units. The inequality representing this constraint is:

Constraint equation.

$$1X_1 \leq 80{,}000$$

To assemble and sharpen the knives and wire cutters Acme has 100,000 labor hours available and it takes 1 hour of labor time for each knife and for each wire cutter. To represent this constraint mathematically we use the following inequality:

Constraint equation.

$$1X_1 + 1X_2 \leq 100{,}000$$

That is, 1 hour times the number of knives produced (X_1) will tell how many labor hours will be used to assemble and sharpen knives and 1 hour times the number of wire cutters produced (X_2) will represent the labor hours used to assemble and sharpen wire cutters. The total must be less than or equal to the 100,000 labor hours which are potentially available.

Finally, we need two more constraints to represent the common sense idea that Acme cannot produce and sell a negative quantity of a product. If the problem is solved by humans using the graphic method to be illustrated in this chapter, these constraints would not have to be stated; they would be understood. But most linear programming problems are solved by computers and the computer must be told explicitly that X_1 and X_2 cannot be negative. These constraints are represented as follows:

Constraint equation.

$$X_1 \geq 0 \qquad \textbf{and} \qquad X_2 \geq 0$$

where $\geq$ means *greater than or equal to.*

Now that we have formulated the objective and each constraint of the Acme problem, the complete formal statement of the linear program problem is shown below:

Linear program illustrated.

Maximize total contribution margin =	**$\$.75X_1$ +**	**$\$1X_2$**			**(1)**
Subject to:					
Knife capacity constraint	**$1X_1$**		**$\leq$**	**80,000**	**(2)**
Wire cutter capacity constraint		**$1X_2$**	**$\leq$**	**40,000**	**(3)**
Labor hour constraint	**$1X_1$ +**	**$1X_2$**	**$\leq$**	**100,000**	**(4)**
Nonnegative output constraint	**X_1**		**$\geq$**	**0**	**(5)**
Nonnegative output constraint		**X_2**	**$\geq$**	**0**	**(6)**

The next section illustrates a graphic solution to this problem.

Graphic Solution of the Linear Programming Problem

To solve a problem graphically, you need one axis for each product. This means that the graph can easily be drawn for a two-product problem. For larger problems a computer program that does not require graphs is used.

Since Acme's problem has only two products, knives and wire cutters, it can be solved graphically. A **graphic solution** to linear programs is illustrated because it helps you understand what a computer does when it solves a larger problem. We will develop a graph to display all possible solutions to the linear program; then we will show you how to pick the best solution, the number of knives and wire cutters to produce and sell in order to maximize the total contribution margin.

The graph shown in part *a* of Exhibit 24-1 has units of knives, X_1, on the vertical axis and units of wire cutters, X_2, on the horizontal axis. The graph is only for positive values of X_1 and X_2 because each axis starts at zero and shows only positive amounts. This satisfies constraint equations (5) and (6) which stated that X_1 and X_2 must be greater than or equal to zero. The shaded area in graph *a* represents the combinations of X_1 and X_2 that satisfy constraints (5) and (6). The shaded area is called the area of feasible solutions. As the other constraints to the program are plotted on the graph the area of feasible solutions is reduced. After equation (2) is plotted on the graph, the shaded area in graph *b* shows the reduced area of feasible solutions. Only the area below the 80,000 unit line is shaded since this constraint equation specifies that it is only possible to produce and sell 80,000 or less knives (product X_1). A feasible solution is one which satisfies the constraints. As far as constraint equation (2) is concerned, any solution which involves selling 80,000 or less knives is a feasible solution. This means, of course, that there are many feasible solutions. The **area of feasible solution** is the area of the graph within (bounded by) the constraint lines.

Feasible solution defined.

The plotting of equation (3) on the graph further reduces the area of feasible solutions as shown by the shaded area in graph *c* of Exhibit 24-1. Finally, plotting equation (4) provides the area of feasible solutions that satisfies all of the constraints in the Acme problem. It is shown by the shaded areas in graph *d* of Exhibit 24-1.

Since the constraint equations in a linear programming problem are all straight lines, it is only necessary to find two points on each line to plot it. To ease our job of plotting, we (1) look at the constraint as an equality and (2) choose the most convenient two points, the ones on the axes. For example, take equation (4); looking at the constraint as an equality gives the equation $X_1 + X_2 = 100{,}000$. Since the sum of X_1 and X_2 must equal 100,000, if X_1 is zero, X_2 will have to be 100,000. Also,

Plotting the constraints.

EXHIBIT 24-1
Plotting the Area of Feasible Solutions for the Acme Knife and Wire Cutter Example

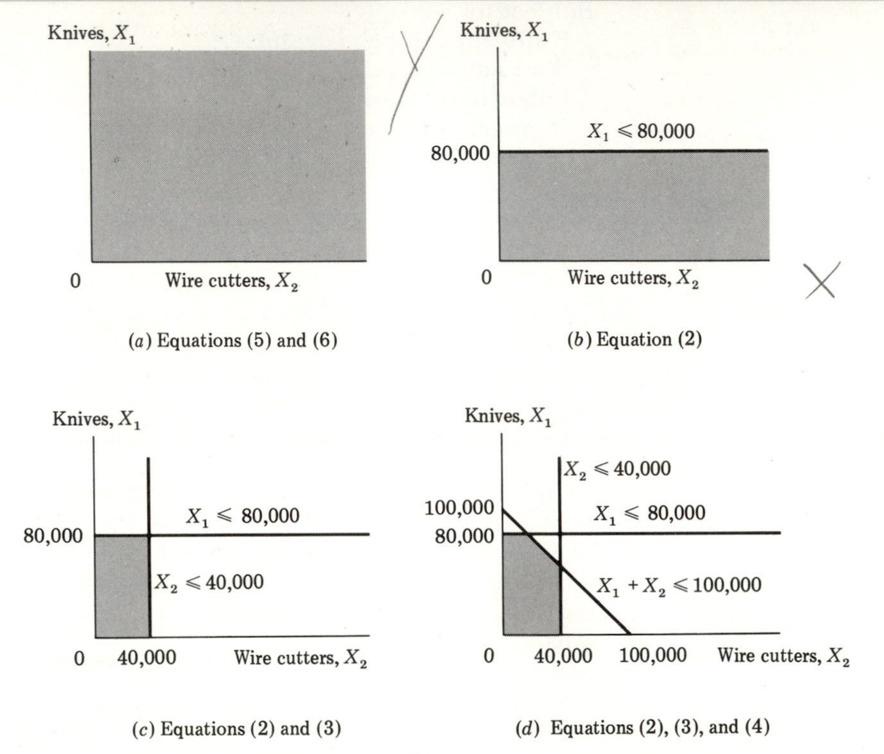

when X_2 is equal to zero, X_1 must equal 100,000. These two points, (0, 100000) and (100000, 0), are enough to permit us to draw the line representing the constraint. After the line of the equality is drawn, we recognize that since this is a "less than or equal to" constraint, any point on the line or below and to the left of the line of the equality satisfies the constraint. Similarly, if the constraint were a "greater than or equal to" constraint, any point on the line or above and to the right of the equality line would satisfy the constraint.

Even though the constraints limit the area of feasible solutions, many feasible solutions remain. Any combination of X_1 and X_2 that falls within the shaded area in graph *d* of Exhibit 24-1 satisfies all the constraints. The remaining problem is to choose the one solution out of the many feasible solutions which results in the most (maximum) total contribution margin as represented by the objective function equation (1).

Mathematicians have proven that the optimum solution to a linear programming problem will be at one of the corners of the area of feasible solutions. Therefore only two steps remain in the graphic solution of the linear programming problem.

1 Calculate the coordinates at each corner of the area of feasible solutions (the coordinates represent the number of knives and wire cutters sold).

2 Calculate the total contribution margin resulting from the number of knives and wire cutters sold at each corner using the objective function.

Location of the optimal solution.

The corner which produces the highest total contribution margin is the optimum solution.

The entire problem is illustrated in Exhibit 24-2 and the possible solutions are summarized below.

	Production Units		Total Contribution Margin
Corner	X_1	X_2	**$.75** X_1 **+ $1.00** X_2
1	0	0	$ 0
2	0	40,000	40,000
3	60,000	40,000	85,000
4	80,000	20,000	80,000
5	80,000	0	60,000

The optimum solution is the one that maximizes the total contribution margin. In this problem Acme should produce and sell 60,000 units of X_1 and 40,000 units of X_2, resulting in a total contribution margin of $85,000.

THE SIMPLEX METHOD

The knives and wire cutter example is a fairly simple problem because it involves only two products and only a few constraints. In fact, since we need an axis for each product, the graphic method is only helpful in two product situations. A three-product situation would have to be drawn in three dimensions (which would be messy) and a four-product situation is impossible to graph. Since most realistic problems involve a larger number of products and many constraints, some other method of solution must be found.

Advantages of the simplex method.

Linear programming became practical for large problems only when the **simplex method** was derived by mathematicians. The simplex method has two main advantages. First, it is easy to program so that computers can make the calculations required to solve the problem. Second, along with the optimum solution, it provides additional information to the accountant and decision maker. You do not need to understand how the simplex method works, but you should understand (1) how the formulation of the problem is modified to fit the simplex method, and (2) how the additional information called shadow prices can be helpful to management.

Problem Formulation for the Simplex Method

The problem formulation is modified for the simplex method by converting the constraints which are inequalities into equalities through the addition of what is called a slack variable. The idea can be illustrated easily. Start with the inequality:

$$3 \leq 5$$

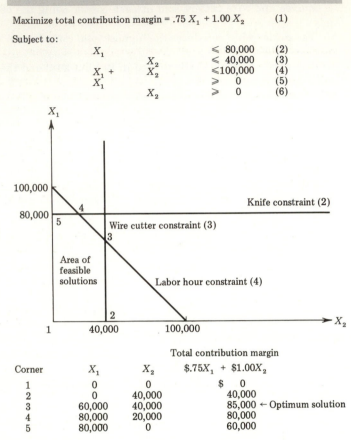

EXHIBIT 24-2
Graphical Solution for the Acme Knife and Wire Cutter Example

Maximize total contribution margin = $.75\,X_1 + 1.00\,X_2$ (1)

Subject to:

$$X_1 \leq 80{,}000 \quad (2)$$
$$X_2 \leq 40{,}000 \quad (3)$$
$$X_1 + X_2 \leq 100{,}000 \quad (4)$$
$$X_1 \geq 0 \quad (5)$$
$$X_2 \geq 0 \quad (6)$$

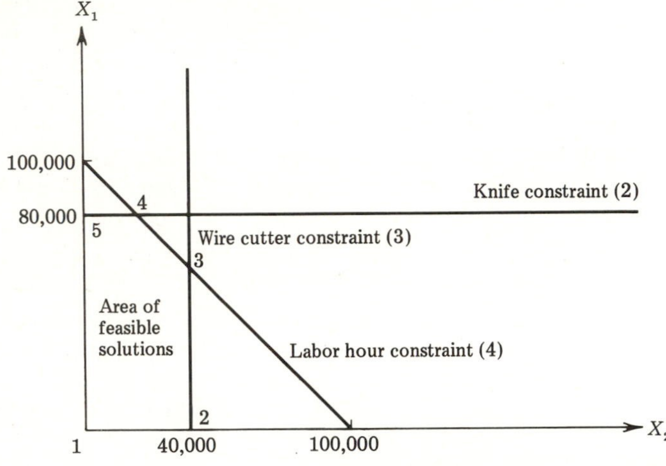

Corner	X_1	X_2	Total contribution margin $\$.75X_1 + \$1.00X_2$
1	0	0	$ 0
2	0	40,000	40,000
3	60,000	40,000	85,000 ← Optimum solution
4	80,000	20,000	80,000
5	80,000	0	60,000

This could be converted to an equality by adding the amount 2 to the left side.

$$3 + 2 = 5$$

It was easy to convert the inequality into an equality in this case, because we were working with two definite numbers, 3 and 5. Now suppose that we are working with a different inequality.

$$a \leq 50$$

We can still convert this to an equality by adding something to the left side, but the amount that will have to be added will change depending on what the value of a is. We handle this problem by adding another variable to the left side.

$$a + b = 50$$

Then as a increases, b decreases, and the equality holds. In linear programming terms, b is a slack variable.

At this point, you might ask yourself, "Why do we want to convert the inequality into an equality?" The answer is that it facilitates the mathematical analysis, and as long as the slack variables do not change the solution to the program, it does not make any difference from the manager's viewpoint. We make sure that the slack variables do not change the solution to the program by putting them into the objective function with a zero coefficient. In the Acme example, it is like adding some products which have a zero contribution margin. Certainly, we will not waste any of our scarce resources producing a product with a zero contribution margin, so including the slack variable will never change the optimal solution. Just one final point before we illustrate the knife and wire cutter problem with the slack variables added. Notice in the old formulation the products, knives and wire cutters, were represented as X_1 and X_2. This is common practice in linear programming. The slack variables will continue this practice and will be called X_3, X_4, X_5, one slack variable to convert each constraint to an equality (other than the nonnegative constraints). You can imagine that in a large problem with many constraints there would be many slack variables. The restated formulation appears as follows:

Simplex formulation.

$$\begin{array}{llr} \textbf{Maximize: TCM} = \$.75X_1 + \$1X_2 + \$0X_3 + \$0X_4 + \$0X_5 & & (1) \\ \textbf{Subject to:} \quad X_1 + X_3 & = 80{,}000 & (2) \\ \quad X_2 + X_4 & = 40{,}000 & (3) \\ \quad X_1 + X_2 + X_5 & = 100{,}000 & (4) \end{array}$$

The simplex method then follows a method similar to the procedure we followed in the graphic solution of the problem. It results in a solution which appears like the one given below.

Simplex solution.

		X_1	X_2	X_3	X_4	X_5		
Variables →		X_1	X_2	X_3	X_4	X_5		
Coefficients in the objective function →		.75	1	0	0	0		
Variables in solution	X_3	0	0	+1	+1	−1	20,000	Quantity of variables in solution
	X_2	0	+1	0	+1	0	40,000 units	
	X_1	+1	0	0	−1	+1	60,000 units	
Shadow prices		0	0	0	−.25	−.75		

This presentation of the solution needs to be explained first and then we will see how the added information called **shadow prices** can be used to aid the accountant and manager in making decisions.

The first row in the simplex solution represents the variables; X_1 represents number of knives, X_2 represents number of wire cutters, X_3, X_4, and X_5 represent slack variables. The second row of numbers restates the coefficients of the **objective function;** in this case they represent the contribution margin associated with each variable.

The variables in the simplex solution to the linear program are shown in the far left column. The variables in solution are X_3, X_2, and X_1. The order of this list is the result of the simplex methods.

The quantity of the variables in the simplex solution to the problem is shown in the far right column. Production of 40,000 wire cutters, X_2, and 60,000 knives, X_1, is the same answer we found graphically. That column also shows 20,000 of X_3, the slack variable for the knife machine capacity constraint. Since it has a zero contribution margin it can be ignored in computing total contribution. It really indicates that we are not producing all of the 80,000 knives that the first resource constraint would have allowed us since we are limited by the other resource constraints. The manager looking at the solution knows that X_3 is not a real product and that there is nothing to produce.

The explanation of the zeros, minus ones and plus ones, and the shadow price row will be explained in the next section which discusses what is called postoptimality analysis.

Postoptimality Analysis

Two pieces of information of particular interest to the manager and accountant can be found by **postoptimality analysis.** The first is the increase (if any) in the objective function, which could result by making more of the constrained factors available. In our example, by how much could the total contribution margin be increased if one more labor hour could be made available? This analysis will be illustrated next. It uses the shadow prices and the plus ones and minus ones in the simplex solution.

The other important piece of information which will also be discussed tells the accountant whether a small change in the contribution margin will change the optimum solution. If a small change in contribution margin will change the solution, the accountant will want to spend considerable effort to make accurate estimates of the contribution margin of each product. On the other hand, if the contribution margin per unit for each product can change over a wide range without changing the optimum solution, a rough (and therefore less costly) estimate of the contribution margin per unit may suffice. We turn now to the first piece of information.

Interpretation of shadow prices.

The Value of Making More of the Constrained Factor Available The shadow prices appearing in the bottom row represent the potential increase in total contribution if the associated constraints could be relaxed by 1 unit. For instance, the −.25 shadow price associated with the slack variable X_4 tells us that if the second constraint [equation (3) representing machine capacity for wire cutters] could be increased to 40,001 units, total contribution margin would be increased by $.25. The minus in front of the $.25 shadow price indicates contribution margin lost by not having that additional wire cutter machine capacity available.

The new solution increasing total contribution by $.25 is calculated by adding the numbers in the body of the simplex solution under the column labeled X_4 to the quantity of the variables in solution as follows:

Variables in Solution	Column X_4		Quantity of Variables in Solution		New Solution
X_3	+1	+	20,000	=	20,001
X_2	+1	+	40,000	=	40,001
X_1	−1	+	60,000	=	59,999

The +1 for the row labeled X_3 means that X_3 will increase to 20,001. The +1 for X_2 indicates that X_2, wire cutters, will become 40,001 units and the −1 for X_1 indicates that X_1, knives, will decrease to 59,999 units. The net effect on total contribution margin will be a $.25 increase in total contribution resulting from a $1.00 increase in total contribution from the sale of one more wire cutter and a $.75 decrease in total contribution from the sale of one less knife.

The −$.75 shadow price associated with X_5 indicates the objective function will increase by $.75 with a 1-unit increase in labor hours [equation (4)]. The increase would occur from increasing X_1 by 1 unit to 60,001 and decreasing X_3 by 1 unit to 19,999.

In most situations, changes in the objective function indicated by the shadow price will be repeated for changes of more than 1 unit—but not for infinite changes in the resource constraints. To determine the range for which the shadow price is a valid indicator of the change in the objective function, assume the initial formulation of equation (3) is altered to read as follows:

$$X_2 + X_4 = 40{,}000 + \alpha$$

If α is carried through all calculations of the simplex method, the final quantities of the variables in solution (appearing at the right side of the solution) would be:

$$X_3 = 20{,}000 + 1\alpha \qquad (1)$$
$$X_2 = 40{,}000 + 1\alpha \qquad (2)$$
$$X_1 = 60{,}000 - 1\alpha \qquad (3)$$

The sign and coefficients for α in the final solution are from the coefficients in the X_4 column, since X_4 is the slack variable for equation (3), the constraint on the number of wire cutters which can be produced. For feasible solutions, the quantities assigned to the variables X_1, X_2, and X_3 must be greater than or equal to zero because of the nonnegativity constraints. Therefore, we ask ourselves, "What is the range of values that α could take without making X_1, X_2, or X_3 negative in the three equations just listed?"

In the first equation α could be −20,000 without making X_1, X_2, or X_3 negative as shown below:

$$X_3 = 20{,}000 + 1(-20{,}000) = 0$$
$$X_2 = 40{,}000 + 1(-20{,}000) = 20{,}000$$
$$X_1 = 60{,}000 - 1(-20{,}000) = 80{,}000$$

In the second equation α could be −40,000 without making X_1 or X_2 negative. However, if α is −40,000 then X_3 becomes negative making this an infeasible solution. The computations follow:

$$X_3 = 20{,}000 + 1(-40{,}000) = -20{,}000$$
$$X_2 = 40{,}000 + 1(-40{,}000) = 0$$
$$X_1 = 60{,}000 - 1(-40{,}000) = 100{,}000$$

In the third equation α could be +60,000 without making X_1, X_2, or X_3 negative as shown below:

$$X_3 = 20{,}000 + 1(+60{,}000) = 80{,}000$$
$$X_2 = 40{,}000 + 1(+60{,}000) = 100{,}000$$
$$X_1 = 60{,}000 - 1(+60{,}000) = 0$$

Based on the above computations α could range from $-20{,}000$ to $+60{,}000$ without making X_1, X_2, or X_3 negative. The original value of the resource represented by equation (3) (wire cutter capacity) was 40,000 units. The shadow price of \$.25 represents the change in total contribution for values of the wire cutter capacity between the following limits:

Range of feasibility for capacity constraint.

$$\begin{aligned} \textbf{Limit} &= \mathbf{40{,}000} + \alpha \\ \textbf{Lower limit} &= \mathbf{40{,}000 + (-20{,}000) = 20{,}000} \\ \textbf{Upper limit} &= \mathbf{40{,}000 + (+60{,}000) = 100{,}000} \end{aligned}$$

The same calculations can be done for equation (4), the labor hour constraint. Adding α to the original formulation results in a final solution of:

$$\begin{aligned} X_3 &= 20{,}000 - 1\,\alpha \\ X_2 &= 40{,}000 + 0\,\alpha \\ X_1 &= 60{,}000 + 1\,\alpha \end{aligned}$$

The range for α would be:

$$-60{,}000 \leq \alpha \leq +20{,}000$$

This means the shadow price of \$.75 would hold for values in the labor hour resource constraint from 40,000 to 120,000 hours.

Accuracy of the Coefficients in the Objective Function Another question that can be answered in postoptimality analysis is, "Over what range can the contribution margins in the objective function change without changing the optimal solution?" The answer to this question provides the management accountant with information about the needed accuracy of the contribution margins in the objective function. For a particular contribution margin, if the solution is highly sensitive (a small change in the contribution margin causes a change in the solution), then additional accounting effort might be spent to provide a more accurate estimate. If the contribution margin can change by a large amount before the optimum solution changes, the manager can feel confident that minor errors in estimating the contribution margins will not lead to the wrong solution.

To calculate the possible changes for product X_1 (knives), refer to the simplex solution on page 685. To determine the change in the contribution margin of X_1 that *would not* change the optimal solution, the ratios of the shadow prices to the coefficients in the row labeled X_1 are calculated. The lower limit is the most restrictive negative ratio and the upper limit is the most restrictive positive ratio. For example, if the ratios ½ and ¼ were calculated ¼ would be the upper limit.[2] The computations for product X_1 are:

$$\begin{aligned} -.25/-1 &= +.25 \\ -.75/1 &= -.75 \end{aligned}$$

Based on these computations the lower and upper limits on the change in the coefficient of X_1 are:

$$-.75 \leq \textbf{change in contribution margin of } X_1 \leq +.25$$

[2] Technically, if no negative ratio exists there is no lower limit. However, when we are dealing with contribution margin we would not produce and sell a product with a negative contribution. If no positive ratio exists there is no upper limit.

The estimated contribution margin of X_1 is \$.75. Combining the \$.75 contribution margin with the lower and upper limits for the change in the contribution margin indicates to management that the contribution margin of product X_1 can vary between \$0 (\$.75 − \$.75) and \$1.00 (\$.75 + \$.25) before the optimal solution would change.

For product X_2, wire cutters, the shadow prices are divided by the coefficients in the row labeled X_2 as shown below:

$$-.25/1 = -.25$$
$$-.75/0 = \text{undefined}$$

Based on these computations the lower and upper limits on the change in the contribution margin of X_2 are:

Range of changes in the contribution that would not change the solution.

$$-.25 \leq \text{change in contribution margin of } X_2 \leq \text{no limit}^3$$

The contribution margin of X_2 can range from a lower limit of \$.75 (\$1 − \$.25) to any upper limit without changing the optimal solution.

To summarize, the main advantage of the simplex method is the additional information provided to management from a postoptimality analysis. The shadow prices indicate the economic value of 1 unit of the capacity constraints. Also, through postoptimality analysis you can see how critical the estimates of objective function coefficients are in determining the optimal solution.

SUMMARY

Linear programming is a mathematical technique that is widely used to aid managers in their decision process. Linear programming can be used in situations in which the manager has a specific objective to maximize or minimize and the objective is subject to a number of restrictions (constraints), and where both the objective and the constraints can be expressed as linear equations.

Linear programs having only two variables can be solved quite easily using a graphic method. More complex linear programs (those containing three or more variables) are solved using the computer programmed for the simplex method.

In addition to providing a problem solution, the simplex method provides managers with information about how (if at all) changes in the objective function coefficients (contribution margins per unit in our example) and the resource constraints (machine capacity and labor hours available in our example) will change the solution. This information guides the accountant in determining how precisely the contribution margins per unit must be estimated, and the manager in deciding if more resources should be made available.

Review Problem

The Frey Company manufactures and sells two products—a toddler bike and a toy high chair. Linear programming is employed to determine the best production and sales mix of bikes and chairs. This approach also allows Frey to evaluate possible

[3] There is no upper limit since there is no positive ratio.

economic changes. For example, management is often interested in knowing how variations in selling prices, resource costs, resource availabilities, and marketing strategies would affect the company's performance.

The demand for bikes and chairs is relatively constant throughout the year. The following data pertain to the two products:

	Bike (X_1)	Chair (X_2)
Selling price per unit	\$12	\$10
Variable cost per unit	8	7
Contribution margin per unit	\$ 4	\$ 3
Raw materials required		
Wood	1 board foot	2 board feet
Plastic	2 pounds	1 pound
Direct labor required	2 hours	2 hours

Estimates of the resource quantities available in a typical month during the year are:

Wood	10,000 board feet
Plastic	10,000 pounds
Direct Labor	12,000 hours

Required

1 Formulate the linear programming model for the determination of Frey Company's product mix to maximize total contribution margin.

2 Determine the optimal solution graphically.

3 Formulate the linear program in a simplex format using X_3, X_4, and X_5 as the slack variables.

(CMA)

Solution

1 Problem Formulation

Maximize total contribution margin = $4X_1 + 3X_2$
Subject to:

$$1X_1 + 2X_2 \leqslant 10{,}000 \text{ (The wood constraint)}$$
$$2X_1 + 1X_2 \leqslant 10{,}000 \text{ (The plastic constraint)}$$
$$2X_1 + 2X_2 \leqslant 12{,}000 \text{ (The direct labor constraint)}$$
$$X_1, \quad X_2 \geqslant 0$$

2 Graphic Solution

The optimum solution must be at a corner of the area of feasible solution. Two steps are involved, finding the quantities of bikes and chairs at each corner and then calculating the total contribution margin generated by producing and selling these quantities.

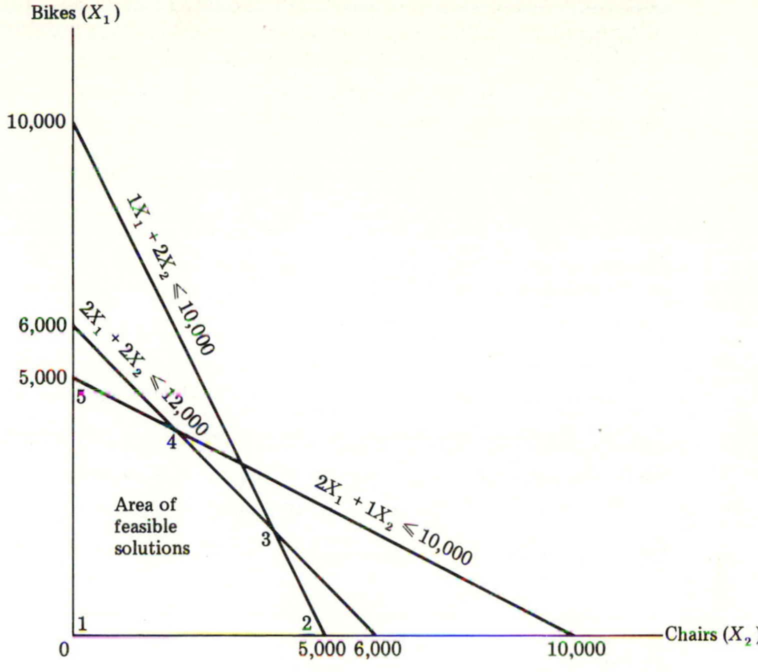

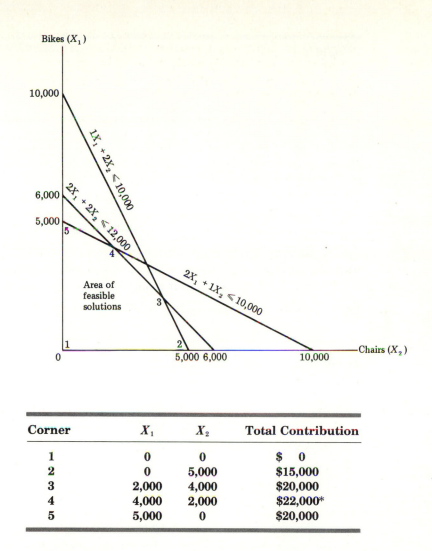

Corner	X_1	X_2	Total Contribution
1	0	0	$ 0
2	0	5,000	$15,000
3	2,000	4,000	$20,000
4	4,000	2,000	$22,000*
5	5,000	0	$20,000

* Optimal solution

3 The simplex formulation introduces slack variables to change the inequalities into equalities. It is shown below:

Maximize total contribution margin $= 4X_1 + 3X_2 + 0X_3 + 0X_4 + 0X_5$

Subject to:

$$1X_1 + 2X_2 + X_3 = 10,000$$
$$2X_1 + 1X_2 + X_4 = 10,000$$
$$2X_1 + 2X_2 + X_5 = 12,000$$

Review Problem

This review problem refers to the situation of the Frey Company described in the previous review problem. A simplex solution to the Frey Company problem would appear as presented on the following page.

Variables in Solution	X_1 4	X_2 3	X_3 0	X_4 0	X_5 0	Values of Solution Variables
X_3	0	0	1	1	− 3/2	2,000
X_1	1	0	0	1	− 1/2	4,000
X_2	0	1	0	− 1	1	2,000
Shadow price	0	0	0	− 1	− 1	

Required

1 Calculate the upper and lower limits for the change in the quantity of the plastic constraint for which the X_4 shadow price will hold.

2 Do the same for the direct labor constraint.

3 Calculate the upper and lower limits over which the contribution margins per unit could change without changing the optimal number of bikes and chairs.

Solution

1

$$2{,}000 + 1\,\alpha$$
$$4{,}000 + 1\,\alpha$$
$$2{,}000 - 1\,\alpha$$

$$-2{,}000 \leqslant \alpha \leqslant 2{,}000$$

$$8{,}000 \leqslant \text{pounds} \leqslant 12{,}000$$

2

$$2{,}000 - 3/2\,\alpha$$
$$4{,}000 - 1/2\,\alpha$$
$$2{,}000 + 1\,\alpha$$

$$-2{,}000 \leqslant \alpha \leqslant 1{,}333$$

$$10{,}000 \leqslant \text{hours} \leqslant 13{,}333$$

3 Contribution margin for product X_1

Ratios

$$-1/1 = -1$$
$$-1/-1/2 = +2$$
$$-1 \leqslant \text{change in contribution for } X_1, \leqslant 2$$

Contribution margin for product X_2

Ratios

$$-1/-1 = +1$$
$$-1/1 = -1$$
$$-1 \leqslant \text{change in contribution for } X_2 \leqslant 1$$

Glossary

Area of feasible solutions The area that contains all sets of values of the variables in a linear program that satisfy all the constraints.

Constraint equations The set of equations in a linear program that restrict the values that can be assigned to the variables.

Graphic solution A solution to a linear program in which the constraints are graphed to define an area of feasible solutions. The optimal solution lies at the corner of the area of feasible solutions which generates the greatest contribution margin or least cost.

Linear programming A mathematical technique used to formulate and solve problems which have an objective and some constraints which can be expressed as linear equations.

Objective function The equation in a linear program that is to be either maximized or minimized.

Postoptimality analysis An analysis of the simplex solution of a linear program to determine how the solution changes with changes in the coefficients of the objective function and the amount of each constraint.

Shadow price A number assigned to each variable not included in the final solution to a linear program. It is a measure of the potential increase in the objective function if the constraint the variable is associated with could be increased by 1 unit.

Simplex method A method for solving linear programs by moving from one extreme point to another until an optimal solution is found. It is normally done by computer.

Questions and Problems

24-1 List four decision situations where linear programming would be the appropriate technique for arriving at a decision.

24-2 What two types of information are provided to managers and accountants from postoptimality analysis?

24-3 Multiple Choice—Problem Formulation Assume the following data for the two products produced by Wagner Company:

	Product A	Product B
Direct materials requirements (liters)		
X	3	4
Y	7	2
Contribution margin per unit of product	$10	$4

If 300 liters of direct materials X and 400 liters of direct materials Y are available, the set of relationships appropriate for maximization of total contribution margin using linear programming would be:

a
$$\begin{aligned} 3A + 4B &\geq 300 \\ 7A + 2B &\geq 400 \\ 10A + 4B &\quad \text{MAX} \end{aligned}$$

b
$$\begin{aligned} 3A + 7B &\geq 300 \\ 4A + 2B &\geq 400 \\ 10A + 4B &\quad \text{MAX} \end{aligned}$$

c
$$\begin{aligned} 3A + 7B &\leq 300 \\ 4A + 2B &\leq 400 \\ 10A + 4B &\quad \text{MAX} \end{aligned}$$

d
$$\begin{aligned} 3A + 4B &\leq 300 \\ 7A + 2B &\leq 400 \\ 10A + 4B &\quad \text{MAX} \end{aligned}$$

e None of the above

(CPA)

24-4 Problem Formulation Watch Corporation manufactures products *A*, *B*, and *C*. The daily production requirements are shown below.

		Hours Required by Each Unit in Each Department		
Product	**Contribution per Unit**	**Machining**	**Plating**	**Polishing**
A	$10	1	1	1
B	$20	3	1	2
C	$30	2	3	2
Total hours available per day in each department		16	12	6

Required Formulate the linear program to determine the daily production levels to maximize the total contribution margin.

(CPA)

24-5 Problem Formulation The Ball Company manufactures three types of lamps which are labeled A, B, and C. Each lamp is processed in two departments—I and II. Total available labor hours per day for departments I and II are 400 and 600, respectively. No additional labor is available. Time requirements and contribution margin per unit for each lamp type are as follows:

	Lamp A	Lamp B	Lamp C
Labor hours required in department I	2	3	1
Labor hours required in department II	4	2	3
Contribution margin per lamp	$5	$4	$3

The company has assigned you as the accounting member of its profit planning committee to determine the numbers of types A, B, and C lamps that it should produce in order to maximize its total contribution margin from the sale of lamps.

Required Formulate a linear program to determine the optimal production level for lamps A, B, and C.

(CPA)

24-6 Problem Formulation and Graphical Solution The Random Company manufactures two products, Zeta and Beta. Each product must pass through two processing operations. All materials are introduced at the start of process no. 1. There are *no* work in process inventories. Random may produce either one product exclusively or various combinations of both products subject to the following constraints:

	Process No. 1	Process No. 2	Contribution Margin per Unit
Hours required to produce 1 unit of:			
Zeta	1 hour	1 hour	$4.00
Beta	2 hours	3 hours	5.25
Total capacity in hours per day	1,000 hours	1,275 hours	

A shortage of technical labor has limited Beta production to 400 units per day. There are *no* constraints on the production of Zeta other than the hour constraints in the above schedule. Assume that all relationships between capacity and production are linear.

Required Graphically determine the optimal solution to maximize total contribution margin.

(CPA)

24-7 Problem Formulation and Graphic Solution Patsy, Inc., manufactures two products, X and Y. Each product must be processed in each of three departments: machining, assembling, and finishing. The hours needed to produce 1 unit of product per department and the maximum possible hours per department follow:

Department	Production Hours per Unit: X	Production Hours per Unit: Y	Maximum Capacity in Hours
Machining	2	1	420
Assembly	2	2	500
Finishing	2	3	600

Other restrictions follow:

$$X \geqslant 50$$
$$Y \geqslant 50$$

The objective function to maximize total contribution margin is \$4*X* + \$2*Y*.

Required Graphically determine the output of *X* and *Y* which maximizes total contribution margin.

(CPA)

24-8 Problem Formulation—Joint Products Company A manufactures two products, *Y* and *Z*. Material *X*, which costs \$2 per unit, is used in the manufacture of *Y* and *Z*. The initial processing of *X* yields 1 unit of *Y* and 3 units of *Z*. At this point in the processing, *Y* could be sold for \$10 a unit and *Z* for \$8 per unit. By adding additional material, *W*, to *Z* and processing it further, it could be sold for \$15 per unit. The additional processing costs for *Z* include \$1 for materials and \$2 for labor. Different machines are used in the processing of *X* and *Z*. It takes .5 hours to process 1 unit of *X* and 1 hour to process *Z*. The machine hours available for processing *X* and *Z* are 10,000 and 5,000, respectively. The sales of *Z before* additional processing are limited to 3,000 units due to market conditions.

Required Formulate a linear programming model of the above problem to maximize total contribution margin assuming sales equal production.

24-9 Problem Formulation and Graphical Solution S. Davis, Inc., has decided to produce and market a diet salad dressing. They have decided that to be marketable each serving must contain no more than nine calories. They have experimented with ingredients and discovered that they can produce the same flavor with various combinations of ingredients.

Each serving must use a minimum of two measures of base. In addition, each serving must use a minimum of 1 measure of flavoring. The total number of measures must not exceed six and must not be below one.

A measure of base has one calorie and costs ½ cent. A measure of flavoring has three calories and costs 1 cent.

Required

1 Formulate the linear program.

2 Graphically determine the optimal combination of base and flavoring to minimize cost.

24-10 Postoptimality Analysis A simplex solution for a linear programming profit maximization problem is shown below:

	X_1	X_2	X_3	S_1	S_2	
X_1	1	0	4	3	−7	50
X_2	0	1	−2	−6	2	60
	0	0	−5	−1	−9	1,200

Assume that X_1, X_2, and X_3 represent products, S_1 is in an equation concerning square feet (in thousands) of warehouse capacity, and S_2 is in an equation concerning labor hours (in hundreds).

Required

1 How many units of X_1 and X_2 should be produced to maximize profits.

2 How much would the organization be willing to pay for 1,000 additional square feet of warehouse capacity? For 100 labor hours?

3 If the organization were able to obtain 200 additional labor hours, would the optimum solution change? Explain.

(CPA)

24-11 Postoptimality Analysis The following is the simplex solution of a linear programming problem which maximizes total contribution margin.

	X_1	X_2	S_1	S_2	
X_1	1	0	−5	3	125
X_2	0	1	1	−1	70
Shadow prices	0	0	−5	−7	500

Assume X_1 and X_2 represent products and S_1 is in an equation concerning labor hours in department 1, and S_2 is in an equation concerning labor hours in department 2.

Required

1 Calculate the range in which the labor hours in departments 1 and 2 can change without changing the shadow prices.

2 Compute the range in which the contribution per unit can change without changing the optimal solution.

(CPA)

24-12 Formulation and Changes in Constraints and Contribution Margin Girth, Inc., makes two kinds of men's suede leather belts. Belt A is a high-quality belt, while belt B is of somewhat lower quality. The company earns $7 for each belt A that is sold, and $2 for each belt B sold. Each belt of type A requires twice as much manufacturing time as is required for a belt of type B.

Further, if only belt type B is made, Girth has the capacity to manufacture 1,000 units per day. Suede leather is purchased by Girth under a long-term contract which makes available to Girth enough leather to make 800 belts per day (A and B combined). Belt A requires a fancy buckle, of which only 400 per day are available. Belt B requires a different (plain) buckle, of which 700 per day are available. The demand for the suede leather belts (A or B) is such that Girth can sell all that it produces.

Required

1 Graphically determine how many units of belt A and belt B should be produced to maximize daily profits.

2 Assume the facts above except that the sole supplier of buckles for belt A informs Girth, Inc., that it will be unable to supply more than 100 fancy buckles per day. How many units of each of the two belts should be produced each day to maximize profits?

3 Assume the same facts as in 2 except that Texas Buckles, Inc., could supply Girth, Inc., with the additional fancy buckles it needs. The

price would be \$3.50 more than Girth, Inc., is presently paying for such buckles. How many, if any, fancy buckles should Girth, Inc., buy from Texas Buckles, Inc.? Explain how you determined your answer.

(CMA)

24-13 Graph Interpretation The cost accountant of the Stangren Corporation, your client, wants your opinion of a technique suggested to him by a young accounting graduate he employed as a cost analyst. The following information was furnished to you for the corporation's two products, trinkets and gadgets:

1 **Exhibit A**

	Daily Capacities in Units			
	Cutting Department	Finishing Department	Sales Price per Unit	Variable Cost per Unit
Trinkets	400	240	\$50	\$30
or				
Gadgets	200	320	\$70	\$40

2 The daily capacities of each department represent the maximum production for either trinkets or gadgets. However, any combination of trinkets and gadgets can be produced as long as the maximum capacity of the department is not exceeded. For example, two trinkets can be produced in the cutting department for each gadget not produced and three trinkets can be produced in the finishing department for every four gadgets not produced.

3 Material shortages prohibit the production of more than 180 gadgets per day.

4 Exhibit B is a graphic expression of linear equations developed from the production information above.

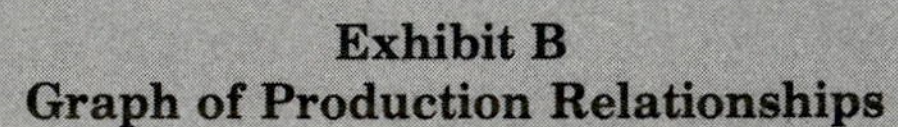

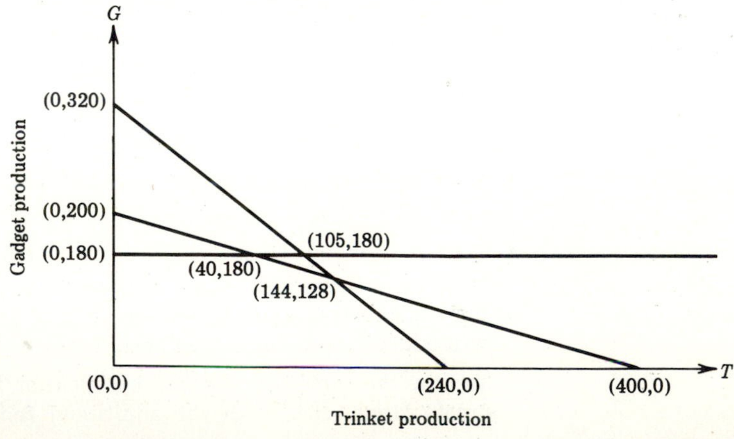

Required

1 Comparing the information in Exhibit A with the graph in Exhibit B, identify and list the graphic location (coordinates) of the:
  a Cutting department's capacity
  b Production limitation for gadgets because of the materials shortage
  c Area of feasible (possible) production combinations

2 a Compute the contribution margin per unit for trinkets and gadgets.
  b Compute the total contribution margin of each of the points of intersections of lines bounding the feasible (possible) production area.
  c Identify the best production alternative.

(CPA)

24-14 Formulation and Revision Based on Regression Analysis The Tripro Company produces and sells three products hereafter referred to as products A, B, and C. The company is currently changing its short-range planning approach in an attempt to incorporate some newer planning techniques. The controller and some of his staff have been conferring with a consultant on the feasibility of using a linear programming model for determining the optimum product mix.

Information for short-range planning has been developed in the same format as in prior years. This information includes expected sales prices and expected direct labor and materials costs for each product. In addition, variable and fixed overhead costs were assumed to be the same for each product because approximately equal quantities of the products were produced and sold.

Price and Cost Information (Per Unit)

	A	B	C
Selling price	$25.00	$30.00	$40.00
Direct labor	7.50	10.00	12.50
Direct materials	9.00	6.00	10.50
Variable overhead	6.00	6.00	6.00
Fixed overhead	6.00	6.00	6.00

All three products use the same type of direct materials which cost $1.50 per pound of material. Direct labor is paid at the rate of $5 per direct labor hour. There are 2,000 direct labor hours and 20,000 pounds of direct materials available in a month.

Required

1 Formulate and label the linear programming objective function and constraint functions necessary to maximize Tripro's contribution margin. Use Q_A, Q_B, Q_C to represent units of the three products.

2 What underlying assumptions must be satisfied to justify the use of linear programming?

3 The consultant, upon reviewing the data presented and the linear programming functions developed, performed further analysis of overhead costs. He used a multiple linear regression model to analyze the overhead cost behavior. The regression model incorporated observa-

tions from the past 48 months of total overhead costs and the direct labor hours for each product. The following equation was the result:

$$Y = \$5{,}000 + 2X_A + 4X_B + 3X_C$$
where Y = monthly total overhead in dollars
X_A = monthly direct labor hours for product A
X_B = monthly direct labor hours for product B
X_C = monthly direct labor hours for product C

The total regression has been determined to be statistically significant as has each of the individual regression coefficients.

Reformulate the objective function for Tripro Company using the results of this analysis.

(CMA)

24-15 Problem Formulation The Witchell Corporation manufactures and sells three grades, A, B, and C, of a single wood product. Each grade must be processed through three phases—cutting, fitting, and finishing—before it is sold.

The following unit information is provided:

	A	B	C
Selling price	\$10.00	\$16.00	\$20.00
Direct labor	5.00	6.00	9.00
Direct materials	.70	.70	1.00
Variable overhead	1.00	1.20	1.80
Fixed overhead	.60	.72	1.08
Materials requirements in board feet	7	7	10
Labor requirements in hours			
Cutting	3/6	3/6	4/6
Fitting	1/6	1/6	2/6
Finishing	1/6	2/6	3/6

Only 5,000 board feet of lumber per week can be obtained.

The cutting department has 180 hours of labor available each week. The fitting and finishing departments each have 120 hours of labor available each week. No overtime is allowed.

Contract commitments require the company to make 50 units of A per week. In addition, company policy is to produce at least 50 additional units of A, B, and C each week to actively remain in each of the three markets. Because of competition, only 130 units of C can be sold each week.

Required

Formulate and label the linear objective function and the constraint functions necessary to maximize the contribution margin.

(CMA)

24-16 Identifying Errors in a Problem Formulation The Elon Company manufactures two industrial products—X-10 which sells for $90 a unit and Y-12 which sells for $85 a unit. Each product is processed through both of the company's manufacturing departments. The limited availability of labor, materials, and equipment capacity has restricted the ability of the firm to meet the demand for its products. The production department believes that linear programming can be used to develop the production schedule for the two products.

The following data are available to the production department.

	Amount Required per Unit	
	X-10	Y-12
Direct materials: weekly supply is limited to 1,800 pounds at $12 per pound	4 pounds	2 pounds
Direct labor:		
Department 1—weekly supply limited to 10 people at 40 hours each at an hourly cost of $6	⅔ hour	1 hour
Department 2—weekly supply limited to 15 people at 40 hours each at an hourly rate of $8	1¼ hours	1 hour
Machine time:		
Department 1—weekly capacity limited to 250 hours	½ hour	½ hour
Department 2—weekly capacity limited to 300 hours	0 hours	1 hour

The overhead costs for Elon are accumulated on a plantwide basis. The overhead is assigned to products on the basis of the number of direct labor hours required to manufacture the product. This base is appropriate for overhead assignment because most of the variable overhead costs vary as a function of labor time. The estimated overhead cost per direct labor hours is:

Variable overhead cost	$ 6.00
Fixed overhead cost	6.00
Total overhead cost per direct labor hour	$12.00

The production department formulated the following equations for the linear programming statement of the problem.

A = number of units of X-10 to be produced
B = number of units of Y-12 to be produced

Objective function to minimize costs:

$$\text{Minimize} = 85A + 62B$$

Constraints:

Material

$$4A + 2B \leq 1800 \text{ pounds}$$

Department 1 labor

$$\tfrac{2}{3}A + 1B \leq 400 \text{ hours}$$

Department 2 labor

$$1\tfrac{1}{4}A + 1B \leq 600 \text{ hours}$$

Nonnegativity

$$A \geq 0, B \geq 0$$

Required

1 The formulation of the linear programming equations as prepared by Elon Company's production department is incorrect. Explain what errors have been made in the formulation prepared by the production department.

2 Formulate and label the proper equations for the linear programming statement of Elon Company's production problem.

3 Explain how linear programming could help Elon Company determine how large a change in the price of direct materials would have to be to change the optimum production mix of X-10 and Y-12.

(CMA)

24-17 Problem Formulation Leastan Company manufactures a line of carpeting which includes a commercial carpet and a residential carpet. Two grades of fiber—heavy-duty and regular—are used in manufacturing both types of carpeting. The mix of the two grades of fiber differs in each type of carpeting with the commercial grade using a greater amount of heavy-duty fiber.

Leastan will introduce a new line of carpeting in two months to replace the current line. The present fiber in stock will not be used in the new line. Management wants to exhaust the present stock of regular and heavy-duty fiber during the last month of production.

Data regarding the current line of commercial and residential carpeting are presented below:

	Commercial	Residential
Selling price per roll	$1,000	$800
Production specifications per roll of carpet:		
Heavy-duty fiber	80 pounds	40 pounds
Regular fiber	20 pounds	40 pounds
Direct labor hours	15 hours	15 hours
Standard cost per roll of carpet:		
Heavy-duty fiber ($3/pound)	$ 240	$120
Regular fiber ($2/pound)	40	80
Direct labor ($10/direct labor hour)	150	150

Variable manufacturing overhead (60% of direct labor cost)	90	90
Fixed manufacturing overhead (120% of direct labor cost)	180	180
Total standard cost per roll	$ 700	$620

Leastan has 42,000 pounds of heavy-duty fiber and 24,000 pounds of regular fiber in stock. All fiber not used in the manufacture of the present types of carpeting during the last month of production can be sold as scrap at $.25 a pound.

There are a maximum of 10,500 direct labor hours available during the month. The labor force can work on either type of carpeting.

Sufficient demand exists for the present line of carpeting so that all quantities produced can be sold.

Required

1 Calculate the number of rolls of commercial carpet and residential carpet Leastan Company must manufacture during the last month of production to exhaust completely the heavy-duty and regular fiber still in stock.

2 Can Leastan Company manufacture these quantities of commercial and residential carpeting during the last month of production? Explain your answer.

3 A member of Leastan Company's cost accounting staff has stated that linear programming should be used to determine the number of rolls of commercial and residential carpeting to manufacture during the last month of production.

- **a** Explain why linear programming should be used in this application.
- **b** Formulate the objective and constraint functions so that this problem can be solved by linear programming.

(CMA)

24-18 Problem Formulation Using Income Statement Data Excelsion Corporation manufactures and sells two kinds of containers—paperboard and plastic. The company produced and sold 100,000 paperboard containers and 75,000 plastic containers during the month of April. A total of 4,000 and 6,000 direct labor hours were used in producing the paperboard and plastic containers respectively.

The company has not been able to maintain an inventory of either product because of the high demand. This situation is expected to continue to the future. Workers can be shifted from the production of paperboard to plastic containers and vice versa, but additional labor is not available in the community. In addition, there will be a shortage of plastic material used in the manufacture of the plastic container in the coming months because of a labor strike at the facilities of a key supplier. Management has estimated there will be only enough direct materials to produce 60,000 plastic containers during June.

The income statement for Excelsion Corporation for the month of April is shown below. The costs presented in the statement are representative of prior periods and are expected to continue at the same rates or levels in the future.

EXCELSION CORPORATION
Income Statement
For the Month Ended April 30, 19X8

	Paperboard Containers	Plastic Containers
Sales	$220,800	$222,900
Less: Returns and allowances	$ 6,360	$ 7,200
Discounts	2,400	3,450
	$ 8,800	$ 10,650
Net sales	$212,000	$212,250
Cost of sales		
Direct materials cost	$123,000	$120,750
Direct labor	26,000	28,500
Indirect labor (variable with direct labor hours)	4,000	4,500
Depreciation—machinery	14,000	12,250
Depreciation—building	10,000	10,000
Cost of sales	$177,000	$176,000
Gross profit	$ 35,000	$ 36,250
Selling and general expenses		
General expenses—variable	$ 8,000	$ 7,500
General expenses—fixed	1,000	1,000
Commissions	11,000	15,750
Total operating expenses	$ 20,000	$ 24,250
Income before tax	$ 15,000	$ 12,000
Income taxes (40%)	6,000	4,800
Net income	$ 9,000	$ 7,200

Required

1 The management of Excelsion Corporation plans to use linear programming to determine the optimal mix of paperboard and plastic containers for the month of June to achieve maximum profits. Using data presented in the April income statement, formulate and label the:

a Objective function

b Constraint functions

2 Explain briefly the underlying assumptions of linear programming.

3 What contribution would the management accountant normally make to a team established to develop the linear programming model and apply it to a decision problem?

(CMA)

PLANNING CAPITAL EXPENDITURES

AFTER COMPLETING YOUR STUDY OF THIS CHAPTER, YOU SHOULD HAVE LEARNED:

1 What a capital expenditure is and the practical limitations on the capital expenditure definition.

2 How present value methods are used to evaluate capital expenditures.

3 How to analyze capital expenditures using net present values, cost-benefit ratios and internal rate of return.

In Chapter 17 capacity costs were defined as those expenditures that provide or increase the productive, distribution, or administrative capacity of an organization. These expenditures are referred to as capital expenditures. The control of capacity costs is primarily accomplished through the careful evaluation of alternatives before long-term commitments are made. In this chapter and the next we will concentrate on the procedures used to evaluate capital expenditures.

DEFINING CAPITAL EXPENDITURES

Under what conditions is a given expenditure a capital expenditure? A **capital expenditure** is any expenditure of cash where the benefit is expected in the form of future cash returns.

Cash Returns

Consider how cash spent results in **future cash returns.**

One way is through the purchase and resale of inventory. The firm spends cash for inventory (either purchasing it or manufacturing it), displays it, and sells it for cash (the outlay or collection of cash is either immediate or after some delay if the inventory is purchased or sold on credit). When the company enters into the operating cycle by purchasing or producing inventory, there is an expectation that when all the inventory is sold and collections have been made from customers, the firm will have more cash than when it began the cycle.

A distinct difference in timing of cash outflows is noted, however, when one compares the retailing or wholesaling situation with the manufacturing situation. The latter requires some kind of producing equipment to transform raw materials to finished goods. This second major form of cash outflow to produce future cash returns involves a relatively long-term commitment to producing equipment.

Is there a difference between purchasing equipment and purchasing inventory? In both cases the ultimate purpose is the same, i.e., to produce cash inflows. The equipment helps to provide cash benefits over quite a long time span, the inventory only at the time of its sale. Inventory is usually purchased in relatively small quantities and held for a relatively short time. As a result, the consequences of making a wrong decision are limited as to time and probably limited as to amount of dollars. But not so on either count in the case of production equipment.

To this point, the future cash return has been considered in the form of a direct cash inflow from customers. There are, of course, other ways in which cash returns can be realized. A future cash return could just as well take the form of cash *savings*.

A firm will often undertake some project which may not directly contribute additional cash inflow from customers but may contribute a future cash return in the sense that it will *reduce* future cash *expenditures*. A prominent example is the purchase of laborsaving equipment. In this situation, spending cash now to obtain the equipment might result in lower future cash outlays for labor. The outlay for the piece of equipment and the series of outlays for the lower labor costs might well amount to less than continuing to spend a greater amount of cash on labor, particularly if one could get some cash for whatever old machinery was being used now.

The firms value is increased by either increasing the cash inflows or decreasing the cash outflows.

Whether the firm's value is being increased by receiving more future cash inflows than otherwise would have occurred, or by paying lower future cash outflows

EXHIBIT 25-1
Effect of Additional Cash Inflows on Cash Balance

Cash

Beginning balance	$600		
Normal cash inflow	220	$200	Normal cash outflow
Added cash inflow	50		
Ending balance	$670		

than otherwise would have been made, it all amounts to the same thing. The value of the firm has been improved. To illustrate this point, consider Exhibits 25-1 and 25-2.

The added cash inflow of $50 results in an ending cash balance of $670 instead of $620. Compare this with Exhibit 25-2. Here there is a cash outflow *reduction* of $50. The effect? An identical ending cash balance.

As far as value added to the firm is concerned, it makes no difference whether it comes as future *additional cash inflows* or future *cash savings*. Perhaps for convenience's sake, *either* additional cash inflows or cash savings can be referred to as *future cash returns.*

Consider again the definition of a capital expenditure. Perhaps there are examples of cash expenditures that are *not* made for the purpose of generating a future cash return. What about wages paid to production employees? This is a cash outflow. Why does the firm employ production employees? They are hired for the purpose of contributing to the cash inflows from the ultimate sales of the product. If the firm has employees who do not at least indirectly contribute to the production of the product, should these employees be on the payroll at all? Take the case of sales employees, or those to whom sales commissions are paid. This is another cash outflow, but one that in most business firms is necessary to generate cash inflows from customers. What about the amounts paid out for office and administrative operations? Again, if the firm is to generate cash inflow from customers on a continuing basis, it must have such functions performed as purchasing, accounting, personnel records, and administration of the various functional areas.

EXHIBIT 25-2
Effect of Reduced Cash Outflows on Cash Balance

Cash

Beginning balance	$600	$150	Cash outflow (normal $200 less $50 cash outflow reduction)
Normal cash inflow	220		
Ending balance	$670		

What sort of things, then, could be excluded? A possible example is the payment of damages in connection with lawsuits. Not much benefit can be foreseen when this type of cash expenditure is imposed on a firm. But even here, it might be argued that the amount of cash paid in settlement of a lawsuit or a judgment was necessary to permit the firm to *continue* to operate and to generate cash inflows. There are probably some cash expenditures whose immediate benefit to future cash returns of the firm is limited. Yet items such as donations, advertising, costs of complying with local ordinances, etc., if *not* made, might materially curtail the firm's future cash inflows.

Practical Limitations of the Definition

In terms of the broad definition set forth earlier, then, any cash outflow from a business firm is a capital expenditure. From a theoretical point of view this is a correct conclusion, and it therefore has some merit; but as a practical matter, business firms just do not treat all their cash outlays as if they were capital expenditures and therefore subject to the sort of analysis which is discussed in this chapter. Some expenditures are treated as engineered costs or managed costs and the analysis procedures of earlier chapters are appropriate. These practical reasons are sound ones, so the definition will be limited on practical grounds, noting however that such limitations are arbitrary.

There is no basic theory outlining precisely what these limits ought to be. As a result, some business firms apply one limit, while others apply different ones. Nevertheless, all could be correct because what constitutes a practical limitation in one business firm might not be one in another. Our definition will therefore be circumscribed by introducing the following three limitations.

Limitations on the definition of a capital expenditure.

1 The cash expenditure is more than some specified minimum dollar amount.
2 The cash returns are expected to continue for more than one year.
3 The cash returns are certain enough in expected amount and timing that management is willing to quantify them.

The first limitation comes into play in cases where it is clear that the improvement in decision making resulting from performing a capital expenditure analysis would not likely be worth the expense of the effort required. For example, the purchase of a pencil sharpener would be a capital expenditure to be sure, and probably employees would get longer use from each sharpening than by whittling and would use fewer pencils. But even if management made the wrong decision, the consequences would not amount to much on either outflow or expected savings counts. With respect to the first limitation, then, the firm should weigh the impact of a wrong decision against the expense of making the analysis. For some smaller firms, a decision requiring an investment of $500 might be worth analyzing. In a very large firm, capital expenditure analysis might be limited to projects having immediate cash outlays of $5,000 or more, since the consequences of making a wrong decision, even a $5,000 wrong decision, are small in relation to (1) the profits of the firm and (2) the expense of analyzing the many projects below $5,000.

The reason for the second practical limitation is that even if there were relatively large dollar amounts involved, a short project time period makes it possible to use a relatively simple analysis without impairing the quality of the decision. For example, if a project were to involve spending $10,000 this month and having a future cash return of $12,000 two months from now, it is obvious that this represents a rather attractive rate of return on the investment—a $2,000 before-tax profit on this transaction. The $2,000 earned on the $10,000 investment is a 20% return earned in only two months. Since rate of return is normally stated on an annual basis, this represents an annual rate of return of 120% (20% divided by two months multiplied by 12 months)! Even if the value increment were not spectacularly high as it is in this case, the short time period makes it relatively easy to see whether the project's value comfortably exceeds the minimum required rate of return. If returns were to continue for more than a year, however, the possibilities that cash returns might not occur in even amounts from year to year is likely. Further, custom dictates that the return be calculated by a compound interest method, something which cannot be done intuitively.

The third practical limitation on the definition is that some kinds of value-producing expenditures may not produce very certain cash returns. For example, the decision to pave the plant parking lot may have considerable merit regarding improvement in employee morale, reduction of absenteeism because of less dust irritation, more efficient heating and cooling because of cleaner surrounding air, more aesthetic value to the community (and thus customers), and so forth, but it would be impossible to determine when and in what amounts these benefits would be received. This is frequently true for advertising, basic research, management development, and other such capital expenditures. But if management cannot quantify the future cash returns, no anaylsis can be performed.

In summary, a capital expenditure is any expenditure of cash where the benefit is expected in the form of future cash returns and where the cash expenditure exceeds some specified minimum dollar amount, is expected to continue for more than one year, and the cash returns are certain enough in expected amount and timing to quantify them.

One final note on the importance of *cash* flows in planning. The overwhelming importance of cash flow predictions for management decision making does not suggest that accrual accounting, as practiced in the preparation of income statements and balance sheets, is inappropriate for some purposes. Although a plan of financial reporting based on discounted future cash flows would likely be superior to the present accrual system of accounting, prediction techniques are not sufficiently advanced to facilitate such a reporting system. As a result, the accrual system is presently the most appropriate one for periodic determination of profit. At the same time, accrual statements, although useful for their purpose, should in no way restrict management in using cash flow analyses in its internal planning for the firm. For planning purposes, management should look at the sequence of cash flows as far into the future as it can reasonably predict.

CAPITAL EXPENDITURE ANALYSIS—PRESENT VALUE

The nature of the analysis underlying capital expenditure decisions will now be examined.

If management is considering any capital expenditure proposal, its value to the firm can be calculated by summing the present values of the future cash returns, discounted at the minimum rate of return.[1] This sum constitutes the *value* of the

[1] The minimum rate of return is also referred to as the cost of capital, the discount rate, or the hurdle rate. The determination of this rate is primarily a finance topic. For our purposes assume the minimum rate of return represents the rate of return that leaves the market price of the firm's stock unchanged. For a discussion of this see Harold J. Bierman, Jr., and Seymour Smidt, *The Capital Budgeting Decision,* 5th ed. New York: The Macmillan Company, 1980.

project. By comparing the value of the project with the cash expenditure necessary to implement it, management can determine whether it will add more to the value of the firm than its required investment. If it does, it should be undertaken. If it does not, it should not be undertaken. (This decision rule applies subject to certain considerations which are discussed in Chapter 26.) Hence, only those capital expenditures will be undertaken which are expected to increase the value of the firm. Most of the remainder of this chapter will be devoted to examining the approaches to the computation of present value.

Present Value Concepts and Calculations

Usually management will not undertake investment projects that are unlikely to yield required returns unless there are compelling reasons of a nonquantitative nature.

How should it be determined whether an investment will yield the minimum rate of return? Perhaps the most obvious approach is to take the amount invested over the life of the project and apply the minimum required rate of return (year by year) to a particular investment. This would give the *opportunity cost* associated with this particular investment. By committing cash to this project, the firm is precluded from committing it to another; management had better be quite certain that they will achieve at least the minimum required rate of return before making the investment.

Assume a project requiring a capital expenditure of $809 will result in the following cash inflows occurring at the end of each year:

Year	
1	$200
2	300
3	500
4	300

If the company's minimum required rate of return is 20%, will this project yield a 20% return on investment?

The cash inflow represents a return on the investment and a return of the investment.

In the first year, the investment is $809. If the project is to earn 20%, the return will be $161.80 for the first year (20% × $809). At the end of the first year a cash inflow of $200 will be received. What must be assumed about this cash inflow? A portion of it is return on investment, and if the amount of cash inflow exceeds the return on investment, the balance is a recovery of part of the initial $809 investment.[2] In this case, return in the first year was calculated to be $161.80. Since $200 will be received at the end of the year, $161.80 of the total represents return on investment and the balance of $38.20 represents a recovery of a portion of the $809

[2] If the required return on investment in any one year were more than the cash inflow during that year, this excess would be added to the amount of the investment for the next year's return calculation.

EXHIBIT 25-3

Year	Average Investment	Total Cash Inflow	Return on Investment at 20%	Recovery of Investment
1	$809.00	$200	$161.80	$ 38.20
2	770.80	300	154.16	145.84
3	624.96	500	125.00	375.00
4	249.96	300	50.00	250.00
5	(0.04)	—	—	—

investment. The investment during the second year will, therefore, be $770.80 ($809 − $38.20). The return on the $770.80 investment at 20% for the second year would be $154.16. The results of this calculation continued over the four years as shown in Exhibit 25-3.

The project thus earns a 20% return on investment while recovering the full $809 investment over the four-year period. Had a large part of the investment been unrecovered at the end of the project (four years), the rate of return on the project would have been *less* than the 20% minimum. Had the project recovered the entire $809 initial investment sometime before the end of the four-year period, the rate of return would have been *more* than 20%.

This method of analysis may be applied to all capital expenditure projects to reveal whether or not the minimum rate of return is being earned. As long as the entire initial investment is recovered over the expected life of the project (including returns), the project has provided a return above the minimum rate. However, there is an easier way of approaching the computations. It is not essential to calculate the change in investment year by year.

Present Value Computation This technique is the **present value** method. Given (1) the minimum required rate of return, (2) the sequence and amount of expected cash returns, and (3) the time period over which they are expected to be received, one can determine a *present value* which represents the amount of value added to the firm by the future cash returns of the project. If this present value is greater than the amount of cash spent to start the project (the investment), then investment in the project can be expected to increase the value of the firm. Here's how the arithmetic works.

Referring to the illustration of Exhibit 25-3, what amount of money is needed *now* to accumulate at 20% interest to the $200 return expected at the end of year

Present value formula.

1? A simple formula does that, $PV = \frac{CI}{(1+r)^n}$, where PV represents present value, CI represents expected future cash return, r represents the required rate of return, and n the number of years the expected cash return is in the future. So the present value of an expected future cash return of $200 discounted at the required rate of return of 20% for one year is $PV = \frac{\$200}{(1+0.2)^1} = \$166.67$. Turning it around the other way, if $166.67 were invested now, by the end of one year the $166.67 plus 20% interest would provide $200. What about the second year? $PV = \frac{\$300}{(1+0.2)^2} = \$208.33$.

Try the last two for yourself. You should get $289.35 for the present value of the third year's expected future cash return of $500, and $144.65 for the $300 of the fourth. The total is, of course, $809.

The difference in approach is that the stream of expected future cash returns becomes the key factor. If the sum of the present values of the stream of expected future cash returns exceeds the cost of investing in the project, the value of the firm will be increased by making the investment. And that is the objective which management strives to achieve in order to maintain the value of the shareholders' investment.

Using the above formulation, $PV = \frac{CI}{(1+r)^n}$, an investor can take any sequence and amount of expected future cash returns, extending over any time period, and fairly easily compute their present value. But since multiplying is handier than dividing (which the above calculation requires) tables have been developed to make obtaining present values even easier.[3]

Present Value Tables Before looking at how, specifically, these tables have been constructed, it might be useful to try predicting how they behave.

There are two factors which will affect present value. One is the period of time involved, and the other is the rate of return, because the amount that could have been earned during the period will depend upon the length of time involved and the assumed minimum rate of return that could be earned in other investments. First, look at the time element. As the time increases during which the firm must wait for the cash inflows, what might one expect to happen to present value? It should go down. This is because the longer the waiting period, the more the return which could have been earned during this period. The present value is the amount to be received at the end of the waiting period minus the return that could have been earned on the present value during the period. Look at the table in Exhibit 25-4, and take any column representing a rate of return, say the 10% column. Move down in that column so that longer and longer waiting periods are involved. As would be expected, the table shows that the present value becomes lower as the waiting period becomes longer.

The same is true for differing rates of return. The higher the rate of return, the

EXHIBIT 25-4
Present Value of $1 Received at the End of the *n*th Year

Year	8%	10%	15%
1	0.9259	0.9091	0.8696
2	0.8573	0.8264	0.7561
3	0.7938	0.7513	0.6575
4	0.7350	0.6830	0.5718
5	0.6806	0.6209	0.4972
6	0.6302	0.5645	0.4323

[3] Complete tables exist as an Appendix to this book. However, the portions necessary to demonstrate their use are excerpted here.

EXHIBIT 25-5

End of	Cash Inflow	Present Value of $1 (10%)	Present Value of Cash Inflow
Year 1	$50	0.9091	$ 45.455
Year 2	50	0.8264	41.320
Year 3	50	0.7513	37.567
Total		2.4868	$124.340

lower the present value. Again the present value is the amount to be received less the return that could have been earned on the present value during the waiting period. The higher the rate, the larger the amount which could have been earned. So, the higher the rate of return, the more that must be subtracted from the ultimate cash inflow to determine the present value. Look again at Exhibit 25-4. Take any row, say the five-year row, and move from left to right so that the rates of return are increasing; the present value is decreasing.

All present value problems can be worked by using a table of the type illustrated in Exhibit 25-4. But there is another kind of table, the *present value of annuity of $1,* which provides a ready shortcut for some problems. An *annuity* is a *periodic* payment of a *fixed* amount which is paid at *regular* time intervals. For example, cash inflows of $1 a year received for each of the next five years constitute an annuity. The fixed amount of $1 is received at the end of the first year, $1 at the end of the second year, and so on to the $1 paid at the end of the fifth year. An expected cash inflow of $260 at the end of one year and another $260 at the end of the second year is also an annuity. In this case, it is a two-year annuity with the fixed amount of $260 a year. However, an expected cash inflow of $400 at the end of one year and $300 at the end of the second year would *not* be an annuity, because the cash inflows are not of a fixed amount. Similarly, an expected cash inflow of $600 at the end of four years is not an annuity, because it is not a *periodic* payment; it is simply a single payment at the end of a certain number of years. But a stream of future receipts, such as projected annual sales of an equal amount for some period of time, would be an annuity. If a stream of expected cash savings from a laborsaving device were determined and the amounts of laborsaving were expected to be the same in each year, the savings from this project would represent an annuity.

Annuity defined.

Exhibit 25-4 may be used to determine the present value of an annuity. It simply involves taking the appropriate present value factors from the table, multiplying them by each year's receipt, and summing the results. For example, suppose that we have an annuity of $50 a year for three years, and we wish to determine the present value of this annuity using a 10% minimum rate of return. Then 10% is our discount rate, and the calculation of the present value is as illustrated in Exhibit 25-5. The present value of each of the three $50 payments has been calculated by multiplying them by the factors for the present value of $1 received at the end of each year from Exhibit 25-4. Summing these, the present value of the annuity is $124.34. As a proof, the three present values of $1 factors may be added, giving a total of 2.4868. The amount of the annuity ($50) multiplied by 2.4868 gives the same present value. Now consult the table in Exhibit 25-6 to

EXHIBIT 25-6
Present Value of an Annuity of $1 Received at the End of Each of *n* Years

Year	8%	10%	15%
1	0.9259	0.9091	0.8696
2	1.7833	1.7355	1.6257
3	2.5771	2.4869	2.2832
4	3.3121	3.1699	2.8550
5	3.9927	3.7908	3.3522
6	4.6229	4.3553	3.7845

find the present value of an annuity of $1, with a three-year period, at the rate of 10%. The answer is 2.4869. If payments of $1 per year are to be made for three years and if the appropriate discount rate is 10%, the present value of this annuity will be slightly under $2.49 (the same figure obtained by summing the individual present value factors from Exhibit 25-4). Therefore, the *present value of the annuity* table is simply a summation of the present value factors for the individual periods from Exhibit 25-4. In what sense, then, is this a shortcut? The present value of an annuity, using the annuity table, can be obtained with only *one* multiplication—simply the dollar amount of the annuity times the factor related to the number or periods during which it will be paid.

A FRAMEWORK FOR CAPITAL EXPENDITURE ANALYSIS

The definition of capital expenditure given earlier suggests that it is a process of spending cash now in the expectation of getting a cash return in the future. The "present value" idea shows that getting back the same number of dollars in the future that he is spending now is not a breakeven proposition for the investor—since he gives up the return that could otherwise have been earned on this cash during the interim period.

The following four steps have general applicability for analyzing any capital expenditure decision:

Steps for analyzing any capital expenditure.

1 Estimate the net future cash returns associated with the project proposal.

2 Determine the present value of the net future cash returns.

3 Estimate the net present cash outlay necessary to implement the proposed project.

4 Compare the present value of the expected future cash returns with the net

present cash outlay and report the results in a meaningful manner to decision makers.

Each of these steps will be treated in turn.

Determine Net Future Cash Returns

The performance of this step suggests the necessity for comparing alternative courses of action. One approach is to estimate what (*a*) the total future cash flows as a result of implementing a proposed project are expected to be and (*b*) the total future cash flows which are expected to exist if the proposed project is *not* undertaken. Then (*c*), the difference between these two streams of future cash flows would be the net future cash returns associated with the project.

Another way of approaching step 1, a way which produces identical results, is to say that the estimated future cash returns associated with the project are those future cash inflows and future cash outflows which would be avoided or forgone if the project were *not* undertaken. In either case, though, it is the expected *net* cash inflows in which we are interested.

Consider the following situation:

New product introduction.

> One product division of Acme Corporation has expected future cash sales of $100,000, employment costs of $60,000, and other operating payments of $30,000 per year. If a proposed project (a new product) is implemented, expected sales will rise to $120,000, employment costs to $65,000, and other operating payments to $35,000 per year for the indefinite future. Exhibit 25-7 portrays the results of an analysis performed to determine the net cash inflows under each of the two approaches.

The results are obviously identical, showing that there is essentially no conceptual difference between the two methods. All that is demonstrated here is that approach A expresses the expected future net cash inflows attributable to the project as *additional* net cash inflow, while approach B expresses the expected future net cash inflow in terms of the amount to be *avoided* or *forgone* if the project is not undertaken. Either method may be chosen.

Estimating net future cash returns in cases in which they are expressed as cash *savings* is virtually identical in process and concept to the forgoing. Again, it is the expected future *net* cash savings with which we are concerned. Consider another alternative-choice situation:

A machine replacement.

> A machine now in use requires $8,300 in labor payments, $300 in power costs, and $150 in property tax and insurance costs each year and is expected to last five more years. A proposed project, assuring equivalent annual output over its expected five-year life, would reduce labor payments to $5,000, increase power costs to $400, and increase property tax and insurance costs to $300 each year. Exhibit 25-8 depicts the outcome of an analysis performed to estimate the net cash savings (or net cash outflow avoided).

Again, the results are identical, and either method may be preferred.

The question of the impact of income tax on determination of cash flows will be dealt with in the next chapter.

EXHIBIT 25-7
ACME CORPORATION
A New Product

Approach A (Comparison of before-project and after-project cash flows:

Item	If Project Undertaken	If Project Not Undertaken	Increase (Decrease) in Cash Flows
Sales	$120,000	$100,000	$20,000
Employment	(65,000)	(60,000)	(5,000)
Other operations	(35,000)	(30,000)	(5,000)
Total net cash inflow	$ 20,000	$ 10,000	$10,000

Increase in net cash inflow attributable to proposed project $10,000

Approach B Avoidable (or forgone) cash flows if project not undertaken:

Item	Cash Inflows (Outflows) Avoided or Forgone
Sales	$20,000
Employment	(5,000)
Other operations	(5,000)
Total net cash inflow	$10,000

Net inflow forgone if project not undertaken $10,000

Determine the Present Value of the Net Future Cash Returns

Having estimated the net future cash returns, the appropriate factors from the present value table(s) should be applied to determine the present values of each year's net cash return. All that remains is the summing of these present values for each year to determine the total present value of the net future cash returns.

> In the case of the machine replacement, assuming a before-tax minimum required rate of return of 20%, the present value of the annuity of $3,050 for five years would be $9,123 ($3,050 × 2.991) before consideration of income taxes.

Estimate the Net Present Cash Outlay

This is the net amount of cash which the firm must spend now to implement a proposed capital expenditure project. An equivalent statement would be "the amount of net cash outlay which could be avoided if the project were not undertaken." Again, this is a net concept, and all cash flows relevant to the project must be considered.

In the machine replacement case, the new machine has an invoice cost of $15,000, expected delivery and installation outlays of $500, and an expected outlay for makeready and first-piece test of $100. The present machine could be sold for $7,000 cash immediately. Exhibit 25-9 presents the analysis of the net present cash outlay.

Again, discussion of the effect of income taxes is deferred until Chapter 26.

Report the Results of the Analysis

There are several ways to compare the present value of the future cash flows with the net present cash outlay. Three will be considered here.

Net Present Value Method The **net present value** method evaluates the capital expenditure by subtracting the net present cash outlay from the present value of the future cash flows. The net present value of the machine replacement proposal is $523 as computed below:

A positive net present value indicates a return greater than the minimum.

Present value of future cash flows	$9,123
Present value of net cash outlay	$8,600
Net present value	$ 523

EXHIBIT 25-8
A Machine Replacement

Approach A Comparison of before-project and after-project cash savings:

Item	If Project Undertaken	If Project Not Undertaken	Cash Savings (Dissavings)
Labor	$5,000	$8,300	$3,300
Power	400	300	(100)
Property taxes and insurance	300	150	(150)
Total cash outflow	$5,700	$8,750	
Net cash savings attributable to proposed project			$3,050

Approach B Avoidable cash flows if project is undertaken:

Item	Cash Outflows Avoided (Incurred)
Labor	$3,300
Power	(100)
Property taxes and insurance	(150)
Net avoidable cash outflow if project is undertaken	$3,050

EXHIBIT 25-9
A Machine Replacement

Approach A Net present cash outlay required to implement the proposed project.

Item	Cash Outlay
Machine	$15,000
Delivery and installation	500
Makeready and first-piece test	100
Total present cash outlay	$15,600
Less: Cash inflow from sale of old-machine	(7,000)
Net present cash outlay	$ 8,600

Approach B Net avoidable present cash outlay if project is not undertaken.

Item	Cash Outlay (Inflow) Avoided
Machine	$15,000
Delivery and installation	500
Makeready and first-piece test	100
Total avoidable present cash outlay	$15,600
Less: Avoidable cash inflow from sale of old machine	(7,000)
Net avoidable present cash outlay	$ 8,600

Since the net present value is positive the rate of return on the machine replacement is greater than the 20% minimum rate of return.

Benefit-Cost Ratio Another way of expressing the results is called the benefit-cost ratio or profitability index. The benefit-cost ratio is calculated as follows:

$$\text{Benefit-cost ratio} = \frac{\text{present value of future cash flows}}{\text{required first year investment}}$$

If all relevant items have been considered and the benefit-cost ratio is one or greater, the project is economically attractive because it promises to yield more than the minimum rate of return. For example, the benefit-cost ratio for the machine replacement proposal is calculated below:

$$\text{Benefit-cost ratio} = \frac{\$9{,}123}{\$8{,}600} = 1.06$$

The internal rate of return is the rate which makes the net present value zero.

Internal Rate of Return A third way of reporting the results of the analysis requires a modification of the method of analysis itself. This third way of reporting is referred to as the **internal rate of return** method.

When a net present value is computed, the amount of that net present value depends on the cash flows themselves *and* on the rate used in determining the present values. The internal rate of return method seeks that rate which makes the net present value of the project zero. Thus, once the relevant cash flow items, amounts, and timing are determined, *any* rate can be used in calculating the present values (step 2).

In the machine replacement case, the net present value was $523 when 20% was used to compute the present value. What would the result be if 22% had been used in the computation? Using 22% the net present value is ($3,050 × 2.864) = $8,735 − $8,600 = $135. The net present value is very close to zero ($135). Thus the internal rate of return on the machine replacement is very close to 22%.

How would the internal rate of return method be used in the decision-making process to determine which alternative is better? By comparing the company's minimum rate of return with the internal rate of return on the project. As long as all relevant items have been considered and the internal rate of return is greater than the minimum rate of return, the project is economically attractive.

Compared with the net present value method, reporting the internal rate of return has the advantage of being expressed as a percentage return, an expression which is more familiar to most business managers than the net present value. It has the disadvantage of not showing how much value will be added to the firm by the investment, and it is more difficult computationally. While computation issues are important in a learning situation, they are of little practical importance since most businesses have access to a computer for making the calculations. Finally, other theoretical arguments favor the net present value method, but a discussion of them is beyond the scope of this book.

ORGANIZING THE COMPUTATIONS IN CAPITAL EXPENDITURE ANALYSIS

The solution of capital expenditure problems calls for an organized approach. One of the many ways of tackling a problem is illustrated in Exhibit 25-10 which starts with the results of step 1 and carries through to step 4.

Exhibit 25-10 has been completed using the data from the machine replacement problem. All the annuity amounts ran for the full five-year life. Had there been some other annuity for a shorter period, it would have been inserted by either lengthening the form or by condensing the data for the five-year annuity. In this problem there were no single payments. A salvage value amount, typical of a single payment, was put in the form at a zero amount to illustrate how such an item would be entered.

SUMMARY

The purpose of this chapter was to examine the analytical framework underlying capital expenditure planning.

A capital expenditure was defined as any expenditure of cash where the benefit is expected in the form of future cash returns. Future cash returns were shown to

EXHIBIT 25-10
Capital Expenditure Analysis Worksheet

Calculating the Present Value of Net Future Cash Returns

Item	End of Years	Cash	Present Value Factor	Present Value of Net Future Cash Returns
Annuities				
Labor savings	*1-5*	*$3,300*		
Power	*1-5*	*(100)*		
Taxes and insurance	*1-5*	*(150)*		
		$3,050	*2.991*	*$9,123*
Salvage value	*5*	*–*	*.402*	*–*
Total present value of net future cash returns (step 2)				*$9,123*

Calculating the Present Net Cash Outlay

Purchase price	*$15,000*	
Less: Trade in or salvage of other equipment	*7,000*	*8,000*
Plus: Installation costs	*500*	
Other		
Makeready & test	*100*	*600*
Total present net cash outlay (step 3)		= *$8,600*

Comparison

Net present value: Step 2 *$9,123* minus step 3 *$8,600* = *$ 523*

Benefit-cost ratio: Step 2 *$9,123* divided by step 3 *$8,600* = *1.06*

take the form of either cash inflows or cash savings. It was demonstrated with the given definition that virtually every cash outflow is a capital expenditure. It would be too time-consuming and expensive to analyze all cash outflows this way. Some practical limitations, therefore, were imposed. Practical limitations on the definition are:

1 The cash expenditure is more than some specified minimum dollar amount.
2 The cash returns are expected to continue for more than one year.
3 The cash returns are certain enough in expected amount and timing that management is willing to quantify them.

Because of the commitment over long time periods, the analysis must be designed to consider the return which could have been earned in other investment opportunities which face the firm. This can be done more conveniently by establishing a minimum rate of return and applying it in present value analysis. The minimum rate of return is usually based on cost of capital analysis. Present value analysis permits estimation of whether the proposed project will yield the minimum rate of return.

This chapter has established the basic framework of present value analysis. A number of useful elaborations, including income tax considerations and the effect of uncertainty on the analysis, are treated in Chapter 26.

Review Problem

Edburr, Inc., is facing the decision of whether to make or buy a particular subassembly used in production of product X. The cost of purchasing would be $12 per unit.

The company owns equipment that can be used only to manufacture this part. The book value and salvage value of this equipment is now $5,000. It will either be used or scrapped. The expected salvage value of the equipment at the end of its useful life three years from now is expected to be $2,000. The part will be made in an adjacent plant which can be rented for $7,000 per year. Other expenses of production will be:

	Per Unit
Direct labor	$3.00
Material	3.40
Variable overhead	1.00
Total	$7.40

In addition, the company will need an average material inventory of $3,000 if it produces the part. It is expected that 2,000 units will be produced each year for three years, at which time the product will be discontinued. Cost of capital is 10%.

Should the company make or buy the part?

Solution

Capital Expenditure Analysis Worksheet

Item	Time	Annual Cash Flow	Present Value Factor	Present Value of Cash Flow
		Make		
Direct labor	1-3	$ 6,000		
Material	1-3	6,800		
Variable overhead	1-3	2,000		
Plant rental	1-3	7,000		
Subtotal		$21,800	2.487	$54,217
Inventory investment	0	3,000	1.0	3,000
Recovery of inventory investment	3	(3,000)		
Salvage value of machine	3	(2,000)		
Subtotal		$(5,000)	0.751	(3,755)
Present value of net cash outflows				$53,462
		Buy		
Purchase price of subassembly	1-3	$24,000	2.487	$59,688
Present salvage value of machine	0	$(5,000)	1.0	(5,000)
Present value of net cash outflow				$54,688

Note: ( ) indicates cash inflow or cash savings.

Edburr, Inc. should make the subassembly.

Glossary

Benefit-cost ratio A measure of whether a capital expenditure will return more or less than the minimum required rate of return.

Capital expenditure Any expenditure of cash where the benefit is expected in the form of future cash returns. Usually the following practical limitations are imposed: (1) The cash expenditure is more than some specified minimum dollar amount. (2) The cash returns are expected to continue for more than one year. (3) The cash returns are certain enough in expected amount and timing that management is willing to quantify them.

Future cash returns Direct cash inflow from customers or others, or future cash savings caused by present cash expenditure.

Internal rate of return That rate which when used in a present value computation results in a zero net present value for the project.

Net present value A measure of whether a capital expenditure will return more or less than the minimum required rate of return.

Present value The present value amount is that amount which will be received at the end of the waiting period minus the return that could have been earned on the present value during the period.

Present value of annuity Present value of periodic payments of a fixed amount paid at regular time intervals.

Questions and Problems

25-1 According to the definition given in the chapter, do the following qualify for the classification "capital expenditure"? Why or why not?

1 Decision to pursue an MBA degree

2 Procter & Gamble's yearly expenditure for advertising

3 Decision to invest $25,000 in developing a computer program to aid in production scheduling

25-2 If a capital expenditure, in addition to incurring outlays and saving outlays, also affects revenue, what additional factors will need to be considered in the analysis of the expenditure which are not necessary when only outlays are involved?

25-3 The present value concept involves discounting future cash flows back to their present value. Why must present value be a part of the analysis?

25-4 Annuity Calculations to Understand the Tables

1 Using only the table for the present value of $1, calculate the present value of a three-year annuity of $50 per year with payments coming at the end of each year. Assume that the appropriate discount rate is 8%.

2 Prove that your answer is correct by using the table for the present value of $1 received annually for *n* years.

3 Answer the question without using any tables or calculations. If the annuity described in question 1 called for payments at the beginning of each year rather than the end of each year, would the present value of this annuity be higher or lower than the annuity described in question 1? Assume that everything else is equivalent, other than the timing of the payments. Explain in words why your answer is correct.

4 Prove that your answer to question 3 is correct by using any tables and making any computations you wish to use to calculate the present value of the annuity described in that question.

25-5 Rate of Return and the Present Value of an Annuity Compute the present value for the following situations with even annual cash inflows. Compare the relationship between the present value and the minimum required rate of return.

	1	2	3	4
Minimum required rate of return (in percent)	8	10	14	20
Cash inflows at the end of each year for next ten years	$2,000	$2,000	$2,000	$2,000

25-6 Present Value Computations with Uneven Amounts Compute the present value for the following situations with uneven annual cash inflows.

1 Assume a stream of expected cash inflows of $800 a year for the first two years, $1,000 for the next three years, and $1,200 for the last five years. Assume a discount rate of 16%.

2 Assume a stream of expected cash inflows of $500 a year for the first nine years, and $900 for the last year. Assume a discount rate of 18%.

25-7 Savings Account Deposits

1 How much should be deposited in a savings account yielding 5% interest compounded annually so that there will be $1,200 on deposit at the end of three years? Assume that no deposits are made to the account after the first deposit.

2 Prove that your answer is correct by calculating the interest over the three-year period.

3 What is the present value of $1,200 to be received at the end of three years at 5% interest compounded annually?

25-8 Investment Choices without the Tables Choose between a variety of pairs of investments, all of which require an initial investment of $10,000. The cash inflows expected from each investment are described in the table given below. The minimum rate of return required is something greater than zero. Without making any computations or using any tables, decide for each of the following four cases: (1) which of the two alternatives is the preferred investment and (2) whether either or both of the alternative investments can be rejected without computations.

- A versus C
- A versus B
- A versus D
- A versus E

Table of Future Cash Flows

End of Year	A	B	Investment C	D	E
1	$+3,000	$+5,000	$+2,000	—	$+5,000
2	+3,000	+4,000	+2,000	—	+5,000
3	+3,000	+3,000	+2,000	$+5,000	+5,000
4	+3,000	+3,000	+2,000	+5,000	−1,000
5	+3,000	—	+2,000	+5,000	+3,000

Note: + means inflow; − means outflow.

25-9 Which New Machine to Buy? Sconapat, Inc., has asked your advice in the purchase of a new machine. Two machines are available which perform the same function. Because of varying patterns of maintenance and spoilage, the future cash inflows are estimated to be as follows:

Year	Machine A	Machine B
1	$10,000	$ 5,000
2	25,000	15,000
3	25,000	20,000
4	15,000	30,000
5	10,000	25,000

Each machine has an initial cost of $50,000.

Required

1 Assuming that the company's cost of capital is 8%, which machine appears more desirable?

2 Assuming that the company's cost of capital is 20%, which machine appears more desirable?

3 Explain the apparent inconsistency in the answers determined in questions 1 and 2.

25-10 Net Present Value and Benefit-Cost Ratio Compute the net present value and the benefit-cost ratio for the following capital expenditure projects.

1 Assume an expected cash outlay of $7,000 at the beginning of year 1, and annual expected cash inflows of $1,000 for the next 20 years. Assume a discount rate of 12%.

2 Assume an expected cash outlay of $15,000 at the beginning of year 1, and annual expected cash inflows of $3,000 for the first two years and $6,000 for the last two years. Assume a discount rate of 18%.

25-11 Differing Patterns of Cash Returns Assuming a minimum rate of return of 10%, which of the following capital expenditure projects should be accepted or rejected? Each is independent of the others.

	1	2	3
Present cash outlay (beginning of year 1)	$12,000	$12,000	$12,000
Cash inflows at the end of year 1	$ 3,000	$ 1,000	$ 5,000
Cash inflows at the end of year 2	3,000	2,000	4,000
Cash inflows at the end of year 3	3,000	3,000	3,000
Cash inflows at the end of year 4	3,000	4,000	2,000
Cash inflows at the end of year 5	3,000	5,000	1,000
Total cash inflows	$15,000	$15,000	$15,000

25-12 Jukebox Purchasing Bilbo, Inc., is considering the acquisition of a fancy jukebox. The cost of the machine is $4,500. The jukebox would probably have to be replaced after four years. At the end of four years, the system will have a salvage value of $200. It will cost an additional $800 to do the wiring necessary to install the remote stereo speakers. The company which sells the machine is willing to service the machine and provide current records for $100 per year plus 20% of the revenue. Alternately, Bilbo can spend $100 to buy tools and $200 to send one of the managers to a service school in order to do their own maintenance. Under this alternative, maintenance expense (including purchase of records) is expected to be $160 per year. It can be assumed that all maintenance expenses other than tools and schooling would be paid at the end of each year. Bilbo expects a 10% return on investment. You may ignore income taxes. Assume that power expense is negligible and can be ignored. The expected yearly revenue is as follows:

Year	
1	$1,000
2	1,800
3	2,000
4	2,200

Required

1 If Bilbo buys the jukebox, should they let the seller of the machine do the maintenance or should they do it themselves?

2 Assume that Bilbo will do the maintenance themselves. Will the purchase of the jukebox result in a 10% return on investment?

3 If a record distributor were to offer the payment of $300 per year to Bilbo for playing its records, would this change your answer to question 2?

25-13 Hopper Company's New Product The Hopper Company is contemplating developing a new product. The following changes are expected to occur if the product is put into production.

Annual sales	$200,000
Cost of goods sold*	115,000
Selling and administrative expense†	45,000
Purchase of equipment	150,000
Decrease in contribution margin from sale of other products	5,000
Increase in accounts receivable	20,000
Increase in inventories	25,000
Increase in current liabilities	15,000
Increase in income taxes	12,000

* Includes depreciation of $20,000.
† Includes depreciation of $10,000 and redistribution of general office expenses of $6,000.

Required

1 Compute the cash flow amounts to be used in the present value analysis for time zero (the present), and for the first year the product would be in production.

2 The company has a cost of capital of 24%. If the product has an expected life of five years, would you expect it to yield a 24% return?

3 As an adviser to management who had no part in developing the amounts shown in the problem, what questions might you raise about the data?

25-14 Improving Production with a New Machine Dorowa Company is contemplating an investment in a new machine to improve the production of a standard product. The machine will, according to engineering reports, reduce maintenance $8,000 per year to $2,000 per year. Production expenses will be reduced from $3.20 per unit to $2.80 per unit. The machine will cost $300,000 and have a useful life of 10 years, with no salvage value after that time. The old machine presently has a book and salvage value of $50,000. It could be used for another 10 years, but will have zero salvage value at the end of that time.

Production will equal sales in all years but year 6, when inventory will have to be increased by 5,000 units to provide an adequate safety stock for increased sales. Current sales are 100,000 units per year; they will increase in year 6 by 20% and then remain at the new level. If the company's minimum rate of return is 20%, should the investment be undertaken?

25-15 Should Botchit Manufacturing Company Make Flubits? Bochit Manufacturing Company buys about 130,000 flubits a year for use in their production. The total cost of the annual supply of flubits when purchased from a supply house is $251,000. For $80,000, Botchit can buy the needed specialized equipment to make their own flubits. The machine would be installed in existing leased plant space. An estimate for manufacturing flubits is as follows:

Annual materials @ $1.15 per flubit	$149,500
Annual direct labor @ $0.50 per flubit	65,000
Maintenance contract for new machine—	
First three years	7,000 per year
Remaining life	11,000 per year
Depreciation	8,000 per year
Foreman for flubit department	13,000 per year
Annual rental of plant space @ $0.50 per square foot	5,200 per year
Annual plant manager expense (based on number of workers)	3,900 per year

The equipment is expected to have no salvage value after a 10-year useful life. Botchit's cost of capital is 20%.

Required

1 Should Botchit make its own flubits?

2 What factors should Botchit's management consider in evaluating the results of the capital expenditure analysis and in reaching a decision?

25-16 Suit City Considers Making or Buying a New Line in Jackets Suit City is considering adding a product line to their store of leather jackets with "that well-worn look." They expect that 13,000 jackets per year can be sold for the next five years, after which the market for this fad may be exhausted. It has discovered that the jackets can be purchased from a military surplus store for $5.50 per jacket. Minor modifications which could be made without any significant investment in equipment would add $1.70 to the cost of each jacket.

Alternatively, with an investment of $40,000 in specialized equipment, Suit City could manufacture the jackets completely from used leather. The equipment would be installed in currently unused space in the basement of the store. The company accountants have made the following expense estimates for manufacturing the required number of jackets per year:

Annual materials	$29,000
Annual manufacturing labor	42,000
Annual maintenance contract for equipment	1,500
Straight-line depreciation per year on equipment	4,000
Annual salary of foreman for the jacket department	8,200
Annual value of store space, @ $0.50 per square foot per year	3,800
Annual general management supervision expense based on the total number of employees of the store	3,700

The equipment is expected to have no salvage value when it is worn out at the end of 10 years. Since the equipment is specialized, it probably cannot be used to manufacture other types of garments. Suit City's cost of capital is 15%.

Required Should Suit City manufacture their own jackets? Explain both the quantitative and other considerations which should enter into management's decision.

25-17 Doing Work for Another Firm Burcam Company purchased a Sharman mill two years ago for $150,000. The manufacturer of the mill estimated the useful life to be 10 years with a salvage value of $15,000 based on operating levels of 8,000 hours per year. The operating expenses are as follows:

Power	$ 500 per year
Lubrication	300 per year
Maintenance and repairs	200 per year
Labor and materials	24,000 per year

The original estimates of useful life and salvage value are still believed to be correct unless significant changes were made in the use of the mill. The mill is used in the production of a variety of products. It is estimated that if Burcam did not have the machine, work presently manufactured on the mill would have been subcontracted to an outside machine shop at $75,000 annually. The company's minimum rate of return is 20%.

Joplin Company has approached Burcam about doing some work which would require the use of the mill. Burcam's engineers estimate that accepting the order would increase the operating rate of the machine such that its useful life would be decreased by two years but the salvage value would not be changed. Revenue minus all expenses except power, lubrication, maintenance, and repair would yield a cash inflow of $15,000 from the contract. Accepting the order would result in a 30% increase in power expense, a 15% increase in maintenance and repair expense, and a 10% increase in lubrication expense. Joplin will supply the raw materials needed for their work and will reimburse Burcam for any additional direct labor. The contract, if accepted, is expected to run for at least six years, and the future annual depreciation of the machine would be adjusted to the new six-year estimated life.

1 Should Burcam accept the additional work?

2 Suppose that the useful life of the mill is limited by obsolescence rather than physical wear of the mill. Would this change your answer? Explain.

26 ADVANCED CONSIDERATIONS IN CAPITAL EXPENDITURES

AFTER COMPLETING YOUR STUDY OF THIS CHAPTER, YOU SHOULD HAVE LEARNED:

1 The impact of income taxes on capital expenditure decisions.

2 The advantage of using accelerated depreciation methods for income tax purposes.

3 What methods are used to rank capital expenditure proposals.

4 Methods to incorporate risk in capital expenditure analysis.

In Chapter 25, a working definition of a capital expenditure was established and the basic method of analysis was studied. In this chapter, three additional major topics are considered: income tax in capital expenditure analysis; analysis in the capital rationing situation, i.e., the situation where the available acceptable projects exceed the currently available funds; and methods of dealing explicitly with risk in capital expenditure analysis.

Since each of these subjects builds fairly independently on Chapter 25, it is possible to study any one of the three without having first covered the others.

INCOME TAX AND CAPITAL EXPENDITURE DECISIONS

How do capital expenditure decisions cause changes in cash income tax payments? To the extent that any capital expenditure decision gives rise to a change in the amount of a revenue or deduction item on the income tax return, the cash amount of taxes to be paid to the government will be affected. It is these changes in the total cash income tax payment which must be a part of the capital expenditure analysis to properly measure the value of an investment alternative.

Income Tax Payments and Other Cash Flows

As a technique for making the adjustments for cash income tax payments, it is usually most convenient to express the change in the present cash outlay and the future cash returns *net* of their income tax effects.[1] Returning to the machine replacement example which was considered in Chapter 25, we find that the future cash returns consisted of the following:

A Machine Replacement

Net cash savings:		
Reduction in labor payments		$3,300
Additions to: Power cost	$100	
Property taxes and insurance	150	250
Cash savings before income tax		$3,050

Labor, power cost, property taxes, and insurance are all deductible items in calculating the required cash income tax payments. Since tax deduction items change, income tax payments will also change. As a result of the labor savings, the

[1] This involves the simplifying assumption that any change in income taxes is paid or saved immediately when the income tax deduction is changed. This is not strictly true, but since most large businesses pay income taxes based on income estimates, it is a reasonable assumption.

A more important assumption is that we ignore the investment credit sometimes authorized by the Internal Revenue Code. The primary effect of the investment is to reduce the net present cash outlay. Since there are so many technical considerations in application of the investment credit, we have chosen not to discuss it. Those who study the subject of income taxes in greater depth should have no difficulty in modifying the analysis of capital expenditures to include the investment credit.

EXHIBIT 26-1
A Machine Replacement

	Before Income Tax Deduction	Income Tax Change (40%)	After Tax
Reduction in labor payments	$3,300	$(1,320)	$1,980
Increase in power cost	(100)	40	(60)
Increase in property taxes and insurance	(150)	60	(90)
Changes	$3,050	$(1,220)	
Increase in cash outflow			$1,830

EXHIBIT 26-2
A Machine Replacement

Net cash savings:		
Reduction in labor payments		$3,300
Additions to: Power cost	$100	
Property taxes and insurance	150	250
Net cash savings:		$3,050
Less: Increase in cash outflows for income tax payments (@ 40%)		1,220
Net cash savings		$1,830

EXHIBIT 26-3
A Machine Replacement

Depreciation reduces the cash outflow for income taxes.

Net cash savings (from Exhibit 26-2)		$1,830
Add: Reduction in tax payments as a result of an increase in allowable depreciation:		
New machine depreciation	$3,120	
Present machine depreciation	1,000	
Additional depreciation	$2,120	
Tax reduction rate	40%	
Cash income savings attributable to depreciation		848
After-tax net cash savings		$2,678

company will have to pay more income tax; but the increased deductions for power cost and property taxes and insurance will save income tax. Since the tax rate is 40%, an increase of $100 in deductions will save $40 (40% of $100) in income tax payments. Therefore, the after-tax cost of the $100 deduction is only $60 ($100 deduction minus $40 income tax savings). The tax impact is illustrated in Exhibit 26-1.

With a savings, income tax deductions are reduced and the income tax payments are increased, so that the *after*-tax benefit is not as great as the *before*-tax benefit. The actual form of the analysis is depicted in Exhibit 26-2.

Income taxes influence the net cash flows.

If a change has the effect of increasing a deduction, it saves income tax payments. If a change has the effect of decreasing a deduction, more income tax will have to be paid.

Income Tax Payments and Depreciation

Depreciation, although not a cash outflow, does influence the amount of income taxes paid. It becomes relevant solely because it represents an allowable tax deduction. And since income taxes are cash payments, any increase in depreciation expense attributable to a proposed project reduces the amount of cash that must be paid as income tax.

> In the machine replacement case, the present machine is being depreciated, straight-line, at $1,000 a year over its remaining five-year life. The new machine being considered is to be depreciated at $3,120 a year over its five-year life.[2]

As Exhibit 26-3 indicates, the amount of the reduction in the tax payment for each year is the product of multiplying the increase in depreciation expense by the tax reduction rate (which is always identical to the tax rate).

Income Taxes and the Present Cash Outlay

So far the illustration has dealt solely with income taxation as it relates to expected future cash returns. But it relates directly to the calculation of the present cash outlay as well. Replacing an old machine with a new one frequently creates a taxable gain or loss which would not be experienced if the replacement were not made. To demonstrate the impact of this element of income taxation, we return to the situation under discussion. The present machine has a book value for income tax purposes of $5,000 and can be sold for $7,000. Exhibit 26-4 shows the tax impact of the $2,000 gain on the sale of the present machine.

The machine replacement promises nearly exactly the minimum required rate of return of 12% on an after income tax basis. The present value of a five-year annuity of $2,678 is $9,654. The present cash outlay computed in Exhibit 26-4 is $9,400, resulting in a net present value of $254. The benefit-cost ratio is 1.03.

Except for the modification for accelerated depreciation methods, this analysis summarizes the effects of income taxes on capital expenditure analysis.

[2] We shall consider the effect of accelerated depreciation methods later.

EXHIBIT 26-4
A Machine Replacement

Total present cash outlay for new machine (from Exhibit 25-9)	$15,600
Less: Cash inflow from sale of old machine	(7,000)
Add: Increase in tax payment as a result of the $2,000 capital gain ($7,000 − $5,000) at a 40% rate of taxation	800
After-tax net cash outlay	$ 9,400

Accelerated Depreciation and Income Taxes[3]

Accelerated depreciation methods assume that a larger part of the depreciation of an asset occurs in the early years of its life, with relatively lower depreciation in the later years. In contrast, the straight-line (or SL) method assumes that the same amount of depreciation occurs in each full year of the asset's useful life. Two methods of accelerated depreciation are widely accepted for both financial accounting and income tax purposes. They are the *sum of the years' digits* methods (SYD) and *twice the straight-line rate applied to the declining balance.*

Accelerated depreciation reduces cash payments for income taxes early in the life of the capital project.

An understanding of present value analysis reveals the potential advantage of using accelerated depreciation methods for income tax purposes. If it is possible to make accurate estimates of useful life, and if income tax rates do not change, the total deductions and total amount of income taxes to be paid are the same regardless of depreciation method. The difference is in the timing of income tax payments. The larger depreciation deductions in the early years will result in lower income tax payments in early years. Lower depreciation deductions in later years will mean higher income tax payments in later years, but the deferring of the income tax payments has a benefit to the firm which can be measured through present value analysis.

A simple example, demonstrating the SYD method of accelerated depreciation, will illustrate this benefit. Any other method could equally well be used; managers should choose the one which will yield the greatest present value benefit. To avoid unnecessary complications, the illustrations here are confined to the SYD method.

As a simple example, suppose a firm is considering the acquisition of an asset with a cost of $1. The asset is expected to have a useful life of four years and zero salvage value. Management has made the analysis of future cash flows on an after-tax basis according to previously discussed methods. In their analysis, they assumed straight-line (SL) depreciation (as was done in Exhibits 26-3 and 26-4).

They wish to consider the use of SYD depreciation and want to know what effect this will have on the present value of the future cash returns. First, the difference in depreciation must be calculated on a year-by-year basis as shown in Exhibit 26-5.

The depreciation deduction allowable under the straight-line method is simply one-fourth of the cost of the asset, or 25 cents per year. The sum of the years' digits (4 + 3 + 2 + 1) is 10, indicating that 40 percent (four-tenths) of the cost is deductible

[3] The discussion of the effect of accelerated depreciation draws heavily on an article by Robert K. Zimmer and Jack Gray, "Using Accelerated Depreciation in Capital Expenditure Analysis," *Management Services,* New York: The American Institute of Certified Public Accountants, January–February 1969, pp. 43–48. Table 3 in the Appendix of this book is also taken from this article.

EXHIBIT 26-5
Depreciation Tax Deduction

	SL Depreciation	SYD Depreciation	Difference
Year 1	$0.25	$0.40	$0.15
Year 2	0.25	0.30	0.05
Year 3	0.25	0.20	(0.05)
Year 4	0.25	0.10	(0.15)
	$1.00	$1.00	$ zero

in the first year, 30% in the second year, 20% in the third year, and 10% in the fourth year. The total depreciation will be the same. The value of the accelerated depreciation results from the deferral of tax payments in the early years of the investment's life.

The value of the tax deferral is found by taking the present value of the difference in tax deductions multiplied by the tax rate. In order to make these calculations we must know the minimum required rate of return that management uses in capital expenditure analysis and the income tax rate. If the required rate of return is 30% and the tax rate is 40%, the calculation can be completed.

In our previous calculations, we applied the tax rate to the depreciation deductions and then calculated the present value. In the next illustration the procedure is reversed by calculating the present value of the depreciation deductions and then applying the income tax rate. Mathematically, it does not make any difference in which order the steps are taken. In order to develop a table which can be used regardless of tax rate, it is convenient to make the present value calculation before the tax rate is applied. The calculation of the present value of the depreciation deductions is shown in Exhibit 26-6. The present value resulting from use of SYD rather than SL depreciation is found by multiplying the result, $0.0697, by the tax rate of 40%. This gives the final result as follows:

$0.0697 × 40% = $0.0279

EXHIBIT 26-6
Calculation of the Present Value of the Differential Tax Deduction

	Difference in Tax Deduction (from Exhibit 26-5)	Present Value of $1 at 30%	Present Value of Differential in Tax Deduction
Year 1	$0.15	0.7692	$0.1154
Year 2	0.05	0.5917	0.0296
Year 3	(0.05)	0.4552	(0.0228)
Year 4	(0.15)	0.3501	(0.0525)
Total present value of differential in tax deduction			$0.0697

The use of SYD depreciation, then, adds approximately 3 cents to the present value of the future cash returns. While the amount is small, remember that this example involves a very small investment (only $1) and a project with a short useful life. As a percentage of the present cash outlay, the use of accelerated depreciation adds 2.19% of the cost of the project to the present value of the future cash returns. This addition could influence the decision in some cases.

Obviously, the use of accelerated depreciation methods adds considerably to the amount of computation required. The amount which SYD depreciation adds to the present value as compared to SL depreciation, however, depends on three factors. They are the total amount of depreciation which will be claimed over the useful life of the asset, the required rate of return, and the income tax rate. Most of the additional computations result from the need to calculate (1) the difference in depreciation on a year-by-year basis and (2) the present value of the difference in depreciation. These two phases of the computation can be done (given a useful life and required rate of return) and put in tabular form. This information is presented in Table 3 in the Appendix of this book. To confirm the computation shown in Exhibit 26-6, look in Table 3 in the four-year row and the 30% column. The figure given is 0.0696, the same as in Exhibit 26-6 except for a rounding difference in the last digit. Table 3, then, provides an easy way to find the amount of present value added to a capital expenditure by the decision to use sum-of-the-years'-digits depreciation rather than straight-line depreciation.

To complete our study of the impact of accelerated depreciation on capital expenditure analysis, let us return to the machine replacement decision, which was last discussed following Exhibit 26-3.

Assume that sum of the years' digits depreciation will be used in the machine replacement example if the machine were purchased. The following facts are relevant to calculating the impact of SYD depreciation on the capital expenditure. The machine expected to have a useful life of five years. Its total cost is $15,600, with no salvage value. The required rate of return is 12% and the tax rate 40%. By using the required rate of return and the five-year useful life, the 12% factor in Table 3 is 0.0541. This factor would be the present value of the difference in depreciation deductions if the total depreciation were to be $1. Since the asset cost $15,600 and is expected to have no salvage value, the total depreciation over the five-year life is $15,600. This together with the tax rate of 40% permits the simple calculation of the present value added through the use of SYD depreciation as:

$$0.0541 \times \$15{,}600 \times 40\% = \underline{\underline{\$337}}$$

This addition to the present value of the future cash flows makes the proposed replacement more attractive than if straight-line depreciation were used. The present value of the future returns has now become $9,991 ($337 plus the $9,654 previously calculated) and the present cash outlay is $9,400.

In summary, then, the effects of income taxes must be considered in capital expenditure analysis—in fact, in all analyses, since managers plan on an after corporate income tax basis. Computing the change in cash income tax payments which will result from the decisions to make investments is sometimes complex, but it is these figures which, once determined, are used in present value computations, just as any other change in cash payment would be. It is frequently easier to adjust the other changes in cash flows for their cash income tax payment impacts and to compute the effect of changed depreciation deductions as a separate item.

CAPITAL RATIONING

In a dynamic firm, investment projects are usually generated at a faster rate than funds can be made available for them; in any year, most firms cannot accept all the projects which will achieve the minimum rate of return. They must, therefore, select the combination of acceptable projects which adds the most to the value of the firm. The usual decision rule would be to accept that combination of projects which maximizes the net present value.

Suppose a firm expects to have $140,000 available for investment in capital expenditure projects. Analysis of five possible projects shows the following:

Ranking of Capital Expenditure Projects

	Present Cash Outlay	Benefit-cost Ratio	Net Present Value
Project 1	$ 80,000	1.40	$32,000
Project 2	50,000	1.28	14,000
Project 3	20,000	1.25	5,000
Projcet 4	40,000	1.20	8,000
Project 5	10,000	1.10	1,000
Total	$200,000		

In selecting capital projects, managers attempt to maximize the total net present value.

As shown by either the **benefit-cost ratios** or the **net present values,** all these projects are expected to achieve more than the minimum rate of return. They are ranked in order of benefit-cost ratio, i.e., project 1 has the highest rate of return, project 2 the next highest, and so on. But the total of these capital expenditures is $200,000. The firm has only $140,000 to invest, and so it must make a selection. Perhaps management can simply move down the list, taking the highest-return projects until the $140,000 is committed. But by accepting projects 1 and 2 they will have committed $130,000 of the company's funds and will not have enough still available to undertake project 3. The possible combinations that will spend the entire $140,000 are projects 1, 2, and 5 or 1, 3, and 4. Which combination will add the greatest possible amount to the value of the firm? Which will result in the greatest net present value?

The net present value is seen to be greatest if the firm undertakes projects 1, 2, and 5. It may at first seem surprising that projects 3 and 4 are neglected, since they are expected to yield a higher rate of return than project 5. Nevertheless, with the constraint of limited funds management adds the greatest value to the firm by choosing projects 1, 2, and 5.

Selecting projects becomes very complex as the amounts of funds and available projects grow. It would be difficult to identify all feasible combinations of projects if, for example, there were 15 or 20 more under consideration. There would probably be a very large number of combinations of ways in which the total funds could be spent.

When a firm faces this situation, it may turn to linear programming techniques. Linear programming is designed to allocate resources in such a way as to achieve a given objective subject to certain constraints. Here the linear programming formulation would be designed to maximize the net present value subject to the constraint that the firm does not commit itself to more present cash outlays than there are funds available.

When short-run capital limitations prevent a firm from undertaking all investments which promise the minimum rate of return, the situation is referred to as **capital rationing.** Capital is only one resource which may be a limiting factor, however. Others are, for example, management, skilled labor, or some necessary raw material. The linear programming approach is very attractive in situations where capital plus other resources are limited, because the formulation permits the selection of the combination of projects which promises to add the greatest value to the firm in view of the limitations that apply. If skilled labor is a limiting factor, the amount of such labor required by each investment project can be formulated algebraically as a constraint and added to the funds constraint previously mentioned. Similar steps can be taken if a needed raw material is available in limited quantities over some future period. Overall, the linear programming formulation is a very useful tool in the selection of a "package" of investment projects in the face of limited resources.

RISK IN CAPITAL EXPENDITURE ANALYSIS

The results of capital expenditure analyses depend on estimates of future cash flows. When estimating future events, the manager can rarely be entirely certain that the amounts of cash flow and their timing will be exactly as anticipated in the present value analysis. Methods of dealing explicitly with **risk**, uncertainty about future cash flows, have recently been applied to capital expenditure analysis but are not widely practiced at present. Indeed, many managers are only now beginning to understand and apply present value analysis.

A starting point in explicitly dealing with risk is to recognize that the cash flow in any future year has several possible amounts. For example, a manager might estimate that the future cash returns in year 4 of some project's life might be $2,000, $3,500, $4,000, or some other value. Usually there would be varying likelihood that each of these cash flows will occur. The manager might estimate the following likelihoods or probabilities:

Cash Return	Likelihood	Probability
$2,000	2 out of 10	20%
3,500	4 out of 10	40
4,000	3 out of 10	30
4,500	1 out of 10	10

If, for each year, the possible cash returns and their associated probabilities are estimated, statistical methods permit the determination of a distribution of benefit-cost ratios (or net present values) and their associated probabilities. The statistical computations quickly become very complex, however.

EXHIBIT 26-7

Project A		Project B	
Probability	**Benefit-cost Ratio**	**Probability**	**Benefit-cost Ratio**
15%	0.30–0.59	5%	0.50–0.79
15	0.60–0.79	10	0.80–0.89
20	0.80–0.99	20	0.90–0.99
15	1.00–1.19	30	1.00–1.09
25	1.20–1.39	20	1.10–1.19
10	1.40–1.59	15	1.20–1.29

In the typical capital expenditure decision there are so many possible combinations of future cash flows with various probabilities that it is impractical to calculate, statistically, the various benefit-cost indices and their associated probabilities. Fortunately, computer simulations using "monte carlo" techniques permit the development of distributions of benefit-cost ratios with associated probabilities which are a satisfactory approximation of the results of an almost impossibly complex statistical computation. Several computer manufacturers have developed the necessary simulation program and have made it available to users of their computers.

Suppose a manager is considering two investments but can accept only one of them. The results of either a statistical computation or a simulation might be presented as in Exhibit 26-7.

If we had calculated only the most likely benefit-cost ratio (the one with the highest probability), project A would appear to be more desirable than project B because the most likely ratio for A falls between 1.20 and 1.39, whereas the most likely ratio for B falls between 1.00 and 1.09. With the additional information generated by the simulation, however, managers can make other observations which may be important in choosing between the projects. The range of benefit-cost ratios for project A is seen to be greater than for project B. Project A has potentially higher value, with its maximum benefit-cost ratio of 1.59; but its minimum ratio of 0.30, if realized, would give it a lower value than B.

Probability concepts are used to evaluate risk in capital expenditure analysis.

Another contrast which can be explicitly evaluated only by this approach is implicit in the question, "Which project has the highest probability of yielding at least the minimum rate of return?" This can be determined from Exhibit 26-7 by summing the probabilities of a benefit-cost ratio of greater than 1.00 for both projects. For project A, the probability that the ratio will exceed 1.00 is 50% (15% + 25% + 10%). For project B, this probability is 65%. It would appear from an analysis of the data that the possibility of high (or low) returns is greater with project A. The possibility for high (or low) returns with project B is not greater, but it appears more likely that project B will at least yield the minimum rate of return.

Given this information, it is impossible to generalize about which project management would choose. If management wishes to try for high returns and is willing to accept the risk of the higher probability of below-minimum rates of return, it might choose propect A. A more conservative management might prefer project B.

Three-Point Estimates

Many firms may feel that they are not yet in a position to use the information generated by the fairly sophisticated analysis outlined above. However, there are several other ways of providing a gauge of varying possible outcomes which can be applied by almost any firm. If the major risk lies in the amounts of future cash inflows, management can obtain a rough measure for an investment project by making several estimates of future cash inflows, but not as many as required by the simulation. If, for example, management is considering a new product line, there might be considerable question about the number of units which could be sold or the price at which they could be sold. In performing step 1 of the capital expenditure analysis, they might estimate a *most likely* figure for future net cash returns but also make a *pessimistic* estimate and an *optimistic* estimate of these returns based on differing estimates of the number of units to be sold. In step 2 of the analysis there would then be three present value amounts, one corresponding to each of the estimates. In step 4, these three present value estimates would result in three benefit-cost ratios.

Acme Corporation was considering a change in production layout in the flexible power tubing operation. This change involved the installation of a proposed new conveyor system for the assembly stage. Since none of the other departments manufactured a similar product, and since no competing manufacturers of flexible power tubing used a similar conveyor system, there was no actual experience in the savings that might result from the installation of the system. The plant engineers provided the following estimates of potential annual future cash savings in material handling and production labor:

- Most likely savings estimate — $ 8,000 per year
- Pessimistic savings estimate — 2,000 per year
- Optimistic savings estimate — 11,000 per year

The cost of the system and its installation was reported to be $20,000. The system was intended to be used for the next four years, at which time a new plan would be constructed to house the flexible tubing operation along with some other production operations. At that time, the conveyor system would probably not be moved, because the cost of removing it would in all likelihood be greater than the cost of the better production systems which would then be available. Since Acme's cost of capital is 13%, the present value and benefit-cost indices of the various possible streams of savings were calculated as follows:

	Annual Savings	Present Value Factor @13%	Present Value of Future Cash Returns	Benefit-Cost Ratio
Most likely	$ 8,000	2.885	$23,080	1.15
Pessimistic	2,000	2.885	5,770	0.29
Optimistic	11,000	2.885	31,735	1.59

Based on this information, Acme's management would weigh its feeling toward accepting risk and evaluate this project compared with others under consideration.

Time-Adjusted Payback

Another major source of uncertainty in some capital expenditure projects is the estimation of the useful life of a project. Shifts in the consumer taste or obsolescence of machinery or equipment can have drastic effects. A machine which is physically in good condition may become obsolete simply because a much more efficient method of doing the work has been discovered. At this point, replacing the physically sound machine may promise a very high rate of return. If this is true, sound management may dictate replacement of an existing machine even though it has not yet been used as long as originally predicted. The rate of return on the machine will then fall short of the estimate management made at the time of the original investment.

No amount of analysis can protect against obsolescence which has already occurred. In evaluating capital expenditures, however, management might wonder how long the machine would have to last to provide the minimum rate of return. Suppose a firm is presently considering the purchase of a labor-saving machine which, according to management estimates, should have a useful life of eight years. The machine will cost \$10,000 and promises net savings of \$3,000 per year. The minimum rate of return is 16%. With this information it can be shown that *if* the machine lasts for eight years, it will provide more than the minimum rate of return:

- Step 1 Future cash returns \$3,000 per year for eight years
- Step 2 Present value factor 4.344 at 16%
  Present value of future cash returns \$3,000 × 4.344 = \$13,032
- Step 3 Present cash outlay
  Investment (given) \$10,000
- Step 4 Net present value \$13,032 − \$10,000 = \$3,032

The investment promises a return greater than 16%. However, the conclusion is based on the estimated useful life of eight years. What will happen if the useful life is only four years? In this case, calculations will show that the net present value is negative \$1,606, indicating that the project will not provide a 16% rate of return. The next question might well be, "How long must the machine be kept in order to achieve the 16% rate of return?" This is calculated rather simply by cumulating the present value of each year's cash returns, as shown in Exhibit 26-8.

Comparing the \$10,000 investment to the cumulative present value demonstrates that by the end of the fifth year the present value of the cash returns almost equals the investment; therefore, if the useful life is slightly more than five years (assuming our cash return predictions are correct), the project will yield 16%. To the extent that the machine lasts longer than this before becoming obsolete, the project will ultimately yield a higher than minimum rate of return. If the machine should become obsolete in five years or less, the project will have failed to achieve the minimum rate of return. When the data is presented in this form, management can decide the likelihood that the machine will be used long enough to provide the minimum rate of return on investment.

A term which is sometimes used for the length of time required to achieve a present value of future returns equal to the present cash outlay is **time-adjusted**

EXHIBIT 26-8
Time-adjusted Payback Calculations

Year	Cash Return	Present Value Factor	Present Value This Year	Cumulative Present Value
1	$3,000	0.862	$ 2,586	$ 2,586
2	3,000	0.743	2,229	4,815
3	3,000	0.641	1,923	6,738
4	3,000	0.552	1,656	8,394
5	3,000	0.476	1,428	9,822
6	3,000	0.410	1,230	11,052*
7	3,000	0.354	1,062	12,114
8	3,000	0.305	915	13,029
		4.343	$13,029	

* Minimum rate of return achieved during Year 6.

Time adjusted payback is the time required to achieve the minimum rate of return.

payback period. In Exhibit 26-8 the time-adjusted payback period is slightly more than five years.

Unadjusted Payback

An **unadjusted payback period** is the length of time required to achieve cash returns equal to the present cash outlay. Present value is not a part of the analysis when this period is calculated. In the illustration summarized in Exhibit 26-8, the present cash outlay is $10,000. Since the future cash returns are $3,000 per year, the present cash outlay will be recovered in 3⅓ years ($10,000/$3,000). Although payback is sometimes used as a criterion for evaluating capital expenditures, there is little to recommend it for the capital expenditure decision. Since it does not take into account present value, it is not directly related to value. In fact, it is easy to find many examples where the project with the shortest unadjusted payback period has the lowest rate of return.

OTHER CONSIDERATIONS

Qualitative considerations sometimes outweigh quantitative analysis in capital expenditure analysis.

To this point we have considered the quantitative analysis of capital expenditures to determine whether or not particular projects promise a required minimum rate of return. However, the rate of return may be only one consideration in reaching a final decision. Occasionally projects are imposed on firms by governmental units. Street improvements may be made and assessed against the company, or public health authorities may require certain changes in operations to improve working conditions or to reduce air or water pollution. In these cases, the rate of return on the project may have little bearing on the decision because the changes must be made to continue in business.

Occasionally, managers will argue that company long-range objectives require current investments whose future benefits are so uncertain that present value analysis cannot be made. Certainly it would be wrong to deny that such investments occur. It may be argued in certain cases that management *intuition* is needed, rather than quantitative analysis. Most managers would, however, subject proposals of this nature to very close scrutiny to make sure that this argument was not an attempt to justify a project where quantitative analysis was, in fact, perfectly feasible and would indicate that the expenditure was not in the best long-range interests of the company.

SUMMARY

Accelerated depreciation and its favorable effect as a tax shield in reducing the income tax payment was examined thoroughly, and a handy way to determine the dollar amount to be added to the present value of expected future cash returns was illustrated, using Table 3 in the Appendix to this book.

Capital rationing, or the case of having more good projects than available capital, was examined, suggesting that the appropriate selection of alternatives would be that combination which produces the greatest present value increase for the firm. With just a few projects to evaluate, this can be accomplished by trial and error; but when there are many, linear programming is essential to find the optimum set of projects.

The use of probability as a risk-evaluating device was examined to show how managers can evaluate a range of probable outcomes with their associated probabilities attached, and make their selections based upon their preferences for various types of risk. Time-adjusted payback and unadjusted payback were examined for the particular contributions they make toward evaluation of risk.

Finally, it was recognized that managers sometimes make capital expenditure decisions based on factors other than the likelihood that the project will yield the minimum rate of return. Care is needed in weighing all factors so that the firm maintains its profitability and, as a consequence, its ability to obtain needed resources.

Review Problem

The Baxter Company manufactures toys and other short-lived fad type items.

The research and development department came up with an item that would make a good promotional gift for office equipment dealers. Aggressive and effective effort by Baxter's sales personnel has resulted in almost firm commitments for this product for the next three years. It is expected that the product's value will be exhausted by that time.

In order to produce the quantity demanded Baxter will need to buy additional machinery and rent some additional space. It appears that about 25,000 square feet will be needed; 12,500 square feet of presently unused, but leased, space is available now. (Baxter's present lease with 10 years to run costs $3.00 a foot.) There is another 12,500 square feet adjoining the Baxter facility which Baxter will rent for 3 years at $4.00 per square foot per year if it decides to make this product.

The equipment will be purchased for about $900,000. It will require $30,000 in modifications, $60,000 for installation and $90,000 for testing; all of these activities will be done by a firm of engineers hired by Baxter. All the expenditures will be paid for on January 1, 19X3.

The equipment should have a salvage value of about $180,000 at the end of the third year. No additional general overhead costs are expected to be incurred.

The following estimates of revenues and expenses for this product for the three years have been developed.

	19X3	19X4	19X5
Sales	$1,000,000	$1,600,000	$800,000
Material, labor, and incurred overhead	400,000	750,000	350,000
Assigned general overhead	40,000	75,000	35,000
Rent	87,500	87,500	87,500
Depreciation	450,000	300,000	150,000
	$ 977,500	$1,212,500	$622,500
Income before tax	$ 22,500	$ 387,500	$177,500
Income tax (40%)	9,000	155,000	71,000
Net income	$ 13,500	$ 232,500	$106,500

Required

1 Prepare a schedule which shows the incremental, after tax, cash flows for this project.

2 If the company requires a two-year payback period for its investment, would it undertake this project? Show your supporting calculations clearly.

3 A newly hired Business School graduate recommends that the company consider the use of the net present value analysis to study this project. If the company sets a required rate of return of 20% after taxes will this project be accepted? Show your supporting calculations clearly. (Assume all operating revenues and expenses occur at the end of the year.)

(CMA)

Solution

1 Incremental after tax cash flow (000 omitted)

	19X3	19X4	19X5
Sales	$1,000	$1,600	$800
Material, labor, overhead	400	750	350
Added rent	50	50	50
Depreciation	450	300	150
Incremental costs	900	1,100	550
Incremental income	100	500	250
Incremental taxes (40%)	40	200	100
Incremental income after taxes	60	300	150
Add back depreciation	450	300	150
Incremental operation cash flow	510	600	300
Salvage value			180
Net incremental after tax cash flow	$ 510	$ 600	$480

Cash outlay for project:	
Purchase price	$ 900
Modification	30
Installation	60
Testing	90
Total	$1,080

2 The project should be undertaken if the criterion is a two-year payback.

19X3	$ 510,000	
19X4	600,000	
	$1,110,000	Payback is in two years, which is greater than cost of $1,080,000.

3 The project should be adopted if a 20% after tax rate of return is required.

Present value of cash flows at 20%			
19X3	.833 × 510,000	=	$ 424,830
19X4	.694 × 600,000	=	416,400
19X5	.579 × 480,000	=	277,920
	Present value		$1,119,150

The present value of $1,119,150 is greater than the initial outlay of $1,080,000; therefore, the project more than satisfies the 20% requirement.

Glossary

Accelerated depreciation A method of depreciation in which larger amounts of depreciation expense are reported in the earlier part of the asset life and smaller amounts are reported in the later years of the asset life. The two most common methods are sum of the years' digits and double declining balance.

Benefit-cost ratio A measure of whether a capital expenditure will return more or less than the minimum required rate of return.

Capital rationing The problem of fitting the various investment proposals to the available investment dollars in such a way that the most value is added to the firm. Applies when capital is limited such that not all proposals which would increase the value of the firm can be accepted.

Net present value A measure of whether a capital expenditure will return more or less than the minimum required rate of return.

Payback—time adjusted The time required for the *present value* of the future cash inflows of an investment project to equal the cash outflow in year 1 (the investment).

Payback—unadjusted The time required for the future cash inflows of an investment project to equal cash outflow in year 1 (the investment). The time required to recover the initial investment, ignoring present value.

Risk The characteristic of an investment that the actual future cash flows may vary from the amounts predicted for the investment.

Salvage value The amount of cash which can be received for an asset when the firm no longer desires to continue using that asset.

Questions and Problems

26-1 Under what conditions, if any, is the *book value* of equipment relevant for an equipment replacement decision? Explain.

26-2 Mr. A. T. Spiro, production manager of the Dixon Engineering Company, was considering replacing a precision milling machine with a new, high-speed machine. Mr. Spiro was unable to understand how the after-tax rate of return could be anything except 60% of the before-tax rate of return if the tax rate applying to his firm was 40%.

Do you agree with Mr. Spiro? Why or why not?

26-3 Value of Accelerated Depreciation Using Table 3 in the Appendix to this book, answer the following questions.

1 What is the combination of useful life and cost of capital which leads to the *greatest* value in using sum of the years' digits depreciation rather than straight-line depreciation?

2 What is the combination of useful life and cost of capital which leads to the *lowest* value in using sum of the years' digits depreciation rather than straight-line depreciation?

3 You are considering the acquisition of an asset costing $15,000 with an expected salvage value of $1,000. The company income tax rate is 40%. Using your answer to part 1 (useful life and cost of capital) what is the maximum economic advantage of using sum of the years' digits depreciation rather than straight-line depreciation?

26-4 Value of Accelerated Depreciation The Gavlor Company has purchased a milling machine costing $45,000 which has an estimated five-year life with no salvage value. In deciding which accounting method of depreciation to use for tax purposes, it is determined that the sum of the years' digits method will cost $500 more to administer than the straight-line depreciation which will be used for book purposes. (Cost consists of setting up depreciation schedules and reconciling tax returns to the books.) The Gavlor Company uses a 10% after tax rate for cost of capital. The expected tax rate is 40%.

Required

Which depreciation method should be adopted for tax purposes? Support your answer with calculations.

26-5 Accelerated Depreciation in Capital Expenditures Ambex is considering replacing a textile machine that originally cost $105,000 and has a book value of $55,000. Annual depreciation calculated on the straight-line basis is $10,000 after allowing for an estimated salvage value of $5,000. The present machine could now be sold for $10,000. The new machine will cost $60,000 and will have a useful life of five years with a salvage value of $8,000 at the end of five years. It would be depreciated by the sum of the years' digits method. The use of the new machine would be expected to result in changes in the following items now appearing in the report prepared on the department in which the machine would be used. None of the numbers given below includes depreciation.

	Old Machine	New Machine
Labor	$26,000	$17,500
Electricity and other operating expenses	6,000	4,500
Share of total plant overhead	13,000	11,000
Repairs	4,000	3,000

Ambex's income tax rate is 40%, and they require a 12% after tax minimum return on investments.

Required

Should they acquire the new machine?

26-6 Accelerated Depreciation in Machine Replacement Lorenz Walk, a cost-oriented member of the management team at the Hard Driving Tie Gears Manufacturing Company, rushed into his supervisor's office to announce: "A new tie gear production machine has just been manufactured, and it should be purchased to replace the machine we currently use." Walk presents the following information to support his position.

	Old Machine	New Machine
Expected life	15 years (new)	10 years (new)
Original cost	$75,000	$105,000
Accumulated depreciation (straight-line method)	25,000	—
Present trade-in value	10,000	—
Trade-in value after ten years	—	5,000
Capacity in units per year	60,000	80,000
Expected output in units per year	50,000	50,000
Production expenses:		
Direct materials	$50,000	$ 50,000
Direct labor	40,000	30,000
Depreciation	5,000	10,000
Overhead: Fixed $10,000 Variable 50 cents per dollar of direct labor	30,000	25,000
Net profit before tax	75,000	85,000
(Tie gears sell for $4 each.)		

Assume that management demands a 20% after tax rate of return on investments; savings from replacement occur throughout the year; depreciation on the new machine would be by sum of the years' digits, while the old machine would continue on the straight-line method; and the loss on the trade of the old machine would have to be added to the cost of the new machine. The tax rate is 40%.

Required

Should the new machine be purchased?

26-7 Choosing between Two Corkscrew Machines with Accelerated Depreciation Your company needs a new corkscrew machine, and there are two types on the market:

Automatic		Manual	
Original cost	$30,000	Original cost	$10,000
Salvage value in ten years	4,000	Salvage value in ten years	0
Overhaul at end of sixth year (charge to expense)	4,000	Operating cash outflows per year	8,500
Operating cash outflows per year	3,000		

Assume an income tax rate of 40%, after tax cost of capital of 10%, and sum of the years' digits depreciation.

Required Which machine should the company purchase? Show all computations.

26-8 Selecting the Better Mixing Machine The On Line Company is considering a new mixing machine for their old standby product, Bamble. The following data outlines the possibilities they are considering. Assume a 40% tax rate, sum of the years' digits depreciation, and a 10% required rate of return.

	New Machine, X	New Machine, Y
Original cost	$38,000	$50,000
Useful life	5 years	5 years
Salvage value	$ 4,000	$ 0
Annual before-tax cash savings	9,000	12,000

Required Which investment should the On Line Company select?

26-9 Replacing "Old Betsy" The Standen Company is considering the acquisition of a new machine to replace "Old Betsy." Old Betsy has a book value and present market value of $2,000 and would continue to be depreciated at $500 per year. Yet the maintenance department believes that Betsy could be used for another *ten* years.

The new machine (as yet unnamed) will cost $18,000 installed, and will go for ten years with no expected salvage value. It is not anticipated that any improved machines (over the one now being considered) will be developed in the next six or seven years.

The new machine is expected to require annual labor of $14,000, while Old Betsy requires $17,800 annually. Assume the sum of the years' digits depreciation will be used, the tax rate is 40% and the minimum required after tax rate of return is 10%.

Required Should this project be accepted?

26-10 Capital Rationing Thunderbird Company has the following five investment projects available:

Projects	Initial Investment	Benefit-cost Ratio	Net Present Value
A	$ 60,000	1.50	$30,000
B	125,000	1.40	50,000
C	50,000	1.30	15,000
D	80,000	1.27	21,600
E	100,000	0.90	−10,000

Required

1 If the total capital available for investment is $140,000, which projects should the company choose?

2 If the total capital available for investment is $200,000, which projects should the company choose?

26-11 Capital Rationing Kiwi Company has $250,000 available for investment in capital expenditure projects. The following projects have been suggested to management, and the values shown below have been calculated. The net present values and the benefit-cost ratios are based on the company's minimum required rate of return of 12%.

Projects	Initial Investment	Net Present Value	Benefit-cost Ratio
A	$ 50,000	$ 5,000	1.1
B	100,000	70,000	1.7
C	60,000	24,000	1.4
D	20,000	10,000	1.5
E	100,000	20,000	1.2

Required

Which investments should the company undertake? Explain.

26-12 Risk in Capital Expenditure Analysis Assume that a certain capital expenditure project requiring an initial cash outflow of $28,000 has a five-year life and a constant annual cash savings throughout the life. Compute three benefit-cost ratios for the project. The cost of capital is 14%. The estimated annual savings and their associated probabilities are given below:

Annual Savings	Probability
$10,000	50%
6,000	30%
12,000	20%

Required

Indicate which of your benefit-cost ratios is (1) most likely, (2) pessimistic, and (3) optimistic.

26-13 Payback or Present Value Analysis? The XYZ Company is preparing its capital expenditure budget for the following year. It is considering two mutually exclusive proposals, each of which would require an initial cash outlay of $60,000. The company has estimated that the net cash proceeds from each proposal would be:

Year	Proposal A	Proposal B
1	$50,000	$30,000
2	30,000	30,000
3	20,000	30,000
4	20,000	30,000
5	20,000	30,000

As only one of the two proposals can be accepted, the treasurer of the company has argued that the decision should be made on the basis of a payback analysis. However, the president of the company believes that the decision should be based on the results of a present value analysis. XYZ's minimum rate of return is 10%.

Required Rank the two proposals as to their desirability.

26-14 Obsolescence and Time-Adjusted Payback Sanderson, Inc., is considering the purchase of a new, electronic atomic dosimeter slicing machine. The cost is $20,000 installed, with an expected useful physical life of six years, and no salvage value. Annual cash savings over the now obsolescent machine are expected to be $15,000 the first year, $12,000 the second, $10,000 the third, and $8,000 thereafter as close-tolerance readjustments become increasingly necessary. The company's tax rate is 40%. Because the new machine's obsolescence is hard to predict, the executive committee has requested a time-adjusted payback analysis.

Required Under what conditions should the new machine be purchased, assuming Sanderson, Inc., requires a minimum after tax rate of return of 16%.

Assume straight time depreciation.

26-15 Payback and Present Value Computations Hazman Company plans to replace an old piece of equipment which is obsolete and is expected to be unreliable under the stress of daily operations. The equipment is fully depreciated, and no salvage value can be realized upon its disposal.

One piece of equipment being considered would provide annual cash savings of $7,000 before income taxes. The equipment would cost $18,000 and have an estimated useful life of five years. No salvage value would be used for depreciation purposes because the equipment is expected to have no value at the end of five years.

Hazman uses the straight-line depreciation method on all equipment for both book and tax purposes. The company is subject to a 40% tax rate. Hazman has an after-tax cost of capital of 14%.

Required Calculate for Hazman Company's proposed investment in new equipment the after-tax:

a Payback period
b Net present value
c Profitability (present value) index
d Internal rate of return

Assume all operating revenues and expenses occur at the end of the year.
(CMA)

26-16 Net Present Value The WRL Company makes cookies for its chain of snack food stores. On January 2, 19X0 WRL Company purchased a special cookie cutting machine; this machine has been utilized for three years. WRL Company is considering the purchase of a newer, more efficient machine. If purchased, the new machine would be acquired on January 2, 19X3. WRL Company expects to sell 300,000 dozen cookies in each of the next four years. The selling price of the cookies is expected to average $.50 per dozen.

WRL Company has two options: (1) continue to operate the old machine, or (2) sell the old machine and purchase the new machine. No trade-in was offered by the seller of the new machine. The following information has been assembled to help decide which option is more desirable.

	Old Machine	New Machine
Original cost of machine at acquisition	$80,000	$120,000
Salvage value at the end of useful life for depreciation purposes	$10,000	$ 20,000
Useful life from date of acquisition	7 years	4 years
Expected annual cash operating expenses:		
Variable cost per dozen	$ .20	$ .14
Total fixed costs	$15,000	$ 14,000
Depreciation method used for tax purposes:	Straight-line	Sum of years' digits
Estimated cash value of machines:		
January 2, 19X3	$40,000	$120,000
December 31, 19X6	$ 7,000	$ 20,000

WRL Company is subject to an overall income tax rate of 40%. Assume that all operating revenues and expenses occur at the end of the year. Assume that any gain or loss on the sale of machinery is treated as an ordinary tax item and will affect the taxes paid by WRL Company at the end of the year in which it occurred.

Required

1 Use the net present value method to determine whether WRL Company should retain the old machine or acquire the new machine. WRL requires an after-tax return of 16%

2 Without prejudice to your answer to Requirement 1, assume that the quantitative differences are so slight between the two alternatives that WRL Company is indifferent to the two proposals. Identify and discuss the nonquantitative factors which are important to this decision that WRL Company should consider. (CMA)

26-17 Expansion of Capacity Wisconsin Products Company manufactures several different products. One of the firm's principal products sells for $20 per unit. The sales manager of Wisconsin Products has stated repeatedly that he could sell more units of this product if they were available. In an attempt to substantiate his claim the sales manager conducted a market research study last year at a cost of $44,000 to determine potential demand for this product. The study indicated that Wisconsin Products could sell 18,000 units of this product annually for the next five years.

The equipment currently in use has the capacity to produce 11,000 units annually. The variable production costs are $9 per unit. The equipment has a book value of $60,000 and a remaining useful life of five years. The salvage value of the equipment is negligible now and will be zero in five years.

A maximum of 20,000 units could be produced annually on the new machinery which can be purchased. The new equipment costs $300,000 and has an estimated useful life of five years with no salvage value at the end of five years. Wisconsin Product's production manager has estimated that the new equipment would provide increased production efficiencies that would reduce the variable production costs to $7 per unit.

Wisconsin Products Company uses straight-line depreciation on all of its equipment for tax purposes. The firm is subject to a 40% tax rate, and its after-tax cost of capital is 15%.

The sales manager felt so strongly about the need for additional capacity that he attempted to prepare an economic justification for the equipment although this was not one of his responsibilities. His analysis, presented below disappointed him because it did not justify acquiring the equipment.

Required Investment

Purchase price of new equipment		$300,000
Disposal of existing equipment:		
Loss on disposal	$60,000	
Less tax benefit (40%)	24,000	36,000
Cost of market research study		44,000
Total investment		$380,000

Annual Returns

Contribution margin from product:	
Using the new equipment [18,000 × ($20–7)]	$234,000
Using the existing equipment [11,000 × ($20–9)]	121,000
Increase in contribution margin	$113,000
Less depreciation	60,000
Increase in before-tax income	$ 53,000
Income tax (40%)	21,200
Increase in income	$ 31,800
Less 15% cost of capital on the additional investment required (.15 × $380,000)	57,000
Net annual return of proposed investment in new equipment	$(25,200)

Required

1 The controller of Wisconsin Products Company plans to prepare a discounted cash flow analysis for this investment proposal. The controller has asked you to prepare corrected calculations of
   a The required investment in the new equipment
   b The recurring annual cash flows

Explain the treatment of each item of your corrected calculations which is treated unlike the original analysis prepared by the sales manager.

2 Calculate the net present value of the proposed investment in the new equipment.

(CMA)

26-18 New Product Introduction The Beta Corporation manufactures office equipment and distributes its products through wholesale distributors.

Beta Corporation recently learned of a patent on the production of a semiautomatic paper collator that can be obtained at a cost of $60,000 cash. The semiautomatic model is vastly superior to the manual model that the corporation now produces. At a cost of $40,000, present equipment could be modified to accommodate the production of the new semiautomatic model. Such modifications would not affect the remaining useful life of four years or the salvage value of $10,000 that the equipment now has. Variable costs, however, would increase by one dollar per unit. Fixed costs, other than relevant amortization charges, would not be affected. If the equipment is modified, the manual model cannot be produced.

The current income statement relative to the manual collator appears as follows:

Sales (100,000 units @ $4)		$400,000
Variable costs	$180,000	
Fixed costs**	120,000	
Total costs		$300,000
Net Income before income taxes		$100,000
Income taxes (40%)		40,000
Net income after income taxes		$ 60,000

** All fixed costs are directly allocable to the production of the manual collator and include depreciation on equipment of $20,000, calculated on the straight-line basis with a useful life of 10 years.

Market research has disclosed three important findings relative to the new semiautomatic model. First, a particular competitor will certainly purchase the patent if Beta Corporation does not. If this were to happen, Beta Corporation's sales of the manual collator would fall to 70,000 units per year. Second, if no increase in the selling price is made, Beta Corporation could sell approximately 190,000 units per year of the semiautomatic model. Third, because of the advances being made in this area, the patent will be completely worthless at the end of four years.

Because of the uncertainty of the current situation, the raw materials inventory has been almost completely exhausted. Regardless of the decision reached substantial and immediate inventory replenishment will be required. The engineering department estimates that if the new model is to be produced, the average monthly raw materials inventory will be $20,000. If the old model is continued, the inventory balance will average $12,000 per month.

Required

1 Prepare a schedule which shows the incremental after tax cash flows for the comparison of the two alternatives. Assume that the corporation will use the sum of the year's digits method for depreciating the costs of modifying the equipment.

2 Assuming that the incremental after tax cash flows calculated in Requirement 1, and the annual incomes for the two alternatives are as given in the following schedule, will Beta Corporation, if it has a

cost of capital of 18%, decide to manufacture the semiautomatic collator? Use the net present value decision rule and assume all operating revenues and expenses occur at the end of the year.

Year	Incremental Cash Flow (000 Omitted)	Annual Income (000 Omitted)	
		Manual	Semi-automatic
1 Beginning	− $110	—	—
1 End	+ 40	$ 24	$ 39
2 End	+ 40	24	39
3 End	+ 40	24	39
4 End	+ 50	24	39

(CMA)

APPENDIX

TABLE 1
Present Value of $1

Years	*5%*	*6%*	*8%*	*10%*	*12%*	*14%*	*15%*	*16%*	*18%*	*20%*	*22%*	*24%*	*25%*
1	0.952	0.943	0.926	0.909	0.893	0.877	0.870	0.862	0.847	0.833	0.820	0.806	0.800
2	0.907	0.890	0.857	0.826	0.797	0.769	0.756	0.743	0.718	0.694	0.672	0.650	0.640
3	0.864	0.840	0.794	0.751	0.712	0.675	0.658	0.641	0.609	0.579	0.551	0.524	0.512
4	0.823	0.792	0.735	0.683	0.636	0.592	0.572	0.552	0.516	0.482	0.451	0.423	0.410
5	0.784	0.747	0.681	0.621	0.567	0.519	0.497	0.476	0.437	0.402	0.370	0.341	0.328
6	0.746	0.705	0.630	0.564	0.507	0.456	0.432	0.410	0.370	0.335	0.303	0.275	0.262
7	0.711	0.665	0.583	0.513	0.452	0.400	0.376	0.354	0.314	0.279	0.249	0.222	0.210
8	0.677	0.627	0.540	0.467	0.404	0.351	0.327	0.305	0.266	0.233	0.204	0.179	0.168
9	0.645	0.592	0.500	0.424	0.361	0.308	0.284	0.263	0.225	0.194	0.167	0.144	0.134
10	0.614	0.558	0.463	0.386	0.322	0.270	0.247	0.227	0.191	0.162	0.137	0.116	0.107
11	0.585	0.527	0.429	0.350	0.287	0.237	0.215	0.195	0.162	0.135	0.112	0.094	0.086
12	0.557	0.497	0.397	0.319	0.257	0.208	0.187	0.168	0.137	0.112	0.092	0.076	0.069
13	0.530	0.469	0.368	0.290	0.229	0.182	0.163	0.145	0.116	0.093	0.075	0.061	0.055
14	0.505	0.442	0.340	0.263	0.205	0.160	0.141	0.125	0.099	0.078	0.062	0.049	0.044
15	0.481	0.417	0.315	0.239	0.183	0.140	0.123	0.108	0.084	0.065	0.051	0.040	0.035
16	0.458	0.394	0.292	0.218	0.163	0.123	0.107	0.093	0.071	0.054	0.042	0.032	0.028
17	0.436	0.371	0.270	0.198	0.146	0.108	0.093	0.080	0.060	0.045	0.034	0.026	0.023
18	0.416	0.350	0.250	0.180	0.130	0.095	0.081	0.069	0.051	0.038	0.028	0.021	0.018
19	0.396	0.331	0.232	0.164	0.116	0.083	0.070	0.060	0.043	0.031	0.023	0.017	0.014
20	0.377	0.312	0.215	0.149	0.104	0.073	0.061	0.051	0.037	0.026	0.019	0.014	0.012

TABLE 2
Present Value of $1 Received Annually for *N* Years

Years (N)	*5%*	*6%*	*8%*	*10%*	*12%*	*14%*	*15%*	*16%*	*18%*	*20%*	*22%*	*24%*	*25%*
1	0.952	0.943	0.926	0.909	0.893	0.877	0.870	0.862	0.847	0.833	0.820	0.806	0.800
2	1.859	1.833	1.783	1.736	1.690	1.647	1.626	1.605	1.566	1.528	1.492	1.457	1.440
3	2.723	2.673	2.577	2.487	2.402	2.322	2.283	2.246	2.174	2.106	2.042	1.981	1.952
4	3.546	3.465	3.312	3.169	3.037	2.914	2.855	2.798	2.690	2.589	2.494	2.404	2.362
5	4.330	4.212	3.993	3.791	3.605	3.433	3.352	3.274	3.127	2.991	2.864	2.745	2.689
6	5.076	4.917	4.623	4.355	4.111	3.889	3.784	3.685	3.498	3.326	3.167	3.020	2.951
7	5.786	5.582	5.206	4.868	4.564	4.288	4.160	4.039	3.812	3.605	3.416	3.242	3.161
8	6.463	6.210	5.747	5.335	4.968	4.639	4.487	4.344	4.078	3.837	3.619	3.421	3.329
9	7.108	6.802	6.247	5.759	5.328	4.946	4.772	4.607	4.303	4.031	3.786	3.566	3.463
10	7.722	7.360	6.710	6.145	5.650	5.216	5.019	4.833	4.494	4.192	3.923	3.682	3.571
11	8.306	7.887	7.139	6.495	5.937	5.453	5.234	5.029	4.656	4.327	4.035	3.776	3.656
12	8.863	8.384	7.536	6.814	6.194	5.660	5.421	5.197	4.793	4.439	4.127	3.851	3.725
13	9.394	8.853	7.904	7.103	6.424	5.842	5.583	5.342	4.910	4.533	4.203	3.912	3.780
14	9.899	9.295	8.244	7.367	6.628	6.002	5.724	5.468	5.008	4.611	4.265	3.962	3.824
15	10.380	9.712	8.559	7.606	6.811	6.142	5.847	5.575	5.092	4.675	4.315	4.001	3.859
16	10.838	10.106	8.851	7.824	6.974	6.265	5.954	5.669	5.162	4.730	4.357	4.033	3.887
17	11.274	10.477	9.122	8.022	7.120	6.373	6.047	5.749	5.222	4.775	4.391	4.059	3.910
18	11.690	10.828	9.372	8.201	7.250	6.467	6.128	5.818	5.273	4.812	4.419	4.080	3.928
19	12.085	11.158	9.604	8.365	7.366	6.550	6.198	5.877	5.316	4.844	4.442	4.097	3.942
20	12.462	11.470	9.818	8.514	7.469	6.623	6.259	5.929	5.353	4.870	4.460	4.110	3.954

TABLE 3
Present Value of Differential between Straight Line and Sum of Digits Depreciation Shield

Years (N)	2%	4%	6%	8%	10%	12%	14%	16%	18%	20%	22%	24%	26%	28%	30%	35%	40%	45%	50%
4	0.0094	0.0177	0.0252	0.0318	0.0376	0.0428	0.0474	0.0515	0.0552	0.0584	0.0612	0.0638	0.0660	0.0679	0.0696	0.0730	0.0753	0.0768	0.0777
5	0.0124	0.0232	0.0326	0.0408	0.0479	0.0541	0.0595	0.0641	0.0682	0.0716	0.0746	0.0772	0.0793	0.0812	0.0827	0.0855	0.0871	0.0877	0.0877
6	0.0154	0.0285	0.0397	0.0492	0.0573	0.0642	0.0700	0.0749	0.0790	0.0825	0.0854	0.0877	0.0896	0.0912	0.0924	0.0942	0.0948	0.0945	0.0936
7	0.0183	0.0335	0.0463	0.0569	0.0657	0.0731	0.0791	0.0840	0.0881	0.0913	0.0939	0.0959	0.0975	0.0986	0.0994	0.1001	0.0996	0.0983	0.0965
8	0.0211	0.0384	0.0525	0.0640	0.0734	0.0809	0.0870	0.0918	0.0956	0.0985	0.1007	0.1022	0.1033	0.1040	0.1043	0.1039	0.1023	0.1001	0.0974
9	0.0239	0.0431	0.0584	0.0706	0.0803	0.0879	0.0938	0.0983	0.1017	0.1042	0.1059	0.1070	0.1076	0.1077	0.1075	0.1060	0.1035	0.1003	0.0969
10	0.0266	0.0475	0.0639	0.0767	0.0865	0.0940	0.0996	0.1038	0.1067	0.1087	0.1098	0.1104	0.1105	0.1101	0.1095	0.1069	0.1034	0.0996	0.0956
11	0.0293	0.0518	0.0691	0.0822	0.0921	0.0993	0.1046	0.1083	0.1107	0.1121	0.1128	0.1128	0.1123	0.1115	0.1104	0.1068	0.1026	0.0981	0.0937
12	0.0319	0.0560	0.0740	0.0873	0.0971	0.1040	0.1088	0.1120	0.1138	0.1147	0.1148	0.1143	0.1134	0.1121	0.1106	0.1061	0.1012	0.0962	0.0914
13	0.0345	0.0599	0.0786	0.0920	0.1015	0.1081	0.1124	0.1149	0.1162	0.1165	0.1161	0.1151	0.1137	0.1120	0.1101	0.1049	0.0994	0.0940	0.0889
14	0.0370	0.0637	0.0829	0.0963	0.1055	0.1116	0.1153	0.1173	0.1180	0.1177	0.1168	0.1153	0.1135	0.1114	0.1092	0.1033	0.0973	0.0916	0.0863
15	0.0395	0.0674	0.0869	0.1002	0.1090	0.1146	0.1177	0.1191	0.1192	0.1184	0.1170	0.1151	0.1129	0.1105	0.1080	0.1015	0.0951	0.0891	0.0837
16	0.0419	0.0709	0.0906	0.1038	0.1122	0.1171	0.1197	0.1205	0.1200	0.1187	0.1168	0.1145	0.1119	0.1092	0.1064	0.0994	0.0928	0.0866	0.0811
17	0.0443	0.0742	0.0942	0.1070	0.1149	0.1193	0.1212	0.1214	0.1204	0.1186	0.1163	0.1136	0.1107	0.1077	0.1047	0.0973	0.0904	0.0842	0.0785
18	0.0466	0.0775	0.0975	0.1100	0.1173	0.1211	0.1224	0.1220	0.1205	0.1182	0.1155	0.1125	0.1093	0.1061	0.1029	0.0952	0.0881	0.0817	0.0761
19	0.0489	0.0805	0.1006	0.1127	0.1194	0.1226	0.1232	0.1223	0.1203	0.1176	0.1145	0.1112	0.1078	0.1043	0.1010	0.0930	0.0858	0.0793	0.0737
20	0.0511	0.0835	0.1034	0.1151	0.1212	0.1237	0.1238	0.1223	0.1198	0.1167	0.1133	0.1097	0.1061	0.1025	0.0990	0.0908	0.0835	0.0770	0.0714
21	0.0533	0.0863	0.1061	0.1173	0.1228	0.1246	0.1241	0.1221	0.1192	0.1157	0.1120	0.1082	0.1043	0.1006	0.0970	0.0886	0.0812	0.0748	0.0692
22	0.0554	0.0890	0.1086	0.1192	0.1241	0.1253	0.1242	0.1217	0.1183	0.1146	0.1106	0.1065	0.1025	0.0987	0.0950	0.0865	0.0791	0.0727	0.0672
23	0.0575	0.0916	0.1110	0.1210	0.1252	0.1258	0.1241	0.1211	0.1174	0.1133	0.1091	0.1048	0.1007	0.0968	0.0930	0.0844	0.0770	0.0706	0.0652
24	0.0595	0.0941	0.1131	0.1226	0.1261	0.1260	0.1238	0.1204	0.1163	0.1120	0.1075	0.1031	0.0989	0.0948	0.0910	0.0824	0.0750	0.0687	0.0633
25	0.0616	0.0964	0.1151	0.1239	0.1268	0.1261	0.1234	0.1196	0.1152	0.1105	0.1059	0.1014	0.0971	0.0930	0.0891	0.0804	0.0731	0.0668	0.0615
26	0.0635	0.0987	0.1170	0.1251	0.1274	0.1261	0.1229	0.1187	0.1139	0.1091	0.1043	0.0997	0.0952	0.0911	0.0872	0.0785	0.0712	0.0650	0.0598
27	0.0654	0.1009	0.1187	0.1262	0.1277	0.1259	0.1222	0.1176	0.1127	0.1076	0.1027	0.0979	0.0934	0.0892	0.0853	0.0767	0.0694	0.0633	0.0582
28	0.0673	0.1029	0.1202	0.1271	0.1280	0.1256	0.1215	0.1166	0.1113	0.1061	0.1010	0.0962	0.0917	0.0874	0.0835	0.0749	0.0677	0.0617	0.0566
29	0.0692	0.1049	0.1217	0.1279	0.1281	0.1252	0.1207	0.1154	0.1100	0.1046	0.0994	0.0945	0.0899	0.0857	0.0818	0.0732	0.0660	0.0601	0.0551
30	0.0710	0.1068	0.1230	0.1285	0.1282	0.1247	0.1198	0.1142	0.1086	0.1030	0.0978	0.0928	0.0882	0.0840	0.0800	0.0715	0.0645	0.0586	0.0537
40	0.0871	0.1212	0.1310	0.1298	0.1240	0.1166	0.1089	0.1015	0.0947	0.0885	0.0829	0.0779	0.0734	0.0693	0.0657	0.0579	0.0518	0.0468	0.0426
50	0.1000	0.1295	0.1323	0.1255	0.1160	0.1064	0.0975	0.0895	0.0825	0.0764	0.0711	0.0664	0.0623	0.0586	0.0553	0.0484	0.0431	0.0388	0.0352

INDEX